Old School Ties

Tim Devlin & Hywel Williams

Old School Ties

Research by Angela Devlin

SINCLAIR-STEVENSON

First published in Great Britain
by Sinclair-Stevenson
7/8 Kendrick Mews
London SW7 3HG England

A CIP catalogue record for this book
is available from the British Library.

ISBN: 1 85619 148 6

Typeset in 10½ on 12½ Linotron Sabon
by Hewer Text Composition Services, Edinburgh
Printed and bound in England
by Clays Ltd, St. Ives plc

Contents

Acknowledgements

The authors would like to thank the following for their advice:

Marcel Berlins, *BBC Law in Action*
Jo Carr, *International Financial Law Review*
Lord Devlin, former law lord
General Sir Anthony Farrar-Hockley, defence consultant
Felsted School Sports Department
Frances Gibb, *The Times* legal correspondent
Sir Paul Kennedy, High Court judge
George Low, Editor *Education*
Brian MacArthur, Assistant Editor *The Times*
Clive Martin, record producer
John Merton, artist
Graham Mather, Director, *Institute of Economic Affairs*
Professor Joseph Needham, Director Emeritus *Needham Institute*
Rabbi Julia Neuberger
Lady Helen Oppenheimer, theologian
Rev Canon Peter Pilkington, former High Master St Paul's School and
    Chairman of the Broadcasting complaints committee
Stuart Rock, Editor *Director*
Kenneth Rose, historian and journalist
Sue Slipman, Director *National Council for One Parent Families*
Carole Stone, TV presenter
Professor Norman Stone, Professor Modern History, Oxford University
Angus Watson, Director of Music, Wells Cathedral School
Lady Victoria Waymouth, interior designer
A. N. Wilson, writer
Sir Peregrine Worsthorne, former Editor *Sunday Telegraph*

We would also like to thank Sebastian Devlin for his help with the
questionnaire and database.

We would also like to thank the following for quotation permission: Chapmans Publishers and Norman Fowler for a short quotation from *Ministers Decide*; Random Century Group and Fiona Pitt-Kethley for nine lines from 'Hate at First Sight' in *Sky Ray Lolly*; Penguin Books and Bill Wyman and Ray Coleman for a short quotation from *Stone Alone* (Viking, 1990 – copyright © Ripple Productions Ltd, 1990); David and Charles and David Shepherd for a short quotation from *The Man Who Loves Giants*; Methuen Books and Brian Cox for a short quotation from *Salem To Moscow*; Redcliffe Press Ltd and Lord Justice Staughton and Sir Allan Green for a short quotation from *When They Were Young*; Pink Floyd Music Publishers Ltd for a short quotation from 'Another Brick in the Wall Part II' by Walters © 1979; Macmillan Publishers and Sir Bernard Lovell for a short quotation from *Astonomer by Chance*; Pelham Books and Fatima Whitbread and Adrianne Blue for a short quotation from *Fatima*. Any inadvertent omissions can be rectified in any future editions.

Introduction

Given the English people's preoccupation with school, it is surprising that this kind of book has not been written before. Only in England can it really matter where one goes to school.

This book has been some time in gestation. At first the idea was to have a plain directory of public schools and famous people. The suggestion came from Bruce Kemble, then education correspondent of the *Daily Express,* now education correspondent of the *Evening Standard.* This doyen of education reporters suggested to the Independent Schools Information Service in the late 1970s that journalists really needed to have a reference book of famous people and where they went to school. The events in November 1990 after Mrs Thatcher's downfall have shown how important schooling can be in national historic events.

Who would have supposed at the beginning of the twentieth century that by the end of it an Etonian education would be such a handicap in the contest for the premiership? It mattered that Douglas Hurd went to Eton and it helped that John Major went to Rutlish Grammar School. In a rather clumsy way Hurd's supporters tried to play his schooling down. What was needed was a lighter, humorous touch — a less dismissive rejoinder of the type Sir Alec Douglas-Home used in 1963 about the 'fourteenth Mr Wilson' which successfully defused the fact that he was himself the fourteenth-generation scion of a privileged family. Instead it was put out that the young Hurd was a farmer's son who grafted for his scholarship to Eton rather than being handed a place on a silver spoon.

Farmer's son he may be, but there was no doubt in Tory MPs' minds that, despite the new found penchant for woolly jumpers, Douglas Hurd to the viewing public personified the Etonian gent. His public persona and previous career of diplomat, mainstream Tory, unflappable Home Secretary, courteous and erudite Foreign Secretary, silver hair and donnish manner, all amplified his upbringing at what is perceived to be the country's most privileged public school. Eton was stamped on him as clearly as if the word had been branded on his forehead. Yet Mr Heseltine's chances were not affected by his public-school background. No one held Shrewsbury against him. If anything, his background was that of a self-made man who had made his fortune – for which he was genuinely respected.

Subconsciously or consciously – but not coincidentally – the British electorate have turned their backs on public-school educated prime ministers. We have to go back nearly thirty years and five prime ministers to Lord Home of the Hirsel to reach the last prime minister who attended a public school. Yet the odds against a state-school-educated Tory prime minister emerging so often from a public-school-dominated Cabinet are overwhelming.

So the arrival at the pinnacle of political power of a Heath and a Thatcher – and indeed of a Wilson and a Callaghan – may be because of a generally held recognition that part of Britain's present difficulties are rooted in a social class structure fostered by a divisive education system. This may have led to a subconscious belief that the prime ministerial saviour will come not from a public school background but from one that will unite all backgrounds. Certainly Mr Major pitched his appeal on a classless society.

Many books have been written about schools and Britain's class system and this is not another one. Although class inevitably plays its part, the focus of this book is on the relationship between the school and the career initially chosen by the pupil. Few books have been written about this and none to our knowledge which concentrates on the successful, notorious and influential.

So the idea that began with a directory went a step further: given a list of schools and famous people who went to them, would any patterns emerge in terms of schools attended and eventual careers chosen?

We would expect Wellington College to turn out soldiers – because it has a military tradition and provides financial help to enable children from military families to attend the school. Army families produce army children. But who could have forecast that such a Conservative bastion as Winchester College would in the first half of this century have turned out so many Labour politicians – Gaitskell, Stafford Cripps, Crossman and Jay – and so many top bankers in the second half? Why did Shrewsbury and Charterhouse produce journalists, Harrow and Westminster actors?

In fact, the best conclusion we can draw from 3,000 and more well-known products of British education is that it is probably coincidence. There are few direct links between any school and a particular career that we could establish apart from Alleyn's School in South London and the theatre (it was founded by the great Elizabethan actor Edward Alleyn and its theatrical tradition was maintained by the late Michael Croft, the founder of the National Youth Theatre); Wellington and the

Army (for the reasons stated above) and Millfield for sport and other specialist schools for art and ballet. By and large the famous musicians in this book have not been educated at specialist music schools.

The choice of the 3,000 or so names in this book is unashamedly and inevitably subjective. The idea for the book had moved from its public-school origins to encompass all schools – independent and state. It would include, for example, pop musicians as well as classical ones and sporting heroes of the present as well as those of the past.

To make our choice we started with the birthday lists in *The Times* and the *Independent* during the calendar year 1990, noting down the names really known to the three of us – the two authors and Angela Devlin, Tim's wife and business partner, the book's researcher. We gave added weight to young people and women mentioned in the lists as it seemed to us that there were greater odds against their being included in them and their inclusion was therefore an especial mark of recognition.

We then checked our list with the names cropping up repeatedly in the national press throughout 1990 and the first half of 1991. We looked out for the numerous newspaper profiles and watched out particularly for the first woman, first black and first anything. We listed more than 3,000 names and the names of their schools (where we could find them in published directories and newspaper reports). If not *the* top 3,000, our directory includes most of the best-known personalities in the country today who were educated in the UK. We decided early on not to include those educated in secondary schools abroad. Our main criteria were that the people chosen should be alive (up until the summer of 1991), well known to the newspaper-reading and TV-viewing public or that they should have made some special national contribution in their chosen job, activity or profession. Some of the famous asked not to be included and we have respected this.

We subdivided the list into broad career categories which led us to the chapter headings in this book. Most categories are straightforward but Public Life (Chapter Eleven) is a broad generic including royalty, trade unionists, civil servants and chief constables, as well as those at the top of charitable organisations. We checked our lists with well-known people in the various categories and tribute is paid to them in the acknowledgements. We found the *Equitable Schools Book 1991* by Klaus Boehm and Jenny Lees-Spalding (published by Papermac) an invaluable guide to the famous people who were educated at the leading independent schools. Sadly there is no equivalent for state schools, and some famous names have not been included simply because we could not discover where they went to school. In a few cases we have entered the general location of the school when we have been able to find it.

We sent out the questionnaire in May 1991 to just over 3,000 people and were amazed to get a more than 50 per cent response. We had in fact predicted a 10 per cent response at best, given that so many people – particularly the well-known – are bothered repeatedly with questionnaires.

This good response shows not just the influence of our publisher, Christopher Sinclair-Stevenson, who personally took the trouble to top and tail each letter (and knew so many people himself), but also the extent to which people are prepared to talk and write about their schooldays. Of the 1,608 who replied, many extended their answers and seven out of ten were happy to be interviewed.

The meat of the book emerged from the responses and in particular those, and there were many, who wrote about events and personalities connected with their school. We followed them up with interviews which went further than, but also concentrated on, the influence of school on their later career.

Some would say that it is not a school's job to influence people in their choice of career or even to prepare them for a particular career – the 'we are not fodders for industry' argument. But we start from the premise that schools cannot be divorced from the charge of preparing pupils for their working lives. Just as they should be preparing them for a world of increased leisure, so they should be educating them and stimulating them for the world of work. Some talented people like David Puttnam, the film director, said of his school (Minchenden Grammar, London) 'I was unconscious – I honestly did not think it had anything to do with me. I was merely condemned to spending a certain number of years passing time and avoiding trouble.' Yet at another grammar school, Northgate in Ipswich, during the same period, Trevor Nunn, the theatre director, found the staff 'unusually interested and talented as well as being encouraging'.

Where there was a failure of the school to relate, how much of this failure was its fault and how much the pupil's? We probably get a one-sided account in this book and a sequel could well be the schools' reactions to some of the tales described.

There have been many changes in British education since the War. One of the facts that emerged from our survey is that quite a few may have been confused by them. We had a number of people replying to us saying that they had been contacted in error since they went to a grammar school rather than a maintained school; we had a few writing to us in similar vein who said they went to a public school not an 'independent' one. How idiosyncratic can nomenclature in an education system become?

We have used *public schools* to describe the top fee-paying schools of which the Heads belong to either the Headmasters' Conference (HMC) or Girls' Schools Association. We have used *independent schools* to describe the plurality of schools which subscribe to the Independent Schools Information Service. We have used *grammar schools* to denote the grammar schools that were maintained by local education authorities and *state schools* to cover the generality of state schools including the old elementary schools, the secondary modern, technical and comprehensive schools.

But whatever the changes, education is a human process: the contact between teachers and taught. For those who were influenced by school towards their chosen career, was it school *per se*, the body of teachers, the headteacher or a particular teacher, their contemporaries or the pupil's family that played the most formative part?

Perhaps the most crucial question asked in our simple list was whether or not on balance successful people were happy at school. This book is about happiness and success at school. It is about why school failed David Puttnam and others like him and succeeded with Trevor Nunn and many more like him. It is about whether success or failure at school – or school at all – really matters. From a simple directory it has evolved into a commentary on different schools at different stages of a turbulent century of education, made up of hundreds of individual secondary school experiences between 1930 and 1980. It is a tale of taken opportunities and missed opportunities. We believe there are simple lessons for the future of the education system from the tales of its past products.

Almost all schools now have prospectuses describing their services. Many of these publications talk about treating each child as an individual. So many claim this that it is in danger of becoming a truism. But this book shows what it means to educate children as individuals and what happens when schools fail to do so.

1 Acting

Chance at school and the release from shyness, illness or private grief often proved with hindsight to be the turning point which set so many future stars on their dramatic road to Damascus.

Of the influence of Harrow on his career Michael Denison told us: 'It was quite unintentional on the part of the school and not recognised by myself as significant at the time.'

Reminiscing a scene which could have come out of a Noël Coward play he said: 'When I was doing my prep one evening at the age of 15, the late Dorian Williams (in those days Harrow's best actor) came into my study and enquired whether I would like to be Aunt Emily in the house play.

'"Why me?" I asked. (I had done no acting anywhere at this point.) "I just thought you might enjoy it," he replied.

'I did and until my voice broke I became Harrow's female impersonator.'

He had found by accident a role – a niche for himself.

As part of a house initiation rite one autumn evening in the early 1950s, in 'Cooks' or 'Du Boulays' as it was more poshly known – one of the Houses on the hill set furthest from Winchester College – the young Tim Brooke-Taylor, aged 13, was thrust reluctantly into the limelight and asked to perform for his supper. The whole house was assembled ready to applaud or jeer, including the housemaster, a rowing enthusiast with yellowing grey hair known as 'Sponge' Walker.

'One of the things which seemed so unfair was that the least capable person was picked on to do something,' Tim remembers. 'I was miserable. My father had just died. I'd come down from the north of England. I was the youngest in the house. The school wasn't part of my family history and I find the whole thing pretty cruel even to this day.

'At prep school I had done a few conjuring tricks. I could shuffle cards then people had to guess the right card – you know the sort of thing. Anyway it went completely wrong and I dropped the cards and everyone laughed. I was mortified. I'm still not sure how much was cruel laughter and how much affectionate.

'Then I tried another trick I had which involved a coin disappearing from a matchbox: it fell on the floor and everyone laughed again even louder when the second trick went wrong. Some instinct made me foul up every subsequent trick as if the "comedy" had been intended.'

The future star of The Goodies remembers to this day 'that sudden satisfying heady feeling as I realised I could make everybody laugh.' Afterwards he was asked to do this act again and again. Like the court jester of old, his role was to make his masters laugh.

Another clown from early childhood was Brian Cox. In his autobiography he says, 'I was regarded by others at St Michael's Junior Secondary School, Dundee – teachers and pupils – as a bit of a clown. My earliest playground memory was of being forced to fight a boy regarded as backward and a simpleton. I shall never forget the look in his eyes as I was being goaded to beat the shit out of him. The only way to avoid both our agonies was for me to turn the whole thing into a joke, so I switched my attention from the unfortunate lad and began grappling with an imaginary opponent, hurling myself on the ground in a frenzy of rage, beating the living daylights out of nothing, reducing everyone around me, including the would-be victim, to hysterical laughter.

'Circumstances from birth had conditioned me to perform. Schoolboy cruelty forcing me to play the fool, I developed a persona which buffeted me against the pains of childhood.' (*Salem to Moscow: An Actor's Odyssey*: Methuen 1991)

'I wasn't that good at anything', Geraldine James told us, 'until I discovered I could make people laugh.' Now perhaps better known for tragic parts in dramas like *Jewel in the Crown,* she says, 'It started with fooling about with a bent pencil and pencil-tin and making the rest of the class laugh.' Becoming a form clown became a niche for her. It was one way of getting over the devastation when her parents divorced. Her friends used to tell her: 'You can't be depressed – you're so funny!'

She remembers the turning point: 'So, aged 12, I was naturally cast as the Artful Dodger in the form play. In those days Downe House (the girls' independent school near Newbury) had form plays in the dining room on Friday afternoons. They removed the large oak table and we rigged up an old curtain on the stage. I was a spikey child with short straight hair. So I found this collapsible hat in the dressing-up cupboard and started performing to the text which was being read out to the whole school. I discovered for the very first time that I could make some 250 girls laugh. I loved hearing a whole audience laughing and have actually spent my whole career trying to re-find that moment and I never have!'

Colin Baker, one of the future Dr Whos, attended St Bede's College, a Roman Catholic grammar school in Manchester, although he lived in Rochdale and had to travel twenty miles a day on four different buses, spending four hours daily on public transport.

'I didn't know anyone when I got to the school and Matron, a benevolent nun, saw me as a boy with a problem and used to tell me to come and have a cup of tea with her at breaktime. I used to entertain her with conjuring tricks. I did a different one every day. So I suppose the performer was always in me.'

But when it came to speaking in debates, he was tongue-tied. 'We used to have a compulsory debating society and if you didn't stand up and say something the headmaster would say: "Haven't heard you saying much lately, Baker!" I was absolutely terrified of speaking in debates. I was always all right saying someone else's words but no good at all with my own words. But in acting, the fact that I was being someone else released me.'

One who never got over his nervousness and had a pronounced stammer until after he left school was Rod Hull of Emu fame who went to Sheerness Secondary Modern School shortly after the end of the last War.

'I was a particularly nervous boy', he told us, 'and suffered from a stutter. In the main my contemporaries were sympathetic, as were the majority of the teachers. But there was one exception.

'My school was mainly sports-orientated (specially boxing which was completely alien to me). This guy was a new chap – I'm not sure that he had any teaching qualifications but he was really the rugby teacher and liked being on the rugby field. If he had to teach any academic lessons he had to create a diversion, partly to cover up and partly to relieve his own boredom.

'This particular teacher would get me to read aloud to the class and if I faltered over a word, the rest of the class had instructions to throw whatever they wanted at me. They threw the books we were doing in class at me and it bloody well hurt both physically and mentally.'

Of course what Rod Hull needed was a good dose of elocution. Miss Edith Clements of Bexhill-on-Sea is the elocution teacher to whom the Thespian world should be most grateful.

'It was she', wrote Dame Wendy Hiller from the hospital bed where she was recovering at the age of 79 from a hip operation, 'who during her weekly visits to the school opened up for me the world of poetry. We also learnt by heart quite a deal of the Bible. We didn't speak of posh accents. One spoke good English. No one was as slovenly or careless in speech as today.' Although she does not remember when or what decided her to go into the theatre, Dame Wendy remembers that her school, Winceby House, Bexhill, did a lot of Shakespeare and that she was a very impressive Macbeth.

Louise Jameson also remembers her elocution teacher with gratitude. 'Mrs Anne Tipping was just brilliant. One day she rang up my mother and said, "Your daughter's got enough talent for private lessons. I'm not touting for business or anything – it's up to you, but she has a love of words and is so responsive." So I went to her for private lessons.

'I had a very bad twitch in my early teens. The doctor told my parents that I should not be put under any pressure, hence Braeside, a private school for Young Ladies in Buckhurst, even though I passed my 11 plus. So my natural tendency towards laziness was fuelled.

'Mrs Tipping wouldn't put up with this. When I turned up for the third lesson in a row without having done any work, she absolutely let rip. Both she and I ended up in tears, but during the course of her tirade, I remember her shouting, "You're so very foolish – you could be one of England's finest actresses!"

'I was astounded that anyone had that much faith in me and it was a real turning point in my self-esteem and therefore in my achievements.'

'Probably the finest 14-year-old Shylock of his generation!' This line in a newspaper review was written about a young Jew of Venice who appeared at the Godolphin Hall, Helston, with locks reaching below the knees – fashioned by enough crepe hair to stuff a mattress – squeaking in a strained unbroken voice.

Whether it was a serious compliment or written with a slight hint of mockery, the local theatre critic on that Cornish weekly inspired John Clark, a schoolboy evacuee from West Ham, to reach for the professional stage and to become one of the country's best-known film directors, Bryan Forbes.'

Fifty years later he recalled with the aid of his memoirs the heady feeling on reading that review:

'From that moment I knew I had to act. But I didn't know how to go about it. So I wrote to everyone I could think of in the *Radio Times* enclosing this ludicrous rave review. The people I wrote to included Tommy Handley, Ben Lyon, Sir Malcolm Sargent and the entire cast of *Happydrome*.

'I had several polite replies but one man said he would see me. This was Lionel Gamblin – the voice of *British Movietone News* and the voice that called "STOP-P-P!!" to London's traffic in the programme *In Town Tonight*. He later told me that the "sheer nerve" of that letter attracted him and he felt he had to see me. I was on his doorstep at the BBC's Bush House immediately after I received his reply.

'He gave me a proper audition and a mike test. For some reason I chose to read Lincoln's *Gettysburg Address*.

'He was obviously impressed. He took me to tea at the Aldwych Brasserie where there was gypsy music playing and genteel matrons up from the country.

'Lionel said there was already an actor called John Clark who played *Just William* – he later married Lynn Redgrave. He told me that Equity, the actors' trade union, forbade two actors of the same name. Then he wrote down alternatives on the back of a menu.

'"What about Forbes? That's an old theatrical name. And yes, Bryan with a Y – that'll look better on the playbills."

'I could already visualize my new name up in lights. If he had suggested that I call myself Nigel Hitler I would have accepted it. So from then on I was Bryan Forbes.'

Gilbert and Sullivan inspired many to great heights. Asked which particular event at school influenced him, Sir Michael Hordern replied: 'The annual G and S production'. He told us, 'At the end of the Christmas term, Brighton College put on a Gilbert and Sullivan opera. Even looking back now as a professional, I can see that we did it very well. It was taken very seriously and indeed took up a lot of time.' His starring roles included the very model of a modern Major General in *The Pirates of Penzance* and the Duchess in *The Gondoliers*.

However, after school he never contemplated becoming a professional actor. He got a job selling desks and blackboards for the Educational Supply Association. He persevered with amateur theatricals and became a professional actor at the age of 25.

Alec McCowen said that there was no consideration or expectation that anyone at his school, Skinners Grammar, Tunbridge Wells, would choose to become an actor. But he had always wanted to act and 'taking part in a school production of *HMS Pinafore* confirmed my choice of career.'

The usefulness of any early performance in public cannot be overrated. Donald Pleasance recalled many theatrical events at Ecclesfield Grammar

School, Yorkshire – a beacon of light after many years of dull backward schooling in Lincolnshire – and in particular 'being elected a Labour MP at a mock election.' Rowan Atkinson said the many school plays he did at St Bees, Cumbria, undoubtedly encouraged him to believe in his ability to perform.

School revues set comedian Bill Oddie on his satirical path. He said: 'At King Edward's, Birmingham, there was a tradition of a school revue – songs and sketches – begun by Nathan Joseph who became a record producer and theatrical impresario. I auditioned for his revue and then I suppose helped to create the tradition by writing and appearing in the second show a couple of years later. This outlet for comedy material and performance gave me a taste which I was able to follow up at Cambridge Footlights and eventually in theatre, TV and radio.'

Tom Courtenay thanks Kingston High School, Hull, for his first experiences of speaking in public, 'mainly reading the lesson in school prayers, which I loved to do.'

There is a biblical background, too, to the training of the future Hercule Poirot. David Suchet recalls: 'The main events at Wellington' (the Somerset public school) 'were being cast in performing the title role in *Macbeth* directed by Mr M. J. Storr – who then pushed me to join the National Youth Theatre – and reading the Bible in Chapel – realising in both cases that I could hold an audience's attention.'

Roy Hudd, Croydon Secondary Tech, wrote: 'We had to write a prayer for "ensemble". I had to read mine to the school. Getting through this made me realise I could face *any* audience.'

Often it took two to bring the acting talent to life. More than half the actors who replied to our survey said they had been influenced by a particular member of staff. At Monmouth School a teacher wrote on Victor Spinetti's report, referring to a reading of *Hamlet* in class: 'He has the dramatic instinct.'

When Ron Moody was at Southgate County School a rather prescient teacher of English said, 'after I had been reading Shylock with more than a hint of character: "There is the only actor in class." I was astonished and a career as an actor was a very remote possibility.'

Who were these discerning and supportive teachers? Miss Evelyn Ward still lives in Cardiff. She was the English teacher at Tenby Grammar

School, which used to be called Green Hill. She discovered Kenneth Griffith.

She put on *Richard of Bordeaux* for his benefit. She remembers: 'Kenneth was quite remarkable. He hadn't done anything significant before that. He had a very good voice. The play was put on in a little theatre which used to be the old cinema and was well received. The local press went to town on Kenneth's performance.' The play had had a West End success with John Gielgud. It was the making of Griffith. Miss Ward told us, 'That play probably did set him on the road to success. He left the school after that and could not be in any more productions. He went to a very ordinary job in an ironmonger's shop in Cambridge and as I said goodbye to him, I added, "For goodness sake don't go joining an amateur group." He took my advice and turned professional.'

Mr Burton was an unfrocked priest who got a job as a drama and divinity teacher at Latymer Grammar School, Edmonton. He was so impressed by a young girl's Bible readings in class that he offered her elocution lessons to rid her of her cockney accent.

Eileen Atkins told *The Times Saturday Review* (22 June 1991): 'I used to meet him in the bus every morning on the way to school and we would separate as we approached the gates. I was too innocent and he was too wise to do anything improper. Yet in a way he was a lover: he opened me up and changed my view of the world. He was brilliant. I became the big cheese in the school drama group; he took me to see *King John* in Regent's Park with my mother as chaperone, of course.'

The article goes on to describe how, sensing her potential, Mr Burton took Miss Atkins to an office typing pool and pointed out forcibly that this would be her fate unless she used her acting talents.

Eileen Atkins wrote to us: 'I wouldn't have known anything about the straight theatre if it hadn't been for my grammar school. My parents only knew that they wanted me to be a tap dancer. There is no one incident – just the fact that one teacher decided to devote himself to helping me. He changed my life. Without him I certainly could not have become an actress!'

Diana Quick was also rescued by a teacher during her time at Dartford Grammar School for Girls. She recounted to us how with a group of other fifth-formers she was caught by her headmistress rehearsing during a private study period for a revue called *The Trials of St Trinian's* which was a send-up of the school.

'The headmistress was very angry and I was called in to see her in her study. She was very reproving and said we should have been working for our "O" levels. But she said that if we promised to leave the play for the moment and concentrate on our exams, we could put it on after the exams were over. I went back and told the mutinous girls and we were all satisfied.

'However, when the end of term came, she absolutely denied she'd ever said such a thing and banned the revue. There was a real mutiny and we all marched out of school on to the playing field. I went home and had a good cry.

'I was all set to leave school when I was 15. I was going to go abroad and widen my horizons. I had done eleven subjects at "O" level and wanted to do English as well as maths at "A" level but the system was too inflexible to allow me to do both.

'I had no careers advice at all and no burning vocation, though I spent my entire time acting. I was doing German, Latin and English at "A" level with Logic as an extra examination subject.'

Diana would undoubtedly have left school had it not been for Mary Davis, a teacher who had helped her with her drama. 'Mary saw that I was bored and she came up to me one day and told me that she had spoken to the headmistress and they had decided to enter me for the Oxbridge exams the next autumn. This was unprecedented but she took charge of me and one other girl and we were removed from formal classes and given two tutorials a week. Then on Saturdays the three of us would go off to London theatres. We often used to go to a matinée in the afternoon as well as an evening performance. We saw everything at the Royal Court and it became my great ambition to work there.'

Meanwhile, her Oxford acting contemporary David Wood, actor, producer and children's writer, was in the Lower VIth at Chichester High School for Boys which had an acting tradition. David puts this down both to the Chichester Festival Theatre and to Mr Norman Siviter, the English master, who was known as Spiv.

'When I was in the Lower VIth, I worked as one of his assistants in the school library. One day Spiv asked me what I was going to do when I left "this dump". I replied that he already knew I wanted to be an actor. He, without dismissing this basic ambition, said I should think beyond that, and work towards becoming a producer/director/creator within the theatre industry, rather than simply act.

'His advice betrayed his own sense of lost fulfilment. He clearly wished he could have had the chance to turn the clock back and enter the theatre himself. He managed partly to satisfy his theatrical nature by directing outside amateur productions, and by becoming secretary of the Friends of Chichester Festival Theatre.

'He subsequently arranged an audition for me to become an extra in the 1966 Festival, when I played a soldier in *Saint Joan* and a policeman in *The Workhouse Donkey*, a wonderful early experience of professional theatre. I am eternally grateful to him for this and indeed I always remembered his advice to widen my horizons, and like to think he would have been pleased with my progress.

'Indeed I know he was. Shortly before he died, I went back to the Festival Theatre to direct my own productions of my plays *The Owl and the Pussycat went to See* and *The Selfish Shellfish*. His gruff greeting concealed, I hope, his pleasure, which he must have found in his other protégés – Howard Brenton, the playwright, David Horlock, the theatre director, and, last but by no means least (although Spiv never lived to see this), Adrian Noble's appointment as Director of the Royal Shakespeare Company.'

Writing about his time at Alleyn's School, Dulwich, before he was expelled by 'Soapy' Hudson, the headmaster, and went to St Paul's, Julian Glover says: 'There was one influence only – Michael Croft. He was entirely responsible for my becoming an actor. Many of us will say the same thing. The school was actually unhelpful at the time. Michael found that I could read aloud well. I auditioned for Mark Antony and got the part. Change of life. *Iolanthe* followed and that confirmed my quite outré decision to become an actor. Hamlet I lost to John Stride, who was the next to leave Alleyn's with the intention of going professional. We are legion!'

Simon Ward told us: 'It was entirely my own decision to name Alleyn's as my first choice school above the more prestigious Dulwich College. A fellow wolf-cub had told me one evening around the camp fire that his brother was at Alleyn's. They did these great plays with a wild party on the last night when everyone got to throw buckets of beer over each other and the staff. That sounded promising to me.

'It seems to me that most schools are a mixture of fun and fear for most pupils. Certainly it was so for me. However, to this day I know that the course of my life was directed by two masters who broke through my crust of apathy and terror and helped me to dare. A little!

'In the six years that Michael Croft taught at Alleyn's before he left to write full-time and to found and run the National Youth Theatre, he had the most profound influence on a generation of boys. An interest in the theatre was born in the most unlikely, and at first often unwilling, pupils. And certainly not just in acting. They became art directors, technicians, dramatists, directors. They work in the film industry in Hollywood and the music business in Europe. They all seem to have retained the down-to-earth practicality which Croft imbued, along with the enthusiasm and the passion.

'The reason why Croft had come to teach at Alleyn's was because Edward Upward was Head of the English Department. He became my house-master and English master. There could be no greater contrast between the two teachers and their methods. Croft would search for his converts among the smokers in the bicycle sheds or from the ranks of the feared 5H; Upward could only speak to the converted and so classes were often painful. Knowing of his friendships with Isherwood, Auden and MacNeice, I was too much the romantic, or snob, to join in the abuse of a gentle, rather broken man and finally I think he came to trust me enough to try to teach me something.'

If teachers were encouraging, how supportive were headteachers? Rita Tushingham at La Sagesse Convent School, Liverpool, put on shows at lunchtime but 'the Mother Superior told me to refrain from doing so as it was not an acceptable way to behave.'

'My headmaster did his very best to put me off my chosen career and it took a long time for my confidence to return,' actor John Hurt told us, speaking of Lincoln School. 'I never fitted into the school and must have been an academic headache at the time. But he was not sympathetic to the arts – or should I say, to those who wished to practise them professionally.'

'I met such resistance over my choice of career,' said Jane Lapotaire, referring to Northgate Grammar School, Ipswich, in the 1950s, 'that it made me even more determined to become an actor.'

But cases of obstructive headmasters and schools are few and far between and sometimes opposition was meant to spare the child a poor performance.

Sir Alec Guinness fell in love with the theatre at the age of 10 or 11. He wrote to us: 'So I suppose I sought out in school life anything that tended towards performing on the whole subconsciously.' But his talent was not immediately spotted at his prep school, Pembroke Lodge, Eastbourne. The headmaster hindered his choice of career 'by refusing to let me be in the school play because he thought I'd never be an actor.'

Sir Alec added in his note to us: 'Or did he *help* by putting iron in my soul?' Of his next school, Roborough School, Eastbourne, he wrote: 'I think they spotted a latent talent. . . .'

One in seven actors who replied to us put down the Head of the school as among the formative influences on their career.

Stan Rees took up his post as headmaster of Pontardawe Grammar School when Sian Phillips was there. 'For a Welsh headmaster he was very witty, jokey and theatrical,' she said. He allowed her time off classes to do broadcasting and even gave her private coaching lessons in English so that she could go to university. Her parents insisted on this before and as a condition of putting her on the stage. 'The whole ethos of this school', recalls Sian, 'was that education was for its own sake and we really believed it – and I still do.'

'As I remember it', says Gwen Watford, 'I entered Bal Edmund School in October 1940 and later progressed to Glenthorne (both in St Leonards-on-Sea). The Principal was Miss Dorothy Catt, who in the four years I was in her care educationally transformed my life. I had studied from the age of six to become a concert pianist, and when at the age of 16 it was found that I did not have sufficient talent to pursue this career Miss Catt re-channelled me into the theatre, and did not rest until I was successfully launched in this field.'

Rula Lenska's experience at the Ursuline Convent, Westgate-on-Sea, illustrates some of the main points of this chapter so far – the influence of the school, the Head and the chance event:
'My English mistress, Sister Mary of the Incarnation, who later became headmistress, had a very definite influence on my career – though I was already well decided on what I was going to be. She encouraged me to start a dramatic club at the school and allowed me to direct while in the Sixth Form.'
Her drama teacher, Rosalinde Boyde, 'gave me a true belief in myself and in my ability and was a brilliant and dedicated elocution teacher. She also encouraged me to explore literature and poetry and stayed a close and supportive mentor until her death two years ago.'
Rula recalls her first 'mini-break' when she was head of the dramatic society. 'I was given the privilege of looking after Jack Warner who came to speak as the guest of honour at our annual prize-giving. He consequently gave me a small part in two episodes of *Dixon of Dock Green* and thus procured me my Equity card.'

However, another actress, Anna Calder-Marshall, found that her convent school – the Convent of the Immaculate Heart of Mary, near Horsham

– was less supportive. She told us, 'The nuns were very shocked that I wanted to act because they believed acting was no way to get to heaven. This made me want to act and increased my spiritual fervour because I didn't believe them. My parents had the greatest influence on my career, because of their outlook and their beliefs and enthusiasm for the Arts. They encouraged my sister and me in verse-speaking and we actually started a drama movement within the school. We practised Stanislavsky improvisations while other kids were playing games. We put on plays. In the end the school was pleased with our efforts.'

Perhaps the most unlikely product and admirer of Catholic schooling is Samantha Fox, the model, page three girl, actress and singer who grew up in Crouch End and attended St Gilda's RC Junior School at the age of 10 and a year later went to St Thomas More RC School.

'At St Gilda's', she told us, 'there was this amazing and trendy priest called Father Dennis who came in to do plays he had written himself. He didn't wear one of those things they usually wear round their necks but instead wore a score of music he'd written.'

When Samantha was 13 at St Thomas More, she came under the influence of her second mentor, Miss Davis, the music and drama teacher, who also taught craft and made clothes and featured Sam in her fashion shows. She inspired her to do music as a GCE option and predicted correctly that she would be famous.

'I always wanted to be a star and was always being told off for day-dreaming and practising signing my autograph. I had these wild dreams about being chased by dinosaurs – especially Brontosaurus Rex – and these dreams gave me ideas for my poems. I had a wild imagination which worried my teachers. All this English helped me in my career because I now write my own songs and am thinking of going back to college.'

A portent of the impending end to her school career came at 14 during rehearsals for the school play – *Grease*. Miss Fox, taking the main female lead, was over-inspired by the sequence in the film where Olivia Newton-John takes her cigarette out of her mouth and looks at John Travolta. Sam did this so suggestively and with such a wiggle of the hips, that she was told to tone it down.

At 16 Samantha appeared topless on Page 3 of the *Sun* a few months after telling her headmaster she was leaving school to take up a modelling career. She is still grateful for the strictness of her RC schools. They taught her self-discipline and for that reason she would send her own children to Catholic schools.

Paul Raymond, the impresario of striptease, is also the product of a convent school. Until the age of seven he was brought up by nuns, before progressing to St Francis Xavier's College, Liverpool, and finally to Glossop Grammar. Although this book concentrates on the secondary school, it is hard to pass over this early influence:

'What I learned from the nuns at the Mount Pleasant Convent (Liverpool) was politeness. I'm a very polite man deep down inside and this is from the nuns. You know what the Jesuits say about giving them a child until he is seven – well, those nuns taught me to walk along on the outside if I took a girl out, and to open the door for women – and I still do those things now. I had a good grounding socially, if not academically.'

Raymond is still a practising Catholic. Although the nuns who taught him might be horrified by his shows, he is not sure that modern nuns today would be. 'We've often had Catholic priests coming to the Revue Bar. At one point they weren't allowed to come to music halls, so they used to come backstage and watch the show from there.'

Nearly 40 per cent of actors in our survey put down 'family' as a formative influence – the second highest percentage of the categories in the book. But sometimes that influence could be a negative one, as in the case of Angela Pleasance, the daughter of Donald Pleasance, whose schooling was nearly sufficiently unorthodox for us to place her in the penultimate chapter of this book.

She wrote to us: 'It is impossible for me to reply to your questions due to the extremely unaverage education I received.' Her formative years were spent in a school (Pinewood School, Hertfordshire) where she boarded from the age of two-and-a-half as her parents were always touring the repertory theatres – which must almost be a record. The school was run on the principles of A. S. Neill.

When, however, we contacted her, she told us, 'I spent my whole childhood determined not to go into the theatre at any cost. To me, to be an actor meant you couldn't be with your parents and you went all over the place.

'The headmistress of Pinewood was an amazing woman called Elizabeth Strachan – "Strix" – who was both a vegan and an atheist. We actually used to run away to go to church because we thought it must be an exciting place if we were not allowed to go!

'It really was a most amazing school full of kids from borstals, kids from all over the world, seriously mental, subnormal kids and emotionally disturbed ones.

'There were about fifty children in this huge rambling Tudor house. Strix could never bear to turn anybody away and in the end the school went bankrupt because she admitted so many children for nothing. The assistant headmistress was Jomo Kenyatta's first wife Edna.

'Strix couldn't afford many teachers so we were taught by girls who had become pregnant and there were always dozens of little babies around.

'When I left Pinewood I was like a female Mowgli. I could climb trees but I could hardly read and was at one stage classified as educationally subnormal. When I sat the 11 plus I wrote only five words and one of them was "March" – I know that because I couldn't spell it.

'So off I went to Hoddesdon Secondary Modern which was supposed to be one of the roughest schools in the country. In fact I was very happy there. It was full of East End overspill kids from London council estates. I had been completely deprived of literature but because of Strix I loved arithmetic.

'I had an extraordinary outlook on life. I had been educated in a free world. People were amazed when I could shin up ropes in a few seconds. I was a rough tearaway and spoke with a cockney accent you could cut with a knife.

'I lived with a family on one of the council estates where the only things to read were magazines like *Woman's Own, Titbits* and *Reveille*. They used to call it "River Alley" and I was 21 before I learnt how to say it properly.

'As I said, I was brilliant at arithmetic. They didn't know what to do with me at school so they used to send me out to measure things – like the river.

'We all had Saturday jobs. Me and my friend Shirl had a job at Woolworths. We felt sorry for the old people and the children who were poor, so we sold them a quarter of a packet of biscuits for a penny. I felt like Robin Hood until the manager discovered the tills were incorrect. He gave us all an arithmetic test which only Shirl and I passed. All the others failed and they got the sack.

'When I was 15 and could leave school legally, I got a job sticking labels on bottles and I wrote to my father saying that this was what I wanted to do.'

Angela's father was horrified and sent her to a progressive school in Swiss Cottage which she hated. She was so backward that she was placed in a class of girls who were two years younger than herself. She failed all six "O" levels, scoring only 10 per cent in maths.

'My education had prepared me for nothing. By this time my father had remarried and my stepmother was a nursing sister so they thought I might like to be a nurse. I went to Chiswick Poly and did a pre-nursing course. I taught myself anatomy and physiology and got "O" levels in them.

'But I didn't want to be a nurse, so I went to France as an *au pair* because I wanted to learn French. While I was there I suddenly thought: "I am going to be an actress."

'I got an interview with Joan Littlewood in Stratford East. I used a false name, I stood on the stage and sang *Tiptoe through the Tulips* in a broad cockney accent. They all clapped and I was asked to come back tomorrow. My father was very upset when I told him I had used a false name and he said, "I would be very honoured if you'd use my name."'

In contrast, there were those who could not get away from their families even at school. *The King and I* star Deborah Kerr told us that her career as an actress and film star was influenced by 'my aunt who taught drama at Northumberland House, Clifton – drama, dance and elocution lessons had a great effect on the choice of my career.' However, despite her aunt, she was not happy at her school.

Susan Hampshire's mother ran a dancing school in Hammersmith. When she realised that her daughter – later Britain's most famous dyslexic – had a learning problem, she established her own school, recruiting Susan's two elder sisters Jane and Ann as teachers. The Hampshire School (recognised by the Ministry of Education) was a day school for boys and girls in the dance studio near Harrods in Basil Street. It had some distinguished alumni: Anthony Dowell, Director of the Royal Ballet, Tony Elliott, founder and publisher of *Time Out,* and Maina Gielgud, artistic director of the Australian National Ballet.

The event that started Susan's showbusiness career happened as the result of chance. Catching a tube one day with her mother, they bumped into a friend in the film business. She asked if Susan might be interested in a film test. She looked exactly like the child needed to play a young Jean Simmons in *The Woman in the Hall.* She got the part and loved every minute of it.

'I was lucky to be in the right place at the right time,' says Roger Law, the puppeteer of *Spitting Image* fame, who grew up in the Fens, a place which he describes as anti-authoritarian, full of peasants rich and poor who had no contact with middle-class culture and values.

'They saw no point to education,' he told us, 'because they knew what they would end up doing in life. In my own case I was kicked out of Littleport Secondary Modern (Isle of Ely) after three years. I had two choices: working (i.e. hod-carrying) or not working. I chose the latter and went to Cambridge School of Art aged 14, with no qualifications except a handful of drawings.

'Of course such a thing would no longer be possible. Nor would the fact that they also taught me some English, history and French while I was there. But I had arrived without the sort of preconceptions which encumbered the better-educated who also attended the Art School. The Principal just gave us books and suggested we read them. For me this was marvellous: I was able to enjoy the things which others had rammed down their throats.'

On the theme of being in the right place at the wrong time, actress Janet Maw wrote: 'At the age of 17 or 18 at Worthing High School for Girls, I was playing Medea in the school production along with boys from the neighbouring boys' high school. It was a large cast and a big responsibility. We were rehearsing the play and on the day of the dress rehearsal – as centre-forward in the Sussex junior hockey team – I was invited to Crystal Palace sports ground for the South of England squad selections.

'Both activities were a passion and I was so torn – I really wanted to attend both events. I chose the dress rehearsal partly because of the role I was playing and partly through no wish to let the cast down.

'With the hockey it was just myself really. However, I'm not sure how much of a career you can have as a hockey player. So I think I made the right choice.'

Sam Walters, Director of the Orange Tree Theatre, Richmond, had to make an equally difficult and, in hindsight, momentous decision. He was captain of cricket at Felsted. A match was cancelled due to rain and rescheduled on to the one day of the year when the school had an outing to a London theatre to see John Neville as Hamlet at the Old Vic.

He told us, 'I rejected this rescheduling as I realised that games were no longer the be-all and end-all for me. At that time my opposition to the new date for the match was an act of rebellion (supported by some masters). The match was not played.'

A sub-plot to the importance of that dramatic chance event is the theme of confidence – the rise in confidence that successful public performance brings.

Roy Castle's confidence was given a boost when he won the cross-country race four years in succession at Honley Grammar School in Yorkshire.

John Wells, the political mimic famous for his impersonations of Sir Denis Thatcher remembers the moment at Eastbourne College when he was caught mimicking Mr Halliday who had a high fluting voice and a very affected way of speaking.

'His punishment was to make me play Mrs Candour in *The School for Scandal,* which I did in exactly the same voice. It was a great success and this had the effect of making me more confident both at work and on stage. My work improved overnight.'

2 The Armed Services

'You English – you are the only Prussians left.'
    (Chancellor Helmut Schmidt
    to Prime Minister James Callaghan,
    Sovereign's Birthday,
    Horse Guards Parade, June 1978)

Governments keep a wary eye on public expenditure; our armed services, however, remain an aspect of public life and the public services which have been generously funded. The present Government's White Paper *Options for Change* has instigated a debate on this country's defence policy in the post Cold War years. That debate was soon sidetracked into a defence of the regimental traditions of the British Army.

The scalpel of modernity clearly has difficulties with the British body politic. Britain remains in many ways an *ancien régime* state, tender-hearted towards the claims of the autonomous, self-governing institution or corporation, the college, the Inn of Court, the regiment. Mrs Thatcher and the rule of the major-generals both foundered on the same rock – hostility towards the centre.

This then is the chapter of predestined institutional man. As General Sir Frank Kitson, ex-Stowe and son of a Vice-Admiral, told us: 'School had nothing to do with my choice of a career. I came from a service family and was destined for the services anyway, school or no school.'

Our survey covers 55 high-ranking officers in the three armed services. Nearly three out of four went to independent schools, and most of them boarded. 84 per cent were happy at school – an average which is one of the highest in the categories in this book. The boys' boarding school was a dominant influence on them, especially Wellington, Winchester, Radley, Sherborne, Exeter School and Haileybury.

Winchester features oddly here, having educated both Field Marshal Lord Carver, who was unhappy there, and General Sir Hugh Beach who said: 'Winchester's ethos was hugely anti-military. That I survived forty years in the Army was due solely to family (three generations of males all in the Army) and the fact that I grew up in 1941.'

One in five of our officers could not think of anyone who had particularly influenced them at school. They were either predestined or drawn by the War into the armed services. Cheshire VC is probably our best-known wartime hero. But Lord Cheshire told us that nothing at Stowe influenced his choice of career: the War came when he was finishing at Oxford.

But many were influenced by particular teachers and by the Officer Training Corps or the Combined Cadet Force, or simply by the discipline of their school to go into the armed services. The combination of these forces at work influenced their choice of career. This fits the pattern of the whole book, with just under half of the entire sample saying that their career was influenced by school.

First, more of predestined man: Vice-Admiral Sir Jock Slater, Allied Commander-in-Chief Channel and Commander-in-Chief Eastern Atlantic in 1991, decided to join the Navy in 1945 when he was seven. The years at Edinburgh Academy and then at Sedbergh did not dim this enthusiasm.

Others decided later to go to the Royal Naval College at Dartmouth and again their careers were predestined. These included Admiral of the Fleet Lord Hill-Norton, a former First Sea Lord who was sent to the Royal Naval Colleges at both Dartmouth and Greenwich. By the time he reached secondary education, he was already committed to a naval career. He told us:

'We've had naval officers in the family since 1600! But my family didn't bring any pressure to bear on me to join the Navy. It could have been a subconscious influence – bred in the bone. And my mother's family lived in Portsmouth. When my father died when I was nine we came to Portsmouth to live with my grandmother and my mother and aunt were enmeshed in naval society. But I don't remember meeting any naval officers and I never went down to the dockyard.

'I'll tell you why I joined the Navy: when I was nine I entered a competition in the *Boys' Own* paper. You had to write an essay called *What I want to be for the Rest of my Life*. I wrote that I wanted to be a naval officer – I don't know why – I'd never heard of any of my mother's naval ancestors, so it must have been in the genes. I won a penknife. So I decided that's what I would do.'

Admiral of the Fleet Sir Henry Leach followed Lord Hill-Norton some seven years later to the two Royal Naval Colleges mentioned above and was also First Sea Lord. His father was a naval officer who had lost two sons in infancy. A third had had to withdraw from the Navy because of ill-health. Sir Henry told us:

'I was the naughty one of the family. I had flaming red hair and a temper to match. I worshipped my father: he was a wonderful man but he was not good at explaining things on which he had made up his mind. He always assumed that I would go into the Navy.

'One day when I was about 11 he came home from one of his expeditions abroad and my mother regaled him as usual with a catalogue of my misdeeds. He replied, as he invariably did, 'Oh well, it'll be all right when he's in the Navy!'

'My mother, whom I also adored, turned on him: "That's all very well but have you ever discussed it with the boy?" My father promised to do so that very night.

'He came upstairs to say goodnight to me. There was no discussion. He switched off the light, left the room and closed the door. Then I think his conscience must have pricked him. He cracked open the door and said, "I take it you've no objection to joining the Navy?" shut the door and went downstairs. "I've had the discussion and it's all arranged," he told my mother. Until then I had always wanted to drive an engine.'

Vice-Admiral Sir Peter Ashmore, Chief of the Allied Staff NATO HQ 1970-1972 and a former Master of Her Majesty's Household, was the son of a Vice-Admiral. He said: 'My future career in the Royal Navy was decided when I left Yardley Court (a prep school in Tonbridge, Kent) to join the Royal Naval College at Dartmouth. My father was at that stage serving as a Commander in the Royal Navy, and my brother, one year older than I, had already gone to Dartmouth and gave attractive reports of some of the activities there.'

Admiral Sir Jeremy Black, Deputy Chief of Staff, Commander-in-Chief Naval Command 1989, was predestined for a career at sea almost two centuries before when his ancestor Captain Westcott was killed in command of HMS *Majestic* at the Battle of the Nile in 1798. 'My career', he says, 'was already decided when I went to the Royal Naval College at Dartmouth as a cadet at the age of 13.'

He wrote to us: 'I was seven years old when war was declared in 1939. I lived in Plymouth and was present for the blitz and was, inevitably, very conscious of the Royal Navy. My father had been at sea in his early life, initially under sail, and later through the First World War. The combination of these two influences gave me an early and strong desire to join the Royal Navy.'

Most of our case histories belong to a senior generation who are now in their fifties, sixties and beyond. Admiral Sir Raymond Lygo explained how at Ilford Grammar School: 'A sense of Empire connected to geography helped my patriotic attitude.'

For many the onset of the Second World War was a crucial event in their choice of career. Their careers were dictated to them by events. They found themselves in the armed services and they stayed there.

'There was a war on, so I joined the Army,' said Field Marshal Sir John Stanier, Former Commander-in-Chief of UK Land Forces, ex-Marlborough, 'To my surprise I found I liked it.'

'Everybody was joining the Services. I came from an army family and the War was on,' said Field Marshal Sir Nigel Bagnall, ex-Wellington College and son of a Lieutenant Colonel.

Marshal of the Royal Air Force Sir Michael Beetham, a Major's son, said: 'I witnessed part of the Battle of Britain and Southern England during the school holidays in 1940. It made me want to join the Royal Air Force, which I did as soon as I left St Marylebone Grammar School in London.'

Air Marshal Sir Denis Crowley-Milling was so inspired by Malvern College's engineering workshop that he started initially as an engineer at Rolls Royce. 'But the War changed all that and I took a permanent commission in the Royal Air Force post-War.'

General Sir Harry Tuzo's plans were also changed by the War. 'My original intention (after Wellington College) was to be a barrister or solicitor – influenced strongly by reading Marjoribanks' *Life of Marshall Hall* and Dicey's *Law of the Constitution*. However, World War II overtook me and I became a soldier for forty years.'

Lieutenant General Sir Hugh Cunningham believes the influence of Charterhouse on his career was negative rather than positive. It was because it did not educate him that he stayed on in the Army, becoming a Deputy Chief of Defence Staff and then Lieutenant of the Tower of London. He said: 'I am afraid my Charterhouse days were largely concentrated on games at which I was quite good. In those days I do not think the school thought of me as a pupil worth much effort on the straight educational side. It was the onset of war in 1939 that led me straight into the Army and to some extent the lack of education that kept me there after the War ended!'

Admiral Sir James Eberle says his career was determined during his days at Clifton Preparatory School. 'My wish to go into the Navy, and thus to the Royal Naval College at Dartmouth, was largely influenced by the War (though in a superficial way) – and by the application for Dartmouth of one of my near contemporaries.'

'It was the approach of war,' says General Sir Anthony Farrar-Hockley. His school, Exeter, had a strong tradition of sending boys to Sandhurst and Cranwell. Opportunities were available to glimpse service life in the tales of the Sandhurst boys revisiting the school, and at the army barracks coincidentally adjacent to its buildings. By the age of 14, Sir Anthony had decided on the life of a soldier:

'What you have to realise too is that for people of my generation the Great War was much closer than the Second World War is to young people today. One of my first memories as a child is of asking my mother why all the traffic had stopped – and that was for Armistice Day. Then there were all the exciting films and books about the war – like *Journey's End* and *All Quiet on the Western Front*.

'Several of our schoolmasters had been in World War I and would talk about it if pressed. Our housemaster had been gassed, poor chap.

'Then by the years 1937 to 1938 it became apparent to most of us that war was coming. We boys heard it in grown-up conversations and saw the Nazi Rallies on newsreels. By this time the masters were taking a grave view.

'Just before I was 16, in the summer holidays of 1940, I went off and joined up as a regular soldier. I wasn't interested in exams and I thought it was a waste of time waiting around trying to pass them when I only wanted to join the Army. You had to be 18, so I concealed my age.

'My mother came along and hauled me out of the Army! But she said she'd never do it again. So the next Easter holidays I went and joined up again, this time for seven years under colours. I looked like a very young 18-year-old: I was about the stature I am now but I had a young face.

'I didn't discuss my decision with anyone. The recruiting officer said I'd better go in on a commission and I'd have to wait for my papers for call-up. But I knew I'd have to produce my birth certificate, so I said I wanted to enlist as a regular soldier.

'That was the best thing I ever did. It meant that I worked my way up through the ranks and was lucky enough, through the rapid promotion of wartime, to be a sergeant by the time I was sent to Sandhurst. By having to go through the mill of a non-commissioned officer I had an enormous advantage. As I tell young officers today, I knew what life was like for the private soldier being ordered around by officers still wet behind the ears!'

When it came, the Battle of Britain had an enormous impact. There were few regrets. Air Chief Marshal Sir Robert Freer said: 'In my last year at school I was in what might then have been known as the "civil service" Sixth Form at Gosport Grammar School. However, the influence of the War in general, and of the Battle of Britain in particular, completely overtook any previous and rather vague notions I had about a career. I volunteered for aircrew training on my 18th birthday, and was accepted. In effect, I joined a queue of men all imbued with the same desire – to fly Spitfires.

'When the time came after the War ended to think again about a career, my mind was already made up and I had no hesitation in accepting the permanent commission. It is a decision I have never once regretted.'

And the War lived on in post-war tales: Air Vice-Marshal Sir Michael Armitage, former Head of Defence Intelligence, said: 'School (Secondary Grammar School, Newport, Isle of Wight) was visited by two distinguished RAF officers, who gave a talk about their World War II experiences, and this encouraged several of us to join the Royal Air Force – which I did.'

General Julian Thompson, of the Royal Marines, a Falklands veteran, believes that his contemporaries at Sherborne did not seek deep motives for their actions. 'At least', he said, 'we did not in those days. We were less sophisticated than today's 18-year-olds. My left and right prop in the House rugby football team joined the Royal Marines as National Servicemen. When my time came to choose, I also joined the Royal Marines but as a regular.'

As the Second World War recedes in the consciousness of the armed services and the yuppie, Trimmer's successor, arrives in the Mess, it is worth investigating what other influences beyond the advent of war might influence a young man to turn to the services for a career.

For Group Captain Niall Irving, who became a familiar face on our TV screens as Gulf War Commander in charge of military briefings, it was the incidental attraction of flying to school in Cyprus!

'My earliest recollection of deciding that I wanted to fly as a career occurred when I started flying to King Richard's School in Cyprus from Libya at the age of 11.'

The influence of the individual teacher has been important for many officers. General Sir John Akehurst, who went to Cranbrook School in Kent, said: 'The teacher who taught my favourite subject, English, also ran the school corps and it was the enjoyment of, and some success in, that which guided me towards the Army.'

Sir John was not happy at Cranbrook – an only child unsettled by attending seven schools in the previous two years, he arrived at 11 and says the bullying by both boys and masters was 'pretty horrific'. He admits he probably invited it by his precocity but by the time it had worn off, after about eighteen months, he had turned into a rebel.

'I was a tearaway who enjoyed taking risks. I was always in trouble with authority. But there was one teacher I related to. His name was Saunders and he taught English, which was my favourite subject. He ran the dramatic society and I acted in a lot of plays. But he also ran the Corps and because I got on with him I did well. He was a caricature of Colonel Blimp – he had that style, even the moustache. He made a lot of people nervous but I discovered that his bark was worse than his bite. I think he saw something in me that wasn't in the others and he promoted me to the top of the Corps. In the House I wasn't even a prefect. You could say I was the sergeant major of the Corps and a private soldier in the House, and I think in fact this caused a bit of bother between the masters.

'Saunders was a very important influence on me. Had I not been promoted in the Corps I might have lost confidence. It was a nice little boost to my ego. But I have to say he wasn't such an influence that I left school determined to be a soldier. I had several jobs – bicycle mechanic and a job at the Midland Bank among them – before I joined up and discovered that I thoroughly enjoyed it.'

Major General Richard Clutterbuck, author of many military books and articles, pays tribute to his maths and English masters at Radley who took unlimited trouble with him and influenced him a good deal as his Housemaster was sick with diabetes and contributed very little. 'One of the masters is alive to this day and remains in touch. The other died (also still in touch) in his nineties.'

The late Admiral of the Fleet Lord Fieldhouse, overall Commander during the Falklands War, said he was totally influenced in his choice of career by his teachers and house officers at the Royal Naval College, Dartmouth.

More light was shed on the Dartmouth system of those days by Lord Hill-Norton. The Captain, the equivalent of the headmaster, was a distant figure:

'I had no knowledge of the Captain at all. You have to realise that in those days a boy of 13 would never speak to the Captain and he would never speak to you. You saw him once a week when he would address you as part of a group and he was about as terrifying and as remote as God.

'As for the officers: you had two officers – a first-term officer for the first two years and a second-term officer for the second two years. I disliked the first and thought the second a dull man. The influence upon me was rather the whole *smell* of the place, the way it worked, its ethos. It was the whole procedure whereby four or five hundred boys were trained to be naval officers as they had been for the last hundred years. Except for the thirty or forty civilian officers everything else was penetrated by the Navy. Everyone was in uniform – the Navy was all around you.'

Seven years later Sir Henry Leach arrived at Dartmouth. He soon became disenchanted:

'I had been at St Peter's, the best prep school in Broadstairs, where I was blissfully happy. I was Head of School and Captain of all the sports teams. In the first year at Dartmouth you were always frightened and hungry, but the novelty of the brass buttons and the comical hat got you through it. But it was then that you started to wonder what the hell this was all about. Being young I was keen to get to grips with the Navy. But the things they taught about the Navy weren't the ones that mattered. You'd have a not very good instructor lolling against a massive model of a ship's forecastle and reading out of an extremely dull seamanship manual for an hour. Or you'd have some decrepit old codger telling you how to tie completely inextricable knots!'

During the War when the better naval officers were called up, things became even worse. 'They were replaced by "dug-outs" – retired men who were nothing like so sparky – but they would do for Dartmouth. One man was absolutely pathetic – about as effective as a cough in a thunderstorm! I remember one famous occasion when he knocked on his own cabin door and stood there for a long time waiting for an answer!'

However, there was one remarkable exception: 'There was a very good officer – a Lieutenant Commander called McKendrick. He had been my term officer and I hadn't liked him at all. I found him austere and abrupt and I had no affinity with him. What none of us realised was that he was a very sick man. He eventually went off and had some dreadful operation – I think it must have been for a brain tumour. The back of his head was chopped off and sewn on again and when he came back to Dartmouth it was still all shaven. He had to walk with a stick because his balance was all wrong and he'd tack all along that great long main corridor from side to side.

'But the amazing thing was, he'd become a different man. He became House Officer and he took part in all sorts of extracurricular things. He would tell us fascinating stories about the Navy and I was gripped by this. It changed everything. Because the War came I only had one term with him before he went off to fight. He made such a pest of himself with the Navy that they let him go to sea on active service and he became the captain of a destroyer. I eventually met up with him when I was Number Two on another destroyer.

'But that man's influence was enough to light a little spark and after that I never looked back. By the end of my time at Dartmouth I was so keen that I used to take manuals on Special Studies – gunning, torpedoing and signals – into church on Sundays and read them during the sermons. I got the top prize for Special Studies when I left – then off I went to sea.'

General Sir David Ramsbotham, Director of Public Relations for the Army during the Falklands War, said that the experience his English master at Haileybury had had of *la vie militaire* was the 'factor that determined my ultimate career'.

General Sir Walter Walker, Commander-in-Chief Allied Forces in Northern Europe 1969-1972, was a close friend of his headmaster and was influenced towards an army career by the 'way Blundell's School was run and the fair discipline it imposed.'

Lieutenant General Sir Anthony Walker said: 'The school [Merchant Taylors'] as an institution did not have a marked influence on me – even in retrospect I cannot detect any strong ethos which the school imparted. However, just at the time (15-16) when I was thinking about a career, my form master was F.K. Paul, later to be headmaster of Exeter School. He was also Commanding Officer of the CCF. I admired him in both capacities and he encouraged me to think positively about the Army.'

Others such as Brigadier Patrick Cordingley, Commander of the Seventh Armoured Brigade in the Gulf War, traced their career back to the influence of the CCF, in his case at Sherborne.

Air Chief Marshal Sir Peter Le Cheminant, a former Lieutenant General and Commander-in-Chief of Guernsey, went to Elizabeth College, Guernsey, where he too was influenced by the flourishing nature of his school's Officer Training Corps.

General Sir Patrick Howard-Dobson wrote: 'I was still at school [Framlingham] when the War broke out and stayed there until June 1940. I joined the Army in 1940 and served until 1981. You could say that my career was dictated to me. On the other hand, I firmly believe that I did reasonably well as a private soldier, as a cadet and then in my regiment very largely due to the training I had at school, not least in the OTC of which I was Company Sergeant Major.'

At most public schools the CCF is now voluntary and this lack of conscription may have had a positive effect, particularly as its focus is now more on expeditions, self-motivated initiative tests and adventure courses. Admiral of the Fleet Lord Lewin was profoundly influenced by his school – Judd School, Tonbridge. 'I took part', he said, 'in a Public Schools Exploring Society Expedition to Newfoundland in 1938. This experience gave me confidence and was a factor in my decision to join the Royal Navy.'

Not all the officers were uncritical about their schooldays. Lieutenant General Sir Napier Crookenden decided on the Army as a career at the age of six. 'The only thing which made me temporarily waver in this decision,' he told us, 'was the Wellington College OTC!'

General Sir Cecil Blacker also wrote to us about Wellington College in none too friendly terms: 'In the 1930s Wellington boys went in large numbers into the Army, and although my parents' (his father was a Colonel) 'already expected me to become a soldier, no doubt the orientation towards the Army did help to make up my mind.

'No doubt I benefited from the education there, but the régime in my day virtually wrote off those going to Sandhurst as far as any cultural or intellectual encouragement was concerned. I suppose this was not a hindrance subsequently in that I have since realised what I missed and have tried to make up for it. Also the rigid discipline of the school tended to stifle initiative and confidence and I have since often felt at a disadvantage with, say, Wykehamists or Etonians. Also, I bitterly regret never having been to university.'

Bitter they may be, but few, as we said before, admitted to being unhappy at school. This small number included Sir Desmond Cassidi at Dartmouth and Sir Alasdair Steedman at Hampton Grammar School (although he is now chairman of the governors of the rechristened Hampton School). Surprisingly, two of the Army's most famous names were not wildly enthusiastic about their schooldays: General Sir Peter de la Billière said he was 'frustrated rather than unhappy' at Harrow. Field Marshal Lord Carver was unhappy at Winchester, though he does not agree with General Sir Hugh Beach that it was 'hugely anti-military':

'It wasn't pacifist or anything. But it was just considered rather infra dig to go into the Army because there was so little intellectual challenge. I had an elder brother who went into the RAF and that was thought even worse. The advantage of my education was that it taught me the Socratic method of questioning everything to start with – *not* to accept what you're told, not just to obey orders. This is vital in the Army. When it comes to war, it is absolutely essential to question everything. You have to ask, Why are we doing this?'

Lord Carver is the antithesis of institutional man: 'I wasn't happy with the institutional life either at Winchester or in the Army. I was not gregarious. I didn't like going round with a crowd. It's all very well to be a good mixer and so on, but you can only get so far that way. One of the criticisms of the typical army officer is that he is terribly nice and gets on well with everybody. But when it comes to a difficult decision – and in the Army you often have to make them – operational or organisational ones – these men are not prepared to be unpopular. I was not a popular boy at Winchester for that very reason. And I didn't much like the other boys. No, I wasn't a leader either. I was quite solitary.

'I wasn't interested in the Army at Winchester. The only reason I went into it was because my father became redundant and there was no money for me to go to Cambridge, even if I got a scholarship. I'd always wanted to be a lawyer or a journalist. But I couldn't afford law training or anything like that.

'I concluded that if you went into the Army you didn't have to work much, you'd have a good deal of spare time and you could live on your pay. My plan was to spend four years there while studying for a profession.

'In fact I passed first out of Sandhurst and got a commission at 19.

My opportunity came because of the war in Egypt. I was a very junior officer in the Seventh Armoured Division. I had a very good memory, a good brain and good physical health and I was in the right place at the right time.'

Does he ever regret not having followed one of his chosen careers?

'No – I have lots of friends who are lawyers and journalists – and thank God I'm not one!'

Most officers are alike in their lack of any sense of missed opportunity, some drifting gently into the Army from National Service. General Sir Richard Vincent, Chief of the Defence Staff, wrote: 'The Second World War was ending as I joined Aldenham School. Returning masters and Old Boys (like General Sir Richard Gale) had a direct influence on the choice I made for National Service and this, in turn, led to my later decision to make the Army my profession. The OTC was well run and, for me, enjoyable, though I did not at the time feel it had any direct influence on my later decision to stay in the Army.

'Perhaps the most influential aspect of life at Aldenham during my time there was the encouragement given by the Headmaster (George Riding) and my housemaster that, in whatever we did, we should develop and encourage a sense of purpose. The Army that I joined in 1950 developed very much the same ethos.'

Others never really emerged from the ethos of discipline. The regimental life was an extension of the house system which they experienced at school and of the patterns of authority which they learnt there. The armed forces were really their only choice for after-school life. Rear Admiral Peter Hammersley said: 'Denstone College had a tremendous influence on my whole character, instilling self-discipline, moral standards, leadership and general self-confidence. Without it, I would probably have had little success in later life. Denstone did not have much influence on my choice of career but had an enormous effect on my achievement in it.'

General Sir David Ramsbotham recalls the inter-house military competition at Haileybury. 'Quite extraordinarily one particular event suggested that the military might be for me. Every year there was an inter-house military competition, based on many aspects of the work done in the Combined Cadet Force which everyone had to join and culminating in a drill and turnout competition. The Head of House had to be away for much of the preparation for this and I had to deputise. Somehow everything gelled and I experienced being part of a well-drilled team, which was exhilarating. The down side was that the Head of House came back just before the competition, insisted on taking charge, did not get the act together and we lost. I learned something about leading and frankly enjoyed the experience.'

Where else could Ramsbotham, a future Commander of the Third Armoured Division, go but into the Army?

Grammar-school boys who became officers also learnt about leadership at school. Wallingford Grammar School was particularly praised by General Sir Frank King, former Colonel Commandant of the Army Air Corps. He wrote that after joining the Army as a private soldier in 1939, 'I discovered that my education was well suited to army requirements: I had developed, as a prefect and captain of sports teams, some leadership qualities; I could communicate confidently and clearly and I had a good basic knowledge of most subjects so that I was soon selected for officer training. A few years later I joined the newly formed Parachute Regiment and felt so at home with the highly motivated members of this organisation that I decided to make the Army my career.

'As a schoolboy I never contemplated a military career. Nevertheless I realise that my education had much to do with any subsequent success and contentment. Above all it taught me to be a good mixer.'

Another grammar-school boy (Southend High School) who ended up in the armed services was Air Marshal Sir Frank Holroyd, Chief Engineer of the Royal Air Force. He said: 'I was good at maths, physics and chemistry in particular and really did enjoy the last two subjects. The physics, and to a lesser extent the chemistry, masters were a particularly strong influence in that they gave me great encouragement and scope for experiments. My father, who was an engineer, and my mother were also influential in my choice of engineering as a career.

'The reason why I chose to pursue it in the RAF is simple – I did National Service there as a Technical Officer. I thoroughly enjoyed it, accepted their invitation to take a permanent commission and here I am today as Chief of Logistics and Chief Engineer of the RAF!'

The greatest tribute to grammar schools – or to any school in this chapter – came from Air Chief Marshal Sir Robert Freer, former Deputy Commander-in-Chief, Strike Command.

He wrote: 'Any success I have had in the past sixty years, in or out of uniform, can in part be traced back to the very thorough basic education I received at Gosport Grammar School. The staff there were a greatly respected and admired group of dedicated, enthusiastic and highly qualified teachers. And their efforts were not confined to the classroom. They spilled over into extracurricular activities and not least of all into well provided and utilised sports fields.

'If the encouragement and insistence on standards by the headmaster and staff added up to what is sometimes pejoratively called élitism, then I believe our country needs as much of it as can be provided.'

Élitist or not, schools often had an overriding, sometimes overwhelming influence on the officers of the recent past. Either that, or the officers' precocity and pre-destiny had an influence, sometimes from an early age, on which schools they attended. Admiral Sir Derek Reffell, Governor and Commander-in-Chief of Gibraltar, answering the question whether school had any influence on his career replied:

'On the contrary, my choice of career influenced the selection of my secondary school!'

3 Art, Design and Fashion

'Introversion turned me to creativity': John Bratby, 'kitchen sink' artist, and subject of a major retrospective at the National Portrait Gallery in 1991, was happy at school, in spite of desperate shyness. 'Some people looking at my paintings think I must be an extrovert figure because they are what you might describe as expressionistic. But I was the opposite of extrovert: the point is that in painting I could be completely free in the expression of my personality – I couldn't otherwise. At school I was never very good at socialising, therefore I devoted my life to creative activity.'

However, for many of our most successful painters, graphic designers, architects, sculptors and interior designers, school has been a struggle. Bratby again: 'The artist's life is a lonely one. If you are not gregarious you are left on your own and this leads you to creativity.' Consequently 40 per cent of the people who responded to our survey in these fields were, unlike John Bratby, unhappy at school – the largest percentage of any category in the book.

If school is a struggle, a lot of self-fulfilment could depend on family influences, entirely separate from school. You would expect David Leach the potter to be influenced by his famous father Bernard, under whom he studied. Norman Hepple the portrait painter was much more interested in what was going on in his father's studio than in the classrooms of Colfe's School, Lewisham:

'My father was an artist and saw that the only ability I had was drawing. He taught me a great deal and sent me to an art school when I was seventeen: henceforth I worked like a madman.'

Sir Hardy Amies, octogenarian royal dressmaker, was happy as a boarder at Brentwood and hated the holidays 'because there were no chums around'. Boarding school taught him 'to manipulate contemporaries' and sent him to France and Germany to improve his linguistic skills. But it was his mother who found him the job which set him on the path to success.

'My mother had worked her way up from being a country girl to the *vendeuse* in a court dressmaker's.' This was a smart establishment that made garments for the aristocracy and the three-year-old Amies loved to play in the stockroom, dressing up dolls in fashionable clothes. He was fascinated by that world and when at the age of 25 he was forced back home from Germany with the rise of Nazi power, his mother 'got me a connection and I was offered a job at Lachasse – a couture house – in 1934.'

Another fashion designer, Bruce Oldfield, thinks he has his foster mother to thank for his career. A Barnardo's boy, he was looked after by a dressmaker. 'I was always drawing clothes and fiddling round with bits of her material,' he told us. 'Only ten years ago I saw my files from Barnardo's and there was a letter from one of the social workers to Head Office. It said, "FM [foster mother] believes boy will be a fashion designer." That was in 1958 and by the time I saw that letter I'd already been a fashion designer for ten years!'

Jane Ray's blazing, jewel-like designs are now appearing on more and more birthday cards and wrapping paper. Ray, currently one of the most popular illustrators of children's books, has only recently begun to recognize some of the sources of her brilliantly coloured pictures.

'It's only in the last two or three years that I've realised that subconsciously I have been influenced by things I saw on childhood holidays: stained glass windows, gargoyles, Roman mosaics. My parents took me to a lot of exhibitions too. My designs are rather ethnic and people always assume I've travelled everywhere but I've only travelled round Europe a bit as a student: I just spend a lot of time at the British Museum! I was at my parents' house last weekend. It's the house I was born in and it has a very distinctive shape with a pointed roof. It was built in 1926 by an antique dealer out of breeze blocks! Anyway it was only last weekend that I realised that the house I always put in my pictures is that house and I just hadn't thought of it before – it was quite exciting to discover!'

Francis Johnson, the great classical architect, who went to Bridlington School, had a far less secure home. His mother died when he was five and his father, remarried to a neurotic and difficult stepmother, became an alcoholic. But Johnson recalled, 'I always knew what I wanted to be and my father encouraged me. I was given Bannister Fletcher's *History of Architecture* and saved my pocket money to buy books on architecture.'

Two other architects, Rod Hackney and Maxwell Hutchinson, current President of the RIBA, had to rely on their fathers for far more than paternal encouragement.

Rod Hackney, architectural mentor of the Prince of Wales, sang the praises of the John Bright Grammar School in Llandudno. But he would never have got there but for his father's efforts.

'I went to the junior school in Bethesda, about thirty miles from Llandudno, where all the lessons were taught in Welsh. I failed the 11 plus and went to the secondary modern. My father, a very proud man from Liverpool – we moved in the War – marched up to the headmaster and said I'd only failed because the exam was all in Welsh! I was of course a fluent Welsh speaker, only speaking English at home, but my father accused the headmaster of being a Welsh Nationalist and the poor man let me sit the exam again and I passed. Llandudno was 99 per cent English and when I got there my English was very poor but my father was delighted!'

Maxwell Hutchinson wanted to be an architect like his father. But he was told at Oundle in the 1960s that he ought to 'go and take a proper degree first'. He told us, 'My father was extremely irritated at this ludicrous proposition: the school hadn't realised that an architect's training takes a full seven years and that there were perfectly respectable degree courses in the subject at dozens of universities! Their attitude raises two important issues: their lack of respect for the professions as opposed to an "academic" career, and their failure to realise the significance of their advice to my career.'

Back in the 1920s, Sir Hugh Casson had even less support at Eastbourne College. 'I was virtually the only pupil in the art school which masqueraded as a branch of the Sanatorium! This was not tremendous in those days. I did not become persuaded towards architecture until I was about seventeen years old.'

This attitude was not confined to the public schools: a resistance to the idea of art and design as a 'proper' career has dogged the steps of British artists in all sorts of schools. So many of them speak of being pushed towards an academic career.

But at her Hertfordshire comprehensive in the mid-1970s Jennie Moncur, the interior designer, was aware of a quite different approach. Sheredes Comprehensive under its charismatic head, Maurice Holt, gave her 'a great sense of the new – a feeling that boundaries were being broken.'

The deliberate flexibility of the curriculum gave her the feeling that anything was possible. Sheredes had only been open three years and it was experimental and, Moncur thinks, the pure ideal of comprehensive education.

'One of the compulsory subjects taken to "O" level was called Creative Art and you had to do cookery, metalwork, woodwork, ceramics and silver work among other things. There was coursework, even in those days, and you were assessed on an exhibition of work you displayed, very much in the same way as you do at art school. Teachers worked as a unit and crossed over from one subject to another. There was quite an excitement about this new form of teaching and it influenced me later. Though I'm best known for my tapestry weaving, I do deal in lots of other forms – I've done linoleum floors, surface decorating, painted work – all sorts of things, and it was the teaching at Sheredes that made me more flexible. The school taught me in the very best manner – it taught me how to learn.'

But at Jane Ray's vast nine-form entry comprehensive, Heathcote Junior High in the London borough of Waltham Forest, she felt swamped. 'I felt that no-one knew who I was and I was aware only of my failures. The nine forms were graded: Grade 1 was university material and if you were in Grade 9 you just went on nice outings all the time. At the age of 11 I discovered for the first time that someone who was good at maths was felt to be a much more valuable person than someone who was going to be a lorry driver and this was quite a shock to me. Art and music were both seen as "recreational subjects" and you couldn't do both – you had to do a certain number of "academic subjects" and this upset me because as well as being keen on art I was quite musical – but I was just an obedient little girl who did what I was told.'

What had happened to the great comprehensive ideal?

Mark Landini, joint managing director of Conran Design, found life at Downside very restricting and enjoyed the 'most escapist elements of school life, like drawing and the workshop.' But though his talents plainly lay in this direction, he was not encouraged.

'I was fairly successful academically and therefore was pushed towards university. I remember a conversation about this with an older pupil who had left school. He asked me what I was going to do after "A" levels. I replied, "Go to university of course." He noticed some hesitation in my reply and said, "Is that what you really want to do?" He asked me what I *really* enjoyed the most in life. I replied, "Drawing." He suggested art school and like a flash of inspiration I knew he was correct. The rest is history!'

Michael Kenny, the sculptor and Royal Academician, found the approach of his school to art very academic. At St Francis Xavier's College in Liverpool there was, he said, 'the minimal amount of art tuition, both in time spent and equipment.'

Howard Morgan, the portrait painter, had a hard time at Fairfax High School, Sutton Coldfield in the 1960s: 'Despite having a rather pronounced gift for drawing I was eventually at about 13 persuaded to give up the option of art at school as I was told I rather unbalanced the achievement standards of my class.' Luckily a friend of his persuaded him to show his drawings to a new art master and he was once again allowed to join the art class. But by then he was 16 and three years had been wasted.

Christopher Lawrence is now a very successful silversmith. But as a borderline 11-plus pupil at Westborough High School he was looked upon as an academic failure. 'I always came top in art and craft subjects and it was accepted that I would take an apprenticeship at the age of 15. I was fortunate in having a good family who recognised where my talents lay, but although I've achieved a certain success in my craft, I shall always have a chip on my shoulder because of my academic inadequacies.'

So many artists speak of having had a fight on their hands: Adrian Henri, polymath painter, poet, singer, songwriter and playwright, and former President of the Liverpool Academy of Arts, loved St Asaph Grammar School in North Wales: 'It was the classic case of a working-class boy from a council house discovering art and literature. But once in the VIth form there was a certain amount of pressure for me to do either English or French at university. I really wanted to study art, so eventually I did a BA Hons in Fine Art.'

Three top fashion designers came under the same pressure. Pascale Smets, Ninivah Khomo and Lindka Cierach were all at convent schools and they all tell the same story.

   At Farnborough Hill Convent as recently as the 1980s Pascale Smets was taken aside by her tutor and told she should do a degree in history and should try for Oxbridge. 'I was very flattered by that and I wavered briefly. But since I was very little I had always wanted to be a fashion designer. I think it's ridiculous that you have to take so much stick, as I did, if you want to go to art school instead of university.'

Ninivah Khomo felt the same. 'I'd always known what I wanted to do. I'd been drawing women wearing clothes I'd designed since I was four! I'd gone on doing it all through junior school and all through the senior school.' But the Convent of the Holy Child, Edgbaston, had other ideas. 'It was a very academic school,' says Khomo, 'and they certainly pushed you towards university. Nearly everyone did an "S" level. The point was for you to get a job afterwards, whether you were happy or not.'

There was also a perception that art schools were dangerous places full of sex and drugs and rock 'n roll. 'It's far too wild,' said Khomo's headmistress. 'You'll never cope.' Khomo and Smets agree that teachers don't know much about art schools and don't understand what goes on there. 'They don't have much contact with them,' says Khomo, 'and they still think they're a bit risqué. They think you're only taught to paint and you have to be one in a million to end up like David Hockney! But our art schools are some of the best in the world and they spawn talent in every kind of design – clothes, furniture – everything.'

Lindka Cierach was actually scared stiff of going to art school and opted instead for a secretarial course followed by a job on *Vogue* then the London School of Fashion. 'I was scared of the drugs scene in the seventies when I was about to leave school. We girls were very naive. I knew nothing about boys at all and I was so unsure and undirected.'

The art teaching at her convent school, St Leonards Mayfield in Sussex, was very limited but in fact stood her in good stead for her eventual career. 'I did nothing but needlework till I was 15, and yes, that's probably where I learned the detail that I now use in my designs. Unlike a lot of designers I still have a passion for sewing and a fundamental knowledge of every stage of a design – making a pattern, cutting, pinning – the lot.'

The nuns at St Leonards can hardly have imagined that the knickers Cierach had to sew for the local orphanage would set her on course for the dazzling dress she designed for Fergie's wedding! 'I also did an excellent history of art course with a marvellous nun – we started with Giotto – and this may well have influenced the dresses I designed later on.'

As well as the knickers, she and her friends were making all their own clothes. 'The sixties was the greatest time. It was all such simple stuff to make – shifts and angel dresses and empire lines – though I was miffed because I couldn't wear them because I had no bosom!'

St Leonards was, she says, academically biased, and she found the work difficult. But she loved the school and still values the self-discipline she learnt there.

Bruce Oldfield liked his Northern grammar school far less. Though he was lucky to have had the early inspiration of his dressmaker foster-mother, he found himself a few years later at Spennymoor Grammar. 'This was the North-East of England and Spennymoor was actually a technical grammar school, so you were pushed towards the scientific and technical subjects.'

Luckily he moved forty miles south and went to Ripon Grammar where he found the liberal art master Tony Smith. 'He's still there nearly thirty years on – I made a speech at the school last year. Tony was one of the lads really and he let me finish off my pottery in the art room instead of doing games which I loathed! He was friendly and easy-going and he gave me quiet encouragement.'

Where pupils managed to break through the barriers and pursue their chosen careers in art and design it was usually through the good offices of teachers like Tony Smith – often, though by no means always, the art teacher. More than half of those who replied said they had been inspired, discovered, supported by one charismatic, dedicated and determined teacher.

Back to John Bratby: when we interviewed him he had just been reading a long letter from his old art master at Tiffins, Harold Watts. Like Oldfield he still keeps in touch. 'He wound up my engine,' says Bratby, 'and set me on track. He came to the school as a very young and enthusiastic master when I was in the VIth Form. The old gentleman who used to teach art was replaced by this young firebrand. He didn't change the art room physically – it was his personality. He made teaching his vocation: he decided he'd try and create a few successful artists and he thinks he's done it – there's me and a few others he considers his successes!'

For the lucky ones like Bratby, good advice was often all they needed to set them on course. Instead of the obstructive university-or-nothing conservatism, some of them found excellent careers guidance. James Butler, the sculptor, had an art teacher at Maidstone Grammar who also happened to be his careers master.

'When I told Mr Fawcett that I wanted to go on to art school he was very much in favour. He told me that even if I never made it as an artist, the few years that I should spend at art school would be the happiest of my life. Well, I have been a professional sculptor now for some thirty years, and he was right. The five years I spent at art school were wonderfully happy ones.'

Dr Dennis Farr had two inspired art masters at Luton Grammar School: A.W. Martin had taught at the Slade, and R.W. Smoothey, who went on to teach at the Royal Grammar School in Guildford, knew all about the Courtauld Institute of Art, where Dr Farr ended up as Director.

Terry Farrell, the architect, was luckier than many others now at the top of that profession: at St Cuthbert's Grammar School in Newcastle, encouraged by a 'legendary art master', Maurice McPartlan, he developed a passion for buildings and went on to get a first-class degree in architecture at Newcastle University.

Another famous architect, Owen Luder, was all set to go to Wilsons Grammar School in Camberwell Green when the War broke out. Wilsons was evacuated but Luder decided to stay and brave the bombing. He had two years of Blitz-disrupted schooling then by a lucky chance fetched up late in 1941 at Peckham School for Girls – temporarily co-educational!

'Miss O'Reilly, the headmistress, suggested I should try for Brixton School of Building – very wise of her because there would be a lot of work for the building industry after the War. In April 1942 I started at Brixton on a three year junior building course – which included practical work as well as theory. I must be one of the few architects who have actually wiped a lead joint, cut stone and laid bricks! After a few months in Brixton my target was to be an architect, and I eventually qualified in 1954. Whatever I have achieved has been despite being denied a grammar-school education, which might have led to university (although few with my background made it that far in those days.) Who knows whether I would have done more or less had I been evacuated with Wilsons Grammar School in 1939?'

Ralph Brown, the sculptor, had the same sort of help at Leeds Grammar School in 1942.

'As I was at school in the War some of the teachers were perhaps more civilised than one would have expected in normal times, when they would almost certainly not have become teachers. The art master hated being there: he should have been teaching in an art school and he did later, when the War was over. He gave me *excellent* advice on how to become an artist – a task which seemed both impossible and ridiculous to me in Leeds in 1942. I did as he advised and it all worked out well.'

But Brown's path was not all smooth: 'The headmaster was an old swine who having explained to me what a *privilege* it had been for me – a working-class scholarship boy – to attend the grammar school finished by telling me that I was bringing no kudos to the school by going on to study *art!*'

John Ward, portrait painter to the Royals and many other distinguished celebrities, had a very different headmaster at his state school, St Owen's in Hereford. He invited us to the lofty splendour of his medieval hall-house studio in Kent:

'I was at a boys' elementary school. You sat the scholarship at 11 and if you passed you went on to the grammar school and if you didn't you stayed where you were. I could never get my act together and I failed, thank God. Staying at that school was the making of me because we had this outstanding headmaster called P. H. Alder-Barratt. It was a small school and he knew every Tom, Dick and Harry in it. He used to tell us wonderful stories. His father had been head printer at the OUP and rescued from an Oxford dustbin one of only five copies of *Alice in Wonderland* that Lewis Carroll had thrown out because he didn't like the first Tenniel illustrations. Alder-Barratt inherited it and when his own daughter wanted to go to Oxford he sold it to finance her.

'He was himself an artist and that's why he recognised some talent in me. He was fascinated by education and believed that the secret lay in finding something that turned you on to it. His philosophy was like William Morris's who told his cook that he could make her son into a designer – and he did! Everyone, he believed, had potential.

'A lot of those boys were very rough but he made sure we started every day with classical music on a wind-up gramophone and were taught singing. We learned a lot of poetry by rote – it was drummed into us. We were failed scholarship boys but there we were, writing essays on Shakespeare's sonnets. He insisted that every boy belonged to the local library and we were sent there to look up the derivation of words.

'Miss Daw the art mistress caned us if we made a mess of a drawing. I remember getting the cane for leaving a line round a lemon! But, like the headmaster, she caned us on the hand, without rancour.

'This amazing headmaster even ran a night school! That school was open from 9 a.m. to 9 p.m. I used to be let in at 8 a.m. as long as I helped the charwoman carry in the coal!

'When I was 15 I was too thick to do anything except art. So the headmaster arranged for me to go to Hereford School of Art. Then he did a really splendid thing. He bought one of my pictures for £3 – an enormous sum of money in those days – and presented it to the local Art Gallery. Imagine how that felt to a 15-year-old boy! I'm afraid it was an awful landscape and it's still there – and I have to see it occasionally because they've now made me a Freeman of the City!

'Alder-Barratt was an exceptional man. We corresponded until he died and he was the first person I phoned when I was elected to the Royal Academy. He said, "You used to say that only happened to *bad* artists!"'

Carl Toms, the stage designer, was much acclaimed for his set for the West End production of *Private Lives* with Joan Collins in 1990. He also has the dubious distinction of having clothed Racquel Welch in *One Million Years BC* ('I made the clothes myself!'). Toms was very unhappy at his school, High Oakham in Mansfield. But he had a perceptive art mistress who encouraged him to go to the Mansfield School of Art, 'where I was blissfully happy for several years, and where I found my major mentor, a young teacher called Hazel Hemsworth.'

Richard Demarco, the artist and director of his own Edinburgh gallery, followed the same path: 'I was fortunate to have at Holy Cross Academy, Edinburgh, an art teacher who encouraged me to follow in the footsteps of one of her students who was five years my senior and who went to the Edinburgh College of Art.' That student was Sir Eduardo Paolozzi, the sculptor.

Jean Muir, the dress designer, was at a highly academic school, Dame Alice Harpur in Bedford. But again, she was lucky enough to have an inspired teacher who encouraged her pupils to look at the works of great painters and it was then an easy step for Jean into the stockrooms of Liberty's.

Teaching art by precept and inspiration turns up in unlikely places. Contrary perhaps to expectations, Sir Oliver Millar, Surveyor Emeritus of the Queen's pictures, says that Rugby in the 1930s was 'a most enlightened and civilised school which encouraged the enthusiasm for pictures and painting and printing.'

In his final year at Mill Hill, Sir Anthony Cox, the architect, read Clough Williams-Ellis's *The Pleasures of Architecture* and it was an important influence. Leeds Grammar sculptor, Ralph Brown, was shown the new (1940) Phaidon edition of Michelangelo's sculpture: 'I would have been about 12, and I remember vividly thinking that it contained pictures of the most beautiful things I had ever seen.' British art plainly owes a lot to the Phaidon Press: Sir Michael Levey, Director of the National Gallery until 1987, still has the Phaidon art books selected as prizes by his headmaster at the Oratory School, 'himself quite a competent artist'.

Comics, not fine art books, turned Michael Foreman on to a career as one of our foremost illustrators. He was lucky to be at Notley Road Secondary Modern in Lowestoft when the dynamic though controversial Michael Duane, later of Risinghill, was headmaster. However, the school in fact played no part in his future career. 'School', he told us, 'was merely an interruption.'

Foreman's mother kept the village shop and he had the run of all the comics and magazines. One of the artists who drew the cover of *John Bull* used to put in hundreds and hundreds of people. Michael copied him: 'The soldiers billeted in our village were all Scottish, so I drew scenes of hundreds and hundreds of people in kilts.'

As you might expect when interviewing artists about their schools, the beauty of the setting played an important part. Francis Johnson described the beautiful situation of Bridlington School in East Yorkshire:

'Its early roots lay in the monastery, Bridlington Priory, a seat of ancient learning and today a piece of superb architecture.'

He now supports numerous societies for conservation: 'My surroundings and the environment generally have ever been paramount to me. I hate what the twentieth century has done in my lifetime.'

Eton influenced architectural historian James Lees-Milne in the same way 'because of the school buildings, Chapel especially'. Michael Manser, another architect and former president of the RIBA, was less impressed with Epsom County Secondary (now Glyn School): 'I realised the school building was bad and sketched amendments!'

But David Shepherd, the wildlife artist, waxes eloquent about Stowe, surely one of the most beautiful schools in Britain. He told us: 'The unrivalled setting of the great house and gardens at Stowe must have a profound influence on any boy who goes there.'

In his autobiography (*The Man who Loves Giants*: David & Charles 1975) he expands:

'The great beauty of Stowe was bound to brush off on anyone with artistic inclinations, however latent, and it certainly shaped my future life far more than I could then know. To anyone who knows it, this must be one of the most beautiful places in England, with its hundreds of acres of magnificent trees, sweeping lawns and vast lakes. Art, for me, was born at Stowe.'

David Hicks, the interior designer, thought the setting of Charterhouse lovely: 'very atmospheric – though it had rather horrible silver birches, and pines, which I loathed. In fact the only things Charterhouse really gave me were manners, discipline, a certain assurance – and a loathing of rhododendrons!' He may, however, have absorbed his sense of theatre from the school chapel.

'It's very impressive – a soaring modern Gothic edifice by Gilbert Scott. It was beautifully lit even then: I love Gothic and I love using dramatic juxtapositions of light and shade and texture in my garden designs – this may have come from those days.'

For another interior designer, Tessa Kennedy, the influence was not so much her school as her weekends in Brighton, where she found an edifice even more impressive than Charterhouse Chapel:

'When our parents got divorced my twin sister and I were sent to our first boarding school, The Downs in Seaford. We were the youngest in the school and I suppose very impressionable. Weekends out were spent in Brighton and the Pavilion turned out to be the biggest influence in my life. I fell in love with it and it started a long affair with colour, fabrics, wallpapers, textures and design. It was the most romantic thing I had ever seen.'

Often it was the general ambience of a school rather than any specific teaching that encouraged the arts. Dartington Hall, the former progressive boarding school in Devon, had a chequered history, ending in its closure in 1987. But for Joanna Drew, Director of the Hayward Gallery, it was just the right school, with 'an exceptional arts, architectural, philosophical and political environment'.

The ultimate liberal education offered by Eton suited Nicky Haslam, a fellow interior designer, very well. It had, he says, 'a unique knack of drawing out an individual's particular talent, and not forcing one to do things like sport that one particularly hated. This, and the total lack of bullying, made one unafraid of the future or of adult life, and did not cast one in a particular mould.'

Although another Etonian, Tom Hustler the photographer, was, he claims, taught by Eton 'that I was bloody useless at everything', he was able to spend the last summer half in the Drawing Schools manufacturing ashtrays 'which I sold in the holidays'. He found his old school invaluable when after national service he became a 'happy snapper'.

'When I took up photography of people as a profession, having failed dismally at everything else, the sobriquet "Old Etonian" was a help in publicity. Many a silly newspaper story started: "Twenty-four-year-old Old Etonian and former army officer, tall, gangling debs' delight Tom Hustler . . . ."'

Harriet Jagger, senior fashion editor at *Vogue* gained the same sort of confidence from going to Marlborough in the late 1970s as one of fifty girls in the VIth form:

'Marlborough opened the door to me: any career at all was thought to be accessible – careers that were never thought possible at the day grammar school in Warwick I'd been to until then. I did Art "A" level – the art department under Robin Child was very good indeed – then I went on to the London College of Fashion because I'd always been interested in clothes.

'Marlborough didn't push me towards that but it was a very broadminded school. It didn't just give you a straightforward "A" level education – it was more like a university, and it gave me the confidence and character to pursue a career which would have been unthinkable had I not moved schools. It made me realise that the type of life you choose is what you make of it yourself.' She appreciated the wide social mix; she now travels a great deal and was well prepared for it by her school: 'Marlborough was so cosmopolitan, with pupils of different wealth, nationality, ability and style.'

Tortington Park near Arundel is now an open prison. 'Not a great change from when I was at school there in the fifties!' said Linda Kitson, the official Falklands War artist. Like Harriet Jagger, Linda was prepared for her travels by her schooling. But her subjects were not lissom catwalk models but yomping squaddies.

'There were icicles on the beds at my school! If you could handle that you could handle anything! It was all a wonderful preparation for the Falklands! It was a very expensive school – more expensive than Eton, where my half-brothers went. It was an odd mixture of girls from diplomatic families and girls from broken homes. There was a great camaraderie because like a lot of the other girls I had been to hell and back at home – anywhere was better than being at home with two alcoholic parents who remarried every holidays!

'There was the feeling of being together in adversity, which of course I also got in the Falklands. The cruelty in that school was appalling. They'd find out what you liked doing best and then they'd forbid it. For instance, I was in the school play, *Charley's Aunt*, and I washed my hair before one of the performances. So I got taken out of the play! You were only allowed to wash your hair once a week – God knows why! Whenever we went out anywhere we had to walk in line and if you were slightly out of line you got punished – as you were for not sitting in a straight line in church! Some of the senior girls were 20-something before they left and there was terrible bullying – not physical brutality but something much meaner – a real sadism. You had to be pretty strong to survive but if you did it was damn' good training.

'But there was also the feeling, very important for any artist, of being alone in a crowd. Being an artist is a very isolated job. I went down to the Falklands on a troopship with 2,000 soldiers and found myself with 10,000 out there and it was marvellous, just like going back to school and being among all those people again.

'How did I become an artist? Oh, nothing to do with school – all they taught you there was how to get out of cars backwards and how to be a lady. The art teacher was an elderly mediocre artist who like all the teachers must have long lost interest in her subject.

'After I left the school I did the Season – there was no question of my having a job. People in my family just didn't work – no one had worked as far back as Victorian times! Anyway, one day when I was in my twenties I was pushing old Sir Stephen Courtauld – the Courtauld Institute, you know – in a wheelchair round his beautiful garden in Zimbabwe. He saw some drawings I'd done of some trees and bushes and he suggested I should go to art school. So I went to St Martin's School of Art, where I took a lot of stick for my accent, clothes, everything I'd learnt about being a lady at Tortington Park. But thank God, that was in the sixties and there really was a social revolution and I cross-decked though I really took a pasting for it. But it all helped when I went down to the Falklands.'

For some artists – cartoonists especially, it seems – school had little if any relevance. Michael Heath (the ubiquitous 'Heath' of the *Sunday Times, Mail on Sunday, Independent* among others) has only vague recollections of his schooling. He says in his *Who's Who* entry that he had 'no education to speak of' and told us that he'd forgotten the names of some of his schools. 'All I could do was draw, so I wanted to be a cartoonist – I could do nothing else.'

Another artist, Beryl Cook, the wonderful apologist for fat ladies, also apologised for being so negative about her schooling at Kendrick Girls' School in Reading. 'I was more or less indifferent and can't recall ever doing any work there or homework. The teachers were in control so there was peace in the classroom for the few who wanted to work and learn while the rest of us were busily engaged in passing notes, drawing or reading comics inside the desks. My greatest ambition was to leave, which I did at 14.' Like Beryl, Serena Sutcliffe of Sotheby's found school – St Michael's, Limpsfield – 'the least interesting part of my life'.

Some artists seemed to become artists almost by default, often because they were anti-academic or anti-sport and found in the art room a blessed sanctuary away from the blackboard or the rugger field.

David Hicks, like Bruce Oldfield, '*hated* sport! I was made to play cricket and I fielded away as far as possible. In my hip pocket I kept Arnold Haskell's *Guide to the Ballet* and I used to lie out on the boundary in the long grass and consult this bloody thing until someone yelled, "Hicks, HICKS! Get UP! There's a catch coming!" I used to try and get out of sport whenever possible and I remember I got my mother to write me a letter to ask if I could do more art and less games, and surprisingly the school agreed!'

Sir Hugh Casson found Eastbourne College 'deeply philistine, dominated by the ethics of sport. Hopeless at games, I was glad to leave.' David Shepherd 'used to invent every excuse to get into the art school where it was altogether a gentler life than the torture of playing rugger. I could not understand the fun of being buried in mud under heaps of writhing bodies and having one's collar bone broken!'

For Raymond Briggs, one of our best-known illustrators for his popular cartoon creations *The Snowman* and *Fungus the Bogeyman*, and for his chilling anti-nuclear fable *Where the Wind Blows*, school sport somehow encapsulates all that he detested about Rutlish School, Merton. He shares his alma mater with John Major (and, Briggs was mischievously delighted to discover, with George Neville Heath, the sadistic murderer!). 'I'm ten years older than Major, so we weren't contemporaries.

'The whole ethos of that school was based on sport. If you're good at sport at a place like that you're a king. I was thought to be a non-sporting wimp because the games they played – rugger, cricket, athletics – weren't *my* sports. I liked Association Football, cycling, table tennis and snooker but they didn't do those.'

Seeing Raymond Briggs in his house in Sussex, surrounded by the artefacts of his success – the Snowman mugs in which he offers coffee, the detailed and beautiful original drawings all round the walls – you are not prepared for the force of his anger against his old school, still strong after all these years.

'I hated it. It was then a brutal place almost entirely run by prefects. We got hit a lot, we were always in detention when the prefects would make us sit absolutely still for an hour. The room was lit with naked bulbs and I've always been touchy about having the light in my eyes. Every time I looked down this bastard of a prefect bashed me over the head.

'I remember one scene so well. A Senior Prefect – a pig with a yellow face like uncooked pastry – stood up on the platform in assembly and cried, "When you come to a school like this you should give up *everything* and *live* for the school!" You only have to substitute the word "state" for "school." . . .

'My parents were so proud of me going to grammar school – nauseatingly so! My dad was a milkman who could use Cockney rhyming slang and Mum was thrilled that I was going to go to a school in this uniform and play this upper-class game, rugger. There weren't many boys from my area at Rutlish. Most of them came from the posher suburbs built in the thirties like Raynes Park and Worcester Park.

'There was a real effort at Rutlish School to get us to talk posh. The previous headmaster had been at the school for about thirty years and everyone was full of awe and admiration for him. He was called Mr Varnish and he was succeeded just before I got there by a Mr Blenkinsop. No, I'm not joking! Blenkinsop was a very tall man with a long face like a chimp. Anyway, this Mr Varnish had written a speech book and we all had to carry this bright blue book around in our left pocket and if you were found without it you got instant detention.

'We had elocution lessons every lunchtime taken by the prefects. There were sentences put in by Mr Varnish for us to practise our vowels. Like "Round and round flew each sweet sound." The joke was that the prefects all talked Cockney too and we'd all solemnly repeat after them, "*Rarnd* and *rarnd* flew each sweet *sarnd*"!

'The prefects wore mortar boards with little tassels and one of these prefects came from what my mum would call a "common" family, really rough, not like us who were respectable working-class. One day when this particular prefect was taking us for our speech lessons some boy dropped something and went to pick it up and this prefect – in charge of our elocution lessons – yelled, "Git back where you woz and git on wiv yer werk!"

'The buildings in this dreadful school were appalling: the corridors were open to the sky and the rain poured in. I was there from 1944 to

1949 and it hadn't been bombed or anything. Most of the staff were elderly, or younger ones the worse for wear after the War. Lots of them kept a slipper in their pockets to wallop you and there was one master who punched boys in the behind every time they bent down.

'I was amazed to find that a Tory prime minister had gone to a school like this. I suppose I was quite pleased in a way – they're usually public schoolboys, aren't they? – except for Mrs Thatcher of course.'

Briggs's ambition to become a cartoonist was entirely private and personal, and influenced by no one at school or at home. 'I did art at school and I was known to be good at art. The art master was a bastard called Jumbo Jenks. He used to jab you on the head with his four fingers all straight and stiff – like this' – he demonstrates the attack on the arm of his sofa – 'it's bloody painful! There was no creative teaching at all. We just did drawing – though actually this training suited an illustrator quite well. I was always keen on being a cartoonist and I used to write off to the papers and ask their famous cartoonists for a drawing. I've still got them – they're collectors' items now, I suppose. Giles sent me a signed print and there's an original of Pip, Squeak and Wilfred.'

The passionate hatred still aroused by Rutlish is more than matched by Ralph Steadman's tangible loathing of Abergele Grammar School and its viciously sadistic headmaster Dr Hughes.

Steadman told Danny Danziger in a *Worst of Times* interview in the *Independent* in 1991: 'He was a real son of a bitch and he destroyed me. It ruined my education. I began to live my whole life in fear of authority and that's stayed with me ever since.'

Most artists and designers seem to have had to put up some sort of fight to convince their schools that their chosen profession was a worthy one, and they emerge from the battle bloody but for the most part unbowed. Perhaps they were sustained by an inner creative life that they knew would win through in the end. Throughout their schooldays, most of them survived not as the anarchic iconoclastic rebels we might expect but as intensely creative and in fact rather well-balanced individuals, even deigning to accept a few school laurels for their skills. The artist Derek Hill won a school drawing prize at Marlborough, as did Nicky Haslam at Eton. Painter Allen Jones was always winning art competitions from infant school up to the end of his time at Ealing Boys Grammar, and even Raymond Briggs mentioned winning 'some sort of prize for art' at the end of his schooldays.

They put up with the slings and arrows of philistine teachers, worried parents (Derek Hill's father made him do 'commercial' art after school) and disastrous career advice and turned it all into their own kind of success. (Derek Hill interpreted the commercial art as stage design and had a splendid time in a Bauhaus-orientated Munich before the War.)

Most of them have survived to review their schooldays with the same sort of wry humour as Norman Thelwell, the definitive chronicler of the schoolgirl gymkhana: 'The art classes at the Rock Ferry High School, Birkenhead, were, I fear, dreary and did not encourage any kind of creative work.' Thelwell's art master expected realism and literal interpretation of his instructions, with no imaginative embellishment: "I told you to draw a dog kennel, boy! I did not tell you to draw the dog. Do it again!"

4 Broadcasting and Journalism

According to Philip Howard of *The Times*, there is an old Fleet Street proverb: 'Heavy the hack with a pack on his back.' (*The Times* 21 September 1991). Journalists, he believes, should be uncluttered by prejudices, otherwise they become bores. They should not accept honours, gongs or titles. They should be oblivious to personal success and unaffected by it. There is therefore no smooth bridge between success at school and a journalistic career.

He told us: 'I do not think it is possible to attach effects to causes as directly as you would like in the matter of choosing a career. Especially not journalism. You fall into it by accident, inertia, instinct and other matters.'

Yet even he admits that he might have been swayed towards journalism by success at Eton. 'I guess that being good at essays and general papers influenced me a bit. I was awarded my King's Scholarship to come to Eton particularly for the essays in my general paper, and I did well in it also for my Trinity (Oxford) scholarship. I was good at amusing examiners with essays – which is one definition of journalism.'

So this is a chapter full of mixtures: of people who drifted and were unhappy at school, often leaving it as soon as they could, and people who were happy and successful at school; of the divide between journalists who learnt their craft in hard apprenticeships or were fired by rebellion, and those who trod the path of success and academia. These met the requirements from the late 1960s onwards for polished graduates to enter what were becoming the more professional careers of journalism and particularly of broadcasting.

BBC Political Correspondent John Cole was educated at Belfast Royal Academy and came from a family with no university tradition. Securing an interview with the editor of the *Belfast Telegraph,* Cole turned up with his school cap in one trouser pocket and a sample essay on the Napoleonic Wars in the other. The editor tested him on the names of railway stations between Belfast and Londonderry and warned him against going to university if he wished to be a journalist.

At the poshest schools, there has long been a distaste for this kind of life. To them, all journalism is gutter. This was no doubt discovered by Geoffrey Archer, ITN's Defence Correspondent, who hated Highgate so much. 'To me it represented the Establishment and blinkered thinking. I think I drifted towards TV journalism as a career in the belief I would find a more broad-minded world.' Or as Brian Hitchen, Editor of the *Daily Star*, ex-Hegginbottom School, Ashton under Lyne, said: 'The most wonderful moment of my life came when I walked out of school . . . now I could get on with living!'

Godfrey Talbot, broadcaster of royal events, left Leeds Grammar School at 16 with few qualifications. He told us: 'My real education began after school when I avidly read and watched people of skills (especially skill in words and art and especially communicators and authors), picked their brains, imitated them, used their words, remembered their stories, tried to mould and model myself on individuals, who were educated and talented as I was not. I left Leeds Grammar School as soon as I could get into the newspaper business. Somehow I wiggled into the old *Yorkshire Post* as an office boy on the commercial side of the paper, simply to get my foot into a newspaper office.'

'If only I could get away from the formal world of education,' thought the young Frank Johnson, author of those brilliantly witty Parliamentary sketches in *The Times*, distinguished foreign correspondent and now Assistant Editor on the *Sunday Telegraph*. 'If only I could get away from the formal world of education I might find things I could do well.'

There was a background of intense competition in the Johnson family in the East End of London. 'My aunt had a son who was two years younger than me and she was always going on about how gifted her son was. She would go round saying: "I'm worried that my son isn't reaching his full potential." This was a way of informing my mother that her son – that's me – was not up to much.'

Things reached a climax when Johnson failed the 11 plus and his cousin passed it. It was a blow to the family prestige. 'I don't know what happened to my cousin. I lost touch with him. The last I heard he was selling fruit from a barrow!'

All Johnson's contemporaries at both his secondary schools – Chartesey and Shoreditch – have similarly melted into his oblivion. 'They went into manual jobs, clerical jobs – either becoming millionaires under Thatcher or in prison or doing dreary jobs.'

'My schools were sink schools. So they turned them into comprehensives. My last year at Shoreditch was the first year of Shoreditch

Comprehensive. So I was an early inmate of a comprehensive school. I was frightened most of the time because I couldn't do lessons. I wasn't good at anything – except from time to time I would have a burst at English or history.'

Interestingly enough Johnson remembers his one moment of success at the end of his first year at secondary school. 'I got a prize – a dictionary – for English. I got shifted into the A Stream as a result of this minor academic triumph. All that happened was that I remained in a slough of despond at the bottom of the A Stream.'

They had to teach him something. 'They did teach us rudimentary English. We had French as well. I was useless at French – completely incapable of finishing a French sentence. The boys who were good at French tended to be the very clever boys who were going to become clerks for the county council or the elect who were chosen to go into banks.

'I did not believe that I was the victim of any injustice because I failed the 11 plus. I took it to be part of life – that if you were not academically gifted or distinguished you went to this type of school. In an ideal world I would be intelligent and academically gifted but for some reason I am not good at lessons. There was nothing I could do about it then.'

But in the order of things life's race had not been run and there was plenty of time to catch up. 'I was ambitious to better myself. For as long as I can remember I wanted to be a journalist.'

Johnson got a job on the local paper in Walthamstow, London, and at the age of 18 was sent to cover a Campaign for Nuclear Disarmament meeting in 1962 when CND was in its heyday. 'I was immediately fascinated by all that was going on at this meeting because there seemed to be this villainous figure called Gaitskell . . . !'

The violence of the political language attracted him. Politicians whom he had previously thought dreary were being described as monsters. His interest and later his career in political journalism took off.

'I got it into my head very early on at school that you did not need any formal academic qualifications to be a journalist. You needed something called *flair*. But I realise now that this is a disastrous thing to recommend to any young chap wanting to become a journalist. The best young journalists I worked with were in fact rather good at school.'

Four out of every ten of the journalists and broadcasters who replied to our survey said that their school influenced them in their choice of career. Perhaps even more surprisingly – in view of the way journalists sometimes slate their schooldays – two out of three journalists and broadcasters were on balance happy at school and some, like Frank Bough, presenter of *Sky News*, were 'embarrassingly happy'. Hugh

Stephenson, Wykehamist former editor of *The Times* Business News and Professor of Journalism at City University, says his schooldays were the 'happiest years of my life'. Ludovic Kennedy knew from the age of 14 that he wanted to write and broadcast and he was happy in his last two years at school: 'Eton did present many opportunities of testing one's skills as a budding writer in the shape of things like the Rosebery History Prize, the Birchall Citizenship Prize and the Annual School Poetry Prize – all of which I entered and some of which I won.'

So why were so many successful journalists and broadcasters happy and where they were unhappy was it their fault or the school's?

The warmest tribute came from those whose schools made them feel like individuals. These tended to be grammar schools rather than public schools.

Gillian Reynolds, writer and broadcaster, says: 'The school' (Liverpool Institute High School for Girls) 'was a small school – 350 pupils – all girls, in the city centre. It took me a 45-minute journey each way each day but its prestige was high and it seemed a privilege to have got in.

'The size of the school made relationships with the staff closer and more useful – teachers knew you and what your record was. It was possible to accommodate individual gifts and aspirations. The attention that was paid to us as individuals gave me great self-confidence and I think formed the basis of my approach to journalism and broadcasting. Encouragement to take part in team and group activities, recognition of effort and fostering of genuinely social attitudes were of the greatest importance.'

The school, she says, is now closed – victim of the 1980s, under the 'Hattonite anti-grammar school régime. Its loss is apparent today with many people (including my son and daughter-in-law) now paying to receive what was once a free education.'

And if all that sounds fairly conventional, nothing could have been more unconventional than Raynes Park Grammar School as seen in retrospect through the eyes of Radio 4's *Brain of Britain* quizmaster, Robert Robinson:

'The headmaster was a monster called Garrett, and the masters were equally peculiar. This was enormously beneficial. I think of them as generating a never-ending supply of anxiety and entertainment, to which I became addicted.

'Everything was open to question. Irony and speculation were so much the climate of the place I didn't even notice, and of course I had no idea that this was unusual. I had never heard of the man – W.H.

Auden – who had written our school song. When T.S. Eliot came to present the prizes he looked like any other old cove, but by the time Rex Warner was teaching me English I'd started thinking I really must read *The Aerodrome* or *The Professor*. When Cecil Day-Lewis not only did a poetry reading but sang as well, accompanied on the Bechstein given to the school by Basil Wright (the one with the burn-mark from Auden's cigarette), I'd begun to realise that by the ordinary standards of our leafy suburb the school had been flown in from Alpha Centauri!'

Where did Frank Muir learn his range of interest in words, their derivation, and the art of punning? At Leyton County High School, in London, it was encouraged and never seen as odd. It was perfectly OK to swot and great chunks of poetry were memorised without resistance from any of the boys at the school.

The headmaster – Dr Couch – a nephew of the great Quiller-Couch – had a plummy melodious voice which no doubt is retained in Frank's subconscious. There was Mr Cohen who taught geography and threatened: 'You'll all end up as clerks.' (Ironically the epitome of success for Frank Muir's contemporaries.) The French master had a sly sense of humour which the boys liked. The gymnastics team toured the Netherlands every year. Musical appreciation classes were excellent and boys performed their own plays. Muir's own was about a mild-mannered man who got mixed up in a jewellery raid – it was light comedy made unintentionally more funny because, like Daisy Ashford, he was dealing with ideas and words he did not really understand – for example: 'His wife was a maiden lady'.

Frank's humour is bred of the air of Broadstairs to which his father, a New Zealand marine engineer, emigrated. The family scraped up enough money to spend the £11 a term needed to send Frank and his brother for their first year of English education to Chatham House School, Kent, where, incidentally they overlapped with Ted Heath, though they never met him.

'We were living in this fun seaside place and I was searching for laughter. I found I could make people laugh and it turned away wrath and brought about respect. People begin to expect you to perform in a certain way and the discipline of having to live up to their expectations was a good thing.

'Nowadays,' says Frank Muir, 'it seems that you have to pay £10,000 a year in order to get as good an education as the one I received. In retrospect I am profoundly grateful for the unbelievable quality of my two schools. It is perhaps a tiny tragedy of this century that that kind of start in life is no longer available.'

Grammar schools had a reputation for grindstone teaching. Not so, according to David Montgomery, Editor and Managing Director of the *Today* newspaper, who talks of the liberal régime at Bangor Grammar School which allowed pupils great freedom of expression. 'We could explore all sorts of avenues well away from the set text, and utter many half-baked thoughts.'

One particular teacher would get them to write their own scripts re-enacting such TV programmes, usually held in low esteem by the educational establishment, as *That Was The Week That Was*. 'This sort of experience', says Montgomery, 'helped to reinforce my desire to be a journalist. It gave me a sense of the thrill in communicating wittily and stylishly.'

Kate Bellingham, BBC2's *Tomorrow's World* presenter, might not have become a scientist had she not gone to a girls' school – The Mount in York. 'I never felt intimidated doing science and maths – "boys' subjects". I can't say science was inspirationally taught but the teachers were extremely dedicated and always willing to give up their spare time. If I had a problem, I could always go to the staff room and teachers would happily give up their coffee break to explain things.

'When I wanted to do Further Maths at "A" level, no-one had done it for about seven years but the teacher re-learned the subject and was quite happy to adapt to my individual needs. Nothing was too much trouble to enable people to realise their full potential.'

There were no school prizes at The Mount – a Quaker school with the Quaker dislike of personal competition – but there were improvement prizes. These awards went to those who had upgraded themselves by more than 10 per cent.

'These were read out at Assembly before the whole school and you really *wanted* one. I remember feeling a bit miffed that because I was very consistent I never got that recognition. But as I went further up the school, I realised that the people who had made this great effort were the ones who needed that encouragement.'

The hankering need for success is the nub of the journalist's stock-in-trade, with the daily comparison of results in competitive broadcasts and journals. It is the warm, long-lasting, oft-repeated 'fix' of The Scoop. Journalists warm to success and yet professionally need to be dispassionate about it.

Stockport High profoundly influenced Joan Bakewell, the TV presenter, and all her subsequent decisions about life. 'It was one of the excellent girls' grammar schools created at the turn of the century. It was staffed by dedicated spinsters (they had to be!) – many of whom had lost fiancés in the Second World War. They were devoted to their *gels*.

'I adored school: it stretched my mind, filled me with curiosity, drive and rewards for effort. I was head of house and head of school. So I learned authority and leadership.'

'School gave me a chance to shine,' says Gordon Honeycombe, the former newsreader, who says he was happy at Edinburgh Academy when he was not afraid. 'I just wanted to be famous but didn't know how. I didn't know which of my talents would bring me the most success. At school I tested those talents, not knowing where they would lead. I always wanted to be a success. It was just a matter of finding the right talents.'

Dominick Harrod, Economics Editor of BBC Radio 4, edited *The Elizabethan* at Westminster and this gave him a taste for journalism. David Jessel co-edited the *Eton Chronicle* with William Waldegrave, and the writer Bel Mooney won the Wiltshire/Somerset inter-schools debate – 'the first time,' she said, 'this little one-horse school [Trowbridge High School] had ever got to the final. I wanted to win.'

Mary Stott, the ex-*Guardian* journalist, wrote an essay on newspapers in the VIth Form at Wyggeston Grammar School, Leicester, and this fired her ambition to follow in her parents' footsteps into journalism. Magnus Linklater, Editor of *The Scotsman*, admits that he was attracted to journalism as a result while at Eton of 'feeding scurrilous gossip to a *Daily Mail* journalist covering the Fourth of June for Paul Tanfield's Diary – and enjoying it.'

While journalists cut their teeth on school magazines, many broadcasters got their first taste of sound waves from performing in school plays. John Craven, ex-BBC Children's TV's *Newsround*, recorded plays on a very early tape recorder at Leeds Modern Grammar School where, appropriately, he remembers playing Biggles.

Richard Baker, the broadcaster and former newsreader, said: 'The school dramatic society gave me the chance to perform in Shakespeare and modern plays at an early age. It was clear from that time that some kind of performing career was probable.'

His first part as a lady-in-waiting in *A Midsummer Night's Dream* did not perhaps augur well for a great broadcasting career. It was a non-speaking part – luckily, because his voice had broken. But then dramatic success at Kilburn Grammar School, founded on the lines of a public school by Bishop Crichton at the turn of the century, came with Enobarbus at age 14, Benedick at age 16, Falstaff at age 17 and then a drink-sodden author in *Tilly of Bloomsbury*.

The secret of success is often the dominating influence of one dedicated teacher. 'Her name', says Margaret Howard, 'was Elizabeth Trembath.' The vowels that made Radio 4's *Pick of the Week* such a long-running success were first taught her by a 'quiet almost spinsterish lady', quite young compared with all the other teachers, who were mainly nuns, at St Teresa's Convent, Sunbury.

'She came in to teach us elocution. We didn't dignify the subject by the name of "drama" in those days. We did do plays but elocution was about the technique of speaking. It is a pity it has become a dirty word because it was not at all about talking lah-di-dah. Elocution was the technique of using your voice properly.

'We never discussed anything like a career while at school. Miss Trembath was far too ladylike. But we were deeply into the art of speaking really well. We were into working out a poem to its absolute perfection. She and I had something going together – we appreciated something jointly. The others were aware of this but they tended to giggle and send it up.'

She left school at 16 and carried on having private lessons with Miss Trembath until she won a place at the Guildhall School of Music and Drama.

Brian Barron, the BBC's Asia correspondent, was inspired to go into journalism by Eric Dehn, the French teacher and his form master at Bristol Grammar School. Eric's brother, Paul, was a successful journalist 'so Eric [who also inspired David Drew the ballet dancer – see Chapter Nine] encouraged my fantasies about journalism. I was very happy to leave school at the earliest possible age – which I did at 16 – to become a junior reporter on the *Western Daily Mail*.'

Blundell's in the early 1960s had an inspired zoology master – appropriately called Joe Panther. His back garden proved to be the Athenaeum where Robert Fox, writer and broadcasting hero of the Falklands War, read the works of Russell, Camus, Sartre, Orwell, Huxley, the Brontës and the beginnings of some serious history.

'It was in his house that I learnt to research and write essays of literary criticism or historical analysis unaided. He was a wonderfully congenial free spirit, eccentric, a bachelor and old-fashioned freethinker. Coupled with the whole ethos of the VIth Form, his influence led me always to question the more outrageous claims of authority. Though it would take years to recognise it, his was the overriding influence which drove me into the world of journalism.'

Tom Burns, former Editor of *The Tablet,* wrote: 'The master (at Stonyhurst) who had most influence on my life was the Rev Martin D'Arcy SJ. He wrote several books of philosophy and theology and introduced me to a little-known and later famous poet – Gerard Manley Hopkins – and to modern writers like T.S. Eliot.'

Sometimes the influence of teacher is intertwined with that of parent. For Alexander Walker, the *Evening Standard*'s film critic: 'It was being read to at home as a child (by mother) and, later, at school (by the English master) that made me realise what words could do. Listening made me an acute writer, for I heard the words inside my own head and wrote them down at once on paper.'

The English master, Cyril Abraham, told Walker: 'Emotion recollected (whether or not in tranquillity) is the essential talent to be cultivated.' Mr Abraham gave him 'an understanding of how words could be used to evoke feelings, to persuade readers and "put myself on paper" with a delight and a comfort and a sense of security that I'd felt (without quite understanding) when I curled up beside my mother in her armchair and begged to be read to.'

Harold Evans, ex-Editor of the *Sunday Times*, caught an infectious interest for English composition from his headmaster W.L. Marsland of St Mary's Road Central School, Manchester, who was a passionate Shakespearean scholar. The young Harold Evans also edited the school magazine at the age of 14. 'This and my success in the history examinations probably began my desire to be a newspaperman.'

Gerald Priestland, ex-BBC Religious Affairs correspondent, writing to us shortly before he died in 1991, said: 'I think it was known that Charterhouse was a literary school, and certainly in my time there were at least two influential literary societies. A number of older and contemporary boys with literary pretensions, and most of the masters – especially the headmaster, Robert Birley (later Headmaster of Eton) – thought essays and the style of one's essays the most important thing. I was profoundly influenced by Birley's insistence that one must be saying something meaningful. His small, marginal notations in red ink: "But does this *mean* anything?" have pursued me through my life and have haunted my journalism healthily.'

Is it possible for a literary tradition to breed journalists? Robert Heller, the financial writer, says of Christ's Hospital (which also produced Bernard Levin): 'The school had a strong bias towards sports, cadet corps and discipline. However, the literary/academic tradition, dating back to Coleridge and Lamb, was very strong and the libraries (school and house) were well stocked. Literary prizes were the top awards and there was an excellent school literary magazine which I edited. A superb teacher stressed the crucial importance of fact-finding analysis and forthright conclusions. So school confirmed my very early ambition to be a writer and nurtured it and pointed me in the direction of journalism.'

Did Shrewsbury do anything to produce the *Private Eye* journalists who first met there in 1951? Richard Ingrams and Willie Rushton edited the school magazine and Christopher Booker and Paul Foot took over from them. How rebellious were they in those days?

Eyewitness accounts suggest that these iconoclasts were really an unwitting part of the Establishment. John Peel, the BBC Radio One disc jockey and pop music critic, was in the Lower Fourth when the *Private Eye* group were prefects:

'The *Private Eye* set were at the top of the school and they were to be avoided like the plague because they were school prefects and very august. They were *very* Establishment – always have been, as *Private Eye* is now really. I always think they fulfilled the same function as I fulfil at the BBC – people could point to them to show how tolerant the school was.

'I remember them bringing out what was really the first *Private Eye*. It was a parody of the school magazine and called *The Wallopian*. In fact I submitted some stuff for it myself but thank God they must have thrown it in the rubbish bin.

'I suppose I was a bit rebellious myself, but it was such low-key rebellion that the school didn't know it was being rebelled against! Your life at a school like Shrewsbury was so hedged about with rules and most of us were quite happy to abide by crazy regulations like not putting your hands in your pockets as you walked along the corridors.

'We had to wear a dark blue suit on Sundays and mine was just a shade lighter than the official school colour and it was double-breasted – that was about the extent of my rebellion!

'It's difficult these days to explain this acceptance of those rules – I can't really explain it to my own children. But both my grandfathers and my father and my brother had been at Shrewsbury and I just thought that Shrewsbury was all there was. I actually failed Common Entrance and was only let in because of my family. It never occurred to me that there was any alternative to the terrible rules and the savage beatings that we had to put up with then. In fact, when I was told that there was no hope of my getting into university, it was as if I'd been given the key to eternal happiness – I thought university would just be an extension of public school.'

Lord Rees-Mogg, Max Hastings, Gerald Priestland, the Dimblebys – David and Jonathan – Peter O'Sullevan and Adam Raphael all went to Charterhouse. However, if there was a journalistic or broadcasting tradition there, little of it seems to have washed off on Max Hastings, Editor of the *Daily Telegraph*, who reputedly feels that 'No day is too short to do an old Carthusian down' and is one of the most successful of those journalists who hated their schooldays.

He told us: 'On the credit side, I was very well taught. It did lay the foundations for a lot of writing which I did later. However, I was one of the last generations of pupils to whom public schools were pretty limited places. I did feel it was a pretty brutal atmosphere. It certainly taught you to be a survivor.'

The school house he lived in was overshadowed by a hill and had dark subterranean areas. There were daft rules about buttons being undone on jackets and Hastings appeared to be a freak and did not conform. 'We went through a trial by ordeal and many children's confidences were snapped and broken at the wheel.

'Ploughing your own furrow at this public school was not perceived to be a good thing. To be happy when I was at Charterhouse was not to be in fear.

'I suppose I was beaten twice a term for this, that and the other. I was always getting found out. It was an overwhelmingly cloistered atmosphere where people from the outside world were like spacemen.'

Occasionally Charterhouse invites him back to give lectures: 'I have always refused. It's not because I bear the school any ill-will at all, and I am always grateful for the education I had, but I could not bear to go and stand in that setting and pretend even tacitly that I had any bond with that place. Up to the age of 17 I really went through hell.

'I have always thought there's a strand of anger in everyone I've known who has been ambitious. It varies against whom or what that anger is directed. Sometimes it is family or friends. In my case my ambition was directed towards proving to myself that Charterhouse was wrong.'

A great deal of devastating journalism may be the result of pent-up wrath and determination from unhappy schooldays.

Lynn Barber hated her school, Lady Eleanor Holles in Hampton, Middlesex, partly because she was from Twickenham, not from classy Surrey, and was one of the scholarship girls among a lot of upper-middle-class girls who seemed thick.

'It was made very clear that our job was to get As at "A" level while the nice pony-riding girls from Claygate could get Ds and could skip homework. My father was a Labour voter, and the school was for Surrey prigs.'

Interestingly – in view of her later career putting down some of the mighty with her pen – Barber remembers: 'I went through a phase in English of terrific debunking – terrific attacks on set books like *Silas Marner* which I don't think anybody should ever have to read. I was attacking for the sake of attacking. Teachers said I would be a more trustworthy critic if I occasionally praised somebody.'

Julie Burchill, novelist and columnist, attended Brislington Comprehensive in Bristol and hated it. But she says she was so rebellious she would have hated any school. By the time she was 14, she was stealing clothes from all the big department stores and selling them at cut-price to the children in the school. She also attacked a teacher with a chair.

'She was called Mrs McIver; she was an English teacher and she was on dinner duty. The girls in this mixed school had to clean up the dining room. That was my very first run-in with sexism. She picked on me at a bad moment and I just saw a red mist in front of my eyes and I picked up a chair and hit her with it and that's all I remember really.'

For this Burchill was suspended and ran away to London and got a job as a shopgirl. 'I got taken back by the police and sent to a social worker. I told her I was "sensitive" and that people didn't understand me. Because I've got this little voice, I got away with it. I never went back to school. I spent the whole time in the public library and I read everything. I worked my way all through the children's section – usual stuff, books on horses and things, then I started on the adult section. I read Huysmans. I may have been a juvenile delinquent but I was a very well-read juvenile delinquent.'

Jilly Cooper, who disliked boarding intensely at Godolphin School, Salisbury, because she was violently homesick, also found an 'Aladdin's cave' of books – everything from Homer to Noël Coward – in her school library, and these and her love of English and history lessons encouraged her to write.

According to a not entirely impartial source – an *Observer* profile – Sir Peregrine Worsthorne, former Editor of the *Sunday Telegraph*, was savagely bullied at Stowe. On one occasion his schoolfellows stuffed him into a laundry basket and hurled it down a steep staircase. He told us:

'The house that I was in must have been the servants' quarters, and I had been led to expect that I was going to this great palace of the Dukes of Buckingham. I thought this would be a palatial life of luxury and comfort. The servants' quarters were about as dark and dank as it was possible to believe. So my first day at Stowe was overshadowed by a feeling of disappointment at being in this slum.'

This house, Grafton, was very rough. Other houses were much better and the headmaster – the legendary Roxburgh – had to his credit advised Worsthorne's mother to wait another term for a vacancy in the house to which his brother had gone. But his mother had ignored this advice, to Peregrine's cost.

'Stowe, being then a new public school (it was founded in 1923), had to take all comers and so accepted people who had neither the intelligence nor the social graces to be accepted by most public schools.'

The housemaster, Major A.B. (Fritz) Clifford, was an admirer of the Prussian Army and had run the Charterhouse school cadet force. He proceeded to try and knock Worsthorne Minor into shape. 'It was a miserable experience for us both – but worse for me than for him. I was very unhappy in my first year. Very bullied. Although he didn't bully me, he didn't stop the bullying.'

The house was so full of children with backgrounds and accents different from his own that he felt he was in a foreign country. 'I did feel as if I was with a lot of savages. I have no doubt that did not make me very popular with my fellow-Graftonians.

'My clothes were different. My mother sent down a tailor to measure me for some suits for the holidays and the measurement was done in the tuck shop. There was a whole lot of Grafton boys – including Colin Welch the journalist – who came and jeered. I remember it was a knickerbocker suit and the idea of having a tailor sent down from London seemed to them a most appalling affectation, while I did not think I had done anything provocative.'

Worsthorne's experience shows that the choice of house was much more important for him than the choice of headmaster or school.

'Roxburgh was such a strong personality and arrogant enough to think that his influence could civilise the entire school. He did have a strong influence on most of the school but there were these outer barbaric areas where Roxburgh's civilising Roman influence did not reach.'

For Worsthorne the unhappiness lasted for two years. He dates the turn-around in his fortunes from the influx of non-professional teachers during the war years. 'You only need one master with whom you click. John Davenport, who taught history, was a marvellous influence and he was absolutely responsible for getting me an exhibition to Cambridge.'

Asked if on balance she was happy at school, Moira Bremner, the TV presenter, put five ticks in the 'No' box. Only after doing a degree as an adult did she discover how able she was. She now suspects that she was a highly gifted child.

'I was a classic product of a time when it was assumed that maths and science were of little importance to "nice girls" who should marry and be kept and not need a real career.

'By the time I reached secondary school (Princess Helena College, Hitchin) my mathematical abilities and scientific curiosity had been repressed by teachers who resented questions and disliked me finishing the maths book when they had asked for only ten sums to be done.

'The relentless pressure to conform 24 hours a day and the exceptionally violent bullying rife in my preparatory boarding school increased the bookish tendency I already possessed as an only child in a very unhappy home. Poetry especially became my solace.

'I learned not to excel, not to try, not to be seen to try, not to use the range of vocabulary which came naturally to me. Not to be myself.'

Maev Alexander, presenter on the TV programme *That's Life*, fell foul of her school, Hutchesons' Grammar School in Glasgow, for daring to want to become an actress – a career even worse than journalism. She has very strong views on the damage done to her by the attitudes prevalent at her school:

'The school from 1953-1965 had probably the best academic record in Scotland. It was largely staffed by single women deprived of husbands by the vicissitudes of war – a crowd of Jean Brodies with none of the vision, charisma or danger, but with Calvinism deeply rooted.

'I was regarded as a self-aggrandising show-off; if I expressed an independent opinion it was perceived as cheek. I was disciplined by the use of deep irony against which few children have any armaments. Young ladies from Hutchesons' Grammar School were expected if clever

– and most were – to go to university, if not clever to go to domestic science college. What they were certainly not expected to do was to go to the Royal Scottish Academy of Music and Drama. My headmistress refused to sign my grant form – so outraged was she by my bringing such notoriety to the good name of Hutchesons'. I am still at 43 trying to throw off the intellectual snobbery and real fear of authority instilled into me.'

Her fellow-presenter Scott Sherrin had an equally miserable time for similar reasons – he was already a child film star and TV personality by the time he went to Boswells Comprehensive, Chelmsford. He told us:

'I left the school in 1988. I wasn't happy at all because I had practically no support there. My TV work, which I had been doing for years, was never mentioned. They all pretended it did not exist. You would think they would have been proud of me but they weren't at all.

'I admit I wasn't a model pupil but it was six of one and half-a-dozen of the other. I feel I was victimised by the teachers. One day I got sent out of the classroom and a teacher came past and asked me what I was doing there. He said this really mean thing, which I have never forgotten: "There's no Oscars to be won here, sonny!"

'Now this really got me, because I had never once mentioned that I was on TV. I did a couple of plays at primary school but I deliberately didn't do any when I started at secondary school. That remark made me out to be a stage-struck affected kid, which I never was.

'There was definitely a race element in these and other comments. Nobody called me a nigger or anything. But it was because I was black and because I was a black who was doing well. It's interesting that a friend of mine – another black guy from a really poor family – got on OK because they could patronise him.

'I never really had any close friends at school. I was a loner. I was just at school for a while before I left and did something.'

Some managed to overcome the adversity of their schooldays. 'On my first day at Bablake (now part of King Henry VIII School, Coventry) at the age of 10, I was singled out twice for being unusually small,' says Donald Trelford, Editor of the *Observer*. 'The first time was in the hall, when the headmaster called me on to the stage and asked me in front of the school how tall I was.

' "Four foot half an inch," I replied proudly. He turned to the congregation and announced to general laughter and applause: "Gentleman, let me introduce Mr Trelford, probably the smallest boy ever admitted to Bablake in four hundred years!"

'The second occasion was in the gym, when we all stripped to shorts and plimsolls and ran round to be inspected by the PT master. A boy called Stubbs, who was unusually fat with flabby breasts, was made to run round with me.' Again Trelford appeared conspicuous by his lack of inches. The PT master said of him to general amusement: "We'll call this one Bruiser."

Trelford told us: 'Looking back on those incidents, which could have had a traumatic effect on a more sensitive soul, I've sometimes wondered if they were what first motivated me to try to excel in sport and to make myself generally prominent in other school activities. I became captain of rugby and cricket and represented the school at tennis and athletics as well as becoming head boy – and, perhaps crucially, editor of the school magazine, where I acquired a taste for writing myself (including poetry which I wrote at speed to fill awkward corners) and for arranging other people's work.'

Some did not simply rise above their schooldays but turned every seeming disaster into triumph. The columnist Miles Kington found himself a Sassenach boy in an alien, fairly traditional, kilt-swirling Scottish Highland school. On the whole he was happy there and he is truly grateful to Glenalmond for the following:

1. for deterring him from ever becoming a teacher;
2. for giving him the experience of having been at a school abroad without having to step out of Britain;
3. for his first entrée into journalism. The school had a very dull magazine. So he and his friends started a rival one which made money.
4. for forbidding pupils to play any form of music except classical or Scottish pipe music. This inspired him to start a jazz band.

He writes: 'On the last day of term, we were woken in dormitories by the bloody school pipe band marching round at about 6 a.m. One term I and the jazz band got up at 5.30 and went round before the pipers, playing jazz to wake people up. It gave me the idea that one could go out and do things one wasn't meant to do.'

In the same vein, Chris Dunkley, of the *Financial Times* and BBC Radio 4's *Feedback*, records his gratitude to Haberdashers' Aske's School, Elstree, for expelling him during the term he was due to sit for a Cambridge University scholarship. 'Had this not occurred I would not have got a job on my local paper, the *Slough Observer*, from which the rest of my career has sprung.'

Jeremy Paxman, the TV presenter, would like to express his appreciation to Malvern College for rusticating him so that he had to return for an extra term during which he won an exhibition to Cambridge University from which all good subsequent things flowed.

Daily Mail gossip columnist Nigel Dempster told us, 'I was happy at Sherborne and even happier when I was expelled after three years.'

'The only influence my school had on my career', says Patrick Stoddart (*Sunday Times* TV critic) of Watford Boys' Grammar School, 'was in telling me I would never have one. The headmaster called my mother in when I was 14 and told her I would be much happier at the secondary modern where I could learn a useful trade.' He left at 16 and went on to a local newspaper.

'Career advice was restricted to an annual address by the headmaster,' we were told by Bill Hagerty, Editor of *The People*. 'When I was 15 (at Beal Grammar School, Ilford), and in response to questioning I told him I wanted to enter journalism, he was scornful and dismissive of my ambition in front of the class. My determination quadrupled on the spot.'

While Bridget Kendall, the BBC's Moscow correspondent, was able to start learning Russian at the age of 14 at the Perse School for Girls, Cambridge, John Timpson, the former co-presenter of the *Today* Radio 4 breakfast programme, is scathing about the uselessness of the education he received at school – compared to the Army.

He told us: 'At Merchant Taylors' there were three "Sides" – Classical, Modern and Science – and a decision had to be made at the age of 13. As I was quite good at arithmetic I was put into Science, where my eventual matriculation in such obscurities as calculus and co-ordinate geometry have proved utterly useless to my career.

'In hindsight I should obviously have gone into the Modern Side and learnt French and German – but who is to know that at 13?

'Consequently the actual curriculum was useless to me in later years, but one of the wartime masters happened also to be a novelist (though I did not know it at the time) and although it was outside normal class activity he gave me some very useful tips on how to write readable English, which have stood me in good stead.

'Other than that, my only useful journalistic experience at school was producing a form newsletter: *Science Div. A – Sidelights* which was almost instantly banned as being an attempt to undermine authority – it was a little caustic about the masters. It then reappeared as the *JTC Jester*, concentrating on the Junior Training Corps, and was again banned for undermining discipline. It did, however, give me useful practice for producing an unofficial army magazine during National Service called simply *Clang*. The Army also taught me how to touch-type, which proved more useful than anything I learned at school – particularly calculus and co-ordinate geometry.'

'The only incident of even peripheral interest', says Anthony Howard, former Editor of the *New Statesman*, 'was the remark of J.T. Christie, headmaster of Westminster, that if I did not pull myself together he could perceive a definite danger that I would end up as editor of the *New Statesman* or something unsatisfactory like that.'

Perhaps it does not matter whether those who went into journalism went with the blessing of their school or whether they grafted their way to success despite their school. The pivot upon which success and happiness at school depended was the encouragement to be an individual rather than the pressure to conform.

Peregrine Worsthorne's unhappy and his happy Stoic experiences typify this. All became bright once he joined the smart set of historians (which included journalist Robert Kee). He said: 'The History set was the stylish social circle. *I wanted their approval and I wanted to be noticed as an individual.*'

5 Business

'I hated school, am rebellious by nature and dislike being told what to do by damn' fools!' comments Sir Maurice Laing, old boy of St Lawrence College, Ramsgate and President of John Laing plc.

Schools have clearly influenced the captains of industry, the barons of business and the counts of commerce, sometimes positively, often negatively. The qualities of drive, ambition, and self-reliance necessary for business success are gifts of personality. Schools have sometimes found these traits of personality difficult to handle.

Many of the individuals interviewed in this chapter, however, arrived at an accommodation (often on their own terms) with the structure of authority encountered in early years. These men and women took what they wanted out of the system and went their way. As the late Sir Charles Villiers, ex-Chairman of British Steel, remarked about leaving Eton: 'I left the herd and never really rejoined.'

There was never any doubt where Maurice Laing would end up. At eight years old he was already marching round the family building sites. Illness, however, persuaded his parents that he should benefit from the sea breezes of Ramsgate rather than go to Mill Hill as was originally intended. St Lawrence was a rugged place but Laing prospered there to the extent of being made the youngest prefect in the school.

The headmaster was unpopular with boys and governors but Laing established a rapport which came in useful when he came into conflict with his housemaster. He went instead straight to the top and when the housemaster tried to pursue him further he told him: 'The matter has been dealt with. Good-day, Sir!'

Laing left school at 17 and started work in the family business at the tail end of the Depression. His father could not by then afford to send both his sons to university and it was his brother who went to Cambridge. He is grateful for this early education in the realities of manufacturing and of how people lived: 'My whole life has been conditioned by that.' The benefits and charitable trusts established by his father continue to receive his full support and he believes that 'it is sordid to have as your sole motive the making of money'. St Lawrence College with its lack of heating or hot water was a good introduction to the austerity of a business trying to move out of recession. He had always been in and out of trouble at school but that also, it seems, bred resilience for the years to come.

Sir Peter Miller, former Chairman of Lloyd's, has spent his life at the heart of the City of London, which Sir Maurice Laing views with some suspicion as a place where too many people make their money too easily. Sir Peter illustrates a theme which will become familiar in this chapter – that of the conventionally successful and competitive public schoolboy, popular with his peer group, who learns the skills of leadership in informal, social ways. He emerges as a consensualist. Rugby, as Miller says, 'fostered the attractions of the "professional" life and taught the logic of thinking.'

He stresses that he found school enjoyable because he was a conformist. Even wrongdoing was a matter of conformity. 'Things like going out at night were usually done in a group.' Individualism only arrived in his last year at Rugby. He seized an advantage and got into the cleverest form, the Upper Bench, as a historian rather than as a classicist: 'This was a very good thing to be because then you were an expert on something they were not experts on.'

He told us, 'Being at school during the war years was like living under a Damoclean sword but it was a good preparation for the realities of army life and beyond. It taught discipline and self-discipline, the need to get the stuff done in time as well as the ability to be comfortable in an ordered framework.' By contrast, 'the rough boys from Tiger Bay found it difficult to get up on time because they were not used to such orderly circumstances at school.'

The great lesson both at Rugby and at Oxford was 'if you persevere enough that will get you a long way.'

Miller was 'lucky enough to find exams easy and that has little to do with intellect really.' Robert Ogilvie, subsequently headmaster of Tonbridge and Professor of Humanity at St Andrews, was in his form, although two years younger. 'He led me to understand what a really clever mind was like and that mine would never be like that. At best it could be a good, possibly very good, second-class brain, never a first-class one.'

Perseverance was therefore a lesson learnt from the small world of the Quad and it could be applied in the later circumstances of adult life. For the time being, Miller made no connection between success at school and his future life: 'My horizons were very limited. I was a very ordinary schoolboy and had no vision about what life could be like. There was little connection with life outside the school or between the growing schoolboy and people earning bread and butter.'

More restless, individualistic, and meritocratic traits have emerged from the grammar-school tradition, the consequences of whose demise are such a theme of this book. Sir Robert Telford, Life President of the Marconi Company, was educated at the famous Quarry Bank School, Liverpool and at Queen Elizabeth's Grammar, Tamworth. He was challenged continually by his headmaster at Quarry Bank to think about why he had come there and what his role was in life. He was being urged to use his talents to help others. School was a diverse experience since he was interested in languages and literature as well as the sciences in which he achieved an effortless success. Maths and physics were a love affair for him and he regarded chemistry as a fascinating detective story.

When Telford moved to Tamworth he found himself doing a project which lasted a whole weekend. An interest in plays continued in Cambridge. These diverse interests were the making of him when he found the doors of the scientific Civil Service closed to him after he got a Third at Cambridge. Marconi only wanted Firsts for their research and development men but were prepared to look for other qualities in their management trainees. At school, as at Cambridge, Sir Robert was 'independent, self-contained but needed to be with people'. He found that his career was made with Marconi for life.

He was lucky, he insists. But what of the 80 per cent of the population, he asks, who are under-trained and not given work up to their capacity? And what of the no-hopers who are churned out of primary schools? Sir Robert's recent report on skills shortages shows that the United Kingdom produces only half of the number of engineers needed in this country. His good fortune was that, coming from a council house, he hit the right school at the right time and, with his interests in jazz, drama, literature and science, could emerge quite as 'rounded' a figure as any public schoolboy of the 1930s.

Sir Archibald Forster, Chairman of Esso UK, spent the war years as a boy at Tottenham Grammar School. Nights would be spent in air-raid shelters, homes destroyed – and two boys were killed by V2s on the school playing fields. 'My one aim was to get to the RAF as a pilot – I didn't think about my career at all.' At the end of the War he just felt lucky to be alive. His parents had 'that working-class zeal that I was not going to go through what they had been through – and that's something I feel very strongly about.'

Tottenham Grammar had a long tradition going back to its sixteenth-century foundation. It had, in Mr Simmonds, a real leader. 'He had a personality and was a leader in the school. There was no doubt about his leadership qualities. He was a model – someone of whom you could say – that's *somebody*.' He could be found everywhere in the school – sometimes sitting in their midst in lessons.

Sir Archibald remembers: 'He was very tolerant of the sort of people we were. We used to make bombs in the chemistry labs and he caught us one day trying to detonate one outside. It went off while he was there. He gave us a lecture on the folly of it – and there were no further repercussions.'

Sir Archibald had always wanted to be a scientist and, although there was a shortage of everything, the school would somehow find the necessary materials even if they had fallen off the proverbial lorry: 'We got a full education in straitened circumstances.' Success came to him easily and he observes the traditional national reserve when he says, 'I have never been conscious of being ambitious. I've just done my best and have been lucky to be in the right place at the right time – which is what most people at the top of British companies will tell you.'

Sir Archibald stresses that Tottenham was more than a centre of academic excellence. There was an atmosphere of all-round dedication. The history master was also the rugby master and everyone had to be in a team however bad they were. 'It was a totally rounded curriculum. I did four sciences at "A" level but you were not allowed just to do that. There was an economics teacher at the school who was a Red. He was a great influence on me and introduced me to business by debating the meaning of money. That did not turn me off business at all.'

The school no longer exists though the building remains near the Broadwater Farm estate: 'It had lots of money behind it but it was closed three years ago because of socialist demagoguery.'

Forster left Tottenham, rarely visited it again and never played a part in the Old Boys' Association. It is perhaps part of the commentary on such schools that they became vulnerable precisely because they were so successful as ladders of social mobility for those who left the area.

Sir Alan Goodison, Chairman of the Wates Foundation, was a member of a talented VIth Form at Colfe's Grammar School, ten of whose members obtained Cambridge scholarships.

'It was the flame of my contemporaries' talent that inspired me, and their sophistication that first abashed and eventually goaded me into emulation.'

Sir Alan is also the only person in this book who recalls the headmaster's secretary as an influence. She would reminisce 'about the Rive Gauche in Paris in the twenties and James Joyce in particular, giving me an idea of life abroad as altogether more exciting than at home.' Possibilities of exploration lay all around him. When a contemporary described César Franck's Symphonic Variations as 'reminiscent of tepid rings of coffee left by dirty cups on café tables' when compared to Brahms' Fourth Symphony, he realised 'that there was a lot more to be explored than I had imagined.'

Sir Frank Cooper, civil servant turned company chairman, sees in Manchester Grammar School just before the Second World War a successful blending of two traditions: 'an exceptional competitive streak coupled with a strong ethos of community and caring for others. You were expected to fight for what you believed in, to compete and do better than others.'

James Birrell, Chief Executive of the Halifax Building Society, left Belle Vue Grammar School, Bradford, when he was 16. Both his parents were teachers but he had an uncle who was a chartered accountant and deemed more glamorous than his father because he travelled more extensively. That was the model that he wished to follow and he had a clear vision about a professional business career by the time he was 15. As many as two-thirds of the top form would leave at 16 for careers in commerce and the professions.

Birrell was always self-motivated, and had to make his own way. He was sent to Belle Vue because neither of his parents taught there. But it did entail a long journey. When he got there he was on his own and knew nobody. He was competitive in an unselfconscious way and there was a certain amount of peer pressure. He certainly got on with people at school. In an implicit way the school, he thinks, taught him this: 'The liberal education of Belle Vue taught you that reason and common sense were the way of the world.' The RAF, in which he was commissioned later on, 'taught you that you can't be a boss and also one of the boys.' At 16 he was looking for a more exciting career than the one which seemed on offer if he stayed at school: by the time he was 21 he had qualified as a chartered accountant.

Sir Ian MacGregor, former Chairman of the Coal Board, has had a more exciting career than most. An earlier scientific training led to a career in general management. When his first company seconded him to a research laboratory because of his technical qualifications and gave staff positions to others, he left. 'My career flowed in the direction of running things and a career in research was incompatible with my ambitions and interests.'

An interest in organisation, however, can be traced to his schooldays at Hillhead High School, Glasgow. Mr Barclay was an inspiring English Literature teacher and 'we went through the whole gamut'. But what really interested him was the history course 'because it gave you an understanding of how the political world had emerged. I was interested in the evolution of our society and in how things had come to be as they are. I was left with an understanding of how things had evolved and I got to understand that things don't happen by accident. Patterns could be seen which followed the economic ambitions of people.'

He was impressed, as an example of this economic determinism, by the invasion of Scotland by the Bronze Age cultures of the Mediterranean peoples. 'That was the advanced technology of the time: they were searching for bronze and I was amazed that they knew where to go and how to get there. The Bronze Age culture did not, therefore, develop in an accidental way and left its impact on Western Europe where the ingredients were developed.'

Sir Ian's parents were 'drivers' and were behind their sons' success. They had to scratch around in order to provide for the education of three sons and a daughter but they never short-changed. Contemporary British education, he thinks, lacks this parental motivation. 'Education is a parental responsibility, not the State's. My parents believed in investing in their children. In the United States parents are similarly acutely ambitious for their children. You start there from a broader base and you're in a materialistic economy and society which means you can buy anything you want. Socialism erodes that. It's like a drug. You end up dependent on other people and the idea of the individual is eroded.'

British schools have often been criticised for their supposed hostility towards vocational and technical education, their bias towards the professions and the eventual 'gentrification of money'. Public schools have been especially vulnerable to this charge.

Sir Campbell Adamson, former Director General of the CBI, thinks that 'the ethos of Rugby tended to militate against my wish to go into industry.' Bob Horton, Chairman of BP, found at King's Canterbury that 'most of my contemporaries, though obviously more clever, weren't really interested in industry. Whereas I, from my family background, was.' The school hindered his career 'by making it fairly clear that the best people went to Oxbridge and into the professions.'

At Blundell's Lord Stokes, Chairman of Dutton Forshaw, made a decision to take an engineering apprenticeship. 'This was regarded as odd and nothing was done to encourage it – rather the reverse. All encouragement in those days was towards a classical education and, funnily enough, the same atmosphere seemed to be pervasive when my son attended the same school.'

Former Chairman of BP, Sir Peter Cazalet, is exceptional in saying that his public school, Uppingham, 'broadened the mind and made jobs in farming, industry and commerce seem to be entirely favourable. It was not an intellectual hothouse, and the fact that it drew boys from a very wide spectrum of backgrounds broadened the options available to those boys.'

However, business leaders also point to the advantages of such schools for their careers in a management sense. They learned lessons in the acquisition of power; they dealt with people and gained leadership skills. As Lord Stokes says, 'Blundell's had a very good effect in making me independent and accustomed to "roughing it".'

At Rugby, Campbell Adamson learned the value of 'guts in adversity'. He says, 'It was a very tough place and you had to stand your corner. If you didn't you were in some difficulty.' He also learned some of the consensual values he brought to the problems of British industry.

'Industry', he notes, 'is a *people* thing, and the values that got you along in a reasonably moral path, your treatment of other people, your views about how you dealt with other people and your treatment of them – all of these were greatly affected by my education.'

When he started in the steel industry he 'was amazed by the lack of consideration for the other man's point of view, the lack of any consultation – and that came from the kind of education and values I learnt at Rugby.'

His school gave him 'a wide view of society and of history'; it taught him that 'everything had been done before anyway'. But it did not inhibit the belief that 'pushing on and change were necessary'.

He comments, 'It's ironic and contradictory, for the British are famous for not enjoying change. But Rugby helped to get me into a liking for change.'

His own transition to Rugby had been a difficult one. He had been head boy of his prep school and was therefore 'too big for my boots'. He actively disliked some of his contemporaries but was resilient: 'The awfulness of school meant that things weren't so bad afterwards.'

Sir Campbell identifies two major episodes in his life when he had to call upon school lessons of guts in adversity. The first was when he was moved from the loss-making Llanwern steelworks to a lesser division. 'Until then everything in my life had been going up. I remember getting over it and thinking: "The only bloody thing to do is – do the next thing better." That was because of my background. I was not going to accept this.'

The second incident was just before the 1974 General Election when Adamson's remarks in an eve-of-poll press conference about the state of the country were blamed by many Tories for their defeat.

'That is now a myth and the myth has nothing to do with what happened. It was a considerable personal hurt – much more so than the first incident. It took me a long time to get over it and to knuckle down again.'

For Adamson the links between education and success are subtle ones: 'If you go to a place like Rugby you are expected to do well afterwards. And so when you do it's not a great thing to crow about. The converse is also true. If you don't do well you should be saying, "What the hell's wrong with me?" That has had an effect on me.'

Some of the success has to do with the content of what gets transmitted, but Adamson lays greater stress on 'the wider surrounding thing, the masters you rub shoulders with.' He has no doubt that his own education helped him start in the steel industry, but for reasons which cast a light on the inadequacies of British industry:

'Until the War British industry was run by small family companies which passed from father to son with a consequent failure to build up a capital base. I got in for snob reasons. They had not known about management trainees but they thought, "We'll take a special interest in this bloke – he's been to Rugby and Cambridge – he's one of us." I liked a lot of them but they had no idea how to manage anything. When I went into steel I had never been into a factory in my life before and I was appalled. The War had interrupted investment and most of the plant had been put in between 1910 and 1920.'

Gentrification of the sons of commerce and business, aided by schools such as his own, played its part in this economic stagnation. 'People owning small steel plants turned themselves into aristocrats straight away. That's the way they managed and operated. They only got down to other things when they were taken over. The Gilbertsons of Pontardawe, for example, expected the whole village to come and sing carols outside the big house on Christmas Eve. Well, 1946 was a bit late for that!'

Adamson remains a defender of much that was done in the name of the corporate State in the 1960s and 1970s and recalls how one of his school accomplishments came very much in useful when he called on Edward Heath, then Leader of the Opposition, in his rooms in Albany.

'Someone must have told him – get to know these people and find out what industry thinks. He asked polite questions but they were obviously questions he was not interested in at all. After about five awkward minutes he said something about music and I said I played the organ and the piano. We finished up playing duets on the piano. The problems of British industry were not mentioned after the first five minutes.'

At Winchester Sir David Barran, former Chairman of the Midland Bank and of Shell, recalls that 'there was a sort of general feeling that if you were reasonably bright you would probably go into the law or the civil service. I was bad at games and I was not in the Corps but I was a natural leader among the friends I made at Winchester. I would always be the one to say "Let's do this."' His housemaster 'gave one a taste for trying everything and it was this general feel, this enthusiasm that was so good. It was a liberal education and the open-plan way of life, having a communal study room and having to sleep in dormitories, was a good thing because you really couldn't be a loner.'

Sir Ian MacLaurin, Chairman of Tesco, also learned to be gregarious: 'The two sports masters at Malvern helped in my development as a team builder.' Though the school helped in another way too: 'Through Malvern I met with the founder and Chairman of Tesco plc who engaged me as a trainee.'

When Wandsworth Grammar School was evacuated Sir Clifford Chetwood, Chairman of Wimpey, found himself living in a boarding house with twenty other boys. There was, he notes, an 'overall development of leadership' – and 'the opportunity to enjoy boarding-school facilities made leadership essential.'

Sir James Cleminson, Chairman of the British Overseas Trade Board, valued the fact that he could spend his last year at Rugby without exams. 'That gave me a very broad education designed to make young men take an interest in a wide circle of subjects.'

Any scepticism about business and industry that these individuals came up against in their schools, therefore, seems to have counted for little.

The opportunity to develop informal skills of management and leadership was more important. In all our case histories, whether learning at school 'how to get the best out of people', or by reacting as strong personalities against meaningless rules, these people evinced a natural feel and taste for authority. They like success.

Yve Newbold, Company Secretary at Hanson plc, went to the Sacred Heart and Blessed Sacrament convents in Sussex. She says that she was a 'difficult, bright, rebellious child and not easy for teachers to cope with'. She told us: 'The most influential person during my school career was my history and Latin teacher who alone recognised and encouraged me.' When she was once commended for an essay which she had worked hard on, 'I realised for the first time the enjoyment of achievement and it never left me.'

Stephen Rubin, Chairman of Pentland, the makers of Reebok trainers, discovered at Canford School 'the unfairness of the promotion system which made me realise that I could rely on no-one other than myself and made me determined to prove that I could succeed.'

Donald Kirkham, the son of a Grimsby fish-merchant, and now Chairman of the Woolwich Building Society, was 'conditioned for respectability', and the technical schools established alongside the grammar schools under the 1944 Education Act gave him his opportunity. He left school at 16 with 'a clear notion that the more I learnt the less I knew'. He was not ambitious much before the age of 11 but thereafter he was 'self-firing' and 'an inferiority complex drove me on.' His education led him to see that ambition should be defined in terms of 'delivering the goods in a professional job.' Kirkham was not concerned with ambition in the sense of keeping an eye on the next step on the ladder. The school prepared him for 'the reality that life is tough and that calm seas don't make a good mariner.'

He emphasises that he is no entrepreneur and dislikes those entrepreneurs who risk other people's money. His education and expectations made him into an 'organisational man' and 'most activity is organisational.' He chose at 11 to go to Grimsby Technical School and into the commercial department where he learnt the fundamental principles of management and administration. There were drawbacks, such as having to give up Latin, but it set him up for a career which left him to work out in the field on his own at the age of 24 with only an office and a secretary. It was a crucial advantage: 'Because you were on your own people began to notice you.'

He might have been 'reticent, introverted and no born leader' but quickly gained 'the confidence that comes from success'. As he has risen he has remained loyal to a principle of individualism. 'I am not an Establishment man and I don't like the diet of conventional wisdom. Leaving school at 16 was the norm in my day. Today everybody is recruited from a university but I think the Prime Minister, who left school at 16, is a good model.'

According to Donald Kirkham 'it is a bad thing not to have a clear sense of what to do at school and in life.' He had this clear sense. Men who espouse conventional saloon-bar wisdom are, in his words, 'left with a sense of their own adequacy'. He, however, always knew that there was more to do. He was taught book-keeping, shorthand and typing and economics in the half of the building that Grimsby Technical School shared with Wintringham Grammar School. There was a commercial, an engineering and a building department. When his class met recently for a fortieth reunion, 'I felt joy at seeing that the class had remained the same: not one member of that class of twenty-four had failed.'

A similar endurance has marked Anne Burdus, the Marketing Director of Olympia and York, who failed the 11 plus and 'worked hard to be transferred from Alnwick Secondary Modern School to Duchess County Grammar in the same town. She observes, unsentimentally, 'This set work patterns which have remained with me.'

Rupert Hambro's patrician banking background made Eton an obvious choice for his education. He remembers the principle of hierarchy which enabled older boys to lord it over younger boys. 'It was like the Japanese – one wanted to be Chairman of the Board because that meant 27 people carrying your bag and when you were Chairman you wanted your own bag-carrier.' This principle of hierarchy, however, is of limited value in life and Hambro is detached about his school: 'Two things change. First, the concept of one's master being "Sir". Then, at 14, an 18-year-old was a god. This changed when one was 26, when there was nobody left in your life who was "Sir". By 30 there was nobody whom you did not call by their Christian names immediately.

'Secondly, personal relationships and friendships are of enormous value, but if you carry on as you were at school – when you have very close friendships and see a lot of each other – then that can affect your success. I notice that my fellow-men who retained their very close school friendships are those who have not succeeded. Those who got out into the world and used their ability to make friendships with others of different ages and generations are those who have succeeded. So – the lesson is to make friends but not allow yourself to be in cliques or to get into a group you can't get out of. When you are at school you don't realise the enormous amount of time, attention and energy it takes to maintain friendships and to work on them. When you leave you realise that if you do spend your time doing that then there's no time for anything else. People who succeed in business tend to be people who don't have great friends.'

School, for Hambro, 'is not something I remember with enormous affection. I have lots of Etonian friends, but not close ones. Some still look as they did then, probably because they have not worked very hard. Others I'm fond of and was fond of at school, but can't persuade others that they are good people. Others leave school and that is the highlight of their lives and they never recover from it.'

He was competitive in the marginal sense of 'wanting to be with the right people and in terms of my place in life. It was important for me to be liked at school – and that did not change till later when I realised that you have to stand up for yourself. I did not become generally competitive until I got married.'

Hambro was a poor sportsman and so he tried other things. For a while he took the leaving photographs of boys. He then bought a 1934 Austin 8 during the holidays, took it back to Eton, took it apart and rebuilt the body. He enjoyed only one form of rowing – bumping fours – because he could actually see the point of trying to catch the man in front. He could not see the point of catching the ball or rowing for miles and then being beaten by someone simply because of bad luck.

His happiest memory is of proving them 'stupid asses' at his prep school when he passed into Eton after the school had written to his father saying that he might not make it. Once he got there the man he was closest to was his tutor, John Marsden: 'He did things for me that others would not do. I was an avid supporter of Spurs and so he took me to the FA Cup Final. He gave me a ticket and said, "I've got a ticket for the other side." I discovered later that he had only the one ticket and had slept the whole way through on the bench outside. It's the sort of thing you never forget.'

Hambro may not have been a rebellious schoolboy but he was not in awe of those set over him. He was once sent to the headmaster for passing a harmlessly dirty joke in the Vice-Provost's dull economics lesson. Birley, 'a distant, bent, cold figure', stopped his leave and said, "Hambro, if you weren't as old and as large as you are I would flog you." "Oh come *on*," I thought.' He became a school hero for a while 'because it was thought extraordinary to have one's leave stopped just for passing a dirty joke.'

Other masters received similar short shrift. 'One just assumed that all masters were queer because they wanted to be surrounded by boys all the time.' The Head of School type who can handle masters and win their approval is similarly dismissed: 'They are often disqualified for success in later life because they feel they've done it all. Their memories linger on and they go back and play cricket. It's very, very exceptional for my contemporaries who were hero-figures at sport and so on to do very well in later life. They are followers but never leaders. They may be partners in estate agents' firms but they don't create anything. Those who do best are the most unlikely figures at school. They don't do well and are not covered with caps and colours. They are late developers and are willing therefore to take risks later on. The risk-takers are the creators – they are the ones who build things. People like Jimmy Goldsmith and Richard Branson. Old English money is always risk-averse.'

Hambro's realisation that school is different and that real life is elsewhere came when he was 16. 'The phrase "so-and-so is in trade" was still around in the fifties and I was puzzled by it because one saw signs saying "tradesman's entrance" on the backs of houses. Then I realised that trade was what made the world go round. A few courtiers might survive on something that evolved from trade but when one looked at the great families one saw that they had either had a windfall and discovered, for example, coal under their land; or that they had become rich by stealing, or by exploiting the weaknesses of others. Others had become rich because they were great entrepreneurs – like those who cornered the market in black crepe when Queen Victoria died. I thought, "Well done them – that shows a lot of forward-thinking and if you make your money that way it shows that you rather deserve to."'

These reflections have only been reinforced by the Thatcher years: 'She showed that there was absolutely nowhere in this country which people could not aspire to reach and feel comfortable in. That was the most wonderful step forward. It destroyed the thing that the public-school system had allowed to continue, the class system, because class revolved around education. Many people who went to Eton thought that they walked out of it a better person than their fellow-men. They had absolutely no right to think that whatever. In many cases they were much worse.'

Janet Cohen, the first woman to become a director of Charterhouse Bank, and now a director in the Corporate Finance department, notes a similar detachment from her old school, South Hampstead School for Girls High. She liked the school: 'It was full of clever children and it was restful' after her removal from 'one of the roughest state schools in the country' where she had been sent by her socialist father. South Hampstead put her 'back in a slot'.

'There were some very good minds there, and I was never jealous but would sit there and think "Ah yes, *that's* it!" '

She liked the competitiveness: 'I am smart – I could see that there were people around who carried greater horse-power, who had cleverer minds. I learned about comparative advantage.'

So she concentrated on what she knew she could do well. She was a linguist and a historian. 'I am a true academic in the sense that I fell for the subject, for the idea. In history it was something about the narrative quality of the subject and the ideas worked for me.' She was 'riveted' by medieval history and twelfth-century monasticism. 'I knew where I was there.'

At Cambridge it was jurisprudence and international law, 'all the theoretical things', that held her attention. 'I have always wanted the whole pattern: I want to see how the whole thing works. My mind goes to what the idea really is. Tell me that and then I'll jump and see where it goes on.' She was impatient with anything she could not do quickly 'and I was pleased to discover that there were some things you could do without busting a gut.' That lesson, however, was not the lesson her school was interested in delivering, and there lay the problem.

'I was always sideways-on to the ethos. South Hampstead and the Girls' Public Day School Trust does not produce flashy women: it produces good women.' The virtuous English sense of honest endeavour at subjects you were never going to be good at, the belief that effortfulness was morally ennobling, was rejected root and branch by Cohen.

She was soon in conflict with her headmistress, Miss Boddington. Cohen was rusticated when she was 15, got bored and led a party roof-climbing. She became head girl despite the fact that she and the headmistress disliked each other.

Being head girl, however, was the ultimate in good, drab jobs. 'I got an inkling there and then of what women are taught: they are taught to be good and to do the drab jobs. Being head girl looked flashy but was a true con. I was an instrument of the organisation and it was a pain. There was lots of responsibility without much flash or power. It was precisely the con up to which we had all been brought. The connection I made, once and for all, was that there were jobs which women did which were boring and jobs which men did which took you out to a wider world and that was where I was going. I was going to cross over that one straightaway.'

Cohen regards herself as eminently 'un-influencable' but also considers that it took her years to rid herself of the school's inhibiting ethical incubus, its insistence on futile, grinding work: 'For years and years I was led to believe that if you could not do something you still had to try.' She realised at school that the ethos was wrong. 'We all knew it was wrong but were terribly influenced by it; it was the sort of thing you could only see out of the corner of your eye.'

In her twenties she was in the United States working for a small company on Defence Department contracts. It was a far cry from the ethical simplicities of South Hampstead. She invented defence scenarios involving whole Latin American countries: 'I got in because, in playing a test game, and using skills undoubtedly developed as head girl, I became President of the country.' When she returned to this country, joined the DTI and spent a frustrating six months working on butter quotas it seemed like a terrible return to the virtuous grind of school. She threatened to leave and went to the Permanent Secretary, Sir Antony Part, who said, 'You're in the wrong place, aren't you?' and got her moved to a more interesting job.

'There was a frightful row. Permanent secretaries are not supposed to do that.' But flash had won the day: 'It took me many years, a second husband and three children to realise that flash: the ability not to mind people shouting at you, and to get on with men, are the most important things.'

The flight from Hampstead socialism to the merchant bank has not been an awkward one in Cohen's case either politically or intellectually. 'It is important to make capitalism work because it is the only thing that does work. When I was young the Labour Party believed that too.' Nor was her school at all hostile to business. 'You don't get that hostility in girls' schools.'

Genteel poverty at home after her father's death was an early object lesson in the need to earn a living, and she thinks it is generally true that business ability, perhaps most forms of ability, are 'governed by the home background and you can't teach it. When I think of the boys I was with at Cambridge – Kenneth Clarke, for example – you could see where they were going and it had much more to do with where they came from than with their schools. Many successes in business and in politics, for example, are eldest children and they are just different.' They have, she thinks, the kind of confidence which enabled her as head girl to take over the headmistress's general knowledge lessons when that luminary was away. 'I would teach current affairs, politics and "whither the future?" stuff.'

Peter Blackman, Chairman of Rowntree UK and Chief Executive of Nestlé UK Ltd, was educated by the Benedictines at Douai, one of their boarding schools. He brings an original light to bear on the question of businessmen's education since he stresses the influence of a distinctive, Benedictine, rounded education. 'It taught us how to treat people and, because responsibility was devolved to the senior boys, we learned inter-personal skills. Responsibility was stressed but also subsidiarity. The attitude towards religion was very liberal for a school in the fifties and a lot of it was done on a voluntary basis.' Since the approach was so pragmatic and Benedictine he kept his feet on the ground as well as receiving an academic education. 'I learnt how to get on with people.'

Sir Michael Caine, Chairman of Booker plc, is, like Janet Cohen, a child of the Hampstead intelligentsia. His father was a civil servant at the Colonial Office and when he left for Hong Kong as Financial Secretary in 1937 Michael could not continue as a day boy at the progressive King Alfred's, Hampstead. Bedales seemed the nearest boarding equivalent and he arrived there with the outbreak of war in 1939. He was 'ambitious academically and ambitious for esteem'.

Caine was not gregarious 'in the sense of loving everybody's company – I had a compact, intimate group.' Because he was an only child and so similar to his father he 'intentionally tried to plough other furrows. Quite deliberately I did not do economics or go to the LSE [where his father had been and where he would return as Director]. I did history and went to Oxford.' Among his Bedales friends, again, 'I'm the odd one out in business.'

He quickly discovered his métier at school: 'Throughout my life I have been successful in management. I was head boy of Bedales for four terms and I liked that part of it. I learnt things.'

As a schoolboy and thereafter he liked the idea of being influential. Knowledge as power and influence attracted him, together with the ability to get things moving. There was a price to be paid for his adjustment to the isolation of boarding-school life: 'September 1939 was when my stammering began.'

The family background was 'classically radical rather than classically left' and it is not, therefore, surprising that he was on Von Hayek's side in the debate held in 1945 at Bedales on Hayek's libertarian, anti-socialist work *The Road to Serfdom*. 'I thought then that he was the answer to everything.' Caine still characterises himself as an old-fashioned liberal in the John Stuart Mill tradition 'combined with bits of Herbert Read's anarchism. It still goes on today, doesn't it – this belief that we've got to be humble? I don't believe that nannies are much good at planning things.'

The great teachers who helped and excited him at Bedales were on the science side and in the English department. Caine sees the Booker Prize sponsored by his company as the direct consequence of his happy experiences in the English department under Barbara and Graham Crump. 'Graham Crump used to teach in front of a wall covered with a time chart of all the authors in chronological order. It was before you every lesson.'

The fascination of history flowed into other subjects, including English and geography. 'There were virile geography teachers whose geography was full of habitat, economics and society rather than wind, rain and rocks. So there was a lot of history in geography.'

These academic concerns echoed world events. 'The War gave a sense of interest and an awareness of other, wider issues in the world.' His 'tremendous absorption' in the War meant that most of his reading was in newspapers and articles: 'I was older than my age.'

There was a good deal of democratic common purpose within Bedales as well: 'We did not do so much sport and we dug potatoes instead: so there was a lot of co-operation between staff and children. There was a feeling that we were all in it together.'

Caine worked with the headmaster in the management of the School Council which brought children and teachers together. He takes a limited view of its value in general: 'It was an excellent educational experience and possibly acted as a safety valve.' Its value for him was that: 'I was really facing issues quite early on', and he remembers thinking that this was the kind of management he enjoyed and wanted to carry on doing. He stresses the school's academic and artistic competitiveness 'although there were near-morons in the school with IQs of 85-90.'

The standard public-school forms of emulation, however, were not around and he concedes that he may have become head boy because he was more competitive than his peers when it came to 'management' and 'leadership'. His decision to join Booker might have been a step away from Bedales values but it reflected his own interests. 'I was not sure what I was entering and I did not really think of it as a business – I saw it as a business operating in the developing world. It was before VSO, Oxfam and all that – so there was an element of those attitudes in it as well. By then MacArthur and MacCarthy had turned me off the

United States, where I had done a research degree and where I might otherwise have stayed. However, I did find as a result of that experience that I was English and not American.'

Caine left Bedales not knowing how unusual progressivism was. 'It was a great shock when I went into the Royal Navy on HMS *Skegness* at Butlin's Skegness Holiday Camp and found myself for the first time in my life in a male society. There was surprisingly little coarseness at Bedales and I only experienced the world of the rugby club dinner later in life.'

He was, he thinks, the product of an unusual form of élitist education which combined the superiority of the public school with the insularity of progressivist élitism. 'We really felt that it was unusual and that was the danger – it led to arrogance and a certain protection from, and non-realisation about, the rest of the world. We felt that we were the best and were shocked when someone from an awful – to us – education system was better than we were.'

Sir Michael doubts the universal applicability of the principles behind Bedales. Those principles were comprehensive ones and were relevant 'for the sensitive, educated children of educated parents. Comprehensive education works well in private schools; it has not worked in the inner city.'

Like so many others in this chapter Sir Michael has been influenced but not moulded by his school and can view it with detachment. Bedales was a long time ago for the Chairman of Booker.

The English tradition of a generalist, non-technical education has equipped many of our subjects for success in management and business. As Sir Michael Caine remarks: 'I have been at many crossroads in my life but I have never been at a crossroads at which it's been hard to make a decision.'

Entrepreneurs are a different matter altogether. Michael Green, Chairman of Carlton Communications, told us that he was unable to become academic at his 'highly competitive school', Haberdashers' Aske's, and he therefore became interested in commerce.

Sir Julian Hodge, born in the same street as the Prime Minister, 'left the council school at thirteen and a half and like John Major had to seek my higher education through night school, correspondence courses and general study.'

Their qualities of wayward creativity may make them unhappy at school even if they do stay on beyond 13. A final minatory comment by Sir Maurice Laing from the commercial perspective of Laing PLC is, however, worth bearing in mind. It may remind us that consensualist managers need entrepreneurs more than entrepreneurs need the managers:

'The old saying "from clogs to clogs in three generations" is, I think, very true. If you are born to wealth you lack the drive to succeed. Only an exceptional person still wants to get to the top if he's born in comfortable surroundings. Stockbroking is easier than commerce: there are no public-school men on my board.'

6 Education and Scholarship

What kind of people teach our children and why do they choose to stay at school and at university? Do they reflect the nature of the society in which we now live? What does it take to be successful in the world of the campus and the cloister, the quad and the classroom?

A cult of the personality has often had a marked influence upon those who fell in love with, or were intrigued by school and decided to stay. These people are easily influenced by role models. Dennis Silk, former Warden of Radley College, 'greatly admired many of my masters at Christ's Hospital and respected their commitment.'

Margaret Maden, now Chief Education Officer for Warwickshire, was in awe of her headmistress, Catherine Moore, at Arnold Girls' High School, Blackpool: 'She was so all-powerful, was everywhere and seemed to know one's inner thoughts. I was worried about not living up to her expectations. In the Blackpool of the 1950s she seemed not to be part of the human race: she looked like Edith Sitwell; she was six feet tall, wore long dresses and had huge rings on her fingers. She really ruled the place with a rod of iron; teachers and pupils were in awe and fear of her.'

When Maden became the head of an inner-city comprehensive in Islington, 'the idea of being everywhere and seeing everything that was going on was very much with me.'

Social ambition was part of Miss Moore's charter for the school: 'She told our parents after we were accepted into the school that it had a tradition of taking girls out of the gutter and making ladies out of them. Our parents accepted this without a flutter. There was a lot of emphasis on the social side and the Head talked a lot about the need to prepare for voluntary work, and the world of good works which went with marriage. She herself, however, was a classic spinster, so there was some dissonance there. Her acme of achievement can hardly have been to join the W I!'

Nonetheless, the 'capacity to stand up, debate, organise meetings and conferences all came from school' and benefited Maden in her career. Miss Moore would not have approved but the same gifts were being deployed in Maden's period as a politically active Young Communist at Leeds University and at the start of her career.

Academically, 'there were low expectations at that school. I was not encouraged to apply to university and the Head exercised much favouritism in that area. She seemed to know, without actually teaching us, who had or had not potential. Of the sixty who were admitted each year, only about fifteen would go to university. We were an élite of sixty, all of whom should have gone to university. Only a small group was expected to go on and that is part of something very English and appalling. More is thought to mean worse; excellence for all means kidding ourselves and letting standards fall.' Half the girls left school at 16 for clerical jobs in banks and offices.

School was a 'stable, closed world with lots of invented traditions' since the Head believed in the power of ritual. 'Her goal for the school was that it should be like a minor girls' public school. She thought that rituals and traditions secured for the school and the girls a stronger sense of purpose and superiority.' The result was a complex, 1930s-type *Mallory Towers* uniform, an abundance of trophies, cups and awards as well as house songs and hymns.

Maden remembers, 'We recognised the Head's birthday and every child in the school would draw a birthday card for her. It was a personality cult gone mad. We had to come in on Sunday evenings and she would read a passage from Synge, Chekhov and Gogol.'

Despite her reservations she can see the point of Miss Moore's rituals: 'I think they are very important in conveying messages and values. A school is a community and a very important one for children because it takes them out of the narrow, personal confines of the family. Morning assemblies at my school were lengthy, ritualistic and very powerful.'

As the head of a comprehensive Maden drew on her old school experience: 'Heads in this country do not get trained so I picked up a lot of behaviour unconsciously from Catherine Moore as a role model.'

Arnold High School, therefore, had been an education in those questions of hierarchy and power which first of all led her to the Left and have kept her in education. 'I was interested in how people acquire power and influence and we were all avid observers of the relationship between the Head and other members of staff – who was in favour and who was not? To whom would Miss Moore speak as she swept out of those ritualistic assemblies? How did the seating arrangements for staff at assemblies and other meetings reflect their influence? We were very aware of corridor behaviour and body language, of who would be stopped and talked to.'

Miss Moore had too much power: 'She was never accountable to anybody, anywhere.' That lack of accountability, she thinks, remains an unacceptable feature of a headteacher's life with obscure judgements based on no more than personal preferences. 'That is not a good message to convey to young people at all.'

At Winchester David Cope, the Master of Marlborough, admired his housemaster Tom Howarth. A subsequent High Master of St Paul's, Howarth was professionally interested in power but in a less parochial, naïve and leaden way than most other headmasters. He was a sophisticated, intellectual *engagé* with an engaging ruthlessness and a direct line to the wider world of events and ideas. Those whom he influenced share some of the same qualities. For Cope, Howarth's teaching was 'colourful, witty, graphic and somehow he seemed to me rather broader, more worldly-wise than anyone else. This was partly because he seemed to have had this dashing career in the War as Monty's ADC and he had a slightly raffish side to his lifestyle. I can remember his teaching about Disraeli which caused me to have a lasting interest in Disraeli and I can remember him on nineteenth-century French history and the French Revolution. He personalised history and had a romantic view of it. Nineteenth century France had so many colourful characters and that caught my imagination.'

Cope's conversations with Howarth in his last year at Cambridge guided him towards his career: 'He said that one of the good things about teaching was that it did not attract charlatans and scoundrels. People who went into teaching were on the whole people of depth and strength of character and moral commitment, interested in ideas.'

Cope taught at Eton, having followed Howarth's advice that he should not do a Dip. Ed. since that might put him off teaching. He felt unsettled, however, in his second year at Eton and joined the British Council. 'I went out to Mexico City under the rather grand title of cultural attaché and then, when I was about 25, I underwent a sort of conversion. I decided that I wanted to be a schoolmaster.' Howarth helped to get him a job at Bryanston and subsequently to become Headmaster of Dover College when he was 28.

James Sabben-Clare, who is now Headmaster of Winchester, was a contemporary of David Cope's in College, the House for scholars at Winchester. He was also touched by Howarth's genius as a teacher. 'As boys we thought he over-dramatised. He snooped out conspiracies.' Nonetheless, 'he was an all-round person, political and down to earth. He encouraged me to be outgoing. He told me that I ought to think of coming back and in time becoming his successor, which by coincidence I actually did. But he said the same thing to other people and it had no particular impact on me at the time.'

Cope was attracted back to school despite receiving 36 strokes of the cane on nine occasions. 'I was set upon by certain prefects who had a down on me and had a sadistic approach to corporal punishment. I was actually beaten by prefects in my first year more frequently than any new boy had been beaten before, it was said at the time.'

Early pain was diminished by subsequent intellectual pleasure: 'We used to spend hours arguing with each other, often about silly things, engaging in an intellectual exercise, almost for the sake of it. Every Sunday after Chapel service we would sit and discuss, dissect the sermon and give it marks, analyse it and discuss whether it had been logically constructed and lucidly expressed. The whole ethos of the place was the power, penetration of thought, and the ability to sort out accurate thinking and clear expression.'

Sabben-Clare is more struck by the fact that 'College was a very curious and not very healthy place in the early 1950s. There were lots of odd people and some later committed suicide.' He was engaged by the teaching of the history of philosophical ideas and ancient history at school but his decision to enter teaching as a career owed much to social and family environment: 'I was inclined to it because I enjoyed my own schooldays, and mainly because I was quite conventional. I fitted in very easily to the school because I enjoyed games. I was well disposed towards Winchester.'

For Cope, on balance, the disadvantages of his education outweighed the advantages: 'It took me a long time after I left Winchester to realise that most people weren't highly intelligent and didn't approach everything from an intellectual point of view. I think we were a bit over-developed intellectually and a bit underdeveloped emotionally.'

His own career has been fuelled less by a love of a subject than by the desire to manage: 'I realised in Mexico City that I wanted to be in charge and I thought I would have a better chance as a schoolmaster of being in charge by the time I was 35 or 40 than I would if I joined a business or the Foreign Office.'

Susceptibility to personality is often a matter of seduction by style. Peter Moore, Professor of Decision Science at the London Business School, was impressed by the sang-froid of one of his teachers at King's College School, Wimbledon, during the War: 'A flying-bomb landed in the school playing field one morning blowing out much of the glass in the classroom. The master (who, unknown to us, was dying of cancer) told us to get under the desks, but he couldn't. After the blast we crawled out unscathed, but the master had some cuts to his hands and face. He sent a boy for a brush and pan and then calmly went on with the lesson on integral calculus.'

Tony Mooney, Headmaster of the Prime Minister's alma mater, Rutlish School in Merton Park, South London, could well have ended up having a political career himself. He was the last Labour alderman in Islington, contested one Parliamentary seat, Epsom and Ewell, and was shortlisted for the Labour nomination for the Bermondsey seat when Peter Tatchell was selected.

The kindness and style of Don Woolhouse, one of his teachers at the Central Technical School in Sheffield, 'made me want to teach'. Woolhouse had been a pattern-maker in the 1930s. When made redundant he had trained as a teacher in his own time in the evenings: 'He knew what limited aspirations we working-class lads had. He drilled into us that we were not failures because we had failed the 11 plus. He called us "Tomorrow's Men". That made me go for it!'

When Mooney's teachers were urging him to stay on at school his parents wished him to leave at 16 and earn money: 'I broke down in tears and my grandparents eventually paid to get me through. I knew, by the time I was 15, that what I was born to was not what I was going to end up with. I was going as far as I could until I said, "Stop."'

He was brought up by his grandparents after his parents separated and it was his grandfather who bought him a Waterman pen and a pocket dictionary when, at the age of 13, he passed the entrance exam and could transfer from the secondary modern. 'I treasured those gifts for years: I had the promise of more control over my own life.

'I liked school because it made me a success.' He was also made its head boy. The old saw that 'education changes lives' is more than a platitude for the son of a bricklayer's labourer.

Mooney's poor "A" levels made it uncertain whether he would come through. He had spent too long in the nets during the summer term playing the Prime Minister's favourite sport. A career as a professional cricketer had seemed to beckon but it disappeared when he discovered he was not good enough. In the meantime he had gone to a teachers' training college and now found himself fallen between two stools, neither a graduate nor a professional sportsman. He decided to come to London to teach and did a part-time first degree at the North London Polytechnic, followed by a research degree at the Thames Polytechnic.

He now finds himself headmaster of a school which was opened in 1895 as a science school for working-class boys. Mooney values his school's blend of 'stability with tradition' and the social combination in Merton Park of 'the middle class with the respectable working class who want their boys to do well.'

For most headmasters and educationists, however, the principle of collegiality, in varying degrees of refinement, has been at work since their schooldays.

James Woodhouse, Headmaster of Lancing and Establishment liberal, may be poles apart from Ted Wragg, Professor of Education at Exeter and officially-sanctioned *Times Educational Supplement enragé*, but they have both been formed by what Woodhouse calls 'the idea of an educational community' at St Edward's, Oxford, and King Edward VII Grammar School, Sheffield, respectively.

At Sherborne, David Summerscale, the Headmaster of Westminster, was 'acclimatised to institutions'. Blundell's gave the uncomplicated David Jewell, Master of Haileybury, 'a touch of the stoicism and humour needed to live in a male-dominated society'.

Canon Peter Pilkington, the former High Master of St Paul's, is a figure unusual in the world of headmasters, and certainly so in the world of the Head Masters' Conference, due to the depth of his schoolboy attachment to the things of the mind.

A taste for the trenchant was evident during his schooldays: 'Mine was a Northern education and the formative event was going to an 1870 Board School in Crook, County Durham, between the ages of six and ten. It was a large stone building with a 1930s housing estate nearby where some of the roughest people in Newcastle lived. Inside the school, however, there was order and peace. The teachers were elderly since the young men were away in the War. It was enormously strict and yet pastoral. It was there that I acquired a love of history. There was a man there called Bell who came from Tynemouth and he made history seem like an endless story – he made it romantic. He took us from 1660 down to the 1715 rebellion. Marlborough and the Old Pretender walked the room when he talked.'

Dame Allan's Grammar School in Newcastle enabled him to learn what historical research really meant. 'Alan Anderson taught me ancient history and how to be sceptical. He never allowed me to make a statement without checking the source. Donald Walker introduced us to European history and politics. He would talk, for example, about the origins of Christian democracy in Europe and about the political parties in Hungary. This was all particularly important for boys from a Northern suburb with a narrow, limited background.'

Pilkington, like his contemporaries, was being trained to see that academic success meant the way forward. Very few of them left school at 16 and many went to the local university at 18. Going to Oxbridge was unusual. 'Many went into practical professions, law and accountancy. There was an emphasis on doing the things that got you a safe corner in a changing world.'

The drive to go to Oxbridge came from Pilkington's headmaster, Wilson, who, in his last year in office, took an interest in the boy's future. 'He had been to Oxford before the Great War. He took me into his study and went through the *University Gazette* with me. This was an exciting, wider world.'

Historical work was a mirror-image of what was going on in Pilkington's own life; broader horizons beckoned. 'I liked political history and history as the study of power. There were none of the Whig lessons about history as the story of liberty: the moral element seemed absent in a Northern historical training!'

History, for Pilkington, meant the study of continuity and he is struck by the way in which 'the England in which I grew up had more contact with the nineteenth century than the England I live in now. Newcastle, for example, had a Literary and Philosophical Society established in the late eighteenth century, in whose library as a boy I spent many hours. It was an England which was less excited by things: there was low inflation and total order.'

One of the few High Tories to have been a member of the Head Masters' Conference in recent years, Pilkington grew up unconscious of deprivation. 'I went to the grammar school as a product of the 1944 Education Act. Many of my contemporaries came from poor backgrounds but I did not see around me people of ability being deprived of opportunity. There were huge opportunities for varied educational provision in Newcastle and hordes of people in my street went to grammar schools. If you did not take these opportunities the attitude, perhaps a rather cruel one, was that there was something wrong with your family.

'There was no bourgeois guilt about me and my contemporaries, but that guilt certainly does now exist in the Head Masters' Conference. There is a widespread guilt there about representing a privileged institution which gets good "A" level results.'

Pilkington feels that public-school headmasters have, at best, a marginal influence in modern England. 'I think that the historical influence of headmasters is overrated; Arnold's myths were of his own making. The influential thing is the style of education which is produced and imitated in the way that the public school structures were imitated by grammar schools at the turn of the century. The idea that public schools train leaders is certainly a mistake. The old school tie is not important in England any more; what matters is money and ability. Those things may be more powerful if combined with an old school tie. But if you have been to Eton and don't have money then you won't have influence. There is no English parallel to the French *grandes écoles*, a band of brothers who are educated together and subsequently exercise influence.'

Another son of the North-East who became a public-school headmaster is Brian Rees, successively Headmaster of Merchant Taylors', Northwood, Charterhouse and Rugby before his early retirement. As with Pilkington, it was the subject that seized hold of him: 'The history master at Bede Grammar School, Sunderland, was a genius. C. J. Wates was small and ginger-haired. He analysed every historical situation with a shrewd diagram, then pottered about opening books, mumbling comments, filling in notes for himself. Once the diagram was there we had to do everything but it was excellent training for university and his methods of note-taking, the skeleton, the double-page (one for quotes and statistics) remained the basis of all my teaching of "A" level and scholarship candidates – though one *had* to teach more to fee-paying pupils!'

School was in some respects an eccentric experience for Rees. He was, for example, the only pupil of both his English and music teachers. A 'large and isolated home' meant that Rees did not belong to coteries of friends, 'so I suppose I was something of an outsider. Things like piano practice took a lot of time' and Rees could share his musical interests with his father, a 'musician *manqué*' who was in other respects difficult: 'He had inexhaustible energy, a flaming temper and a great jealousy of me.'

Ahead, however, lay a history scholarship to Trinity, Cambridge, in the company of Douglas Hurd and Lord Mackay and the *mondain* world of the glittering prizes. It is a background which equips him for the role of iconoclast. 'I think times are going to be hard for the public schools. Despite the horrors of state education the younger generation do not see the social advantages of independent education. How can they if half the pupils come from Singapore and Hong Kong? I think the 1990s will see a recrudescence of the grammar schools in different forms – especially with opting-out gathering pace. Furthermore the public schools have avoided publicity so much over the last few years that they really have been forgotten about.'

These, however, are self-consciously dissident voices far removed from the conventional, corporatist pieties of most public-school headmasters.

The fact that one has been a Head Boy may disqualify one from eminence in most other professions. Here, however, those consensual values seem to be a *sine qua non*. For Donald Crichton-Miller Fettes was 'a happy world to which I would be happy to return', The 'supremely happy' Head of School returned as Headmaster.

A headmistress like Ena Evans, of King Edward's School for Girls, Birmingham, is out on a limb compared with her male colleagues, when she stresses the connections between her schooling and the wider world. 'I was surrounded at Queen's, Chester, by women who had a real commitment to liberal education and wanted through it to give substance to their hopes for a better world in the immediate post-war years.'

Donald Naismith, the innovative Director of Education at Wandsworth, is one of the few discontented educationists. He left Belle Vue Grammar School, Bradford, with 'a restricted view of the world'. It is a complaint which is echoed by James Woodhouse, who felt 'quite critical of the enclosed atmosphere and the lack of privacy' at St Edward's School, Oxford.

For John Rae, doyen of radical headmasters with an instinct for the eyecatching headline when he was Head Master of Westminster, Bishop's Stortford College closed as many doors as it opened. 'It helped in the sense that it provided me with models of good schoolmasters. It hindered in the sense that there was no careers guidance whatsoever, which may have meant that I did not seriously consider another career.

'I suspect I really did go into teaching *faute de mieux* after my fourth year at Cambridge. I went to the Appointments Board. They suggested I should meet a chap who, I later learned, was from the Secret Service. But I had no idea from the meeting that a career in Intelligence might be beckoning. Then a job came up at Harrow. I think I really went into teaching for nostalgic reasons because I'd read about idealised boyhoods and enjoyed schoolboy books like *The Hill*.

'Walter Strauchan, the French and German teacher, switched me – and a lot of other philistine types like me – on to literature. Bishop's Stortford at that time was a fairly bread-and-butter philistine school – fond of sport, particularly rugby. That was its ethos. Walter Strauchan was rather a fish out of water. He wrote poetry, translated contemporary French poetry and was a friend of Henry Moore. He was at odds with the general sporting ethos of the school. He opened our eyes to contemporary literature, art, calligraphy and of course sculpture since Henry Moore lived nearby.'

Charles Mellow was another influence for the good. He was 'an eccentric bachelor who taught Latin and English in a very old-fashioned way but communicated a real enthusiasm for what he taught and gave me a love of Shakespeare. He was short with white hair swept back, and had fought in the Great War. We all assumed his eccentricity was because he was shell shocked, though there was no evidence for this. If you got something wrong he would lock you up in a cupboard in the classroom. This was greeted as a great deal of fun, until one day the headmaster walked in with a couple of parents and there were strange sounds emanating from inside the cupboard.

'Arthur Evans, the headmaster, was a very decent man but a very weak headmaster. Nothing happened as a result of the cupboard incident. Later on I drew some conclusions from this, the main one being that it doesn't do to be too nice as a headmaster. He should have expelled me and a lot of others like me: we used to terrify inexperienced wartime masters in a way that should have been firmly handled. One master who taught us had escaped from a German concentration camp and we consistently reduced his lessons to total chaos. Mr Evans used to plead with us to be more lenient and to remember what had happened to this master. I don't think at the age of 15 we cared very much whether he'd been in a concentration camp or not. Evans should have told us that if we didn't stop bullying this man we would be chucked out.

'I simply learned from this that you cannot run a school and be too tolerant and too weak because in the end everybody suffers. So if people thought I was a bastard at Westminster, then Arthur Evans was partly responsible!'

An instinct for the institutional life has sometimes been communicated by schools which were free of stress and competition. Sheila Browne, Principal of Newnham College, Cambridge, and a former Senior Chief Inspector of Schools during the 1970s and early 1980s, enjoyed the democratic style of the co-educational Ranelagh School in Bracknell. Life there was 'competitive and generous with no gender roles' and 'a pupil-run school council even at the end of the 1930s. The curriculum was broad with no differentiation by gender. Because of their need to service small numbers with a broad curriculum the staff insisted on a great deal of individual learning by pupils from an early stage. As a result one learnt to cope.'

Sir Christopher Ball, a former Warden of Keble College and now a Fellow of the Kellogg Foundation for Continuing Education, was a boy at St George's, Harpenden: 'Intellectually, the school was not outstanding, but it does not seem to have mattered. I loved it – still do with its boarding, co-educational, Anglican and artistic ethos.'

For Margaret Pringle, now Head of Holland Park, learning at Holton Park Girls' Grammar School was 'relaxed, stress-free, a matter of individual fulfilment, accompanied by very positive, enjoyable relations with my peer group. I learned to love learning but it was in a collaborative rather than a competitive environment.'

The force of idealism, the ethical strand in English education, remains strong. For good or ill, many have seen in education a means of changing the world. Anne Sofer, the Chief Education Officer of Tower Hamlets, for example, found that St Paul's was 'strongly moralistic about the "duty" to serve the community. I subsequently regarded this as both oppressive and patronising – but I am sure it has played a part in getting me where I am.' Margaret Pringle realised towards the end of her time at school, while rehearsing a school play, 'how talented this group of pupils was and how few of them were thinking of going on to higher education. Our education system seemed to embody an enormous waste of talent and potential. Idealistically, I wanted to do something about it.'

One of the classic functions provided by education is that of the ladder of social mobility. Sir William Taylor's discovery of the influence of the ladder was a random matter. The future Vice-Chancellor of the University of Hull (who retired in 1991) failed the 11 plus. When he was 13 he transferred, like Tony Mooney, from a secondary modern to a technical school where he followed courses in bricklaying and building construction: 'The event that shaped my career was discovering in the back of a pocket diary a reference to vocational counselling provided by the National Institution for Industrial Psychology. A relative made the arrangements, I had myself tested and sent the results with a personal letter, to the Chief Education Officer for Kent. It was solely as a result of this that I secured a transfer to a grammar school.'

The inner drive continued at Erith Grammar School where he had to do all the work for the Higher School Certificate, the ancestor of "A" levels, in nine months. He was a year older than his contemporaries and the Army were not willing to defer his call-up: 'I worked practically alone in a small room in an annexe to the school, visited from time to time by members of staff. Learning to work on my own has been invaluable to me.' Taylor had got on his bike.

Alan Smithers is now Professor of Education at Manchester University and well known for his strictures on an education system which gives 'the ordinarily intelligent child a poor deal. About 16 per cent of the age group are picked out by "A" levels and educated to a high standard on degree courses. The other 84 per cent of the age group are at some stage cast aside.'

Smithers himself, however, has benefited from this system. The son of a Billingsgate fish porter, he was naturally good at puzzles and passed the 11 plus to enter Barking Abbey Grammar School. His mother prevented him from leaving at 16 to join the bank and 'I developed a love of learning at school: it opened up opportunities for me.'

King Edward's, Birmingham took Sir Edward Parkes from 'a craftsman background' and 'widened my options'. The future Chairman of the Committee of Vice-Chancellors learnt from the senior physicist at his school the need for 'action as well as contemplation'. Sir Edward's story reminds us of one of the two great asymmetrical truths which apply to the education of future educational leaders. Grammar schools created opportunities for them: boys' public schools restricted those opportunities.

Wherever they found themselves, educational administrators clearly started early. Their characteristic interest in the process rather than the content of education has deep roots. Sheila Innes, Chief Executive of the Open College, valued the teamwork at Talbot Heath School, Bournemouth, and draws on those memories as a manager. Love of other people's attention, so important for the successful teacher and administrator, is also an early bloom. David Styan, Chairman of the Government's Task Force on School Management, was 'asked to read in a whole school carol service. I remember the whole school looking at me and then realising that I could command attention, and wanting to do it again.'

The successful educational administrator needs a range of enthusiasms wider than those which can be provided by his (or her) chosen 'field'. Sir Wilfred Cockcroft is the author of an epoch-making Government report on the teaching of mathematics in schools. He is also a former Vice-Chancellor of the New University of Ulster. His time at Keighley Grammar School was dominated by 'the public life of sums and the private life of the novel'. He was 'hooked on the printed word', a taste he shared with his colleague Philip Larkin when he was Professor of Pure Mathematics at Hull. When bemoaning the reading habits of the contemporary undergraduate Cockcroft recalls Larkin telling him, 'Yes, Bill, do you know they can actually take socks out of the drawers without reading the newspapers?' Cockcroft 'realised that I could not live just with maths. I had to read half a novel before settling down to homework.' It amounted to the recognition of a wider world.

Without maths, however, Cockcroft conceded, 'nothing else would have happened' in his career. 'The ability of my maths teacher, George Cadman, to get me the Balliol Williams Exhibition in maths' was the foundation stone. Cadman had a joint degree in French and maths from Sheffield, came out of the First World War with trench foot and stayed at Keighley Boys' Grammar School for most of his career. For eight years in the 1930s he enjoyed a dazzling period as a teacher preparing boys for Oxford and Cambridge scholarships. In one year he added the top maths scholarship at Trinity to his line of successes. 'He said later that he himself never understood the phenomenon,' remembers his old pupil. 'He just could not go wrong. Balliol would even write to him asking who his candidate would be.'

Cockcroft enjoyed the element of apprenticeship in being taught by Cadman. 'It was like watching a craftsman at work and thinking that I could get there. My father was the ultimate craftsman with his hands – as a plumber, coppersmith and carpenter. I could never aspire to that but I could get to first base with maths. I don't know where it all came from; the ball just went straight to the boundary.'

Cockcroft did not understand the nature of Pure Maths, or the philosophy of the subject, and the notes made in Sheffield University in 1914 which were the basis of Cadman's teaching were in many ways misleading. That, however, did not matter. Cadman had got Cockcroft to grasp the heart of the matter. 'You won't get Trinity, Bill – but I will get you Balliol.'

War interrupted Balliol and when Cockcroft returned, 'I realised that I had lost the facility at maths. The speed and efficiency of mind was gone.' He got a good second rather than a first. 'That brought home to me that the way I had done maths at school was not maths at all. I had to ask my own questions instead of asking somebody else's.' Great bodies of theorems had to fit together not just as individual theorems but as a unit. Undoubtedly, he had been spoon-fed at school but 'the man was a good trainer and by the time he got to me he knew what he was about.'

Cockcroft benefited in a wider way from the classic boys' grammar school atmosphere 'where all was possible'. His father had to be persuaded that his son should stay on at school after 16. Once that bridge had been crossed Cockcroft could specialise avidly. He was a County Minor Scholar: 'There were six or seven of us and we stuck together collecting each other on the way to school.' The boys who left at 16 entered the local clerkocracy of Keighley: 'The school served the town in that way, as well as discharging its meritocratic function as a promoter of talent. It was a meritocracy and there was no social snobbery at all.'

He felt at home in school: 'The business of an ordered existence was very important to me. It really mattered to me that I should know where I was.' The eternal verities of school life with its comforting timetable reflected the values of the town in which he felt equally at home: 'It was an unquestioning society without being deferential.' Cockcroft and his contemporaries were being educated for a society in which they would all be professionals: 'That was the assumption.'

The death of the grammar schools, Cockcroft notes sadly, has meant the rise of 'an inverse snobbery which says that "Oxford and Cambridge are not for the likes of you."' His school taught him no such fatalism. It gave him an 'opportunity to understand that the world is about fighting to get things right. You do have to fight: things are never easy. I had to fight to get my sums right.' School had equipped him for a career which has always stressed the need to 'move with a particular tide' and to respond creatively to opportunity.

Sir Claus Moser, the Warden of Wadham College, Oxford, is within a tradition of British thought which stresses the need for a 'broad' education. He benefited, at the progressive Frensham Heights, from a 'broad education which led me to the social sciences'. The powerful, obsessive qualities of most scholars, however, have led them to dissatisfaction with a diet of thin gruel at their schools. Scholars need their subjects and benefit from specialisation.

Dame Rosemary Murray, for example, a former Vice-Chancellor of Cambridge University and President of New Hall, received the traditional broad education at Downe House but was frustrated by the 'poor teaching in sciences and maths'. The historian Sir John Plumb was encouraged at Alderman Newton's Grammar School, Leicester, but thought that from a technical point of view the teaching was 'pretty poor.' Sir Albert Sloman, Essex University's first Vice-Chancellor, was inspired at Launceston College, Cornwall, by 'a visit to the school by the best-known scholar in the field of Hispanic Studies.'

Neil Cossons, who is now Director of the Science Museum, hated his first few years at Henry Mellish Grammar School, Nottingham, but enjoyed the VIth-Form years of specialisation: 'My performance improved accordingly.'

The seeds of scholarship owe little to the ancestral voices of institutional thought and respond to a powerful inner drive. The scholar's inspiration is that 'pursuit of excellence' which the philologist Professor Sir Randolph Quirk has noted as the characteristic of Douglas High School, Isle of Man. Alan Borg, Director General of the Imperial War Museum, became a historian because he was visually responsive: 'Daily attendance in Westminster Abbey led to my interest in medieval architecture.'

At the Glasgow Academy Norman Stone, future Professor of Modern History at Oxford and Thatcherite scourge of the *bien-pensants*, was always a 'kings, battles and foreign countries man'. When he was 11 he was writing spoof history books: 'I invented a country and I wrote its history. There were genealogical tables and it was all a spoof on the old *Cambridge Modern History*.' The geographically remote countries of Central and Eastern Europe, whose histories he would subsequently write, appealed partly because of the attraction of something a long way from home.

For Stone, the Academy and Trinity College, Cambridge, are 'the only two educational institutions of which I can say, hand on heart, that I was entirely happy with them and they with me.'

Hillhead High School, the standard middle-class grammar school in West Glasgow, would not take him because of his poor maths, and so he arrived at the Academy, his fees paid for by his father's squadron after his death in action in 1942.

At the Academy there was 'inspired teaching by people who helped to get your teeth into that learning process.' Christopher Varley was an astonishing French teacher whose pupils include Jeremy Isaacs, the first Controller of Channel Four and now General Director of the Royal Opera House, and Neil MacGregor, Director of the National Gallery. Stone was linguistically adept and benefited from the fact that the Academy had 'an extraordinary modern language machine to get you to Cambridge'.

The school was 'enlightened' in that it allowed him to give up science when he was 14. 'It meant nothing to me,' he says. He could therefore spend more time on his German. 'They were very generous-minded. They never forced me to get bored by English social history, a subject by which I am still, to some extent, bored rigid. I could do genealogical tables of the Hapsburgs from memory and that's a more interesting occupation, and probably more important for a historian, than totting up the numbers of farm labourers in Northamptonshire.'

Stone was the product of a world of implicit Presbyterianism and very quiet Sundays. He was aware of a Calvinist world view which meant that in the sixteenth century all Scots were either drunk or reading the Bible but 'it did not mean anything to me until I wrote *Europe Transformed* in my late thirties.'

His abiding memories are of the gulf between where he was and where he wished to be. It was a gulf which the Academy helped him to cross: 'I can remember the idea of colour and of painting dying on me when I was six or seven and reading a line, uncomfortably, "Too provincial to have a sense of aesthetics". That struck. The fact of England mattered a great deal at the Academy. It was always there in your consciousness of place and you were conscious of being on a trampoline which would get you over the border. A lot of the Glasgow Academy was geared to arriving in the South. If you were a high-flier you were going to Oxbridge and not to Glasgow.'

The Academy also fulfilled a social function: 'It was a glorious place locally.' In the inter-war years the school had been 'a finishing school for the sons of the rich' and was academically undistinguished. Other local schools, such as Allan Glen's, shared these aspirations: 'They gave people better manners, taught them how to speak properly and gave them the chance of a more interesting life. They took a hammer to those other schools when they removed their social character and proletarianised them.' The Academy's social cachet, supplemented by intellectual strength in the post-war years, fitted into a pattern which applies to 'any school which has ever been any good on the continent of Europe from Galway eastwards. Social aspiration is as important as curricular reform: you might as well be blunt about it.'

At school, edges were softened. Stone played Claudius in a school production of *Hamlet* opposite Neil MacGregor. The future historian of the Eastern Front in the First World War was 'a blob in the Corps. Jock Carruthers would turn me into the enemy so I could sit in the bush and light thunder-flashes. They were characters, you know, those teachers, with endless eccentricities and very good informalities.'

Politically, Stone was growing away from his mother, a provincial radical Gladstonian who was now turning towards Labour. The son was developing as a 1950s romantic Churchillian with a pronounced competitive edge: 'I was competitive from the age of nine or ten onwards and was always very aware of intellectual competitiveness. I had three or four to pace myself with but there was a good spread of people with all sorts of interests. People found their own level. It pleases me to see the boys in the B and C classes ending up quite rich because it shows that education is not necessarily about making money. I was very much tolerated there and was hugely popular at the end. They cheered me to the skies at the prizegiving when I left with a scholarship. In the gradations of decibels I was only beaten by Jeremy Isaacs.'

David Vaisey, Bodley's Librarian at Oxford, is another scholar who associates scholarship with the bourgeois ascent. His 'origins were from a rural, agricultural – what would now be called "disadvantaged" – community. Rendcomb College (in Gloucestershire) opened my eyes to undreamed-of possibilities – scholarship, books, universities, culture, heritage. Without it I would now probably be working in a factory in Swindon or driving a combine-harvester, instead of directing one of the great libraries of the world.'

Others have been struck by the fortuitous school experiences which shaped their scholarship. Professor Malcolm Fraser, Chairman of the Business Technical Education Council (BTEC), was a 'typical late developer' who had a sudden conversion when he was in the C stream at Christ's College, Finchley, and decided that he was as good as the others. 'The Combined Cadet Force taught me leadership and gave me confidence. The reason for the conversion was success in chemistry because of the imposed discipline and confidence gained in the cadets.'

Christopher Hill, the historian and former Master of Balliol, was 'a bit bolshie' as a boy at St Peter's, York. These were tendencies encouraged by his headmaster, 'a complete sceptic who was good at turning things on their heads, asking difficult questions and puncturing platitudes.' Hill had embryonic left-wing views at school. Marxist ideological purity would be an undergraduate development of the 1930s. For the time being he was content with Shavian scepticism about the established order and a restless mood of being 'generally agin' the government. I was very hostile to some things about the school. Day boys were looked down upon as members of the lower orders. At first I was a day boy and then I became a boarder because we lived four miles away.' His contemporary at school, C. Northcote Parkinson, of Parkinson's Law, was a sardonic reinforcer of Hill's schoolboy style. 'I was turned on to the things of the mind by reading history and literature – and especially by reading Shaw.'

Domestic conditions contributed to his bookishness and provided him with something to react against. 'My parents were seriously well read. My mother was a frustrated intellectual, a hockey-player and a feminist *avant la lettre*.' She had a more liberal outlook than Hill's father although she was unpolitical. His father had voted Liberal until 1931 because they were still the party of Temperance; thereafter he voted Conservative. 'I was interested in Labour because my parents were not.'

Equipped with these conventional patterns of bourgeois dissidence

Hill left school convinced that 'if something was universally accepted then it was untrue'.

Christopher Hill was unusual in learning intellectual dissidence from his headmaster. Few heads have the taste or the talent for such dangerous adventures. They can, nonetheless, change the direction of a scholar's life.

The headmaster of Chigwell in Essex, a school which 'in effect only offered classics at university entrance level', favoured Oxford, according to the philosopher Bernard Williams. 'Going there rather than Cambridge led directly to my doing philosophy.' The headmaster of Edmonton Latymer School told Dr John Horlock, Vice-Chancellor of the Open University, to apply to Cambridge. When he was 15, Gerald Fowler, Rector of the East London Polytechnic, asked his headmaster at Northampton Grammar which university he should apply to and received the oracular reply, 'Oxford, my dear boy! All the best people do.'

Dr A. L. Rowse, the great Elizabethan historian, is unburdened by doubt: 'Without St Austell Grammar School I should not, as a working-class boy, have known about Oxford or scholarships to get there.' He was a boy at the school during the First World War and the immediately succeeding years: 'I owed everything to the headmaster, a public-school and Oxford man, who got my schoolboy poems published at the time in successive volumes of *Public School Verse*. He also sent in essays of mine which won prizes from the English Association and from the Navy League. The first was literary, the second historical. This set me on an academic and writing career. I owe all that to my school, a day grammar school.'

Headmasters may encourage and pontificate but the individual scholarly teacher is more likely to affect intellectual development, the way a scholar actually thinks. Lord Blake was moulded as a historian at King Edward VI School, Norwich, by the senior history master who also happened to be his father. Sir Keith Thomas, President of Corpus Christi College, Oxford, won the Brackenbury History scholarship to Balliol from that great nursery of historians, Barry County Grammar School, when he was 17: 'I did not originally plan to include history among the subjects I would offer for the Higher School Certificate. But I was intercepted on the way to the room where I had to declare my choice by the relatively recently arrived history master, Teifion Phillips. He persuaded me to stay with history: it was he who pointed me in the direction of Oxford and

Balliol; and it was his inspired teaching which made it possible for me to get there.'

Another academic knight, Sir Roy Strong, shares the widespread indebtedness to the grammar-school tradition which moulded British scholarship from Erasmus to Shirley Williams.

Former Director of the Victoria and Albert Museum, Strong started unpromisingly at Edmonton County Grammar, the school which also educated Norman Tebbit. His disadvantages were legion: 'I was always the odd man out, wore glasses, was cripplingly shy and a late developer.' He only went to Edmonton because he was not thought bright enough to get into Latymer.

Strong still feels social resentment: 'I loathed the class into which I was born and really disliked my father. I was enormously introspective and all I wanted to do was paint, create toy theatres and a private world.' He was passionately interested in history and art but there was no trace of those interests in his home. While his father was a sales representative for a firm of hatters, his mother 'had endless dreadful jobs to keep the family going.'

Education could alleviate this gloom: 'The belief in education came from my mother whose father was of Quaker extraction. So you get there the continuity of a nonconformist belief in education.'

Strong might not have gone to the better grammar school but he was a late developer and 'the point is whether you can continue to develop. So many of those who shone at everything at the grammar school have sunk without trace.'

Millais' *Boyhood of Raleigh* and *Between Two Fires* – a portrait of a Puritan sitting between two wenches – might have been the only two paintings at home but his mother took him to see the great exhibitions of the immediate post-war years when the National Gallery was reopened. The calendar was also kind to him because he was born in August and he had the stimulus of being taught in the company of those who were up to a year older than him.

He found that he was increasingly good at exams and 'I always knew that, however bad I might be at some things, I could apply myself to most things. If I was determined enough to do something then I would do it.'

At his own request he did History of Art in the VIth Form and the poor art master had to keep on reading Bernard Berenson's *Italian Painters of the Renaissance* in order to keep ahead of him. He failed "O"-level French but needed it for university entrance. With extra tuition from his teachers he got through.

Strong's teachers all seemed to be left-wing, to ride bicycles and to be inspired by the socialist vision of what education would lead people to. The school's social spectrum was considerable: 'There were the respectable lower middle classes as well as the really working-class children of Edmonton and I am moved to tears by what those teachers did for those children. They were socially inept and their parents had no aspirations for them. At least my mother had aspirations for us.'

Miss Staples ran the VIth Form and 'being admitted to it was rather like being admitted to a sacred temple which you must never betray. There was no Latin taught at the school and two of us needed it in order to read Arts subjects at university. Every evening we would sit down with Miss Staples and do a Latin lesson and that was how we got through. It was all unpaid.'

His history teacher, Jane Henderson, would leave the grammar school early on Monday evening and attend the graduate seminars of the Elizabethan historian, Sir John Neale, at the Institute of Historical Research. 'So I was learning about Elizabethan history from someone who was actually doing it herself. She inspired my love of Elizabethan England. I could take things in to show her, like a drawing of a man in a doublet or of an Elizabethan lady, and would never be made to feel silly. I had a passion for the portraits of Elizabeth I. There was only one catalogue of them and it was in the British Library. It was published in 1894 and consisted of 120 pages of close Victorian typesetting. She copied that out entirely by hand for me so I could have a copy. It was the most extraordinary act.' This was the basis of Strong's first book, *The Portraits of Queen Elizabeth I.*

The school was co-educational but 'girls were not developed then. If a girl appeared in school wearing a brooch it would be ripped off her. Girls sat on one side of the classroom and boys sat on the other. There were some sexually predatory boys but I was underdeveloped. The fundamental fact about school was that we were all brought up to be competitive. It was not done in a bad way. Miss Staples would sit at the front of the class with tears in her eyes if anyone let the side down. It was an act of betrayal. You had failed people's expectations and expectations were very high for you. I was very shocked when I went back to do a Speech Day and discovered that no-one was allowed a prize. All of that had completely gone.

'I nearly did not get into the VIth Form. At 14 there was a move to take me out of school because it was known that I had a flair for drawing and a cartoonist wanted an assistant. I also remember a traumatic interview at school when we were all interviewed about jobs. I said I was artistic and was told, "Why don't you start work with textiles?"'

Strong had a narrow escape. His elder brother had had to leave school 'because the family was utterly penniless. By 1953, however, things were easier and no questions were asked as long as I did not ask for a penny.' The results of his Higher School Certificate were so extraordinarily good that 'it was possible to go on at school as long as I kept clear of my father.

'I did not conceal being clever at school. There was a nasty little bit to me which thought, "I'll get it back on all those butch, macho, sports-playing sods." It was my only weapon against them.'

Strong's scholarship evolved from an interest in the early history of dress. Originally he had wanted to be a stage designer. It made sense to read all of Coward's plays: 'I did that *very* quietly.'

Those, however, were ambitions which were difficult to achieve from a modest background. 'I knew nobody as a lead into that world and I was hopelessly crippled by shyness when I went to draw at Hornsey School of Art on Saturdays.' He came first in a London schools' competition to design sets and costumes for a production of *The Winter's Tale*. 'I still have great bale-loads of costumes and designs. I went to see John Gielgud and Diana Wynyard at the Phoenix Theatre and suddenly I could understand every word and could draw every set for it.'

Shakespearean passions could lead him in other directions. Reading A.L. Rowse and C.V. Wedgwood was 'just marvellous for me at school. They were terribly despised when I was an undergraduate but they could write and that became my ambition as well. I wanted very much to belong to the great tradition of historical writing, of writing history for everybody. I wanted to be read because history was about humanity and human beings. In a similar way in the museum world I have wanted to open doors to people.'

None of these things arrived without a fight. Dame Frances Yates, the Renaissance scholar, gave Strong a direct response once when he said he could not do a certain topic because it impinged on another discipline. 'You have a trained mind: you take the book from the shelf.' He says, 'I never looked back after that and I owe that Renaissance tradition that you can apply yourself to anything to my school. I owe it a great debt because I was a basically competitive spirit and they added to it a belief in application and hard work. There was a degree of that Renaissance tradition in the old grammar schools.'

Versatility, however, withers easily. Most people, according to Strong, including scholars, undergo a 'continuing narrowing' after their schooldays. 'My extraordinary luck was that I was able to continue to develop. Mr Woodward, the art master, once said to me, "I know what you will end up as – Director of the National

Portrait Gallery." He made it sound as it it was a fate worse than death. But I did end up doing that job at the age of 31. He had great foresight.'

Scholars have little time for the institutional ethos; the counter-suggestibility of the intellectual sees to that. Schools, however, can clearly make or mar the conditions which make a scholarly career possible in the first place. There is a resonant irony in the fact that the educational system of the English, a race given to anti-intellectualism, promotes a degree of specialisation at first-degree level which is unique in Europe. It is important to get on that fast-track early on in the game and the successful scholar's gratitude to his school reflects that fact.

Roger Scruton, Professor of Aesthetics at Birkbeck College, speaks for many in recalling how his school made him 'seriously believe in the intellectual life'. First impressions of the Royal Grammar School, High Wycombe, were, however, less exalted: 'I was terrified because I had heard of initiation ceremonies, based on public-school traditions of bullying. I never liked the school very much and the headmaster, Tucker, was a figure of fun and ridicule. I never got on with him and I ended up being expelled because I burned down the school stage. Although very quiet, I was never very accommodating towards the authorities and I thought that the power structures at school paid insufficient attention to people like me, the introverted and possibly talented. Perhaps your average aesthete just feels spontaneously, and unjustly, that the surrounding world is too obviously concerned with the more obvious forms of worldly prowess.'

In retrospect, however, Scruton esteems his school 'because it brought me into contact with a variety of opportunities. The masters were cultivated, intelligent people who took teaching seriously. They did not just follow the curriculum but also oversaw the moral and intellectual development of the boys in their charge.

'My physics master, for example, had been Assistant District Chief Commissioner in Iboland, Nigeria. He introduced me to Beethoven, anthropology and drink, three civilising influences. The chemistry master had served with the forces in Germany after the War; he introduced me to Heine and Goethe and made me want to learn German.'

Scruton was doing scientific 'A' levels but was intellectually restless and, by the time he was 16, asking questions to which science could give no answers. The first broadly philosophical book he read was Oswald Spengler's *The Decline of the West* when he was 15; works by Sartre, Kierkegaard and Heidegger soon followed on the reading list. 'The first philosophical question I asked myself was about the existence of God.' There were other questions, however, to be asked: 'We had a society at school called "The Thirteen", to which I was finally admitted. The image of culture as a source of authority was important to me. Reading F.R. Leavis was a huge influence in persuading me of the seriousness of culture and in persuading me that this contained more that was of value than all the scientific texts I had read. I liked George Eliot's *Middlemarch*, for example, because of its depth, reality and seriousness, the fact that these characters were more concerned with more important issues than people are in ordinary life.'

High seriousness, once encountered, did not go away. Scruton was not aware of public events in the 1950s and was apolitical as a Cambridge undergraduate. Once he came into contact with French Marxism in 1965, however, as a lecteur in a French university during the run-up to 1968, he could identify the enemy. The embattled Charles de Gaulle was seen through Leavisite spectacles first worn in the Royal Grammar School: 'He was the first public figure I really admired. I liked the combination of authority with culture and the fact that he represented an idea of France, a moral and spiritual idea, which was more than just material well-being.'

Scruton's family upbringing, however, had been socialist. 'My family were all Labour voters for whom Conservatism represented class privilege. There was a lot of family tension about my being in the grammar school in the first place. My father was a primary schoolmaster of working-class origins. He had considerable resentment against the grammar-school system and against my having opportunities which he had not had.'

At school, however, Scruton was seizing all possible opportunities to educate himself into an alternative vision of England and Englishness. 'I was confirmed into the Church of England when I was 15 without my parents knowing. They would have been horrified. It was a religious and a cultural statement about my sense of belonging to England as it should be. It was part of a search for order.'

The social order he was looking for was one which would combine stability with flexibility: 'My aspiration was not classlessness; I have never believed in that. Classes are natural provided there is enough mobility between them both upward and downward. I'm all in favour of seeing people toppled and others taking their place. There must, however, be stability; a class system can only work if there are traditions of politeness, courtesy and *noblesse oblige*.'

Scruton's search for order grew out of the 1950s grammar school. His own old school may survive but the system has been dismantled, the victim, according to Scruton, of English class obsessions: 'I am a beneficiary of the English love of education and the grammar school was an attempt at spreading the best of English education as widely as possible. Egalitarianism has destroyed education by making it subservient to social engineering. What I got at school was an education and that is what people from the lower orders were getting in England from the beginning of the last century. The end of the grammar schools has put us back in the eighteenth century when the only educated people are those who can afford it, or those who are well placed socially and have books at home.'

Sir Geoffrey Warnock, former Principal of Hertford College, Oxford, and Sir Peter Strawson, Oxford Professor of Metaphysical Philosophy, are unusual in their professed lack of indebtedness to their schools. It is perhaps no accident that both are philosophers, scholars in a subject which is rarely taught in schools. At Winchester, Sir Geoffrey 'never thought of becoming an academic'.

Sir Peter won an Oxford scholarship in English from Christ's College, Finchley, 'but the switch I immediately made from English to Philosophy was not related to any influence I associate with my schooldays.'

Dame Kathleen Ollerenshaw, the mathematician, is more typical among scholars in her recollections of the power exerted by school on the growing mind. The visual appeal of mathematics was primary in her case since 'all, in the good old days, went on the blackboard'. Her family was bewildered by the strength of her response but Ladybarn House School in Manchester was more understanding. The school was a Montessori experimental school for six-to-13-year-olds: 'I can truly say that I won my scholarship to Somerville from what I had learnt before the age of 12; in particular to use imagination and ingenuity, because often the required method was not available in books or in the ordinary school curriculum.'

St Leonards School in St Andrews was less of an influence and found it difficult in the 1920s to conceive of a girl having a career as a professional mathematician. An enlightened housemistress, however, gave her a copy of H.W. Turnbull's *The Great Mathematicians*, after which there was no turning back: 'I knew that I must specialise in mathematics, with no conceivable alternative.'

Scholars lust after knowledge for its own sake and the schools which breed them need to give them room to breathe. Richard Cobb, the great historian of the French Revolution, was happy at school at Shrewsbury but hated 'my horrible house'.

Street, his housemaster, 'was thought to be a tremendous classical scholar, but his idea of housemastership was to let the bullies run the house. They were an appalling lot, mostly Unitarians from Liverpool like Street himself. There were three nervous breakdowns in my year alone and some people had to leave for a year. They never worried me because I was devious and tough; I was a survivor. I would read Thomas Hardy, for example, but would conceal the book in yellow Crime Club dust-jackets. I did not even mind being beaten. They would run at you along the corridor and hit you hard but I thought to myself – "You buggers, I can stick this out." I have found that kind of public-school stoicism very useful in later life. It taught me deviousness which I think is a very useful quality. I held my own counsel at school. I greatly enjoyed wrecking the system.'

Cobb won his school colours as a runner and this, combined with his scholarly abilities and survival qualities, made him a force to be reckoned with in his last year at Shrewsbury. 'I profited from that combination but they got me out in the end. I telegraphed Hardy, my headmaster, and the monster, Street, from Oxford to say I had got an award. They telegraphed my parents saying, "We feel that Shrewsbury has done all it can for Richard and that Shrewsbury and Richard should now part company."'

Cobb was fortunate as a historian in being taught by Murray Senior who arrived in the middle of one term in 1933 straight from Christ Church. Senior 'put history on the map and I transferred from the Classical side. He gave us tutorials and would have us up in pairs to his House, give us sherry and we would then return to our houses at nine o'clock. This enraged the housemasters, including mine. There was a built-in opposition at the school which consisted of housemasters opposing everything under the sun – a dreadful lot. Senior was an arrogant man and was sacked from two disastrous headmasterships after leaving Shrewsbury, but he had just that measure of eccentricity which appeals to schoolboys. Of the nine of us on the History side, eight got Oxbridge awards in my year.'

Eccentricity was in the air and the masters played up to it. 'Dick Sayle's desk in his classroom had a hole in it surrounded by a painted eye through which he would communicate with you over the top of the desk. Brook, the French master, had an electric contraption consisting of traffic lights. If he wanted to interrupt the reading of some obscure, boring nineteenth-century essayist, the amber and then the red light would go on. Dawson, the Ancient Historian, had a wooden leg which stuck up at right angles when he sat down so we would all sit with our legs in the air. Captain Banks, who taught English extremely well, was amazingly drunken. He had an awful first period to teach before breakfast at 7.30. We would swing the lights as he came into the room and you could see him going green.'

The great point was that these men 'were characters – you could identify with them and that made them good teachers.'

Senior fed Cobb's feeling for continuity in history related to recognisable topography: 'Frontiers fascinated me – I thought in terms of frontiers. I would look out from the Shrewsbury playing fields, see the bluish hills in the distance and think, "That's Wales".' Later on, his tutor at Merton, Idris Deane Jones, would remind him that, 'You can't understand anything in English history from the Conquest to the Elizabethan Settlement unless you look at the March. That's where it all happens and what happens in London follows on from that.' The topography of Cobb's schooldays helped equip him for that understanding.

Senior introduced Cobb to the works of the historian, Sir Lewis Namier. 'This was very exciting for me because it was the first time I had related English and European history to a region. Namier's *England in the Age of the American Revolution* had a chapter on the Shropshire gentry and there they still were, Captain Sir Offley Wakeham and the like, still on the governing body.'

Contemporary enthusiasms also flourished in his schooldays. Once again, Murray Senior was an influence: 'He was very keen on current affairs and he got me, for example, to do a report on the 1933 Spanish elections. He used to get the Soviet fortnightly news from the Soviet Embassy and would read that.

'The school would show lots of those worthy Soviet films with solemn subtitles. *Frozen Banks*, for example, explained the progress of old people cutting their way through mounds of ice and snow in order to build a canal. This created chaos in the audience because it was taken as a reference to Captain Banks and the ice in his whisky! We were very receptive to things happening in the Soviet Union and thought that they were good on the whole.'

These enthusiasms spread among boys whose originality and brio rivalled that of the masters themselves. 'George Rudé the historian was seven years older than me and had been Head of my House – he was an early public-school Communist. John Alexander was with me on the history side and was later on the Central Committee of the Communist Party. Nigel Heseltine was the son of the musician who adopted the name Peter Warlock. He was a Welsh Nationalist and established and edited a newspaper called *Wales*.

Another friend on the History side was Eric Dehn who, as a Bristol Grammar School housemaster, inspired so many boys.

It is only appropriate that the school which spawned *Private Eye* should also have produced one of the great iconoclasts of modern historical writing. Cobb's hatred of system, theory, prigs and self-righteous wielders of authority took root during his schooldays. Fortified alike by his contemporaries and his teachers, and despite the Liverpool Unitarian gang, he survived and flourished at Shrewsbury.

As in so many other cases the future scholar emerged from his chrysalis, weaned at his school by a combination of social tolerance with intellectual structure and discipline.

7 The Law

More than two-thirds of the higher judiciary, according to Marcel Berlins, the legal commentator, went to public schools and Oxbridge. Most come from comfortable middle-class homes. 'Although there are now moves towards a more open appointments procedure,' he told us, 'it is doubtful how many from outside a fairly close circle would actually aspire to a life on the Bench or relish life in an Inn of Court.' The same narrow background was almost as common, he said, for the lower ranks of the judiciary.

Until recently the same has been true of the Bar – the breeding ground for the judiciary. We were told that matters are improving as the Council for Legal Education, set up by the Inns of Court to train would-be barristers, has more applicants from polytechnics graduates in England and Wales than it has from Oxbridge.

But how far can schools play a part in this democratising process, which many, including Lord Scarman, feel is necessary? At school Law as a career is one of the most popular options. But this may not have been the case ten or twenty years ago. There are only one or two cases in this chapter when the decision to go to the Bar comes down during schooldays like a blinding flash on to a gilded youth. Lord Scarman may be one rare example, for his first thoughts towards Law may have been inspired, he says, by winning Radley College speech prize in 1930.

For most who answered our survey, however, it is more a question of drifters and grafters. There is a marked division between the top public-school products who drifted into the Law and the direct grant and grammar-school products who grafted their way into it. Of all the categories in this book, lawyers seemed to be the least influenced by school in terms of their career and also in terms of life generally.

'I was neither unhappy nor happy,' says Lord Devlin of his days at Stonyhurst, 'just bored.' Perhaps this was a portent of his decision years later to end continuous active service as a Law Lord at the comparatively tender age of 58. In his last term at school he discussed what he was going to do with a friend called Rooney. Devlin was going to go into the Church like his two sisters and one of his brothers. Rooney, who became a Jesuit, rather fancied going into the Law!

John Mortimer, who loathed Harrow, said that it had no influence on his choice of the Bar as a career but it did give him a hatred of the upper classes and a feeling that all public schools should be abolished. Mortimer, Judge Stephen Tumin, Her Majesty's Inspector of Prisons (St Edward's, Oxford) and Lord Donaldson, Master of the Rolls (Charterhouse), were among the few lawyers to admit to being unhappy at school.

Roy Amlot QC was advised by his headmaster at Dulwich after an appalling "A"-level result 'that in no circumstances should I contemplate going to the Bar.' And a senior judge who asked to remain anonymous said his Scottish public school did its damnedest to persuade him that he would be quite unsuitable for the Law but this attitude only spurred him on.

Faced with a form about their schooldays, most lawyers who went to public schools are unlikely to be verbose, prone to be a little pompous, usually cautious yet at the same time unable to resist filling it in. This chapter could almost have been a succession of one-liners like the following from two successive Lord Chancellors, who both said (as did Lord Shawcross, ex-Dulwich) that no-one in particular had influenced them at school:

'It [Eton] was admirable in every way': Lord Hailsham.

'It [Westminster] awoke my interests in the benefits of study': the late Lord Havers.

Hugh Peppiatt, Senior Partner at Freshfields, one of the City of London's top firms of solicitors, epitomised the actual effect of public school when he ticked the box acknowledging the influence on him of Winchester but qualified the tick with the phrase: 'in the general sense that it set a tone which pointed boys like me in the kind of direction I took.'

Another Wykehamist, Lord (Eustace) Roskill – the former judge and Lord of Appeal – said: 'I always knew what I wanted to do but my education at Winchester did much to enable me to do what I wanted.'

When Michael Beloff QC, ex-Eton, got a first from Magdalen College, Oxford, he thought perhaps he was bright and there came a rush of blood to his head which made him consider teaching.

But he told us: 'I was drawn to the Law inevitably because of the simple perception of others that I was likely to be best off in the Law. I debated a lot. I was President of the Union. I was likely to be good at the Law.'

Would Judge Tumin's parents now be asking for most of their money back from St Edward's, Oxford, if they could read their son's words? This expert on prisons wrote of the five years' time served at his old school: 'Other than in providing a good library, the school played very little part in my education. Teaching suffered from masters still being away at the end of the War or unsettled.'

Judge Tumin's decision to go into the Law came largely from the influence of his father, who was a barrister. Undoubtedly family connections were responsible in some cases for today's glittering legal careers. But the influence of family was mentioned by only 29 per cent of those who responded – slightly below the average for this book.

David Tench, head of the Consumers' Association's legal department, owes his legal career entirely to his father. He wrote: 'I was somewhat dim at school [Merchant Taylors', Northwood] – partly because of some chopping and changing due to the War. I was 17 before I took the old School Certificate and did not do very well. So I was not judged able enough to be considered for university or any kind of career involving qualifications. My father was, however, convinced that I could become a solicitor, a notion (because he was something of a snob) which he greatly favoured. He persuaded me – but not the Merchant Taylors' School – that this was something of which I was capable. He turned out to be right, and they were wrong. I was a late maturer, one who was not identified as such by the school, but by my father. My subsequent qualifying (quite well) into the legal profession and my later career owe virtually nothing to my schooling.'

It would be unbalanced to give an impression of there being no detailed bouquets for the public schools, particularly the former direct-grant ones: Lord Mishcon, who went to the City of London School, said: 'The School Debating Society in which I took a prominent part encouraged a love of advocacy as well as an interest in social problems and political affairs.'

Anthony Lester QC, a product of the same school, wrote in similar vein: 'The liberal tradition at CLS in the 1950s made me aware of the new independence movements in the Commonwealth, problems of racial and religious prejudice, and the importance of rational discourse. My sixth-form teachers steered me towards university when I might have gone without. Debating and (minor) acting were important activities for me.'

And the Catholic schools also provided their fair share of lawyers: the Christian Brothers spotted Rodger Pannone, the 1993 President of the Law Society, when he was at St Brendan's, Bristol, as an ideal candidate for the priesthood. He had the right balance of idealism and commonsense to run a working-class parish. But he disappointed them, joined the Labour Party at the age of 17, and after a year as a schoolmaster, became articled to a small law firm. The idealism is still there but it operates in favour of disaster victims and has brought him to the forefront of his profession.

Mrs Pauline Crabbe JP, Britain's first black woman to become a magistrate, attended Highgate Convent. She said: 'The education at this convent was of a very high standard. Amongst other advantages it fostered my love of reading and enabled me to develop a truly catholic taste in literature and a wide range of other subjects.

'The school had a brilliant elocution teacher who taught me to make the fullest use of my voice. I believe that although this did not directly affect my choice of career, it opened many doors to me that would otherwise have remained closed to a black woman.'

'I enjoyed debating,' said Sir Michael Nolan, the Appeal Court judge, 'and the headmaster (of Ampleforth) suggested that I try for the Bar.'

St Francis Xavier's College had a strong debating society. The Jesuits valued good speech, said Sir Bernard Caulfield, the former High Court Judge – the one who later described Jeffrey Archer's wife Mary as 'fragrant'. 'My headmaster's comment in my first school report is imprinted on my mind: "Bernard should take more trouble to improve his speech."'

There are plenty of links between acting at school and later advocacy. Few are better expressed than by Lord Justice Staughton, who wrote about his schooldays in *When They were Young* in aid of CLIC, the children's cancer trust, as follows:

'My acting career at school had variety at first. Later it settled into a pattern – some say it has never stopped.'

At the age of ten he played Doll Tearsheet in *Henry IV Part 2*. It was an unsuitable part because his voice had broken but he was not old enough to understand what the lady was up to. He would have preferred to have been Justice Shallow. At 16 he appeared in Eton's production of *Macbeth*.

He wrote: 'Timothy Renton (Macbeth) selected the three most disorderly boys in the school as First, Second and Third Murderers: Stephen Egerton (KCMG – Ambassador to Italy), Neil Ascherson the journalist and myself. Unfortunately the props department thought that a squawk of the clarinet would do for the "owl that shrieked" and the audience rocked with laughter. Besides Banquo, our instructions were to kill Fleance (Tam Dalyell); but Shakespeare let him escape.'

By the time he was 18 the die was cast with two lawyers' parts on speech day. 'The first was Cicero declaiming on self-defence in *Pro Milone*. It was marvellous stuff for a jury:

"*Non potestis hoc facinus improbum judicare, quin simul judicetis omnibus, qui in latrones inciderint, aut illorum telis aut vestris sententiis esse pereundum*. (If you convict my client you will decide that everyone who is set upon by robbers must perish either by weapons or by your verdict)."

'The second was Serjeant Buzfuz in *Pickwick Papers* – a prolix, bombastic and unconvincing lawyer. So the child is father to the man.'

Sir Allan Green, former Director of Public Prosecutions, wrote to us saying: 'I took part in a number of school and house plays (at Charterhouse) and so acquired a taste for "performing in public" which barristers and actors plainly share.' This was written before the King's Cross incident.

But in *When They were Young*, mentioned above, he recalls a delightful lesson in justice at his prep school, Hazelwood. 'On one occasion a boy stuffed a rag down a lavatory and blocked it. Parry (the headmaster) threatened to beat the whole school if the culprit did not own up. He waited in vain for a confession and then proceeded to carry out his threat.

'When my turn came, he candidly acknowledged that I couldn't have been responsible since I had a perfect alibi: I'd been in hospital, having ruptured myself lifting the school tea urn. Nevertheless, he had said that he would beat everyone and he did. This convinced me that justice is elusive.'

Sir Allan first got the idea of a career at the Bar when he accompanied a litigious grandfather to court. His counsel on that occasion was Leonard Caplan – then a rising junior – whose 'urbane tenacity' impressed Green enormously.

A visit to Winchester Assizes switched on the young Tom Denning. Lord Denning, the best-known grammar-school product to scale the peaks of the Law, told us that Andover Grammar School had no influence whatsoever on his going into the Law. He was all set to study mathematics at Magdalen College, Oxford, and teach thereafter. He took a vacation job teaching maths at Winchester College and decided that he did not want to teach the subject all his life.

'I popped into the Assizes and sat in the public gallery and watched counsel during a case. I said: "Surely I can do as well as he" and I went back to Oxford and changed to Jurisprudence.'

There are a few examples of visits by lawyers to schools influencing those who listened to them. Sir Ivan Lawrence, the QC and Tory MP, remembers a talk by a Recorder – Eric Neave KC – at Brighton Hove and Sussex Grammar School, while Judge Nina Lowry remembers being taken to the local assizes when she was at Bedford High School.

But while most lawyers from public schools drifted into the Law, we found only one from a grammar school who talked about drifting:

'I never did choose a career,' says Sir Robert Jennings, President of the International Court of Justice, who was educated at Belle Vue Secondary School for Boys, Bradford. 'Things just worked out as they did. That I believe is probably true of most people. I went to Cambridge, however, though none of my family even knew what a university was and could not really afford it, through the influence of one superb teacher who taught me that to be at Oxford or Cambridge was the finest thing that could happen to you. He went to Birmingham University and I suppose that he imagined most of it – but he did teach me to love the poems of Matthew Arnold: and who can do that without at least loving the idea of Oxford?

'I read Law because I was bored with history, which was not very well taught at my school (though the history masters were very nice chaps who became friends.) I knew no Law, so did not realise that that, like everything else, would have its boring patches too.'

John Hayes, Secretary General of the Law Society, was another lower-middle-class lad who had his sights raised towards the Law both by poetry and by his teachers at Morecambe Grammar School. He had a particularly poetic journey to his legal Damascus. He said: 'Grammar school led people like me with no other member of the family having gone to university into feeling special and having a special goal.' The precise flashpoint came when he was 15 and analysing the meaning of *Saul* by Robert Browning:

'I cannot remember the poem at all now. Our set books for "O" level were Browning and Tennyson. A master called Fred Siddle gave us this long poem to look at. We all read through it in class. No-one understood a word of it. He set it for homework for a weekend. I really tried to work it out. It was a challenge. It was the first time I realised that maybe being a lawyer would not be a bad thing. I cracked it. If I could crack *Saul*, I could crack anything. I could crack the Law.'

His previous idea had been to become a teacher. This was influenced by a history master called Taylor. 'He was regarded as a bit of a roué among masters. It was he who always seemed to go out with the French assistante. He used to show her Morecambe's illuminations. He owned an Austin A35 and you got an image in your mind that it would not be a bad life going back to school, having this little car and quite a bit of home life.'

However, his parents – his father who worked as a signals inspector on the railways and his mother who ran a corner shop – impressed on him that school teaching was just going back to school and he would never break out.

'Doing history with Taylor first gave me an interest in writing structured essays. I was useless at science, but the thing about writing a history or an English essay was that you had to use logical arguments to reason with. I applied these to science and found that using logical arguments helped me to get marks for the most elementary descriptions of scientific experiments. I began to think of Law as a subject in which you would be solving problems in a way that had some human effect.'

However, once his sights were lifted towards Law, he was afraid to lift them too high: 'I thought probably the big private firms of solicitors would be full of people from public schools. I must be destined for a boring legal job. I used to read the advertisements for corporation lawyers in the local paper. You soon learned of the progression. It seemed boring and safe enough. You went in as assistant, the next rank was called senior assistant, the rank after that was chief assistant solicitor, and then there was deputy town clerk. The top was town clerk.'

He thought: 'That's part of the ladder that I could go up.' He used to read his mother's magazines and remembers that in the romantic short stories corporation lawyers were boring chaps – not very good-looking and not very interesting.

He said: 'I thought – that's me. Someone who has a reasonably high standing in the community. I would know what was going on but would not be aiming too high.'

Years later – Worthing Borough Council, Nottingham Borough Council, Somerset County Council and Warwickshire's Chief Executive later – John William Hayes has climbed through the progression listed in his mum's magazines and now has one of the most influential jobs in the Law as the 'new broom' in the Law Society since 1987. He can even list one of his recreations in *Who's Who* as 'idleness'.

At the age of 14, Anne Mallalieu, the future barrister and baroness, had wanted to read dairying at Reading University and become a farmer. Instead she went to Cambridge and became the first woman President of the Union.

No previous girl at Holton Park Girls' School, Wheatley, had gained a place at Oxbridge and only a very small number had gone on to university from this small country girls' grammar school.

Lady Mallallieu says, 'The staff were of an exceptionally high calibre (dons' wives from Oxford) who gave a great deal of inspiration and praise for even limited academic success. They encouraged me to aim high without giving me any sense of failure if I failed to make it. Had I attended a larger school with more of an academic background, I feel I might well have settled for something less.'

Professor Brenda Hoggett QC, the Law Commissioner, was also encouraged at Richmond High School, Yorkshire, to become the first girl to aim for Oxbridge and to read Law at Cambridge. The encouragement came from her headmistress.

Sir Gordon Borrie, the former Director General of the Office of Fair Trading, was not turned on to the Law by poetry or by his headmaster but his sights were raised by the way current affairs were dropped into the history lessons at the John Bright Grammar School, Llandudno. Sir Gordon's father was a solicitor and his uncle and grandfather were lawyers, so there was a fair amount of family influence behind him when the family moved to North Wales.

Sir Gordon said: 'Combining family influence and school influence, the big thing really was an influence of something broader which I would call Public Affairs.'

The history master, I.T. Davies (he never knew his Christian name), 'used to finish off history lessons in the senior forms with a run-down on current events like the civil war in Greece or what was to happen to Germany after the Second World War. I was absolutely fascinated by those sorts of things and I used to read and acquire myself, because they didn't come into the home otherwise, magazines that have now ceased to exist like *News Review* which used lots of photographs and had lots of foreign news. The end of the Second World War and the combination of this particular master and his interest in world affairs, and the family influence, meant that I was interested in the Law, not as something that solicitors did in, as it were, back rooms, but more as leading to public affairs, a political career.'

Had he gone to public school and Oxbridge (rather than Manchester University), would he have been a greater success at the Bar?

'I had a very modest practice in the mid-1950s. Insofar as I lacked connections and might have had more had I been to Oxbridge, then possibly I might have done better.'

But then he thinks of Sir Robin Day – Brentwood, Bembridge School (Isle of Wight) and Oxford, where he was President of the Union. 'Robin Day didn't find the Bar very satisfactory and did not do very well at it. Yet we all know from his work on the BBC and so on what an effective cross-examiner he is. Obviously he found the Bar terribly slow and difficult. He was a sort of impatient fellow like me. He felt he just couldn't bear to see his twenties and thirties going by, not getting any work. Then the opportunity came in his case to be a newscaster and to be in public affairs. I'm sure he never looked back.'

However, Sir Gordon does believe the Bar and judiciary tend to be a self-perpetuating oligarchy and this is only slowly being broken down: 'The organisational divide into chambers means that there is a very strong personal element in terms of how you get into the right chambers and so on. It is the heads of chambers and the senior people in them who are important and they in effect are self-perpetuating to a degree that works through into the judiciary as well. Whom does the Lord Chancellor ask who are the appropriate people to become judges in the Queen's Bench Division? He asks the senior judges there and they are largely Oxbridge and so the thing is self-perpetuating. But it is of course breaking down gradually.'

One person who is keen to open up access to the legal profession, and who is in a position to do so, is the 1992 Chairman of the Bar Council, Sir Gareth Williams. He went to Rhyl Grammar School and, unlike Sir Gordon Borrie, entered the Welsh language stream as his father was a Welsh-speaking primary school headmaster and lay preacher. Williams senior was the headmaster of the first Welsh language school in Wales.

The school had an extremely dedicated headmaster called Bertram Evans, who taught modern languages, fought in the First World War and was decorated after Gallipoli. The young Williams had a choice between studying Welsh or French and kept on with his Welsh. 'When it came to sitting the scholarship examination for Cambridge, you had to do a modern language. Welsh was not regarded as acceptable. So Mr Evans had to teach me French in a year, which he did by taking me for two extra lessons a week in his study in his spare time.'

Sir Gareth knew from the age of eight or nine that he was going to do Law. 'I always knew I was going to be a barrister. Don't ask me how. There was no family connection with the Law at all.' He was the only pupil at his school to study for Cambridge. After Cambridge he did his pupillage in Pump Court in the Temple and then used a Welsh connection, through Bill (later Mr Justice) Mars-Jones, to go into practice at the Bar in Swansea.

He believes that with paid pupillage, mini-pupillage for sixth-formers to spend a week at the Bar, the barriers to the Law are crumbling quickly. This is a view shared by his predecessor Anthony Scrivener who, when he was Vice-Chairman of the Bar Council, introduced the first mock trial competitions for schools, for which regional contests now attract 1,000 pupils.

A mock trial was one of the reasons why Anthony himself, a grant-aided pupil at a direct-grant grammar school (Kent College, Canterbury), first decided that the Law would be the career for him.

He recalls: 'It was a huge occasion – attended by the whole school and organised by a down-town firm of solicitors. They wrote the script. The offence was a public mischief – a very rare offence and so not entirely suitable for the occasion. I remember I was leading counsel but whether it was for the defence or prosecution, I am not certain.'

He had been a child prodigy in terms of height but not in terms of academic prowess. He was six foot two inches tall at the age of 12 and very competitive. But the competition was in sport where his long legs took him to third place in a cross-country run in which the whole school took part. His long reach made him a devastating bowler and batsman and he excelled at both cricket and rugby.

He said: 'I concentrated entirely on sport. My academic work was abysmal. I was almost always at the bottom of the B stream. But I respond to personalities I can get on with.'

At the age of 14 or 15, Mr (Sydney) Haynes, took him for history. Anthony Scrivener can even remember that in his first history lesson Mr Haynes said, 'History is the story of chaps and chapesses . . .' The lessons were fun and Anthony was interested.

'All of a sudden from coming bottom I came top. English became fun and I did well there too. I joined the debating society and shone there as well.'

One of the debates was 'This House believes in Fairies.' The future QC convinced his sceptical teenage audience that life would be so dull without fairies, that they had to believe in them! They did and he won.

About this time and before his work began to improve, he decided, he does not remember quite how, that he would become a barrister. He confided this ambition to Mr Haynes, who said that with the appalling 'O' Level results he was likely to get, Scrivener had not a chance in hell of going to the Bar unless he raised his sights.

'I was so influenced by him that I did. I came from bottom to top. I worked from morning to night. My family was staggered. Sport had to take second place.'

One problem was maths where his 'O' level mock scores hovered around an average of 7 per cent. In a desperate measure to improve this modest score, he was allowed to drop science subjects completely, and in three months did eight lessons of maths a week – some on his own in the library, and he passed comfortably thanks to a sergeant-major type disciplinarian of a maths teacher called 'Daddy' White.

The final hurdle – a legacy of the B stream – was a complete absence of Latin. Without Latin 'O' level, no admission to a Law degree. In a year he did Latin from scratch with private coaching – in his spare time for no extra money – from 'Sparks' Spencer, the music and Latin teacher, who owned an open-roofed car and an electric organ, and once took them all carol-singing in Canterbury with the organ in the back of the car when they got stuck in a blizzard. But he had better success teaching the young Scrivener Latin because he passed *cum laude*.

Scrivener says: 'It is less true today that you need money to start at the Bar, than it was then. What you did need was plenty of luck and you had to plan it. I had to work in the canning factory in Faversham. I worked there with other Law students, including the Nicholls twins (Colin and Clive), who are both now QCs. In fact, we put the wrong dye in one day and turned the peas out red by mistake.'

Another grafter, who passed into the top stream of Holyrood Senior Secondary School, Glasgow, was Helena Kennedy QC, whose father was a despatch hand and parcel binder at the *Daily Record*.

She said: 'I was due to go to Glasgow University to read English. Most Scottish students live at home when they go to university. My parents, who had both left school at 14, expected me to go there and then to take up a career in teaching. It was a good job for a woman.

'But I did not do it for two reasons: I wanted to leave home and I did not want to end up as a teacher. My older sister had married someone who did Law at Glasgow University and that gave me the idea.'

She went down to London to the Council for Legal Education. She thought she might study for the Bar examinations for a year and then do a degree. But once started, she was determined to finish the course.

She said: 'Students who come from working-class backgrounds see education as a way to a job. I did not want my parents to continue supporting me. Although I got a small grant, it was not a full one because Scotland disapproved of my working away from home. I was always hard up. I worked during the summer holidays and in the evenings. I worked in an employment agency interviewing people who wanted to be secretaries. I worked in restaurants and I taught Bar Final failures.'

She was influenced by two teachers at school. 'I was the only girl in my year to do Greek. I tend to want to do things that other people don't do and I know that this was one of the reasons why I chose Law. I virtually had private tuition from the classics teacher – John Lavelle. He took a real interest in me. I'm sure I got the idea of studying away from home from him.

'The other person who influenced me was my form mistress and namesake – Miss Moira Kennedy. She was a kind of Miss Jean Brodie. She led a glamorous independent life. It became clear to me that to be an educated woman was not the same as being a stuffed shirt. She was an important role model in my life. She took us on walking trips in the Highlands, ski-ing trips on the Cairngorms and sailing. I would never have done these things otherwise. My parents were urban types.'

Looking back on her decision to do Law from a working-class background, she says it was exceptional: 'It is very much a question of aspiration. The Law for most working-class kids seems a world apart – outside of the possible. My mother was fearful about me going to London. She would have been far happier if I had taught. That was in her ken. As for "eating dinners" – only the English could think up a thing like that! However, my dad was actually quite proud of me. But my education drew me away from home.'

Now she feels an obligation to go to schools, to talk and to demystify the Law. 'The only way to change would be to have a Bill of Rights and to instil in people a notion of their rights – the rights of citizenship – and this would put them in touch with the Law.'

Patricia Scotland, Britain's first black woman QC, attended Walthamstow Senior High School for Girls. According to an interview in the *Evening Standard* (10 July 1991), she was told by a careers teacher that she was setting her sights too high in going for a law career. Since she had a Saturday job in Sainsbury's, she was advised to apply for a job there. Undeterred, she applied for a London University external degree, became a pupil at the Council of Legal Education School of Law and was called to the Bar at 21.

Patricia was aware from the age of seven that it was assumed that one day she would be going to university. One day her brother came back from school with a 99 per cent pass in Latin. Her parents wanted to know what had happened to the other 1 per cent. Her father was keen on literature and gave her Zola and Dostoevsky to read when she was ten.

She is quoted in the article by Pauline Peters: 'We always had lots of fun in our family. We used to have great philosophical discussions until late at night about things like Marxism or social work. If I had any problems with my school work, there was always somebody at home who had already excelled at maths or physics or whatever.'

One school holiday waiting for her 'A' level results, she worked in a solicitors' office and decided there and then that Law was to be her career.

There are dangers that lack of money and now increasingly (with both the Bar and the solicitors' branch of the profession) the lack of the right class of degree might deter talent from a career in Law. But lack of money actually drove Janet Cohen the merchant banker into Law: 'I chose to be a lawyer because I desperately wanted a good, highly paid, male career. I am the only child of a widow.'

One quality which Janet Cohen, Patricia Scotland and Helena Kennedy share with Lord Denning and the other heroes and heroines who in this chapter struggled for their place in the Law, is ambition.

Lord Denning said: 'Of course, going to a grammar school was not an advantage. In those days it would have been a help to go to Eton, Winchester or Harrow. They did not like grammar schools much at university. But I was highly ambitious and ambition will get you anywhere.'

8 Literature

Schools have been powerful presences in modern English literature. Evelyn Waugh's *Decline and Fall* seized on the irrationality, cruelty and arbitrariness of school life. School contemporaries recur in Anthony Powell's *A Dance to the Music of Time*. Widmerpool, the most memorable bore in English fiction, is last seen as an elderly jogger in a grotesque parody of the cross-country run where he first appears.

Cyril Connolly's *Enemies of Promise* blames the afflatus of premature schoolboy glory for a failure to achieve one's potential in later life. Alan Bennett's play *Forty Years On* presented public schools as an aspect of the heritage industry, and as part of modern England's antiquarian, anti-serious, anti-modernist charm. Sex in the hothouse has been investigated by David Benedictus in *The Fourth of June*, by Michael Campbell in *Lord Dismiss Us*, by Simon Raven in his sequence of novels *Alms for Oblivion* and by Alec Waugh in *The Loom of Youth*.

The vein originally mined by Thomas Hughes in *Tom Brown's Schooldays* may by now have assumed some louche forms, but there is no denying its richness. Among contemporary writers, William Boyd seems set to continue the exploration.

Schools can provide writers with their subject matter but in a wider sense can provide them with the neuroses, the hatreds, the absurdities and the inspiration which will inform their work.

Fiona Pitt-Kethley's collections of verse, *Private Parts* and *Sky Ray Lolly*, draw heavily on her experiences at Haberdashers' Aske's Junior and Senior schools. In *Hate at First Sight* she describes her feelings about the school:

> *Our form-teacher in her twin-set and pearls*
> *was round-faced and always smiling*
> *as the Iron Maiden of Nuremberg.*
> *each day I met the furnace of her hate.*

'I wasn't as unhappy at the Upper School because by then I didn't expect anything of it,' says Pitt-Kethley. 'I was cynical about school and I accepted that I had to go there.'

She had won a scholarship to the school and her parents could not have afforded the fees. Nonetheless: 'I always hoped to get expelled. I was always thought to be very naughty but I didn't really do anything that terrible. I was sent to a psychiatrist at the age of seven for writing "bum" on my desk – and I only used a soft pencil – I didn't even carve it!'

> *My Head, Miss Harold, five foot square in grey,*
> *was deeply disappointed that the shrink*
> *she had me sent to certified me sane.*
> *(At seven, I'd written 'BUM' upon my desk,*
> *and that, in Old Harry's view, meant madness.)*
> (*Sky Ray Lolly*: Abacus 1986)

'In the Upper School I was labelled the wickedest girl in the school but I was quite religious, so that made me quite restrained sexually.' She had read Dante and Milton at home and so was 'bored out of my mind' at school. 'I learned absolutely nothing at the Junior School. I knew it all already.'

Writing poetry, for Pitt-Kethley, is a form of therapy and a way of dealing with her memories of snobbishness at school:

'I'm a profoundly mean person. Everything in life has to be used and I must get my value out of everything. So if I have a bad experience I put it to professional use. I say, "I sold that poem for fifty quid" and that makes me feel I've got my money's worth out of it. I am strongly motivated by revenge – though not to get my revenge on specific teachers. They weren't really worth it. They were poor screwed-up people.'

Travel writing, as in the cases of Graham Greene and Robert Byron in this century, has been a way of expressing in code your feelings about your own country. Jonathan Raban's scepticism about his England and its values, especially in the 1980s, has been obvious in his books about other countries. Disillusion with England set in early and he regards his time at King's School, Worcester as 'an intensive five-year education in cruelty'.

He says now, 'It taught me a kind of survival, but at a grim cost. At 49 I still feel warped by the experience. The gulag of the school at that time still sometimes figures in my dreams and the brutality of that experience does not diminish.' In Raban's view, his schooldays had 'a profoundly negative influence on my subsequent career.'

Brian Aldiss, the science-fiction writer, was 'severely unhappy at Framlingham' and believes that the school should have been closed.

Sebastian Barker, the poet and Chairman of The Poetry Society, is another creative spirit at odds with the institution. Both his prep school and King's School, Canterbury in those days had 'dreadful aspects' to them 'mainly to do with the potential for sadistic acts against defenceless boys and sexual molestation on a pretty serious scale.'

He told us, 'I would in one instance have been raped if a slightly more working-class boy had not come to my rescue.'

Romantic love entered his life for the first time during his summer holidays from King's. 'Unfortunately I wrote it all down in a series of long letters to a friend from school, mixed in with very precise details of the love affairs between the older boys at the school, who were all senior monitors, and the prettier younger boys. My friend's mother, from good old Bromley, found the letters and sent them to the headmaster, Canon Shirley. He was unamused. Fortunately all the boys' names were in a simple numerical code which couldn't be broken. I was threatened with a beating, but Shirley was honourable enough not to force me to decode my revelations.'

Barker learnt 'that people are very dangerous indeed and that friendships and group identification are vital to survival. I saw too that there was no knowing where the next evil act might break out, though it would probably be amongst the disgruntled. I did in fact see an eight-year-old boy being raped. It is as clear and large as life to this day. Such schools taught me an excessive and vital caution, which was undoubtedly a significant key in my development as a poet.'

The explorer and travel writer Robin Hanbury-Tenison left Eton with 'a determination never to lead an institutionalised life again'. So strong was this determination that he abandoned his original intention to be a regular soldier. 'An inner strength was forged out of solitude and misery, which has made the rigours of exploration pale in comparison.'

Jack Higgins (the *nom de plume* of the novelist Harry Patterson) left Roundhay School, Leeds, at 16 after a series of unhappy experiences. 'The Head used the cane and believed in the virtues of rugby, whereas I had already discovered the truth about sportsmanship in the changing-rooms when the captain of school rugby and captain of Yorkshire Colts gave me a good hiding for bringing him down with a tackle. It was the only one of my career and prevented not only his try but his House winning the championship.'

On another occasion, 'The Head told me that I would never amount to anything.'

The one bright spot in this bleak environment was a woman, Dorothy

Quarton, who 'allowed us to do creative writing in literature lessons and who called me back one evening to say, "I think you could be a writer." That sustained me for many years and became an ambition in an otherwise pretty lousy life doing boring jobs.'

In *Another Country* the playwright Julian Mitchell produced a classic study of the connections between political and sexual secrecy and deception. His material is to be found within that 'general ethos' which he has been 'struggling to resist ever since leaving Winchester'.

Novelist Rosie Thomas thinks that 'Everything I have achieved since leaving school has been a contradiction of the preparation for life I was given at Howell's School, Denbigh.'

Thomas told us, 'At this very muscular, philistine and old-fashioned girls' school we were not encouraged to develop any individuality or display any eccentricity. Routine and regimentation were the norm, together with a kind of hearty games-players' indifference to anything "soppy" or "arty". As a rather diffident, awkward and sensitive scholarship girl who had suffered the death of my mother, I was oppressed by my inability to fit in with a horde of jolly girls from affluent Cheshire families. I ignored all my own inclinations towards literature and poetry and solitude and tried to be like everyone else. I hated Howell's, without ever realising quite how profoundly.'

Another novelist, Alexander Stuart, confronted the 'pompous head-master' of his school, Bexley Grammar, 'who thought he was in control of a nineteenth-century public school. He gave me a focus against which to direct my energies and a face for the value system which I still find unacceptable.'

The uses of adversity, however, are many: 'In the sixth form I made an 8mm short film, starring a female pupil from the school, about a girl who committed suicide after an involvement with drugs. The film attracted some press attention and horrified my headmaster. It also won me a chance to direct for BBC TV.'

Jon Silkin, the poet, was expelled by his headmaster, the famous Jilkes of Dulwich College. He played truant at the age of 17 and was discovered.

'Jilkes, a cold man, caned me in his study, though I should have resisted but I didn't. Then he said, "You have no use for this school, so this school has no use for you."'

Poetry got hold of Silkin when he was 15 and at Dulwich. He hated the way he was taught poetry by rote. 'We had to learn a bit and remember who wrote it. Appalling! There was no attempt to understand it.'

School only seemed to confirm Silkin in his 'outsider' status: 'I saw a horrific incident of a boy being publicly caned for being in bed with another boy – he was fourteen or fifteen – before being expelled.'

He was also becoming alienated from his parents. He fell out with his father 'when I was about 15 because he wanted me to be a solicitor like him. My mother got very angry with me and said, "If you don't stop writing this poetry I'll come up and destroy it!" And I said, "If you do that I'll kill you." And I meant it because poetry was the only thing in my life – except girls.

'Fear,' he explains, 'was deeply ingrained in my parents. They were middle-class Jews who had been working-class Jews and they were always frightened.' Their desire for a safe profession for their son was a reflection of that fear. 'The English,' says Silkin, 'are a rather frightening people. You have to be English or nothing.'

The author of a classic feminist study of the Virgin Mary, *Alone of All Her Sex*, was cast as the Virgin in the school nativity play at St Mary's, Ascot, and told that 'in order to be worthy of the part, I should imitate Mary in every particular.' Marina Warner recalls that her school gave her 'a language and a whole system of thought which has been an inspiration for my subsequent work as a writer.' Beryl Bainbridge is similarly indebted to the Arts Educational School, since it made her realise that 'I would never make a ballet dancer.' Not only was she very well taught – her social horizons also widened since 'I mixed with people from an entirely different social class and that opened my eyes.'

She had joined the school after being expelled from Merchant Taylors', Crosby for 'writing a dirty story and illustrating it, so one can see I was fairly artistic from an early age.'

Competitiveness and sometimes counter-suggestibility emerge as a key element in the school experience of many writers. Alan Garner, celebrated as a children's author, especially for his book *The Weirdstone of Brisingamen*, praises the teaching method at Manchester Grammar School.

'It was based on Plato's methods, on question and provocation. They would issue a ridiculous statement which was wholly plausible and wait for someone to refute it. It was the principle of *advocatus diaboli*. The school continues to instil the concept of excellence, in the absolute and for its own sake, yet manages to do so by fitting the school to the boy rather than by making the boy conform to the school. The elderly schoolmasters of the war years gave us Victorian teaching of intellectual rigour.'

Garner remembers: 'In my time there was a boy of 15 who really thought he was a train – a steam engine. This boy used to go round with his feet shuffling and his arms outstretched, chuffing along, and to get him into a classroom took several minutes. The staff and several of us boys would have to change the points so he could come in backwards – then the points would have to be changed again and he'd have to be put on a turntable to get him into his desk. No-one told him to snap out of it: it was all part of this acceptance thing.'

Relief from intellectual work was provided by Wilf the caretaker: 'There were 1,400 boys in the school and Wilf knew the name of every one. If any boy had a problem he went to Wilf. He was working-class like most of us but he was very intelligent and he could interpret emotional and academic stress in our terms. If a member of staff realised a boy was upset, he'd go along to Wilf to find out what was the matter. He was the father-confessor to both boys and staff and he saved me hours of misery.'

Alan Plater, the playwright, is another product of a Northern grammar school who values independent thinking and behaviour. Kingston High School, Hull, was, he tells us, 'a very independent school. My generation produced everyone from actors like Tom Courtenay and John Alderton to professional soccer players and probably the leading Shakespeare scholar in the land – Stanley Wells.'

Many writers are conscious of the way their school environment accommodated them. D.J. Enright's physics master at Leamington College 'observed how miserable I was when taking his subject at Higher School Certificate and persuaded the Head to let me take English instead.' The headmaster was the school's one teacher of English and although he did not take classes because he was busy with administration, he made an exception for Enright: 'I became his one and only class.'

Rosemary Anne Sisson, novelist and scriptwriter, found Cheltenham Ladies' College 'a place of great interior freedom within an apparently rigid framework. That tall, ugly, stooping, brilliant Greek teacher, Miss Rackham, kept me behind after class to scold me for a careless piece of work, and then, when she saw that she had reduced me to tears, cried, "Oh my dear! Do you think I would bother if I didn't think you were worth it?" To know that someone thinks you have a special quality is something which is desperately important to every writer.'

Hopeless at maths, Sisson once wrote on a piece of homework, '"This took two hours!" Miss Shaw replied: "I'm not surprised. You have done everything twice". Quite right. Writers have to learn to write again and again, but really it's better to get it right the first time.'

Sir Stephen Spender thinks that the teaching at University College School, Hampstead was indifferent. 'When I was there no boy, apart from one or two scientists, seemed to get a scholarship at Oxford or Cambridge – none of my contemporaries really distinguished himself in any way in later life.'

He is grateful, however, for the flexibility of the school's structures, its 'liberal and sympathetic atmosphere, its public-spirited headmaster' and the absence of bullying. The greatest individual influence on Spender was that of 'a very bright teacher of English and history called Geoffrey Thorp who was a Fabian, politically and artistically active as well as open-minded about sex. He encouraged me a great deal.'

A. Alvarez, like Sir Stephen, has influenced modern English letters both as critic and as poet. Oundle was indulgent enough to establish a VIth Form in English on his behalf at a time when the subject was not taught in the school. Alvarez's career was shaped by 'a wonderful guy called Harry Cauldwell. One day he produced a poem by John Donne for us to comment on. It was *Witchcraft by a Picture*. I was about 15 and had never heard of Donne. I don't think I understood the poem but I kind of fell in love with it. It seemed mysterious and beautiful, yet full of energy. What got me above all was the tone of voice: argumentative, exasperated, heart-broken. For me it was *le coup de foudre*. I thought – this is what I want out of life.'

Alvarez had been sent to Oundle because it was a good science school and he had originally wanted to be a scientist: 'I swiftly discovered that I was no good at physics and chemistry, so I became a linguist.' Despite Oundle's special arrangements on his behalf he failed the Oxford scholarship at his first attempt. 'I spent all my time boxing and playing rugger and did very little work.'

When Alvarez arrived at Oundle he describes himself as 'a spoilt little Jewish intellectual who looked like Franz Kafka: I left with a 17-inch neck!' Oundle turned him into an unusually sporty intellectual and 'it gave me the habit of exercise which I still have.'

The argumentative nature of Donne mirrored the condition of the schoolboy who, like so many literary intellectuals, found himself at odds with the authorities. 'I was very nearly thrown out of Oundle.

When I was in the VIth Form and a school prefect and Head of my House, a new headmaster arrived – G.H. Stainforth, otherwise known as Gus. Stainforth decided I was a disruptive element – which was probably true. He wanted to take the school by the neck and shake it a bit, so he organised the younger masters to spy on the older ones. I christened these power-hungry young toadies The Gustapo, a joke that went round the school in about two minutes.'

Since Alvarez was known to visit a pub eight miles away with two of his friends, Stainforth set a trap. However, 'that evening there was a recital I wanted to hear.' And so he said no when his friends asked him to come with them as usual. Stainforth was at the concert. 'I saw him looking at me very gimlet-eyed and I wondered why. I discovered soon enough: he had sent one of his Gustapo to the pub and when my friends came out of the door at ten o'clock there was this gung-ho master on his knees in the mud with a flashlight. His first words were, "Where's Alvarez?" I was told by my housemaster that if I had been there all three of us would have been expelled.'

It is hardly surprising that so many writers record a sensitivity to their environment. This sensitivity can lead the writer in embryo to the conviction that he is not where he should be. The novelist Peter Dickinson, for example, says that 'Eton reinforced an already existing uncertainty about my place in the social structure, the sense of not-quite-belonging.'

More positively, though, he notes that the school 'allowed for much greater nonconformity than many public schools. In a more rigid set-up I might have become a sort of crypto-dropout (without the nerve to drop out properly). The ambience, the myth, may have given me a mistaken belief that whatever I did eventually do I'd be accepted as being unusually good at it. The heavy diet of Latin and Greek must have had some effect, negatively, by not spoiling anything else for me; positively perhaps by making me unafraid of long sentences.'

Anita Brookner records no ambiguity in her feelings about James Allen's Girls' School, 'an entirely innocent and immensely restful' place which was an escape from a home 'full, over-full of adult emotions'. She enjoyed the various rituals of school life: 'It was a dreamy active time, in an attractive pre-war outer suburb – a time capsule. Although I was at school throughout the War I felt quite safe there.'

Lady Rachel Billington, novelist daughter of Lord Longford, was also happy at More House, a London Catholic day school for girls. It had twenty-seven pupils when she arrived there and 'it has left me with a romantic leaning towards the small independent school'.

Her education was in many ways 'narrow and shallow. The school was in two houses in the Cromwell Road and had very few facilities. We were taught no sciences and I had the choice of doing a maximum of seven "O" levels.' She is grateful, however, that the school left her with space for development:

'As a writer it left me relatively virgin territory for entering the world. What the school taught me was to be rather individualistic: there was no particular conformity about it. In fact Reverend Mother used to go round pushing us out of line when we lined up to go into lessons. She used to say, "You're all sheep. Get out of line!"'

Joan Aiken is another writer who feels indebted to the ambience of a small school, in her case, Wychwood School, Oxford. It had only eighty girls when she went there. 'When the school amalgamated with Oxford High in 1941 I couldn't take it so I left.'

Wilfred Thesiger's prose and photographs record an extreme sensitivity to the beauty of remote landscape. It was a sensitivity which was present when, as a boy at Eton, he refused to accede to his tutor's suggestion that he should move to another study. He was too attached to the view of Windsor Castle from the window.

Thesiger is a traditionalist who has used his sense of tradition and ceremony in order to live among the Bedouin, the Marsh Arabs and the Masai. It is the same sense which has given him 'a dislike of interference with other cultures, of others putting on our clothes.'

He explains: 'Eton made me into a traditionalist and that helped me and gave me the ability to adapt myself to years of living in the desert with the Bedouin. I could live with them and be accepted by them.' Even being birched was grist to this traditionalist's mill since it was conducted in such a ritualistic way: 'It was like an execution on Tower Hill – and I was rather glad of that.'

The son of an ambassador to Addis Ababa, Thesiger always knew that he would return to Africa as a member of the Sudan Civil Service. He was obsessed with returning to Abyssinia and his boyhood reading at school, in Kipling, Buchan and Conrad, nourished this need for adventure.

'I was unhappy at my prep school since I did not know the conventions. I had never seen a football, knew nothing of cricket but knew all about tiger hunts. At nights, when I was lonely, I would imagine myself back in the delegation looking at the mountains. I therefore arrived at Eton suspicious – even of friendly people – and the ability to get on easily with people only arrived when I was at Oxford.'

The fact that he had his own room meant that he was given the space to develop his own self-assurance. 'I missed out on the crowded dormitory, could select my friends and develop along the lines I wanted without too much interference from others.'

This interplay between detachment and involvement has characterised Thesiger's dealings with the various tribes among whom he has spent his life – Etonians, Bedouins and Marsh Arabs. In each case he has valued being part of a community. College chapel at evensong was an aesthetically satisfying act of self-identification although he could not say the creed and rejected religious belief early in his Eton career.

At first he felt excluded both at his prep school and then during his early years at Eton. This feeling may explain why 'my heroes right up to the Gulf War have been the men on the opposite side. My brother told me to read *Prester John* at prep school. It was written at the turn of the century and yet the hero of the book is black. I identified completely with Laputa.'

The hothouse aspects of boarding school life can be crucial to a writer's development, as Sebastian Barker recalls:

'My contemporaries showed me the grounds of human interchange. My friends made these grounds worthwhile and sowed the seeds of passion. The entire phenomenon of boarding produced a pent-up energy in me as a young man.

'Hearing the *Song of Songs* in Canterbury Cathedral and reading Shakespeare's sonnets in our dingy studies instilled the first awakening to the depths of love and language, which were crucial to my decision to give my life over to poetry. The psychological environment of the King's School, despite all evidence to the contrary, was sympathetic to the germinations and hatchings of poetry. I was best known as a rugby player but that did not mean that I did not show my fellow players my first attempts. I did show them, and their encouragement and reaction still seem to me like a spur to action. Those guys were tough but I saw that poetry could pierce their marvellous adolescent defences, if it wasn't sentimental or pretentious.'

Perhaps the most constricting aspect of boarding-school life for a writer is the lack of private space and time, the ubiquitous organisational mania of the run-of-the-mill boarding school. Writer Gillian Tindall thinks that her school punished her 'desire to quarry out time and privacy'. But another novelist, Rose Tremain, has a happier tale to tell of her 'liberal arts-dominated' girls' school, Crofton Grange in Hertfordshire, also attended by actress Sarah Miles.

'The commodity in greatest abundance was time. What to do with it. How to use it creatively, so that one didn't die of boredom.'

Her school experiences led directly to her success as a novelist and radio dramatist. 'I was allowed to write two plays, act in them, design the sets, paint the scenery, design and make the costumes. I'm quite certain these early successes in a closed but encouraging environment helped me to stay on course as a writer in the early, difficult years.'

The school, which has now closed and become a golf club, had only eighty-five girls and science and languages were poor. 'You were allowed to give up any subject you didn't like. I gave up maths and Latin at 13.' However, drama was encouraged and Tremain left the school with 'the notion that I could become a writer'.

Her first play at school, about two girls who were thrown out of their families and went to London to work as cleaning ladies, 'succeeded in making people laugh a lot and I enjoyed that feeling.' Her second, about a melancholy circus clown, was also effective: 'I enjoyed having the power to move people. But the whole emphasis was on not wasting time – to waste time was presented as an evil thing. Even in the quiet half-hour after lunch we had to do something, like listening to music or doing needlework. I soon cottoned on to the idea that the best way of making use of weekends was to be involved in drama.'

Encouragement and the force of example clearly mattered greatly to a large number of literati. The publisher and man of letters Nigel Nicolson feels that he owes a lot to Robert Birley, his teacher at Eton.

'Excitability was part of his genius as a teacher. He would enact the parts of the people he was teaching about. For example, when talking about the Sicilian expedition of 420 BC he would be a galley slave, then a hoplite, then he would be in the caves and quarries of Sicily. He had such diverse interests: clothed crucifixes, of which there are only twelve examples in the world, was one of them. I went with him once to Berlin. We went past all the prettier pictures in the Gallery and I was only allowed to look at one picture, a self-portrait by Rembrandt. He made me happy and gave me intellectual pleasure.'

Encouragement, however, came in many other forms as well: 'There is no question about what was the happiest moment of my entire life. I was sitting at lunch with some forty others and the captain of the house football team passed behind me and dropped into my lap the cap with my House colours. No event in later life can match that pleasure. It was far better than being elected MP for Bournemouth, though games are not my forte.'

'Success is so important to little boys and the lack of it damages their morale. Most schoolboys are frightened of getting into trouble because of failing a test or something like that. Later on you realise that it's not important but at the time you are frightened of wrongdoing or of being made a fool in class because of a wrong answer at which others would roar with laughter. I really dreaded corporal punishment.'

Nicolson would be caned by Charles (later Sir Charles) Villiers, former Chairman of British Steel, as his Head of House. He did not see him again until the Tolstoy trial when he was giving evidence for Tolstoy and Villiers was testifying for Lord Aldington. 'You could be caned for trivial reasons and it is outrageous that it went on for so long. There was real sadism involved since it took place in the library with only six senior boys present. The other five watched the beating. It was discipline through fear.'

Nicolson was torn at Eton between a guilty acknowledgement of the reality of snobbery at the school and dislike of the actuality of working at one of the school's boys' clubs. He went to the Slough club:

'We always loathed it. We did not care to confess to the master that we hated it – but we did.' Nonetheless, he also hated the way Cockney accents were laughed at:

'One felt one came from an élite school and I felt ashamed about that. I knew I belonged to that world and it was fraudulent to pretend that I didn't. I never go back to Eton now and the social side of it now seems to me pretty horrible.'

These are unsurprising views for a son of Bloomsbury to hold. Nicolson thinks that he was more influenced intellectually by his home than by his school.

His father, the diplomat and biographer Harold Nicolson, was very interested in his son's progress. 'He followed my progress in history and, when I was in the Headmaster's Division and studying Aeschylus' *Seven Against Thebes,* he read the whole book so he could talk to me about it when I got home.'

School was therefore to be contrasted with the holidays and he did not want to mix school with home. School homosexuality was 'rampant. We all did it and slept with each other. Housemasters knew about this but did not know how to handle it. There was no shame about love affairs between boys but there was a shyness about girls.'

Another aspect of the ethos was that one had to break the rules in order to work. 'There was a terrible English philistinism in the House about anyone trying to work and so you had to work under the bedclothes with a torch at night. You would never admit to working.'

Nicolson, like so many in this chapter, was aware of a gap between the values of his school and those of a wider world. He finds it difficult to name any of his contemporaries whom he admires:

'It's such a narrow band to choose from. I have never liked a person because he's an Etonian and I have not helped a person or been helped by a person because he's an Etonian. I don't think the OE network is really very important. There's a general public school fraternity which might get you a job but there's no more to it than that. I might say, "I was at Balliol". I wouldn't say, "I was at Eton." After all, Bloomsbury admired achievement and it is no achievement to have been born into a particular family and to have gone to Eton because one's parents could afford the fees.'

David Lodge's encouragement at St Joseph's Academy, Blackheath, took a very specific form. He is now both a novelist and a literary critic and his academic development was clearly prefigured:

'A new English teacher took over my class when I was 14 or 15. He set us the task of writing a long essay on the techniques of poetry. I had never reflected on literary techniques before. I researched the essay at the Deptford public library and received a high mark and warm encouragement from the teacher. I date my serious interest in literature from that event.'

The interest of a single teacher's personality can indeed change the pattern of a pupil's life. Barrie Keeffe, the playwright, 'would be working in a factory now if it hadn't been for Barry Davies who taught him English at East Ham Grammar School. 'All these years later I can still hear him acting out *Henry IV Part I* to a spellbound class of East End kids. He made Shakespeare thrilling – he changed my life. He encouraged me to write. At first I wanted to be an actor. Mr Davies suggested I write plays featuring the parts I would like to play.'

Alun Owen is another playwright who started out with acting ambitions. When his school was evacuated to Cardigan during the War he came across the dramatic figure of the Welsh writer Gwyn Thomas who was then teaching Spanish at Cardigan County School. He impressed Owen as a remote, fascinating figure.

At Kingswood School, Bath, Anthony Thwaite, poet and director, was struck by the personality of W.G. Ingram:

'A rather fierce, rather grim, certainly complex man. A great enthusiast and sportsman (which I was not). I was rather in awe of him. One day he read us some Old English riddles, in translation, and talked about them. I took some interest in them: they didn't sound like "poetry" and they linked up with my archaeological interests. For prep we were set to write such a riddle-poem ourselves. I wrote several and when Ingram handed them back he judged mine to be much the best. So I knew I was a poet – and immediately I began voluntarily to write and read poetry. I don't think he liked me and we were never friends. But I owe a great debt to him.'

Alan Ayckbourn attributes his early desire to be an actor to Edgar Matthews, who taught at Haileybury and organised the school play tours during the holidays to Holland, the USA and Canada.

Michael Frayn was 'rescued' by an English master at Kingston Grammar School. 'The school didn't make me want to be a writer: I'd wanted to be one long before I got to it. But it did rescue me from the rather low water I was in after the death of my mother. I had sunk to the bottom of the class and become the form clown (which I suppose had a certain influence on my later outlook in itself).'

Frayn's interest in work and thought was caught again by a particular English master, 'and through him refocused on literature and writing'. An interest in languages and literature was strengthened by the master who taught him French and German in the VIth Form.

The novelist Emma Tennant is indebted to St Paul's since it 'led me to learn how to translate a gift which had lain solely in oral story-telling into written stories and novels.'

She told us, 'Starting from when I was about two I had this odd habit which my family called "walking about". I used to walk round out of doors where we lived in this pretty remote bit of Scotland, carrying a twig and telling these stories. I've no idea what they were about except that my mother said that they contained lots of people.

'This went on until I was about 14. It stopped because one rainy day I was walking about my room – indoors I didn't use a twig, I'd use an old Penguin paperback book whose spine I'd broken – and I'd be talking about all these imaginary people. It was to do with character and dialogue and where they went but it had no plot.

'On this day we had people staying in our house and they overheard me and they stood outside the door and giggled and I stopped after that. I never talked about it to anyone for years. But I heard that Madame de

Staël used to do the same thing – she was always waving a stick about too. Until then I rather kept quiet about it – I thought it was a sign of madness!

'Miss Jenkinson at St Paul's took this strange thing that was given to me at birth and brought discipline into my writing. She was laconic – a retiring and rather restrained woman of few words – but her burning interest got through to us. She could make you see the point of reading a Shakespeare play and could make you want to go on and read more.'

Apart from Miss Jenkinson, Tennant found St Paul's 'rather repressive and strict and I was glad to leave.' Science-fiction writers like J. G. Ballard showed her the way into her first proper book. Until then she was writing naturalistic novels which didn't suit her. In a recent novel, *Sisters and Strangers* (1990), Tennant returns to her oral roots, with the story of a Cornish grandmother who guides two little girls through the seven ages of woman in fairytale form.

For some writers an education in a combination of subjects is an important element in their success. Nigel Calder, the science-fiction writer, attributes his success to the fact that Merchant Taylors' provided him with 'a good grounding in science combined with inspired teaching of English literature'.

James Herriot (*nom de plume* of J. A. Wight) also straddled subjects. At Hillhead High School, Glasgow he took Scottish Highers in English, French and Latin and then went on to veterinary college.

His English master, John Gibb, was the teacher who most influenced him and 'his teaching of literature undoubtedly inspired me in my second profession as an author.'

Alan Ross, the publisher and editor of the *London Magazine*, is one of those upon whom contemporaries had a great influence. 'Romantic friendships' were the key events of his schooldays at Haileybury. Michael Frayn writes that one particular school friend was 'the most powerful influence on the way I came to see the world'.

Writer and critic Kay Dick was struck by 'the mature and cosmopolitan' nature of her contemporaries at the Lycée Française de Londres: 'In my class once there were about a dozen with nine different nationalities.' The fact that the school was mixed was a good thing and 'did not affect homosexual, bisexual or heterosexual behaviour. Everyone took such matters as quite natural.

'We were admittedly a trifle snobbish culturally: there was great stress on intellect and great encouragement to shine. We were more adult in our cultural and social attitudes than our English contemporaries. One was naturally encouraged by marvellous professors – one of whom taught Racine as only the gods can – and by contemporaries. I wrote several bad novels and loads of inept poetry.

'Of course we had our peer groups. I went straight into *troisième*. We just about tolerated some people from lower grades while others were ignored in the corridors. We were a very high-spirited crowd immensely conscious of our potential.'

School magazines can be an outlet for creative energies and a means of pacing oneself against contemporaries. Wolf Mankowitz started a magazine called *Troll* at East Ham Grammar and wrote most of it himself. Alexander Stuart 'edited and published an inter-schools "underground" magazine called *Toad* which had a successful first issue but which never appeared again owing to the threat of expulsion.' It is clear that, however great the opposition between the structure and the individual, schools can force writers to creative acts of self-definition. As David Benedictus puts it: 'If it hadn't been for Eton I should not have become a writer, or at least, not a published one.'

Competitiveness and the need to prove that others were wrong emerge in many cases. Francis Durbridge became a playwright having seen the end-of-term play at Bradford Grammar. 'I thought I could write a better one.' Peter Nichols received no encouragement at Bristol Grammar: 'Perhaps the fact that they never let me appear in the official school plays strengthened my ambition to act and write plays.'

The 'vindictive midget of a careers mistress' at South Wigston Girls' High strongly advised *Adrian Mole* creator Sue Townsend to become a telephonist. On a more positive note, however, her school taught her an important truth:

'I used that cliché "cottonwool clouds" and missed winning an essay competition. The winning essay was dreadful but my Brodie-like teachers knew I could do better and wanted to teach me a lesson.'

The lesson of self-discipline in writing, if not in behaviour, is one of the most important of the functions a school can discharge for a writer. Alice Thomas Ellis is 'absolutely' indebted to Bangor County Girls' Grammar School:

'The mistresses were all well qualified. Some were spinsters; some were married. They were all very competent. They did not allow you to get away with sloppy grammar, sloppy language, faults of expression, misspelling. We used the old parsing books and although I could never parse then, I never get my grammar wrong now: I learned it all without ever having to learn how to do it. They were on to everything – using long words, or too many adjectives.

'There was structure, discipline, self-discipline and a lot of culture. It was orderly and peaceful; in a way it was rather like heaven although I didn't see it like that at the time. Now I wish that every child could have such a schooling. I was very fortunate. I was born at the right time.'

Story-writing arrived early, at the age of seven when she was at the elementary school in the village of Penmaenmawr near Bangor. An ability to draw emerged at the same time and her teachers there encouraged her.

'I was very indulged. It sounds conceited but it is true to say that they knew I was an individual.'

Writing imaginatively stopped at the grammar school because Alice was reading books like *War and Peace* and there was little time left over for writing. Painting was a more therapeutic activity and so she continued to paint.

She admired rather than liked her teachers and she left school with a horror of the bluestocking.

'The girls who went to university were tiresome in appearance and demeanour – they were priggish, serious and stuffy.'

Liverpool Art School seemed a better bet for one who knew that she had to get away to a wider world. At school she was keen on asserting her difference and liked the exclusivity of her own gang of friends: 'We didn't talk about literature, we teased people. It was important to have your own image at school – otherwise you were just another dreary girl in a hat and gymslip.'

She thinks now that 'it was wonderful, marvellous, essential to be at a single-sex school. If you are going to compete you are better off competing with your own sex. The distractions aren't there.'

The poet and art critic Edward Lucie-Smith also benefited from the intellectual structures of his school. At King's School, Canterbury, he was 'groomed and trained like a little thoroughbred'.

The headmaster, Canon Shirley, was, says Lucie-Smith, 'a fixer openly interested in success. Like a racehorse trainer spotting a two-year-old he spotted in me an exam-passing machine. I just thought that they were fun and I had no conception of failing an exam. I was a baleful child and I'm not sure that I would like myself, looking back. I was a pet of his: he used to have one or two in each year. He would have long conversations and he would keep me dangling.'

The conversation's subject-matter would be gossip, with Shirley asking Lucie-Smith, 'What d'you think of so-and-so, m'dear?'

'I liked his complexity: he could be alarming but not monolithic. It was possible to have a relationship full of light and shade with him. He was more independent and authoritative than normal headmasters. He had taken over a school which was near bankruptcy and had struck a hard bargain with the Chapter, forcing them to give him a canonry in case the school collapsed. He chose masters and boys whom he thought would be successful and I would be exhibited to parents from a distance. "Look at the sort of boy who can survive with me" or "Look how peculiar we can get" was the point.

'I never knew what I wanted to be at school. I just knew what I wanted to do at any given moment. At school I was a success and I knew I was a success. I was not conceited about it. I just knew it in a placid, level-headed, way.'

Examination efficiency was also a feature of Monica Dickens' life at St Paul's: 'Success at that gave me a confidence that has stuck with me.' It meant that she could feel able to embark on writing a book or an article. The fact that 'the stuff had to be turned in on time' was a good grounding for a career spent among books and newspapers.

Susan Howatch reminds us that writers' true interests are more likely to lie in the organisation of their own experiences and thoughts rather than those of others. 'Being head girl of Sutton High School', she told us, 'made me never again want to have anything to do with running another institution. I had to make a speech at the prize-giving to around 1,500 people. I vowed afterwards never to make another speech.'

Her decision that she would never seek to be the leader of a group was useful since it helped her rule out various careers. 'It confirmed that all I really wanted to do was write novels. Which I did.'

Very few writers seem to have taken the ethos or values preached by their school at all seriously once those values started to extend beyond academic matters and towards areas of social control or belief. The case of Simon Raven is an ambiguous one since he was expelled from Charterhouse. He is happy to record, however, that he 'received the education appropriate to someone who would wish to become a cultivated gentleman.

'What I did not wish to become, therefore, was a barrister, a businessman, or in any case whatever, a politician. Thus everything was ruled out except leisure (not rich enough); scholarship (not patient and accurate enough to be a don); soldiering (tried and failed) and the arts which I attempted, as a novelist, with pleasure and modest competence.'

This profession of faith, however, it is fair to note, owes more to an educational philosophy based on classical humanism and the study of the Ancients than it does to the conventions of public school ethics.

On his first day at Rugby A. N. Wilson found himself placed in the highest form:

'The Upper Vth was an invention of the headmaster, Walter Hamilton. It got you through "O" levels by the time you were 14; you did no science, just maths, English language, history, Latin and Greek – and mainly Latin and Greek. My first lesson was on Euripides' *Iphigenia in Aulis* and I did not understand a word. I felt jolly thick surrounded by Dragon schoolboys. My second lesson was Hamilton teaching *The Aeneid*. We were given scissors by the headmaster's secretary and had to cut the glossary out of the back of the book. I could not imagine how you could puzzle out those Latin lines without a glossary.'

Timothy Tosswill, the English master, though formidable, was a profound influence: 'He never praised anything I wrote. I did not find that at all discouraging – one just kept trying to please him. The essays would be returned covered in red ink and accompanied by sneering little grunts. All the comments were negative but it made one want to do better and nobody complained.

'In some ways he corrupted me. He opened my eyes to the possibility that there was a wonderful world somewhere or other which was not bourgeois. "Bourgeois" was one of his great terms of contempt. Tosswill was a great name-dropper; he always implied that he knew Auden rather well and MacNeice better – as well as Graham Greene and Evelyn Waugh. Some of this was true and some of this was fantasy. Philip Toynbee was a real friend of his, for example, and had been a boy at Rugby with him. He would invite some of these people to his literary club and one wanted to be in such a world although the reasons for that desire might not be particularly worthy. Tosswill injected Bohemian chic into my life. He was actually quite hard-line Left himself, apart from the fact that he approved of public schools and all they stood for, including games and freemasonry. He liked cliques – something that possibly linked his left-wing politics with his love of public schools. He probably thought of himself as a neo-Stalinist and he went on strike when the National Union of Teachers called a strike.'

Approval and inclusion within his circle was only extended by Tosswill at the end of a selected boy's time at school:

'One revered him without admitting to oneself that one did. There is a strong element of badinage in that kind of relationship with a schoolmaster and that is presumably why it works. One is absorbing an awful lot when one imitates somebody like that. I cannot remember anyone ever speaking in one of his lessons. He gave us pseudo-lectures after which you would be tested on what he told you. While all of this was going on he would be pouring scorn on our heads about people paying fees rather than going to state schools.'

Tosswill may have liked cliques but his protégé had no circle at school, although he does not remember ever being lonely.

'My memory is of spending a lot of time on my own reading. I had got "A" levels out of the way early when I was 16; between 16 and 18 I read all of Dickens and Dostoevsky. I was reading more than I have done at any other stage of my life.'

Wilson's enthusiasms were eclectic in the manner of teenagers: 'At the same time as I was being excited about socialism and the simplicity and absolutism of Tolstoy I also became very High Church and would slip out to services in the town. St Oswald's was so High it felt like going to a pornographic shop. Holy Trinity was Prayer Book Catholic; they rang gongs at the moment of consecration as if dinner was being served. It was all very mysterious and oriental.'

Wilson had concluded that he had a vocation and made jokes all the time about religion because it was so important to him:

'Jack McDonagh was the Assistant Chaplain and he used to hear my confession. He was an Irish Anglican and therefore high in doctrine and low in practice. He was also very alcoholic. When preaching a sermon in Chapel he once said: "If it were not for Jesus Christ I would drink myself blind." He then collapsed in the pulpit as he said it.'

McDonagh was intellectually important since he had a sense of doctrine and its implications. There were other influences in this area: "I was addicted to Cardinal Newman's *Apologia*; I liked both the romantic self and the Catholic objectivity. I liked to think that it all hung together, that it cohered. I was attracted by the romance of a figure like Newman and, by implication, the romance of anyone's religious journey. Newman was a romantic who knew that he should not be one – and I think that was true of me too.

'I thought I was *au fait* with politics and joined the Labour Party when I was 15. It is very difficult to explain why one adopts views and especially so for an earlier self when I assume that one only adopts views in order to be irritating. I hoped that it would irritate my housemaster or my father. I daresay I thought that my politics represented a passionately felt defence of the underprivileged. But anyone can defend any position, can't one? I got bored and disillusioned with Labour and I then slithered into an indifferentism; many would say that was a form of Conservatism.

'When I was at school I thought that the class system was wicked rather than absurd. Now I see it as absurd although I think it still hangs too heavily upon us.'

Wilson recalls how fascinating it was to meet Jews for the first time at Rugby and how shocked he was by the casualness with which they accepted the fact of anti-semitism: 'The rudeness was appalling. One friend of mine had a friend whom I thought was his enemy. For two years he persecuted him mercilessly in front of the others. I only discovered later that he was his lover.

'Romantic friendships were universal at Rugby and the patterns of emotional life paralleled those of the outside world. There was a certain amount of love, a certain amount of romantic friendship and then of sex, sometimes casual and sometimes involving love affairs. The only difference from the outside world was that it was exclusively homosexual. The sex was accepted among the boys and a blind eye was turned to it. It was not an orgy – it simply went on all the time as it does in ordinary life. Homosexual sex was joked about but then so was everything else. It was decided that some boys were "queer" but I am not sure that that even meant homosexual. Every boy I knew either had such feelings or expressed them. The expression was not always sexual and people had crushes on each other all the time. In my house you would spend fifty per cent of the time talking about whom you had a crush on or who you thought had a crush on you. I remember hour after hour sitting around discussing these questions. Moreover, they really were interesting questions for some reason. Within this framework you would discover lots of things that you had in common with other boys, reading or whatever. It is a peculiar preparation for life but I don't think that it is a bad one. I don't think it scars anyone.'

Wilson 'loved the life of the House, the silliness and all the gossip about sex and about the masters. I liked my friends to be good-looking, gossipy and to share my kind of jokes. If you are in an institution like that you form friendships which are not based on anything else which is held in common other than the fact that you all happen to be there. It is like ending up next to someone on a train; you are happy to share the journey but would not want to talk to them if you met them somewhere else.'

Wilson survived, adapted and prospered within an institution whose oddities he appreciated and whose mechanisms could be subverted intelligently. 'Mr Gordon Jones was in charge of games and he also taught me Greek. I knew that he was supposed to beat me if I did not turn up for games and also that he would be hideously embarrassed by that. I cut games, he had to beat me but he could not do it again. I never played games again.'

Particular events have had a profound influence on writers' imaginations. Alice Thomas Ellis and the poet George Macbeth (at King Edward VII, Sheffield) both described the importance of hearing poetry read aloud.

'We were made', said Thomas Ellis, 'to read and learn chunks of stuff by heart and discouraged from reading rubbish.'

The late George Macbeth, writing to us just before his death, remembered 'hearing poetry – Masefield's *Reynard the Fox* – read aloud by the English teacher.'

But the Liverpool poet Roger McGough found English literature classes dull at St Mary's College, Crosby: 'I gained an interest in poetry in drama and elocution classes where I enjoyed reciting poems and doing choral verse.'

A more unusual event might have affected the playwright Bernard Kops at Stepney Green Jewish School: 'The one time I played cricket I was hit on the head by a cricket bat. Subsequent concussion might have changed my life. Certainly from that moment on I appeared to behave differently from my four sisters and two brothers and eighteen cousins!'

The education of some writers simply passed them by as being a matter of no great moment. The experience offered them little of any use.

Colin Wilson was an outsider at Gateway Technical Secondary School, Leicester. His mother gave him a chemistry set for his 11th birthday and this triggered an interest in science. By the age of 12 he was reading Eddington, Jeans and popular books on Einstein. He surged ahead in chemistry and physics, was known by his schoolfriends as 'The

Professor' and found that, 'my status as an "intellectual" gave me a sense of uniqueness'.

His discovery of Shaw, however, changed his life and he decided to be a writer rather than a scientist.

'But there was no-one to encourage me. Mr Harris, whom I much admired, dismissed Shaw as an exhibitionist.'

Wilson became a lab assistant after he left school at 16 but was sacked after a year when the headmaster realised that he had lost interest in science. His education was an independent, solitary matter:

'No-one suggested a scholarship to a university, which is probably just as well – it meant I plodded on totally alone and wrote *The Outsider* out of the experience. School is only a good experience if you are "ahead" of the others in some way, as I was. Auden said that the purpose of education is to induce as much neurosis as the student can take without cracking – and I am inclined to agree. Too much plain sailing makes for mediocrity.'

Ian Curteis, the TV playwright, is another writer for whom schooling, at Iver Council School and Slough Grammar, was an irrelevance. The 'old-style learning' of the council school, 'four-square and comforting – spelling by rote' stuck in his mind.

Slough Grammar, however, was 'ill-disciplined chaos with the masters unable to cope with a tide of barbarity. I remember one committed suicide. I was always about place 28 or 29 out of a class of 31, except for English, and emerged with relief at the end.'

Real education, reading 'all the great Eng. Lit. books', and preparation for university proceeded during his two years working in a factory on Slough Trading Estate.

Others waited and bided their time, aware that the world was a bigger and more interesting place than school. Nigel Calder at Merchant Taylors', Northwood, felt 'socially debilitated by separation from the generality of mankind and from the opposite sex.'

Frederick Forsyth's 'dislike of Tonbridge School, or more particularly of the house that I was in, caused me only one ambition – to get out as fast as I could. I therefore swotted as hard as I could, passed every exam they could throw at me and left just after my 17th birthday with huge relief.'

Many writers echo Joanna Richardson's assertion that writing is a matter of temperament and is therefore little affected by school. She had been writing since the age of eight, long before she arrived at The Downs, Seaford, and so 'my choice of career was perhaps inevitable'.

Robert Nye 'already knew my destiny as a poet and novelist' when he arrived at Southend High School. Although grateful for 'the good instruction in grammar' he left the school at the first legal opportunity.

V. S. Pritchett 'wanted to be a writer when I was about eight or ten'. The excellent teaching of foreign languages at Alleyn's School, Dulwich, was valuable to him as a traveller but the strongest personal influence on him was that of a master at Rosendale Road School in Dulwich: 'W. W. Bartlett was haphazard. He made us write stories and disregarded the official programme.'

The critic and writer David Daiches is another who 'wanted to be a writer from the age of about eight. The school [George Watson's, Edinburgh] had no influence in this determination.'

Michael Frayn had wanted to be a writer long before he arrived at Kingston Grammar. Victoria Glendinning, educated at St Mary's, Wantage, and somewhat improbably, Millfield, tells us that 'I was happy/unhappy in much the same ratio as nowadays. It's not school so much as one's own temperament. The influence was pretty negative. I did not want to be like they wanted me to be.'

Jessica Mann, the crime novelist, seems unusual in the degree of environmental influence she attributes to her school, St Paul's. This was partly because she was there from 1943-1955 ('far too long') but also because 'it turned me, the daughter of German Jewish immigrants, into an apparently 200 per cent Brit – which is what all immigrants' children need – and I'm glad of it.' St Paul's gave her not only 'the ineradicable St Paul's voice' but also the confidence that she could choose, and have a career – 'neither at all usual in the 1950s'.

Academically motivated day schools have had the greatest beneficial influence on writers. The poet and critic Donald Davie describes how Barnsley Holgate Grammar in 'a depressed and run-down industrial town in the North Midlands in the Depression fostered respect for the arts because it left us in no doubt that the arts, far from being handed to us on a plate, had to be worked for if we were to profit by them.'

Maureen Duffy's life would have been entirely different, she thinks, had she not attended Trowbridge Girls' and Sarah Bonnell High Schools: 'We were encouraged to read, to write both poetry and prose and, as girls, to believe that anything was possible.'

She received 'an excellent liberal humanist education' and there was 'a continual growth from when I entered my first secondary school at ten, which countered a home life of misery and deprivation in my early teens, and then the extreme loneliness after my mother's death.'

Margaret Forster says that hers was a 'classic case of a working-class girl, with no books at home, being encouraged and inspired' by her school, Carlisle County High for Girls. 'I adored school and it was vital in my general development.' Her reading was guided, her writing 'endlessly praised' and her 'horizons in general lifted'.

Author of the much-praised children's book, *The Machine-Gunners*, Robert Westall gives us, in his portrait of Tynemouth High School, an account of the world we have lost:

'I loved every minute of my High School: the gloriously eccentric architecture (municipal Jacobethan in garish red and yellow brick); the pompously idealistic school song (which I can still sing); the elaborate uniform with its yellow piping and the gowns of the masters. It seemed to be the very Kingdom of Heaven to a foreman-fitter's son off a council estate. More to the point it delivered me to university where I could compete on equal terms with the sons of wealthy men.

'The headmaster, Major Joseph Smedley, never preached but treated us to his thoughts of the day. Two quotations give the quality of the man.

On the fickleness of fortune: "One morning in 1917 my CO said to me, 'Smedley, I'm going to recommend you for promotion and an MC.' By 4 p.m. the big German push had started, my CO was dead and I was a prisoner of war in a German cage."

'To my mother on the occasion of my wanting to become a journalist: "Madam, if he becomes a journalist he will take to drink and be dead by forty. I recommend that he follows another more respectable career, and freelances at journalism in his spare time." (Which is exactly what I did.)'

The chemist who persuaded all the best boys on the arts side into doing science rather than Latin, the English master who is the hero of

Westall's first novel, *The Machine-Gunners*, the master who controlled school debating with just two gestures of the face – all of these remain vivid presences in Westall's memory.

'The school was a finely-honed educational tool that was eventually destroyed for political, non-educational reasons.'

9 Music

'We don't need no education . . .' sang Pink Floyd in 1980. But the band's drummer Nick Mason qualified as an architect, with a degree and a year's office experience under his belt before embarking on his pop music career.

Even architecture as a career was considered pretty shocking to his careers master at Frensham Heights. 'And he was horrified when I mentioned film school! And as for pop music! – Well – in the fifties and sixties there was a perception that rock 'n roll was an alternative to working on the railways!'

Schools in general seem until very recently to have been suspicious of music – rock or classical – as a career: presumably they recognised how precarious a future in any of the arts can be and perhaps they felt a duty to their paying customers, the parents, to provide a safer option. The musicians – singers, instrumentalists, conductors, dancers – that we interviewed for this chapter often met with the same sorts of obstacles as the artists, architects and designers in Chapter Three.

Nick Mason was luckier than most. 'The liberal attitudes, the spirit engendered at Frensham and the friends I made there enabled me to go into rock 'n roll. Had I gone from my prep school to a traditional public school I could never have made the very radical change I did: it would have disappointed everyone too much.'

Pink Floyd's greatest hit, 'Another Brick in the Wall,' is still used as backing to TV programmes about sink schools and quoted in tabloid press stories about falling standards in state schools. In fact, says Mason, this is a complete misconception. 'Roger [Waters] who wrote it had been at a Cambridge prep school and the song was anti all that sort of academic regimentation. If you remember, the video that went with the song showed private schoolboys in uniform being forced through a mincer!'

Many musicians found themselves being forced through the academic mincer and turned into university fodder. It was the same story in music as in art and design: teachers who had themselves gone through the academic mill of seven years at secondary school and three years at university came into teaching blinkered against wider career options.

'Little polite rows of toffee-headed robots,' John Lennon once said, 'That's all any of the teachers were after.'

Arwel Huw Morgan, English National Opera star, left Ystalyfera Grammar School in the Swansea Valley to read chemistry at university. 'It was quite the wrong decision, but the school was academically inclined and pupils who had an aptitude for science were pushed in that direction with no questioning as to whether it was a wise career choice. I eventually found my own way into singing.' Another singer, bass-baritone John Shirley-Quirk had the same problem at the Holt School in Liverpool: 'My dominant influence was the chemistry master, Mr Milnes – with the result that I went on to read chemistry at Liverpool University. If I had been informed that there was indeed such a thing as a career in music as a performer then perhaps the timing of my career might have been different.'

Gwynne Howell, Principal Bass at Covent Garden, was another late starter on the career ladder. Though he competed for Pontardawe Grammar School in eisteddfodau it took him until he was 30 to become an opera singer. He first followed the accepted path to a good solid job: 'I qualified as a town planner. On reflection all the music began at school – it just took a few years for it to ignite into a career.'

English National Opera singer, Jane Eaglen, had no encouragement from her Lincoln grammar school to apply to music college: 'My headteacher wanted me to attend university and I was actively discouraged from becoming a professional singer.' And it was the music mistress at De La Warr School in East Grinstead who told another opera star, Josephine Veasey, that she would certainly not become an opera singer!

However, there are some who found academic rigour both a prop and a challenge.

David Drew is now a top choreographer with the Royal Ballet, but he is still grateful for the education he received at Bristol Grammar School in the 1950s.

'My mother and father were very clear about my having an all-round education as something to fall back on if I didn't make it as a dancer and they were very far-sighted in this, for which I'm most grateful. There was a very cultured ambience at the school: plenty of music – I was introduced to Shostakovich as well as Gilbert and Sullivan;

my appreciation of poetry was widened, yet there was an enormous emphasis on sport, athletics, army cadet training and activities of all kind, including drama. I was Katharine in *The Taming of the Shrew*, landing me ever afterwards with the dreadful nickname Drew the Shrew!

'It was amazing the huge number of things we found time for. The grammar schools went by the old Greek idea of education – a broad-based education which truly stimulated the eager adolescent – and I swear they were right. It also got me through three "A" levels when I was only just 16, so the purely academic side was never allowed to suffer. I wish all young people had equal access to such a fine education. I sent my own son as a day boy to St Paul's in the belief that it's as close an approximation to a grammar school as you can get these days.'

Drew is one of the few ballet dancers in our survey who did not attend a vocational school such as the Royal Ballet School, Sadler's Wells or Elmhurst. Had this ever been a disadvantage?

'Certainly not at that time,' he says. 'The technical requirements on young dancers then were not nearly so high. Actually we are now at a turning point – a lot of people are saying we've gone too far down this road and have produced dancers who are too technically specialised. Maybe we should now concentrate on making them more rounded – on developing the total person. But in my day if a young male dancer had all his limbs and didn't trip over himself he was fine – compared to what the poor buggers have to do nowadays! Now they're brilliant – astonishing!'

Dame Beryl Grey, the great ballerina and former director of the London Festival Ballet, also believes that dancers – and indeed all performing artists – should have a fully rounded education. 'I do feel that a school like Elmhurst, which is totally geared to the ballet, is OK for those very talented in dance. But if you decide at 18 that it's not for you, then it's rather a problem. I ran the Arts Educational School in the mid-sixties for two years and I do think that school gives a generous all-round arts education. Whatever you do, it's vital that you should be made to feel an integral part of the whole arts scene.'

Like David Drew, Dame Beryl feels she was lucky to have had 'a normal education in a wonderful school'. At the age of nine she won a unique nine-year scholarship to Sadler's Wells and her parents moved to London specially so that she could attend an academic direct grant grammar school – Dame Alice Owen's – just opposite Sadler's Wells Theatre. 'The headmistress, Miss Bozman, was a fantastic, most enlightened woman who went on to be head of Manchester High School for Girls. All doors were open to you at that school and you never felt restricted in any way. Although I went to ballet school at 4.30 each day, apart from that my schooling was normal'

The school proved remarkably flexible when during the War it was evacuated to Kettering. There were no good dance teachers in the town and after six months, though she kept up her daily exercises, Beryl had almost given up the idea of dancing and was thinking of becoming a doctor when 'a commanding telephone call came from Ninette [de Valois] saying not all of London was being bombed and I was to come back to the Wells.'

Miss Bozman allowed Beryl to miss Friday school so that she could travel down to London on the 7.30 a.m. train, dance all Friday and Saturday, and come back on Sunday – and this went on for 18 months.

However, most dancers we spoke to had attended vocational schools and were glad of it. Another great Dame of dance, Merle Park, was happy 'after initial homesickness' at the Royal Ballet School. David Bintley, principal dancer and resident choreographer at Covent Garden, had chosen his career before entering the same school and thereby achieved his ambition to join the company. Darcy Bussell, at 21 currently the Royal Ballet's youngest principal dancer, was there more recently, though she first attended the Arts Educational School. 'They were specialised schools in my career,' she says, and she was happy at both. Ballerinas Alfreda Thorogood and Antoinette Sibley and Christopher Gable, now artistic director of the Northern Ballet Theatre, felt just the same about the two great London ballet schools.

Viviana Durante came to the Royal Ballet School from Rome for her final year. 'I hated it,' she says. She plainly found it difficult to accept the passive behaviour and uniformity that she claims are demanded by the school's rigorous training.

Nonconformists like Durante are not always likely to fit in easily at vocational schools for music and dance. Violinist Nigel Kennedy had not at the age of six developed the punk style that has done much to send his records to the top of the charts. But at that age he was auditioned for the Yehudi Menuhin School and he started boarding there at seven, practising four hours a day. For years he begged to be taken away. He was shy, introspective and not even musically outstanding. At the age of 11 he would have been removed but for Menuhin's interest and faith in him.

Clare Francis, the novelist and round-the-world yachtswoman, was miserable at the Royal Ballet School. It was the 'brick in the wall' problem all over again:

'The atmosphere was oppressive and ruthless. The pupils were there to be turned into dancers, and no other talents were valued or particularly encouraged, although there was a full "O"-level syllabus taught. "A" levels were not available – I did mine at an "A"-level college later – and alternative/fall-back careers were neither discussed nor considered. The school was a production line, pure and simple.'

The staff were to blame and Clare's bitterness is still apparent as she speaks of it today: 'They enjoyed their power and exercised it according to whim, power politics and what we then called favouritism but which we might now recognise, in some cases, as having distinct homosexual overtones.

'The place did nothing for one's self-esteem or confidence, and, since I had very little of either in the first place, I emerged with a feeling that I was good for very little – which wasn't far from the truth!'

The rigour of the training has, however, helped her indirectly in her two subsequent careers:

'The only thing it did for me was teach me that hard, grinding toil was the sole path to success – something I have applied in my sailing and writing careers. After training as a dancer, a 736-page novel is a mere continuation.'

The same anger emerges in Sir Michael Tippett's recent autobiography, *Those Twentieth Century Blues* (Weidenfeld 1991). A classics scholar at Fettes, he appreciated the quality of his piano lessons but abhorred the bullying of younger boys by older ones. Finally he was so traumatised by having to stand up in front of the entire school and give an account of the sexual habits of his fellow-pupils that for decades he blocked the school out of his mind and refused to acknowledge that he had been there. He completed his schooldays happily at Stamford Grammar School.

Like Clare Francis, many of our most successful musicians were given the impression that they were academic failures – but for them music was an escape route.

Sian Edwards, one of the few top women conductors, is to become Musical Director of English National Opera in 1993. She told us, 'Oxford High School had a very active music department which became the focus of my schooldays very early on. As I was a failure academically this was all the more important to me as a place where I could do something I enjoyed.'

But the blinkered academic approach dogged her school life too. Sadly, she had little careers guidance – an aberration surely surprising in so excellent a school.

'The amount of practical guidance I was given at school in music, as to how to go about studying, where to train after school, how to become acquainted with the music profession, was very much left up to me and I wish now I had had firmer direction from teachers. I was a difficult and I suppose rebellious pupil, however, so I guess it's not entirely the fault of the staff that I was left on my own in this area!'

Opera singer Teresa Cahill was much luckier at Notre Dame, her East End grammar school. She told us, 'My convent grammar school in Southwark was of utmost importance to my future life and career. I came from a very poor working-class family in Docklands with no money for books, music or holidays. My secondary school education was the key that unlocked the door to everything that I've achieved and to a classless position in society. I was taught how to behave and how to work. This was a *true* socialist attitude – what your father did for a living was never an issue.' She is scathing about comprehensive schools: 'I don't think the comprehensive schools have helped the situation at all. In these days of ever increasing unemployment I think it's vital that people are not ignorant as well as unemployed. That leads to hopelessness and violence. We need to level people up educationally, not down. I get very annoyed with the low standard of education of the full-time students coming to the Guildhall these days. They have no repertoire, they haven't read anything, they are sloppy. When I was 12 I had been taken to all the Robert Mayer concerts and had a good basic education.'

Cahill's mother wouldn't allow her to 'talk Cockney'. 'There was the dividing line of the 11 plus and if you passed and went to the grammar school you got a new set of friends who didn't speak Cockney. I had a friend whose father was a concert pianist and he heard me sing an aria from *Figaro*. He told me: "Your voice is quite small but it's an unusual colour." He introduced me to a Hungarian conductor and he said I had a voice of unusual beauty. This is what I mean by the levelling-off process that takes place in a school like that. You didn't meet concert pianists and Hungarian conductors in Docklands.'

Michael Kaye, Director of the City of London Festival and former general director of the South Bank Concert Halls, feels exactly the same about his East London School, West Ham Secondary:

'I was particularly lucky to have found, in the East End of London, a school with an enlightened and liberal headmaster and a staff which was progressive and open-minded. They succeeded in opening up for us – mainly children of working-class parents – a world of thought, literature and culture that might otherwise have passed us by. They not only showed us that such possibilities existed but convinced us that they were accessible – more, that they were our rights. Although I left school at 15 they gave me the confidence to tackle anything with optimism and convinced me that no intellectual task would be too difficult. Bryan Forbes [see Chapter One] is another ex-pupil who has spoken very warmly of his experiences there. We were very lucky.'

Teachers – progressive and open minded like Michael Kaye's – are the key to everything. When Dame Ruth Railton, founder of the National Youth Orchestra, set up her own school, the National Junior Music School, in 1946, she was absolutely convinced 'that it is the quality of teachers and example given to the right talent that matter – and it works.' She went to St Mary's School in Wantage from 1927 to 1933 and the headmistress, a nun, had an intuitive gift:

'She seemed able to acquire outstanding visiting staff. We had a Russian ballerina – after five years with her I could have gone straight to Diaghilev in Paris. Then there was Gwyneth Thorburn, Head of the Central School of Speech and Drama. We had her every Monday. And lots of visits from famous musicians. It was the quality of these people that influenced me – and the quality of their talents and their work. My admiration led me to follow their standards. I had no use for the mediocre!'

Outstanding teachers are legion in the replies we received from musicians. The late singer Alfreda Hodgson (Levenshulme High School), and opera stars Jane Manning (Norwich High School) and Jean Rigby at Elmslie Girls' School in Blackpool all spoke of splendid music staff.

Boy Friend composer Sandy Wilson at Harrow loved 'learning to play the piano from a very sympathetic teacher, Mr Ebdon, who, at the end of lessons, would play over the current song hits I had bought.' Ian Wallace at Charterhouse had an equally enlightened musical director: 'Although he had a very highbrow outlook on music he didn't frown on my love of popular songs, but brought classical repertoire to my notice.' Pop singer Barbara Dickson found the music teaching at Woodmill High School, Dunfermline, stimulating and interesting. Simon Rattle went to Liverpool College. His earliest teacher, Douglas Miller, was quick to recognise his talent: 'Simon seems to have a direct line to the composers,' he said.

Sir David Willcocks, Musical Director of the Bach Choir, has fond memories of the late Douglas Fox, the remarkable Director of Music at Clifton College, still a legend among Clifton schoolboys to this day.

'He was destined for a great career as a world-class concert pianist, having won all the top London piano prizes. At 20 he went off to the Great War and lost his right arm in battle. His career was shattered. He took up teaching, first at Bradfield and then at Clifton. He played the organ and conducted left-handed – both brilliantly. He was a very shy and diffident man but we boys all admired him so much and felt so sorry for him that he had a great influence on us and he managed to get the whole school singing.'

It was not always teachers in the music department who opened the door to a career in music. The composer and conductor Michael Howard found the chaplain at Ellesmere a great help. 'He spent an infinite amount of time leading me to understand the place of the church musician in a liturgical context.' The new art master, Eric Waddams, who arrived in Howard's third year was also an important influence. 'He had been a choral scholar at King's, Cambridge and founded a glee and madrigal society, using me as rehearsal pianist and additional bass.' Philip Langridge, the ENO opera singer, was taught to sing by the history master at Maidstone Grammar in the lunch hour.

For Graham Jenkins, Musical Director of Glyndebourne Touring Opera, at Dulwich the outstanding influence was 'an English master with an obsession for Fred Astaire, whose daydream was to dress up in top hat and tails and to waltz in from West Dulwich station to give an oration on the importance of Fred Astaire and Busby Berkeley musicals. He left a profound impression on me!'

The great Royal Ballet choreographer Sir Kenneth Macmillan was also keen on Fred Astaire and Ginger Rogers. Inspired by their films, he organised his own dancing tuition at the age of 12 and found the only ballet teacher in Great Yarmouth, Phyllis Adams. It was when he was looking through her copy of *Dancing Times* at the age of 15 that he saw the advertisement that would change his life. It offered scholarships at Sadler's Wells Ballet School. He got one and had to tell his headmaster at Yarmouth Grammar School that he was leaving.

At assembly on the last day of term the Head proudly announced the triumph and Macmillan's carefully kept secret was out. 'I was mortified,' he told Peter Crookson in *The Times Saturday Review*. 'I fled the school that morning and never went back. In a place like Yarmouth I had to keep my dancing a secret because they would have thought it appalling. There was no other boy in either of my dancing schools before I came to London. It creates a kind of schizoid state in a person.'

David Drew at Bristol Grammar had the same problem. 'Being a known ballet dancer in *any* school at that time – the early fifties – was *not* easy,' he told us. Drew found his salvation in his housemaster, Eric Dehn, a remarkable man also remembered fondly by Brian Barron, the BBC's Asia correspondent [see Chapter Four].

'He was a short man but a big character. I took a lot of stick for being a ballet dancer and was bullied unmercifully. I didn't cope with bullying very well. I couldn't deflect it with humour as some people can: I didn't find it very humorous. I was definitely the boy that others love to hate because I won festivals and eisteddfodau – yes, they had them in Bristol as well as Wales – and got my "A" levels at 16 – I was the youngest in the class. I was also physically very slight though now I am six foot and rather portly! Eric Dehn was a man with a great sense of humour and very sensibly he took me under his wing, but not too obviously so. He just let it be known that he understood and he was very supportive. Just by his manner and interest he showed me that there was a more cultured and artistic side to life.'

Peter Jonas, Managing Director of the English National Opera, did not get much encouragement in music at Worth, with one notable exception: 'There is no question that my life in music and opera was in some way inspired by the Abbey organist Dom Thomas, an ageing, tobacco-stained and avuncular monk who would launch into one of the great Bach Preludes and Fugues after each Mass. The world he opened up was a rare one at Worth, for aside from Gregorian Chant and Father Thomas's baroque efforts the school was distinctly philistine and unmusical in my day. However, Gregorian Chants and Bach are by no means bad kernels of a start in music and, if you have nothing else, you drink them with a youthful eagerness of appetite that nurtures real knowledge. So I guess I must offer thanks for that.'

The idea of Worth, so praised for the beauty of its setting, as a philistine place is surprising. But our survey charts most spectacularly the enormous changes in the attitude of the educational establishment to music and the arts in general – revealed in both state and public schools.

The conductor Norman Del Mar had set his heart on being a musician, 'as far back as I can remember'. That said, 'Marlborough was probably a bad choice for the sort of boy I was, with its emphasis on sport and the Army, both of which were anathema to me.'

Michael Gough, Director of the Royal College of Music, who went to Chigwell School, says: 'Public schools were not equipped in the 1940s to cater for musically gifted children. I was only interested in becoming a concert pianist but when I boarded for a short time I found piano-practising facilities inadequate.' Philip Jones, Principal of Trinity College of Music, had no such problems at Battersea Grammar and Cotham School, Bristol. 'At both my schools I had inspired music teachers who worked in their spare time to foster music and musicians in the school.'

The practice facilities at Wells Cathedral School are now first-rate, but Angus Watson, Director of Music there, remembers that at his own school, King Edward VI, Norwich, there was very little music. Michael Brener, Director of another of our great music schools, Chetham's, however, found his old school, Bishop Vesey's Grammar in Sutton Coldfield, very flexible, allowing him to take a half day off in the VIth Form to attend music college part time.

Osian Ellis the harpist found that Denbigh Grammar School actually appointed a new music teacher especially to teach him "A"-level music – he was the first pupil in his school to study the subject – in 1945.

There were other worthy exceptions: Sir David Willcocks remembers: 'Clifton in 1934 was one of the few independent schools that offered a music scholarship and I was fortunate in being awarded such a scholarship. This enabled me to study piano, organ, and enjoy excellent facilities for practice, as well as receive first-class instruction and encouragement.'

John Lanchbery, the conductor and composer who wrote the score for the film *The Tales of Beatrix Potter,* is profoundly grateful to Alleyn's School, Dulwich: 'It shaped my career: the Director of Music fought for me, the sympathetic headmaster allowed him to win, and I switched in the VIth Form from classics to music, winning from the school an open scholarship to the Royal Academy of Music. I cannot sufficiently thank Alleyn's School for all it did for me.'

The changes in recent years have been enormous and younger musicians chart them clearly. Mark Elder, Musical Director of the English National Opera, and Mark Wigglesworth, at 23 his predicted successor as a top conductor of the next generation, were both at Bryanston, which also produced conductor John Eliot Gardiner and composer Robert Saxton. Elder says he was 'encouraged to make the most of my gifts' there and was happy.

Mark Wigglesworth's explanation for Bryanston's success is a combination of flexibility and trust. 'It was the atmosphere created there: you were not peculiar whatever you wanted to do. The rest of the school didn't think it at all strange if someone wanted to spend all his time in the music department. This was exactly the same with everything – woodwork, cricket, whatever you did they made you feel it was important. Everyone treated everyone else with respect.

'From the very beginning there was a flexible timetable like a university. You had lots of free time even at the age of 13. Because people trusted you, you did your work on time.'

As part of his "A"-level course, the school took the brave step of allowing the 16-year-old Wigglesworth to conduct the full school orchestra in a public performance – never having conducted before at all!

'I don't remember being particularly fazed by it – not as frightened as I was when I played the piano! We played a Mozart symphony and it must be the worst ever performance of that work. But it was very well received and I think the people in the orchestra enjoyed it – it was a bit of variety and they were very supportive. No, I didn't dominate them! You have no power at all as a conductor – you can't make those musicians do anything unless they want to. Anyway, I was very small – too small for tails – though I do remember we all dressed up in something different.

'There was an enormous amount of music in the school and this allowed me to gain a great deal of experience at an early age.'

Soprano Emma Kirkby was just as impressed with the excellent music provision in both her schools – Hanford School, Dorset and Sherborne Girls' School – and for similar reasons. 'Music was well organised and well taught and a large proportion of pupils took part – it was considered normal and enjoyable to do it. Thus someone like myself without any stunning instrumental talent could still be given plenty of music-making opportunities.'

Gradually the pre-war philistinism was receding and music was beginning to lose its image as a purely recreational subject.

Often a single, dazzling event made all the difference to a musical pupil and was the catalyst to a career.

Julian Lloyd Webber as a 13-year-old pupil at University College School heard Rostropovich play the cello for the first time. He also had a good new teacher 'and generally determined that there was nothing else I would rather do.'

Composer Robert Simpson was at Westminster City School when he heard Beethoven's Pastoral Symphony for the first time on the radio from the Proms. 'I didn't know what had hit me' he says, 'I went out of the house and walked around in a daze for hours.'

Often participation in school music started a career. Philip Langridge of the ENO was at Swattenden Secondary Modern School, his first secondary school, 'when the music master showed me a violin and suggested that I join his violin class. That single event changed my life.'

At Christ's Hospital conductor Sir Colin Davis was given a clarinet so that he could play in the school military band. For Richard Hickox, Musical Director of the City of London Sinfonia, the turning point in his career was taking part in a performance of Walton's *Belshazzar's Feast* at the Royal Grammar School, High Wycombe.

David Pountney, the immensely successful production director of the ENO, has revolutionised productions at the Coliseum. Maybe this had something to do with the large amount of theatre and music he was able to participate in at Radley.

At Farnham Grammar School Dr Jeffrey Tate, principal conductor of the English Chamber Orchestra, 'performed many unusual and – for the fifties – daring pieces. My love of musical theatre began then.'

Musicians, like some of the actors we interviewed, had their first experience of opera with Gilbert and Sullivan at school. Soprano

Felicity Lott specially enjoyed the performance of *The Sorcerer* when Pate's Grammar School for Girls in Cheltenham joined with the boys' grammar – 'my first experience of opera'.

Gilbert and Sullivan combines theatre and musical performance, and this perhaps is why it appealed to so many top musicians at school. Theatre was often the door into a musical career. Julian (*Salad Days*) Slade found himself in 1948 playing Prince Hal in the first theatrical production ever to be staged in Eton's School Hall.

'My brilliant contemporary John Barton succeeded against all odds in overcoming the stubborn resistance of the authorities and obtained permission to put on one performance only. The play was *Henry IV Part 1* with Barton as an electrifying Hotspur. I was lucky enough to be promoted from Lady Percy to Prince Hal at a week's notice. The play was a triumphant success and paved the way for Eton to abandon prejudice and now, in the present day, to have a flourishing theatre of its very own. *Henry IV* was one of the most exciting nights of my life and decided me that my future lay in the theatre.'

Eton is near enough to London for trips to concerts and theatres, and for similar accessibility the location of a school was important for many musicians. The fact that Westminster School was in central London enabled David Lloyd-Jones, artistic director of Opera North, to attend many top-quality musical and theatrical performances.

Others were more interested in taking part. Martin Neary, Organist and Master of Choristers at Westminster Abbey, was at the City of London School and sang with the Chapel Royal Choir. He attended great occasions like the opening of the Festival Hall and the Coronation.

The late Stephen Oliver the composer, whose recent new opera *Timon of Athens* was widely acclaimed, was more influenced by his early education at St Paul's Cathedral School than by his secondary education at Ardingly College.

'Although I was often frightened and unhappy there, for children of 13 and younger are crueller than teenagers, in my experience, I was there exposed to the daily recitation of great literature and music, which handed my profession to me on a plate.' He was a choirboy at St Paul's Cathedral and remembers singing through the psalms, 'the most poignant, searching analysis of the agonies of the human heart – nothing could be more operatic.' He saw his first opera, *Cosi fan tutte*, at the age of 17, but by then he had already written four of his own.

Even outside London, the choir schools produced satisfied customers. George Guest, Cambridge University organist, was a pupil at Chester Cathedral Choir School, and Stephen Cleobury, another Cambridge organist and Director of Music at King's College, attended King's School, Worcester, as did his brother Nicholas, the conductor. Stephen Cleobury told us, 'I would simply point to the value to individuals, and to our national musical life, of the choir schools.'

Michael Howard had decided by the age of six to be a cathedral organist because of his outings, like Teresa Cahill's, to the Robert Mayer children's concerts and his visits to Westminster Abbey, St Paul's and Southwark Cathedral. Howard comes from a family of musicians. His father was, he told us, 'a foundation principal in Sir Thomas Beecham's Philharmonic, and viola of the International String Quartet, thinly disguised in Christopher Isherwood's *Lions and Shadows*. My aunt was Director of Music at Bedford High School for Girls.' This aunt was a great influence: it was she who 'during her free weekends and holidays, gave me my first piano lessons.' She also took him on his musical excursions in London.

Family outings like these to theatres, concerts and great cathedrals were mentioned by several musicians. But we were surprised to find that family influence was important to fewer than one third of those who replied.

One of those who is grateful to his family is Osian Ellis the harpist, who said that though he was happy at Denbigh, 'my major influences came from my home environment. My mother played the harp and sang; my father (a Welsh Methodist minister) sang and gave lectures on Welsh poetry and song; my brother and sisters and I took part in concerts from an early age.'

Dr Carl Dolmetsch the recorder impresario, of the great Dolmetsch family of recorder makers and players inevitably mentions family as an influence. Both the Lloyd Webber brothers, as one might expect, acknowledge a great debt of gratitude to their father, Dr William Lloyd Webber, an outstanding organist and Principal of the London College of Music.

Their mother too was a top-rank piano teacher, with John Lill among her pupils. But it was Andrew's Aunt Vi who was the greatest influence on him. She knew many of the stars of West End musicals in the fifties and Andrew went to see them on stage as a small child. By the age of eight he was producing his own musicals in a model theatre he had built himself.

At Westminster he wrote two more musicals and did badly in his "A" levels. He was advised by the school not to try for Oxford but got in anyway. He won a scholarship to Magdalen on the strength of a paper on Victorian architecture, and he says he can still name all the important Victorian buildings in the City – a product of his wanderings through the streets on games afternoons! After a year at Oxford he left. Still only 17, he had met Tim Rice and written a musical about Dr Barnardo.

Lloyd Webber successfully straddles the worlds of classical and pop music, with the academic training he received at Westminster and, after Oxford, at the Royal College of Music. He does not seem to have suffered from the anti-music academic straitjacket that afflicted so many other top musicians.

But if some found it hard to break out of the straitjacket into the classical concert hall, the world of rock music was a double anathema. The shock-horror reaction of Nick Mason's careers teacher was typical, particularly in public schools.

Bruce Dickinson, lead singer of heavy metal band Iron Maiden, has few good words to say for his alma mater, Oundle. He told the *Independent on Sunday* in January 1991:

'It was the most illiberal place on the planet. Whacko! Mass floggings over minor practical jokes. Eventually I was expelled for pissing in the headmaster's dinner.'

But he told us that he did appreciate the access the school gave him to extracurricular activities like drama. And maybe Oundle had something to do with his success as a novelist and world-class fencer.

Public schoolboys like Dickinson are unusual in the world of rock 'n roll: people like Peter Gabriel of Genesis (the band formed at Charterhouse), Mike d'Abo of Manfred Mann (Harrow), Tom Robinson (Friends' School) and Pink Floyd's Nick Mason are, says Dickinson, 'as rare as university graduates in the football league'.

When they were there, they were out to shock, though DJ John Peel admits that at Shrewsbury the extent of his rebellion was wearing a suit that was a shade lighter than the official school suit [see Chapter Four] and playing loud records of Gene Vincent and Little Richard.

Luckily his housemaster, the late R. H. J. Brooke was 'an odd and enchanting man, a genuine character in a place where lots of people were trying to be characters.' He quite approved of Peel disturbing people listening to Stravinsky in the library next door. 'I suppose he was only about the age I am now – early fifties – though at the time he seemed a man of infinite age. He realised I was never very academic, never going to make any mark in the house. People younger than me were made house monitors and I must admit I was hurt by this. It was a great insult and such a public one. But Mr Brooke encouraged me to be my own man. If I ever get round to writing a book I will certainly dedicate it to him.'

Mike d'Abo, ex-Manfred Mann, was a hit among his contemporaries at Harrow. One of those was Hugh Montgomery-Massingberd of the *Daily Telegraph* who recalls d'Abo's 'legendary glamour':

'In order to avoid the tedium of the Combined Cadet Force he charmed the authorities into letting him conduct weekly alternate sessions in italic handwriting and jazz appreciation.' Here was someone who could loosen the straps of the academic straitjacket. Massingberd remembers: 'The highlight of the week was the pop show d'Abo and his cronies performed on Saturday nights. Even when he unwisely attempted to sing the excruciating Cliff Richard hit, "The Young Ones", the jeers were tinged with affection, not to say awe.'

Academic aspirations cast aside, d'Abo left Harrow and formed The Band of Angels. Two years later the group had turned professional and was delighting the deb circuit, cashing in on the alma mater by wearing Harrovian straw hats.

Dusty Springfield sang for the debs too. When she was 15 and still at St Anne's Convent in Ealing, her brother Tom was playing in smart venues in Draycott Place and the supper clubs of the West End.

'I used to go and join him and sing with him at the debs' parties.' She says she 'blundered through this kind of life with total innocence, and the debs' mothers were all very nice to me and would take me upstairs and feed me. I'm not sure if the nuns knew or not. Anyway, they'd given up on me by then.' Dusty freely admits she was never very academic. 'Algebra! That was the stuff of nightmares!' Her father, a great lover of classical music and a keen amateur pianist, might have hoped for his children to go down that road. But Dusty braved the wrath of the nuns and formed a group at school.

'We sang things like "St Louis Blues" and lit the stage with purple lighting. Actually the nuns thought it rather amusing – it was the lay staff who walked out!'

Dusty took the project seriously, however: for her it was an early career move: 'I knew I was going to be a singer and I was the only one in the band who took it seriously. The only problem was getting the other girls to rehearse. They were only interested in going off to be radiographers or getting married.'

We found this 'go for it' mentality, the absolute faith in one's own talent against the disapproval of sceptical teachers, turning up in all sorts of schools. State schools often regarded rock 'n roll as a dangerous aberration likely to lead to the undermining of staff authority. Morrissey, ex-The Smiths, expressed his resentment of his school in the song *The Headmaster Ritual*; only faith in his own ability saw him through.

Robert Smith, lead singer of The Cure, now fills stadia all over the world, with impresarios queueing up to stage his concerts. But his first public performance at St Wilfrid's RC Comprehensive in Crawley met with enormous opposition:

'It was self-organised and promoted and took place after school in the Assembly Hall. The continual battles I had with the older more authoritarian teachers before and particularly after this rather riotous affair strengthened my resolve no end!'

The school had an 'elitist orchestra-only mentality'. It was a far cry from his first secondary school, Notre Dame Middle School, where there was 'a very open music room – pupils were encouraged to try out different instruments.' But opposition breeds resolve and Smith told us, 'In a strange way, the former was as encouraging as the latter!'

It is interesting to speculate whether including pop music in the GCSE syllabus has made life easier for today's embryo rock singers, or whether an element of rebellion is a prerequisite for success. We asked Colin Johnson, Manager of The Stranglers, controversially brought in in 1991 to advise on the content of music courses in the National Curriculum. But he says that he had himself met a wall of academic non-comprehension in the other members of the advisory committee.

'I was called in by Angela Rumbold – she wanted input from the pop music scene. There were sixteen people sitting round that table and not one of them was interested in pop music at all except me and Mike Batt. Some of them were younger than me – I'm 50 after all – but I found them very set in their ways. Their attitude seemed to be that rock music is anti-social and if it's allowed in schools the pupils will get out of control. This was the attitude when I was at school and I honestly don't think anything has changed much. I resigned after just two meetings.'

In January 1992 new National Curriculum guidelines concluded that the emphasis should be upon learning about great composers from the Western tradition: earlier working party reports suggesting African drumming, football chants, pop and reggae were rejected, though Lennon and McCartney, Fats Waller and Duke Ellington were still thought appropriate.

Simon Rattle said this reversal was the greatest single blow to the advancement of music in his lifetime. The combined orchestras of Britain said it was horrifying and devoid of professional authority to deprive children of hands-on experience in making music, and to revert to making them learn arid lists of the names of composers exclusively rooted in the European classical tradition.

But maybe a sense of alienation at school is necessary to create a ready empathy in an adolescent album-buying public. If new bands were patted on the back by liberal teachers, perhaps they would produce music too anodyne for teenage tastes.

Current Rolling Stones gigs may well be attended by middle-aged fans, many of them parents themselves, but in their heyday they were hardly family favourites.

Bill Wyman found plenty to alienate him from his family and his school. In his recent autobiography *Stone Alone* (with Ray Coleman: Penguin 1991) he describes the trauma of trying to reconcile his own working-class background in Penge with the middle-class ethics of Beckenham and Penge Grammar School: his accent alone caused problems. Just before his "O"-level exams his father wrote to the headmaster and insisted on Bill leaving school for a job at a bookmakers. 'I kept that letter because it marked my life: having to leave school was a bitter blow to my confidence.'

Roger Daltrey of The Who found himself at the wrong school too. He says his world was shattered when he passed the 11 plus and went to Acton Grammar School. He told Jane Ferguson in the *Daily Telegraph* last year, 'It was only a mile up the road but the division in society was unreal. Before this I had not been aware of social divisions. It was horrendous, like being thrown to the lions. They even sang in different accents!' He was eventually expelled for smoking, after annoying the teachers for four years by humming 'Heartbreak Hotel' during lessons and daydreaming about owning a guitar.

Mark E. Smith of The Fall has mixed feelings about his grammar school in Whitefield, Manchester, where he too was ridiculed for his accent, 'being one of the three per cent allowed from poor areas'. But, he told us, 'Stand Grammar School no longer exists and in retrospect that's a shame as it taught children like myself what Britain was all about. I've come to the conclusion, coming into contact with a lot of young people, that comprehensive schools are a disgrace. The 20-25 year olds I meet in North Manchester can't spell, know no history and have been brainwashed by hippies!'

Whether they went to public schools or state schools, grammar or secondary moderns, the vast majority of musicans we questioned – 78 per cent in fact – said they were happy at school. Whether they were given the wrong careers advice or were the subjects of peer-group taunts, or whether their schools backed their judgement and engendered an atmosphere of mutual respect, the talent of these artists gave them the will to succeed.

Anyone who saw Philip Langridge's splendid Aschenbach in *Death in Venice* in 1992 at Covent Garden must feel shocked when he says, 'At none of my three schools was music as a career considered a particularly brilliant idea. Certainly I had no encouragement at home.'

But a beaming optimism shines through most of the replies we received. Musical talent, like the talent of artists and designers, will out, it seems, even unsupported by family or teachers.

Opportunity is a key to the success of musicians – the opportunity to perform, whether as soloist or in a group. And so many of them saw their chance and seized it with both hands.

Top jazzmen Kenny Ball at Mayfield School in Ilford and Terry Lightfoot at Enfield Grammar School, Middlesex, were both inspired by schoolfriends who formed jazz bands and took the opportunity to join in.

Meanwhile in Wales Shakin' Stevens was winning the hearts of his teachers and classmates, seizing the opportunity to perform at the drop of any hat:

'I can vividly recall entering a competition and winning first prize as a rock 'n roll singer. The word soon went round that I was able to sing and consequently I was asked to participate in further musical events. Frequently my teacher would ask me if I would sing for the class when school work was completed – I guess they were my first public performances.'

Harry Webb was a boy who loved being part of the drama society at Riversmead School in Cheshunt. Taking a once in a lifetime opportunity he played truant one day and got up at 5 a.m. to go to Kilburn and see Bill Haley and the Comets at the Gaumont Cinema. Back at school next day his prefect's badge was removed and his teacher bet him a box of chocolates that in ten years' time he wouldn't even remember the name Bill Haley. Those ten years passed: Haley was the established king of rock 'n roll and Harry Webb had become Cliff Richard.

Thomas Hicks left Bacon's Boys' School in Bermondsey destined to be a bell-boy at the Savoy. At 15 he preferred the idea of being a waiter on a ship and ran off to sea. After eighteen months he found himself back on shore, laid up with spinal meningitis in Guy's Hospital. Opportunity knocked when a busker taught him a few chords on the guitar and Thomas Hicks was soon calling himself Tommy Steele.

Billy Bragg, too, looked set for a pretty dull life on the factory floor. He only managed one "O" level at Park Secondary Modern in Barking. The subject was English and he got an A, which goes a long way to explain his success as a left-wing lyricist. But the event which shaped his future even more strongly was the visit to the Ford body plant in Dagenham, where Bragg and all his classmates were taken on a visit. 'This is where you'll all be working shortly,' their teacher told them. Enough to knock the optimism of the most confident talent. But 'Not me!' thought Billy and that was the turning point in his career.

Perhaps Dame Beryl Grey is right. 'Talent is very short on the ground,' she says. 'And talent will out if it's there.'

10 Politics

'You will be of the House of Commons as soon as you are of age,' wrote Lord Chesterfield to his son Philip Stanhope on 5 December 1749. 'You must first make a figure there if you would make a figure . . . in your country.'

The Bruges Group may fear that real power is slipping away to Brussels but for most British politicians Lord Chesterfield's dictum remains true. The drama of the House of Commons as the cockpit of the nation continues to inspire even when the reality is more likely to be tedium enlivened by farce.

Politics is a later rather than an earlier choice of career. Dreams of political glory, however, start young, as this chapter will show. Ideologies begin on the hearth; schools can fortify them. How have schools affected the membership of 'the best club in London'? Stamina, gregariousness, assertiveness, persistence, the readiness to give up a private life for a public one: these are the well-established characteristics of a political and governing class at any time and in any country. How have British schools affected the changing faces of British politics and politicians in the late twentieth century as they meet with triumph and disaster 'and treat those two impostors just the same'?

They seem to have been a very happy bunch at school as they talked, debated and encountered teachers with developed political interests. Few of them were Nature's head boys and they were always aware of a wider world than that of school.

A large number of politicians describe how, in the words of John Biffen, 'love of history aided political enthusiasm'. Sir Rhodes Boyson thinks that walking the hills of the early Industrial Revolution with his history teacher at Haslingden Grammar School made him into a historian and politician. John Butcher's left-wing history teacher at Huntingdon Grammar 'stimulated my interest in right-wing ripostes'. Sir John Cope at Oakham got 'a feeling for history which ultimately propelled me gradually into politics.' Lady Falkender, at Northampton High School, was influenced by the teaching of nineteenth century economic and social history and by a renegade French teacher who was the socialist daughter of a Tory MP.

For such politicians an interest in public affairs started with the ability to make connections between past and present and with the realisation that all history is contemporary history. Many a historian may be a failed politician but many a politician is also a historian *manqué*.

John Biffen arrived at Dr Morgan's Grammar School, Bridgwater, on a county scholarship: 'It had been established in 1723 and, although it had been a private school, it became a grammar school under the Education Act of 1944. I was always conscious of being in a grammar school.

'For me there was always a connection between being a politician and being a historian, though no particular connection between being a Conservative and being a historian.'

The most important element in his Conservatism was the fact that he was deferential to his home background of low-key, covert Conservative sympathies. Awareness of current affairs grew as a part of his response to the War and this awareness in turn fed his historical interests: 'With all the changes in Central Europe I am now glad of the historical training I received.'

Biffen was emerging as a historian at a time 'when the British Empire was still at its full stretch. The defeat of Britain seemed inconceivable and the possibility of defeat never registered with me. History made me feel that I was on the winning side.' He 'loved being at the ringside of history' in those war years in Somerset: 'My commitment to the Conservative Party was ferocious and I would go round with the local milkman breaking up Labour meetings.'

School reinforced these beliefs. Jack Lawrence, his history master, was a radical but 'this aberration made no difference to my awe and respect for him.' Lawrence's politics were, in any event, 'kept discreetly out of the classroom.' Biffen once wrote a shallow essay on Frederick the Great: 'I compared his bureaucracy to the regulated misery of Labour Britain. My essay was returned with a C grade and a warning not to engage in such nonsense again.'

Biffen lived on a remote farm and travelled in to school by bus. He only really went beyond the village for the first time when he was 17. He was going to Cambridge and knew that he had to change at St Albans. The West Country boy arrived at Paddington and asked at the booking office for a sleeper from St Albans to Cambridge. It was the end of innocence.

Of the politicians in this survey, almost half went to independent schools – either boarding or day. The 20 per cent who went to state grammar schools include some well-known names in the current

Labour Party: Frank Field (St Clement Danes Grammar); George Galloway (Harris Academy, Dundee); Austin Mitchell (Bingley Grammar); Dale Campbell-Savours (Keswick Grammar); George Robertson (Dunoon Grammar); Dennis Skinner (Tupton Hall Grammar) and Lord Donoughue (Northampton Grammar). John Biffen, Sir Rhodes Boyson and Sir Bernard Braine are all grammar-school boys, of an older generation, in the Tory Party. Bill (now Lord) Rodgers, a former Labour cabinet minister and founder of the SDP, is a product of that nursery of political and public talent, Quarry Bank Grammar School, Liverpool.

He is indebted to a school which encouraged a breadth of interest. He ended up doing four subjects for his Higher Certificate, for example, because of the school's broadmindedness. The school owed its success, he believes, to a headmaster who put on it the imprint of a public school. It was divided into houses and there was a major role for prefects. The desire to achieve came from the school rather than from the home. Although there were books at home 'we were not brought up to believe in education. Life at Quarry Bank was about achievement and not about competition. For the headmaster, competing against one's peers amounted to the wrong set of values. We had to do well but it was not acceptable to push others down in the process.'

R.D.B. Roberts, his history teacher, was an important political influence. 'He was passionate about social and economic history, a member of the Left Book Club and an archetypal 1930s man. He got me to Oxford. Liverpool University would not take me because people were returning from the War. I was 17 and would have to wait. So Roberts said, "Why not try the Oxford exam?" I sat at a table, he got the entrance papers and I wrote.'

What Rodgers wrote about was nineteenth century social, economic and political history with lots of political theory of the Mill – Bentham variety.

He was also making explicit connections between history, politics and his environment. 'The roots of my socialism and of the values I hold today lie in seeing children without shoes sitting outside the pub as I travelled into school on the trams. It all began therefore with experience. To that, school added intellectual confirmation.'

Being at school during the war years made him aware of the outside world but: 'I was very fully aware of the political scene in Europe even before 1939. I knew all about the Balkans and the tensions there, for example.' By the time of the 1945 election when he was 16 he was writing to the Communist, Labour, Liberal and Commonwealth parties for information.

Rodgers's career as a vigorous heckler at political meetings was by then well launched: 'I was once complimented by the chairman of a Conservative meeting and invited to attend the next meeting of the Young Conservatives. They were pleased that I was politically active and I always remember that when someone heckles me.' Oratorical qualities were clearly there at school as well, since he was due to play the role of Brutus, the ultimate political agoniser, in a school production of *Julius Caesar*. Eventually, however, Derek Nimmo pipped him to the part.

The politician who was a member of the Labour cabinet which enforced near-universal comprehensivisation felt guilty about selection, even as a boy: 'When I left as one of the ten per cent who went to grammar school I thought of the rest. The better ones went to the technical schools and the rest did nothing for three years until they could leave school. I thought it odd that I should go on and be educated and that they should not.'

Nonetheless Rodgers retains a nostalgia for the values of the boys' grammar school: 'I remember as a government minister visiting Manchester Grammar in order to speak. I was met at the station by a young master in a tweed jacket and the keen questioning of the boys brought it all back to me.'

Former cabinet minister Peter Walker (Latymer Upper) and Shaun Woodward (Bristol Grammar) are both products of independent day schools and stress the open, 'classless' nature of their education. As Walker says, 'When you see a Rolls in the City it's possible that both the chauffeur and the man in the back are wearing Old Latymerian ties.'

Walker's organisational skills started early. He founded 'Walker's Anti-Labour League' and wrote its manifesto. In 1945 when he was 13 the League was dropping leaflets in socialist households.

Like Rodgers, he attended the meetings of parties other than his own because he was so fascinated by the business of elections: 'The public library in South Harrow was run by the deputy headmaster of the local primary school I attended. I went to him and said, "Give me two books each on Socialism, Liberalism and Conservatism."' Shaw's *Intelligent Woman's Guide to Socialism* was no match for the *Financial Times* which Walker was reading every day on the tube going into Hammersmith from Harrow. 'Mr Stollery, the maths teacher, gave examples from the *FT* for working out stocks and shares and so I started buying it.'

Walker enjoyed his political arguments with the English master, Mr Sharp, a humorous socialist who ran debating at the school and admired Shaw. It was, however, another English master, Mr Parrish, 'who taught me how to think. Parrish provoked thought in a big way.' A Roman Catholic, he founded a philosophical society which met after school and he got Walker to read literature and philosophy.

Like most Conservative politicians since Winston Churchill, Walker prefers to play down his schoolboy academic achievements: 'I did the homework, passed the exams but did not do a lot more than that.' He was certainly clever enough for the headmaster to intervene with his parents when they were moving to Gloucester and tell them that he should stay at school since he was university material. 'But my parents knew nothing about university.'

In any event, Walker was 16 and clear about the advantages of getting a matriculation and setting off on a professional career rather than going to university. He left without any conviction that there was anything fundamentally wrong with British society: 'Here was I, the son of a factory worker, and doors were opening to me. My father hated working in a factory – it was dirty and dangerous work.' Matriculation opened the way to a middle-class existence on £1,000 per annum.

Inevitably, his political interests were reflected in his school history, but the history teacher, a dour and biased socialist, was a problem. He would put Walker at the bottom of the class on the basis of his usual term-time work; more objective marking in end-of-term exams found Walker top of the class: 'I remember writing a vast 120-page essay on Gladstone and Disraeli which was, of course, pro-Disraeli. I got a low mark for it and was told by my teacher: "I am interested in history and not in prejudice."'

A Conservative of a younger generation, Shaun Woodward, the former TV producer who is now the party's Director of Communications, started badly at Bristol Grammar School: 'I was quite unhappy. I did badly in the first-year exams and so I went into the bottom stream. That determined the whole course of my education to "O" level. I had a real sense of being pedestrian. I behaved quite badly and my behavioural pattern reflected the way the school had pushed me to the margins. There was a watershed, however, when I slammed a door very hard. I had not meant to hurt anyone but I did hurt someone. I was summoned to the headmaster's study, along with my father, and told that I would be out unless things improved.'

After this incident Woodward 'worked hard because I wanted to be valued, to be worth something. I fluffed the early entry exam to Cambridge and lots of people must have thought, well, he was in the bottom stream and that's what he's really about.'

It was the influence of strong individuals which kept the flame of

Woodward's ambition alight: 'I adored those teachers who gave me support and the seventh term in the VIth Form for Oxbridge candidates was wonderful. There were no rules and you could read what you liked. English as a subject was a good way of breaking the rules, of looking at a poem, for example, and seeing the thinking behind it.'

Politically, Woodward was interested in power, and 'Shakespeare's history plays were fascinating because they dealt with power.' History was the study of concepts rather than of individuals, though Cromwell and the English way of managing a revolution excited interest. 'The idea of the revolution in electoral reform and its effects really affected me.'

Bristol Grammar School might have been a quasi-public school but Woodward is swift to point out that it was in tune with the grammar-school tradition of a social mix: 'Had I gone to public school perhaps I would not have developed the ability to feel at home with someone of any background.' Social ease with his contemporaries, however, was not an easy achievement in Woodward's case:

'I was fat as a boy, was unfit and played sport badly. Those things detached me from my peers and I spent a lot of time between the ages of 11 and 16 feeling an outsider. When I was 16 I decided that that was not how my life was going to be and I turned my life around.'

Woodward became Captain of his House but in an unconventional way which ensured that he continued to feel something of an outsider. 'I used my interest in theatre (as a producer of school plays) to get me there: my housemaster was annoyed but had no alternative to making me head of house. I knew that he felt like that and I minded the fact that other people knew how he felt.' When Woodward achieved his goal, 'I felt a sense of triumph but not a sense of belonging.' It was perhaps an important element in the political education of one who 'sympathised with people who wanted to challenge things'.

Ian Mikardo also relishes a challenge. A key figure in modern Labour Party politics, he feels considerable bitterness at having been denied the education at Portsmouth Grammar School which might have sent him to Oxford. His mother's ambition that he should be a rabbi dictated otherwise and his school day was divided between the secular education at Portsmouth Secondary School and theological education at the Jews' College attended by eight boys. At the former his education was lopsided and the only subjects he took for his School Certificate were English, French, maths, applied maths and further maths. By 16 his maths was already of degree standard. Meanwhile, the Jews' College provided him with a diet of 'archaic, idiotic dogma'.

Satisfied neither with dogma nor with the vocational education at Portsmouth Secondary, Mikardo's was a 'lively mind, reaching out'. The moment of his secular revelation came in 1922 at the age of 14 when he read R. H. Tawney's *The Acquisitive Society* and discovered an account of justice which cut more ice than anything offered by the Prophets.

The Principal of the Seminary was 'a crook and a phoney', a Fagin-like figure who used qualifications which belonged to his brother. Nonetheless Mikardo clearly learnt something from him: 'On Jewish feast days he would preach. He was excellent in Hebrew but in Yiddish he was a combination of Isaiah and Demosthenes.'

Mikardo preached himself on one occasion but the authorities frowned on his mischievous exposition of the thesis that many traditional Old Testament villains were the victims of slander. 'In another sermon I said that the patriarch Jacob, much hailed as a great entrepreneur, was really a petty crook who had mistreated and cheated his brother and father-in-law. All the time I was trying to resolve doubt. At 15 I was told that Spinoza had proved the existence of God. So I read, in Latin, the *Ethica*, the *Tractatus Logicus* and the *Tractatus Theologico-Politicus* – and was not convinced.'

Mikardo was exceptional in his political and theological restlessness. 'At school, boys accepted their political lot. My English master, Mr Thomas, saw this: he was political and that got me into politics. He was a lovely man with no special qualifications. When you came in in the morning he would take a really good look at you to see that you were all right.'

In 1924 Mikardo was the Labour candidate in the mock General Election organised at the school by Thomas. 'Because I did well I was invited to speak in the election campaign itself. I liked it. I was saying things that were meaningful to me.' Politics were now dominating everything. At school they determined his reading so that by 15 he had read all of Byron, so engaged was he by Byron's radicalism. He was enchanted by Swift, 'the Tawney of his generation'. He absorbed details about the French Revolution, 1848 and the Chartists. The dynastic histories of monarchs bored him but he loved Shakespeare's history plays since they dealt with power, rebellion and intrigue. Soon he would be in London moving amongst Bolsheviks, Mencheviks, Anarchists and Syndicalists.

By the age of 11 he knew 'that there were people who were not fulfilling their potential because they were living under the shadow of a rainy day.' Later intellectual revelations about political activity were built on these earlier personal experiences.

Ken Livingstone also thinks that his contemporaries accepted their lot too readily: 'When I go to Eton or Harrow to speak I am amazed at the boys' confidence when they say, "If I were Chancellor . . ." At their age we would have been frightened of going into a bank!'

Livingstone was cheeky, disruptive and well organised: 'If I had a bad report I would stop on my way home, buy erasers and change it. If my parliamentary colleagues who can't stand me could see a film of me as a boy they would say that I am today exactly what I was then.'

At school he was a loner and his membership of any group was always heavily qualified. He would never join the Boy Scouts but would happily join a gang throwing stones at them. The parliamentary Just William reflects that: 'Those were more innocent days: trouble meant stealing Dinky toys not drugs. Nowadays I would have got into more trouble.' His confidence as a boy only worked within a narrow circle and he left school worrying about whether he could do the things that adults were expected to do.

Things had started well. 'He's been excellent,' said the teacher at St Leonard's Church of England Primary School when Mrs Livingstone arrived to collect the infant Ken at the end of his first day at school. 'He's just stood in front of the class and entertained them with stories.' He had the essential political ability to speak in front of strangers. But he failed the 11 plus and went to a vast comprehensive school, Tulse Hill, (now closed), with a 13-form entry.

There too he started well. This was mainly due to the poet and writer Philip Hobsbaum who was his inspirational form-master and English teacher. 'He was a dramatic teacher and the most dramatic influence on my childhood. In my first year he developed me more than at any other stage in my education. He was thought to be very revolutionary – we did impromptu plays in mid-lesson and he ran school newspapers. In the first three weeks of that autumn term, 1956, he got us debating the Suez crisis. My first political speech opposed Suez and the invasion of Hungary. He made me aware of politics rather than a man of the Left. That came later.'

When Hobsbaum appointed him the Liberal candidate in a mock election Livingstone had to go home and ask, 'What's a Liberal?' – a disadvantage which did not stop him from doing well in that election. From Hobsbaum he learnt what confidence was: 'He had a huge personality. I admired and wanted that confidence and that use of language.' Hobsbaum was no trendy 1960s liberal but a man with a fiery commitment to the proper use of English. He was 'what every teacher should be, never boring, and he led by enthusiasm. If every teacher was like that we would have too many clever people to know what to do with.'

Livingstone dates his educational decline to the end of his third year at the school when Hobsbaum left: 'As his influence waned, I tailed off, became disruptive and was always in trouble. I played truant.'

He was one of the smallest boys in the school and sport was out of the question but he found that he could take on the school bullies by using words. He would use humour to defuse the situation. His greatest school interest was in science and he was obsessed by astronomy. If he had an ambition at all, it was to become the character played by his parliamentary colleague, Andrew Faulds, in *Journey into Space*. When he left school he was in limbo: 'I was likely to be "difficult", possibly a scientist working on his own – and I would have liked that. Certainly no-one could have predicted a political career.'

Ken Livingstone's parents were working-class Conservatives, albeit with original touches. His father was 'sympathetic to the Soviet Union and hostile to the United States since he resented our being stripped of the Empire.' His mother had been on the stage and had generous views about those 'who had exotic sexual lives'. The son was 'a classic working-class reactionary who favoured hanging and opposed premarital sex though I was prepared to make an exception in my own case. My broad view on politics was that of H. G. Wells in *The Shape of Things to Come*. I saw all politicians as venal characters, liars and deceivers. I thought that the world should be run by scientists – this was before I met any.'

Livingstone's energies remained unfocused: 'I was a gadfly and my role was to annoy everybody. I was always in a group but I was never the leader. I was "Brains".'

Exams were not for him: 'I was midway between John Major and Neil Kinnock.' He had no university expectations: 'I accepted that I was in the great mass; I never expected not to be in that mass.' He was aware of class and knew what a BBC accent was but had no sense of inferiority: 'If anything, we laughed at the upper classes. I was happy where I was – but I was also frustrated – I desperately wanted to be an adult. I did badly because I was rebelling against the rules. If I could not see the logic behind a rule I would not obey it – and most rules at school were ridiculous.' If he was not given free time he would create it by playing truant.

Twenty-five years on, 'Brains' is still ploughing a lonely furrow. Politics, after all, is the art, not only of the possible but also of the clubbable. For Livingstone, however, 'The veneer of the House of Commons is a real joke and I refuse to take that system seriously. There's no power there; it's a cross between a rubber stamp and street theatre.

Patronage works against any independence of spirit. It's painful not to have the approval of others, but I'm prepared to live without it.'

Ken Livingstone thinks that his school failed him because it did not abandon the grammar-school aspirations which survived the comprehensive reorganisation. Those aspirations were doomed to failure since 'Dulwich and Alleyn's creamed off the academics'. The headmaster had been the deputy at Dulwich College and 'he thought that he could turn us into grammar-school kids. It just did not work because there was no grammar-school material there. They did not develop the non-academic side of the school as they should have done. Keeping order and making sure that there wasn't a riot – that, not education, was the priority.'

English confusions about class, in Livingstone's view, muddied the educational waters because: 'Our class system was seen to be inexorably linked with streaming and selection, and that was not true of Germany. I am no longer opposed to selection and streaming – provided we get all kinds of education catered for in the same building.'

In the 1980s politics was governed by memories of the political and economic failures of the 1960s and 1970s and by the need to break out of a debilitating consensus. As the political class reflected on the social disorders of those years a new consensus emerged. It emphasised economic liberalism, the minimal State and competition. As Mrs Thatcher's press secretary, Sir Bernard Ingham soon became associated with the new values.

'One of the great things about getting into trouble', he remarks ruefully about the Westland affair, 'is that voices come winging in from the past saying, "We hope you're all right." The English teacher who taught me *Julius Caesar* rang up in the middle of it all and said, 'I hope I can say that I'm part of your success." "That's the nicest thing anyone's said about you for months," my wife said.'

Ingham rebuffs any romantic cliché of the journalist as outsider. 'I was never an outsider,' he says emphatically, and this may be why he found the political aspect of his job so congenial. It was in any event 'pure chance' that he became a journalist and that a job became available: 'though I had always had a feeling and a hankering after it.'

School certainly did not instil in him a craving for national success but he owed a great deal to Hebden Bridge Grammar School. It gave him 'an outlook on life and on the arts – I played the violin, for example, in those days.' School was all the more necessary since 'I did not have much encouragement at home. My parents suffered from the limited horizons of the working classes.'

Ingham failed the 11 plus since he was not properly prepared at his elementary school. He was given a good grounding but was not crammed for the exam. He eventually arrived at the grammar school because his parents paid for him to go. He did well once he got there, he thinks, because of the broad grounding of his earlier education. He 'had not been trained like a puppet to pass tests.'

The headmaster, Herbert Howarth, 'made quite a lot of the material that came before him', and Ingham stresses Howarth's concern with a general education which meant that one had to persevere with all subjects. Contemporary education, he believes, quite apart from getting back to basics, needs to 'give a broad general education which is not concerned with pouring doctrine into people's ears but with stretching and broadening their minds. My teachers were an entirely beneficial influence on me whereas my parents were something of a wet blanket.' All influences, however, combined to emphasise that it was 'important to succeed – whatever that meant – at school because you were not going to work in a mill or a factory.'

Sir Bernard shares with Mrs Thatcher roots in a provincial, dissenting culture and he emphasises the role of those roots in her success. In the 1990s as Mrs Thatcher's premiership becomes a historic memory, the search continues for persuasive answers to perennial questions of authority and consent. How have the values and aspirations of two current members of the Conservative cabinet reflected their education?

David Hunt, Secretary of State for Wales, was a day boy at Liverpool College, a predominantly day school 'for the sons of Liverpool gentlemen'. It was in Sefton Park, a part of Toxteth, and was his local school. It was not inevitable that he should be a Tory but his powerful grandmother Mrs Fletcher-Hunt had decided 'that I should do something in the world'.

He was an active schoolboy, a secretary of the dramatic, the debating and the choral societies. He was secretary of an all-Liverpool Schools Playgoers society and wrote a history of the College's cadet force. 'I had a challenging school life and I had to work quite hard. When I was working for my "A" levels I got a duodenal ulcer and that was quite a problem. I was always being spurred on. I joined the Liverpool Mosley Crusaders, which was a Bible reading class and I went with them to Europe. Politically, Europe was very much my issue.'

Despite this record his headmaster was sceptical about Hunt.

Mr Collinson complained of Hunt's 'impertinence and intolerance' in his school report and he concedes that he used to speak his mind and was 'quite difficult to handle'. Scepticism, however, only stiffened Hunt's resolve. He was one of a group of boys who disputed the school's conventional wisdom, and because of that fact 'the school did consciously instil in us the desire to achieve something.' His contemporaries included Richard Stilgoe, the musican and lyricist; Nigel McCulloch, the new Bishop of Wakefield; Bernie Faulk, the journalist, and Guy Edwards, the racing driver who pulled Nicky Lauda out of his car's blazing wreckage.

Hunt did not return to the school while Collinson was alive but was asked by the College Council to read the lesson at his memorial Service. 'I remembered it was his favourite lesson, the opening verses of the Fourth Gospel: "And the Word was made Flesh . . ." He always read it with the correct intonation and it was a great challenge to me to read it. I wonder what his feelings would have been had he looked down. Perhaps he would recognise that I had made some progress. Certainly because of him I wanted to succeed more than I would otherwise have done.'

Adversity had schooled the future Secretary of State and school history reinforced his brand of Tory liberalism and European enthusiasm. 'I really enjoyed the Napoleonic era and the revolutions of 1848. I was very struck by the way in which the history of Europe moves in phases and how events in one country mirror those in another. There were concerted developments and that certainly affected my views on the need for Europe to be more united.'

Social concern came to David Hunt through his father, who was known as 'the dockers' friend' among ship owners because 'he had always been of the view that the dockers were very badly treated.' When he was 17 the school gave him an opportunity to demonstrate that social concern in a concrete form. 'My father was upset about the slum clearances in Liverpool and seeing all the streets mowed down. From the top of Goodison Park and Everton, looking down, you could see rows of condemned streets which nobody wanted to leave. The inhabitants told the council that all that was needed was to mend the damp and build inside loos but the council enforced their move to green field sites.' Hunt and a schoolfriend decided to make a film because they were so angry about municipal socialism 'and we filmed ourselves interviewing these people'. His housemaster encouraged him in that venture and the film was submitted at the Montreux Festival in the school film category.

'I enjoyed George Watson's,' says Malcolm Rifkind, Secretary of State for Defence, 'but I would not regard my schooldays as the happiest days of my life. There was a streak of indolence in me and I should really have got better grades in my Highers. I identified the minimum necessary to get me to university and I settled for that.' He knew while he was at school that he was a Conservative and formed his own political party with its own manifesto in order to fight a mock election at school. His views were 'progressive, mainstream Conservatism'.

His was not a cerebral brand of politics and he stresses the sheer fun of it all: 'fun in the sense of being relevant to the great issues of the day.' It also brought excitement: 'People and events were interesting and I came to the conclusion that the adult world was a more exciting place than that of childhood.'

Advocacy was an important part of Rifkind's politics. He remembers speaking against apartheid in a school debate. That was indeed his view but the important thing was that this was a subject he was called upon to speak about and he had therefore to prepare his brief.

Robin Morgan was an influential history teacher who would start the lesson by studying the issues of the day in that morning's newspaper and therefore link current affairs with history. Historically, Rifkind was stirred by great moments such as the unification of Germany and of Italy. 'There was something romantic about this that appealed to me.'

Rifkind left school young at the age of 17 and with an emerging sense that he wanted to be a politician. 'Mine was an Edinburgh world, comfortable without being rich, and I lived at home with my parents both at school and at university.' This seemed reasonable enough at the time but within a few years Rifkind decided that he needed wider experience and lectured for two years in Rhodesia so that he could travel in Africa. He thought that he was returning to a career at the Scottish Bar but other longings were taking root: 'Politics has to be in the blood – and you have to be stimulated by that kind of life. The great thing is that you can get into a position in which you exercise responsibility at a much earlier age than in other professions.'

Labour MP Austin Mitchell has not tasted the responsibilities of ministerial office, and seems unlikely to do so. His independent mind has ensured that he spends his parliamentary life out on a limb. Bingley Grammar School was 'a working-class Summerhill. You did what you wanted.' Mitchell, therefore, 'drifted through school and there was no suggestion that you should do anything – and I didn't particularly want to do anything.'

The school prepared its pupils for the cosy, uncompetitive, common-culture world of the Yorkshire of the 1950s. 'It was a community school and people were happy with it as it was. It gave a good grounding but not a set of expectations. I didn't want it to do more.'

Education at Mitchell's school was simply 'a nice river to drift down and that is how education should be. I was turned down for a job at 15 so I stayed on at school and that led on to university.' It was suggested that he apply to Oxford or Cambridge but the only master who had been to Oxford had been there thirty years previously. Mitchell was therefore sent to look up the University Calendar in Bradford Reference Library. The calendar was so complicated that he could not understand it and so he went to Manchester.

He was small, hated sport and therefore missed 'the benefits of so-called character-building'. On cross-country runs he would walk to the CND milk bar in Bingley and pretend to return exhausted. He was always ill for rugby.

Mitchell went on CND marches with his history teacher, who was a founder member of the Bradford CND, and with John Braine, then a librarian in Bingley. Politics, however, was a latent interest. He was the Liberal agent in the school's mock elections in 1950-1951. At the time he had a part-time job delivering meat for a local butcher. He would go round with a yellow rosette on his meat-round and people would wonder what the colour stood for. Was it a health warning for the meat?

At Bingley Grammar there was a marked distinction between 'the academic who discovered sex later on and the non-academic who discovered it earlier and was provided with a reason for leaving.' Very few went to university and only about three went from Mitchell's year. It was difficult even to get to Leeds, and none went to Oxford or Cambridge. Mitchell is forced to concede 'that that was a service the school could have provided far better than it did.'

Jack Straw, the Shadow Education Minister, was a scholar and a boarder at Brentwood School, after his parents separated. He felt different from his contemporaries and did not let any of his friends know for two years that his parents were divorced. He was conscious of living in a council maisonette and, because he lived some way away from the school, could conceal the fact. 'I had picked up the idea that being on the wrong side of the tracks was not a good idea.'

Even as an 11-year-old he 'made a point of expressing my political views'. In the Vth Form he ran a poll of his fellows in order to get a copy of the *Manchester Guardian* delivered to his House. The generous allocation of time for medieval history meant that there was plenty of time left over for the discussion of contemporary politics under an inspiring history teacher. Medieval history, moreover, was a good choice because 'you were unencumbered by facts' and dealt with a limited corpus of material. His kind of history and politics dealt with 'the interplay of large forces' and he specially liked the sense in medieval history of looking at the pattern of a whole development in a detached way. 'That kindled fire for me' and he enjoyed medieval politics as the 'interplay of big personalities'.

As the son of strong Labour supporters, Straw was brought up in a faith. 'You don't have to think that hard about why you support the party you do if you are brought up that way.' Nonetheless he was further radicalised by the experience of talking about past and contemporary politics in the History Sixth. 'It was 1960-1963 and we captured the spirit of the times.' By the time he was in the VIth Form he was thinking seriously of a political career.

Radicalisation, adds the Labour revisionist, meant 'taking a very black and white view of the world', and his history teacher once reproved him for being so vituperative about those he disagreed with in an essay. He was, however, genuinely interested in the way institutions worked and was fully integrated into the structure as head of house and deputy head of School. He was interested in seeing how a 'smooth and liberal headmaster, an ambassador rather than a hands-on manager', managed a school which was 'a series of baronies'.

A sign of things to come arrived when Straw won the Civics prize at the age of 13. The headmaster was keen on 'Citizenship' and involved in the Council for Education in World Citizenship. In September 1959 Straw found himself involved in a political gimmick when he spoke in piping tones at the local Labour candidate's adoption meeting. 'That was when I first thought of being an MP.'

When, after Brentwood days, he went to Leeds, he discovered that it was 'just right for me socially. I fitted in very well. At Brentwood I made myself fit in. I am a social animal but I was never sure that I was part of it.' An emotional trauma just before his "A" levels meant that he had to retake his exams a year later. After Leeds he ran the National Union of Students at a time when 'there were big issues around and I had to think hard' – an echo perhaps of that love of the broad sweep he got out of medieval history.

Straw's accommodating tone and emphasis on the co-operative virtues show how easily his Anglican public school ethics have found a home in the reformed Labour Party. He himself, as he notes, exists in a world where one is more likely to succeed if one learns the boarding-school lesson of successful concealment. His final comments have more than a ring of the Deputy Head of School about them:

'When I came into the House twelve and a half years ago I was struck by the odd mixture of parliamentary politics. At one level it was all very individualistic and competitive. But at another level it needed a high degree of co-operation. A criticism often made in this place is that "X is a loner". Being too competitive is not a plus point in the competition.'

Some have been led to their politics by a more straightforward alienation than Straw's. Labour MP Joe Ashton was ridiculed at High Storrs Grammar School because of his accent and lack of a school uniform. The teachers mocked him. 'This was in 1945, the first year of the 11 plus when the first really poor kids got to grammar schools. We were not welcome. It probably turned me into a rebel.' It was difficult doing homework in a two-up, two-down slum: nonetheless, resolution in the face of adversity is an important political attribute. 'Eventually I achieved my ambition and became an award-winning Fleet Street columnist and Labour MP. So it didn't turn out too badly, did it?'

Another rebel, Rupert Allason (spy story writer Nigel West), resented the fact that Downside would not recommend him for a commission. 'They destroyed the CCF for me because it was run in such a half-hearted way: the monks were just incompetent.' By the age of 16 he was a 'fully-fledged rebel. I responded very badly to being told to do things as opposed to being asked.'

The result was that he spent his time 'bending the rules and manipulating things to my advantage. For example, we were not allowed out of the grounds into the local villages and towns. I invented an "A" level geography project which was a survey of a local town, Wells, so that I could go to the cinema twice a week. I learnt that you got special privileges as captain of a school team. Since there was no school sailing team I started my own, made myself captain and awarded myself the privileges of a captain of school team.'

Downside, says Allason, was a 'bleak, unpleasant school with pointless regulations. It made me rebellious, sceptical, inherently anti-Establishment, iconoclastic and virulently anti-pomposity. I find it ludicrous to see people prancing around giving themselves airs and graces.'

It was the 1960s, the era of flower-power, and Allason got the franchise to sell the underground newspaper *International Times* in the school. He has turned into a dissident of the right rather than of the left. 'The Left like state control: I prefer control by the individual.'

Allason is happiest as an Opposition politician and has never been a team player. Hence his refusal now to ask planted questions or to 'congratulate people on insignificant speeches'. He will rarely sign early-day motions: 'I take a very old-fashioned view of politics and of the Commons. I have no wish to be a minister and the idea of being driven to work every day in an Allegro fills me with horror and despair.'

The effect of being flogged so regularly at school has been to turn him 'mildly anti-Catholic and mildly anti-organised religion'. Downside was a tough, public place with little privacy. 'None of the teachers inspired me and I liked none of them.'

None the less it taught Allason how to be anti-Establishment and sowed the seeds of his interest in intelligence and security. While he was at Downside he read an account of a Dutch intelligence officer who was seized by the Germans. 'It was very candid about the role of an intelligence officer. Some said that this man was dead but I was convinced that he was alive. Years later I found him and did a programme for the BBC about the incident.' Another influence was one of the monks who had been a spy. Dom Joseph Coombe-Tennant would give an annual talk about his escape as an officer in the Welsh Guards from a POW camp. 'He became a spy afterwards, though he never mentioned that in his talk. He was a great friend of David Cornwell (John Le Carré) who used to come and see him.'

Tam Dalyell's Etonian individualism adorns the benches of the Parliamentary Labour Party. His dissent on the sinking of the *Belgrano*, the Westland Helicopters affair and the *Spycatcher* case has been systematic. He has been fortified by that 'certainty that one is right and that the rest of the world is wrong' which he sees as the defining difference between an Old Etonian and the rest of mankind. There were intimations of dissent at school: 'I knew that I was a Scot and that the world of English high society, of the Quorn and the county families of Northamptonshire and Leicestershire was different.'

Having emerged from a prep school which had never sent anyone to Eton before, Dalyell clearly felt that he had something to prove and entered for the Latin prose competition which he won 'much to the consternation of people from Ludgrove and places like that'.

Dalyell's house, under the housemaster Tom Brockway, the brother of Fenner Brockway, the Labour Member for Eton and Slough, seems to have been something of a political nursery. It produced Tory MPs Winston Churchill and Michael McNair Wilson as well as Nicholas Ridley. 'I had no dislikes in my house and many friends – though Nick Ridley was a bit rough with the cane. Nick was a superb schoolboy painter; Wilfrid Blunt, the drawing master, used to say of him that he was more talented than his grandfather, Edwin Lutyens.'

The Eton of 1945-1950 was 'a very serious place and I was never a schoolboy in the sense I might have been in another school. We were treated like undergraduates. There were masters around who had a very adult view of the world.'

And there was, of course, the headmaster, Robert Birley: 'I was one of his favourites and saw much of him after leaving school. He was always interested in Eton's dissenters, of whom I was one.' Dalyell's housemaster was a difficult man, 'a mixture of great kindness and total duplicity'. But Birleyesque high-mindedness was the dominant ethos. 'You worked very hard. You were told that you were privileged and that this country had to be rebuilt after the War.'

He specialised in science and languages, which may be responsible for that 'training in fact' in which he thinks most MPs are lamentably deficient. Intellectual stringency within an unconstrained school framework clearly suited Dalyell well and he is an appropriate political heir to Birley's moderate Fabianism. He played chess at prep school and at Eton. 'The finest accolade of my life was when *The Times* printed Dalyell v. Kasparov on the occasion of Kasparov's challenge to seven clerks, seven peers and seven MPs.' He was, nonetheless, powerless after Kasparov's first move.

As a writer he is indebted to standards of prose composition that he learnt from R. C. Martineau and Walter Hamilton at Eton. They are teachers he shares with Sir Robert Armstrong, the former Secretary to the Cabinet, who for Dalyell 'epitomises the pinnacle of verbal skill in the English language'.

Dalyell's intellectual security enables him to be 'very relaxed' about the fact that his parliamentary career has been such a lonely one. 'I did not set out like that – it just worked out that way.' He brings a chess-player's mind to bear on political issues and, on issues such as devolution, he delights in posing mutually exclusive alternatives rather than in offering a diet of political fudge. As a schoolboy Dalyell once read a paper on Gladstone's view of laughter to the Lyttelton Essay Society. He has brought the same quixotic spirit to the great issues of our time.

Our female politicians are more likely to have been head girls than the men are likely to have been head boys. They may correspond more closely to Janet Cohen's description of the 'good' rather than the 'flashy' woman. (See Chapter five.)

In the Prime Minister's Private Office, Judith Chaplin, former head of the office and now Conservative MP for Newbury, recalled how she sewed a great tapestry while she was at Wycombe Abbey: 'I am not a seamstress but if you were sewing that was the one time you were allowed to sit and think. What I disliked about boarding school was that you had to follow the rules the whole time and do everything in a very regulated way.' She feels indebted to the school but 'I didn't actually enjoy being there. I would have preferred to have been allowed to be more academic. It was a conformist school and they did try to stop you from growing up and having your own views.'

She also insists, however, that Wycombe was not unusual in that respect and at that time: 'We conformed and all wrote to a high standard – but ideas were very much developed for you.' In maths, for example, 'I could do it because I had been taught to do it by example but I did not understand the principles, in the sense of really knowing them, until I had to teach my own children.'

Chaplin may have been intellectually frustrated but she also stresses the importance of the school's ethical code in developing her political views. 'You were expected at school to contribute very widely. I think that you have to indoctrinate people in the belief that they are fortunate and have a duty to others and that you should contribute back. That's a good ethic and is the reason why people go into politics.'

Her father broke with the family tradition in deciding to send his daughter to a boarding school and she sees the post-war period in which she grew up as one of great social change. At school she was interested in the whole process of social change and it was therefore all the more frustrating that she seemed endlessly to be studying the Wars of the Roses rather than the two World Wars. Chaplin's particular abilities needed a more flexible structure than the school was able to provide: 'I enjoyed two different things which you were not allowed to enjoy together – maths as well as history and English.' It was a natural progression to Economic History at Cambridge and an interest in how economics interacts with culture and class.

Is there such a thing as a distinctively feminine political approach? Chaplin thinks there might be: 'Women want to get on with the job. I am not sure whether that is a basic male/female difference or whether, given the difficulty of getting in at all, the sort of women who do get in tend to be that kind of person. Probably the latter, I think. Women in politics, after all, are relatively older and have done other jobs.'

She also dislikes the way in which our party system results in 'a tendency to present it all in extreme terms. Confrontation is tiresome when you are trying to get a job done and the job is that of trying to achieve the kind of society you want.'

If Jack Straw has become more sceptical about the ability of schools to effect social change Chaplin remains convinced that schools can and should contribute to the kind of large-scale social change she first became interested in as a schoolgirl: 'I totally agree with H. G. Wells that it is a race between education and chaos; there are whole swathes of problems in this country which could be solved if we got rid of our culture of educational bureaucracy.' In the 1990s, therefore, schools' task will be to prepare children for a more flexible society than the one Wycombe Abbey prepared its girls for in the 1950s. 'The biggest problem in our schools is that we don't allow competition and don't really recognise the fact of different abilities and the fact that you can't change those abilities.'

She adds, 'A Senior Inspector of Schools once said to me that she had never been to a school where she had had to say, "You are pushing these children too hard". I think that is a damning comment.'

As Lynda Chalker also demonstrates, women politicians are no exception to the general rule that our views of schools reflect not only our own educational experiences but also our views of the kind of society we want to live in: education is necessarily political.

Baroness Chalker, Minister for Overseas Development, has no doubt that there is a link between school, home and future success. 'School gives you the mechanism of good organisation and presentation. Basic principles and tenets come from both the school and the home. The best schools can give you rules which are not there in the home. Schools can't change a basic character but they can enhance the positive: if you have a bent for organisation, they can improve on that. If you have an enquiring, philosophical mind, schools can enhance that.'

There is no doubt that Chalker was awesomely well organised at Roedean. 'I didn't mind being organised either – but I wanted to know where I stood. What were the rules of the game? I found lots of rules absurd but by the VIth Form I found myself showing age, which is to say that I saw the rules were there for a reason.'

Zerbanoo Gifford, Community Relations Adviser to Paddy Ashdown and Liberal Democrat candidate for Haslemere in 1992 also values the discipline she was taught at Roedean. 'The Asian approach is so different. I was taught to be logical at school and that's very important in later life. I know that if I have to do an article I have to get down to it now.'

She was the first Asian girl to go to Roedean and she values it because it taught her 'the norms of another society'. She told us, 'I was taught the importance of being able to make small talk. Most Asians are very bad at that. I am now very good at clubbing, at saying nothing of consequence. To me it is a waste of time, but it has to be done and I know how to do it. I am at ease in both communities, the British and the Asian.'

She knew that she had rarity value at Roedean and was expected to be ill-disciplined. 'The British are very good at rules and regulations. I don't really care. I run if I want to get from A to B. I have always been punished but have also been indulged.'

Roedean really taught Gifford that education involved relating to others: 'That really is what education is all about. At Roedean they really studied you and brought out the best in you. I am a team person, which they liked very much, so I played centre in lacrosse. I liked doing everything, defending and attacking and running around the pitch. They were very perceptive about my personality.'

Her politics reflect her lacrosse while her views on the role of women in politics echo those of Judith Chaplin in some respects: 'Women are more conciliatory and are lateral thinkers whereas the English logical mind is quite masculine. Men simply see the steps which are needed to get to the end result: women don't go through the system, they just want the end.'

Her approach to people and public issues has always, therefore, been feminine, but Roedean changed the way she thought and taught her that 'your original thoughts are more important than the ability to quote which is so highly valued among Asians. You had to work it out and that makes you original. That's a priceless lesson to learn. All my teachers valued original thought. For example, when I had to write an essay on the importance of selling ideas I used the idea of Eve selling the idea of the apple and a good time to Adam. They liked that because it was the expression of an old thought in an original manner.'

Gifford regards herself as a team player but is also aware of the disadvantages. 'If you want to succeed in Britain you can do it in one of two ways: either by being a complete original so that people think you are outstanding; or by not rocking the boat. Highly motivated people can end up not being valued because they rock the boat and the Establishment then closes ranks.'

Another reservation is that public schools are too public. 'They occupy your whole time and don't set much store by being reflective. When people leave them they can find it is difficult to occupy themselves.'

As a public and political figure she has a horror of being introduced as 'Zerbanoo Gifford who was educated at Roedean'.

'When I ask people like Dimbleby why they do it, they reply, "We have to put you into a context." What they mean is, if I'm wearing a sari, they have to explain why I am producing these thoughts and in this speech. It's a statement. It means: "Don't worry, she's one of us, we educated her."'

Despite these remarks an awareness of the clannish qualities of English public life and an ability to play the game by the rules she has described are clearly qualities that Gifford values enormously. She may say that public schools teach people not to challenge the status quo but by her own account she was taught at Roedean that if she wanted something done she should not rely on others but do it herself. This, she thinks, is the very lesson that Asians in Britain should learn so that they can challenge negative images of themselves in British public life.

In the last analysis her account of public school ethics and what Roedean did for her has a familiar ring: 'I learnt about the underplaying of your talents, that superiority should be natural and that you would be put in your place if you bragged about it. You should come top automatically. The popular people at school were the relaxed and naturally superior. It means that when someone comes into a room you know whether they've got it or not.'

This chapter written a century ago would have been crowded with aristocratic names. The absence of the Cecils, the Russells, the Cavendishes is a commentary on the politics of upward ascent which has been a main theme of this chapter. Comparatively few of the 'great' or Clarendon Schools have been mentioned here.

The Secretary of State for Education and Science John Patten went to a state voluntary aided grammar school. Gillian Shephard, Secretary of State for Employment, is a grammar school girl, and Home Secretary Kenneth Clarke went to Nottingham High School. Environment Secretary Michael Howard is a former head boy of Llanelli Boys' Grammar. Chief Secretary to the Treasury Michael Portillo was at Harrow County School and David Mellor, Secretary for National Heritage is a Swanage Grammar School boy. Their success has been fuelled by their own competence and by the sight of others' incompetence. As Norman Fowler (King Edward VI Grammar School, Chelmsford) recalls of politicians visiting Cambridge: 'Some suffered terrible stage fright and needed a couple of stiff drinks before they were ready for the fierce Cambridge audience. Others were simply unimpressive. There is nothing like getting close to politicians to make politics appear more accessible.'

Mr Major's rise to power marks yet another stage in the story of meritocratic openness in England. It remains to be seen whether the lesson to be drawn from his ascent is that British schools have failed many able children or that education does not really matter after all and that talent will out.

11 Public Life

Voluntary activity and public-spirited endeavour are enduring nineteenth century legacies to late twentieth century British life. Those who 'have done the State some service' without being party-political have served on quangos and public bodies. They have worked for voluntary organisations, interest groups and charities. Trade Unions, the Civil Service and the Foreign and Commonwealth Office have provided them with careers. British suspicion of the State remains powerful even in the age of the Welfare State. Lady Bountiful, however, is still a recognised, and sometimes admirable, type, while Sir Humphrey Appleby has become a national institution.

Public life attracts the conventionally great and the good as well as the bolshie. Both display civic virtue in either a conventional or a dissident form. The great and the good can be subdivided into two further categories. Those who offer uncomplicated assertions about *noblesse oblige* belong to an older generation and observe a seamless web between the traditions of their education and their subsequent lives. Others, however, were taught constructive, critical scepticism by their schools. They tend to be the products of grammar schools whereas the members of the first group have imbibed a public-school ethos. Grammar schools often put their pupils on to a fast academic track and opened their eyes to opportunities that they would not otherwise have seen.

The now elegantly Bohemian Duke of Devonshire was 'shamefully lazy' and 'unbelievably dirty' at Eton. He would steal away to the race-track: 'I ran the school book until the Duke of Norfolk put me out of business.'

He had been 'blissfully happy' at Ludgrove, his prep school: 'That is said to be one of the great signs of mediocrity — that you should be happy at your private school.' He had been so intensively coached for Eton that he was over-placed and was therefore always struggling academically in the school.

Looking back, the Duke now thinks that the régime should have been a less *laissez-faire* one, one less naturally suited to the indolence of 'four generations of Cavendishes who did not get a single colour between them.' None the less, he also sees the advantages of the system: 'I did love it because it really was a university. If you did not want to work you were left in peace. In my day there was room for everybody at Eton.'

What some might regard as the clannishness of English society is, to Andrew Cavendish, simply 'a way of making friends'; he made a lot of school friendships and has kept them. The system's consequences are disarmingly viewed: 'If you wanted to get a message around from Her Majesty the Queen to the dustman you could do it in no time through people who knew each other at Eton.'

Public service was, however, more a matter of family than of school influence. The Whiggish flame of the Cavendishes was kept alight by his father with the belief in 'improving the lot of the underprivileged as long as it does not interfere with one's own wealth.' There were the High Tory convictions of the Cecils, to whom he was related through his mother: 'They were High Church and convinced that the aristocracy knew best'. School was an irrelevance within such a nursery of the public spirit and rumours of a world elsewhere were slow to arrive. 'We had very little bad language at home. We lined the cortège in Windsor Castle at George V's funeral and I was absolutely amazed by the language of the soldiers and sailors. That did open my eyes.'

Racing apart, it was an innocent education: 'The worst thing that could be done was to drink white port in back rooms. I had no emotional friendships at school and nobody made advances to me. I was, after all, a very dirty schoolboy, and have always been perhaps over-aggressively heterosexual.'

This picture of a blissfully Woosterian indifference to schooling was only overshadowed by the approaching clouds of the Second World War: 'I had some excuse for my idleness both at Eton and Trinity. From 1936 onwards every thinking person of my generation was aware that war would take place.' The decade's urgency reinforced hereditary insouciance about school.

The Marchioness of Anglesey was similarly unaffected by school. Her interest in public issues started when she saw unemployed Welsh miners singing for money outside houses in Eaton Terrace. 'I also travelled on top of an open tram over Battersea Bridge when my father explained to me how much money many of those living on the other side of the bridge had to manage with on the dole.' These were profounder influences than anything offered by Francis Holland School.

Less patrician public servants were more easily influenced by their schools' ethos. Sir Brian Young, Chairman of Christian Aid and a former Chairman of the IBA and Headmaster of Charterhouse, indulged in 'the admiration of schoolmasters' at Eton. Nicholas Hinton, Director of Save the Children Fund, is thankful for the range of activities he engaged in at Marlborough 'as an alternative to the Corps from which I was sacked (until being reinstated on becoming a prefect) for being so hopelessly unmilitary.' During the school holidays he worked at an approved school for young offenders.

Alastair Service, General Secretary of the Family Planning Association, discovered at Westminster School a heightened sensitivity to his environment: 'The buildings started my interest in Parliament and love of architecture and old buildings.' An associated feel for public life led to his work as a legal reformer.

The Earl of Longford is a more original example of the interaction between the individual and his environment. He was 'not unhappy' at Eton but the roots of his principled altruism, the sense that he is himself an outsider, go deep. 'Some say I became a Socialist because I didn't get into Pop [Eton's exclusive social and debating society]. Others say it was because I was concussed at a point-to-point or at a Mosley meeting.'

He was an athletic boy and 'lived for years for the moment when we won the House Cup at football and I led the winning team in. Basil Dufferin [the Marquess of Dufferin and Ava], my friend at school, always said that I was hissed when I led in the team but I was too elated to know whether I was hissed or not.'

As the youngest boy in the school when he arrived he had always been ahead and therefore, 'I had assumed that I would be Captain of the Oppidans. I would then automatically be a member of Pop.' Both prizes eluded him when a boy in the year ahead stayed on for an extra year. In other respects as well, Eton was not as successful an environment for the young Frank Pakenham as Oxford would prove to be:

'I had been very clever at my prep school and I didn't work at Eton because I felt that I didn't have to. I thought that I would automatically go to the top.'

When he got to Oxford he found that he had fallen behind both in Classics and History. If he wished to make a mark he needed to find a new subject where he, with others, could start from base. He found it in PPE, the School of Modern Greats, in which he got a First and later became a don.

As a young man he espoused a romantic conservatism which he now regards as unreflective. Even this attenuated form of political consciousness escaped him at school and at home. As a boy he was unaware that Sir Robert Peel was his great-great-grandfather.

In his last year at Eton, in 1923, he went along to the Political Society, with the intention of making his mark by saying something amusing. 'I asked the visiting speaker whether he thought that Mr Winston Churchill had a political future. I suppose it was rather like asking whether Enoch Powell has a political future.'

Longford evolved from Conservatism and Anglicanism towards Socialism and Catholicism but is aware of the religious continuities which underpin his active public life. His headmaster, Cyril Alington, was 'a tremendous Christian influence in Chapel. When the issue of religious education came up for debate in the House of Lords two years ago the old Alington people – Hailsham, Home and myself – were very vocal.

'I remember a missioner who came to preach in Chapel about his work. He would say, "It's not your money I want: it's you, my dear fellows, I want."' Political alignment with the Left came much later in 1936 when he joined the Labour Party. '"Socialist" may not be a word that means very much now but I am still on the side of the underdog.'

These, however, were feelings of exclusion for which he had been prepared at school: 'I was not bullied but I was not, and have never expected to be, popular.' He was aware, as a schoolboy, that being Irish meant that he was different and his world was not that of the great county families. 'I did not go and stay with them during the holidays.'

His housemaster, Wells, was a strong character, an athlete, a fine scholar and an eccentric. 'He once ran out of Glyndebourne after the first few minutes of the opera with his fingers in his ears, shouting, "Stop that caterwauling!"' Wells taught the young Pakenham a philosophy of stoicism and of guts which he admired and whose remains may be found in his habit of weekend jogging.

Fortitude of a moral kind has been a characteristic of Lord Longford's public life. It has been sustained by his sense of detachment from the aristocratic milieu of his education and upbringing.

Once a week he would visit the Eton Manor Club, a working boys' club, which was partly run by his bachelor uncle, Arthur Villiers, a banker with Barings. 'After my father died he was my closest relative and I used to stay there. It was there that my social conscience developed. I did not feel that there was a great barrier between myself and the other boys there. We played games and this is a great catalyst and means of communication. My uncle also took me to see boys in the East End. They were not really poor but were healthy working-class boys. I did not feel sorry for them: I simply felt a sense of kinship with them.'

Bruce Kent, Vice-President of CND, was, however, less happy about the London charitable settlement supported by his school, Stonyhurst:

'We used to go down to this settlement very much in the spirit of meeting the servants – like a kind of Lord Bountiful. We were taught that we were the cream of society. For example there was a Catholic grammar school at Preston only about ten miles away but we never went near it: we only had dealings with the other Roman Catholic public schools.'

Kent, whose parents were Canadian, had been evacuated to Lower Canada College in Montreal, and the three years he spent there made him nonconformist. 'It made me think about things. But I became very conformist afterwards at Stonyhurst.'

There was little in his schooldays to prefigure his future commitment to nuclear disarmament. The school was 'establishment and militaristic' and Kent enjoyed the Officer Training Corps as much as the next boy:

'No-one ever refused to take part – it was just part of life like the Latin classes, and I quite enjoyed it and became a sergeant.

'I was fond of the school: it gave me personal piety and establishment values. In fact it was *because* of these, not despite them, that I later joined CND. As a traditional Roman Catholic I couldn't understand why the bishops of the fifties and sixties weren't saying anything about nuclear warfare – which is the violation of everything the Church teaches about the just war.'

He remembers all too well the bombing of Hiroshima when he was 16: 'It was the summer holidays of 1945 and I was standing on the corner of Marylebone Road and Baker Street when I read the news on a newspaper hoarding and I thought, "Wonderful – it's the end of the War!" Like most people then I believed exactly what I was told – that the Japanese were guilty and that it was the right way to end the war. I only started to become critical of nuclear warfare much later after reading what Archbishop Thomas Roberts and others wrote in the *Catholic Herald*.'

Colonel John Mayo believes that 'the religious aspect of life at King's College, Taunton had a profound effect' on him and certainly influenced his choice of a second career as Director General of Help the Aged.

Christopher Brown, Director of the NSPCC, touches upon a common theme when he writes of the 'commitment to public service' at Hertford Grammar School: 'The headmaster had a major influence upon boys in their teenage years, recognising that there is more to life than making the maximum amount of money in the shortest possible time.'

Sir John Banham, former Director General of the CBI, echoes these orthodoxies of the public service: 'Both my parents were fundamentally uninterested in making money: they believed in contributing to the wellbeing of the people around them, my father as a surgeon and my mother through the social services. I must have been a bit pompous as a boy but I knew that I had been lucky and that I had better do something with that luck.'

Although he has never traded on being an Old Carthusian he feels a greater indebtedness to Charterhouse than his near-contemporary there, Max Hastings. 'I feel gratitude for the sense of values I learnt there, whether Max recognises them or not. I learnt that one has obligations that arise from the opportunities that came through no effort on my part. I learnt lessons that are a good guide to life, including the one that winning is better than losing and that cheating is worse than both.'

Self-effacing consensualism made Banham a successful honourable schoolboy. 'I was one of those irritating people – I was good at games and I got by academically.' He was aware of his privileges but he did not consider that school was a cloistered environment: 'On the contrary, I thought of it as an open environment.' Obligation and public service might now be old, unfashionable phrases, 'but I do not think that they are unfashionable sentiments – many people feel them.' They were an implicit part of the air he breathed as a schoolboy.

The environment nurtured his self-confidence: 'I had a sense that education was not something that ended when you left school. I felt that I was on a conveyor belt and that I would naturally go on to Cambridge. I don't know why I thought that – but I did. It was my assumption and not my family's – they had always gone to Oxford. I didn't think of life as a career. I just knew the kind of things I was interested in and the kind of life I would like to lead in the future.

'I have never been interested in making money for its own sake.' On the other hand he feels no kinship with the mentality of the *rentier*. 'Charterhouse did not turn me off the idea of making things.' And there was no disdain for such matters in his family either.

He was, however, very greatly affected by the classic public-school idea that 'teamwork is important'. 'I got used to the idea that a good team of mediocre individuals, if organised properly, can do better than a lousy team of outstanding individuals. It is unquestionably true in business that effective teamwork is a better way of organising ordinary people to do extraordinary things by helping and motivating them. Erratic individualism can't do that.'

There is a clear continuity with the schoolboy who was competitive at games, 'preferred winning to losing', was captain of various school teams, and conventionally reticent about any idea of academic competitiveness. His happiest school memories include being one of the first group in a cross-country race for the whole school.

The grown man observes that: 'I have been very fortunate in ways that I can't claim the credit for, and have always believed that you should put in more than you take out. That's what every doctor I know believes and most of my friends believe that too. It is what being a professional, in the best sense of the word, means. At the Audit Commission I was creating an institution which would make a contribution and have a life of its own after I am part of history.' Before he left the CBI, his ambition was to leave it better equipped to do its job: 'If we all do that we contribute to the sum total of human happiness.'

Religion at school was a part of this communal code. 'I took it reasonably seriously without being obsessed by it. Theology was never a special interest but I liked the feel of Chapel. It reminded you that there was more to life than making a pile of money.' As headmaster, Brian Young was a pervasive influence: 'You could see there what a class act looked like. He personified a kind of excellence which is good for everybody to rub up against.'

Banham is a *locus classicus* of the developed public-school professional ethos at its most revealing and admirable. Local Management of Schools will, he hopes, be a means of 'creating a public-school ethos in state schools'. When the time came for him to leave Charterhouse Banham discovered the extent of his popularity within a community he had made his own and which claimed him as his own: 'It had never occurred to me that I was popular and I was surprised. It was kind of agreeable, I suppose.'

Senior civil servants and diplomats are the modern heirs to that tradition of service to the State first exemplified by the medieval clerks trained at Oxford and Cambridge. They owe much to their environment. Sir David Hannay, Ambassador and the UK's Permanent Representative to the EC, thinks that 'the Winchester tradition of public service' influenced his choice of career 'by instilling the idea of service to the community'.

Diplomats do, however, record a higher than average curiosity about the outside world while at school. Sir Antony Acland, Ambassador to Washington and now Provost of Eton, attributes this to the fact that he specialised in French and German at Eton. Sir Ewen Fergusson, Ambassador to Paris, notes 'the value put on public service' at Rugby. The 'frequency of visitors to the school and discussion reinforced an existing interest in international affairs', since he was born abroad and was much travelled.

Sir Nicholas Fenn, Ambassador to Dublin, strikes a moral note in assessing the influence of his Methodist boarding school, Kingswood, Bath, on his career: 'The school taught me, through history and travel, that the world mattered and that peace was not a natural state but something to be worked at. The headmaster taught me the relevance of the Christian Gospel to the travails of the world and fired my ambition to do something about it.' John Gray, Ambassador to the OECD and a former Ambassador to the Lebanon, is unusual among this group in saying that his school, Blundell's, had no influence on his career: 'When I left school I had no inkling that I might finish up in my chosen career.'

It is perhaps unsurprising to find that Sir Anthony Parsons, a former Ambassador to Iran and a diplomat with a reputation for teasing the orthodox, was uninfluenced by his school: 'I don't think about it much. King's, Canterbury, was irrelevant to my career which was shaped by the War. Had there been no war, I would have gone up to Oxford, read Greats and then, who knows? As it was I came home eventually in 1948 having learnt Arabic in Palestine. Back to Oxford where I read Oriental Studies for obvious reasons. My family had been Army or Indian Political for generations.'

No such family influence directed the footsteps of Sir Peter Middleton to the Permanent Secretaryship of the Treasury. When he was a boy at Sheffield City Grammar School he was not even aware of the existence of the Civil Service. Although he was happy at school it was uncertain whether he should stay on at 16 or start work. His father, however, who manufactured brushes for Sheffield's cutlery industry, had a profound belief in education and persuaded him to stay at school.

Sir Peter found himself a member of a small VIth form which also included Roy Hattersley: 'Being part of a small group had its advantages and it meant that we got to know each other very well.' A love of numbers started early and shaped his career. He read economics at Sheffield University, aided in part by the careers advice of an otherwise distant headmaster, and afterwards researched in statistics at Bristol University. 'I went to Bristol partly because I thought it might be a good way of avoiding National Service.' The Army, however, would not be denied and he ended up in the Pay Corps after Bristol days, 'with very clever people, mostly accountants, who had not been to university.' By then he had learnt that his forte was the interpretation of statistics. 'The calculator saved my life. I could not add up, was no good at arithmetic but loved algebra. I would probably never have finished university had I not been allowed to use a calculator.'

Middleton drifted into the Civil Service. This most contemporary of mandarins who has advised chancellors of the exchequer from Callaghan to Major left school with his options still wide open and his expectations of a wider life heightened. Within the Civil Service he found no evidence of a liberal-humanist, anti-business conspiracy. Snobbish arcadianism about 'trade' is, he maintains, a southern phenomenon, if it exists at all.

School was certainly no Arcady and was all the better for not being so: Middleton's school was co-educational and in the centre of the city: 'You could go and see Sheffield play during the lunchtime.'

Middleton, the open-minded meritocrat, describes himself as being mainly affected by what he is doing at any particular moment rather than the kind of person who develops long-term career plans. Having left the Treasury he is now Deputy Chairman of Barclays de Zoete Wedd. His education clearly served him well as a school in realism. It encouraged no cultural barriers and he found himself in a world where the old barriers were coming down. As he says, 'Throughout my time in the Service I was never asked which university I attended.' He was launched on and prepared for a flexible world of ceaseless change, a world in which adaptability was the crucial element in success. The traditional verities of public service were being forged anew in the crucible of change.

Peter Joslin, Chief Constable of Warwickshire, has a brusque way with those who rely too readily on the vocabulary of public service in explaining their career choices. 'I had no sense of public service when I decided to join the police force and I take it with a pinch of salt when people tell me at interview that they have that sense. The ethos is more likely to develop as you progress within the service.'

Joslin's father, a detective-sergeant, profoundly influenced his choice of career. 'He seemed to have a quality of life and a wonderful combination of family and professional life. He taught me about mixing with people; he had both authority and a good social life.'

The appeal of that authority must have been reinforced at an early age when at King Edward VI, Chelmsford, his son's school, he arrested one of the masters who had been fiddling the National Savings.

By the age of nine Joslin had decided that he wanted to be a policeman: 'At that time there were no qualifications needed and so there was no pressure on me to succeed academically. I left school at 16 and the senior masters thought that I was wasting a good education by joining the police force.'

Joslin was one of a group of 'high-spirited and memorable boys at school. We were also, however, difficult and needed discipline. The master who did us most good was an ex-Army officer who came to us during the War. We liked hard men and had no respect for the weak.'

Nigel Fanshawe, an Eton housemaster, arrived as headmaster in Joslin's last year at school. 'He tried to get us to play rugby and we were a soccer school so we didn't take to that. I think he was happy to see his fourth and fifth years go. We had had a fair bit of freedom before he came.'

Joslin's eyes were firmly fixed on the outside world. 'My crowd moved with people from other schools at the Chelmsford Youth Centre and that was rare. Nobody in my circle moved without consulting me. At the age of 16 I was serving with adults on the committee of the Centre.'

There were brighter boys around at school 'but they have often not made it because they lack the social skills. The ones who went on to university have tended to get stuck in tedious jobs. Most of my friends, however, have got to the top of their professions.'

Like his near-contemporary at the school, Norman Fowler, Joslin is an admirer of his school. It clearly provided an amenable *Boys' Own* world for one whose future was already mapped out for him. 'We felt that we were very much boys together, all the more so since there was a much smaller sixth form at the school in those days.' When he now returns to his old school Joslin's message is a familar and to some a comforting one: 'I tell the boys that success is not necessarily academic success.'

Constructive sceptics among the public-spirited include Martin Rosenbaum, Director of End Physical Punishment of Children (EPOCH). At University College School, Hampstead, 'the slogan that you should question everything you are told rather than accept it automatically was part of the accepted wisdom of the school.' There was no causal effect between school and career but, as with so many others in this chapter, school was an enormously ethical experience 'which helped to make me the sort of person I am. School life made me the sort of person who would campaign for social change.'

Elizabeth Hoodless, Director of Community Service Volunteers, is similarly enthusiastic about the headmistress of Redland High School, Bristol, who 'had an immense range of friends and contacts to whom we were sent to discuss our ideas about careers from the age of 14 onwards. We were involved in volunteer work from 11 onwards and the school started careers education at five when we were made to analyse our strengths, weaknesses and value systems. We were trained to succeed at everything we resolved to do: organising Christmas parties for disadvantaged children when we were 11, organising homes and clothes for Hungarian refugees at 15, demonstrating against apartheid when we were 18. We were introduced to lobbying at 12. Above all we were taught to handle power: to spot it, grasp it and use it for good.'

A less strenuous ethical and virtuous approach at Wimbledon High School for Girls awoke the social conscience of Valerie Packenham, now Director of Fundraising for the Samaritans: 'One of my form mistresses took great interest in the childish caricatures I drew and suggested that this might be a future career. She brought me many examples to emulate, mostly political. I am not a cartoonist but her efforts did serve to awaken my social and political consciousness at the age of 13.'

June O'Dell, Deputy Chairman of the Equal Opportunities Commission, was a 'destructive and disruptive child' at Edgehill Girls' College. 'If not checked in such an understanding manner, I would have committed offences of ever-increasing seriousness, the classic cry for attention. From the school I absorbed the lesson that with enough determination much can be achieved.'

Lady Marre, Chairman of the Marre Committee on the future of the legal profession, says that Chelmsford County High School for Girls was a non-competitive place in the 1930s. 'There were no places or prizes for individuals, but encouragement for groups (either classes or houses) to compete in drama, music and sport. There were no punishments. We were encouraged to learn how to speak in public and how to use our voices.'

Two headmistresses gave the girls 'better understanding of the wider world, and encouraged debate about the wider political issues. War, fascism, pacificism, were our concern and this encouraged political awareness.' The school helped her to acquire 'an enquiring mind and tolerance, as well as that essential quality for a life devoted to good works, experience of managing by consent.'

Graham Mather, former Director of the free-market think tank, the Institute of Economic Affairs, is an example of the post-war grammar-school meritocracy in public life. He has been associated with consistent scepticism about the competence and validity of government intervention in business and other areas of civil life. In the Vth Form at Hutton Grammar School, Lancashire, Mather flirted with Communism for the same reasons that led him eventually to the intellectual right, an interest in the machinery of politics and the levers of institutional power. There was nothing romantic or anarchic about his reaction: 'I was very interested in how institutions run and how you get ideas to work in institutions.' This meant that he was more of a Leninist than a Marxist and this reflected his intolerance with the 'confusions and the muddle and the institutional failure of 1970-1974.'

Hutton Grammar School, however, was relentlessly normal and stable. 'The school atmosphere was liberal and accommodating; you could test outrageous theories and ideas.' Mather's school was a community school, one in which the masters were also significant local figures. They had names like Harry Wilkins, they wore tweed sports jackets, had gruff exteriors and were mostly graduates of the Northern universities.

In the 1930s gentrification had been the order of the day when the school was rebuilt in minor public-school Georgian by a headmaster with big ambitions. Colonel Hinds had a gardener who was also his chauffeur. He established a boarding house and 'consciously elevated the school beyond being a county grammar school.' From 1662 to 1928 the school had been relatively undistinguished and it slipped back to that condition after the Hinds period. Mather's time at the school coincided with the headmastership of John Nelson, who 'brought an independent style back to the school in an understated, gentle way without airs and graces.'

Mather appreciated the style but the school and the society it served were immobile and unimaginative. A master, younger than the rest, taught VIth Form history and 'without him I would not have gone to New College'. The school was 'receptive and broadly geared to Oxbridge but there was no idea of doubling or tripling the three or four who got in every year – and that could easily have been done.'

The school's constituency was only marginally professional and parents tended to be in middle management. This, in Mather's view, made for an unquestioning environment. 'Hutton Grammar School was deferential to whichever headmaster it got. It accepted Hinds in the 1930s but it would also take the decisions of the Lancashire Education Committee, God help us, as Holy Writ, and anything which came from the DES was cast in concrete.' Abolition and comprehensivisation were the inevitable consequences: 'If I had been a governor of that school I would not have allowed that to happen.'

It was a 'flattened-down school' which spawned some marginal bullying and teasing 'directed towards anything brighter or distinctive'. Nonetheless, the school was worth getting into and Mather's parents, more articulate and active than most, moved house when their son was five in order to get him into the right catchment area for the primary school which would prepare him for entrance: 'In some sense, therefore, the system was manipulated by keen people but it lacked a leadership core group.'

Escape from this environment seemed a priority and Mather's parents were 'powerfully, determinedly certain that I would break out of the Lancashire system into which they had been trapped.' His father, with a 'journalistic, colourful and vigorous mind', was keen that his son should be a lawyer. Thereafter it was a process of continuous emancipation with the headmaster telling his father that he should not be confined to being a solicitor in Preston: 'That was the next stage that had been pencilled in and that would have been a disaster.' It was also his headmaster who told his parents that he should not go to a local Northern university. Unlike others in his environment Mather would obey the Parkinsonian law of the flow of talent to the south.

'I was in a benevolent network with eyes being kept on me. It was difficult to go back to inertia.' The necessary ambition and dynamism which would get him off the treadmill of limited local aspirations occurred in the VIth Form. Here he benefited from that 'premature specialisation' which fashionable opinion laments as a key feature of English education. He was identified on the Oxbridge fast track and was 'more closely supervised. There was a clear attempt at a broadening of horizons so one changed gear and having got into that one never got out of it. I realised that it was as much fun to be energetic and dynamic as the other way round.'

He might well have been an 'impossibly dogmatic' VIth-former but consoles himself with the thought that: 'To say anything interesting and clear it is likely that you have to simplify and narrow out the irrelevant'.

The dogmatic lawyer's manner which Mather first developed at school 'can be too powerful unless leavened by some form of self-imposed doubt. My first employer said to me, "You must get off the dogmatic tramlines and see all sides to a question." I went home and thought, "Am I really like that?" It's a good quality to have, though, if you are running a think tank. Few of them are run by those who can see all sides to a question.'

Mather has played a part in the generation of a mass of convictions in the 1980s, a decade which reacted against the lack of convictions in the public life of the 1970s. Mather emerged from a school which lacked an aura and an atmosphere strong enough to equip its old boys with a definite ethos. This had, however, its advantages as well as its disadvantages. It meant, for example, that one did not have to suffer from the inhibitions of a Wykehamist: 'At New College it was clear that Wykehamists were much more affected by something. What it was was very mysterious – it equipped them with tortured personalities. They displayed great intelligence but also a great reluctance to draw lines and to come down firmly on one side of an argument or to risk offence to the recipient by so doing. I found them a shock to the system and I don't think it was brash provincialism on my part. It did disable great chunks of the mechanism in the area in which I eventually operated – those uncertainties caused problems.' Mather's school was representative of middle England in a post-war vacuum. It left him with a *tabula rasa* on which to inscribe his own reaction to the disabling uncertainties produced by that vacuum.

Other products of grammar schools feel indebted to them for an open-minded, enquiring education which eventually led them to careers in public life. Sir Rex Richards, who is now a Director of the Leverhulme Trust, ended up reading chemistry at St John's, Oxford, because his headmaster 'travelled to Oxford, and in the science area waylaid people and asked which was the best college for chemistry. He was told St John's, put me in for the examinations, and I got an exhibition; just enough, with a county scholarship, to make it possible for me to go to Oxford. So I owe a lot to Colyton Grammar School, then with 200 boys and girls, in Devon countryside serving several villages and little towns. I don't think they had sent anyone before to Oxford.'

Doreen Massey, Director of the Family Planning Association, found that Darwen Grammar School, Lancashire, 'opened up the possibilities' for her since she came from a working-class home. 'Two French teachers took an enormous interest in me and helped me to develop cultural and aesthetic interests. There was a gradual process of development which was in contrast to my background.'

Sir John Johnson, Chairman of the Countryside Commission, was taught at Manchester Grammar School by men 'in their thirties and early forties, back from the War, full of experience and eager to impart knowledge. They fired my zeal to learn and gave me a desire to see the world beyond Britain. The camps and treks organised by the school laid the foundations of my countryside interests.'

Two academic members of the House of Lords also owe their careers and earlier advancement to their grammar schools. Lord Harris of High Cross, Chairman of the Institute of Economic Affairs, is an old boy of Tottenham Grammar School and was distressed at its recent closure. Lord Griffiths, a former Head of the Policy Unit at Number 10 Downing Street, is now the Chairman of the School Examinations Assessment Council. Dynevor Grammar School in Swansea 'created great intellectual curiosity and I became very interested in public affairs through studying history.'

The radically discontented in public life contain both the disenchanted, middle-aged-to-elderly public-school male as well as the dissident, radical, often younger female. David Astor, the former Editor of the *Observer* who is now Chairman of the Council for the Protection of Rural England, records a fastidious detachment from Eton where he learnt three great truths: 'First, there were a lot of people waiting around to become Old Etonians. Second, Authority and Establishment must be challenged: just because it's there does not mean it is right. Third, it is necessary to spend time alone.'

Sir Geoffrey Chandler, a former Director General of the National Economic Development Office has reacted against that ethos which others in public life have found so congenial: Sherborne was 'a negative influence' since it provided 'an education and internal culture totally alien to any realities of the world in which one would ultimately live.' It therefore obscured 'any thought in an admittedly late developing child of what he could or might wish to do in life.' This was no doubt responsible for the passion he put into making Industry Year a success in 1986.

Jim Rose, Chairman of the Runnymede Trust, 'very much disliked' Rugby where he was 'certainly a failure. Oxford was a liberation in every way. Rugby had a negative effect on my development, perhaps because I was a scholar and the Arnoldian system of prefects stopped bright young scholars entering the VIth Form until they were 16. Upon entry you then automatically became a prefect whether you were suitable or not.'

Alec Dickson, the founder of Voluntary Service Overseas, feels that much of the motivation behind his work 'was a reaction against what I had experienced at Rugby. I saw it as essential to convince the young people among whom I was working that one cared for them personally and believed in their ability to help others. These were not feelings I ever experienced in my five years at Rugby. The staff withheld their friendship from us as a deliberate act of policy and the school denied us the chance to share the thinking of men who had chosen to be teachers. The aseptic atmosphere banished the display of deep feelings in human relations.'

Not one of the four chaplains made a spiritual impact on him: 'Not one sermon did I hear which moved me. The one outside speaker who riveted us was William Temple, then Bishop of Manchester and later Archbishop of Canterbury: he did not speak down to us but made us feel that our faith was of the utmost importance.

'The gymnasium was a place of dread and penitence' presided over by an ex-Royal Navy commander who was 'allergic to laughter'. Academically, 'the teaching was asphyxiatingly dull and I cannot recall any moment in a classroom when I was excited emotionally or intellectually by some new insight into poetry or history or science and least of all in Scripture. The last two terms were, intellectually and academically, a wilderness.'

John Edmonds, General Secretary of the General Municipal Boiler-makers and Allied Trades Union, educated at Christ's Hospital, is a representative of a new breed of trade unionist who has benefited from the extension of education in modern Britain. He approaches trade unionism in the spirit of a professional administrator rather than as a class warrior. Christ's Hospital, however, was for him quite as unhappy an experience as Rugby was for Dickson: 'The school was an interlude between a happy home life and adulthood. Christ's Hospital was a school which pretended to classlessness but was governed by middle-class values that were unfamiliar to me when I arrived and not particularly attractive to me when I left. I can now hold cutlery properly but try to remember that there are more important things in life than table manners – a view contradicted by my life at Christ's Hospital.'

Other trade unionists had happier times at their more modest schools. Moss Evans was encouraged as a debater by one of his teachers at Church Road Secondary Modern School, Birmingham: 'Pat Collins would ask us to state our views on a topical issue. After testing our views he split us into two groups: those for and those against. In nearly all cases I was chosen to lead a group, and was given time to present the argument and lead the debate. He taught us the rules of debate. There was strict discipline; if you committed an offence, you were instructed to fetch the cane and the punishment book.'

Lord Murray was happy at Wellington Grammar School, Shropshire, and a former headmaster whom he met later in life 'opened my eyes to the possibility of a trade union career' which would lead to the General Secretaryship of the TUC.

For Lord Scanlon, the former General Secretary of the AEUW, however, Stretford Elementary was an unhappy experience: 'Fear of unemployment and the need to make a contribution to the family income were the factors in career choice.' Sid Weighell, the former General Secretary of the NUR, found his education at Northallerton Church of England School in Yorkshire 'dull and repetitive. One of my teachers told my parents I was lazy but the basic fault of my school was the lack of stimulation, which was probably due to the surroundings together with the manner in which subjects were taught.'

Stan Mendham, Chief Executive of the Forum of Private Business, hated his school, felt an outcast and was regularly beaten up by the other boys. 'I never recovered from being evacuated to Hertfordshire at the age of four-and-a-half. When I went to Downhills Central School, Tottenham, at the age of eleven-and-a-half, I was mentally shattered, cross-eyed and I stuttered terribly. I was also very slight in stature and suffered from having a very bright brother who had gone through the school five years before me and who had been brilliant.

'I came bottom of the whole school in spelling tests every year. We were the first group to take the new GCE examinations. I failed every one dismally at the age of fifteen-and-a-half.

'It was only after I signed on for the RAF that they discovered that I was the brightest in the aptitude tests and they offered to sponsor me through Cambridge University.'

This adverse school experience, he says, and the subsequent realisation that he had after all been quite bright, turned him into a campaigner. He now leads the fight for small businesses against exorbitant bankers and late payers of debts. His brother, who has since died, never really made a success of his career.

With Diana Warwick, General Secretary of the Association of University Teachers, we return to the 1990s' world of the administrative trade-union official who could as easily, and more probably, be found sitting in the Treasury as on a picket line. As a head of house in St Joseph's College, Bradford, she 'became involved in organising a citywide meeting of senior pupils to discuss common concerns: an early indication perhaps of an interest in collectivisation.' She goes on, 'It was always acknowledged that I should go to university and have a career but I had no clear career path in mind when I left school, except an unfocused determination to do well and "prove myself".'

Radical women in public life represent a period in British history, the post-1960s, when radicals gave up hope of large-scale institutional reform of British society. Instead, they have directed their energies towards a more politicised view of voluntary activity and pressure groups and a more sceptical view of their schooling than any other group of individuals encountered in public life.

For example, Sue Slipman, Director of the National Council for One-Parent Families, was expelled from Stockwell Manor Comprehensive: 'It gave me a nose for trouble and a commitment to bending rules' as well as making her aware of 'the need to work positively to open up opportunities for disadvantaged people.'

Erin Pizzey thought the Mother Superior at Leweston Manor Convent, Sherborne, was 'such a bitch that I became an anarchist at a very early age. It gave me an abiding dislike of the whole English establishment.' Mother Superior's method was 'to break the spirits of all the girls so that they became Mother Eleanor acolytes. I chose not to co-operate in this. She had an iron control over absolutely everyone but I chose not to co-operate in this control and I opposed her at every stage. I attached myself to an extremely wealthy girl whom I knew they wouldn't dare to expel and when I was 11 or 12 I used to climb out on the roof with this girl and we would stay there until they had to get the firemen to get us down.'

Pizzey was at boarding school because her parents were living abroad. Actresses Joanna Lumley, Nicola Pagett and Jenny Agutter are similarly strong-minded and successful women who have emerged from the crucible of a boarding-school education as the daughters of expatriates. As Pizzey notes: 'In those days parents abroad might not see their children for years at a time. I used to go to a holiday home for public-school children who couldn't go home because their parents were abroad. The reason I was brave enough to be such an anarchist is that Mother Eleanor and I were stuck with each other. In 1949 my parents were both under house arrest during a Communist uprising so there was simply nowhere to expel me to!'

One crucial event led her towards her eventual career as the founder of the first Battered Wives Shelter. 'A girl told me she had been raped by her father. The nuns called the parents in and expelled the girl. The terrible outrage was that nobody in authority believed this girl. The nuns scarred both me and the girl for life.'

Dianne Hayter, Chair of Alcohol Concern, 'would never set foot in Penrhos College again. I have nothing but distaste and dissatisfaction for my school.' Professor Ruth Lister, a former Director of the Child Poverty Action Group, defied her school, Moreton Hall, Shropshire, when she decided to read sociology at the University of Essex. Jane Goodsir, Director of Release, the drugs rehabilitation charity, reacted against Christ's Hospital at that time: 'Many injustices and instances of inhumane behaviour occurred.' She was also uncomfortable with the hothouse atmosphere of Oxford High School for Girls: 'There was a drugs raid at the school: I was not involved but it did seem very unjust and I suppose that influenced me.' At both schools, 'you really had to conform, or face quite a bit of injustice and labelling. That has influenced me and I am concerned about sticking up for people who don't really conform to the rules.'

Jane Tewson, who founded the charity Comic Relief, was hindered in her development at Headington School with its endless detentions. She then went to Lord Williams' Comprehensive, Thame, and 'had fantastic involvement with the local community – which I'm sure led me into my current job.'

Two further radical voices have issued from the convent and left their mark on contemporary public life. Lady Helen Brook, founder of the Brook Advisory Centre for birth control, developed 'my natural independence of outlook and imagination despite the religious discipline, and contrary to the intentions' of her convent school, St Leonards Mayfield in Sussex, 'I was always a bit of a rebel. I could never see any point in being a martyr and I certainly believed that what happened in this life was very important. It all led me to the realisation that women had to be allowed to make their lives more tolerable by being able to space their children. Not all the nuns at school would have been all that horrified at what I went on to do.'

Julie Kaufmann, Press Officer to Children in Need, discovered that the Ursuline Convent, Wimbledon, offered no careers advice except in teaching, typing and taking the veil: 'Role models were restricted to Mary, Mother of God, or to the Saints. "Be good, sweet child, and let who will be clever" was embossed in gold on my pencil case. So I became a nurse rather than a doctor, having learned to cultivate modesty and to stifle ambition – for the time being at least.'

Sheila Kitzinger, the writer who specialises in educating women about childbirth, was told by her headmistress at Bishop Fox's Girls' School, Taunton, that she would never get into Oxford 'because no-one from that school ever went there: I made up my mind that I would go to Oxford.'

She loathed 'the petty rules, the exercise of autocratic authority, the systematic destruction of girls' vitality and inner confidence – compared with the freedom and political and social debate that I experienced at home. This led me to want to find out about human behaviour, the social pressures on individuals and groups to conform, the causes of violence and why human beings behave as they do. This led me to social anthropology.

'Miss Lloyd nurtured my love of writing but she also challenged my values and beliefs. I turned up at school wearing a pacifist badge. Miss Lloyd took me for a brief walk round the hockey field, asked me to explain what I believed and finally announced, "We must clip your wings, Sheila. We must clip your wings." I was never allowed to announce any political beliefs again at school. I felt a sense of burning injustice.'

The experience was also, however, a creative one and 'strangely empowering since it fuelled anger and determination not to be crushed. I was determined that institutions like this school should never crush the things I believed in most passionately.'

Early choices for figures in public life are often incidental to their final careers. Sometimes this may be because their fame is the result of a decisive shift of attitudes both in themselves and in the world at large.

Sir Colin Buchanan, the urban planner, was educated at Berkhamsted under 'a brutal régime' and left the school at 16 'owing to family financial difficulties'. He has discovered that public consciousnesss has caught up with his choice of a profession and made a public figure out of him.

Others, however, are more likely to have courted publicity actively, bowed to destiny and found that destiny has repaid them the compliment. Their careers have not been straightforward and they are frequently pursuing second careers. Dr John Beishon, for example, was educated as a scientist at Harrow County Boys' School but uses other gifts as Director of the Consumers' Association.

Schools' influence on these people can be seen to have been a matter of inculcating mentalities, attitudes, the development of social concern and a sense of the public weal. The effect of educational experiences on such beliefs may be more powerful and profound than is the case with one's choice of livelihood. In no other chapter in this book has the ethical code of school, whether assimilated or rejected, been of such importance. The result has been the creation of distinctive personalities whose activities and concerns have flowed from their whole being. As Lord Longford explains: 'When people ask me why I do what I do I can't explain it. I feel rather like one of the offenders I visit in gaol when I ask them, "Why did you do it?"'

HRH the Prince of Wales was also born to do what he has to do. He has an ambiguous relationship with his Gordonstoun schooldays but his public pronouncements are inescapably marked by the holistic, neo-Christian, communal moralism which was Kurt Hahn's legacy to the school.

Dr Michael Shea, former Press Secretary to HM the Queen and now Director of Public Affairs at Hanson plc, had only two terms under Hahn as headmaster when he was a boy at Gordonstoun. 'I had come from a state school on a scholarship and was therefore aware of how eccentric a place it was. One master employed by Hahn to teach geography, was arrested by the police in the middle of a class because he was a complete impostor. He was one of the most popular masters there.

'My parents sent me to Gordonstoun because they were impressed by Gordonstounians' ability to survive as individuals and by the absence of packaging. My contemporaries were very diverse. There were Sikhs and Ethiopians, Sudanese as well as some Germans whose parents had died at the hands of the Nazis.' Living conditions lived up to the famous Spartan reputation: 'at the beginning of the spring term once I woke up with snow on the pillow. It was probably hoar frost but it seemed to be snow!'

The school was a strongly ethical place. 'We ran a fire service as well as coastguard service. Once we were called out as volunteers when an elderly monk disappeared. You grow up when you discover a dead body in the undergrowth when you are 16.'

There was a system of trust to be observed in punishment. 'Some forms of punishment consisted of being told to walk by oneself and the boys were trusted to observe that punishment themselves. People did rubbish the system but they tended to be the throw-outs from other schools.'

Shea was 'at the bottom of the physical level' but he learned about self-reliance at Gordonstoun. 'National Service was dead easy compared to school.'

The great disadvantage was the low academic standards at Gordonstoun, which meant that Shea had to go to a crammer after he left school in order to gain entry to Edinburgh University. 'The thought of doing well academically was not part of my world as a boy at Gordonstoun. That, however, did not stop many of us from doing well academically later on.'

Versatility has been a feature of Shea's character as a diplomat, an author, a servant of the Crown, a businessman and now as a Visiting Professor at Strathclyde University. 'I have always had two or three careers and in the new world of employment that is the kind of adaptability you need.'

The versatility is part of the Hahnian ethic and, Shea points out, makes the school an especially suitable training ground for members of the Royal Family who often, *faute de mieux*, have to be generalists: 'The Duke of Edinburgh has a very brilliant mind but, as he says himself, he has been forced to butterfly around, being Colonel-in-Chief one minute, and opening a university the next. He's never been allowed to get on to one subject. For both Prince Charles and the Duke, pursuing their own ideas all over the place is an inevitable part of the role forced upon them by society. It is an unfortunate fact that the Royal Family are obliged to be generalists. In that respect, however, a more traditional school would not have been as useful to them as Gordonstoun.

'Gordonstoun has also democratised the Royal Family since it is neither snobbish nor élitist as a school. It is a very casual place. It was like that when I was a boy there and it is like that now.

'Prince Charles, although not very excited by the place, also says there is a lot of mythology about his hating Gordonstoun. I think it will be a pity if his sons go to Eton and into the Etonian mould. I don't think that is helpful to the monarchy.'

The Prince of Wales's reservations about his old school do not stop his views from having a distinctly Hahnian tinge to them. As Shea points out, Laurens van der Post, the Prince's most influential adviser, has much in common with Hahn's views. 'I think', says Shea, 'that it was very good for the Royal Family to go to Gordonstoun because to critics it was eccentric and to aficionados it was mind-forming.'

Gordonstoun is unusual among British schools since it operates under the banner of an educational ideology, albeit one that stresses a diffuse, ecumenical religion and an unstratified approach. In Shea's opinion, 'The ideology worked for many boys.'

He himself was not a gregarious boy but was encouraged by his English master to write creatively at school. Thoughts of what he would do with his future in a career sense were, however, far removed.

'None of us ever thought of going into business when we left school. I had a friend who was, inevitably, going to go into his family's timber business but I was never sure what people's parents did – or I was never curious about that. The ethos was professional and the feeling was that you would be of service.'

One form of service that came Shea's way had less of a Gordonstoun link than appeared at first sight: 'When I was appointed to the Palace as Press Secretary many said it was because of Gordonstoun. I knew the Prince of Wales slightly because I had been around the States with him. I went to Windsor for lunch after my appointment and the Prince called out across the room, "At last we'll outnumber the Old Etonians here!" The Queen, who had done the interviewing, said, "Were you at Gordonstoun?" She was very upset because she had a photostat of my CV and the bottom line of one of the pages had been cut off so the fact that I had been to Gordonstoun was missing. She did not actually know – so there was no question of her having appointed me on that basis.'

Gordonstoun, although remote, had to look outwards; it was part of its philosophy and besides, its Royal connections forced that role upon it. That made it, in Shea's view, different from other Scottish boarding schools. 'They have always been traditional and inward-looking; they have not advanced Scotland in the way they should have done. Loretto, Glenalmond and Fettes have been tight little backwaters producing imitation Englishmen. Fettes was the Eton of Scotland in my day but its products were going into a very small network of lawyers, financial advisers and so on. It is a pity that so many of Scotland's best people have had to go South and that Scotland's boarding schools have not matched up to her day schools. Scottishness at Gordonstoun was a positive, outward-looking thing.'

This lack of the cloistered mentality may explain why, in Shea's view, the old-boy reunions are such low-key affairs. It is not a school for the old school tie.

Tempora mutantur et nos mutamur. Public figures need to be able to read the signs of the times and to respond to them. As subjects become citizens and acquire charters to enforce their rights, as public bodies become more accountable and public services more diverse as well as privatised, it is likely that the activities of the individuals described in this chapter will become increasingly important. Lady Bountiful and, more importantly, her radical daughter, will be with us for a while yet.

12 Religion

Our survey covers writers on religious affairs as well as prominent clergy. Nearly two-thirds of them attended independent schools. One quarter attended state grammar schools. Only 12 per cent of the sample said they were unhappy at school, making this category one of the happiest. School influenced clergymen more than any other category in this book except Education: 71 per cent said they were influenced by school in their choice of career.

The Anglican Establishment is represented by Eton, Rugby, Lancing and King's, Canterbury. Merchant Taylors', with four representatives including two former Archbishops of Canterbury – Lord Coggan from its school at Northwood and Lord Runcie from its school at Crosby – is the star among independent day schools. Lord Runcie told us: 'An OTC inspection was coming at Merchant Taylors', Crosby. The inspecting officer asked me what I wanted to be. I was stuck for a reply and blurted out, "The Church!" I hadn't thought much about it before.'

The Roman Catholic Establishment is represented by Downside, Ampleforth, Stonyhurst and Beaumont. There are now more Roman Catholics than there are practising Anglicans in Britain and our survey has an 18 per cent RC representation.

This chapter focuses on the different school influences of the Roman Catholic and Anglican clergy and the intellectual influences on rabbis and evangelicals which led them to their teaching vocations.

A small number of our correspondents were educated at seminaries. In their day some resembled a cross between an Offenbach opera and Stephen Daedalus's school in Joyce's *Portrait of the Artist*. Francis Walmsley, Roman Catholic Bishop of the Forces, is critical of the way in which St Joseph's, Tunbridge Wells, 'hindered my normal development and left me innocent and unaware of much that I should have known and experienced.'

Richard Holloway, the Anglican Bishop of Edinburgh, decided at the age of 14 that 'I had a vocation to the ministry and I was sent to a monastic institution called Kelham in Nottinghamshire where the Society of the Sacred Mission took about thirty boys from poor backgrounds and educated them. The thing that influenced me most about Kelham was the general ethos. It was an all male monastic community with no servants, so that it was completely self-sufficient. This meant that in addition to one's studies and the usual sports, one spent a lot of time scrubbing and polishing floors, peeling potatoes and mucking out pigsties.

'The other thing that greatly influenced me was the high level of eccentricity found in many of the fathers and brothers who were members of the community and actually taught us. I don't think even one of them was a qualified teacher, so their methods were wildly unprofessional and there was a high failure rate among the students. But those of us who survived developed a peculiarly Freudian and deeply subconscious relationship with the place. This was probably best expressed in a little verse crafted by one of the brothers. The chapel at Kelham had a large dome and we spent a great deal of our lives beneath it. The verse went:

> We give our lives, we give our all
> Beneath this great big tennis ball.'

An emphasis on order, authority and obedience has characterised many of our Roman Catholic contributors. Father John Coventry, now a distinguished Jesuit himself, tried to escape from the Jesuits at Stonyhurst by declaring that he wished to be a secular and not a religious priest. The headmaster 'replied that God had given me some brains and the Jesuits would give me a good education whereas the bishops wouldn't. I then came quietly.'

Cardinal Basil Hume leads the Roman Catholic witnesses to the communal power of Christianity when he remembers 'the monastic community' at Ampleforth, the school where he was a boy, teacher, housemaster and Abbot. He also pays tribute to 'the first-class teachers'. Dom Aidan Bellenger, Headmaster of Downside, writes of the 'creation of a sense of purpose and vision' at Finchley Catholic Grammar School, where he saw, 'the advantages of a Catholic community'.

The Provincial of the Dominicans, Timothy Radcliffe, thinks that Downside introduced him 'to a large multi-coloured world'. He was shown 'that one should never simply accept the conventional nature of reality. Many of the monks communicated a calm benevolence towards all human folly and a fundamental optimism about human beings.'

While at Downside, he was moved by 'an experience of beauty, early in the morning, in the Abbey Church. It still affects me.'

The Roman Catholic Bishop Emeritus of Manchester Grammar, Leeds, the Right Reverend Gordon Wheeler, still remembers vividly a school trip to Paris where on Easter Day 1926 he attended High Mass in Notre Dame Cathedral.

Dom Henry Wansborough, who is now Master of St Benet's Hall, Oxford, was picking a first rugby XV one evening at Ampleforth with the coach, Father Basil, now Cardinal, Hume:
'He had to interrupt to go to compline in the monastery. I and one other boy went along too, and sat in the dark church while the monks sang in the lighted choir. As the Abbot went round at the end blessing the monks I really appreciated that it was a genuine family dedicated to an important purpose.'

Dom Philip Jebb is an extreme instance of the institutional man as a boy, a monk, a master and then, until recently the Head Master at Downside. His vocation was not always clear: 'I could not make up my mind between careers as a boat-builder, an archaeologist or an astronomer.'
But he admits, 'I wanted to find out what went on in the monastery. And after holding the monks in cheerful, friendly and gentle contempt during my school career, I came to realise at the end of my time as a pupil that they did have a sense of purpose and a moral stability lacking to most others I knew outside my family. I did not expect to stay permanently as a monk but after six months I found I wanted to.'
The monastic vow of obedience determined his choice of career: 'As a monk I was sent under obedience to get a degree at Cambridge and then taught in the school. I was simply told to do the various jobs, such as housemaster, deputy head, headmaster – and while I have been happy enough doing such work, I would never have *chosen* to do it.'

Dr Giles Mercer, the first lay headmaster of Stonyhurst, found the beginnings of his own vocation as a boy at Austin Friars, Carlisle. It was a 'small Catholic provincial boarding school where there was an all-pervasive sense of belonging to a community based upon fundamentally shared assumptions. I imbibed, half-consciously or unconsciously, the ideal of teaching as a vocation not merely as a job.'
Mercer also discovered the cultural power of Christianity at his school. The Irish priests were 'the most educated people I have come across. They showed me an Irish world that looked at Britain in a different

way and a Church that was supranational. I remember feeling that I was being introduced to a great cultural tradition. When I went up to Cambridge, to my astonishment, I found myself rather better educated than many from "great public schools".'

The Roman Catholic Archbishop of Cardiff, the Most Reverend John Ward, was profoundly influenced by the 'daily rhythm of liturgy and religious education' at Prior Park, Bath. It was wartime and he remembers nights spent in air-raid shelters and the school itself being bombed. There was of course 'concern for fathers and other family at the Front, but the Christian Brothers managed to convey a stability in their lives. They tried to make sense at a time of uncertainty and confusion. They were great men and fostered vocations – for marriage, priesthood or religious life. I can't recall any single big event that influenced me: daily life was an event.'

A dissenting note in this litany of indebtedness is struck by Father Michael Hollings. Now a parish priest in Bayswater, he was for many years the Catholic Chaplain at Oxford University. At the Jesuit-run Beaumont College, he says, 'I learnt the hard way to be separated from home in an alien society which I resented.'

Hollings disliked school and 'developed a love/hate relationship with religion.' His life was changed by a boyhood illness: 'I developed a heart weakness and had some time off school and at home. We lived near Oxford and I had a temporary tutor in North Oxford so got to know something of tutoring and the Oxford system.' When war broke out, he was due to return to school. 'But I persuaded my mother to let me try to get into Oxford instead: the combination of sickness, dislike of school and attraction to Oxford changed the course of my life.'

Roman Catholics have preserved a strong sense of identity and a deep interest in denominational education despite Vatican II and its traumas. Meanwhile, some Anglican clergy have been afflicted by a *crise de foi sociale* as a result of their schooling. David Sheppard, the Bishop of Liverpool, for example, told us that at Sherborne School he reacted against 'the whole set of values and assumptions with comparatively little questioning of staff and boys, and the limited social class from which we all came.'

R.M.C. Jeffery, the Dean of Worcester, also kicks against the traces: 'I was only a mediocre person in a school, St Paul's, which was really only interested in high-fliers. Academic matters only came alive for me at university and the school did nothing to help me get there. My experience has led me to be strongly opposed to all forms of private education.'

Three Etonians were aware of the difficulty of reconciling a privileged education with a social conscience. Simon Barrington-Ward, Bishop of Coventry, loves great schools 'too much to want to lose them and yet Eton helped me to want a different kind of society and education for everyone, less divisive and more comprehensive. Strangely enough I was encouraged in learning to have a critical view of our society there and free to debate and examine radically all of my assumptions. I was concerned to break free from the very "Establishment" of which I was inexorably being made a part by being there. I still feel this inherent contradiction in my whole being.'

Ronald Bowlby, formerly Bishop of Southwark, 'was at Eton during the War when it was being opened up to new influences in a number of ways. The Christian faith was clearly important in the lives of several teachers whom I admired and one in particular, a temporary wartime member of staff rather different from most of the others, put the idea of ordination into my mind.'

Simon Phipps, formerly Bishop of Lincoln, is another Etonian who found that the school 'fostered and developed a general sense of social responsibility to do something useful for one's fellow-men, not just "make money".'

Hugh Montefiore, a former Bishop of Birmingham and now Assistant Bishop of Southwark, was converted to Christianity from the Judaism of his background as a result of having a visionary experience in Rugby School chapel. 'After my conversion the school found me so religious that I was too hot to handle and I was prepared for confirmation by the Rector of Rugby rather than by the chaplain, whom I was not close to.'

Conversion alienated Montefiore from orthodox public-school religion. Yet in other respects he remains a characteristic example of the English public-schoolboy as bishop. Membership of the First XV coexists with guilt about privilege. Classical scholarship marches hand in hand with uncertainty about the continued role of the Established Church.

Montefiore was influenced by Roger Roberts in the classroom. A future headmaster of Blundell's School, from which post he was sacked, and Editor of the *Church Times*, Roberts 'was pleasantly radical and gave us intellectual curiosity. He made us unfrightened to ask questions.' Roberts also influenced Patrick Rodger, former Bishop of Oxford, and helped him make his decision to become a priest.

'When a bloated bishop preached a sermon one Sunday,' Montefiore remembers, 'Roberts deflated the arguments the following day and detected flaws in them. This impressed us as boys. He saw education as something more than just vocational.'

Other masters, by their value and style, showed that tradition was important. They 'induced enthusiasm' and introduced Montefiore to the power and the appeal of the institution.

'Some saw Hugh Lyon, the headmaster, as a silly little man after the grandeur of his predecessor, Vaughan.' Montefiore, however, co-operated gladly with his liberal Christian headmaster. Lyon and other masters awakened social concern among the boys by taking them on tours of the unemployed areas during the Depression of the 1930s. 'We needed to have our eyes opened because we did not know how others lived. International awareness was fostered by visits to the League of Nations Union in Geneva.'

Rugby might have been a tough place for Montefiore with school lessons taking place before breakfast during the summer months. None the less it was also a time of awakening for him. 'I was five years younger than my brothers and I was released at school. I disliked nothing: even fagging was quite fun with boys breaking their legs as they ran down the stairs in School House. It all initiated me into the idea of community. The school taught me to work hard and I have been a workaholic ever since I read in one half term report that I was "careless and slapdash".'

The atmosphere of the school was one of 'unquestioning conservatism' and there were no party politics in Montefiore's schooldays. 'Unemployment would be raised in a non-party-political way. But I was moderately aware of public affairs and I remember when we were reading Demosthenes in the class, Roberts would point out the parallels between Philip of Macedon and the dictators of the thirties.'

Sometimes the outside world would come to the school: 'Lyon would invite boys to breakfast so that they could meet his guests such as Harold Nicolson and William Temple, later Archbishop of Canterbury, who was then Chairman of the Governors. Temple would impress by the depth of his personality and his cheerfulness, qualities which were on view during his amazing speeches on Speech Day.'

Like Alec Dickson [see Chapter Eleven] Montefiore found Temple a bright light in the world of Rugby religion which seemed 'stiff, formal and cold. My Christian friends were more important to me than the ethics of public-school religion. Christianity was a private relationship with God and I did not discuss it a great deal. I was impressed by individual Christians who came to speak at the school. Confirmation in those days was the passing-out parade of the Church of England; it was Christianity as duty rather than as religion. Christianity was then something taken for granted; it is now more participatory and the Church of England is warmer and in better heart.'

A more unhappy consequence of this development, in Montefiore's view, is that the Church of England has now been marginalised in the national culture: 'it is now more like a club.' This is perhaps an inevitable consequence of the fact that we are now 'less disposed to think of our culture as naturally Christian. Public-school assumptions about the inevitable predominance of Western Christian culture have faded.' For Montefiore Archbishop Carey is a representative figure since he has emerged from a milieu in which Christianity is neither natural nor inevitable.

Another leading Southwark churchman to be influenced by the power of personality while at school is the Very Reverend David Edwards, the Provost of Southwark, who recalled for us the appeal of one of the century's most colourful headmasters at King's School, Canterbury.

'I remember meeting Fred Shirley for the first time as a fag in my first year at King's. The school had been evacuated to a hotel on the Cornish cliffs and I was being prepared for confirmation at the time. My job was to wake my House and I was therefore reading the Bible early one morning while sitting near the clock on the landing of the hotel. Fred came along to take the early service, saw me there and took an interest in me from then on.'

'I realised at an early stage that he was not a saint. He enjoyed talking to selected boys and gossiping about other boys and masters. He lent me books and encouraged me as a historian. When I was in the Army on National Service he wrote me letters once a fortnight in his own hand and he was very proud of me when I became a Fellow of All Souls. A number of us were treated as favourites, much to the fury of masters who felt they were being undermined and gossiped about. He took those boys more seriously than staff. He was very interested in success and was the classic case of a boy who had had a struggle. He was the son of a carpenter in Oxford and had gone to St Edmund Hall, then a very cheap college. He was still heavily in debt when he left Oxford for things like bread and butter.'

Shirley had been a very successful headmaster of Worksop College. Under his headmastership the school's finances and numbers had improved and he was appointed to King's, Canterbury in order to repeat that success at a time when the school faced bankruptcy.

'I was very aware as a boy that these were extraordinary times in the history of the school. Shirley was very proud of what he was doing at King's and he communicated to the boys and partly to the staff a Victorian belief in hard work that was rather Thatcherite. Shirley had risen from nothing to be Canon of Canterbury and it was as if he was saying, "You can do likewise."

'King's is now a more prosperous and a less dramatic school than it was in those days. Children there now are more comfortably off and they would probably see Shirley as vulgar, which, in a sense, he was. He had a competitive edge to him and he stood apart from the consensual public-school ethic. Indeed, he was suspended from membership of the Head Masters' Conference after he had persuaded Worksop boys and masters to follow him to King's, Canterbury. That was totally against the code. He was pre-eminently "not one of us". But he took a delight in playing members of the HMC at their own game and beating them. He was really laughing at them all the time. Clergymen especially disapproved of him. He was capable of cutting corners in money matters and was a kind of Maxwell. There was a camp quality to King's under Shirley and there was a lot of theatricality on the cheap. School at times was like an *opera buffa*.'

One of the features of King's under Shirley was that 'scholars were not persecuted. I lived my own life. I did not have to do games and there were a number of other boys like that.'

More importantly, however, Shirley persuaded Edwards that academic success was important. There was no-one else on the staff to switch him on and 'I never did an hour's science though I pontificate like the next man about the relationship between science and religion. I had to choose between science, Greek and German for school certificate and followed Fred's advice when he said: "Gentlemen do Greek."'

The relationship was not entirely one-sided. Shirley had done a thesis on Hooker for a London PhD while he was at Worksop. When he arrived at Canterbury he decided that he wanted to be an Oxford DD and he revamped his old work with some new material. He got Edwards to comment on the drafts and eventually got the Oxford degree.

Edwards was being shaped by Shirley as a historian and as a churchman. He had been brought up in Egypt, and 'because I grew up outside the English historical scene it interested me from afar. Moreover, because of Fred's influence I became interested as a historian in the question of leadership. When I wrote a book on leaders of the Church of England reviewers said I was too interested in the top people: I needed to do more sociology. But intellectual and spiritual leadership is what has interested me as a writer and a churchman.'

As a schoolboy, Edwards liked living within a settled framework and especially the framework of the cathedral which the school adjoined. He saw Canterbury for the first time at the funeral of William Temple, a dramatic occasion which left an indelible impression.

He decided while at King's that he would definitely be ordained. It was a decision that he stuck to although it astonished people in the Army and at All Souls where he was the first Fellow to be ordained since Alington in 1911. Many were disappointed at All Souls and thought that they had wasted a Fellowship on him. 'But the Warden, John Sparrow, a wistful Wykehamical non-believer, was kind to me and specialised in young men who were confused.' Shirley might have been a Disraelian bounder but his magic had woven a powerful spell around his young protégé.

The future Bishop of Winchester, John Taylor, was grateful for the influence of a few masters who gave him 'a strong feeling for music and literature and a certain style of thought and relationship which determined the way I have tried to do things rather than the choice of things to do. The school [St Lawrence's, Ramsgate] strengthened and clarified my somewhat romantic valuation of the missionary vocation.'

Monkton Combe, also like St Lawrence's 'an evangelical foundation,' made Graham Leonard, the future Bishop of London, 'question the assumption that I should be ordained. As a result I went to Oxford to read natural science rather than to Cambridge to read classics as planned.'

Stephen Sykes, the Bishop of Ely, remembers his relief when he discovered at the same school that the Book of Jonah 'was intended as a novel. It came as a profound relief to discover that I need not swallow the whale!'

At the Belfast Royal Academical Institution and the Methodist College, Belfast, Archbishop Robert Eames, Primate of All Ireland, imbibed 'the general atmosphere of responsibility for people which gave me an early desire to serve the community.'

The Most Reverend George Noakes, until recently Archbishop of Wales, recalls the 'close family spirit' of Tregaron Secondary School 'where pupils and staff were most supportive of each other'.

Family as well as scholarship influenced Basil Mitchell, former Professor of the Philosophy of Christian Religion at Oxford. In the 1930s, at King Edward VI, Southampton, Mitchell was grateful for the stimulating VIth Form, for the headmaster who persuaded him to learn Greek and for the three or four teachers who 'talked with me as an equal out of hours'.

But it was his mother's illness that most affected him: 'My mother was bedridden and this meant that my own and my sister's friends met in her room and argued constantly. The room became a focus for a lively group of contemporaries.'

However, Professor Dennis Nineham, a former Warden of Keble College, Oxford, and Regius Professor of Divinity at Cambridge, can see in retrospect that he 'was fairly grossly bullied and repressed by a staff-parent combination' at the same school:

'I was an only child and I had this extremely strong-minded – no, *fantastically* strong-minded – mother who was determined that I should do well academically. I was taught by the Senior Master who also had a very strong personality indeed. He was an expert at getting good results out of boys and an astonishing number of his pupils ended up as Fellows of Oxford and Cambridge colleges. I strongly suspect that this master and my mother were in cahoots about me. Neither of them had any compassion for children or any idea of how children felt.

'Several of us in my year were thinking of taking holy orders so we formed a sort of mutual encouragement society. We were persuaded of this in about the fifth year but it was nothing really to do with school. It wasn't as uncommon then as it might be now for boys to think of going into the Church. All these boys got their motivation from several different local churches.

'On the other hand, three of us were taught by this very powerful Senior Master who was positively anti-religion and I suppose you could say that he stiffened our resolve to take holy orders.

'He was a very strange man. He had been knocked about a lot in the Great War and he offered us a mixture of dismissive Freudianism and Marxism – an odd combination. But he was a good scholar and in fairness he always said, "Well, if that's what you really think, you must do what you feel is right."

'However, the school was a good old grammar school founded in 1553 and it was extremely good at getting boys into Oxford and

Cambridge – it had been doing it for 400 years. The trouble was that it did rather regard boys as Oxbridge fodder and to a certain extent we were victims of the school's thinking.'

Other Anglican Establishment liberals, however, owe a lot to their schools. For Stanley Booth-Clibborn, the Bishop of Manchester: 'The Christian life of Highgate School was undoubtedly a major influence in my life, and in my eventual decision to seek ordination.'

David Jenkins, the Bishop of Durham, was 'greatly influenced by an agnostic, but deeply socially concerned, master at St Dunstan's, Catford.' Jenkins decided to be a priest at the age of 15 but before that he had been inspired by a powerful sermon from a preacher who came and talked to the school after visiting China. Jenkins went to bed that night and said a prayer because he felt he was converted. He remembers wondering if this feeling might be like a New Year's resolution that might wear off.

At Stamford School, Philip Goodrich, the Bishop of Worcester, discovered the roots of his dislike of 'Christian sectarianism and fundamentalism. Commitment to Christ should be there but it should not exclude others or distance them.' Goodrich's headmaster, John Duncan Day, was 'almost a clerical Field Marshal Montgomery'. The Second World War covered all his time at Stamford 'and had its poignant yet exhilarating moments. It put a premium sometimes on seriousness.'

Bishop Peter Ball, the Bishop of Lewes, pays tribute to 'the whole atmosphere and style' of his school, Lancing College. His twin brother, Bishop Michael Ball, who is now the Bishop of Truro, was only ordained in 1971. Michael was 'aware of the religious life' at Lancing where 'worship was beautifully done. I was surrounded by beautiful Catholicism but there was nothing preciously high-church about it. There was a sense of mystery and of beauty and in a strange way one was caught up in the feeling of worship. It was a passive involvement. It was community rather than individual fulfilment that was emphasised. Perhaps public schools in those days over-emphasised the community-minded but now personal fulfilment has taken over. At Lancing in my time the balance was about right. There was little individual fagging at school and we swept the communal rooms not the individual ones in the houses. The individual was the lesser thing.

'There was fear in the school, as there was in society as a whole then: authority had an influence upon you and could terrorise you. Nobody enjoys fear. I disliked the Corps and nobody much liked it. There was the fear there of people shouting at you. But although there was physical harshness at Lancing there was little physical punishment. The headmaster was a gentle man and there was a subconscious feeling at Lancing that you were part of a corporation – the Woodard Corporation – which was bigger than the school itself.

'The public schools have stood for service to others; that is part of their charter. That element of service has doubtless influenced the bench of bishops. I am myself a 24-hour-a-day man, a duty man. That makes you paranoid about work and gives you a guilt complex.'

Lancing gave Bishop Ball a scientific training as well as a historical understanding. When at Cambridge he read both natural sciences and history. 'I liked maths and because I have a retentive memory I found that I could do science, which in those days involved a lot of rote learning. I found it fascinating when you could see a pattern emerging. My education was enjoyable and a useful cocktail: as a priest I found that ability to analyse and to relate to other kinds of thinking very useful.

'I was not a political animal at school but we did debate social questions endlessly. I was more influenced, for example, by the question of whether British colonialism was right and by the question of the abolition of capital punishment than I was by politics.'

Ball's thoughts about contemporary Christian education reveal some classic Anglican dilemmas. 'I am not sure that I want the Church to influence state education directly. We need Christian teachers and not Christian schools and the Church has to see a divine angle in all subjects. The question is not so much "Do we teach Divinity?" as "Do we teach other subjects with a God-ness in them?"'

This means that opting-out should not be a policy of church schools: 'The Church of England is the servant of the nation and I do not want a ghetto approach with a wall around our Christian faith. We should not turn our gifts into possessiveness. I can't support that.'

Scholarship rather than public affairs concerned Lord Coggan as a schoolboy. He was concentrating on getting to Cambridge: 'The happiest day of my life was the day I got the telegram telling me that I had won an exhibition to St John's College, Cambridge. I could feel wings growing.'

When the former Archbishop of Canterbury was a boy at Merchant Taylors' School, it was the only school in the country with a Hebrew class. 'At the age of 16 I switched from the modern side – from doing

German and French – to doing classics and Hebrew. Languages were always my cup of tea. I loved them. Words have always been a delight and I liked accuracy in thought and the good discipline involved in the mastery of grammar and syntax.'

Coggan as a boy, was, 'naturally shy' and found mixing difficult. He was solitary, introspective and asthmatic. The fact that he could not play games added to his shyness. By the time he was 15, however, he knew that he had to be ordained since he had seen his local parson at work in a roughish area of London. His mother was quietly devout and was happy that this was the direction her son's life was taking. His father, a businessman, was less approving since he had hoped that his son would follow him into the City. 'But he was very silent on these things.'

The arrival of a new headmaster, Spencer Leeson, changed Coggan's life. 'He was an invigorator and I opened up because of the influence of his personality on me. Leeson stopped the teaching of Hebrew but in other respects his influence was a beneficial one. Many teachers were old and past it; Leeson brought new life with a range of extracurricular activities. He moved the school from its site in the centre of London to Northwood and it became more middle-class because of its catchment area when it moved out of central London.'

John Lang, the Dean of Lichfield, and Canon Bryan Green, of Birmingham Cathedral, were also influenced intellectually in their Christianity by Merchant Taylors'. For Lang, 'Merchant Taylors' was especially important to me because I came from an unhappy, though stable, home.' For Lord Blanch, former Archbishop of York, Alleyn's School, Dulwich, 'provided a classical education which was to prove invaluable in my later studies for the ministry.'

Douglas Feaver, the former Bishop of Peterborough, learnt at Bristol Grammar School how to work rapidly and perhaps secretly, 'a habit I have never entirely lost. It was tacitly and generally assumed that work was the purpose of being there and that nothing was beyond reason and reach.'

Lady Oppenheimer, the moral theologian, felt that Cheltenham Ladies' College gave her 'a notion of excellence as something worth struggling for. I think I owe to the College a concept of scholarship as truly important as a training in the craft of putting words together. The College found out what aptitudes people had and set them on the way towards fulfilling them.'

Social conscience drew Ronald Preston, Professor of Theology at Manchester, to economics at Borden Grammar School, Kent, because he wanted 'to understand the economic mess' from 1919 onwards.

Bill Westwood, the Bishop of Peterborough, was brought up as 'a migrant English boy in the North Wales of the 1940s. The choice of vocation was easier within a community where such choices were honoured.' At Grove Park Grammar School, Wrexham, 'there was an interest in ideas, talk, reading, music and radio as well as sport, girls and the War.'

At Gillingham Grammar School, David Silk, the Archdeacon of Leicester, discovered the origins of his love for 'the culture and the language in which Christianity first spread. A Christian sense developed alongside a sense of history and an appreciation of the centre of European culture.' Discussion on the works of Plato led to a conviction about the eventual truth of Christianity and a feeling for philosophical method and logic.

Ossett Grammar School in Yorkshire gave Mrs Elaine Storkey, Director of the Institute of Contemporary Christianity and a leading evangelical, 'a love of ideas, of exploration of these ideas in drama and debate. I was convinced on leaving school that I wanted to be an academic, but one who would communicate widely and help others to make ideas their own.' This regular contributor to *Thought for the Day* was the only non-Sixth Former to be a candidate in the school's mock election in 1959. 'I suppose I was already the token woman. I lost the election but the exciting experience of trying to persuade the whole school with argument remained.'

Another striking annual feature of school life was the play which the headmaster wrote each year for the pupils to perform for the town. 'The plays explored the themes of incarnation, sin and redemption.'

But it was through a local tragedy that she found her real vocation: 'As school Head Girl I had to attend the funeral of a second-year boy killed in an accident. The devastation of his parents and the confusion and pain amongst his friends drew from me a great desire to help them find a path through grief.'

A fellow Radio Four broadcaster, Rabbi Lionel Blue, came to religion indirectly through his history teacher at Westminster City School:

'He had a great influence on me, because he was serious about history and he communicated that seriousness to me. I think we both felt that history was personally important to us. I was a very uncouth child and I liked him because this didn't seem to bother him. Because of him I went on to read history at university and history led me to religion. So it was this teacher who led me indirectly to become a rabbi.'

There was no rabbinical tradition in Lionel's family: 'My grandmother was pious and before the War we used to separate the milk and the meat. But then we were bombed and the bombs blew the milk into the meat and that was the end of all that!'

His history teacher used to send him to the local library to fetch library books for him: 'I used to wait until he brought the books back, then I'd get them out after him. I read every book he read, and in this way I discovered all sorts of authors. At the age of 13 or 14 I'd read Macaulay – that was the rational part of my reading – and some odd authors like Charles Williams – that was the strange part. Williams was a Christian writer and poet. He was different from anyone else I had read and he sat me back on my haunches. This history master also introduced me to the better sort of historical novel, and through him I remember reading a critique of Marxism which planted the first seeds of doubt. It made me realise that everything was much more complex than I'd thought.

'I wasn't happy at either that school or at Hendon County where I went next. I couldn't have been happy at any school – I was too confused and disoriented. There was no counselling system at that time and I was going through a mental crisis during puberty. I didn't know whom to talk to: I had lost the ability to relate to people.

'The library was my haven: I haunted it – it was my home. I used to go there after school and stay there till it closed. I shut myself up in the world of books and that was my education: my real school was the library.'

Julia Neuberger also reflects the rise of the rabbi to public prominence 'as a member of the chattering classes. South Hampstead High School was great for very academic children like me; it has had a profound influence on how I have developed my career in, for example, reviewing, talking about music, teaching, and being "articulate".'

Rabbi Neuberger explained, 'When I said I belonged to the chattering classes I meant the Left of Centre British Establishment into which I was born. My parents were pretty Left and we lived in Hampstead. I went to school with the daughters of politicians. There was a liberal atmosphere.

'There are now thirteen of us female rabbis. It wasn't a struggle for me to be accepted at first because at that time it was felt to be right for women to become rabbis. But I have found it more difficult the more senior I've become. It hasn't been easy chairing my male colleagues. They were quite happy about allowing female rabbis but I think they found me daunting.

'I'm sure that the toughness I needed to survive is due to my education at South Hampstead High. The thing about that school and about most Girls' Public Day School Trust schools is that they treat you as if it is possible that you can do absolutely anything at all that you choose. They teach you not to be defeated by difficulties. You are taught to solve problems either by stamping your foot or by negotiating. We were taught not to use feminine wiles but to be fairly aggressive – or at least *very* assertive. It was a jolly useful training but it caused problems later for some girls who went to those schools. When they emerged they found that there were still blocks that they could not negotiate – a lot of organisations are still very much run by men.'

Rabbi Sybil Sheridan loved Bolton School and identified fully with its ethos. The school laid great emphasis on public service and despite its very high academic successes seemed to value most those individuals who entered the caring professions. 'When I left I had no doubt that that was the best thing one could do.' However, it was pure chance that she opted for "A"-level Religion which set her on course for her career:

'I had difficulty finding a third subject that I was any good at. At a presentation of "A"-level courses the RE teacher mentioned Biblical archaeology. I happened to be interested in archaeology and so chose the subject. The two years' study opened up an area of thought that seemed quite wondrous to me then, and I have been fascinated by religion – all religions – ever since.'

Rabbi Jonathan Romain knew that he wanted to be a rabbi by the time he arrived at University College School, Hampstead. The staff gave him 'models of character traits which I admired and wanted to emulate such as their integrity, their ability to teach and transmit ideas and values they considered important and put others at ease.' Rabbi John Rayner 'was a German-Jewish refugee in an English and Christian public school, Durham School, during World War II. I was helped by the tolerance and courtesy of all my teachers and most of my fellow-pupils. The headmaster's very liberal Christianity influenced me to become a very liberal Jew and ultimately a rabbi.'

Nearly three-quarters of our sample of the religious were influenced in one way or another by school: for the rabbis, teachers were especially important. As Julia Neuberger puts it, 'The word *rabbi* means "teacher": it is essentially a teaching role and is not the same sort of vocation as the clergy of the Church of England or the Roman Catholic Church.' For the Catholics, inspiration for their vocation came not just from their teachers but from the whole religious community of their schools.

Thomas Hobbes once described the Roman Catholic Church as 'the ghost of the deceased Roman Empire sitting crowned upon the grave thereof'. A contemporary observer might be drawn towards a similar parallel between the Church of England and the death of Empire as Anglican priests discover in social conscience a new justification for the social role which accompanies the fact of Establishment. The panoply of ecclesiastical pomp and power which meant so much to a Fisher, archetypal public-school headmaster, or to a Lang who used to dress up as an archbishop as a small boy, does not figure among the early aspirations of our Anglican correspondents. They, like the rabbis, were more influenced by the power of individual teachers who awakened in them a sense of social responsibility and of service to the community.

13 Science

Specialisation suits scientists and is a precondition of their success. Conventional establishment wisdom may lament the specialisation of British education. Nonetheless, our survey of leading scientists could only discover four who were unhappy at school: Professor Richard Lacey at Felsted, Sir Nevill Mott at Clifton, Dr Antony Storr at Winchester and the astronomer Heather Couper at St Mary's Grammar School, Northwood. All the others found that the intellectual and institutional structures of school life complemented their strong intuitive feel for science.

Sir Derman Christopherson, a former Master of Magdalene College, Cambridge, and Vice-Chancellor of Durham University was happy 'on balance after the first two years' at Sherborne. He strikes the chord characteristic of most scientists in recalling how his headmaster 'advised that my work in the first year or two suggested that I should choose scientific subjects. By choosing subjects which were congenial to me I was able to pass the necessary number of "O" levels to enable me to enter the Sixth Form at the age of 15.'

Few scientists' energies were diverted to non-scientific areas during their schooldays. Dr John Horlock was unusual in recalling how 'a mock election tempted me towards politics' at Latymer Grammar School, Edmonton: 'An engineering degree course at Cambridge showed me what I was good at.' Earlier interests, however, may survive in his present incarnation as Vice-Chancellor of the Open University. The obstetrician and gynaecologist Dame Josephine Barnes is similarly unusual in recalling a social dimension to her vocation: 'I wanted to be of service to the community and that's why I became a doctor. This is something that was certainly taught us at Oxford High School for Girls in the 1920s.' No other scientist, however, offers aspiration towards secular priesthood. About a third of those who responded attended independent schools. Nearly half attended state grammar schools which inspire the customary threnodies. Dr Pauline Cutting, the heroine of the Palestinian refugee camps, represents a younger generation of those entirely educated at a comprehensive school. Patrick Moore and Miriam Rothschild were educated by private tutors. Chemists are well represented in the survey and 25 per cent of the scientists in our sample are women.

Predestination has played its part among most of them. Sir Fred Hoyle 'already knew the broad features of my intended career at 11, when I first attended Bingley Grammar School.' Sir Aubrey Trotman-Dickenson, Principal of the University College of Wales, Cardiff, 'intended to be a scientist before going to Winchester. Winning the school science prize with a project that was published in the *Journal of the Chemical Society* confirmed a commitment to scientific research.'

The influence of particular teachers, however, ensured that scientific potential could be translated into concrete achievement. Dr Derek Roberts, Provost of University College, London, would have left Manchester Central High School at 16 were it not for the 'intervention of a maths teacher who persuaded my parents that I should go into the VIth Form and on to university.' At Mount Grace Comprehensive School, Potters Bar, Pauline Cutting 'stubbornly wanted to apply for veterinary science but my headmistress cleverly steered me into applying for medicine'. After the 1929 crash Lord Butterfield ceased to be a boarder at Solihull School and became a day boy. The future Master of Downing College, Cambridge, found 'several masters who encouraged me to pursue my inclination towards a medical career: two helped me in the scholarship to Oxford which started me off.' At the liberal-minded University College School, Hampstead, Professor Eric Ash, Rector of Imperial College, discovered enthusiastic scientists and mathematicians: 'Two of them were post normal retirement age but were carrying on during the War.'

At Queen Elizabeth Grammar School, Wakefield, a German Jewish refugee boy whose parents had died in the concentration camps met T.W. Gibling, the chemistry master. Sir Hans Kornberg, now Master of Christ's College, Cambridge, arrived in England at the age of ten in 1939 without a word of English. Socialisation and anglicisation proceeded apace while Kornberg boarded at 'an old-style grammar school where you were rapped over the knuckles with the ruler and shouted at from time to time.

'Gibling was a small, fierce, bald man. One side of the bowl of his pipe had a dent in it because he always lit it with a bunsen burner. Gibling agreed to "take me on" and to try to get me from scratch to

Higher School Certificate level in two years. He also allowed me to spend spare time in the school laboratory by making me one of his lab assistants. This started me on the road to chemistry and biochemistry.' He emerged from school with a realisation of how much depends on teaching methods and on the teachers themselves.

Kornberg is the product of a system of scientific apprenticeship which harks back to the nineteenth century. It therefore seems appropriate that he should be an advocate of that pragmatic, flexible experimentation which helped make Britain the workshop of the world. The post-war years in British science have, in his view, left an ambiguous legacy. On the other hand, they witnessed the emergence of science as a professional activity. Before then 'it was something gifted people might indulge in but not something that you would take seriously'. This advance has to be offset against an excessively theoretical scientific approach during the same period. For Kornberg, knowledge as an end in itself is not a valid universal scientific approach. In the same vein, he disapproves of the British cult of the educated generalist who can turn his hand to anything, a system, as he puts it, of 'highly paid managers moving from firm to firm'.

Professor Arnold Wolfendale, the Astronomer Royal, came under the influence of A.N. Leaning, the physics master at Stretford Grammar School. 'He was very keen on practical hands-on experiments, had green fingers and made the experiments work – which his predecessor had not always done. Mr T. Whittaker, the head of the VIth Form and a mathematician, was another influence, an impressive and severe man who was interested, like many mathematicians, in music.' Indeed, a scientific approach ran like a golden thread throughout the school as a result of the influence of the headmaster, Albert Dakin, a distinguished mathematician who was the author of a famous textbook. He was a grand patriarch and the headmaster who had founded the school. The headmaster of Wolfendale's elementary school, St Michael's, Flixton, was another mathematician and a powerful influence: 'It was indeed a great day when I got my scholarship from St Michael's to Stretford Grammar; it was the first for five years and the top class got a half-day off to celebrate.'

Stretford, an all-boys grammar school 'in a fairly mixed area', made a physicist out of Wolfendale. It was a development which could only occur because he was taught maths, 'the language of science', so very well. The absence of the grammar of that language in contemporary education alarms him: 'At the universities we can cope with lack of knowledge but not with the lack of a language. I realise that maths is a difficult subject to teach and we have downgraded it a lot and seized on the more interesting areas to inspire the young. But the other side of the coin is that we are just not teaching maths. I am a traditionalist and I believe in learning tables, formulae and the facts of maths. I am anti child-centred trendy learning. You can't expect children to discover everything for themselves – there are just too many things to find out. They must learn maths as the language of science, just as you would learn any language.'

Despite these traditional statements Wolfendale harbours aspirations which, for many, are incompatible. Can science education be both broad and deep, both wide and rigorous? Wolfendale is aware of the contradictions as the educational metaphors jostle for prominence. Like some others he hopes that circles can be squared and incompatibilities reconciled: 'I think there's a lot to be said for combined science at school. Those who attend university are only a small fraction of the population and I do like the idea of an overall rounded education.'

Sir Philip Randle, Professor of Clinical Biochemistry at Oxford, shares in the common indebtedness to an individual teacher. At King Edward VI Grammar School, Nuneaton, 'a particular science teacher interested me in science, made it clear that he believed I had ability, and lifted me from indifference.' Professor John Thoday, Emeritus Professor of Genetics at Cambridge, said that at Bootham School in York 'the logical demonstration classes given by the physical science teacher, Mr Livesey, had a profound effect on my choice of genetics.' At Barrow Grammar School, Lord Lewis, Professor of Chemistry at Cambridge, was 'impressed and encouraged by a staff member who was dedicated to his chemistry'.

Professor Denis Noble is Professor of Cardiovascular Physiology at Oxford and one of the founders of the *Save British Science* campaign. At Emanuel School in South London he was taught by 'a superb team. The great strength of Mr Hurst, the chemistry master, was to be able to enthuse about the subject while going on with the demonstration. I remember his demonstrations so vividly. There was an element of showmanship in it but he made you realise that there was something very serious behind it. He would show us that what we were doing was the basis of some industrial process. He would show us the relevance of it all. He captured the spirit of the subject but he was down to earth – he'd say, "What you just did in that test tube is the process whereby your father's silver cutlery was electroplated." Or "That's how your photographs were developed." He got it across to me that science was a serious business but that it certainly wasn't boring. W. G. Garrad, the physics master, was quieter with less showmanship but he taught us rigour – that a scientist has to think rigorously – and if you did so you were rewarded. He also taught some of us that there was a lot more than just science to be considered in life.'

Emanuel, for Noble, was a good school partly because, through its clubs, debating and poetry societies, it tried to bridge the two cultures. The experience underlies Noble's belief that 'doing just three "A" levels is a bad idea. You can still be rigorous but you need not teach such a volume of science. I also think that the divide between the sciences is lessening: the subject divisions between them are not what they were. Look at modern molecular biology. It is absurd to keep them separate and actually I think it's the teachers who are holding back the trend to merge the sciences because it's easier to keep them separate. Many of us have come to see that it is not good for Britain that scientists should be hived off separately. We can see that the world of politics and the civil service is full of people who lack the benefit of a scientific background.'

Noble became a scientist because of his teachers' enthusiasm. It was an enthusiasm and a scientific solidarity which survived the end of school days: 'When we all left in 1955 the science VIth Form set up the *55 Club*. It consisted of about forty pupils and we kept it going for about fifteen years after we left. About twenty five to thirty of us would turn up at each meeting for the pleasure of seeing what had happened to colleagues. We invited the masters as guests: I was the Secretary and I still have the minute book. When I became an FRS in 1979 two of my science masters attended the ceremony with obvious and justified pleasure.'

Despite his espousal of the latest wisdom on the need for a 'broader' education Noble remains in other areas a scientific traditionalist. Like Wolfendale he is aware of the contradictions: 'I prefer the *baccalaureat* but having said that I would like to keep some way of identifying high-flyers at an early age, and of making sure that they could go at the speed they wanted. Emanuel used to do this. It depends on what suits the individual. Perhaps it did suit Ruth Lawrence to go up to Oxford so young – it would entirely depend on what she wanted. In general it seems to be not a bad thing to allow most bright people to go on as far as possible. In some areas of science people achieve outstanding things at an early age, especially in maths and science and even in my own area of physiology.'

Since the Nobel Prize started, Noble points out, Britain has had a total of 36 winners. 'We have not been doing so well in the Nobel Prize stakes in the last few decades; this may not be the be-all and end-all but it is an indication. Up to my generation there was no question about our distinction. Lack of funding is only part of the problem.' There is also, he observes, an increasing cultural resistance to science which is reflected in the diminishing percentages of "A" level candidates in scientific subjects.

Sir Richard Bayliss, a former physician to Her Majesty the Queen, shares Noble's anxiety: 'In world medicine', he believes, 'we are sinking fast and I hope it won't be without trace. It's the thing now to get money from the big pharmaceutical industries but the trouble with that is that it is result-orientated. My friend Lord Rothschild created a great furore when he said all research should be end-orientated and must either make money or benefit someone. The trouble is that discoveries are often made entirely by chance when you are looking for something quite different and those are often the discoveries that benefit most people.'

These worries were far removed from Sir Richard's scientific education at Rugby where 'we had an absolutely inspired biology teacher called Peter Falk. He was the most inspired teacher I ever worked with. I shall never forget how once I was dissecting a dogfish and it was not at all like the book. Falk said: "This is nature and you'll find that human beings are not like the book either". His whole teaching was inspirational. He approached everything with a fresh mind: "Let's see what we can learn about this worm – is it male or female I wonder?" Of course we didn't know that worms are hermaphrodite – we'd never heard of such a thing! He taught us never to accept anything as 100 per cent certain because nothing ever is. You never say that something never occurs because you can then discover it has occurred in the Galapagos Islands or somewhere. He had a totally enquiring mind.'

It was many years before Baylis realised the nature of the path his education had taken with specialisation from the early age of 14, though he still did Latin and French. He also continued with Art under 'the famous Talbot Kelly who did all the posters for the London Underground.'

Very few successful scientists appear to have had to fight against the odds in order to get to where they are today. The recollections of Lord Dainton, Chancellor of Sheffield University, are unusual in recording a struggle. The Central Secondary School in Sheffield was scientifically well-equipped and attracted well-qualified staff: 'This was in part because they had opportunities of teaching students for external degrees at night school in the same premises.' There was, however, one exception to the rule: 'I developed a desire to go to Oxford to read chemistry partly because of the appointment of a bad chemistry master who inspired little confidence and whose lessons I cut. Instead, I went to a nearby public reference library. This parting was certainly good for me and possibly also for him. I went my way to Oxford and he went his way to educational administration, ultimately becoming Sir Percy Lord, Chief Education Officer of Lancashire.'

Scientists fall in love with a technique and a particular way of looking at the world at an early age. As Sir Hans Kornberg insists, 'In science, method and technique matter more than facts. I always tell my students that it is important to know what experiments *not* to do.' The all-consuming nature of that intellectual passion explains the hermeneutical nature of the scientist's life and interests. It is hardly surprising, therefore, that so few scientists enlarge on the connections between their science and other aspects of their education. Denis Noble was unusual in being influenced at school by his history and English teachers. At Forfar Academy, Sir Douglas Black, Professor of Medicine at Manchester, found that 'my contemporaries socialised me'. This, however, is a lonely voice among scientists in finding the fact either valuable or noticeable. Most appear innocent of the public, political and cultural changes which constituted the context of their education.

The best schools for scientists have adapted themselves to the particular, obsessive needs of the gifted scientist. At Cardiff High School Professor Brian Josephson 'had a fairly advanced understanding of mathematics at an early age and the school assisted my progress by giving me books to look at and exam questions to try on my own. After a time I reached the level of the VIth Form and attended their lessons.'

Schools which were less accommodating caused scientists to define themselves by opposition. Professor Richard Lacey is now Professor of Microbiology at Leeds and a prominent commentator on issues such as salmonella and BSE: 'I have a high profile and have been controversial; I was like that in my schooldays too.' At Felsted, 'the Headmaster and housemaster seemed to contribute nothing but oppression. Being demoted in house order on account of being bad at games made me concentrate on work.' Lacey was in full-scale rebellion against 'this nonsense about house spirit. I could not care less if my House won at sport but games were the major criteria of success at that school.

I resented having to do exercise for the sake of it. What really got up my nose was that if you were discovered not to have done your PT during break, for example, you had to run three miles along the road, and I thought this was a complete waste of time. I was told that I was an unpleasant influence and that I had the wrong attitude. When I was 15 it came to the crunch: my parents were summoned and told I wasn't the sort of person they wanted at the school. My parents told me plainly that the alternative was the local secondary modern, which was pretty awful.' Lacey had to stay but the decision 'caused quite a family rift which lasted until only about ten years ago. Nothing could have been worse than the misery I went through for so many years. I frequently wrote to my parents but they did not help.

'The trouble with Felsted was that most boys there had secure careers in things like farming and stockbroking without their having to do anything. There were very few people who needed to make their own mark in the world and the school was not at all academic. Only two of us ever went to Oxford or Cambridge.'

Yet in the science department at Felsted 'there was an atmosphere of optimism' with enthusiastic science teachers who 'did everything for you. The biology master, Mr Sturdy, explained things in the context of the real world. You would start with a fairly mundane process, you would go on field trips, come back and look at things under the microscope and then he would show their relevance in the real world.

'When Sturdy and Lee, the chemistry masters, marked your work they would make legible constructive comments, not just a score, or ticks and crosses. I now do the same with students' work and I realise how much more effort it requires to explain where someone went wrong.

'The facilities at Felsted were not that modern but that did not matter since the boys had individual attention and space. You don't need modern equipment so much as space to do your own thing. We worked as individuals instead of having to double up and share equipment and results. This creates a pattern of individual discipline, of responsibility for your own results. Shared problem-solving is not as satisfactory a method of teaching.'

The individualism, therefore, which was frowned upon elsewhere in Felsted was allowed to flourish within the narrower confines of the laboratory. Lacey emerged from his school with scientific commitment. As he observes contemporary science education he notes a now familiar dilemma: 'I think that combined science is an awful idea. You just end up with the lowest common denominator. At the same time, I don't think that it is a good idea to be committed to the narrowness of three science "A" levels. In science, everything you do until your mid-twenties is only preliminary. But we must remember that only 10 per cent of students will become serious scientists. The other 90 per cent will take a minor role or will leave science altogether. So we should keep a general, broader approach too. Do we want more people educated to a moderate standard, or just a few educated to a high standard? We must decide.'

Sir Nevill Mott FRS, the Cavendish Laboratory physicist, is another scientist who disliked the 'games-based, anti-intellectual atmosphere' of his school. The teaching of chemistry and physics at Clifton College was indifferent: 'The chemistry master was chiefly interested in the Arabic origins of chemistry – which would interest me now but not then.' Unsurprisingly, therefore, Mott 'came up through the maths ladder rather than physics or chemistry. The maths teacher at Clifton spotted my talent when I was about 14 and pushed me on.'

Sir Nevill is very clear that 'physicists and chemists are extremely different kinds of people' and that therefore the idea of combined physics and chemistry is necessarily superficial. 'I think that a talented child needs to be exposed to a pure physicist or a pure chemist. I don't mind being called élitist; it is a word we should use as a term of praise. Such élitism has ensured that the British excel in some branches of physics; we are at least as competitive as Germany or France.' Can such excellence survive the introduction of a more demotic style of scientific education? Sir Nevill notes the desirability of both having your cake and eating it in the best of all Panglossian worlds: 'I am not keen on early specialisation. Schools should offer "A" level courses but also a more practical course for those who are good with their hands. People like the chap called Bill in every laboratory on whom we all depend. There should be more time for subjects outside science but it is also true that you have to make time for biology as well if you are doing physics and chemistry.' How all these things are to be achieved remains an enigma: 'I remember discussing it at the Royal Society two decades ago and we did not come up with any answers then.'

Sir Christopher Cockerell, the inventor of the hovercraft, insists that 'there is a huge difference between engineering and science. Scientists fiddle around with bits of paper; engineers are entirely different animals: we make useful things.' His own distinctiveness was always evident. 'Gresham's got in the way like hell with the things I wanted to do. I had to go and play games which I disliked, though I did like rifle shooting. The school did not approve of me. They liked orthodox people. In fact school was a beastly nuisance and had no influence on me in an orthodox academic way. I could design things and I knew how things worked but otherwise I was a dud. There was no engineering though there was practical work on carpentry and things like that.' He managed to get into Cambridge but 'there was no opportunity to write anything exciting in the entrance exams.'

Free time at school was Cockerell's salvation. He read books on 'engineering and wireless, as it was called in those days' and made his first wireless set at prep school at about the age of 12. 'I was the only boy at Gresham's with a wireless and constructed many sets thereafter.'

Cockerell's family background was an unusual one for an engineer; it helped him to avoid the malign effects of the great divide between the sciences and the humanities. 'There should be no specialisation at all up to the age of 18. An engineer loses so much under the present system. I was lucky; my mother was an artist and I have inherited her creativity. My father was head of the Fitzwilliam Museum in Cambridge and I now collect Greek coins and artefacts as a hobby.

'The other boys at Gresham's were only interested in sport and in knocking each other about. Luckily it was a school with studies and I shared with a very clever but quiet boy; we used to read the books we wanted.' The narrowness of Gresham's education did not suit the young inventor, who was dismissed as a dud. Yet when he joined Marconi he 'whizzed to the top: after two years I was at the head of one of the eleven sections in the company. This does not come out of a narrow academic world.' It was the breadth of his interests that enabled Cockerell to build 'exciting navigational equipment for our bombers during the War.' One of his inventions 'automatically recorded the signals from the enemy coastal radar stations so that their positions could be plotted very accurately, enabling them to be bombed to extinction a few days before D Day.'

Sir Bernard Lovell, the former Director of Jodrell Bank Experimental Station, was another schoolboy who was obsessed by electronics and gadgetry. At Kingswood Grammar School, which had opened only two years before he went there, Lovell was 'a regular reader of the weekly wireless journal and had built equipment that would transmit as well as receive.' In his autobiography, *Astronomer by Chance*, he says that during homework spent on other subjects 'my spirit yearned for the wireless gadgetry that surrounded me. I had one desire – to leave school and expand my father's business into these new and fascinating activities.'

His headmaster, however, thought that he showed scientific and mathematical ability, despite being ranked near the bottom of his class.

His father was persuaded that the boy should stay in school. There was another, profound influence: 'A friend of my father's called to consult him on a religious topic. His name was Champion, a mathematics master in another school, and that evening he showed me the elegant way to deal with a problem in dynamics that had utterly confused me for the past hour. Those moments in the company of Champion had released an elementary mathematical insight and such confidence that for the rest of my schooldays mathematics was never a problem.' A school visit to the Physics Department at Bristol University confirmed him in his vocation: 'That lecture room held all the gadgets and devices that represented my idea of paradise.'

Seeing how things work, taking them apart, collecting and classifying them: these are powerful scientific impulses as the scientist seeks to discover, or impose, order in the created world. Dr Ruth Jarrett of the Leukaemia Research Unit at Glasgow University, for example, used to love watching her mother in the kitchen disembowelling the chicken: 'I was fascinated by how the parts of the body worked and by the chicken's anatomy.'

Jarrett moved from a comprehensive school with good facilities but poor teaching at the age of 13. The fact that her next school, Westbourne, a private girls' school in Glasgow, had poorer science facilities did not matter: 'In my mixed comprehensive the boys dominated the science lessons; there were only four or five girls in my physics class. Whereas, of course, we were all girls at Westbourne School and plenty of girls did physics.'

The school also suited Jarrett for the familiar scientific reason that she wanted to specialise and at her comprehensive 'it was impossible for me to do a combination of physics, chemistry and biology for Scottish highers.' Her new school fed her curiosity.

'When I was still under five I used to love to go to post-mortem rooms at the vet school with my father and see what the different parts of the animals did. It wasn't morbid fascination, it was curiosity to see how things worked. The time I enjoyed most at Westbourne was when our rather eccentric physics teacher decided we had done enough coursework and could do things that interested us. So a group of three of us girls set out to disprove Millikan's experiment to prove the charge on electrons. We never managed to disprove the theory but we thoroughly enjoyed trying; it was the flexibility we liked.'

The similar experimental spirit of Mrs Thatcher's chemistry don at Somerville, Professor Dorothy Hodgkin OM, was obvious by the time she was nine. She lived in lodgings while her parents were in the Sudan and she attended Sir John Leman School in Beccles. When she was nine, however, 'my mother took me to visit the Wellcome Laboratories. I was shown gold panning and set out to pan the bottom of the stream running through our garden. I isolated a black mineral and subsequently took this to the soil chemistry lab of the Wellcome Laboratories which helped to identify it as ilemonite. After this, Dr Joseph, the soil chemist, gave me a box of surveying equipment for testing minerals in the field. I made many experiments with these at home.'

When Sir Vivian Fuchs, a former Director of the British Antarctic Survey, was a boy at Brighton College in the 1920s geology was not taught as a subject at the school. This, however, did not stand in his way: 'When I had passed for Cambridge I still had a term left and the senior chemistry master got hold of one of the first geology textbooks and said we would learn it together.' Previously Fuchs had found relations with Mr Pryce-Jones difficult: 'I was interested in chemistry but I found him too pernickety; lines had to be drawn exactly two centimetres in from the side of the page and so on. So I was always bottom of the class. Then one day he got ill and a new master took over and I got the prize. When Pryce-Jones came back he was horrified. After that, however, he became very helpful and gave me the idea of geology.' The subject suited a zeal for classification and collection: 'As an only child I collected everything, things you are not allowed to collect now, birds' eggs, butterflies, moths, knots of wood. I had aquaria where I kept newts and tadpoles. I loved to acquire things; I kept them in lists and books, I had trays for foreign coins, including Roman ones. Sometimes I would display them.'

Other kinds of scientists were seduced by more theoretical intellectual pleasures. For Lord Flowers, a former Vice-Chancellor of the University of London, the discovery of the power of pure mathematics was the great event of his time at Bishop Gore School, Swansea. Sir Brian Pippard, Emeritus Professor of Physics at Cambridge, thinks that: 'The main thing is to be taught not to be sloppy, to be analytical, to ask "What does that mean?", to be rigorous, to take information seriously. You can do all that in any science at all; it doesn't matter at all which science pupils learn. The great thing is to get someone turned on.

'It all lies in the quality of the teacher. It does not matter what method a good teacher uses: he will know what is best to turn the child on.' Flexibility is all. Nonetheless, there are traditional reservations to be expressed: 'I do think that there is a great danger in child-centred learning. It's ludicrous to imagine that a child can find out for itself scientific ideas that took great minds years and years of research to discover. I was taught physics by a martinet called W. C. Badcock, and I wish there were more martinets around.'

Sir Brian 'was brought up in a perfectly ordinary classical curriculum at Clifton until I did School Certificate at 14.' Although the son of an FRS 'it was only when I went on to Higher Certificate that I got fascinated by science. Once I got started I was very excited. One of my father's colleagues was Professor Maurice Travers, Professor of Physical Chemistry at Bristol. Travers would take me to the labs when I was about 15. He was one of the great pioneers of low-temperature research. He had isolated Argon, Krypton and Xenon and I found this idea very exciting indeed. Travers told me that my maths was not good enough for me to read physics. Nevill Mott was passionately switched on to mathematics at Clifton; I was only adequate. So I went to Cambridge to read chemistry in 1938. The War came and my tutor called me and said: "If you don't want to be called up I should switch to physics; they want chemists but they don't seem to want physicists." Well, anything to avoid being called up – and so I switched. Within a week I knew that physics was what I wanted to do for the rest of my life.'

One of the notorious penalties of abstraction is a failure to communicate. The astronomer and astro-physicist Jocelyn Burnell, however, was fortunate in her physics teacher at the Mount School in York. 'Being a girls' boarding school, it was not strong on science. But Mr Tillott who had been brought out of retirement for the second time made everything very clear and showed us how easy it all was.' She was also fortunate in her father, 'an architect with very catholic tastes who crossed the boundaries between the arts and sciences. He brought some books on astronomy home from the library when I was in my early teens.'

Professor Heinz Wolff, Director of the Brunel Institute for Bioengineering, is, perhaps, the best known of those who communicate across the difficult terrain of the no-man's land of the two cultures: 'Science for the citizen and maths for the citizen should be core subjects so that people can understand the issues of today.' These advantages, however, he thinks, should not be bought at the expense of the traditional scientific rigour: 'We have gone too far on the empirical child-centred learning idea. The Government is beginning to realise that a problem has been created by the movement away from didactic teaching. Teachers feel that they have to keep their pupils interested and amused. They are therefore tending to let the fundamentals of science teaching drop out of the bottom. Schools must teach the fundamentals, otherwise pupils will never understand anything. I don't think much of the idea of combined science and, as for "A" levels being broadened, you would have to have four-year undergraduate courses which would cause enormous financial problems.'

Wolff proved he understood the fundamentals of physics at the City of Oxford Boys' School. 'The physics master was a chap called Bodey, a pillar of the Church and a master of sarcasm. He was also Deputy Head and very understanding when I missed my time fire-watching and instead spent it inventing an electromagnetic machine that turned the laboratory lights on and off once a second. It was a not very funny joke but it so impressed the management that I understood the principles of electromagnetism that they took no action.'

When it came to the supply of scientific materials the spirit of wartime improvisation could also appear pretty wayward: 'I shall never forget the excitement when a large crate of ex-War Department electronic material arrived, a huge crate full of things like cathode ray tubes. They had been dumped nearby and local schools had permission to come and collect them before bulldozers crushed them. This stuff was sold at a penny a pound. So the heavy stuff with a lot of iron in it was more expensive!'

For Professor John Yudkin enthusiasm is the key to the communicator's success: 'It doesn't matter if you are taught physics or chemistry or biology. All pupils need is a good teacher who is enthusiastic about his subject. The secret of good teaching is to have the facility to explain even the most complex things at the level of your pupils' understanding. I have spent a lot of time talking to adults with an aversion to science, probably because of the way they've been badly taught. When I used to come home from the labs doing quite complicated research I was able to explain it to my wife so that she understood, even though it was really quite specific: you do not use jargon.'

Nutrition, Yudkin's subject, proved to be one of the boom subjects of the 1970s and 1980s in terms of the public awareness of scientific issues. Yudkin has benefited accordingly as a broadcaster and commentator, but he told us, 'I may have a high profile now but I was always very shy at school and I still am. The only reason I have a high profile is because nutrition is a very fashionable subject and because I have this ability to communicate, the facility to enthuse and explain complex ideas in lay terms.'

It was a quality which Yudkin discerned in his biology teacher at school: 'He created enthusiasm.' Hackney Downs School had been one of the London City Guild Schools but was taken over by the LCC in 1905. 'The area was mixed and fairly poor; some people paid fees if they could, and about three-quarters of the boys could. I was a scholarship boy. The list of Oxford and Cambridge scholars was in the front hall and they were very proud of it; they got one or two scholars every couple of years.'

Yudkin was a persistent schoolboy scientist. 'Long before I did science at school I was already doing experiments at home and my poor mother was always complaining of holes in the sheets.' The arrival of a chemistry set when he was ten was a great event but it came without a set of instructions. 'The set was bought from a shop the other side of London; I walked all the way to the shop to get the instruction book but they didn't have one. They said that they would get it by that day the following week. I walked there again. No book. I did this journey again and again for six weeks.'

Patience was also the secret of success with fireworks at school: 'We took days to make the cardboard tubes rolled up round pencils, then we would stuff the chemicals down inside. The fireworks either would not light or they would quietly fizzle down the tube until they finally fizzled out.' Yudkin had greater success at a parents' evening when he was in the Science Sixth: 'The biology teacher told me he would like me to show the parents a small pond animal through a microscope. I was so enthusiastic that the parents would not go away and a small crowd gathered around me.'

Yudkin is more hostile to early specialisation than most other scientists but joins the consensus in being against 'too much child-centred discovery learning. You can't assume that children have any instinct for science and maths. Some degree of formal teaching is imperative. You can have a degree of learning by self-enthusiasm but you must make a balance. Otherwise some children might emerge very advanced in some subjects and not do anything in others.'

Scientists, like other scholars, need space at their schools. They are not in awe of tradition or of an inherited structure of enquiry and belief. The only authority that counts is that of scientific reason. Professor Joseph Needham, the former Master of Gonville and Caius College, Cambridge, is unusual among scientists in the extent of his indebtedness to an educational tradition, in his case that of Oundle and its scientific headmaster, F. W. Sanderson. Needham's distinctiveness, however, goes further. He is the author of a multi-volume history of science in China, a Christian Marxist, lay reader and philosopher of science as well as a biochemist. He has pursued those wider interests which have been a wistful aspiration for most other scientists as they gloomily contemplate their relegation to a Dr Strangelove-like status in the public mind.

'Sanderson often used to say: "You should think spaciously, my boy, spaciously." Again, he would say: "You'll be all right, my boy, once you have found your obsession." All this turned out to be extremely true in my own case. *Science and Civilisation in China* is an example of thinking spaciously and China has been my obsession for many years.'

Scott Fitzgerald thought the rich were different: the obsessive quality of science makes scientists just as different from the rest of us. Enquiry rooted in a sense of wonder at the created world can appear an unworldly occupation. The professional scientist has an awkward relationship with mainstream culture and education in Britain. Northern anorak-wearing chemists called Colin continue to provoke derision. Britain's most famous scientist, Stephen Hawking, incarcerated in a wheelchair, feeds the popular macabre fantasy of the scientist as a form of disembodied intelligence, remote and alienating. The story of scientists' education offers us less myth and more realism. If the obsessions of scientists are to flourish they need the creative challenge of a stimulating environment. In that respect they are no different from the rest of us.

14 Sport

Mens sana in corpore sano: Juvenal's phrase has been used by the public schools to justify plenty of healthy exercise to nurture lively minds. The grammar schools aped the public schools. Success on the sporting field has only recently become less important than academic success. So we would have expected top sports people to have been greatly influenced by the opportunities for sports and games at their schools. It therefore came as a surprise to find that only 38 per cent of top sporting professionals think that their school had any influence on their choice of sporting career. Indeed, many had made it to the top despite their schools. Only in the areas of Law and Business does school have less of an impact on career choice.

There are several reasons for this. The first and most important is that to a greater extent than in any other of our professional categories, sportsmen and women are born to sport. To be a great sportsman often requires dedication from the family as well: 45 per cent of sporting people acknowledge the influence of their families – the largest percentage in the book. But the school's attitude towards sport was often ambivalent: sport was fine as an amateur activity but not as a professional career. The job of education was to prepare pupils for a life including a career beyond the precarious tightrope of competitive sport and while schools are keen to promote team games, many until recently have not encouraged minor sports if they take pupils away from the school teams. These then are the conflicts between sport and school which will be illustrated in this chapter.

The sporting heroes and heroines of most schoolchildren are top-earning professionals often augmenting their salaries by endorsing brand name T-shirts and trainers. But to many schools the ideal still seems to be the gifted amateur, the gentleman player untarnished by filthy lucre: there is still a suspicion of the professional. Equestrians suffered most from this prejudice.

Sir Mark Prescott, the Newmarket racehorse trainer, told his careers master at Harrow that he wanted to be a professional jockey. The response was typical: 'Stunted and stupid. I can't think of anything better!'

Willie Carson at Riverside School in Stirling told us emphatically that no-one at school had the slightest influence on his career. In defiant capital letters he added 'SELF!' Belmont Abbey, the Catholic school in Hereford and Worcester, had no influence either on Peter Scudamore, though he says he was happy there. He was deputy head boy and he admits that he still says a Hail Mary at some fences and an Our Father at others!

At Northallerton Grammar School, Alex Greaves, the female jockey, said: 'As you can imagine, racing wasn't a subject ever touched on in the school curriculum.' And though Grand National winner Richard Dunwoody is grateful to Rendcomb College for teaching him independence and self discipline, no one there had any influence on his choice of career. He was captain of a couple of rugby, hockey and cricket teams and knew he wanted to be a professional sportsman 'and fortunately I was good enough to become a jockey though no-one at the school had a deep interest in racing.'

Champion three-day eventer Virginia Leng was unhappy at Bedgebury School in Kent and denies that it had any influence on her – rather surprising for a school that these days actively encourages equestrian sports.

Schools have traditionally backed the team game and until quite recently there was little choice other than hockey, football or rugby in the winter, cricket or netball or sometimes tennis in the summer. Only latterly, *pace* Millfield, have they really encouraged individual or minority sports. Of our 134 interviewees, 50 were at the top of these: athletics, squash, tennis, golf. And only 12 felt that school had any influence on their career decision.

No-one at Inverkeithing High School influenced snooker star Stephen Hendry. And boxers Henry Cooper and Dave 'Boy' Green emerged unaffected from their schools in Bellingham and Cambridge. Nor did Chay Blyth become a sailor as a result of Hawick High School nor Stirling Moss a racing driver as a result of Haileybury, nor even Graham Gooch a cricketer as a result of his education at Norlington Junior High School, Leytonstone.

Shot-putter Geoff Capes is now a governor of his Lincolnshire secondary school, George Farmer County in Holbeach. 'A lot has changed since I left in 1964,' he told us. But at the age of 13 he was so angry with the school and its headmaster Mr Fathers – nicknamed Daddy-O – that he put out a statement in the *Spalding Guardian* in protest. He can no longer recall the exact words but remembers his indignation:

'I was 13 years old and doing well at the Holbeach Athletics club. I had been winning races from the age of six or seven in the annual local sports gala and I was at this time the youngest member of the club. Anyway Daddy-O found out and he suspended me from school sport. I was in all the school teams by this time – athletics, cricket, basket ball – you name it. I won the school prize for physical education too.

'The headmaster was trying to make a point. The sports master Gary Cook wasn't very happy! They had to reinstate me when they found they couldn't do without me!'

Capes was the son and grandson of farmworkers and was expected to follow suit. But paradoxically the obstacles that were put in his way at school made him all the more determined to succeed in a sports career.

'When I was 13 I said publicly that I would represent England and the deputy head called me in and said that if I ever did, he would eat his hat. I've met him since and he swears he never said that! But by the time I was 13 my coach was the international hurdler Stewart Storey, now the BBC athletics commentator, and I went to the All England championships when I was 14.'

Lucy Soutter also had her first big success at 14. In 1982 she won the British under-16 Open – the Wimbledon of squash. Although they congratulated her in Assembly, teachers at her school, Charlton Park Convent in Cheltenham (now the co-educational St Edward's), were mystified as to why she would want to spend Saturday afternoons playing her individual sport instead of joining in school hockey and netball matches – though she did play in the hockey team whenever possible. She had to be very strong-willed indeed:

'My sports teachers gave me a lot of encouragement with my tennis: often they would come and watch me play in tournaments outside school hours. However, squash was my biggest love and the sport at which I did best. But I didn't feel I received the same amount of encouragement or support there. To be fair, I believe this was because squash was only regarded as a sixth form sport, and to have a first-year student playing in her lunchtimes and competing nearly every weekend as an individual, rather than being part of a school team, was maybe hard to understand.

'Of course no-one knew I'd make a career of squash then: it seemed strange to them that a girl of 11 should be so single-minded. The squash courts were only half a mile from the school but no-one else from the school went there. I had to have two distinct sets of friends – one lot at school and another lot at the club. I was the only girl in the school playing squash and I couldn't go to parties or shopping on Saturdays – so the other girls thought me a bit strange.'

By 1987 Lucy was British number one and world number two. She is grateful to her school for its support as she hauled herself up the professional ladder: 'When I was in the finals for the British Open I was sent a big bouquet saying "From the sports department and all at Charlton Park – wishing you all the best!"'

Tennis star Anne Hobbs was far less happy at another Catholic private school, The Hollies Convent Grammar in Manchester. She told us, 'My school had very poor sports – absolutely no tennis – although I was very motivated in netball at school for many years. I left school at 16 after "O" levels to take up full-time tennis in London.'

The current National Head of Training at the Lawn Tennis Association is Richard Lewis. He found Goff's Grammar School at Cheshunt 'particularly negative towards tennis. I consequently left at the earliest opportunity despite being in the A stream.' Like Geoff Capes, Lewis turned negative to positive. 'One particular member of staff was very negative about my prospects as a player and this became a great source of motivation for a number of years. I enjoyed proving him wrong!'

Pat Smythe, the great show jumper, was at Talbot Heath in Bournemouth. Uncompromising in her candour she says, 'I did not like school. I felt I had a more responsible job at home.'

Pentathlete Richard Phelps was more specific in his criticism of Brockworth Comprehensive. 'As an up-and-coming modern pentathlete I was depressed by the lack of enthusiasm and knowledge of staff as to how much training was needed to reach international level. It took a lot of persuading to get ten minutes off assembly in the morning because I would be coming back from swimming training. It was the same with trying to get time off to do competitions.'

Golf in English schools, unlike Scottish schools, has always been a minority sport if it was offered at all. Nick Faldo said that his school, Sir Frederick Osborne in Welwyn Garden City, had no influence at all on his golfing career and Tony Jacklin, remembering his Scunthorpe secondary modern, agreed.

Katrina Douglas, the Ladies' Golf Champion, is grateful to St Brandon's, the independent girls' school in Bristol, for the confidence and security she found there. But the school was not as flexible as she and her father would have liked when it came to sport versus studies: Katrina went on a family holiday in Scotland after "O" levels and a friend of her father's gave her a golf lesson. The two men were so impressed at her performance on the driving range that they asked her if she would like to have a year off playing full-time golf before embarking on her "A"-level course.

'I knew that I could go back and study at any time but in sport you don't have that option – age is much more important. My father wrote to the school outlining his intentions but they could only see him ruining my education. He suggested an American-style schedule which could combine golf and study but the school refused and I left at Christmas after a term's notice.' There were apparently no hard feelings and Katrina continued to play hockey for St Brandon's and stayed friends with her former classmates and some teachers. But an interesting compromise between academia and sport had been rejected.

Laura Davies has had 15 tournament wins so far in her golfing career, including the British Open in 1986 and the US Open the following year. But when she was about to leave Fullbrook School in Surrey the headmaster warned her, 'You'll need to find a proper job of course. You'll never make enough out of golf.'

That was in 1980 and since then Davies has won nearly half a million pounds from tournaments and probably double that sum through sponsorship and other earnings.

Adrian Moorhouse at Bradford Grammar also found 'there was an obvious conflict at school' because of his swimming. The master in charge of swimming had been a competitive swimmer himself and gave up a lot of his time to coach Adrian. Generally the school was helpful when he had to go away for competitions; the headmaster even reorganised his "O" level exams. But 'some teachers had a problem with me missing lessons to compete abroad. Being at an all-boys school with the major sports being team-oriented rugby and cricket it was not easy.' At the age of 14 he had more problems with his out-of-school swimming club and one master suggested he went to Millfield. However, 'I didn't take his advice and went to Leeds swimming club half an hour away from home and that's where I still train.'

Some schools were even more co-operative. At Clifton High School for Girls Jo Durie's PE mistress was 'very into tennis and I was put into the first team at a very young age – playing girls older than me, which helped me cope later.' The school allowed her days off for tournaments, lessons and training.

Nearly a third of the 134 sports people who replied to our survey were indebted to a particular teacher. Veteran cricketer Alec Bedser remembers his teachers at Monument Hill Secondary, Woking, for their interest.

Welsh fly-halves Gareth Davies and his brother Jonathan went to Gwendraeth Grammar School, Llanelli, alma mater of the great Barry John. Gareth told us, 'I am indebted to one or two members of staff who were most supportive and influential in my development. They helped develop a feeling of self-confidence, a belief in my own ability, which was crucial for a miner's son from a nearby mining community which erred on caution and introspection.'

Another Welsh grammar school boy, Tokyo Olympic gold medallist athlete Lynn Davies, said of Ogmore Grammar, Mid-Glamorgan: 'The small grammar school I attended had an excellent sporting tradition and the PE master in particular, Mr Royden Thomas, was very keen and enthusiastic. He was the first person really to influence my career.'

At the Marist Convent in Paignton Sue Barker, now working for the Sky sports channel, was lucky in both of her PE teachers. One of them, Mrs Chadwick, 'got me going in tennis: she ran the local club that I belonged to from the age of eight.'

Mrs Chadwick was a gifted teacher. 'She had an excellent way of encouraging you. She'd write off to the LTA for their special tests. If you rallied ten balls you'd get a badge, then if you managed twenty it would be a certificate and so on. These were mini-goals and you really wanted them. If you missed a day's practice you wouldn't get a badge. Encouragement was everything. All my success in tennis really goes back to the achievements Mrs Chadwick made me get.'

The other PE teacher, Mrs Emburey, invited a top tennis coach to the school to spot tennis talent. This was Arthur Roberts who became Sue's own coach and took her to the top of the tennis ladder. 'When I was 12 I won the Under-14 event at Exeter and earned a bit of money. Arthur said to me, "Success doesn't taste too bad, does it?" and I said, "Too right it doesn't!" From then on I felt that going out to parties didn't seem nearly as good as winning a tournament!'

Cricketer Rachael Heyhoe Flint has reason to be grateful to Mary Greenhalgh, who arrived to teach PE at Wolverhampton High School for Girls when Rachael was in her second year.

'Before she came no-one was very interested in cricket. She was an Angela Brazil type figure – a real schoolgirls' heroine, very fit and good-looking. Our greatest rival was Bilston High School in an industrial district of Wolverhampton. Those of us who got most runs got more doughnuts for tea. In my last year I managed to get two centuries although some of the boundaries were fairly limited. If you hit the wall of the school building full toss, you were given a six. I was trying to win a bet that I could break the windows of either the library or the music block, but I never managed it. Seriously though, it was Mary Greenhalgh who inspired me. In 1954 she took us to Edgbaston to watch an international women's cricket match and I realised then that cricket was the game for me. For one thing it meant I could travel all over the world – and I have!'

Another cricketer, Norman Cowans, impressed the maths master, Paul Lukas, at Park High School in Stanmore.

'A group of us were keen on cricket and we found a lot of bats in the school basement. They must have played cricket at one time but the sports master wasn't keen on the game. Anyway I persuaded my mates to form a team. There was a cricket ground a few hundred yards down the road but we needed a member of staff to supervise us. Mr Lukas was so impressed with our enthusiasm that he agreed to do it. After that he gave up his breaks and lunchtimes to coach us. It was he who recommended me and a few others for the Harrow schools cricket week.'

England cricketer Angus Fraser also found at Gayton High in Harrow and Orange Hill Senior, Edgware, 'teachers who were keen to take pupils out to play cricket midweek and on Saturday mornings.' Fellow-cricketer Alan Wells found 'one or two members of staff' at Tideway Comprehensive, Newhaven, 'very supportive when they realised I had the potential to be a cricketer.'

Paul 'Gazza' Gascoigne was happy at both his schools, Breckenbecks Junior High and Heathfield Senior Gateshead and he is grateful to one of the staff. But fellow Spurs star Gary Lineker declared that it was his family rather than anyone at Leicester Grammar who influenced him; while England captain Bryan Robson felt he was influenced equally by his family and by the staff at Birtley Lord Lawson Comprehensive.

England scrum half Richard Hill praised Bishop Wordsworth's Grammar in Salisbury. 'The school was very much involved in competitive sports. Although facilities were not great, many good sportsmen were produced due to the time and commitment exercised by the PE department. Rugby was particularly strong.'

Rugby master John Oates was the moving force behind England players Rory Underwood and Rob Andrew – close friends and contemporaries at Barnard Castle School in the Yorkshire Dales. He remembers them both as 'outstanding athletes and exceptional sportsmen'.

Of all the teachers described the most exceptional in her dedication is surely Margaret Whitbread, the coach and adoptive mother of the javelin champion Fatima Whitbread. Mrs Whitbread, ironically the PE teacher at St Chad's, the deadly rivals of Fatima's thousand-pupil comprehensive, Culverhouse, was the spur and inspiration for her career. But Fatima was first attracted to the javelin by the story told in a classics lesson of the Greek heroine Atalanta whose javelin killed monsters. She described how she felt in her autobiography *Fatima* (with Adrianne Blue: Pelham Books 1988):
   'Atalanta had grown up like me without a normal family – she was abandoned as a baby and suckled by a bear. But she became a heroine, the greatest woman athlete of the ancient world. My ambition was to be a great sportswoman like her.'
   A few weeks later, when Fatima turned up at the local playing field to try out the javelin she was shocked to find Margaret Whitbread was the javelin coach. But from that moment there grew a remarkable relationship that ended with her adoption by the Whitbread family and her stunning success as a world-class thrower.

The heady taste for success described by Sue Barker was the spur to many a sporting career. Barker remembers the great day when the tiny Marist Convent beat all the great schools, even the mighty Millfield, to win the Aberdare Cup – the national girls' schools tennis team trophy.
   'It was very exciting. It was held on the clay courts at Wimbledon

and it was wonderful to go there and win, especially for such a small school. The whole school felt involved when we won. They couldn't come and watch because we only had one school bus. But afterwards at assembly the teacher read out the results and we became little celebrities. I remember a great round of applause went up and the Aberdare cup was shown around and all the local press came – it was quite an occasion!'

Denis Compton's cricket career was set by the remarkable 114 runs he scored at the age of 14 for the elementary schools – he went to Bell Lane School Hendon – against the public schools at Lord's in 1932. John Emburey at Peckham Manor represented the South London schools and 'at the end of the season my figures were 18 wickets for 30 runs – an average of 1.66.' Footballer Billy Wright scored 10 goals in a great 13-nil victory for Madeley Modern School.

Recently retired Wales rugby captain Paul Thorburn would rather forget the massive 104-nil defeat that Hereford Cathedral suffered at the hands of Christ College, Brecon. Years later he shared a room with Robert Ackerman in France when he got his first cap for Wales. Ackerman had starred for Christ College in the fateful game and fortunately did not remember fly-half Thorburn!

Most of the great team players found that the team game was only part of a wider and richer education. Most sports lead to a comparatively early retirement and many are grateful that their education equipped them for another career. Cricketers Chris Tavaré and Paul Downton at Sevenoaks are cases in point. Tavaré told us: 'Two teachers gave me the enthusiasm, interest and inspiration to pursue both cricket and zoology. As well as a career in professional cricket I have spent two winters working for the Ministry of Agriculture, Fisheries and Food.' Downton agrees. Sevenoaks, he says, 'encouraged sporting excellence whilst maintaining a high degree of academic commitment.' Fellow-cricketer Chris Broad at Colston's School in Bristol says 'it helped having a full education which included sport.'

In other words, schools are not doing their job if they concentrate only on sport – a career that rarely lasts a lifetime. Athlete Roger Black did not choose athletics as a career until he had left Portsmouth Grammar. 'My chosen career at school was medicine. The school encouraged me to participate in all sports and never pressured me into athletics, which was honourable on their part since I was obviously talented in this area. The school gave me freedom of choice which I usually took against athletics. For example, I chose to participate in a school play instead of competing at the English Schools Athletics Championship.'

Like ballet dancer David Drew in Chapter Nine, Black realised how precarious his chosen career could be, and how vital it might be to have the benefit of an all-round education. David Gower at King's School, Canterbury, had the best of both worlds – a top academic education and 'being at a school where sporting facilities were of a high standard, and where sports were given above average attention.'

Clare Wood, 1987 Wightman Cup Player, found the right balance too at St Bede's near Eastbourne. 'Although my chosen career was non-academic I was still given support by the school to pursue tennis. They helped me find a balance between studies and practice which gave me the best of both worlds.'

Chris Bonington, the mountaineer, said: 'University College School provided an open liberal education which gave me the confidence/freedom to help make my choices. The influence was not so much direct as a background influence.'

The great Welsh rugby legend, J. P. R. Williams, became an orthopaedic surgeon – and thanks Bridgend Grammar School as well as Millfield for his second career. Another rugby-playing medic is Tommy Kemp who captained England in the 1940s. He was about to leave Denstone College in the 1930s when medicine was considered a wise option against the vagaries of the Depression.

His career decision was finally clinched after a scare when he feared that a heart murmur might prevent him playing any more games. So awful was this prospect that when in the school holidays the murmur was pronounced innocent, Kemp was so impressed by the cardiologist who gave the welcome news that 'this most memorable event raised my estimation of the medical profession and endorsed my decision to study medicine!'

Olympic hurdler Alan Pascoe began his athletics career at Portsmouth Southern Grammar 'supported by the PE staff and headmaster. This led to the opportunity to gain a unique insight into the business of sport as well as the sport itself. This has ultimately been of value to me in my second career – originally I lectured in Physical Education.'

A disarmingly honest comment came from Ian Wooldridge, now a *Daily Mail* sports columnist. 'A scholarship to Brockenhurst Grammar

School happily brought me under the influence of an English master of outstanding inspirational ability. I was as thick as five planks at everything other than cricket, but he encouraged me to write. It has now kept me just above the breadline for forty years!'

Even humbler was the late John Arlott, in whose glowing obituaries it was said that he could have turned his hand to most things. He started in the police force and then went on to the BBC. But he remembered the day at school when he went to watch Jack Hobbs in a Test at the Oval. 'It set a spark alight which has never died,' he told us. 'It made me, though, a commentator, not a player – and conscious of my own deficiencies.'

And Peter West is grateful to Cranbrook School in Kent – where he was Head of School and captain of most of the sports teams – for the 'solid educational background which might have served me well in several careers. The one the school and my parents planned for me – Civil Service after university – did not materialise – probably on account of my falling short of required standards and certainly of my failure to work hard enough!'

Henrietta Shaw hit the headlines after leaving Harrogate Ladies' College by becoming the first woman Cambridge cox in the Boat Race. But her subsequent career has been with television documentaries. The career of another oarsman, Daniel Topolski, followed a similar pattern. His recent book *Dark Blues*, exposing the ruthless competition of the Boat Race, aroused some controversy and he is well known as a former Oxford coach and current commentator on the race. In fact, far more of his life has been devoted to travelling and writing about his travels.

'I did row at Westminster and then at Oxford but it was only ever a sideline – a ridiculous passion. The thing was, I never had any money for travel, but my rowing got me to places on free trips and I took advantage of this.'

In fact, Topolski began rowing long before he got to Westminster. He was a day boy until the age of 11 at the French Lycée and he lived in a big house overlooking Regent's Park.

'I started rowing on the boating pool at Regent's Park Lake when I was about eight. My mother was very keen on fresh air. She was always pushing me out into the Park. My father used to take me on the boats. Then, at the age of 11 or 12, I began helping the men who looked after the boats. I got about £7 a week, quite a lot for those days. I used to help to varnish a battered old shell which had been a good racing boat and I really learned to row on that. It used to delight me to go out late in the evenings after school – and then I'd work there in the holidays as well. My parents would have preferred me to be playing football or something traditional – my father, as an émigré Pole, was entranced by English traditions and that's why he sent me to Westminster.

'I made some wonderful friends at the Lake. The manager, Frank Nightingale, came up daily from Molesey. His right hand man was George, an ex-army officer. Then there was Johnny Gale, a rough character who used to get into pub fights – they all came from the Paddington area. One of the biggest tragedies I remember was when he was working on a building site and he fell off and was in hospital for four days before he died. These were my very close friends though apart from our work together our worlds never mixed. They called me Danny and I think they regarded me as the little nob from the big house across the Lake. But they stopped me becoming a little public school creep by showing me this earthy part of British life. My mother was a bit worried about the way I spoke – if I said, "I'm going over the Park", she'd get upset and say, "*INTO* the Park!"'

Round-the-world yachtsman Robin Knox-Johnston was also messing about on the river before he went to Berkhamsted Boys' School. 'I had decided on a career before I went to Berkhamsted. Although rather far from the sea, we did have the Grand Union Canal running through the town, where I launched my first boat, a canoe, at the age of 14. It sank!'

Nothing at school happened to change Robin's choice of career, even the scathing comment of the maths master on a piece of work he had handed in. 'He just said, "Knox-Johnston, if you ever go to sea I am going to emigrate to Switzerland!" The next piece of work just had, "By air!"'

Families, far more than schools, influenced the career choice of sportsmen and women: the dedication of sports star families is well documented and just under half of our replies bore that out.

Athlete Kathy Cook was happy at the Hurst School, Baghurst, and at Queen Mary's VIth Form College in Basingstoke: 'But my parents were the ones who probably influenced and helped me the most.' Tennis player Ann Jones said the same thing and added with characteristic no-nonsense brevity: 'Career mapped out – school made no difference.'

Lucy Soutter began playing squash at the age of six 'because Mum and Dad played squash all through the winter.'

Sue Barker, like many other sports stars, recognises with gratitude the debt she owes to her parents. 'They had to sacrifice a lot – they gave up everything for me. I was the youngest of three and it was terribly difficult for them. I had to be taken to tournaments and if they didn't take me I just couldn't go. And I had to be driven one-and-a-half hours to the practice courts. My father, who was an area manager – a salesman for a brewery – used to fit his working day round me, so that the last jobs of the day were near my school and he could come and pick me up and drive me to my training.'

Often parents had been distinguished sportsmen and women themselves. Paul Thorburn's father had played for Cardiff University and Cardiff Rugby Club and used to take Paul and his two brothers to internationals at Cardiff Arms Park and Twickenham. Alex Greaves's mother had been one of the first female jockeys and has worked for the past twenty years as a trainer in the stables where Alex now rides. Her father was a show jumper and eventer and Alex was in the saddle by the age of four. Lester Piggott began his apprenticeship at the age of 12 with his father, who insisted that he make up the school hours lost on the racecourse with a tutor at home. Lester rode his first winner at 12 and by the age of 15 he had won 52 races.

Cricketer John Lever also had keen parents. 'My Dad enjoyed cricket. He was one of a large family who was kicked out of school at 14 to work in a butcher's shop. He loved the game but it was too expensive for him to play. But he saw to it that I was never short of equipment. My parents have supported me all the way through. Mum came to watch all the early games I played for the Ilford Schools side and Dad worked all hours so he could pay my subscriptions to the cricket club and all the other expenses – though he never earned much money.'

Both of Ian Botham's parents played cricket and Ian was already a prodigy in both cricket and football by the age of nine. But Botham Senior used to tell him: 'It's the next success not the last one that matters.'

Rachael Heyhoe Flint's father Geoffrey Heyhoe 'was a good club cricketer and he was especially good at the theory of cricket. He had represented his college as a student and he became Director of PE for Wolverhampton Borough Council.'

Rachael had been playing cricket 'from the year dot' and rumour had it that she could score a cricket match before she could read a sentence. When she was 11 she went to watch her father playing for the Technical College. The team was one man short and she was soon co-opted at number 11. 'The pads reached to my waist and the bat felt like a tree trunk, but the men were kind enough to bowl me a few slowish half-volleys and to everyone's surprise I managed to score two or three undefeated runs and save the game.'

She remembers too that her father played in the Fathers' Match at Wolverhampton Girls' High. He was wicket-keeping and she was batting for the other side – but he could not refrain from coaching her after each stroke, to the great amusement of the spectators.

'I lacked nothing in the way of support and encouragement and my parents were, I believe, genuinely pleased at the sporting direction I had chosen. My father would often spend hours bowling at me in the garden.'

Parents, no doubt, will continue to support their offspring with the immense dedication praised in so many of our replies.

But what of the schools? Many top professionals triumphed in spite of poor facilities and lack of enthusiasm from their teachers. Indeed, Graham Fowler never played cricket at all at Accrington Grammar, 'so I never realised its pitfalls nor benefits!' It never held Fowler back and he is able to joke about it.

Others, however, are now beginning to express serious concern. The cricketer Neil Fairbrother 'only played a couple of games a year' at Lymm Grammar. 'Hardly inspiring!' is his wry comment.

John Lever was lucky in that Dane County Secondary sent its cricketers to indoor coaching facilities at Ilford. There was also Mr Pearse, the art master, who had played cricket for his club and was quite a good batsman. 'We had bowling in the playground for which they even put up a net – they really made an effort.'

Even at Highlands Junior School, Mr Cummings, the head teacher, would encourage his team to spend hours bowling at a set of stumps marked up on the playground wall. 'I got into the team at the age of ten and I felt a little bit different,' remembers Lever. 'The rest of the school would watch as I bowled, and I remember Mr Cummings throwing the cricket ball high into the air for us to catch.'

He comments wistfully, 'I don't think there is so much cricket being played in playgrounds today. The bottom line is an interest shown in cricket by teachers willing to play and to run school teams – something which is sadly lacking these days. Cricket takes up a lot of time. It's one of the longest games. Cricket clubs are now providing more and more facilities for colts' cricket. Clubs have to a large degree taken over the problems and responsibilities of cricket in the state school sector.'

Another problem he identifies is the training provided by the colleges. 'Many of the PE teachers coming out of places like Loughborough are athletics coaches – they are not ball-orientated. I have done cricket coaching in various parts of Essex and some of the PE coaches have to be coached in cricket themselves. In Essex some of the public schools have ex-professional cricketers as coaches on their staff and that is an ideal situation.' He himself teaches PE at Bancroft's School, Woodford Green.

Lucy Soutter too noticed sadly that 'most of my squash contemporaries come from private education, which is a pity.'

But this public/state school divide seems to affect team games most. Norman Cowans agrees with John Lever. 'I think it's a pity that all the new young cricketers seem to be coming from private schools where they have staff committed to promoting the game. The trouble is that cricket suffers especially in state schools because it takes up so much time outside school hours.'

Cowans also thinks that the clubs are taking over to right this wrong: 'At the moment all the onus is on the clubs. A kid hasn't got much of a chance to play cricket in a comprehensive unless he belongs to a club.' And private sponsorship is taking a hand too. 'I work for an investment company that sponsors coaches to go out into schools in every region – they also sponsor the England team's training. This is the way things will have to go in the future.'

Rachael Heyhoe Flint dates the decline in girls' school cricket from the time when comprehensive education spread and, as part and parcel of it, co-education. 'When I was at Wolverhampton High there were ten or twelve nearby girls' schools playing cricket. Now there are only 30 cricketing girls' schools in the whole country. When a school becomes co-educational and there are limited PE facilities, inevitably the cricket goes to the boys.'

Rugby too is beset with recruitment difficulties. Paul Thorburn finds it depressing that a lot of comprehensives in the Rhondda have stopped playing the game altogether.

Even the mighty Gwendraeth Grammar became a mixed comprehensive in 1983 and rugby there has been declining ever since. Twenty-seven-times-capped Jonathan Davies said that at the school, 'from the age of 11 all I wanted to do was to play rugby. But youngsters don't want to do that any more.' Deputy Headmaster Huw Morgan blames television: 'Pupils are less dedicated to rugby than they were. They are now regarding sport as a spectator rather than a participatory activity.'

Back to Paul Thorburn: 'Rugby is now hit by a lot of problems. Unlike the England team, the Welsh rugby team doesn't have many public schoolboys. There is a move away from competitive sports in the comprehensive schools and the teachers' strike hasn't helped either. It's also possible that because Wales hasn't been very successful lately, kids are turning to other sports. In my day you didn't have much choice: it was only rugby and cricket. Now there are so many more opportunities – shooting, golf – it's easy for a child to get out of the major team sports if he doesn't like them. Another factor may be that kids see so much sport on offer on TV – ice hockey, squash – even football – and they want to have a go.'

The clubs may have to take the lead in rugby too. 'The senior clubs are worried about this decline and they are taking over the coaching in a lot of schools.'

Geoff Capes disapproves of the clubs taking over coaching. 'The local clubs look to the schools to supply sportsmen and women. PE teachers are not doing their jobs properly. Sports men and women have to start early. The teachers have to train them and spot their talent – it's often too late otherwise.

'The state schools are losing out on this. The public schools are supplying the talent – look at the England rugby team – nearly all public school. The state schools are getting rid of 70 per cent of British talent in sport!

'I think there's a load of bull talked about sport in schools these days. All this rubbish about not having competition! There's so much emphasis placed on success in exam results but to my mind that puts a lot more stress on children than competition in sport. If they feel that way about competition in sport they should ban exams as well.

'PE teachers who won't take team matches are pathetic – it's the Dark Ages syndrome! A lot of them must be failed sportsmen themselves. They're complete charlatans!'

Former England Association Football manager and national coach Bobby Robson wonders whether there are still the teachers who are willing and capable of spotting and training talent. He told us: 'The school that I went to, Waterhouses Secondary Modern in County Durham, was at that time keen on sport. There were only two: football in the winter and cricket in the summer – and the girls played netball or hockey. The PE time was therefore spent on one subject and not spread over many sports as is the case now. Through that system I was able to play quite a lot of schoolboy football. That stimulated me and helped put me "on my way" – together with the help I received from a very enthusiastic sports teacher who spent time AFTER school hours to help and encourage boys to play football.'

Robson concludes sadly: 'Those days and teachers have gone now.'

15 Unorthodox

'Learned precious little anywhere. Never passed an exam. Never got a degree.'

The words of best-selling novelist Mary Wesley sum up the education of those listed under 'Unorthodox' in the index at the back of this book. Some of the most successful people in the country never went to school. So in what ways if any did they miss out as a result of having no formal schooling or a highly unusual one?

Several had governesses – Mary Wesley had at least 16! They were either aristocratic or exceptionally talented children – prodigies like the Menuhins. Miriam Rothschild was taught by her father. Patrick Moore was often ill. Wendy Toye's schooling was the stage. Others left school early – either by their own design like Lucy *Castaway* Irving who ran away from school at 13, or by the design of the school – like Eddy Shah whose parents were asked to remove him from a series of establishments. Or Oliver Reed who only admits in his *Who's Who* entry to attending Ewell Castle, Surrey but who is said to have been expelled from more than a dozen schools.

Reed finds himself in illustrious company: singer Marti Caine's nomadic family life sent her to fifteen schools, designer Mary Quant went to thirteen, and writers Jill Tweedie and Penelope Mortimer went to nine and five respectively, while another writer, Gillian Tindall, declared her schools were too numerous to mention. SDP founder Shirley Williams went to eight different schools. Her father lectured in political science in England and North America, and Shirley followed him around.

Mary Wesley is by her own admission a late developer – an author whose first best-seller was published after she reached her seventies. In her youth it was, she says, 'quite usual for girls to be brought up by governesses, like the Mitfords. My brother did the usual thing of being sent to Eton and Oxford. I must say I was never at all envious of him – in fact I rather despised him though I don't remember why; he was rather an amiable character. I did tag along behind him on his fishing and birdwatching expeditions, but I didn't learn anything from him at all.

'My mother had been brought up by governesses herself. Education was thought to be totally useless for girls, who were just waiting to be married. I was brought up to look after men – and God they do need it, don't they? I've been writing since I was 18, but other things got in the way, like falling in love.'

Nevertheless, even in the early part of the century, Wesley's education was rather out of the ordinary.

'I started having governesses from the age of three. The reason for that was my brother. My mother had the idea that he must be able to speak French before he went to prep school. She knew how appallingly languages are taught in English schools. So when I was only three-and-a-half my beloved nanny was given the push and my brother and I started on this series of foreign governesses.

'These governesses – I think I can count sixteen but there may have been more – weren't much more than rather jolly *au pair* girls – French, Swiss, Italian, Danish – if they lasted a year that was good going. They would chatter away in their own language and I grew up speaking French and Italian. I even used to dream in French till I was in my thirties. But I didn't learn any verbs or anything like that at all. And I never learned any English grammar either. My editor still has to put all the punctuation in for me even now.

'I didn't like those girls at all. I remember screaming at one of them, "I won't talk to that woman!" and my mother saying I was absolutely bloody.

'The trouble was, these girls weren't educated themselves. We did get sent a curriculum from a thing called PNEU [Parents National Educational Union] two or three times a year but we didn't stick to it of course.

'I do think I missed out a lot socially through not going to school. I was absolutely terrified of other people. We moved around a lot so I never had the chance to make friends. My parents lived in twenty-seven different houses in their first twenty-five years of marriage. As soon as Mother got settled in to one house, she'd hear of somewhere nicer. In those days it was easy to rent houses unfurnished. They had all their silver and glass and linen and furniture and they just moved about from house to house.

'I realised pretty early that I was totally uneducated – partly through the boyfriends I had. There were plenty of men in those days who thought girls shouldn't bother with education, but I had rather left-wing boyfriends who kept saying, "How ignorant you are!" They'd thrust books at one – Bertrand Russell – that sort of thing. In the end I got rather fed up with this so I went to the LSE and clocked on to courses in international politics and anthropology, which still very much interest me. But I was really educated by my boyfriends, lovers and husbands. My second husband was wonderful at educating me. He never said how ignorant I was – he just answered any question that I asked and I got a lot of information that way.'

When Wesley was 14 her father was in India and her mother decided to join him there. Mary was sent to school for the first time.

'My mother just dumped me in a home school on the south coast. A home school was one where you could stay in the holidays. I stayed there for eighteen months and I hated it. I just couldn't understand what was going on.'

The following year she went to Queen's College, Harley Street – also the alma mater of Penelope Gilliatt and Anna Wintour – and now speaks rather wistfully of the two happy terms she spent there – though hardly for purely educational reasons:

'I loved it because no-one knew what I was doing and I only did what interested me. There was a wonderful teacher called Émile Cammaerts who taught French literature and he latched on to me because I spoke French. I did Greek and history too. But the best part of it was being allowed to go about London on my own when I was about 15 or 16.'

Relationships with fellow pupils were still a problem. 'I had no friends. It was so difficult just getting to know the other girls. I was terrified of women. I thought them all extremely sophisticated and I was very shy until my late twenties.

'I was always writing, but I threw everything away – poems, stories, several novels. The person who got me going was Antonia White. She was my godmother and one day I showed her something I'd written. We were always desperately short of money and she suggested I try writing Mills and Boon stuff. Well, I was hopeless at that but I went on and finally got it right.'

Women *d'un certain age* and of a certain class may always have had the option of a governess. Betty Kenward – the recently retired gossip queen Jennifer of *Harpers and Queen* 'Jennifer's Diary' told us she 'never went to school at all.'

In fact, she went only to finishing school in Brussels at the extraordinarily early age of twelve-and-a-half. 'The other girls were all at least four years older than me, but that was because I had a cranky mother!'

Until then, however, Betty had governesses – one in London and two in the country. She had two brothers who at first shared the governesses.

'There were no pre-prep schools in those days – I'm talking about the year 1910 or thereabouts. When my brothers went off to prep school and then to Winchester I was terribly lonely. All my meals were brought to me in the schoolroom by a children's maid. It was also her job to pick up my riding clothes if I left them on the floor. When I was about eight and had lessons all day the governess would have lunch in the schoolroom with me. But it was a solitary existence. I used to long for the holidays when my brothers would come home.'

Life was not all work, however. 'I'd much rather go riding than do my lessons – I'd been taught by the grooms. My second governess in the country was Miss Webb. Dear Webbie – she had a woolly hat and she used to ride up from the village on a bicycle. Anyway, Webbie and I had this splendid arrangement. If I heard the hounds baying anywhere near, I'd want to be off to the Meet. So she'd always manage to have a convenient dentist's appointment or a sick grandmother – just in case my parents found out I'd missed my lessons. This went on for years and they never found out. You can't imagine now how remote we were from our parents in those days.'

Betty's father set her on course for her ultimate career on the *Tatler* and finally on *Harpers and Queen*.

'My mother couldn't care tuppence about me. She never wanted a girl. I was never close to her, though I was to my brothers and my father. He was a busy man but he thought it important that I should go to see the best of everything. He took me to see Pavlova dance and to the best tennis matches with people like Suzanne Lenglen. And we went to the best race meetings, the best polo and to Cowes.

'My father gave me a very good piece of advice which stood me in good stead in my job. It was, "Keep your eyes and ears open and your mouth shut"! He knew an enormous number of people himself. When I got to the *Tatler* I didn't know what to do at all. So he used to take me out to lunch at Claridges at least twice a week and help me. He gave me a very different sort of education – a social education, I suppose you could call it.

'It was extraordinary that I was sent off to finishing school so young. The idea was for me to learn French. I'd done some French with my governess – I remember we had a pink book called *French Without Tears*. The trouble was, I learned French in Brussels with a Flemish accent – just like an awful Cockney accent here!'

Like Mary Wesley, Betty Kenward found relationships with women a problem:

'I was absolutely terrified of the older girls and this is one way I feel I missed out tremendously in not having gone to school. One of my greatest problems has been dealing with other women. I had no sisters and as I said, I wasn't close to my mother. So I've always found it hard to deal with difficult women. Whenever I've come across them I just couldn't cope. They tell me that's the sort of thing you learn at school.'

Surely 'Jennifer''s solitary childhood was quite at odds with the hyper-social career for which she became a household name?

'Yes, that's absolutely right. I really believe that because I was alone so much as a child – in the country for hours on end with my pony and my dogs – my job has been absolute agony at times. Even now, after 47 years, I still sometimes get to a door and feel I just can't go in.'

What had she missed out on educationally?

'There are *masses* of things I feel I missed. I'd *love* to have been properly educated. I know that 1066 was the Battle of Hastings but that's about all I know about history. I don't know any literature at all! I keep *frightfully* quiet about that! I suppose I'm self-educated to a certain extent. And then I did no sport.

'But really I've been very lucky. People have to go and get degrees before they can do a job like mine these days.'

The experience of novelist and scriptwriter Elizabeth Jane Howard runs parallel to that of Betty Kenward. But her perception of her education is very different, probably due to the extraordinary quality of her governess.

Like 'Jennifer', Howard had brothers who went to conventional schools and indeed she started at one herself. But it was 'a horrible day school' where she was bullied from morning to night. After four terms she was allowed to leave and Miss Cobham, her mother's old governess, was summoned.

Miss Cobham was by no means in the first flush of youth but like all the best teachers she was still learning. At the age of 70 she won a gold medal for the History of Art and was so enthusiastic about the subject that when the Chinese Exhibition arrived in London in 1936 'we had no lessons for a fortnight – we went to it every day!'

This, however, was rare. The tutorial day was structured with lessons five days a week from 10 a.m. to 1 p.m. and homework to do as well. There was none of the paucity complained of by Betty Kenward. Elizabeth Jane was learning Latin and Greek from the age of nine and had soon read the whole of Shakespeare. She was allowed to choose a special subject each term: one of them was Egyptology which ended up lasting the whole year.

Best of all for a future novelist was the encouragement she was given in her writing. No-one in the family was at all interested, though her grandfather 'had written a book about trees'. But Miss Cobham laughed at all her jokes and let her go on writing all the time, at the possible expense of algebra!

When three other children joined the group they included painter John Saxton who like Howard had his priorities clear even from this early age. 'At the age of 13 he had already been to eight schools and was expelled from the last. But Miss Cobham could manage him. He drew all the time, just as I wrote all the time.'

Perhaps because of her three fellow-pupils, Howard feels none of the social deprivation described by Mary Wesley and Betty Kenward. She had dozens of cousins as well as her brothers to play with. But at the age of 16 she realised she had to leave home.

'I was desperately homesick if I even went out to lunch. I wanted at that time to be an actress, so something had to be done. I asked to go away to boarding school and a finishing school run by twin sisters near Beaconsfield was found for me. The first term was absolute agony – but after that it was all right.'

Her only regret is that she did not keep closely in touch with Miss Cobham who afterwards retired in Hove. It was the War, and Hove seemed awfully far away. 'But I sent her my first novel and I've written about her in my books' – repaying a debt of gratitude for a good education.

Illness was the reason for astronomer Patrick Moore's education by tutors. He told us, 'I had a great deal of illness during my boyhood. I managed one term at prep school, and at 13 took Common Entrance for Eton and passed it. Unfortunately I was ill again before term started, so I never went and had to finish things with tutors. I passed my School Certificate and Matric at 15, and at 16, when the War broke out, I admit I faked my age and the medical to get into the RAF and fly.'

Did this solitary childhood lead him to the solitary science of star-gazing? Possibly, but then any day boy could have begun the way Moore did. His mother was 'slightly interested' in astronomy and at the age of six he found one of her books about it. He resolved to identify a new constellation every night and invested his 6d pocket money in a star map. Out in the garden that first night he had no trouble in finding several constellations. But when his mother called him in at bedtime he was quite lost in the pitch dark. He used the Plough to get his bearings, found his way to the tennis net and after 15 minutes to the back door. After that he was hooked for life!

Education at home is a tradition in the Cecil family and Lady Rose Cecil, still only in her thirties, stayed behind when her brothers went off to Eton. She was, she says, 'always very lonely' and is not sure how good her teachers were. The Rothschilds too sent their son off to Harrow but their daughter Miriam, now the distinguished naturalist and biologist and Fellow of the Royal Society and holder of six honorary doctorates, stayed at home.

Her father Charles Rothschild was himself a great botanist and entomologist who inspired in his small daughter the same enthusiasms. He did not like schools and hated examinations which he thought were bad for everybody.

'I *hated* the idea of school. My sisters went, though only much later in life – and I didn't like the sound of it one bit. My mother didn't believe in sending girls to school at all really. My father's hatred of exams was legendary. I once met Professor Gardiner, my father's zoology professor at Cambridge, and he said my father had been the most brilliant student he'd ever had but he only got a poor third because he was such a nervous examinee. Everything went out of his head when he saw an exam paper. He wouldn't put me through the same misery.

'Funnily enough I found that I was a wonderful examinee. When I finally took myself off at the age of 17 for evening classes in zoology at Chelsea Polytechnic they gave me an exam to do and I found that, unlike my father, all the ideas came *into* my head when I sat down to an exam and I easily came out top!'

Did she, we wondered, regret never having had a chance to prove herself in the academic world?

'Not at all! I think exams are *impossible* – they're criminal! They don't tell you anything about a person. When I was teaching at a school for a short time I refused to give the children exams. I'd give them three weeks to look things up. Yes – I suppose I was rather modern. I think I was probably the inventor of coursework!'

Miriam never learnt anything from a book. She used to go for walks with her father and share his passion for natural history.

'You have to realise that for me as a child, biology and natural history were a part of life. We had no set lessons. On walks with him from a very early age I'd learn the names of trees and identify what birds were singing. I had a wonderful childhood and the only tragedy was my father's death when I was 15. After he died I couldn't bear to have anything to do with natural history for two years because that was what we'd done together.'

Fortunately for the scientific world, she was shaken out of this torpor by her brother Victor who came back from Harrow with the holiday task of dissecting a frog.

'I was so fascinated that it latched me back on to natural history.'

There was some formal teaching in the shape of Miss Joyce, an elderly governess who used to arrive in a pony and trap and stay for a couple of hours every day.

'We did do things like history, though I never got further than the Saxons because the end of term would arrive and the next term we'd start on the Romans all over again!'

Miriam, brought up with her own three siblings and numerous Rothschild cousins, was never lonely, though there was no social life for children outside the family until she was about 15, when the tennis tournaments and house parties began.

'I was never a solitary child and I was never shy! I was always rather contemptuous of shy people – I thought they were far too interested in themselves. I was far too curious to be shy. At dances in those days you'd have to sit out if nobody asked you to dance and I didn't mind that in the least because I was busy watching people. I was pretty scornful of those girls that went and hid in the lavatory!'

She sent her own children to day school. 'Certainly not to boarding school! Dreadful places! Winston Churchill said of the Navy that it was "rum, sodomy and the lash". I used to say that boarding schools were the same, but without the rum!'

Would she have followed a different career had her father not interested her so early in natural history?

'Oh, I don't think I've *had* a career! I was lucky that my hobby was my amusement and it happened to lead to some quite useful scientific research, that's all! I had a serenely happy childhood and the education I had was absolutely wonderful!'

Those who lack the formal structure of the conventional school day must surely develop self-discipline, and this is a quality that Wendy Toye possesses in abundance. The theatre director who produced the 1992 Sadlers Wells revival of *The Sound of Music* needed it for her long and distinguished career as dancer, choreographer, actress, theatre, film and opera director.

Miss Toye was one of the host of stage children – that special category who even today have a fragmented, often tutor-directed education designed to fit round their professional lives.

She spoke to us in one of her brief spells of free time between rehearsals of *The Sound of Music* – following the pattern her life has taken from her earliest childhood.

'I started dancing at the age of three-and-a-half. My first appearance was a solo dance in a charity performance at the Albert Hall, and at five I was there again in a ballet. I was called The Pocket Wonder.

'My mother was extremely strict. She was a Scot and very well educated like most Scottish girls then, though she was of quite humble origin. She insisted on my having a governess from the age of five and I had the same one until I was 15.

'She was a wonderful woman called Miss Cockell and she seemed very old to me but then most people do when you're only five. I remember teaching her bézique and she taught me French and history as well as the three Rs.

'My lessons with Miss Cockell had no set pattern – they could be anywhere at any time, though I had to put in the same number of hours each day. I might have dance classes in the morning and lessons in the afternoon, or the lessons might be from 8.30 till 11 before an afternoon rehearsal and an evening show. And this included weekends.'

Toye's mother was the motivating force in her life: 'My mother played a tremendous part in my artistic education. Every time the Diaghilev company came to London she managed to take me to it, from the age of five – I don't know how she did it.

'I suppose she saw something special in me and wanted me to go as far as I could in dancing. She's wasn't a pushy theatrical mother at all.'

But there is a twinge of regret in her voice now for what must have been a kind of social deprivation: 'I really had very little time to play. I did mix with other children but it was always in a working relationship at the dance classes. And all the other girls were much older than me. I was often in shows where I was the only child. Yes, I suppose I was a bit of an Infant Phenomenon. I had classes with Ninette de Valois – that certainly gave me self-discipline. I was in the Royal Ballet by the age of 12.'

Wendy's mother had the monopoly of ambition in the family. Her father took no interest, and never once came to see her in a show. 'He preferred to stay at home and read.' Her brother went to school and university 'and had a normal education'.

But by the time she was 14 and had her name up in lights outside the old Alhambra Theatre, she must sometimes have longed for a little independence. 'Theatrical children have to have a chaperone – I know – I've got 14 children in *The Sound of Music*! Even in those days you had to be chaperoned and my father refused to let anyone chaperone me except my mother.'

Educationally as well as socially there are obvious disadvantages to this kind of childhood and Toye is conscious of those too.

'Not having been to school didn't at all affect my career – you didn't need Matric or "A" levels or anything to get a job in those days – I wouldn't stand a chance now! I've had a wonderful, fascinating life. I've never stopped working and I couldn't really say I'd missed out. It would be so ungrateful. But if I had my time over again I'd like to have had a good education. You can never compensate for that – for the insecurity – however hard you try. For instance, if I've had to do a historical piece in the theatre I've had to do so much homework. It would come naturally to someone who's been properly educated. I must say I've never quite understood my mother for not making sure I had a proper education.'

There are those who for various reasons rejected the 'proper education' offered them by their parents. Eddy Shah, the newspaper magnate who smashed the power of the print unions, then launched and lost *Today,* had a confused childhood. From the age of four he lived with his grandparents, first his maternal ones in England, then with his father's parents in India. When he was 11 his father, a Persian lawyer, rented a house in Surrey, and he went to live with him there. His father operated a strict educational régime for Eddy, his only son. 'I was hammered with education,' he told Elisabeth Dunn in the *Telegraph* magazine in 1991. 'Because I never worked hard at school my dad used to sit me down and really put me through my stuff – grilling me all Sunday morning.' During these sessions he would be questioned on a book he had been allocated to read the previous week – writers like Jack Kerouac and Thomas Wolfe.

Finally he was packed off to boarding school, first to a now defunct prep school, then to Gordonstoun. He told Lynn Barber in the *Independent on Sunday* in 1991: 'I just became a rebel. I was thrown out of Gordonstoun twice, thrown out of a grammar school, almost thrown out of a secondary modern and then thrown out of a crammer.'

He realises now that 'It was just me trying to be noticed.'

Lucy Irvine became famous for her book *Castaway* after answering an advert which read 'Writer seeks "wife" for a year on tropical island.' Before that she had been a monkey-keeper, charlady and stonemason's mate among other things – a 'university of life' training that began when she ran away from Lady Eleanor Holles, the pukkah Hampton girls' school, at the age of 13. Like Shah she puts her rebellion down to family influence.

Lucy's own family split up and by her own admission her home life while at Lady Eleanor Holles was terribly disturbed.

'I was not happy towards the end of the period I attended that school, but would hesitate before saying that this was because of anything that was happening at school. I ran away from lots of schools and I wouldn't like to blame any of them, except that they weren't a refuge for me when my family split up. There was never anyone I could open up to there. But whenever I ran away I was really leaving home, not the school.'

She seems to have coped well enough in adult life; she has flourished in several jobs, and survived with an impossible writer on a desert island. But she points out, 'They were all fairly isolated jobs.'

She compares her own education with her eldest son's. 'The main thing I missed by ducking out so early was social integration. I never learned to be part of a team. My eldest child is now six. He's been at school a year now and he's learning it already, going round in groups – all that sort of thing.'

Several writers had a fragmented education: Barbara Cartland went to five schools, as did Penelope Mortimer, whose schools ranged from Croydon High to St Elphin's School for the Daughters of the Clergy. Journalist Jill Tweedie was also at Croydon High, then ran an amazing gauntlet of eight other schools including Roedean, Benenden, St Paul's, Sherborne and Cheltenham – qualifying her to write her own mini Good Schools Guide. She was, she says, happy at all of them, winning various in-school and national awards for essays and poetry which helped by 'making me feel writing needn't be just a private activity which you did and then stuck in a drawer. Some people out there were interested . . . .'

Another writer, Gillian Tindall, ended up at Oxford after a series of schools which she says are 'too numerous to list'. For family reasons she went through a series of starkly contrasting schools and the sudden changes made her a misfit in all of them.

'I found myself always socially misaligned. It felt as if everyone else had a book of rules except me.

'The awful thing about being a child is that you don't know enough to form a proper opinion. You might have a wild perception that something is wrong, but if you're a misfit, as I was everywhere, you think it's your fault. You can't believe that the adults are wrong. The early fifties were a time when a complete lack of adult accountability was tolerated. But even I couldn't help noticing that the norms of the adults in these schools I went to were utterly different.'

Two consecutive schools were poles apart from each other and from the 'decently agnostic, middle-class home of a medical publisher' that she came from:

'After the War, in the late forties and early fifties, there were numerous potty little schools that sprang up. It so happened that we lived in Sussex near two of them and I went to both. There was this ultra-progressive one like a hippie commune where everyone showed off and said, "Let's take all our clothes off and talk about sex." Some of the pupils never set foot in a classroom at all. It was all rather like *Lord of the Flies*. Even then A.S. Neill's ideas were old hat because the Victorian repression they were meant to combat had all disappeared anyway.'

Luckily she was a day girl there. 'I couldn't bear to have been there 24 hours a day. I don't think it dawned on my mother that there was a kind of child abuse going on. But she did realise that I wasn't learning a thing. So she decided to send me at the age of 11 to a revolting conventional little girls' boarding seminary.'

This change necessitated 'a good slug of academic teaching'. So Gillian had at least one idyllic golden summer in the 'interminable unchanging grey that was my school life'.

She was tutored by the local vicar, 'a dear man who had been a master at Lancing before retreating into country vicardom. He was at that time tutoring thick rich boys for Common Entrance in maths, Latin and English grammar. I was two years younger than these great oafs and he thought I was a dear clever little thing compared with them. He used to give us home-made lemonade each morning break and I'd play ball with these great boys.'

The idyll was quickly over. She was soon at a 'rotten little school which I would rather not name where the teaching of English was *degradingly* awful. "Oh *Keats*! *Feel* the sensuous rhythms, girls!"'

Here, she says, 'the creepy "Have you given your souls to Jesus, dear little girls?" kind of low church religion was almost as bizarre as the weirdo ideas of the progressives.'

But it was the illogicality, the endemic injustice of the school that Tindall really abhorred.

'For instance, there was a dearth of bathrooms so we all smelt – but we were also nagged all the time by the matrons for smelling! It was also the absolute phoniness and hypocrisy of the place that riled me. We all had to get dressed up for dinner – but then there was absolutely nowhere to go *after* dinner except a draughty classroom!'

The contrast with the hippie commune was stunning. Needless to say, Gillian didn't fit in there any better. She tried to take refuge in writing – she'd always written poems and novels since she was small. There was compulsory hymn practice every morning but Gillian had been told to shut up because she was singing out of tune. 'Perhaps if Gillian Tindall would stop singing we'd be able to hear the others!'

'It seemed to me preposterous therefore that I should have to attend, so I used to bunk off and sit in a freezing classroom and write a bit more of my novel.'

But the hideous illogicality of the school triumphed. 'When I was discovered the novel was torn up in front of me.'

We wondered whether these traumas stiffened the sinews for the struggle for self-discipline that is always a writer's lot. Tindall has her doubts:

'I suppose that when I had a young baby and my husband was working very hard and couldn't help, I was, because of this ghastly experience, better equipped in my desperate struggle to quarry out time for my writing. But I still don't believe that this validates the experience.'

However, she has never used the awful vicissitudes of her schooldays as material for her books. Some things, she says, hurt too much and go too deep to write about. 'And after all, what's life for if not to recover?'

Gillian Tindall was just as solitary in the midst of her peers at school as Mary Wesley and Betty Kenward in the schoolroom with a governess. But unlike them, her solitude did not last. 'I had a dim apprehension that there was life beyond school and I longed to be part of it. Throughout my schooldays I was an incognito grown-up. As soon as I escaped when I was 15 I found to my delight that I had no difficulty in making friends at all.'

Actress Juliet Stevenson values her many friends but says that her fragmented schooling has affected the way she approaches relationships.

She told Ann McFerran in the *Sunday Times Magazine* in 1990: 'I moved countries, schools and sometimes even languages every two years. I had a very happy childhood, but I recognise that I tend to go into a relationship with the subconscious expectation that it will end.'

Ironically, she believes that this has helped her in her profession: 'I love the fact that you concentrate so fully on something for a while, then you leave it behind and move on.'

Inventor genius Sir Clive Sinclair is another 'multiple-schooler' whose education may well have shaped his career. The search for privacy, often a problem in boarding education, was vital to Sinclair. His father, who ran a small machine company, went broke when Clive was 11 and the boy attended 13 different schools, forcing him to rely on his own company rather than on a constantly changing group of friends. The fact that he sought refuge in his books and his inventions, which must have influenced his subsequent career.

Phil Cooper must be the only ex-drug addict and street poet to address Etonians in their own Chapel. He is now becoming a familiar face in top public schools throughout Britain, where he regularly speaks to pupils warning them of the dangers of drug abuse. But sometimes it is all he can do to cross the threshold.

'I have this real dread of going into places of education. I hardly attended school at all after I got into hard drugs at the age of 12.

'I lived with my mum and grandmother and even then I hated school. I always wanted to learn from my own experience – whether it was climbing over a garden wall at the age of six or going to prison a few years later.

'I remember exactly the day when this drugs thing started. I was seven. I didn't want to go to school and I was playing my usual tricks, throwing a tantrum and screaming. I remember my mother screaming and saying she'd go and fetch the headmaster to take me to school. I didn't believe her but when I heard him downstairs with her I ran into the bathroom and I took a little bit of every medicine and pill in her bathroom cabinet!

'The headmaster dragged me downstairs and shoved me in his car. All the way back to school he lectured me about being a busy man and all that stuff. He stood me in the middle of the classroom and all the kids were told this is what would happen if they bunked off school. They all started making fun of me and calling me names. Then I vomited all over the boy next to me!

'I was back in that headmaster's car and in no time he was giving my mum a bollocking for sending me to school ill!

'That's when I realised the power of drugs.

'When I was 12 I registered at Our Lady of Lourdes, a Catholic secondary modern in Southport. Straightaway I got in with some older boys, told them about my medicine trick and pretty soon I was into their drugs scene. So at the age of 12 I was injecting speed and I was on hard drugs till 1979 when I was 29.

'I remember my only school report. It said, "There is nothing to say about Phil Cooper except that he has had 144 days off." In the four years I was registered at that school I only spent 25 days there. I was in and out of drugs and I only went when I felt like it.'

Could some teacher have intervened at that stage and somehow discovered the potential that Phil has now developed in his anti-drug poetry books that have sold in thousands and in his charismatic one-man performances? Perhaps he might have been noticed by the English staff:

'The one time I used to go into school was for the English exams. I'd find out the day of the English language exam from my mates in the street and I'd go in for that. What I liked was that you had to write a story. One time, I hadn't been in that school for about six months, so I got some crazy looks when I turned up. We were asked to write a story about a boy being adventurous. When the exam was marked my friends told me I got 50 out of 50!

'The thing I really regret is not learning reading and writing and maths properly. Because of that I have signed contracts I shouldn't have signed, and I'm frightened by things like schedules and bank balances. I know that I am now successful but when I first meet headmasters I realise that they underestimate me for not being very well educated. Then I must admit I get a little bit of pleasure when after my sessions they compliment me for being able to communicate with young people.'

Phil Cooper thinks he was hindered both academically and socially by attending secondary school so infrequently. But the overwhelming impression from our straw poll of those who had an unorthodox education is that the lack of social know-how was of greater detriment to them than the lack of academic teaching. Somehow, they could catch up on the latter and make good, but the lack of the former has hindered them all their lives.

16 The Real Old School Tie

The Rt Rev Peter Selby, Suffragan Bishop of Kingston-upon-Thames (ex-Merchant Taylors'), wrote: 'I have received the Sinclair-Stevenson questionnaire. I find the idea that I should answer such questions to a total stranger with no information on how the material will be used or without any assurance of confidentiality extraordinary.'

More than 1,600 of the 3,000 plus people selected did, however, fill in their forms and only a handful asked for their answers to be kept confidential. Many wrote extensively about their schools. About 1,000 agreed to be interviewed and we spoke to more than 170 of them. Schooling, it seems – or the lack of it – is a matter too personal not to be openly and voluntarily discussed.

Their replies provide a snapshot of the influence of schools on the careers chosen by the famous during the middle part of the twentieth century. They also indicate whether those people were on the whole happy at school and which were their most formative influences in terms of headteachers, teachers, contemporaries and families. It should enable some conclusions to be drawn on what makes a good school and what really is the nature of the 'old school tie'.

The 1,594 (excluding the 14 with an unorthodox education), drawn from the great, the good, the influential and the notorious who replied to our survey, mainly attended the long-established independent and grammar schools. Half of the sample were educated at established independent schools – most of them at what used to be called the boys' and girls' 'public schools'. A further eight per cent attended the semi-independent grammar schools – known as 'direct-grant schools' – because they received some of their money direct from the government. Such schools include Manchester Grammar School, King Edward's, Birmingham, and Bradford, Bristol and Leeds grammar schools. They have since the mid-1970s been fully independent.

Just under a third (30 per cent) of those chosen in our survey attended grammar schools, maintained by local education authorities. Most of these were phased out by circular 10/65 in the ten years after 1965 under which the Labour Government asked local education authorities to submit plans for comprehensive education. But some authorities, notably

Buckinghamshire, Kent and a few Outer London boroughs, have resisted this request, and there are some 150 grammar schools left.

The remaining 11 per cent attended secondary schools of various sorts – secondary moderns for those who failed or did not take the 11-plus examination, secondary technical schools and the old elementary schools, including many of the central schools in London and elsewhere. Many of these left school at 14. About seven per cent attended schools which might have been termed state comprehensives when they were at the school.

More than three-quarters of those who went to independent schools boarded at them. The first half of the century may be looked back upon as being the apex of boarding education in Britain. The second half of this century saw it steadily decline year by year until now boarders are about a fifth of the present child population at independent schools. Although there are a considerable number of scholarships and bursaries for boarders, most come from monied families. As we move to the end of the twentieth century, some 40 per cent of those who achieved fame, fortune or notoriety during it went to boarding schools attended now by fewer than two per cent of the nation's schoolchildren and some 50 per cent went to independent schools which educate about ten per cent of the nation's secondary schoolchildren. About seven per cent came from comprehensives which some 90 per cent of the nation's children now attend. Such is the imbalance between the schools that educated the famous in the past and the schools most children attend today.

The dominance of the independent school and particularly of boarding varies from profession to profession as can be seen from the following table. Nearly two-thirds of those who went into the armed forces, and more than half of those who went into public life, business and the Church went to boarding schools. The table shows first the average for the 1,594 who replied and then the percentages for each of the chosen career paths in this book.

Although, as we explained in the introduction, we set out to include as many women in our total as possible, we found that of the 1,594 who replied only some 335 or 21 per cent were women. We were sad that there were not more women but took some heart from the fact that there was a similar proportion of women to men in the 1992 New Year Honours List. A comparative breakdown with the table above showed that women were less likely than the men to be sent to independent schools (44 per cent as compared to 52 per cent) and much less likely to be boarders at them (29 per cent compared to 44 per cent).

Just over half of some of the most successful men and women in

Career	Independent	Boarding
Average	*50%*	*41%*
Acting	38	25
Armed Forces	71	65
Art Design and Fashion	46	39
Broadcasting and Journalism	49	41
Business	64	59
Education	39	29
Law	58	47
Literature	55	42
Music	43	33
Politics	45	38
Public Life	70	63
Religion	61	52
Science	37	28
Sport	40	29

Britain – some 53 per cent – said their school had had no influence at all on their choice of career. This proportion was virtually the same for boarders and day pupils and across all types of school and across both sexes. It is interesting to compare it with a Gallup Poll survey of 1,500 adults published in 1992. This showed that 40 per cent of those surveyed said that their education had been of no use at all in preparing them for their present jobs. Perhaps careers education in schools has improved, but the replies we received from down the ages do not suggest that the improvement is very noticeable.

The Winchester of the 1920s, in Sir David Barran's view, lacked careers advice and encouraged the general feeling that bright people would go into the Law, the civil service or the Army. These remarks were echoed by Will Wyatt, Managing Director of Channel 4, who told us that his education thirty years later at Magdalen College School, Oxford 'did not encourage the idea that the commercial or industrial world was one for a bright young lad to aspire to.'

James Birrell, Chief Executive of the Halifax Building Society, who emerged post-War from Belle Vue Grammar School, Bradford, said: 'The careers master tried to be helpful but had no real knowledge outside the world of academia.' Some twenty years earlier, Sir Robert Jennings, the international lawyer, who had drifted into Law from the same school, made much the same point.

The schools were not just against careers in business. They frowned on professional careers in the arts, journalism, sport and almost all the categories in this book except education, religion and science.

The arrival of comprehensive education does not seem to have brought the two worlds of school and work closer so far as we can judge from the fairly limited number of comprehensive school-educated pupils in this book. Charles Donald, editor of *Viz* magazine, was at Heaton Comprehensive, Newcastle, from 1971-1978. He said: 'The school was so lacking in careers advice, and the advice I received so unimpressive, that it led me to question whether or not I should completely ignore it. So I did.'

Elizabeth Coldwell, editor of *Forum Magazine,* said of Clifton Comprehensive School, Rotherham: 'The careers advice was quite limited, both in counselling while in the Vth Form and between doing "O" levels and going into the VIth form. They remained convinced that I should go into teaching for no other real reason, I think, than that various members of my family were teachers. I'm sure a lot of people go into the wrong career because of the wrong advice from teachers.'

Does it matter? Helen Couper, the astronomer and broadcaster, said: 'I was told by my careers mistress – who being Head of Latin had a great knowledge of the outside world – [at St Mary's Grammar School, Northwood] that: "in order to be an astronomer, one had first to make a discovery". That completely put me off and as a result my first job was in fashion retailing.'

Yve Newbold, company secretary of Hanson plc (who attended two convents in Sussex: see Chapter Five), decided to go into the Law, and rather fancied becoming a barrister after she saw a film in which Margaret Lockwood played a young barrister – looking marvellous in a wig and gown. She said proper careers advice might have made a difference. 'My true loves are anthropology and philosophy and help in recognising that and building on it (neither subject was even mentioned at school) would have possibly meant a different career direction. But hard to say. So many imponderables at work. I do actually like what I'm doing.'

Three-quarters of those who went on into careers in education were influenced to do so by their schools. Some from the independent schools did so because they could not think of any better career and others were uplifted towards teaching from their grammar schools (see Chapter Six). But schools also influenced most of the churchmen and scientists in this book – seven out of ten of the former and six out of ten of the latter.

The profession least affected by the influence of school was the Law, where only 29 per cent of respondents said that their schooling had influenced them in their choice of profession. Law is not generally taught as a subject at school. Mary Sabben-Clare, wife of the Headmaster of

Influence of school on career chosen:

Career	% influenced
Average	47
Acting	45
Armed Forces	47
Art Design and Fashion	40
Broadcasting and Journalism	41
Business	34
Education	75
Law	29
Literature	43
Music	45
Politics	48
Public Life	54
Religion	71
Science	61
Sport	38

Winchester College, who teaches Law at the school, said that it might encourage more students to consider a legal career if Law were to be taught in schools. More importantly, she said that contact with the Law as a subject at that age had deterred a few who might have been unsuitable for it from becoming lawyers.

How important is the headmaster or headmistress in the school? The famous were asked: 'Who of the following influenced you most at school?' This question was not intended to be answered in the singular and almost all those who replied to it put down a number of different people. But the headteacher did not figure as largely as we expected. He or she is not the most formative influence on the successful in schools. Fewer than one person in five mentioned him or her as being among the 'most influential' on their own development.

Famous women are more likely to be influenced by their headmistress than famous men by their headmaster. A quarter of the women in our survey mentioned their headteacher as a formative influence as opposed to a sixth of the men. There was only a slight difference between those who boarded and those who were day pupils – 20 per cent of day pupils as opposed to 18 per cent of boarders mentioned the headteacher.

Praise for headmasters came mainly from the older generation and, not surprisingly, from academics such as Sir John Habakkuk, the distinguished historian and former Vice-Chancellor of Oxford

University, and his fellow academic – also a distinguished historian – Asa Briggs, who said that at Keighley Grammar School in the 1930s he was particularly impressed by the way 'the headmaster was able to influence my own mother and father'. Douglas Feaver, former Bishop of Peterborough, looking back to his time at Bristol Grammar School (1925-1932), said: 'The chief glory of this school was the respect all had for J.E. Barton, the headmaster.' The influential headmasters like Canon Shirley and Robert Birley are figures of the past and they clearly do not make them like that any more.

Did the respect wane as the century progressed? The average size of secondary school increased rapidly during the twenty years after the end of the War. The headteacher has become much more of an administrative figure and a personnel director rather than an educator. Many headteachers no longer teach. In boarding schools the housemaster (and sometimes the housemistress) has often a greater personal influence on pupils than the headmaster, as Sir Peregrine Worsthorne found to his cost (see Chapter Four). Many pupils only really came to know their headteacher when they stayed on at school for a seventh term in their VIth Form to study for Oxbridge entrance exams. But now that this practice has been discouraged by both universities it has been discontinued.

Across the career boundaries educationists were likely to be the most heavily influenced by their headteachers. They were their role models as described in Chapter Six and nearly one in three (31 per cent) of those in education and scholarship mentioned their headteacher. Just over a quarter (26 per cent) were influenced by their headteacher in the areas of science and religion. A quarter of business people were also impressed by headmagisterial power.

The categories where the headteacher seems to have had the least impact were: broadcasting (12 per cent), music (12 per cent), sport (13 per cent), and, surprisingly in view of those headteachers mentioned in Chapter One who took budding thespians under their personal wings, acting (15 per cent). All these came below Law (16 per cent).

This book is full of testimonials to individual teachers. More than four out of ten (42 per cent) of those who replied found that a particular teacher, or in a few cases two teachers, had the most profound influence on them rather than the teachers in their schools as a whole. The whole teaching staff was mentioned by 31 per cent of those who responded. The proportion of those who were influenced by a particular teacher varies between 38 per cent of those at boarding schools and 44 per cent at day schools and between 43 per cent of men and 36 per cent of women.

Influence of headteacher on percentage of pupils

Category	Head's influence
Average	*19*
Acting	15
Armed Forces	20
Art, Design and Fashion	22
Broadcasting and Journalism	12
Business	25
Education	31
Law	16
Literature	19
Music	12
Politics	18
Public Life	24
Religion	26
Science	26
Sport	13

'Without one teacher who "opened me up" I would never have gone into acting' says Eileen Atkins (Chapter One). No-one expressed it better than the artist John Bratby, talking about his old mentor Harold Watts at Tiffins Boys' School, Kingston, (Chapter Three): 'He wound up my engine and set me on track.' The references in this book are legion. The interest of an individual teacher has been crucial to the success of so many well-known people.

The influence of the single teacher is shown as being most important by artists and designers, actors, and musicians ahead even of educationists. Among future lawyers and members of the armed services it does not appear to have been so important as the influence of the teaching staff as a whole. In brackets we have put the corresponding percentage for all teachers.

One in six of those who replied put down the influence of contemporaries as being one of the foremost influences of their schooldays. This influence was stronger among men than among women, with one in five men mentioning contemporaries as being most important compared to one in seven women. Contemporary ties are much stronger in boarding schools than day schools with 25 per cent of boarders feeling that they were most important as compared to 12 per cent of day pupils. There was little variation across careers, but the importance of such links was felt most by business people: a third of those who boarded mentioned their contemporaries. Musicians and scientists were least susceptible to their contemporaries' influence.

Category	Particular teacher	All teachers
Average	42	*(31)*
Acting	49	*(21)*
Armed Forces	25	*(35)*
Art, Design and Fashion	52	*(25)*
Broadcasting and Journalism	43	*(27)*
Business	30	*(36)*
Education	47	*(38)*
Law	45	*(36)*
Literature	48	*(24)*
Music	51	*(35)*
Politics	39	*(42)*
Public Life	40	*(24)*
Religion	42	*(42)*
Science	30	*(43)*
Sport	30	*(25)*

The Oxbridge scarf is probably more important to success than the Old School Tie. We had expected a much higher return for the influence of contemporaries among independent and boarding school pupils. As Nigel Nicolson observed (Chapter Eight) it was Balliol not Eton that was important as far as networks and jobs were concerned.

Category	Influence of contemporaries
Average	18
Acting	16
Armed Forces	18
Art, Design and Fashion	19
Broadcasting and Journalism	17
Business	26
Education	19
Law	14
Literature	17
Music	11
Politics	16
Public Life	21
Religion	20
Science	11
Sport	20

Major General Sir Richard Clutterbuck, who went to Radley, told us: 'I became aware and remain convinced that the boy at boarding school instantly develops a second personality from the one he continues to have with his family at home and it is the school personality which in the main becomes the man.'

The idea of involving the family more in the education of the child was advocated with the publication of the Plowden Report in 1967. But it is much easier to make this possible at day schools than boarding schools and the responses in this book reflect this. The overall average of those who said their family were a formative influence during their schooldays was 31 per cent. The percentage for day pupils was 36 per cent, while that for boarders was considerably lower at 26 per cent.

But there is also a marked difference between successful men and women. 39 per cent of the women in our survey mentioned the influence of family while at school as compared to 29 per cent of the men.

The people most influenced by their families later went into sport, followed by acting (showing that the advice to Mrs Worthington about not putting her daughter on the stage was not always followed) and interestingly religion, where the family influence was mentioned by Basil Mitchell and Dennis Nineham in Chapter Twelve. Those least influenced by family went into the armed services – despite the dynasties of serving officers (see Chapter Two):

Category	Influence of family
Average	*31*
Acting	38
Armed Forces	24
Art, Design and Fashion	32
Broadcasting and Journalism	27
Business	31
Education	25
Law	29
Literature	26
Music	32
Politics	34
Public Life	26
Religion	38
Science	28
Sport	45

Nearly eight out of ten (78 per cent) of those who replied to our survey considered themselves on balance to have been happy at their schools. Cynics will say that those who were happy at school will be the more prepared to fill in forms about their schooldays – and there may indeed be something in this. We encouraged a few waverers who contacted us over the telephone to fill in their forms because of the 'debt' they owed their schools. But in more than a fifth of cases – a significant percentage – respondents were willing to indicate that they had not been happy on the whole at school, showing that there was no reluctance to do so. Many people found the question hard to answer. A few gave the schools the benefit of the doubt. But we would argue that had the whole sample replied, we would not have received a very different answer.

From 1970 until the mid-1980s at any rate most people, while being dissatisfied with the education system as a whole, were actually satisfied with the education provided by particular schools. Most of the people mentioned in this book attended school during the years before the 1960s when the so-called 'public school revolution' hit the independent schools and before 1969 when the first Black Paper criticisms hit the State sector. There was a general consensus of opinion that schools were doing a good job. This feeling only began to ebb in the late 1960s when many other factors caught up with the end of the 'never had-it-so-good' affluent era.

Some respondents answered the question on happiness at school with both a 'Yes' and a 'No'. These included a few like Lord Roskill, the former judge, who said that although he was unhappy at Winchester, he did enjoy his later years there.

Some, particularly of the older generation, found the question surprising: the late Ronald Eyre, the television and theatre producer who was at Queen Elizabeth Grammar School, Wakefield, at the end of the last War, said, 'The school provided the plank that got me out of family coal-mining to Oxford. Nobody told me we were supposed to be *happy* as well.' While Rosalie Crutchley, the actress, who told us that she had got little joy or anything else of benefit from Francis Holland School (Graham Street), London, said: 'We never considered being happy at school. It was just something you had to do.'

There were marked career variations from 92 per cent happiness of those who went on into education to 60 per cent of those who went into art, design, or fashion careers, in some cases frustrated by their schooldays.

Category	% Happy
Average	78
Acting	74
Armed Forces	84
Art, Design and Fashion	60
Broadcasting and Journalism	67
Business	87
Education	92
Law	84
Literature	69
Music	78
Politics	81
Public Life	71
Religion	88
Science	85
Sport	88

More successful men appear to have been happy at school than successful women. Nearly four out of five men said they were happy at school as compared to three out of four women.

There is a significant difference between boarding and day pupils. Day pupils were happier than boarders. The percentage of happy day pupils was 84 per cent as compared to 74 per cent of boarders. In view of some of the remarks about boarding, however, it is quite a surprise to find that three out of four were happy at their boarding schools.

How do individual schools compare in terms of the numbers in the book and the proportion of those who replied who were happy? There were 11 top public schools from which we received at least ten replies. Etonians top the list with 180 people in our survey and with 86 who replied to it. Winchester (50), Rugby (42) and Westminster (37) follow some way behind with the rest of the pack. We have listed the 'first eleven schools' in terms of the number of their replies and the percentages at the end refer to the percentage of those who replied who were happy. Anything over 78 per cent has been asterisked as above average in terms of our survey.

Most people who went to Eton felt they had to add something about the experience in a way not felt by those at other top public schools. And most of it was unsolicited enthusiasm for the school. The authors of this book – an Old Wykehamist and a Rugby beak, not the most natural Etonian allies – have had to admit to its Old Etonian publisher that the enthusiasm and sometimes self-analytical nature of the replies

School	Numbers	Replies	Happy	% of Replies
Eton	180	86	73	85*
Winchester	50	26	19	73
Rugby	42	28	22	79*
Westminster	37	20	18	90*
Charterhouse	36	16	8	50
Harrow	32	19	15	79*
Marlborough	28	13	10	77
St Paul's	26	10	7	70
Wellington	24	10	7	70
Stowe	24	10	9	90*
Sherborne	22	14	13	93*
TOTALS	*501*	*252 (50%)*	*201*	*80*

were impressive. Several Etonians fastened on to the privacy of having your own study from the start. This encouraged individualism according to Viscount Weymouth, the Lord of Longleat, and Tom Hustler the photographer. The Hon David Astor learnt that it was necessary to spend time alone.

There was not so much unsolicited enthusiasm about the replies from those who went to Westminster – but we were struck by the theatrical link of those who had been there: Sir John Gielgud and Sir Peter Ustinov head a cast including Peter Brook, Simon Gray, Andrew Lloyd Webber, Nigel Planer, Stephen Poliakoff, Imogen Stubbs, and Donald Swann. We suppose some might add Tony Benn as well. This, to a less extent, was true also about Harrow which educated Michael Bogdanov, Michael Denison, Edward and James Fox, John Mortimer, Simon Williams and Sandy Wilson.

Wykehamists were often critical of their school either consciously or subconsciously, as in this reply received from Professor Lucas, the lay Christian philosopher, who wrote: 'I was so well taught that I was always at a great advantage in any competition and in life generally.' And then he went on to say: 'It is possible that Winchester made me too *modest* [our italics] thereby ruling out a career in politics, where pushiness is a *sine qua non*. . . . Certainly Winchester imbued me with fairly stringent standards, and ensured that I never contemplated Chartered Accountancy or anything *ejusdem generis*.'

Rugby is distinguished in this book for being the butt of the longest diatribe (three typed pages) received against any school – public or private. It came from Alec Dickson, who founded Community Service Volunteers. One haunting comment based on a quotation from Kurt Hahn, the founder of Gordonstoun, stands out: 'The aim of schooling he (Kurt Hahn) remarked should be to make the brave gentle and the gentle brave: that kind of thing played no role at Rugby in my time,' according to Dickson. But many, including Sir Oliver Millar found Rugby an enlightened place long before it was fashionable for public schools to be enlightened.

Supporters of Charterhouse might take heart from the fact that it is often the admitted fault of the pupil rather than the school if someone is unhappy during his schooldays. David Hicks, when asked by us why 'apart from his loathing of rhododendrons' he was unhappy at Charterhouse, replied: 'I wouldn't have responded to any mass collection of human beings. I didn't like the Army any better.'

In terms of happiness at school, successful women educated at the top girls' independent schools were not on average as happy as the successful men at either the top boarding or leading day schools. Seven out of ten of them were happy at their schools as compared to eight out of ten at the top boys' boarding schools and nine out of ten at the top boys' day schools. The average of 72 per cent is below the 73 per cent average for women covered by this book.

School	Numbers	Replies	Happy
St Paul's	18	6	4
Roedean	8	5	3
Oxford High	7	5	3
The Mount	6	5	4
St Mary's, Wantage	6	5	3
South Hampstead	6	3	2
Cheltenham Ladies'	5	2	2
Downe House	5	5	4
North London Coll	5	1	1
Wycombe Abbey	5	2	2
Benenden	4	1	1
Talbot Heath	4	3	2
TOTAL	79	*43 (54%)*	*31 (72%)*

Apart from Princess Anne (from whom we had an indirect non-reply) our survey included only three others who were educated at Benenden: Liz Forgan of Channel 4, Baroness Ryder and Joanna Foster of the Equal Opportunities Commission. The surprise inclusion in the above top girls' schools list is perhaps the Mount School. This Quaker school in York was praised by Kate Bellingham, the *Tomorrow's World* presenter, and by Jocelyn Burnell, the astronomer, as well as by Dame Judi Dench, the actress, who told us: 'It was just their attitude at the Quaker schools. They encouraged you to have your own individual ideas. It wasn't a sausage machine. I've met Mount girls all over the world – so much so that it's become a joke with my husband and daughter – and they are so varied in their ideas and feelings. It was the idea of the individual at the Mount. They found out what you were jolly good at and they fostered it.'

More than one successful woman in ten who replied to our survey attended a convent school. Convent-educated girls include Yve Newbold the business woman, Margaret Beckett the politician, Sue Barker the tennis player, actresses Eileen Atkins and Anna Calder-Marshall, writers Marina Warner and Rachel Billington, Anne Leslie the journalist and Anne Robinson the broadcaster, Fay Maschler the cookery expert, fashion designers Ninivah Khomo and Pascale Smets, Dusty Springfield, the pop singer, and Samantha Fox, the model. Compared with the totality of the girls' schools, they appear neither more nor less happy (74 per cent were happy as compared to 73 per cent) but they were more influenced in terms of their career (57 per cent as compared to 47 per cent). They were more likely to board and more willing to be interviewed about their schooldays.

Erin Pizzey, who had such an anarchic reaction to Leweston Manor Convent, has a theory about the advantages of boarding education for girls which may explain why so many convent-educated girls have been successful. She said: 'A lot of them become very powerful women, especially those whose parents were abroad. These women had no real childhood – they had to grow up almost immediately because they never really knew their parents and could not be vulnerable. Boarding-school girls don't find it so difficult making relationships with men because they are not used to kowtowing to men. They refuse to make the men in their lives central. They have spent their formative years interacting with other girls as equals and they are used to seeing the all-powerful roles taken by women.'

Every chapter in this book, whether it be concerned with artists, journalists or lawyers, has sooner or later come up with good citations about grammar schools. Their alumni often express regret at the demise of the grammar schools. There is a striking testimony in their favour from the successful.

At Quarry Bank High School, Liverpool, the lead given by the headmaster of the time was praised both by Sir Robert Telford and by Lord Rodgers. Sir Robert, the son of a farmer who went bankrupt in the Depression, was there in the twenties and Quarry Bank got him to Cambridge. Telford's headmaster had established the school in 1922 when he came from being a housemaster at Shrewsbury, and he stayed there until 1947. In the thirties, the young Bill Rodgers was equally impressed by the same headmaster's emphasis on 'character'. Rodgers told us: 'The ethos was to help every boy make the most of himself and to take great care with those who fell behind or got into trouble.' Actor Derek Nimmo agreed that although the school was organised like a public school 'it was more about achievement than about competition.'

Quarry Bank also educated celebrities as diverse as former Beatle George Harrison, soccer manager Joe Royle, architect James Stirling and former Labour cabinet minister Peter Shore. As Lord Rodgers said, 'It was a wide experience of life. A grammar-school education like mine was a wonderful experience. But perhaps I was just very lucky.'

Maybe luck came into it. If so, many successful people were equally lucky, no matter where they were brought up. The grammar schools flourished, from Edinburgh to Swansea, from Leicester to London's East End. They rescued children from the poorest homes and set them firmly on the first rung of their career ladder.

The London and suburban grammar schools were much praised. The old Grocers' Company school, later renamed Hackney Downs School when in 1905 it was taken over by the LCC, was in a fairly poor area but had a board with a list of its Oxford and Cambridge scholars in the front hall. Its old boys include names as various as actor and director Steven Berkoff, and Harold Pinter, Lord Goodman and Sir Alfred Sherman as well as darts star Eric Bristow and nutrition expert Professor John Yudkin.

Not far away, Kilburn Grammar has educated journalists like Bernard Shrimsley, who edited both the *News of the World* and the *Mail on Sunday*, and *Financial Times* journalist Samuel Brittan; entrepreneur Jarvis Astaire, Oxford Law don Professor G. H. Treitel, and Max Morris, former president of the National Union of Teachers. Another famous old boy, Richard Baker, told us, 'I think the grammar schools were entirely a good thing. My father was a plasterer who was often out of work in the thirties and even when he worked never earned more than £3 a week and so it was a great struggle. If you passed the scholarship at 11 you were able to go to the grammar school whether your parents had any money or not.'

Opera singer Teresa Cahill said the same about Notre Dame, her London Docklands grammar school: 'I came from a very poor working-class family in Docklands with no money for books, music or holidays. My secondary education was the key that unlocked the door to everything that I've achieved and to a classless position in society.'

Further north of the Thames, West Ham Grammar was turning out people of such diverse talents as Michael Kaye who has been involved in so many London music projects, and Bryan Forbes who has achieved success in all three of his chosen careers of acting, directing and writing.

Watford Grammar School produced ten names in the index of our book – the largest number for any state grammar school. They included Andrew Davis, the musical director, and two company chairmen – Ian Prosser of Bass plc and James Watson of the National Freight Corporation.

The great Welsh and Scottish grammar schools produced generations of distinguished alumni – our list for Holy Cross Academy in Edinburgh includes a Cardinal, an actor, a sculptor, a seamen's trade-unionist and a car-tyre tycoon. While the list from Dynevor Grammar School, Swansea, ranges from Sir Harry Secombe to Lord Griffiths, former head of Mrs Thatcher's policy unit and Chairman of the Schools Examination and Assessment Council.

Many experiences in this book do not confirm the 'grindstone' stereotype that grammar schools were only about hard academic work: Actress Cheryl Campbell attended Francis Bacon Grammar School in St Albans: 'The thing that helped me most was the acknowledgement of the importance of art at school, in fact, the arts in general. School plays, the choir and an orchestra, along with a good art department and good interesting teachers, were the most important things to me.'

Robert Westall, on receiving our questionnaire, penned a two-page letter to the publisher, referred to in Chapter Eight. It began: 'Thank you for your circular, which aroused such a storm of memories in me that, should I be typical, I am sure your book will go like a bomb'. He echoed the thoughts of many in his graphic description and concluding expression of regret that 'these finely-honed educational tools were destroyed for political non-educational reasons.'

There is praise too for the old elementary school from its more successful products. Two quotes from those who climbed to the top of the journalistic tree come to mind:

Louis Heren, confidante of United States presidents and one of the most distinguished foreign correspondents that *The Times* has had, began life as a messenger boy for that newspaper. He went to St George's, London. 'My school was an LCC central school in the East End. I wasn't bright enough to get a scholarship to a secondary school. It was a good school and I am grateful to a number of teachers – Miss Nixon who guided my reading; Mr Miller who broadened my horizons; Mr Rees who introduced me to Beethoven and Mozart, and Mr West, an unsuccessful Communist candidate for North Kensington, who fed my radicalism. Bring back the old LCC and central schools.'

Marjorie Proops ('Dear Marge' of the *Daily Mirror*) told us: 'My period at Dalston County made it plain, not only to my teachers and my parents, but also to me, that I would have no future whatever in anything in which academic skills were required. But my artistic and creative talent was discovered and encouraged. One particular teacher encouraged the only talent I had. Miss Stainsby changed my life.'

As a result Marjorie went on to Hackney Technical School to study anatomy and life drawing. Later, at the age of 17, working in a 'grotty' office in Wine Court, Fleet Street, for a freelance fashion artist, her fashion sketches came to the notice of Hugh Cudlipp, then Features Editor of the *Daily Mirror*.

Perhaps it is surprising that the comprehensive flagships – Holland Park, Kidbrooke, and the early comprehensive schools in Wales yielded so few of the names in this book: only TV correspondent Polly Toynbee (Holland Park) and Glenys Kinnock (Holyhead).The bulk of the people who responded to our survey were educated before the 1960s when the comprehensive movement really got under way. Others would argue that the comprehensive ideal was to concentrate on all children, not just those who were likely to be successful. But throughout this book the comprehensive ideal gets a battering.

However, some comprehensive schools were praised – particularly by those who found a refuge in them after switching from other schools. Jane Tewson, Founder of the charity Comic Relief, wrote: 'As someone unable to distinguish between B and P I didn't enjoy spending endless detentions writing "but" and "put" out 100 times each. Having left Headington School (the girls' private school in Oxford) I went to Lord Williams' School, Thame – a comprehensive – as one of seven girls. 'It was brilliant to be taught not for exams but for interest. I had fantastic involvement too in the local community, which I am sure led me into my present job.'

Jennie Moncur, the interior designer, is one of the most enthusiastic of those who attended comprehensive schools. 'Sheredes Comprehensive', she said, 'taught in the very best manner – it taught me how to learn.'

The flexibility of her comprehensive was praised by Glenys Kinnock who went to Holyhead Comprehensive School. She told us: 'I attended a comprehensive and know that the non-selective system helped me as I was what is often described as a late developer. At the beginning of my fourth year, I was able to drop maths and it meant that I could concentrate on subjects I could manage. I subsequently passed 7 "O" levels – very unexpected.'

From this book there would appear to be four overriding hallmarks of a happy and successful education – flexibility, individuality, trust and the encouragement that gives pupils the feeling that anything is possible.

The flexibility that Glenys Kinnock observed about her comprehensive is a theme that is often repeated in this book – whether it allows a future teacher and politician's wife to drop mathematics (which would not be allowed under today's regulations about the core curriculum) or a budding barrister like Anthony Scrivener to drop science in order to concentrate exclusively on maths. Flexibility allowed Rod Hackney to try again for the John Bright Grammar School in Llandudno – although it took some good-natured bullying of the headmaster by his father. When he eventually arrived there, better late than never at 14, he found it 'everything a school should be'.

Unfortunately there is a less attractive aspect to education, a stolid and unbending rigour which is the very quality so attacked by adherents of comprehensive education. Best-selling author Rosie Thomas told us what it felt like to be at Howell's School, Denbigh. 'At this very insular, philistine and old-fashioned girls' school, we were not encouraged to develop any individuality or display any eccentricity. Routine and regimentation was the norm.'

Adrian Juste, Radio One disc jockey, on Guthlaxton Grammar School: 'The whole thing was a six-year non-event. I hated every minute of it! Because I did not conform to their normal stereotype, I was regarded as a troublemaker.'

The school that can manage to make each pupil feel special by making him or her feel like an individual wins great praise. The great schools like Manchester Grammar with 1,400 boys could manage it 'by fitting the school to the boy rather than by making the boy conform to the school', as writer Alan Garner put it. Eton, as we have seen, comes across as a school for the individual. This begins with privacy, mentioned by so many Old Etonians. In no other public school does the new boy of 13 have a room of his own. The paint in Eton's corridors of power may be flaking to an extent that would shame an inner-city comprehensive; there may be great chunks of plaster missing from the billiard-room walls. But the privacy afforded by one's own study has a civilising power beyond price and may go a long way to explaining why nine out of ten OEs said they were happy at school.

The converse is to feel that you are mediocre. Alec Dickson, in his diatribe against Rugby, said: 'Academically I was a nonentity – and I wasn't much good at games either, so I did not arouse the interest of the staff.'

Bryanston, a comparatively new public school, is remarkable in our survey for the number of distinguished musicians it produced (see Chapter Nine). Conductor Mark Wigglesworth made a special phone call: 'I'm interested in talking to you because I did enjoy Bryanston and I want to give something back. It was the atmosphere created there: you were not peculiar in whatever you wanted to do – they made you feel it was important. Because people trusted you, you did your work on time.'

Soprano Jane Manning has still not forgiven Norwich High School for their lack of trust in her. She told us, 'I was never made a prefect and was constantly made to feel inept socially (partly my own fault). I could never understand why, since everyone remarked on my straight shoulders and back (including my classmates), I never received a deportment badge. I always felt discriminated against.'

This book has shown the importance of giving confidence in adolescence. We have seen again and again how one chance remark, one word of praise, has changed the ambience of a school for a pupil and often pointed them towards a particular career or life interest.

A typical illustration of this was given by Alastair Service, General Secretary of the Family Planning Association, describing one triumph at Westminster. 'One essay I wrote was picked out and read out by Jumbo Wilson as an outstanding example of atmosphere given in writing about a place – that little incident gave me ambition to write and the realisation that I had some talent for it.'

Writer Maureen Duffy said of her two schools, Trowbridge High School, Wiltshire, and Sarah Bonnell High School: 'We were encouraged as girls to believe that anything was possible – a university, a career.' Charles Denton, the journalist, speaking of Reading School – a boarding and day grammar school – said: 'Reading School for me was an easygoing humane institution which nevertheless managed to instil in me the belief that everything is possible in life.'

The secret of successful schooling, as illustrated by the experiences in this book, is the secret of any personal relationship. It is all about giving encouragement, a sense of confidence, making that person feel special. But the person has to respond to the teaching. It needs both the teacher with the time and dedication and the Renaissance school, the school which is prepared to try anything to enthuse its pupils.

The grammar schools which provided so much extracurricular encouragement have been decimated (literally a decline from more than 1,500 to 150). There has been a serious and steady decline in boarding education. Boarding schools are more easily able than day schools to find the time to draw out their pupils. The comprehensive schools are filling the void left by the grammar schools, secondary moderns and the boarding schools. They have to balance pastoral care – the care and concern for every child – with the needs of a national curriculum. Flexibility and individuality have to co-exist with national benchmarks and increasing emphasis on public examinations.

The British have less faith in their education system than any other nation in Western Europe. Only 37 per cent expressed confidence in a *Reader's Digest* Eurodata report in 1991 compared to 71 per cent in the former West Germany, 63 per cent in France and 77 per cent in Denmark, Switzerland and Finland. Sir Claus Moser, Warden of Wadham College, Oxford, has said that Britain is in danger of becoming the 'least educated of the advanced nations'.

Sir John Banham, former Director-General of the CBI, hopes that local management of schools will restore in each school an ethos that has been lost. The process of opting out of local education authority control could also give a school a sense of personal identity. The overall organisational differences between secondary schools have largely been eradicated so that the comprehensives are offering a supermarket model of the larger school, co-educational, fully day and non-selective. The independent schools too are going rapidly down the roads of becoming fully day and co-educational. If they are to be distinctive, the distinguishing style and ethos has to emanate from an individual rather than from a committee at the top. Yet it would appear from this book that the personal influence of the headteacher has been, and is, on the wane.

As for the teachers, years of trade unionism have altered the profession into one where rights have been demanded by teachers and duties laid down by governments. Teacher strikes and sanctions have sapped morale. The School Teachers' Pay and Conditions Document of 1987 laid down the number of hours to be worked each week. A survey by the Assistant Masters and Mistresses Association in 1992 showed that teachers work longer hours, but their time in larger schools is spent more on administration and meeting the requirements of the national curriculum than teaching in the classroom. There have been so many changes recently in education. Is there the time or the goodwill for teachers to stay behind evening after evening to help their pupils? Do we pay them enough to expect it? Do their pupils want it? Or do *Neighbours* and *Eastenders* come in between?

'Those days and teachers have gone now,' said Bobby Robson, England's former football manager, in the context of encouraging the sporting professionals of the future. But the remarks apply in a far wider general context. Good teachers make good schools. But it is the individual teacher with whom the pupil clicks that counts far more than the influence of the headteacher, the school's teachers as a whole, school contemporaries or the influence of one's family. We have lost count of the number of remarkable teachers mentioned by those who replied to our survey. They abound in every chapter of the book. Some, like the great Michael Croft of Alleyn's School, founder of the National Youth Theatre, achieved national fame in their own right. Others live on only as incidentally named catalysts to their famous protégés – like Eton's John Marsden who gave up his football ticket to Rupert Hambro while he himself slept through the match on a park bench outside the ground.

Some were as caviare to the general, like the gentle 'rather broken' Edward Upward, friend to Auden, Isherwood and MacNeice, who also became a friend to the young Simon Ward; or the ladylike Miss Trembath who shared the secret of perfectly spoken poetry with Margaret Howard while other girls giggled all around. It took forty years and a university professorship for microbiologist Richard Lacey to realise the hours required for his science teachers at Felsted to mark his work constructively rather than with simple ticks, crosses and grades.

Others were beacons of inspiration, shining still down all the years: like the dazzling Peter Falk at Rugby whose retirement dinner included sixty doctors who had all been led to study medicine by his biology classes. Or the legendary Dr Douglas Fox at Clifton, cruelly cheated by the Great War of his right arm and his career as a concert pianist, who got the entire school singing as he conducted and even played the organ with his left hand.

Or, as quoted in Chapter Eight: 'That tall, ugly, stooping, brilliant Greek teacher, Miss Rackham,' who kept Rosemary Anne Sisson behind to scold her after class and who, when she realised she had reduced her pupil to tears, cried, 'Oh, my dear! Do you think I would bother if I didn't think you were worth it?' To know that someone recognises one's special quality is desperately important to an adolescent.

The real old school tie is not a piece of material, nor is it a link with a building or body corporate. The lasting influence of an old school tie is likely to be that crucial link with one individual teacher. That link more than anything else at school has inspired the famous of today.

Index of Former Students

Abbott, A.C. - *Senior designer BBC TV; Dulwich*
Abbott, Diane - *Labour MP; Harrow County Girls' GS*
Abse, Dannie - *Poet, physician and surgeon; St Illtyd's College, Cardiff*
Acheson, Prof Sir Donald - *Fmr Chief Medical Officer DHSS; Merchiston Castle, Edinburgh*
Ackland, Joss - *Actor; Cork GS and Dame Alice Owen's*
Ackner, Lord - *Law Lord; Highgate*
Ackroyd, Peter - *Journalist, novelist and biographer; St Benedict's, Ealing*
Acland, Sir Antony - *Diplomat, British Ambassador, Washington; Eton*
Adams, Douglas - *Writer; Brentwood*
Adams, Richard - *Author* Watership Down; *Bradfield*
Adamson, Sir Campbell - *Former Director General of the CBI; Rugby*
Adeney, Martin - *Broadcaster; Monkton Combe*
Adie, Kate - *Correspondent BBC TV News; Sunderland Church HS*
Adriaenssens, Rosy - *Principal Officer Save the Children Fund; Parliament Hill Girls' GS*
Agnew, Rudolph - *Chair TVS; Downside*
Agnew of Lochnaw, Sir Crispin - *Explorer and Herald; Uppingham*
Agutter, Jenny - *Actress; Elmhurst Ballet*
Aiken, Joan - *Writer, especially children's books; Wychwood, Oxford*
Airlie, The Earl of - *Lord Chamberlain The Queen's Household; Eton*
Aitken, Jonathan - *Minister of State for Defence; Eton*
Aitken, Maria - *Actress; Sherborne Girls*
Akehurst, General Sir John - *Former NATO Commander; Cranbrook*
Alderton, John - *Actor; Kingston HS, Hull*
Aldiss, Brian - *Science fiction writer; Framlingham and West Buckland*
Alexander, Bill - *Associate Director RSC; St Lawrence College, Ramsgate*
Alexander, Maev - *Presenter* That's Life; *Hutchesons' GS, Glasgow*
Alexander, Rt Rev Mervyn - *RC Bishop of Clifton; Bishop Wordsworth GS, Salisbury and Prior Park College, Bath*
Alexander of Weedon, Lord - *Chair National Westminster Bank; Brighton College*
Alexandra, HRH Princess - *Heathfield*
Allan, Andrew - *Director of Programmes Central Indep TV; Tynemouth HS*
Allan, Julia - *Sculptor; St Helen's, Northwood*
Allason, Rupert - *Conservative MP; Downside*
Allison, Ronald - *Former press secretary to HM the Queen; Weymouth GS and Taunton's, Southampton*
Alliss, Peter - *Golfer and TV commentator; Queen Elizabeth's GS, Wimborne and Crosby House, Bournemouth*

Allott, Paul - *Cricketer; Altrincham GS*
Allsopp, The Hon Charles - *Chairman Christie's; Eton*
Alvarez, A. - *Writer; Oundle*
Ambler, Eric - *Novelist and screenwriter; Colfe's GS*
Amery, Lord - *Former Conservative MP; Eton*
Amies, Sir Hardy - *Fashion designer; Brentwood*
Amis, Sir Kingsley - *Writer; City of London* and *(5 terms as an evacuee)*
      Marlborough
Amiss, Dennis - *Cricketer; Old Know Road, Smallheath, Birmingham*
Amlot QC, Roy - *Barrister; Dulwich*
Anderson, Eric - *Headmaster Eton College; George Watson's, Edinburgh*
Anderson, Lindsay – *Film and theatre director; Cheltenham College*
Anderson, Dr Robert - *Director British Museum; Woodhouse GS*
Anderton, James - *Chief Constable Greater Manchester; Wigan GS*
Andrew, Rob - *England rugby player; Barnard Castle*
Andrews, Anthony - *Actor; Royal Masonic*
Anglesey, The Marchioness of - *Chair Broadcasting Complaints Cttee; Francis*
      Holland and *St James's, West Malvern*
Ansell, Col Sir Michael - *Director Horse of the Year Show; Wellington College*
Anthony, Evelyn - *Novelist; Sacred Heart Convent, Roehampton*
Appleby QC, Elizabeth - *Barrister; Dominican College, Brewood, Staffs* and
      Wolverhampton Girls' HS
Archer, Geoffrey - *ITN Defence Correspondent; Highgate*
Archer, Lord - *Author and politician; Wellington, Somerset*
Archer, Lord - *Former Solicitor General, Labour MP; Wednesbury Boys' HS*
Arden, John - *Playwright; Sedbergh*
Arden QC, Mary - *Barrister; Huyton College*
Armitage, AVM Sir Michael - *Former Head of Defence Intelligence; Newport GS,*
      Isle of Wight
Armstrong, Pamela - *ITN newscaster; Ashford Girls', Kent*
Armstrong, Lord - *Former Cabinet Secretary; Eton*
Armstrong-Jones, Lady Sarah - *Artist; Bedales*
Arnold, Geoffrey - *Cricketer; Elliott Comprehensive, Putney*
Arnold, Sir Thomas - *Conservative MP; Bedales*
Ascherson, Neal - *Journalist Independent; Eton*
Ash, Professor Eric - *Rector Imperial Coll of Science & Technol; University*
      College Sch
Ashcroft, John - *Former Chair Coloroll; Upholland GS*
Ashcroft, Michael - *Head of ADT, UK largest car auction co; Norwich GS*
Ashdown MP, The Rt Hon Paddy - *Leader Liberal Democrats; Bedford*
Asher, Jane - *Actress and writer; North Bridge House* and *Miss Lambert's PNEU*
Ashley, Sir Bernard - *Chair Laura Ashley Holdings plc; Whitgift, Croydon*
Ashley, Lord - *Former Labour MP; St Patrick's Elementary, Widnes*
Ashmore, Admiral of the Fleet Sir Edward - *Former C in C the Fleet; RNC,*
      Dartmouth
Ashmore, Vice Admiral Sir Peter - *Chief of Allied Staff NATO; RNC Dartmouth*
Ashton, Joe - *Labour MP; High Storrs GS*
Ashton, Laraine - *Model agent; Farmhouse, Wendover*
Aspel, Michael - *TV presenter; Emanuel*
Aspinall, John - *Director Howletts Zoo, Kent; Rugby*
Astaire, Jarvis - *Boxing entrepreneur, Deputy Chair Wembley; Kilburn GS*
Astor, The Hon David - *Director, former editor, Observer; Eton*

Astor, The Hon Hugh - *Director Hambro's plc; Eton*
Astor, David Waldorf - *Chair Council Protection Rural England; Eton*
Astor of Hever, Lord - *Company director; Eton*
Atherton, David - *Conductor; Blackpool GS*
Atherton, Mike - *England cricketer; Manchester GS*
Atholl, The Duke of - *Landowner; Eton*
Atiyah, Sir Michael - *President The Royal Society, Master, Trinity, Cambridge; Manchester GS*
Atkins, Eileen - *Actress; Latymer GS, Edmonton*
Atkins MP, Robert - *Minister of State, N. Ireland; Highgate*
Atkinson, Rowan - *Actor; St Bees, Cumbria*
Attenborough, Sir David - *Broadcaster and naturalist; Wyggeston GS, Leicester*
Attenborough, Sir Richard - *Actor, producer and director; Wyggeston GS, Leicester*
Aukin, David - *Head of Drama Channel 4; St Paul's*
Auld, Sir Robin - *Judge, Brixton riots enquiry; Brooklands College*
Awdry, Rev Wilbert - *Author* Thomas the Tank Engine; *Dauntsey's*
Ayckbourn, Alan - *Playwright; Haileybury*
Ayres, Gillian - *Painter; St Paul's Girls'*

Bacon, Frances - *Artist; Dean Close, Cheltenham*
Badel, Sarah - *Actress; Poles Convent, Herts*
Baelz, Very Rev Peter - *Dean Emeritus of Durham; Dulwich*
Bagnall, Field Marshal Sir Nigel - *Former ADC General to HM The Queen; Wellington College*
Bailey, Sir Brian - *Chair TV South West, Dep chair Channel 4; Lowestoft GS*
Bailey, Norman - *Baritone; East Barnet GS*
Bailey, Paul - *Novelist and critic; Sir Walter St John's, London*
Bainbridge, Beryl - *Writer; Merchant Taylors', Crosby Arts Educational*
Baker, Colin - *Actor; St Bede's College, Manchester*
Baker, Dame Janet - *Opera singer; The College for Girls, York*
Baker, Rt Rev John - *Bishop of Salisbury; Marlborough*
Baker MP, The Rt Hon Kenneth - *Former Home Secretary; St Paul's*
Baker, Mary - *Director Barclays Bank; Rothesay House, Edinburgh and St Mary's, Wantage*
Baker, Richard - *Broadcaster and author; Kilburn GS*
Bakewell, Joan - *Broadcaster; Stockport Girls' HS*
Baldry, Tony - *Former Under Secretary State, Environment; Leighton Park*
Ball, Sir Christopher - *Founding Fellow Kellogg Foundation; St George's, Harpenden*
Ball, Johnny - *Children's TV presenter; Bolton County GS*
Ball, Kenny - *Jazz trumpeter; Mayfield, Ilford*
Ball, Rt Rev Michael - *Bishop of Truro; Lancing*
Ball, Rt Rev Peter - *Bishop of Gloucester; Lancing*
Ballard, J.G. - *Novelist; Leys, Cambridge*
Bamford, Sir Anthony - *Chair and Managing Director of JCB; Ampleforth*
Bamford, J.C. - *Inventor JCB excavator; Stonyhurst*
Bancroft, Lord - *Former Head of the Home Civil Service; Coatham*
Banham, Sir John - *Former Chairman CBI; Charterhouse*
Banks, Tony - *Labour MP; Archbishop Tenison's GS*

Banks, Gillian - *Registrar General England and Wales; Walthamstow Hall, Sevenoaks*

Bannen, Ian - *Actor; Ratcliffe College*

Bannister, Sir Roger - *4-minute miler; neurologist; City of Bath* and *University College Sch*

Barber, Chris - *Jazz band leader; King Alfred, London* and *St Paul's*

Barber, Lynn - *Columnist* Independent; *Lady Eleanor Holles*

Barfield, Dick - *Chief Executive Standard Life Assurance; Great Yarmouth GS*

Barker, Sebastian - *Chair The Poetry Society; King's, Canterbury*

Barker, Sue - *Tennis player, Commentator Sky Sports Chl; Marist Convent, Paignton*

Barkworth, Peter - *Actor; Stockport GS*

Barlow, Sir William - *Chair BICC plc; Manchester GS*

Barnes, Carol - *TV newscaster; St Martin in the Fields Girls HS*

Barnes, Dame Josephine - *Obstetrician and gynaecologist; Oxford HS*

Barnes, Rosie - *Former Liberal Democrat MP; Bilborough GS*

Barnett, Corelli - *Historian; Trinity, Croydon*

Barran, Sir David - *Former Chairman Midland Bank; Winchester*

Barratt, Michael - *Radio and TV broadcaster; Rossall* and *Paisley GS*

Barrington-Ward, Rt Rev Simon - *Bishop of Coventry; Eton*

Barron, Brian - *BBC Asia correspondent; Bristol GS*

Barron, Derek - *Chair and chief executive Ford Motor Co; Beckenham and Penge GS*

Barron, Sir Donald - *Former Chairman Rowntree Trust; George Heriot's, Edinburgh*

Barry, Rt Rev Patrick - *Former Abbot of Ampleforth; Ampleforth*

Barstow, Josephine - *Opera singer; Minchenden GS*

Barstow, Stan - *Novelist and scriptwriter; Ossett GS, Yorkshire*

Basham, Brian - *Founder, MD Broad Street PR company; Catford Secondary*

Bates, Alan - *Actor; Herbert Strutt GS, Derbyshire*

Bateson, Professor Patrick - *Provost King's College, Cambridge; Westminster*

Battishill, Sir Anthony - *Chair Board of Inland Revenue; Taunton* and *Hele's, Exeter*

Baughen, Rt Rev Michael - *Bishop of Chester; Bromley GS*

Bawden, Nina - *Writer, especially children's books; Ilford Girls' County HS*

Baxter, Keith - *Actor; Newport HS*

Baxter, Raymond - *Broadcaster and writer; Ilford County HS*

Bayley, Professor John - *Literary critic; Eton*

Bayliss, Sir Richard - *Former physician to HM The Queen; Rugby*

Beach, General Sir Hugh - *Former Director Council for Arms Control; Winchester*

Beacham, Stephanie - *Actress; Sacred Heart Convent, Whetstone*

Beale, John - *Chief Education Officer, West Glamorgan; Dynevor GS, Swansea*

Beardsley, Peter - *England football player; Longbenton HS, Newcastle*

Bearsted, Lord - *Deputy Director Hill Samuel, Chair Dylon; Eton*

Beatty, The Earl - *Landowner; Eton*

Beaufort, The Duke of - *Chair Marlborough Fine Art; Eton*

Beaumont, Bill - *Rugby player; Ellesmere*

Beaumont-Dark, Sir Anthony - *Former Conservative MP; Cedarhurst, Solihull*

Beaverbrook, Lord - *Chr Beaverbrook Fndn; Charterhouse*

Beck, Rev Brian - *Secretary The Methodist Conference; City of London*

Beck, Sir Edgar - *Former Chair John Mowlem; Lancing*

Billington, Lady Rachel - *Writer; More House, London*
Bingham, Rt Hon Lord Justice Thomas - *Appeal Court Judge; Sedbergh*
Bingham, The Hon Charlotte - *Writer; Haywards Heath Priory*
Binney, Marcus - *President SAVE Heritage protection; Eton*
Bintley, David - *Principal dancer, choreog Royal Ballet; Holme Valley GS and Royal Valley*
Birch, Peter - *Chief executive Abbey National; Allhallows*
Birch, Reginald - *Chair Communist Party of Great Britain; St Augustine's Elementary, Kilburn*
Bird, Dickie - *Test match umpire; Raley's, Barnsley*
Birley, Mark - *Nightclub owner Annabel's; Eton*
Birrell, James - *Chief Executive Halifax Building Society; Belle Vue GS, Bradford*
Birt, John - *Deputy Director General BBC; St Mary's College, Crosby*
Bishop, James - *Editor* Illustrated London News; *Haileybury*
Bishop, Sir Michael - *Chair British Midland Airways; Mill Hill*
Black, Sir Douglas - *Physician & prof medicine Manchester Un; Forfar Academy*
Black, Sir James - *Prof of analytical pharmacology London; Beath HS, Cowdenbeath*
Black, Admiral Sir Jeremy - *Former Deputy Chief of Defence Staff; RNC, Dartmouth*
Black, Roger - *Athlete; Portsmouth GS*
Blackburn, Peter - *Chief Executive Nestlé UK, Chair Rowntree; Douai*
Blacker, General Sir Cecil - *Former Adjutant General MOD; Wellington College*
Blackstone, Baroness - *Master Birkbeck College; Ware Girls' GS*
Blair MP, Tony - *Opposition employment spokesman; Fettes*
Blake, Lord - *Historian; King Edward VI, Norwich*
Blake, Peter - *Painter; Gravesend Technical College*
Blanch, Rt Hon the Lord - *Former Archbishop of York; Alleyn's*
Bland, Christopher - *Chair LWT; Sedbergh*
Blank, Victor - *Chair, Chief executive Charterhouse Bank; Stockport GS*
Blashford-Snell, Col John - *Explorer, Direc Gen Operation Raleigh; Victoria College, Jersey CI*
Bleasdale, Alan - *TV scriptwriter; Wade Deacon GS, Widnes*
Blom-Cooper QC, Sir Louis - *Fmr Chair The Press Council; Seaford College*
Bloom, Claire - *Actress; Badminton and Arts Educational*
Bluck, Duncan - *Chair, British Tourist Authority; Taunton*
Blue, Rabbi Lionel - *Writer and broadcaster; Westminster City and Hendon County GS*
Blunkett, David - *Labour MP, Shadow Local Govt minister; Royal National College for the Blind*
Blyth, Chay - *Round the world solo yachtsman; Hawick GS*
Blyth, Sir James - *Director and chief executive Boots plc; Spiers*
Boardman, Lord - *Director National Westminster Bank; Bromsgrove*
Boateng, Paul - *Labour MP, TV presenter; Apsley GS, Hemel Hempstead*
Bogarde, Sir Dirk - *Actor; University College Sch and Allan Glen's*
Bogdanov, Michael - *Artistic Director English Shakespeare Co; Harrow*
Boksenberg, Professor Alexander - *Director Royal Greenwich Observatory; Stationers' Company*
Bolam, James - *Actor; Bede GS, Sunderland and Bemrose, Derby*
Bolt, Robert - *Playwright; Manchester GS*
Bolton, Eric - *Former Senior Chief Inspector of Schools; Wigan GS*

Braine, Lord - *Former Father of the House of Commons; Hendon County GS*
Bramall, Field Marshal Lord - *Former Chief of General Staff; Eton*
Bramall, Sir Ashley - *Former Labour MP; former chair GLC and ILEA; Westminster* and *Canford*
Bramall, Margaret - *Vice-Pres Nat Counc One Parent Families; St Paul's Girls'*
Branagh, Kenneth - *Actor and director; Meadway Comprehensive, Reading*
Brandon of Oakbrook, Lord - *Law Lord; Winchester*
Brandon-Bravo, Martin - *Former Conservative MP; Latymer Upper*
Brandreth, Gyles - *Conservative MP, author, broadcaster, journalist, producer; French Lycée, London* and *Bedales*
Branson, Richard - *Entrepreneur - Virgin Atlantic, Records; Stowe*
Bratby, John - *Painter; Tiffin Boys', Kingston-on-Thames*
Brearley, Mike - *Cricketer; City of London*
Bremner, Moyra - *TV Presenter and homecare expert; Princess Helena College, Hitchin*
Brener, Michael - *Director of Music Chetham's Music School; Bishop Vesey's GS, Sutton Coldfield*
Brenton, Howard - *Playwright; Chichester HS*
Bresslaw, Bernard – *Actor; Coopers Company*
Brett, Jeremy - *Actor; Eton*
Brett, Simon - *Writer; Dulwich*
Bridge of Harwich, Lord - *Law Lord; Marlborough*
Brien, Alan - *Journalist; Bede GS, Sunderland*
Briers, Richard - *Actor; Ridgeways*
Briggs, Lord - *Provost Worcester College; Keighley GS*
Briggs, Raymond – *Illustrator and writer; Rutlish*
Brighouse, Professor Tim - *Professor of Education Keele University; Lowestoft GS*
Brigstocke, Baroness - *Former High Mistress St Paul's Girls'; Abbey, Reading*
Bristol, The Marquess of - *Director Bristol Estates; Harrow*
Bristow, Eric - *Darts player; Grocers Company GS, Hackney Down*
Brittan, Sir Leon - *Vice Pres Commission of the EC; Haberdashers' Aske's.*
Brittan, Samuel - *Economist, Financial Times journalist; Kilburn GS*
Broackes, Sir Nigel - *Chair Trafalgar House; Stowe*
Broad, Chris - *Cricketer; Colston's, Bristol*
Bron, Eleanor - *Actress; North London Collegiate*
Brook, Lady - *Founder Brook Advisory Centre birth control; St Leonards Mayfield*
Brook, Peter - *Producer; Westminster* and *Greshams*
Brooke MP, Rt Hon Peter - *Former Secretary of State for Northern Ireland; Marlborough*
Brooke of Ystradfelte, Baroness - *Former Chair the Conservative Party; Queen Anne's, Caversham*
Brooke-Taylor, Tim - *Actor and comedian; Winchester*
Brookner, Anita - *Novelist; James Allen's Girls'*
Brooks, Liz - *Admin Director the Dyslexia Institute; Oxford HS*
Broome, David - *Show jumper; Monmouth*
Broome, John - *Chair Alton Towers; Rossall*
Brophy, Brigid - *Author; St Paul's Girls'*
Brophy, Michael - *Director Charities Aid Foundation; Ampleforth*
Brown, Christopher - *Director NSPCC; Hertford GS*
Brown, John - *Publisher Viz magazine; Westminster*

Burton, Charles - *World circumnavigator via N and S Poles; Millfield*
Burton, Humphrey - *Artistic director Barbican, TV producer; Judd, Tonbridge*
Busby, Sir Matt - *Football manager; St Bride's, Bothwell*
Bush, Dr Alan - *Conductor, prof composition Roy Coll Mus; Highgate*
Bussell, Darcey - *Ballerina Royal Ballet; Arts Educational and Royal Ballet*
Butcher, John - *Conservative MP; Huntingdon GS*
Butler, James - *Sculptor; Maidstone GS*
Butler, Professor Marilyn - *Professor English Lit King's, Cambridge; Wimbledon Girls' HS*
Butler, Hon Sir Richard - *Former President NFU; Eton*
Butler, Sir Robin - *Secty to Cabinet, Head of Civil Service; Harrow*
Butler-Sloss, Rt Hon Dame Elizabeth - *Lord Justice of Appeal; Wycombe Abbey*
Butt, Michael - *Director BAT Industries plc; Rugby*
Butterfield, Lord - *Former Master Downing College, Cambridge; Solihull*
Butterworth, Lord - *Vice Chancellor Warwick University; Queen Elizabeth's GS, Mansfield*
Buxton, Cindy - *Film maker; New Hall, Chelmsford*
Byatt, Antonia - *Writer; Sheffield Girls' HS and Mount, York*
Bygraves, Max - *Entertainer; St Joseph's, Rotherhithe*

Cadbury, Sir Adrian - *Former Chair Cadbury Schweppes plc; Eton*
Cadbury, Dominic - *Chief executive Cadbury Schweppes plc; Eton*
Cadbury, George - *Chair Emer Internat Planned Parenthd Fdn; Leighton Park*
Cadbury, Peter - *Chair Preston Estates, George Cadbury Trust; Leighton Park*
Caesar, Canon Anthony - *Domestic Chaplain to HM The Queen; Cranleigh*
Cahill, Teresa - *Opera singer; Notre Dame HS, Southwark*
Caine, Marti - *Singer and actress; Hatfield House Lane Secondary Modern*
Caine, Sir Michael - *Chair Booker; Bedales*
Caine, Michael - *Actor; Wilson's GS, Peckham*
Cairncross, Frances - *Editor the Economist; Laurel Bank, Glasgow*
Calcutt QC, David - *Barrister, Master Magdalene, Cambridge; Cranleigh*
Calder, Finlay - *Captain British Lions; Daniel Stewart's, Edinburgh and Melville College*
Calder, Nigel - *Science fiction writer; Merchant Taylors'*
Calderwood, Alan - *Chief Education Officer Cleveland; Perth Academy*
Calder-Marshall, Anna - *Actress; Conv Immaculate Heart Mary, Billingshurst*
Callaghan, Lord - *Former Labour Prime Minister; Portsmouth Northern Secondary*
Callow, Simon - *Actor; Oratory*
Calman, Professor Kenneth - *Government Chief Medical Officer; Allan Glen's*
Calman, Mel - *Cartoonist; Perse, Cambridge*
Campbell, Cheryl - *Actress; Francis Bacon GS, St Albans*
Campbell, Menzies - *Liberal Democrat MP; Hillhead HS, Glasgow*
Campbell, Naomi - *Model; Italia Conti Stage*
Campbell, Penelope - *Hockey international; Maynard*
Campbell-Johnson, Rev Michael - *Provincial Superior British Jesuits; Beaumont*
Campbell-Savours, Dale - *Labour MP; Keswick*
Cannon, Tommy - *Comedian; Henshaw Secondary Modern, Oldham*
Cant, Brian - *Children's TV presenter; Northgate GS, Ipswich*
Capel, David - *Cricketer; Roade Comprehensive*

Capes, Geoff - *Shot-putter; George Farmer Comprehensive, Holbeach*
Cardiff, Jack - *Film director; Medburn, Hertfordshire*
Carey, Most Rev George - *Archbishop of Canterbury; Bifrons Secondary Modern, Barking*
Carey, Sir Peter - *Chair Dalgety plc, Direc Morgan Grenfell; Portsmouth GS*
Carling, Will - *England rugby captain; Sedbergh*
Carlisle, Mark - *Former Education Secretary; Raley*
Carman QC, George - *Barrister; St Joseph's College, Blackpool*
Carmichael, Ian - *Actor; Scarborough College and Bromsgrove*
Carmichael, Sandy - *Most capped Scots rugby forward; Belmont House*
Carnarvon, The Earl of - *Former racehorse trainer to HM The Queen; Eton*
Caro, Sir Anthony - *Sculptor; Charterhouse*
Carpenter, Harry - *Sports commentator; Ashburton, Croydon and Selhurst GS*
Carrington, Lord - *Diplomat; Eton*
Carson, Willie - *Jockey; Riverside, Stirling*
Carter-Ruck, Peter - *Solicitor; St Edward's, Oxford*
Cartledge, Sir Bryan - *Principal Linacre College Oxford; Hurstpierpoint*
Carver, Field Marshal Lord - *Former Chief of Defence Staff; Winchester*
Cass, Sir Geoffrey - *Chair Royal Shakespeare Company;, Queen Elizabeth GS, Darlington*
Cassels, Sir John - *Former Director General NEDDY; Sedbergh*
Cassidi, Admiral Sir Desmond - *Former Flag ADC to HM The Queen; RNC, Dartmouth*
Casson, Sir Hugh - *Architect; Eastbourne College*
Casson, Lady - *Architect and designer; Wychwood, Oxford*
Castle, Baroness - *MEP, former Labour Minister; Bradford Girls' GS*
Castle, Enid - *Principal Cheltenham Ladies' College; Hulme Girls' GS, Oldham*
Castle, Roy - *Entertainer; Honley GS, Yorkshire*
Cater, Sir Robin - *Former Chair Distillers Co; George Watson's, Edinburgh*
Catherwood, Sir Fred - *Industrialist, Former Chr British Institute Management; Shrewsbury*
Caulfield, Sir Bernard - *High Court Judge; St Francis Xavier's College, Liverpool*
Causley, Charles - *Poet and broadcaster; Horwell GS and Launceston College, Cornwall*
Cavanagh, John - *Fashion designer; St Paul's*
Cayzer, Lord - *Financier; Eton*
Cazalet, Sir Peter - *Chair APV, former Chair BP; Uppingham*
Cazenove, Christopher - *Actor; Eton*
Cecil, Henry - *Racehorse trainer; Canford*
Cecil, Jonathan - *Actor; Eton*
Chadwick, Very Rev Professor Henry - *Master Peterhouse, Cambridge; Eton*
Chadwick, Lynn - *Sculptor; Merchant Taylors'*
Chadwick, Rev Professor Owen - *Church historian, Chancellor E Anglia Univ; Tonbridge*
Chalfont, Lord - *Chair The Radio Authority; West Monmouth*
Chalker, Baroness - *Minister for Overseas Development; Roedean*
Chalmers, Judith - *TV presenter; Withington Girls' HS, Manchester*
Chalmers, Sandra - *Radio producer; Withington Girls' HS, Manchester*
Champion, Bob - *Jockey; Earl Haig, Guisborough, Yorks*
Chandler, Sir Colin - *Managing Director Vickers; St Joseph's Academy, Blackheath*
Chandler, Sir Geoffrey - *Industrial Advis RSA, fmr direc NEDO; Sherborne*

Channon, Rt Hon Paul - *Former Secretary of State Transport; Eton*
Chaplin MP, Judith - *Former political adviser to John Major; Wycombe Abbey*
Chapman, The Hon Rhiannon - *1st female director The Industrial Soc; Tormead*
Chapple, Lord - *Former Gen Sec Electricians, Telecom and Plumbers Union; St John's Road, Hoxton, N London*
Charles, Caroline - *Fashion designer; Sacred Heart Convent, Woldingham*
Charlton, Bobby - *Footballer, Director Manchester United; Bedlington GS, Northumberland*
Charlton, Jackie - *Footballer, Manager Ireland team; Bedlington GS, Northumberland*
Charteris, Lord - *Chair National Heritage Memorial Fund; Eton*
Charteris, Leslie - *Author The Saint; Rossall*
Chasty, Dr Harry - *Director of Studies Dyslexia Institute; Royal Belfast Academical Institution*
Chataway, Rt Hon Christopher - *Former athlete and MP, Company director; Sherborne*
Checkland, Sir Michael - *Director General BBC; King Edward's, Birmingham*
Cheshire VC, Lord - *Founder of Cheshire Homes for Disabled; Stowe*
Chesterton, Sir Oliver - *Consultant Chestertons Chtd Surveyors; Rugby*
Chetwood, Sir Clifford - *Chair Wimpey plc; Wandsworth GS*
Chichester-Clark, Sir Robin - *Former Minister of State, Employment; managmt consultnt; RNC, Dartmouth*
Chilver, Lord - *Chair England China Clays; Southend HS*
Chisholm, George - *Trombonist; Strathclyde, Glasgow*
Cholmondeley, The Marquess of - *Landowner; Eton*
Chope, Christopher - *Former Under Secretary of State for Transport; Marlborough*
Christian, Terry - *TV presenter; St Bede's RC GS, Manchester*
Christie, Sir George - *Chair Glyndebourne Productions Ltd; Eton*
Christie, Linford - *Athlete; Henry Comprehensive, Fulham*
Christopherson, Sir Derman - *Former Master Magdalene College, Cambridge; Sherborne*
Churchill, Winston - *Conservative MP; Eton*
Cierach, Lindka - *Fashion designer; St Leonard's Mayfield*
Clapton, Eric - *Guitarist and singer; St Bede's Secondary Modern, Woking and Hollyfield Road, Surbiton*
Clark, The Hon Alan - *Former Minister Defence Procurement; historian; Eton*
Clark, Felicity - *Director Royal Opera House Covent Garden; Downe House*
Clark, Jim - *Motor racing driver; Loretto*
Clark, Sir John - *Former Chair Plessey; Harrow*
Clark, Sir Robert - *Chair United Biscuits, Director TSB; Highgate*
Clarke, Arthur C. - *Science fiction writer; Huish's GS, Taunton*
Clarke, Sir Ashley - *Chairman Venice in Peril Fund; Repton*
Clarke QC MP, Rt Hon Kenneth - *Home Secretary; Nottingham HS*
Clarke, Neil - *Chair British Coal; Rugby*
Clary, Julian - *Entertainer; St Benedict's, Ealing*
Cleese, John - *Actor; Clifton*
Clemence, Ray - *Footballer; Lumley Secondary, Skegness*
Clement, John - *Chair Unigate Group; Bishop's Stortford College*
Cleminson, Sir James - *Chair British Overseas Trade Board; Rugby*
Cleobury, Nicholas - *Conductor; King's, Worcester*
Cleobury, Stephen - *Director Music King's College, Cambridge; King's, Worcester*

Cool, Phil - *Entertainer; St Augustine's Secondary, Chorley*
Cooling, Wendy - *Head of Children's Book Foundation; Blyth GS, Norwich*
Cooney, Ray - *Theatre producer; Alleyn's*
Cooper, Derek - *Author, broadcaster and journalist; Raynes Park GS and Portree HS, Isle of Skye*
Cooper, Sir Frank - *Civil Servant and company chairman; Manchester GS*
Cooper, Henry - *Boxer; Athelney Street, Bellingham*
Cooper, Jilly - *Novelist and journalist; Godolphin, Salisbury*
Cooper, Leo - *Publisher; Radley*
Cooper, Phil - *Our Lady of Lourdes, Southport*
Cooper, Roger - *Businessman and Iranian hostage; Clifton*
Cope, David - *Master, Marlborough College; Winchester*
Cope MP, Sir John - *Paymaster General; Oakham*
Cope, Wendy - *Poet; Farrington HS, Chislehurst*
Copley, John - *Opera producer; King Edward's, Birmingham*
Corbett, Ronnie - *Comedian; James Gillespie's, Edinburgh and Royal HS, Edinburgh*
Corby, Sir Brian - *Chair The Prudential; Kimbolton*
Cordingley, Brigadier Patrick - *Commander 7th Armoured Brigade Gulf War; Sherborne*
Coren, Alan - *Writer and broadcaster; East Barnet GS*
Corfield, Sir Kenneth - *Industralist, former President Institute of Directors; South Staffs College*
Cormack, Patrick - *Conservative MP; Havelock, Grimsby*
Corrigan-Maguire, Mairead - *Co-founder The Peace People, Nobel Prize '76; St Vincent's, Belfast*
Cossons, Dr Neil - *Director The Science Museum; Henry Mellish GS, Nottingham*
Cotton, Bernard - *Manager GB hockey team 1992 Olympics; Hitchin GS and Northampton GS*
Cotton, Bill - *Director Noel Gay TV; Ardingly College*
Cotton, Fran - *Sports commentator; Newton le Willows GS*
Couper, Heather - *Astronomy broadcaster and author; St Mary's GS, Northwood*
Courtenay, Tom - *Actor; Kingston HS, Hull*
Couve de Murville, Most Rev Maurice - *RC Archbishop of Birmingham; Downside*
Coventry, Rev John - *Catholic theologian; Stonyhurst*
Cowans, Norman - *Cricketer; Park HS, Stanmore*
Cowdray, Viscount - *Landowner; Eton*
Cowdrey, Chris - *Cricketer, Tonbridge*
Cowdrey, Sir Colin - *Cricketer; Tonbridge*
Cowley, Professor Roger - *Professor experimental philosophy Oxford Univ; Brentwood*
Cowling, Maurice MP - *Fellow Peterhouse Cambridge, Conservative historian; Battersea GS*
Cox, Baroness - *Deputy Speaker House of Lords; Channing, London*
Cox, Sir Anthony - *Architect; Mill Hill*
Cox, Professor Brian - *Professor Eng Lit Manchester University; Wintringham Secondary*
Cox, Brian - *Actor; St Michael's Junior Secondary, Dundee*
Cox, Sir Gordon - *Chemist; City of Bath*
Cox, Mark - *Tennis player; Wyggeston GS, Leicester and Millfield*
Cox, Martin - *Producer Radio 4 FM; Eton*

Crabbe, Pauline - *First black woman magistrate; Highgate Convent*
Craig, Amanda - *Writer; Bedales*
Craig, Marshal of RAF Sir David - *Former Chief of Defence Staff; Radley*
Craig, Wendy - *Actress; Yarm GS, Yorkshire*
Cram, Steve - *Athlete; Jarrow GS*
Cranborne, Viscount - *Defence Minister; Eton*
Cranbrook, Viscount - *Head of Nature Conservancy Council; Eton*
Craven, Gemma - *Actress; Loretto and St Bernard's Convent, Westcliff on Sea*
Craven, John - *TV presenter; Leeds Modern GS*
Crawford, Michael - *Actor; St Michael's College, Bexley and Oakfield, Dulwich*
Crawley, Aidan - *Former Chair LWT; Harrow*
Crewe, Quentin - *Writer and journalist; Eton*
Crichton, Charles - *Film director; Oundle*
Crichton-Miller, Donald - *Former headmaster of Taunton, Fettes, Stowe; Fettes*
Crick, Professor Bernard - *Biographer, lecturer in politics; Whitgift, Croydon*
Crick, Professor Francis - *Molecular biologist; Mill Hill*
Crickhowell, Lord - *Chair National Rivers Authority; Westminster*
Crine, Simon - *General Secretary The Fabian Society; Weston Super Mare GS and Broadoak Comprehensive*
Critchley, Julian - *Conservative MP, broadcaster, journalist; Shrewsbury*
Croft, David - *TV scriptwriter Dad's Army etc; Rugby*
Croker, Ted - *Former Secretary The Football Association; Kingston Technical College*
Crook, Frances - *Director Howard League for Penal Reform; Camden Girls' HS*
Crookenden, Lt Gen Sir Napier - *Former GOC-in-C Western Command; Wellington College*
Crosbie, Annette - *Actress; Boroughmuir, Edinburgh*
Crowley-Milling, Air Marshal Sir Denis - *Former Principal Air Attaché Washington; Malvern*
Crowther, Leslie - *Comedian, TV presenter; Thames Valley GS*
Crutchley, Rosalie - *Actress; Francis Holland*
Cryer, Bob - *Labour MP; Salt HS, Shipley*
Cubitt, Sir Hugh - *Chair Lombard North Central; RNC, Dartmouth*
Cuckney, Sir John - *Chair Royal Insurance, 3i Group plc; Shrewsbury*
Cudlipp, Lord - *Former Chair IPC; Howard Gardens, Cardiff*
Cunningham, Lt Gen Sir Hugh - *Former Lieutenant Tower of London; Charterhouse*
Cunningham, Dr Jack - *Labour MP; Jarrow GS*
Cupitt, Rev Don - *Dean Emmanuel Cambridge Divinity lecturer; Charterhouse*
Currie, Edwina - *Conservative MP; Liverpool Institute Girls': HS*
Curry, John - *Skater; Solihull*
Curteis, Ian - *TV playwright; Slough GS*
Cushing, Peter - *Actor; Shoreham GS and Purley County Secondary*
Cutting, Dr Pauline - *Surgeon, Palestine refugee camps; Mount Grace Comprehensive, Potters Bar*

D'Abo, Jennifer - *Former Chair Ryman; Hatherop Castle, Gloucestershire*
D'Abo, Mike - *Singer, ex-Manfred Mann; Harrow*
Dacre, Lord - *Former Regius Professor Modern History, Oxford, and Former Master, Peterhouse, Cambridge; Charterhouse*
Dacre, Paul - *Editor Evening Standard; University College Sch*

Daiches, Professor David - *English Literature scholar; George Watson's, Edinburgh*

Dainton, Lord - *Chemist, Chancellor Sheffield University; Central, Sheffield*

Dalglish, Kenny - *Footballer, former manager Liverpool; High Possil Secondary*

Dalton, Vice Admiral Sir Geoffrey - *Secretary General MENCAP; Reigate GS*

Daltrey, Roger - *Singer ex-The Who; Acton GS*

Dalyell, Tam - *Labour MP; Eton*

Dance, Charles - *Actor; Widey Technical, Plymouth*

Daneman, Paul - *Actor; Haberdashers' Aske's and Sir William Borlase's, Marlow*

Daniel, Paul - *Musical director Opera North; King Henry VIII, Coventry*

Daniels, Paul - *Magician; Sir William Turner's GS, Coatham, Redcar*

Dankworth, John - *Jazz musician; Monoux GS*

D'Argy Smith, Marcelle - *Editor Cosmopolitan magazine; Westcliff Girls' HS*

Darling, Alistair - *Labour MP; Loretto*

Davenport, Nigel - *Actor; Cheltenham College*

David, Joanna - *Actress; Altrincham GS*

Davie, Professor Donald - *Poet; Barnsley GS*

Davies, Rt Hon Denzil - *Labour MP; Queen Elizabeth GS, Carmarthen*

Davies, Dickie - *Sports commentator; William Ellis, Highgate and Oldershaw GS, Wallasey*

Davies, Gareth - *Wales rugby player; Gwendraeth GS*

Davies, Garfield - *Trade Unionist Shop Workers; Heolgam Secondary Modern*

Davies, George - *Former chief executive Next stores; Bootle GS*

Davies, Geraint - *Controller BBC Wales; Cardiff HS*

Davies, Howard - *Controller Audit Commission; Manchester GS*

Davies, Hunter - *Writer and journalist; Creighton, Carlisle and Carlisle GS*

Davies, Jonathan - *Wales rugby player; Gwendraeth GS*

Davies, Laura - *Golfer; Fullbrook County Secondary*

Davies, Lynn - *Athlete gold medallist '64 Tokyo Olymp; Ogmore GS*

Davies, Sharron - *Swimmer; Plymstock Comprehensive and Kelly College*

Davis, Andrew - *Musical Director Glyndebourne Opera; Watford Boys' GS*

Davis, Sir Colin - *Conductor; Christ's Hospital*

Davis, Sir John - *Director The Rank Foundation; City of London*

Davis, Steve - *Snooker player; Abbey Wood, London*

Davis, William - *Author, journalist and broadcaster; City of London*

Davison, Peter - *Actor; Winston Churchill County Secondary*

Dawson, Anthony - *Physician to HM The Queen; Wyggeston GS, Leicester*

Dawson, Peter - *General Scty Prof Association Teachers; Bishop Gore GS, Swansea*

Day, Sir Michael - *Chair, Commission for Racial Equality; University College Sch*

Day, Sir Robin - *TV and radio journalist; Bembridge, Isle of Wight and Brentwood*

Day-Lewis, Daniel - *Actor; Sevenoaks and Bedales*

Day-Lewis, Sean - *Journalist and author; Allhallows*

De Bellaigue, Sir Geoffrey - *Surveyor of the Queen's works of art; Wellington College*

De Burgh, Chris - *Pop singer; Marlborough*

De Ferranti, S.B. - *Former Chair Ferranti plc; Ampleforth*

De Freitas, Phillip - *Cricketer; Willesden HS, Brent*

De Grey, Roger - *President Royal Academy of Arts; Eton*

De La Billière, Gen Sir Peter - *Cdr SAS Falklands War, Cdr Gulf War; Harrow*

De La Tour, Frances - *Actress; French Lycée, London*

De Peyer, David - *Direc Gen Cancer Research Campaign; Rendcomb College*
De Savary, Peter - *International entrepreneur; Charterhouse*
De Villeneuve, Justin - *Discoverer and mentor of model Twiggy; Tottenham Commercial College*
Dean, Brenda - *General Secretary SOGAT; Stretford Girls' HS*
Dean, Letitia - *Actress; Sylvia Young Theatre*
Dean, Sir Patrick - *Director Taylor Woodrow and former HM Ambassador, Washington; Rugby*
Dear, Geoffrey - *Chief Constable West Midlands Police; Fletton GS, Huntingdon*
Dearing, Sir Ron - *Chair Universities Funding Council; Doncaster GS*
Deedes, Lord - *Former editor Daily Telegraph; Harrow*
Del Mar, Norman - *Conductor; Marlborough*
Delaney, Shelagh - *Playwright; Broughton Secondary*
Delfont, Lord - *Chair Trusthouse Forte; Rochelle Street, East London*
Dellal, Jack - *Chair Allied Commercial Exporters Ltd; Heaton Moor College, Manchester*
Delvin, Dr David - *TV, radio and magazine doctor; St Dunstan's, Catford*
Demarco, Richard - *Artist, director Edinburgh art gallery; Holy Cross Academy, Edinburgh*
Dempster, Nigel - *Gossip columnist; Sherborne*
Dench, Dame Judi - *Actress and producer; Mount, York*
Denison, Michael - *Actor; Harrow*
Denning, Lord - *Former Master of the Rolls; Andover GS*
Dennis, Major General Alastair - *Secretary Imperial Cancer Research Fund; Malvern*
Dennis, Very Rev John - *Bishop of St Edmundsbury and Ipswich; Rutlish*
Denton, Baroness - *Businesswoman; former rally driver; Rothwell GS*
Denton, Charles - *Chief executive Zenith Productions; Reading*
Derby, Lord; *Landowner; Eton*
Deuchar, Patrick - *Chief executive Royal Albert Hall; Christ's Hospital*
Devlin, Lord - *Former Law Lord; Stonyhurst*
Devonshire, The Duke of - *Landowner – Chatsworth; Eton*
Dewar Donald MP, - *Shadow Scottish Secretary; Glasgow Academy*
Dews, Peter - *Theatre and TV director; Queen Elizabeth GS, Wakefield*
Dexter, Ted - *Chair England Committee TCCB; Radley*
Dick, Kay - *Writer and critic; French Lycée, London*
Dickens, Geoffrey - *Conservative MP; East Lane, Wembley*
Dickens, Monica - *Writer, founder of USA Samaritans; St Paul's Girls'*
Dickinson, Bruce - *Rock singer Iron Maiden; Oundle*
Dickinson, Peter - *Author; Eton*
Dickson, Alec - *Founder VSO; Rugby*
Dickson, Barbara - *Pop singer; Woodmill HS, Dunfermline*
Dilley, Graham - *Cricketer; Dartford West Secondary*
Dimbleby, David - *Broadcaster and newspaper proprietor; Charterhouse*
Dimbleby, Jonathan - *Broadcaster, journalist and author; Charterhouse*
Dimmock, Peter - *Commentator, Vice President ABC Video; Dulwich*
Dobbs, Michael - *Novelist; Hertford GS*
Dodd, Ken - *Comedian; Holt HS, Liverpool*
Doll, Sir Richard - *Medical epidemiologist; Westminster*
Don, Robert - *Theatre and opera designer; Bell Baxter HS, Cupar, Fife*
Donald, Chris - *Founder and editor Viz magazine; Heaton Comprehensive, Newcastle*

Donaldson, David - *Portrait painter; Coatbridge*
Donaldson of Lymington, Lord - *Master of the Rolls; Charterhouse*
Donohoe, Peter - *Pianist; Chetham's*
Donoughue, Lord - *Former Labour policy adviser; Northampton GS*
Dooley, Wade - *England rugby player; Bolton*
Dotrice, Roy - *Actor; Dayton and intermediate schools, Guernsey*
Dougall, Robert - *Broadcaster and writer; Whitgift, Croydon*
Douglas, Katrina - *Ladies' golf champion; St Brandon's, Bristol*
Douglas, Margaret - *Chief political adviser BBC; Parliament Hill Girls' GS*
Douglas, Professor Mary - *Anthropologist; Sacred Heart Convent, Roehampton*
Douglas, Sue - *Journalist Sunday Times; Kingston Girls'*
Douglas-Hamilton MP, Lord James - *Under Secretary of State Scottish Office; Eton*
Douglas-Home, William - *Playwright; Eton*
Dowell, Anthony - *Director The Royal Ballet; Hampshire Sch, London* and *St Saviour's Hall, Knightsbridge*
Down, Lesley-Ann - *Actress; Professional Children's*
Downey, Sir Gordon - *Chair FIMBRA; Tiffin Boys', Kingston on Thames*
Downton, Paul - *Cricketer; Sevenoaks*
Drabble, Jane - *Deputy MD BBC; Plympton GS, Devon*
Drabble, Margaret - *Author; Mount, York*
Drabble, Phil - *TV commentator; Bromsgrove*
Drew, David - *Ballet dancer, choreographer Royal Ballet; Bristol GS*
Drew, Jane - *Architect; Croydon Girls' HS*
Drew, Joanna - *Director The Hayward Gallery; Dartington Hall*
Drummond, John - *Former Controller Music BBC Radio 3; Canford*
Drury, Rev John - *Biblical scholar; Bradfield*
Du Cann, Sir Edward - *Chair Lonrho plc; Woodbridge*
Du Cann QC, Richard - *Barrister; Steyning GS*
Dudley, William - *Stage designer RSC, Royal Opera; Highbury GS*
Duff, Sir Anthony - *Diplomat and intelligence expert; RNC, Dartmouth*
Duff, Mickey - *Boxing promoter; Rabbinical Sch, Northampton*
Duffy, Maureen - *Author; Trowbridge Girls' HS* and *Sarah Bonnell HS for Girls*
Dummett, Ann - *Former Director Runnymede Trust; Guildhouse, Pimlico* and *Ware Girls' GS*
Dummett, Professor Michael - *Wykeham Professor of Logic Oxford Univ; Winchester*
Dunkley, Chris - *Journalist and broadcaster; Haberdashers' Aske's*
Dunlop, Frank - *Director Edinburgh Festival; Kibworth Beauchamp GS*
Dunn, Richard - *Chief Executive Thames TV; Forest, Essex*
Dunnant, Sarah - *Presenter The Late Show; Godolphin and Latymer*
Dunstan, Rev Prof Gordon - *Emerit Prof Moral Theology King's, London; Plymouth Corporation GS*
Dunwoody, Gwyneth - *Labour MP; Fulham County* and *Notre Dame Convent, Battersea*
Dunwoody, Richard - *Jockey, Grand National winner; Rendcomb College*
Durbridge, Francis - *Playwright and author; Bradford GS* and *Wylde Green College*
Durham, Sir Kenneth - *Chair, Unilever; Queen Elizabeth GS, Blackburn*
Durie, Jo - *Tennis player; Clifton Girls' HS*
Dyke, Greg - *Chief Executive LWT; Hayes GS*

Evans, Robert - *Chair British Gas plc; Old Swan College, Liverpool* and
     Blackburn GS
Eve, Trevor - *Actor; Bromsgrove*
Everett, Rupert - *Actor; Ampleforth*
Ewart-Biggs MP, Baroness Jane - *Labour Party spokesperson Home Affairs;*
     Downe House
Ewing, Winifred - *Scottish National Party MP; Queen's Park, Glasgow*
Exton, Clive - *Playwright and scriptwriter; Christ's Hospital*
Eyre, Richard - *Theatre, film and TV director; Sherborne*
Eyton, Audrey - *Diet writer, F-Plan diet; Blackburn HS*
Ezra, Lord - *Former Chair National Coal Board; Monmouth*

Faber, Thomas - *Chair Faber and Faber; Oundle*
Fairbairn, Sir Nicholas - *Conservative MP; Loretto*
Fairbrother, Neil - *Cricketer; Lymm GS*
Faithfull, Baroness - *Chair All-Pty Parlty Group for Children; Talbot Heath*
Faldo, Nick - *Golfer; Sir Frederick Osborne, Welwyn*
Falkender, Lady - *Columnist; Northampton HS*
Fallon, Michael - *Former Under-Secretary of State for Education; Epsom College*
Fantoni, Barry - *Cartoonist and* Private Eye *journalist; Archbishop Temple*
Farmer, Tom - *Founder and Director Kwik Fit Tyres; Holy Cross Academy,*
     Edinburgh
Farquharson, Rt Hon Lord Justice Donald - *Appeal Court Judge; Royal*
     Commercial Travellers'
Farr, Dennis - *Director The Courtauld Institute; Luton GS*
Farr, Sir John - *Former Conservative MP, Campaigner Birmingham 6; Harrow*
Farrar-Hockley, Sir Anthony - *Defence Consultant and lecturer; Exeter*
Farrell, Terry - *Architect; St Cuthbert's GS, Newcastle*
Fashanu, John - Wimbledon centre forward, Direc Kiss FM; Attleborough
     Secondary, Norfolk
Faulds, Andrew - *Labour MP and film actor; King Edward VI, Louth, Daniel*
     Stewart's, Edinburgh and *Stirling HS*
Faulk, Bernard - *Journalist; Wellington College*
Faulks, Sebastian - *Journalist; Wellington College*
Fawkes, Wally - *Cartoonist; Sidcup Central*
Feaver, Rt Rev Douglas - *Former Bishop of Peterborough; Bristol GS*
Fellows, Sir Robert - *Deputy private secretary HM The Queen; Eton*
Fenn, Sir Nicholas - *HM Ambassador to Dublin; Kingswood, Bath*
Fennell QC, Desmond - *High Ct Judge King's Cross Fire report; Ampleforth*
Fenner, Dame Peggy - *Conservative MP; LCC Brockley* and *Ide Hill, Sevenoaks*
Fenwick, John - *Chair Fenwick of Bond Street; Rugby*
Ferguson, Alex - *Manager Manchester United; Govan High Senior Secondary*
Ferguson QC, Richard - *Barrister; Methodist College, Belfast*
Fergusson, Sir Ewen - *Diplomat, HM Ambassador to Paris; Rugby*
Fermor, Patrick Leigh - *Writer; King's, Canterbury*
Ferry, Bryan - *Pop musician; Washington GS, Co Durham*
Ffrench-Beytagh, Rev Canon Gonville - *Writer, fmr Dean of*
     Johannesburg; Monkton Combe and *Bristol GS*
Field, Brigadier Anne - *Dep Cdt WRAC, Chair W London Lloyds Bank; Keswick*
     and *St George's, Harpenden*
Field, Robin - *Chief Executive Filofax plc; Sherborne*

Field, Frank - *Labour MP; St Clement Danes GS*

Fieldhouse, Admiral of the Fleet Lord - *Former First Sea Lord, Chf Defence Staff; RNC, Dartmouth*

Fielding, Fenella - *Actress; North London Collegiate*

Fielding, Yvette - *Presenter* Blue Peter *Children's TV; Braeside, Buckhurst* and *Hillcrest GS*

Fiennes, Sir Ranulph - *Explorer; Eton*

Findlay, Ian - *Former Chair Lloyd's; Fettes*

Finlay, Frank - *Actor; St Gregory the Great, Farnworth*

Finney, Albert - *Actor; Salford GS*

Firth, Peter - *Actor; Hanson, Bradford*

Fish, Michael - *Radio and TV weather man; Eastbourne College*

Fisher, Mark - *Labour MP; Eton*

Fitt, Lord - *Former SDLP MP; Christian Brothers', Belfast*

Fitzgerald, Penelope - *Novelist; Wycombe Abbey*

Flanders, Dennis - *Landscape artist; Merchant Taylors'*

Flint, Colin - *Principal Solihull College Technology; Scarborough HS*

Floud, Professor Roderick - *Provost City of London Polytechnic; Brentwood*

Flowers, Lord - *Former Vice Chancellor Univ of London; Bishop Gore GS, Swansea*

Floyd, Keith - *TV personality; Wellington, Somerset*

Foale, Marion - *Knitwear designer; Ilford Girls' County HS*

Follett, Ken - *Author; Harrow Weald GS*

Fookes, Dame Janet - *Conservative MP; Hastings and St Leonard's Ladies' College* and *Hastings Girls' HS*

Foot, Lord - *President UK Immigrants Advisory Service; Forres, Swanage, Bembridge, Isle of Wight*

Foot, Rt Hon Michael - *Former Labour Leader; Forres, Swanage* and *Leighton Park*

Forbes, Hon Sir Alastair - *President Court of Appeal Falkland Is; Blundell's*

Forbes, Anthony - *Joint Senior Ptner Cazenove Stockbrokers; Eton*

Forbes, Bryan - *Film director; West Ham GS*

Ford, Sir Brinsley - *Former Chair National Art Collection; Eton*

Foreman, Michael - *Illustrator and writer; Notley Road Secondary Modern, Lowestoft*

Forgan, Liz - *Director programming Channel 4; Benenden*

Forman, Sir Denis - *Deputy Chair Granada; Loretto*

Forman, Nigel - *Under Sec of State, Education and Science; Shrewsbury*

Forrester, Rev Professor Duncan - *Prof Christian Ethics Edinburgh Univ; Madras College, St Andrews*

Forster, Sir Archibald - *Chairman Esso UK; Tottenham GS*

Forster, Margaret - *Novelist and biographer; Carlisle County Girls' HS*

Forsyth, Bruce - *Entertainer; Latymer GS, Edmonton*

Forsyth, Frederick - *Novelist; Tonbridge*

Forsyth MP, Michael - *Minister of State Employment; Arbroath HS*

Forte, Lord - *Chair Trusthouse Forte; St Joseph's College, Dumfries* and *Alloa Academy*

Forte, Rocco - *Chief executive Trusthouse Forte; Downside*

Forth MP, Eric - *Under Sec State Education and Science; Jordanhill College, Glasgow*

Foster, Joanna - *Chair Equal Opportunities Commission; Benenden*

Foster, Brendan - *Athlete; St Joseph's GS, Co Durham*

Foster, Neil - *Cricketer; Philip Morant, Colchester*
Foster, Sir Norman - *Architect; Burnage GS, Manchester*
Fowlds, Derek - *Actor; Ashlyns Secondary Modern, Berkhamsted*
Fowler, Professor Gerald - *Rector East London Polytechnic; Northampton GS*
Fowler, Graham - *Cricketer; Accrington GS*
Fowler, Rt Hon Sir Norman - *Chairman Conservative Party; King Edward VI,
      Chelmsford*
Fowles, John - *Writer; Bedford*
Fox, Edward - *Actor; Harrow*
Fox, James - *Actor; Harrow*
Fox, Sir Marcus - *Conservative MP; Wheelwright GS, Dewsbury*
Fox, Sir Paul - *Chair Channel 4; Bournemouth GS*
Fox, Robert - *Broadcaster; Blundell's*
Fox, Samantha - *Actress; St Gilda's RC Junior, Hornsey and St Thomas More RC
      Senior, Wood Green*
Foxley-Norris, ACM Sir Christopher - *Chairman Battle of Britain Association;
      Winchester*
Francis, Clare - *Novelist; round the world yachtswoman; Royal Ballet*
Francis, Dick - *Novelist; Maidenhead County Boys'*
Francis, Sir Richard - *Director General The British Council; Uppingham*
Francome, John - *Jockey, Channel 4 presenter; Park Senior HS, Swindon*
Fraser, Angus - *England cricketer; Gayton HS, Harrow and Orange Hill*
Fraser, Lady Antonia - *Writer; St Mary's Convent, Ascot*
Fraser, General Sir David - *Former ADC General to HM The Queen; Eton*
Fraser, Professor Malcolm - *Chair BTEC; Christ's College, Finchley*
Fraser, Murdow - *Chair Young Conservatives; Inverness Academy*
Frayn, Michael - *Journalist, playwright, novelist; Kingston GS*
Frears, Stephen - *Film director; Gresham's*
Freeman, David - *Solicitor D J Freeman & Co; Christ's College, Finchley*
Freeman, Rt Hon John - *Former MP, journalist, Ch London Weekend;
      Westminster*
Freeman MP, Roger - *Minister for Public Transport; Whitgift, Croydon*
Freer, ACM Sir Robert - *Former Deputy C-in-C Strike Command; Gosport GS*
French, David - *Director RELATE marriage guidance group; Sherborne*
French, Dawn - *Comedienne; St Dunstan's, Plymouth*
Freud, Sir Clement - *Writer, broadcaster, former MP, cook; St Paul's*
Friel, Brian - *Playwright Dancing at Lughnasa; St Columba's College, Derry*
Frink, Dame Elisabeth - *Sculptor; Convent of the Holy Family, Exmouth*
Frisby, Terence - *Playwright, actor, producer; Dartford GS*
Frith, Donald - *ex Secretary HMC; Whitgift, Croydon*
Frost, David - *TV presenter and producer, author; Gillingham GS and
      Wellingborough*
Fry, Christopher - *Dramatist; Bedford Modern*
Fry, Dame Margaret - *Chair Nat Union of Conservative Assocs; Tavistock GS*
Fry, Stephen - *Comedian and scriptwriter; Uppingham*
Fuchs, Sir Vivian - *Former Director British Antarctic Survey; Brighton College*
Fullerton, Fiona - *Actress; Elmhurst Ballet*

Gable, Christopher - *Artistic direc Northern Ballet Theatre; Sadler's Wells Ballet*
Gabriel, Peter - *Singer ex-Genesis; Charterhouse*
Gall, Sandy - *Foreign correspondent, newscaster ITN; Glenalmond*

Gloucester, HRH The Duchess of; *St James's, West Malvern*

Glover, Jane - *Conductor; Monmouth Girls'*

Glover, Julian - *Actor; St Paul's*

Glover, Stephen - *Former editor* Independent on Sunday; *Shrewsbury*

Goddard QC, Ann - *Barrister; Grey Coat Hospital, Westminster*

Goddard, Liza - *Actress; Farnham Girls' GS and Arts Educational*

Godden, Rumer - *Novelist; St Monica's and Moira House, Eastbourne*

Goehr, Professor Alexander - *Professor Music Cambridge University; Berkhamsted*

Goff of Chieveley, Lord - *Law Lord; Eton*

Golding, Sir William - *Novelist; Marlborough GS*

Goldring, Mary - *Economist and broadcaster; Our Lady's Priory, Sussex*

Goldsmith, Harvey - *Entrepreneur; Christ's College, Finchley*

Goldsmith, Sir James - *International businessman; Eton*

Goldsmith, Walter - *Former Marketing Director Trusthouse Forte; Merchant Taylors'*

Gollancz, Livia - *Chair Victor Gollancz publishers; Kensington HS and St Paul's Girls'*

Gooch, Graham - *Cricketer; Norlington Junior High Sch, Leytonstone*

Goodchild, Stanley - *Chief Education Officer Berkshire; East Howe Bilateral and Bournemouth GS*

Goodhart QC, Sir William - *Barrister; Eton*

Goodhew, Duncan - *Swimmer; Millfield*

Goodison, Sir Alan - *Chair The Wates Foundation; Colfe's GS*

Goodison, Sir Nicholas - *Chairman TSB Group plc; Marlborough*

Goodman, Lord - *Former Master University College, Oxford; Grocers Company GS, Hackney Down*

Goodrich, Rt Rev Philip - *Bishop of Worcester, Stamford*

Goodridge, Rosemary - *Hockey international; Maynard*

Goodsir, Jane - *Director RELEASE drugs rehabilitation; Oxford HS, Christ's Hospital and St Clare's Hall, Oxford*

Gordon, Hannah - *Actress; St Denis Girls', Edinburgh*

Gordon, Sir Alexander - *Architect; Dynevor GS, Swansea*

Goring, Marius - *Actor; Perse, Cambridge*

Gorman, Teresa - *Conservative MP; Fulham County*

Gormley, Lord - *Former trade union leader; St Oswald's RC, Ashton*

Gough, Brandon - *Chair Coopers and Lybrand accountants; Douai*

Gough Matthews, Michael - *Director Royal College of Music; Chigwell*

Gourlay, Sir Simon - *President National Farmers' Union; Winchester*

Gow, General Sir Michael - *Former GOC Scotland, Govnr Edinburgh Castle; Winchester*

Gower, David - *Cricketer; King's, Canterbury*

Gower, Professor Jim - *Solicitor, Prof. Emeritus Southampton; Lindisfarne College*

Gowing, Professor Margaret - *Professor History of Science Oxford; Christ's Hospital*

Gowrie, The Earl of - *Chairman Sotheby's; Eton*

Grace, Nickolas - *Actor; King's, Chester and Forest, Essex*

Grade, Lord - *Chair The Grade Company; Rochelle Street, East London*

Grade, Michael - *Chief executive Channel 4; St Dunstan's, Catford*

Graham, Alistair - *Director The Industrial Society; Royal GS, Newcastle upon Tyne*

Graham, Rt Rev Andrew - *Bishop of Newcastle; Tonbridge*
Graham, Duncan - *Chair National Curriculum Council; Hutchesons' GS,
    Glasgow*
Graham-Smith, Sir Francis - *Former Astronomer-Royal; Epsom College* and
    Rossall
Granger, Stewart - *Actor; Epsom College*
Grant, Alistair - *Head of Safeway Stores; Woodhouse Grove, Yorkshire*
Grant, Russell - *TV astrologer; Harefield, Middlesex* and *Abbotsfield, Hillingdon*
Graveney, David - *Cricketer; Millfield*
Graves, Rupert - *Actor; Wyvern Comprehensive, Weston*
Gray QC, Gilbert - *Barrister; Scarborough HS*
Gray, Cardinal Gordon - *Former Archbishop St Andrews, Edinburgh; Holy Cross
    Academy, Edinburgh*
Gray, John - *Ambassador to OECD; Blundell's*
Gray, Linda - *Opera singer; Greenock Academy*
Gray, Simon - *Playwright; Westminster*
Grayson, Larry - *TV presenter; Manor Park, Nuneaton*
Greaves, Ms Alex - *Jockey; Allertonshire GS* and *Northallerton GS*
Greaves, Jimmy - *Former footballer, commentator; Kingswood Secondary,
    Hainault*
Green QC, Sir Allan - *Former Director of Public Prosecutions; Charterhouse*
Green, Father Benedict - *Theologian; Eton*
Green, Benny - *Jazz musician, writer and broadcaster; St Marylebone GS*
Green, Rev Canon Bryan - *Evangelical; Canon Emerit B'ham Cathedral;
    Merchant Taylors'*
Green, Dave "Boy" - *Boxer; Cromwell Chatteris, Cambridgeshire*
Green, Sir Kenneth - *Director Manchester Polytechnic; Helsby County GS,
    Cheshire*
Green, Lucinda - *Three-day eventer; St Mary's, Wantage* and *Idbury Manor,
    Oxfordshire*
Green, Michael - *Chair Carlton Communications; Haberdashers' Aske's*
Green, Michael - *Controller Radio 4; Repton* and *Barnsley GS*
Green, Sir Peter - *Former Chair Lloyd's of London; Harrow*
Greenbury, Sir Rick - *Chair, chief executive Marks & Spencer; Ealing GS*
Greene, Graham Carleton - *Director Jonathan Cape publishers; Eton*
Greene, Sarah - *Actress; Grey Coat Hospital, Westminster*
Greengross, Lady - *Director Age Concern; Brighton and Hove HS*
Greenslade, Roy - *Former editor* Daily Mirror; *Dagenham County HS*
Greenwood, Ron - *Former Manager England Assoc Football Team; Alperton*
Gregson, Sir Peter - *Permanent Secretary DTI; Nottingham HS*
Grey, Dame Beryl - *Former Artistic Dir London Festival Ballet; Dame Alice
    Owen's*
Griffith, Kenneth - *Actor; Tenby GS*
Griffiths, Lord - *Law Lord; Charterhouse*
Griffiths of Fforestfach, Lord - *Former Head No. 10 Policy Unit; Dynevor GS,
    Swansea*
Griffiths, Derek - *Actor; Acland Burghley, Comprehensive*
Griffiths, Sir Eldon - *Former Conservative MP; Ashton-in-Makerfield GS,
    Nr Wigan*
Grimond, Lord - *Former leader Liberal Party; Eton*
Grimshaw, Nicholas - *Architect; Wellington College*
Grinstead, Sir Stanley - *Chair Reed International, ex-Grand Met; Strodes, Egham*

Groom, Major General John - *Director Guide Dogs for the Blind; King Charles I, Kidderminster*

Groves, Sir Charles - *Assoc Conductor Royal Philharmonic Orch; Sutton Valence*

Guest, Douglas - *Organist Westminster Abbey; Reading*

Guest, George - *University organist Cambridge; King's, Chester*

Guinness, Sir Alec - *Actor; Roborough, Eastbourne*

Gummer MP, Rt Hon John Selwyn - *Secretary of State for Agriculture; King's, Rochester*

Gummer, Peter - *Founder, Chair Shandwick PR co; King's, Rochester*

Gunn Thom - *Poet, visiting lecturer Berkeley, Calif; University College Sch*

Guscott, Jeremy - *England rugby centre forward; Ralph Allen Senior, Bath*

Habakkuk, Sir John - *Former Vice Chancellor Oxford University; Barry GS*

Habgood, Anthony - *Chief executive Tootal; Gresham's*

Habgood, Most Rev Rt Hon John - *Archbishop of York; Eton*

Hacker, Alan R. - *Clarinettist and conductor; Dulwich*

Hackney, Rod - *Architect; John Bright GS, Llandudno*

Hagerty, Bill - *Editor* The People; *Beal GS, Ilford*

Hague, Prof Sir Douglas - *Chair Metapraxis Management Consultants; Moseley GS and King Edward's, Birmingham*

Haig, The Earl - *Painter; Stowe*

Hailsham, Lord - *Former Lord Chancellor; Eton*

Hale, Professor Sir John - *Historian; Eastbourne College*

Hale, Kathleen - *illustrator and author; Manchester Girls' HS*

Halford, Alison - *Assis Chief Constable Merseyside Police; Notre Dame Convent GS, Norwich*

Hall, Sir Peter - *Director; Perse, Cambridge*

Hall, Rt Rev Peter - *Bishop Suffragan of Woolwich; Queen Elizabeth GS, Blackburn*

Hall, Willis - *Playwright; Cockburn HS, Leeds*

Halliday, Simon - *Rugby international; Downside*

Halpern, Sir Ralph - *Former Chair Burton Group plc; St Christopher's, Letchworth*

Halsey, Professor A.H. - *Oxford sociologist; Kettering GS*

Halstead, Sir Ronald - *Deputy Chair British Steel; Lancaster Royal GS*

Hambling, Maggi - *1st artist in residence National Gallery; Hadleigh Hall and Amberfield*

Hambro, Charles - *Chair Hambros plc; Eton*

Hambro, Rupert - *Banker, director Daily Telegraph; Eton*

Hamilton MP, Rt Hon Archie - *Minister of State for Defence; Eton*

Hamilton, Willie - *Former Labour MP, anti-monarchist; Washington GS, Co Durham*

Hamlyn, Paul - *Founder Hamlyn publishing group; St Christopher's, Letchworth*

Hammersley, Rear Admiral Peter - *Director Brit Marine Equipment Council; Denstone College*

Hammond, Martin - *Headmaster Tonbridge School; Winchester*

Hamnett, Katharine - *Fashion designer; Cheltenham Ladies' College*

Hampshire, Susan - *Actress; Hampshire Sch, London*

Hampson, Dr Keith - *Conservative MP; King James I GS, Bishop Auckland*

Hampton, Christopher - *Playwright; Lancing*

Hanbury-Tenison, Robin - *Explorer and travel writer; Eton*

Hayklan, Stephen - *Chair Wiggins Construction Co; Christ's Hospital*
Hayman, Helene - *Politician and broadcaster; Wolverhampton Girls' HS*
Hayter, Lord - *Deputy Chairman House of Lords; Leys, Cambridge*
Hayter, Dianne - *Chair Alcohol Concern; Penrhos College*
Hayward, Biddy - *Theatre producer; Sacred Heart Convent, Tunbridge Wells*
Hayward, Ron - *Former General Secretary Labour Party; Bloxham*
Healey, Edna - *Writer; Bell's GS, Coleford, Gloucestershire*
Healey, Lord - *Former Deputy Leader Labour Party; Bradford GS*
Heaney, Seamus - *Oxford Professor of Poetry; St Columba's College, Derry*
Heath, Sir Edward - *Former Prime Minister; Chatham House, Ramsgate*
Heath, Michael - *Cartoonist; Fawcett Secondary Modern, Brighton*
Heaton, Very Rev E.W. - *Dean of Christ Church, Oxford; Ermysted's, Skipton*
Hebditch, Max - *Director Museum of London; Yeovil*
Heffer, Simon - *Journalist, Dep Ed* Spectator; *King Edward VI Chelmsford*
Heilbron, Dame Rose - *Former High Court Judge; Belvedere, Liverpool*
Hele, Warwick - *Former High Master St Paul's & Chairman HMC; Sedbergh*
Heller, Robert - *Editor* Finance *magazine; Christ's Hospital*
Hemery, David - *Athlete; Endsleigh, Colchester*
Hemmings, David - *Actor and producer; Glyn College, Epsom*
Hemmings, Eddie - *Cricketer; Campion, Leamington Spa*
Henderson, Sir Denys - *Chair ICI; Aberdeen GS*
Henderson, Sir Nicholas - *Diplomat, former Ambassador to Washington; Stowe*
Hendry, Stephen - *Snooker player; Inverkeithing HS*
Henri, Adrian - *Poet, musician, artist; St Asaph GS, North Wales*
Henry, Hon Mr Justice Denis - *High Court Judge Queen's Bench Division; Shrewsbury*
Henry, Lenny - *Comedian; Dudley*
Henson, Nicky - *Actor; Charterhouse*
Hepher, Michael - *MD British Telecom; Kingston GS*
Hepple, Norman - *Portrait painter; Colfs GS, Lewisham (destroyed War)*
Heren, Louis - *Journalist and author; St George's, London*
Hermon, Sir John - *Former Chief Constable Royal Ulster Constab; Larne GS*
Heron, Patrick - *Painter; St George's, Harpenden*
Herriot, James - *Writer – Vet books; Hillhead HS, Glasgow*
Hertford, The Marquess of - *Landowner – Ragley Hall; Eton*
Heseltine MP, Rt Hon Michael - *President of the Board of Trade; Shrewsbury*
Hesketh, Lord - *Government Whip House of Lords; Ampleforth*
Hetherington QC, Sir Thomas - *Former DPP, Head Crown Prosecution Service; Rugby*
Hewish, Professor Antony - *Radio astronomer; King's College, Taunton*
Heyhoe Flint, Rachael - *Cricketer; Wolverhampton Girls' HS*
Heylin, Angela- *Chair, chief executive Charles Barker PR; Apsley GS, Hemel Hempstead*
Hichens, Antony - *MD Consolidated Goldfields, Chair Caradon; Stowe*
Hickox, Richard - *Conductor, Dir City of London Sinfonia; Royal GS, High Wycombe*
Hicks, David - *Interior designer; Charterhouse*
Hicks, Maureen - *Former Conservative MP; Ashley Secondary and Brockenhurst GS*
Hickson, Joan - *Actress; Castle Bar, London and Oldfield, Swanage*
Higgins, Jack - *Novelist; Roundhay, Leeds*
Hill, Sir Brian - *Chair Higgs and Hill Building Co; Stowe*

Holroyd, Air Marshal Sir Frank - *Chief Engineer Royal Air Force; Southend HS*
Holroyd, Michael - *Writer; Eton*
Holt, Thelma - *Theatre producer; St Anne's Girls' College*
Home of the Hirsel, Lord - *Former Prime Minister; Eton*
Honeycombe, Gordon - *TV presenter; Edinburgh Academy*
Hoodless, Elizabeth - *Exec Direc Community Service Volunteers; Redland HS, Bristol*
Hooker, Professor Morna - *Professor Divinity Cambridge University; Guildford County Girls' GS and Copthall GS for Girls, Mill Hill*
Hope, Rt Rev David - *Bishop of London; Queen Elizabeth GS, Wakefield*
Hopkin, Sir David - *Chief Metropolitan Stipendiary Magistrate; St Paul's*
Hopkins, Anthony - *Actor; Cowbridge GS*
Hopkins, Antony - *Composer and conductor; Berkhamsted*
Hopkins, Michael - *Architect new Glyndebourne concert hall; Sherborne*
Hordern, Sir Michael - *Actor; Brighton College*
Horlock, Dr John - *Vice Chancellor Open University; Latymer GS, Edmonton*
Hornby, Derek - *Chair Rank Xerox UK; Canford*
Hornby, Richard - *Chair Halifax Building Society; Winchester*
Hornby, Sir Simon - *Chair WH Smith plc; Eton*
Horton, Bob - *fmr Chair BP; King's, Canterbury*
Hoskins, Bob - *Actor; Stroud Green Secondary, London*
Hoskyns, Sir John - *Chair Burton Group plc, ex-Director General IOD; Winchester*
Hounsfield, Sir Godfrey - *Engineer, inventor X-ray scanner; Magnus GS, Newark*
Howard, Alan - *Actor; Ardingly College*
Howard, Anthony - *Political journalist; Westminster*
Howard, Elizabeth Jane - *Novelist; Unorthodox*
Howard, Margaret - *Radio presenter; St Mary's Convent, Rhyl and St Teresa's Convent, Sudbury*
Howard, Professor Sir Michael - *Historian; Wellington College*
Howard, Michael - *Composer and conductor; Ellesmere*
Howard MP, Michael - *Environment Secretary; Llanelli GS*
Howard, Peter - *Editor Jane's Defence Weekly; Dialystone Lane, Stockport and Woodseats County, Sheffield*
Howard, Philip - *Journalist The Times; Eton*
Howard-Dobson, General Sir Patrick - *Quartermaster-General; Framlingham*
Howatch, Susan - *Novelist; Sutton Girls' HS*
Howarth, Alan - *Conservative MP, former Education Minister; Rugby*
Howe, Lord - *Former Deputy PM;Winchester*
Howe, Lady - *Former Dep Chair Equal Opportunities Commission; Bath HS and Wycombe Abbey*
Howell MP, Rt Hon David - *Former Secretary of State for Transport; Eton*
Howell, Gwynne - *Principal bass Covent Garden; Pontardawe GS*
Howells, Anne - *Opera and concert singer; Sale County GS*
Hoyle, Professor Sir Fred - *Astronomer; Bingley GS*
Hudd, Roy - *Actor; Croydon Secondary Technical*
Huddleston, Most Rev Trevor - *Chair Internat Defence, Aid South Africa; Lancing*
Huebner, Michael - *Lord Chancellor's Department; Rugby*
Hugh Smith, Andrew - *Chair International Stock Exchange; Ampleforth*
Hughes, Nerys - *Actress; Howell's Denbigh*
Hughes, Bill - *Chair Scottish CBI, Grampian Holdings; Firth Park GS, Sheffield*

Jackaman, Michael - *Chair Allied-Lyons; Felsted*
Jacklin, Tony - *Golfer; Doncaster Road Secondary Mod, Scunthorpe*
Jackson, Betty - *Fashion designer; Bacup and Rawenstall GS, Lancashire*
Jackson, Dr Caroline - *Conservative MEP; St Clare's, Penzance*
Jackson, Prof Daphne - *Professor Physics Surrey University; Peterborough County GS*
Jackson, Glenda - *Actress and Labour MP; West Kirkby Girls' GS*
Jackson, Michael - *Head of BBC TV Arts and Music; King's, Macclesfield*
Jackson, Paul - *Chair and Chief Executive Noel Gay TV; Gunnersbury GS*
Jackson (Jak), Raymond - *Evening Standard cartoonist; Lyulph Stanley Central*
Jacobi, Derek - *Actor; Leyton County HS*
Jacobs, Clive - *Broadcaster; Berkhamsted*
Jacobs, David - *Radio and TV broadcaster; Belmont College, Devon and Strand, Brixton*
Jacomb, Sir Martin - *Chair Barclays de Zoete Wedd; Eton*
Jacques, Martin - *Editor Marxism Today; King Henry VIII, Coventry*
Jaffe, Professor Michael - *Director Fitzwilliam Museum, Cambridge; Eton*
Jagger, Harriet - *Senior fashion editor Vogue magazine; Warwick GS and Marlborough*
Jaine, Tom - *Editor Good Food Guide; Kingswood, Bath*
James, Rt Rev Colin - *Bishop of Winchester; Aldenham*
James, Rev Canon Eric - *Chpln HM The Queen; Direc Christian Actn; Dagenham County HS*
James, Geraldine - *Actress; Downe House*
James, Mark - *Golfer; Stamford*
James, P.D. - *Crime novelist; Cambridge Girls' HS*
Jameson, Derek - *TV and radio presenter and commentator; Mount Pleasant Senior, Hackney*
Jameson, Louise - *Actress; Braeside, Buckhurst*
Jameson, Susan - *Actress; Surbiton Girls' HS*
Janner, The Hon Greville - *Labour MP; St Paul's*
Jarratt, Sir Alex - *Company Chairman (Prudential, Midland); Royal Liberty GS, Essex*
Jarrett, Dr Ruth - *Head AIDS research unit Glasgow Univ; Westbourne Girls', Glasgow*
Jarvis, Fred - *Former Gen Sec National Union of Teachers; Plaistow Secondary, West Ham and Oldershaw GS, Wallasey*
Jarvis, Martin - *Actor; Whitgift, Croydon*
Jason, David - *Actor; Northside Secondary*
Jay, Peter - *Economics Editor BBC; Winchester*
Jay, Sir Anthony - *TV scriptwriter Yes Prime Minister etc; St Paul's*
Jay, Lord - *Former President Board of Trade; Winchester*
Jayston, Michael - *Actor; Becket GS, Nottingham*
Jebb, Dom Philip - *Former Headmaster Downside; Downside*
Jeeps, Dickie - *Former Chair The Sports Council; Bedford Modern*
Jefferies, Lionel - *Actor; Queen Elizabeth's GS, Wimborne*
Jeffery, Very Rev R.M.C. - *Dean of Worcester; St Paul's*
Jefford, Barbara - *Actress; Taunton Girls'*
Jeffrey, John - *Scotland rugby player; Merchiston Castle, Edinburgh*
Jellicoe, Earl - *Chair Medical Research Council; Winchester*
Jenkin, Lord - *Former Secretary of State for Energy Environment; Clifton*
Jenkins, Clive - *Trade unionist; Port Talbot Central*

Kalms, Stanley - *Founder, Chair Dixons Stores; Christ's College, Finchley*
Karlin, Miriam - *Actress; South Hampstead HS*
Katin, Peter - *Concert pianist; Henry Thornton GS, Clapham*
Kaufman, Gerald - *Labour MP, former Shadow Foreign Secretary; Leeds GS*
Kaufmann, Julie - *PR Offr Children in Need, ex-Gingerbread; Ursuline Convent, Wimbledon*
Kavanagh, P.J. - *Writer; Douai*
Kay, Sir Andrew Watt - *Regius Professor Surgery Glasgow Univ; Ayr Academy*
Kaye, Michael - *Director City of London Festival; West Ham GS*
Keane, John - *Official war artist Gulf War; Wellington College*
Kearton, Lord - *Chemist, Chancellor Bath University; Hanley HS*
Keating, Frank - *Sports columnist the* Guardian; *Belmont Abbey, Hereford and Douai*
Kee, Robert - *Author and broadcaster; Stowe*
Keeffe, Barrie - *Dramatist; East Ham GS*
Keith, Penelope - *Actress; Annecy Convent, Seaford and Webber Douglas, London*
Keith of Kinkel, Lord - *Law Lord; Edinburgh Academy*
Kellett, Sir Brian - *Chair Port of London Authority; Manchester GS*
Kelly, Graham - *Chief executive Football Association; Baines GS*
Kelsey, Linda - *Editor* She *magazine; Woodhouse GS*
Kemble, Bruce - *Education correspondent* Evening Standard; *Dulwich*
Kemp, Rt Rev Eric - *Bishop of Chichester; Brigg GS, Lincs*
Kemp, Jeremy - *Actor; Abbotsholme, Staffordshire*
Kemp, Peter - *Second Permanent Sctry Cabinet Office; Wellington College*
Kemp, Dr Tommy - *Rugby player, physician; Denstone College*
Kempson, Rachel - *Actress; St Agnes Convent, East Grinstead and Colchester Girls' HS*
Kendall, Bridget - *BBC correspondent Moscow; Perse Girls', Cambridge*
Kendall, Kenneth - *Broadcaster; Felsted*
Kendrew, Sir John - *Molecular biologist; Clifton*
Kennedy, Charles - *LD MP; Lochaber HS, Fort William*
Kennedy QC, Helena - *Barrister; Holyrood Senior Secondary, Glasgow*
Kennedy, Joanna - *Senior engineer Ove Arup; Queen Anne's, Caversham*
Kennedy, Ludovic - *Broadcaster and writer; Eton*
Kennedy, Nigel - *Violinist; Yehudi Menuhin*
Kennedy, Tessa - *Interior designer; Oak Hall, Haslemere*
Kenny, Sir Anthony - *President British Academy; fmr Master of Balliol St Joseph's College, Upholland*
Kenny, Michael - *Sculptor; St Francis Xavier's College, Liverpool*
Kent, Bruce - *Vice-President CND; Stonyhurst*
Kent, HRH The Duke of - *; Eton*
Kent, HRH Prince Michael of - *; Eton*
Kenward, Betty - *Jennifer, Jennifer's Diary (no school); Unorthodox*
Kermode, Prof Frank - *Professor English Literature; Douglas HS, Isle of Man*
Kerr, Deborah - *Actress; Northumberland House, Bristol*
Kettley, John - *TV weather man; Todmorden GS*
Keys, Bill - *Trade unionist; South London GS*
Khan, Imran - *Cricketer; Royal GS, Worcester*
Khomo, Ninivah - *Fashion designer; Holy Child Convent, Edgbaston*
Kilroy-Silk, Robert - *TV presenter; Saltley GS, Birmingham*
King, Lord - *Chair British Airways; Hascombe, Surrey*

Landini, Mark - *Joint Managing Director Conran Design; St George's, Weybridge and Downside*

Lane, Lord - *Former Lord Chief Justice; Shrewsbury*

Lane, Sir David - *Former Chair Commission for Racial Equality; Eton*

Lane, Graham - *Vice Chair Newham Education Committee; Handsworth GS*

Lane, Margaret - *Novelist and biographer; St Stephen's, Folkestone*

Lang MP, Rt Hon Ian - *Secretary of State for Scotland; Rugby*

Lang, Very Rev John - *Dean of Lichfield; Merchant Taylors'*

Langdon, David - *Cartoonist Punch, Sunday Mirror; Davenant GS, London*

Langford, Bonnie - *Actress; Italia Conti Stage*

Langridge, Philip - *Opera singer English National Opera; Maidstone GS, Maidstone Technical College and Tunbridge Wells Technical College*

Langtry, Ian - *Education Officer Assoc of County Cncls; Coleraine Academical Institution*

Lansbury, Angela - *Actress; South Hampstead HS and Webber Douglas, London*

Lapotaire, Jane - *Actress; Northgate GS, Ipswich*

Larkins, Wayne - *Cricketer; Bushmead, Huntingdon*

Lasdun, Sir Denys - *Architect; Rugby*

Lash, Professor Nicholas - *Professor Divinity Cambridge University; Downside*

Laslett, Peter - *Academic innovator; Watford Boys' GS*

Lavender, Ian - *Actor; Bournville Boys' Technical, Birmingham*

Law, Roger - Spitting Image *puppeteer; Littleport Secondary Modern, Isle of Ely*

Lawley, Sue - *Broadcaster; Dudley Girls' HS, Worcester*

Lawrence, Christopher - *Silversmith; Westborough HS*

Lawrence QC MP, Sir Ivan - *Barrister, Conservative MP; Brighton, Hove and Sussex GS*

Lawrence, Josie - *Actress; Rowley Regis Sixth Form College*

Lawrence, Murray - *Chair Lloyd's of London; Winchester*

Laws, John - *First Junior Treasury Counsel; Durham*

Laws, Dr Richard - *Director British Antarctic Survey; Dame Allan's, Newcastle*

Lawson, Dominic - *Editor* Spectator; *Westminster*

Lawson, Mark - *Journalist* Independent; *St Columba's College, St Albans*

Lawson, Lord - *Former Chancellor of the Exchequer; Westminster*

Laycock, Malcolm - *Head of programming Jazz FM radio; Bradford GS*

Le Carré, John (Cornwell) - *Novelist; Sherborne*

Le Cheminant, ACM Sir Peter - *Lt Governor The Bailiwick of Guernsey; Elizabeth College, Guernsey*

Leach, David - *Potter; Dauntsey's*

Leach, Admiral of the Fleet Sir Henry - *Fmr Chief Naval Staff and First Sea Lord; RNC, Dartmouth*

Leach, Rosemary - *Actress; Ludlow HS, Shropshire and Oswestry Girls' HS*

Lean, Ferelith - *Founder Glasgow Mayfest; Westbourne Girls', Glasgow and Craigmount, Hawick*

Lee, Christopher - *Actor; Wellington College*

Lee, Sir Desmond - *Former HM Winchester, President Hughes Hall Cambridge; Repton*

Lee, Laurie - *Poet and author; Stroud Central*

Leeming, Jan - *Newsreader and TV presenter; St Joseph's Convent, Abbey Wood, Kent*

Lees, Sir David - *Chair GKN plc; Charterhouse*

Leese, John - *Former editor* Evening Standard; *Bishop Vesey's GS, Sutton Coldfield*

Lloyd, Sir Nicholas - *Editor Daily Express; Bedford Modern*
Lloyd, Sir Richard - *Chair Hill Samuel; Wellington College*
Lloyd, Robert - *Opera singer; Southend HS*
Lloyd Webber, Sir Andrew - *Composer; Westminster*
Lloyd Webber, Julian - *Cellist; University College Sch*
Lloyd-Jones, David - *Conductor, Artistic Director Opera North; Westminster*
Lloyd-Jones, Sir Hugh - *Regius Professor Greek Oxford University; French Lycée,*
       London and *Westminster*
Loach, Ken - *Film and TV director; King Edward VI GS, Nuneaton*
Lobeck, Ron - *TV weather man; Barry GS*
Lodge, Professor David - *Novelist, Professor English Birmingham; St Joseph's*
       Academy, Blackheath
Logue, Christopher - *Poet; Prior Park College, Bath* and *Portsmouth GS*
Longford, Lord - *Writer, former Lord Privy Seal; Eton*
Longford, the Countess of - *Historical biographer; Headington*
Longland, Sir Jack - *Former Director Education Derbyshire and broadcaster;*
       King's, Worcester
Longley, Ann - *Headmistress Roedean; Walthamstow Hall, Sevenoaks*
Lorimer, Hew - *Sculptor; Loretto*
Lott, Felicity - *Soprano; Pate's Girls' GS, Cheltenham*
Loughran, James - *Conductor Laureate Hallé Orchestra; St Aloysius's, Glasgow*
Lovell, Sir Bernard - *Former Director Jodrell Bank Experimtl Stn; Kingswood,*
       Bath
Lovelock, Professor James - *Chemist; Strand, Brixton*
Lowe, ACM Sir Douglas - *Former Director of Ordnance; Reading*
Lowe, Chris - *BBC newscaster; Haileybury*
Lowe, Chris - *Head Prince William Upper School; Oundle Wolstanton GS,*
       Newcastle under Lyne
Lowe, Chris - *Pop singer Pet Shop Boys; Arnold, Blackpool*
Lowery, Nigel - *Designer English National Opera; Addey and Stanhope, London*
Lowry, Lord - *Former Lord Chief Justice N Ireland; Royal Belfast Academical*
       Institution
Lowry, Her Honour Judge Nina - *Circuit judge; Bedford HS for Girls*
Lucas, John - *Lay Christian philosopher Fellow Merton College, Oxford;*
       Winchester
Luce, Richard - *Former Conservative MP; Wellington College*
Lucie-Smith, Edward - *Poet and art critic; King's, Canterbury*
Luder, Owen - *Architect; Peckham*
Lumley, Joanna - *Actress; St Mary's Anglican Convent, Hastings*
Lumsden, Sir David - *Principal Royal Academy of Music; Dame Allan's,*
       Newcastle
Lunghi, Cherie - *Actress; Arts Educational*
Lush, Peter - *Manager England cricket team; Brighton College*
Lustig, Robin - *Radio 4 journalist; Stoneham, Reading*
Lyell QC MP, Sir Nicholas - *Attorney General; Stowe*
Lygo, Sir Raymond - *Former Chief Executive British Aerospace; Valentine's,*
       Ilford and *Ilford County HS*
Lyle, Sandy - *Golfer; Shrewsbury local*
Lymbery, His Honour Judge Robert - *Commons Serjeant; Gresham's*
Lynam, Desmond - *Sports commentator; Varndean GS, Brighton*
Lynn, Jonathan - *Director and author Yes Prime Minister; Kingswood, Bath*
Lyons, Bernard - *Former Chair UDS group; Leeds GS*

Mann, Rt Hon Sir Michael - *Lord Justice of Appeal; Whitgift, Croydon*
Mann, Rt Rev Michael - *Former Dean Windsor; Harrow*
Manning, Jane - *Soprano; Norwich HS*
Mansell, Nigel - *Racing driver; Hall Green Bilateral*
Manser, Michael - *Architect; Epsom County Secondary*
Mansfield QC, Michael - *Barrister, Counsel for Birmingham Six; Highgate*
Margolyes, Miriam - *Actress; Oxford HS*
Mark, Sir Robert - *Former Commissioner Metropolitan Police; William Hulme's
        GS, Manchester*
Markland, Anna - *Concert pianist; Chetham's*
Marks, Vic - *Cricketer; Blundell's*
Marland, Michael - *Head North Westminster Community School; Christ's
        Hospital*
Marquand, Professor David - *Professor Modern History Salford Univ; Emanuel*
Marre, Lady - *Chair Cttee on Future Legal Profession; Chelmsford County
        Girls' HS*
Marriner, Sir Neville - *Conductor, Direc St Martin in the Fields; Lincoln*
Marsh, Lord - *Chair Newspaper Publishers Association; Jennings, Swindon*
Marsh, A.W. - *Musical director The Old Vic; Chetham's*
Marshall, Sir Colin - *Chief executive British Airways; University College Sch*
Martin-Jenkins, Christopher - *Cricket commentator; Marlborough*
Maschler, Fay - *Cookery writer; St Teresa's Convent, Dorking and St Catherine's,
        Bramley, Surrey*
Maschler, Tom - *Former Chair Jonathan Cape publishers; Leighton Park*
Masham of Ilton, Baroness - *Chair Cttees on drug, alcohol, crime, AIDS;
        Heathfield*
Mason, Air Vice Marshal Anthony - *Former Air Secretary; Bradford GS*
Mason, John - *Daily Telegraph cricket correspondent; Colston's, Bristol*
Mason, Monica - *Senior principal dancer Royal Ballet; Royal Ballet*
Mason, Nick - *Pink Floyd drummer; Frensham Heights*
Mason, Peter - *Former High Master Manchester GS; King Edward's, Birmingham*
Massey, Daniel - *Actor; Eton*
Massey, Doreen - *Director Family Planning Association; Darwen GS, Lancashire*
Mates, Michael - *Minister of State Northern Ireland; Blundell's*
Mather, Graham - *Former General Director Instit Economic Affairs; Hutton
        GS, Lancs*
Mather, Victoria - *Journalist and broadcaster; Sacred Heart Convent,
        Woldingham*
Mathew QC, John - *Barrister; Beaumont*
Matthews, Lord - *Former owner Express Newspapers; Highbury GS*
Matthews, Sir Stanley - *Former footballer; Wellington, Hanbury*
Maude, The Hon Francis - *Former Financial Secretary to the Treasury; Abingdon*
Mavor, Michael - *Head Rugby School, former Head Gordonstoun; Loretto*
Maw, Janet - *Actress; Worthing Girls' GS*
Mawhinney MP, Dr Brian - *Minister of State for Health; Royal Belfast
        Academical Institution*
Maxwell, Ian - *Former Chair Mirror Newspapers; Marlborough*
Maxwell, Kevin - *Former Chair Maxwell Communication Corporation;
        Marlborough*
Maxwell Davies, Sir Peter - *Composer and conductor; Leigh GS*
May, The Rt Hon Sir John - *Former Lord Justice of Appeal, Enquiry Guildford
        4; Clifton*

Merricks, Walter - *Assistant Secretary General Law Society; Bradfield*
Metcalfe, Stanley - *Chair Ranks Hovis McDougall plc; Leeds GS*
Meyer, Sir Anthony - *Conservative MP; Eton*
Michael, George - *Pop singer; Bushey Meads, Herts*
Michelmore, Cliff - *Broadcaster; Cowes Senior, Isle of Wight*
Michie, Professor Donald - *Artificial Intelligence Scientist; Rugby*
Middleton, Sir Peter - *Deputy Chair Barclays de Zoete Wedd; Sheffield City*
Midwinter, Dr Eric - *Director Centre for Policy on Ageing; Sale County GS*
Mikardo, Ian - *Former Labour MP; writer; Portsmouth Southern Secondary*
Miles, Dillwyn - *Herald Bard National Eisteddfod of Wales; Fishguard County*
Miles, Dame Margaret - *Former Head Mayfield School, Putney; Ipswich Girls' HS*
Miles, Sarah - *Actress; Arts Educational and Crofton Grange, Herts; Roedean*
Milford, Lord - *Painter, Member of Communist Party; Eton*
Milford, Rev Catherine - *Moderator, Movt for Ordination of Women;Headington*
Milford Haven, The Marquess of - *Landowner; Gordonstoun*
Millan, Rt Hon Bruce - *European Commissioner; Harris Academy, Dundee*
Millar, Sir Oliver - *Surveyor Emeritus the Queen's pictures; Rugby*
Millar, Sir Ronald - *Playwright; former speech writer Mrs Thatcher; Charterhouse*
Miller, Jonathan - *Former artistic director The Old Vic; St Paul's*
Miller, Geoff - *Cricketer; Chesterfield GS*
Miller, Sir Peter - *Former Chair Lloyd's of London; Rugby*
Millichip, Bert - *Chair Football Association; Solihull*
Milligan, Spike - *Writer, humorist (after schools in India); S E London Polytechnic*
Mills QC, Barbara - *Director of Public Prosecutions; St Helen's, Northwood*
Mills, Hayley - *Actress; Elmhurst Ballet*
Mills, Sir John - *Actor; Norwich GS*
Milne, Alasdair - *Former Director General BBC; Winchester*
Milroy, Rev Dominic - *Headmaster Ampleforth; Ampleforth*
Mirman, Sophie - *Founder, MD Sock Shop, Tie Rack; French Lycée, London*
Mishcon, Lord - *Labour Spokesman House of Lords; City of London*
Mitchell, Adrian - *Writer; Dauntsey's*
Mitchell, Andrew - *Conservative MP, Vice-Chair Conservative Party; Rugby*
Mitchell, Austin - *Labour MP, broadcaster; Bingley GS*
Mitchell, Professor Basil - *Former Prof Philosophy of Christian Religion Oxford; King Edward VI, Southampton*
Mitchell, Julian - *Writer, TV playwright; Winchester*
Mitchell, Warren - *Actor; Southgate County*
Mlinaric, David - *Interior designer; Downside*
Mo, Timothy - *Novelist; Mill Hill*
Moberly, Sir John - *Diplomat; Winchester*
Mogg, General Sir John - *Adjutant General; Malvern*
Moncur, Jennie - *Interior designer; Sheredes Comprehensive*
Money-Coutts, David - *Chair Coutts Bank; Eton*
Monkhouse, Bob - *Comedian and TV presenter; Dulwich*
Montagu, The Hon David - *Chair Rothmans International; Eton*
Montagu of Beaulieu, Rt Hon Lord - *Conservative peer, founder Beaulieu Motor Museum; Eton*
Montefiore, Rt Rev Hugh - *Assis Bishop Southwark, former Bishop B'ham; Rugby*

Mountbatten of Burma, Countess - *Vice Patron Burma Star Association; Miss Faunce's PNEU, London*

Mowlam MP, Dr Marjorie - *Labour front bench City spokesperson; Coundon Court Comprehensive*

Moynihan, The Hon Colin - *Minister for the Environment; Monmouth*

Mugglestone, Simon - *International athlete; Colston's, Bristol*

Muir, Frank - *Writer and broadcaster; Chatham House, Ramsgate and Leyton County HS*

Muir, Jean - *Fashion designer; Dame Alice Harpur, Bedford*

Mulcahy, Geoffrey - *Chief executive Kingfisher; King's, Worcester*

Mullett, Tony - *Head Nat Criminal Intelligence Service; Moat, Leicester*

Mullin, Chris - *Labour MP, Campaigner for Birmingham Six; St Joseph's De La Salle, Birkfield*

Mulvey, Robert - *HM Cademuir School for Gifted Children; Sheffield City GS*

Mummery, Hon Mr Justice - *High Court Judge Chancery Division; Dover GS*

Murdoch, Dame Iris - *Novelist and philosopher; Badminton*

Murless, Noel - *Keeper of the Queen's Racehorses; Wrekin College*

Murphy-O'Connor, Rt Rev Cormac - *RC Bishop of Arundel and Brighton; Prior Park College, Bath*

Murray, David - *Chair Murray International; Rangers FC; Fettes and Broughton HS*

Murray, Jenni - *Presenter Radio 4 Woman's Hour; Barnsley Girls' HS*

Murray, Dame Rosemary - *Former Vice Chancellor Cambridge Univ; Downe House*

Murray of Epping Forest, Lord - *Former General Secretary TUC; Wellington GS, Shropshire*

Musgrave, Thea - *Composer; Moreton Hall, Oswestry*

Mustill, Rt Hon Lord Justice Michael - *Appeal Court Judge; Oundle*

Nairne, Sir Patrick - *Chancellor Essex University; Radley*

Naish, David - *Leader National Farmers Union; Worksop College*

Naismith, Donald - *Director of Education Wandsworth; Bell Vue GS, Bradford*

Napley, Sir David - *Solicitor; Burlington College*

Neame, Ronald - *Film director; University College Sch and Hurstpierpoint*

Nearey, Martin - *Master Choristers Westminster Abbey; City of London*

Needham, Professor Joseph - *Director Emeritus Needham Research Institute Cambridge; Oundle*

Needham, Richard - *Minister of State Trade & Industry; Eton*

Neil, Andrew - *Editor Sunday Times; Paisley GS*

Neil, Ron - *Director Regions BBC TV; Glasgow HS*

Neill QC, Sir Patrick - *Warden All Souls Oxford; Highgate*

Nerina, Nadia - *Ballerina; Sadler's Wells Ballet*

Neuberger, Rabbi Julia - *Writer and broadcaster; South Hampstead HS*

Neville, Oliver - *Principal RADA; Price's, Fareham*

Neville-Rolfe, Marianne - *Director Civil Service College; St Mary's Convent, Shaftesbury*

Newbold, Yve - *Company secretary Hanson plc; Sacred Heart Convent, Hove and Blessed Sacrament Convent, Sussex*

Newman, Nanette - *Actress and writer; Sternhold College, London and Italia Conti Stage*

Newmarch, Mick - *Chief executive Prudential Corporation; Tottenham GS*
Newport, Phil - *Cricketer; Royal GS, High Wycombe*
Newsam, Sir Peter - *Director London Institute of Education; Clifton*
Newton MP, Rt Hon Tony - *Lord President of the Council; Leader of the
    Commons; Friend's Saffron Walden*
Nicholas, Sir David - *Former Chair ITN; Neath GS*
Nicholls, Rt Hon Lord Justice Donald - *Appeal Court Judge; Birkenhead*
Nichols, Peter - *TV playwright and film scriptwriter; Bristol GS*
Nichols, Rt Rev Mgr Vincent - *Gen Sec RC Bishops' Conference; St Mary's
    College, Crosby*
Nicholson, Sir Bryan - *Chair The Post Office; Palmer's Grays, Essex*
Nicholson, Emma - *Conservative MP; St Mary's, Wantage*
Nicholson, Mavis - *TV interviewer and presenter; Neath County Girls' GS*
Nicholson, William - *Playwright; Downside*
Nicolson, Nigel - *Author; Eton*
Nightingale, Ann - *TV presenter; Lady Eleanor Holles*
Nimmo, Derek - *Actor; Quarry Bank HS, Liverpool*
Nineham, Rev Professor Dennis - *Former Warden Keble College Oxford; King
    Edward VI, Southampton*
Noakes, Most Rev George - *Former Archbishop of Wales; Tregaron Secondary*
Noakes, Michael - *Portrait and landscape painter; Downside*
Noble, Adrian - *Director RSC; Chichester HS*
Noble, Professor Denis - *Professor Cardiovascular Physiology Oxford; Emanuel*
Noble, Richard - *World land speed record holder; Winchester*
Nolan, Sir Michael - *Appeal Court Judge; Ampleforth*
Norden, Dennis - *Scriptwriter and broadcaster; Craven Park, London and City of
    London*
Norfolk, The Duke of - *Premier RC layman; Ampleforth*
Norman, Barry - *TV presenter, journalist and author; Highgate*
Norman, Rev Dr Edward - *Dean of Chapel Christchurch Canterbury; Chatham
    House, Ramsgate*
Norton, Erica - *Assis Chief Constable Leicester Police; Newarke Girls' GS,
    Leicester*
Norwich, John Julius (Viscount) - *Writer and broadcaster; Eton*
Nott, Rt Hon Sir John - *Chair Channel Tunnel Commission; Bradfield*
Nott, Rt Rev Peter - *Bishop of Norwich; Bristol GS*
Nunn, Trevor - *Theatre director; Northgate GS, Ipswich*
Nursaw, James - *HM Procurator General, Treasury Solicitor; Bancroft's*
Nuttall, Professor Desmond - *Dir Centre for Educational Research LSE; Bradfield*
Nutter, Tommy - *Savile Row tailor; Camrose, Edgware*
Nye, Robert - *Writer; Southend HS*

Oakley, Robin - *Political Editor The Times; Wellington College*
Oaksey, Lord - *Racing correspondent and commentator; Eton*
Oddie, Bill; *Actor; Halesowen GS and King Edward's, Birmingham*
Ogilvy, The Hon Sir Angus - *Company director; Eton*
Ogilvy, David - *Chair PP Advertising; Fettes*
Oldfield, Bruce - *Fashion designer; Spennymoor GS and Ripon GS*
Oliver, Rt Rev John - *Bishop of Hereford; Westminster*
Oliver, Stephen - *Composer, especially opera; Ardingly College*
Olivier, Tamsin - *Actress; Bedales*

Ollerenshaw, Dame Kathleen - *Educationist; Ladybarn House, Manchester* and *St Leonards, St Andrews*

Oman, Julia Trevelyan - *Designer; Luckley, Wokingham*

Onslow, Rt Hon Cranley - *Conservative MP; Harrow*

Opie, Iona - *Folklorist; Sandecotes, Parkstone*

Oppenheim, The Hon Philip - *Conservative MP; Harrow*

Oppenheim-Barnes, Baroness - *Former Chair Consumer Council; Sheffield Girls' HS*

Oppenheimer, Sir Harry - *Former Chairman of Anglo-American Corporation; Charterhouse*

Oppenheimer, Sir Philip - *Chair The Diamond Trading Company; Harrow*

Oppenheimer, Lady - *Writer, moral and philosophical theology, Cheltenham Ladies' College*

Orbach, Susie - *Feminist writer; North London Collegiate*

Organ, Bryan - *Painter; Wyggeston GS, Leicester*

Ormond, Richard - *Director National Maritime Museum; Marlborough*

Orr, Chris - *Artist and print maker; Beckenham and Penge GS*

Osborne, John - *Playwright and actor; Belmont College, Devon*

Osbourne, Ozzy - *Singer; Birchfield Road School, Birmingham*

Oswald, Admiral Sir Julian - *First Sea Lord and Chief of Naval Staff; RNC, Dartmouth*

Oulton, Sir Derek - *Former Permanent Sec Lord Chancellor's Dept; St Edward's, Oxford*

Owen, Alun - *Playwright and screenplay writer; Cardigan County* and *Oulton HS, Liverpool*

Owen, Lord - *Co-founder SDP, fmr Foreign Secretary; Bradfield*

Owen, Thomas Arfon - *Director Welsh Arts Council; Ystalyfera GS, Swansea*

Owen, Ursula - *Joint MD Virago; Cultural Adviser Labour Pty; Putney Girls' HS*

Oxford, Sir Kenneth - *Former Chief Constable Merseyside; Caldecot, Lambeth*

O'Brien, Sir Richard - *Former Dir Manpower Services Commission; Oundle*

O'Connor, Tom - *Comedian; St Mary's College, Crosby*

O'Dell, June - *Dep Chair Equal Opportunities Commission; Edgehill Girls' College*

O'Donovan, Kathy - *Finance Director BTR; Portsmouth Southern GS*

O'Neill MP, Martin - *Labour MP; Trinity Academy, Edinburgh*

O'Neill, Terry - *Photographer; Gunnersbury GS*

O'Sullevan, Peter - *Racing commentator; Charterhouse*

O'Toole, Peter - *Actor; St Anne's, Leeds*

Packenham, Valerie -*Director fundraising The Samaritans; Wimbledon Girls' HS* and *North Walsham Girls' HS*

Padmore, Elaine - *Opera singer, Director Wexford Fest Opera; Newland HS, Hull* and *Arnold Girls' HS, Blackpool*

Page, Annette - *Ballerina Royal Ballet; Royal Ballet*

Pagett, Nicola - *Actress; Beehive, Bexhill on Sea*

Paige, Elaine - *Singer; Southaw Girls' Secondary*

Paisley, Rev Ian - *Democratic Unionist MP; Ballymena Model* and *Ballymena Technical HS*

Palin, Michael - *Writer and actor; Shrewsbury*

Palumbo, Lord - *Chairman The Arts Council; Eton*

Pannone, Rodger - *Solicitor specialising in disaster cases; St Brendan's, Bristol*

Paolozzi, Sir Eduardo - *Sculptor, RCA tutor in ceramics; Holy Cross Academy, Edinburgh*

Park, Dame Merle - *Director Royal Ballet School; Elmhurst Ballet*

Parker, Sir Eric - *Dep Chair & Chief exec Trafalgar House; Priory Boys' GS, Shrewsbury*

Parker, Geoffrey - *High Master Manchester GS; Alderman Newton's, Leicester*

Parker, John - *Chair and chief exec Harland and Wolff; Belfast College of Technology*

Parker, Sir Peter - *Former Chair British Railways Board; Bedford*

Parkes, Sir Edward - *Chair Cttee Vce Chancellors & Principals; King Edward's, Birmingham*

Parkin, Leonard - *Broadcaster; Hemsworth GS, Yorks*

Parkinson, Lord - *Former Secretary of State for Transport; Lancaster Royal GS*

Parkinson, Michael - *TV presenter, interviewer and writer; Barnsley GS*

Parsons, Sir Anthony - *Former HM Ambassador to Iran; King's, Canterbury*

Parsons, Nicholas - *Broadcaster; St Paul's*

Pasco, Richard; *Actor; King's, Wimbledon*

Pasco, Rowanne - *Religious editor TV AM; Dominican Convent, Chingford and Ursuline Convent, Ilford*

Pascoe, Alan - *Olympic hurdler; Portsmouth Southern GS*

Patten, Rt Hon Chris - *Governor Hong Kong; St Benedict's, Ealing*

Patten MP, Rt Hon John - *Education Secretary; Wimbledon College*

Pattinson, Rev Sir Derek - *Former Sec Gen General Synod Church of England; Whitehaven GS*

Paxman, Jeremy - *TV presenter and reporter* Newsnight; *Malvern*

Payne, Nicholas - *Director Opera North; Eton*

Peach, Dennis - *Former Chief Charity Commissioner; Selhurst GS*

Peacock, Professor Sir Alan - *Economist; Dundee HS*

Peake, David - *Chair Kleinwort Benson; Ampleforth*

Peake, Dame Felicity - *First director WRAF; St Winifred's, Eastbourne*

Pearl, Dr Valerie - *President New Hall Cambridge; King Edward VI Girls' HS, Birmingham*

Pearlman, Her Honour Judge Valerie - *Circuit judge; Wycombe Abbey*

Pearman, Johnny - *Leader Wakefield Education Committee; Thornes House, Wakefield*

Peel, John - *Disc jockey,* Observer *pop music critic; Shrewsbury*

Pennington, Michael - *Actor and writer; Marlborough*

Pennock, Lord - *Director Morgan Grenfell; Coatham*

Penrose, Professor Roger - *Professor Mathematics, Oxford University; University College Sch*

Peppiatt, Hugh - *Solicitor Senior Partner Freshfields; Winchester*

Perry, Lord - *Former Vice Chancellor Open University; Ayr Academy and Dundee HS*

Perry, Lady - *Director South Bank Polytechnic; Wolverhampton Girls' HS*

Perry, Fred - *Tennis player, now coach and commentator; Elementary school*

Peters, Mary - *Athlete; Ballymena Academy, County Antrim and Portadown College, County Armagh*

Pettifer, Julian - *Broadcaster; Marlborough*

Phelps, Richard - *Pentathlete; Brockworth Comprehensive*

Phillips, Baroness - *Labour peer House of Lords; Marist Convent, Paignton*

Phillips, Leslie - *Actor; Chingford and Italia Conti Stage*

Phillips, Captain Mark - *Olympic horseman; Marlborough*

Phillips, Sian - *Actress; Pontardawe Comprehensive*
Phillips, Tom - *Painter, writer and composer; Henry Thornton GS, Clapham*
Phillis, Bob - *Chief executive ITN; John Ruskin GS*
Phipps, Rt Rev Simon - *Former Bishop of Lincoln; Eton*
Pickles, His Hon Judge James - *Former Circuit Judge; Worksop College*
Pickup, Ronald - *Actor; King's, Chester*
Piggott, Lester - *Jockey; King Alfred's, Wantage*
Pigott-Smith, Tim - *Actor; Wyggeston GS, Leicester* and *King Edward VI,
     Stratford upon Avon*
Pile, Stephen - *Journalist; Clifton*
Pilkington, Sir Alastair - *President Pilkington plc; Sherborne*
Pilkington, Sir Antony - *Chair Pilkington plc; Ampleforth*
Pilkington, Canon Peter - *Former High Master St Paul's and Chair Broadcasting
     Complaints Commission; Dame Allan's, Newcastle*
Pimlott, Stephen - *RSC director; Manchester GS*
Pincher, Chapman - *Journalist; Darlington GS*
Pinker, Sir George - *Former gynaecologist to HM The Queen; Reading*
Pinter, Harold - *Playwright, actor and director; Grocers Company GS, Hackney
     Down*
Piper, John - *Painter; Epsom College*
Pippard, Professor Sir Brian - *Emeritus Professor Physics Cambridge; Clifton*
Pitman, Jennifer - *Racehorse trainer; Sarson Secondary Girls'*
Pitman, Mark - *Jockey; Wycliffe College, Gloucester*
Pitt-Kethley, Fiona - *Poet; Haberdashers' Aske's Girls'*
Pizzey, Erin - *Founder 1st battered women shelter Chiswick; Leweston Manor
     Convent, Sherborne*
Planer, Nigel - *Actor; Westminster*
Plastow, Sir David - *Chair Vickers plc; Culford*
Plater, Alan - *Playwright; Kingston HS, Hull*
Platt QC, Eleanor - *Barrister; Hove County Girls'*
Pleasence, Angela - *Actress; Hoddesdon Secondary Modern* and *Chiswick
     Polytechnic*
Pleasence, Donald - *Actor; Ecclesfield GS*
Plouviez, Peter - *General Secretary Equity; Sir George Monoux GS*
Plowden, Lady - *Educationist; Downe House*
Plowright, David E. - *Former Chair Granada TV; Scunthorpe GS*
Plowright, Joan - *Actress; Scunthorpe GS*
Plowright, Rosalind - *Soprano; Notre Dame HS, Wigan*
Plumb, Sir John - *Former Master Christ's College Cambridge; Alderman
     Newton's, Leicester*
Poliakoff, Stephen - *Playwright; Westminster*
Polkinghorne, Rev John - *President Queens' College Cambridge; Elmhurst GS
     and Perse, Cambridge*
Pollen, Arabella - *Fashion designer; Hatherop Castle, Gloucestershire*
Pope-Hennessy, Sir John - *Art historian; Downside*
Popplewell, Hon Sir Oliver - *High Court Judge Queen's Bench Division;
     Charterhouse*
Porritt, Jonathan - *Former Director Friends of the Earth; Eton*
Porter, Eric - *Actor; Wimbledon Technical College*
Porter, Sir Leslie - *President Tesco; Holloway County*
Porter, Lady - *Former Leader Westminster Council; Warren, Worthing*
Porter, Thea - *Fashion designer; Fernhill Manor*

Portillo MP, Michael - *Chief Secretary to the Treasury; Harrow County*
Portman, Lord - *Landowner; Eton*
Postgate, Professor John - *Microbiologist; Kingsbury County, Middlesex*
Potter, Dennis - *Playwright; Bell's GS, Coleford, Gloucestershire*
Potter, Hon Mr Justice Mark - *High Court Judge Queen's Bench Division; Perse, Cambridge*
Pountain, Sir Eric - *Chair Tarmac plc; Queen Mary's GS, Walsall*
Pountney, David - *Production director English National Opera; Radley*
Powell, Anthony - *Writer; Eton*
Powell, Sir Charles - *Former foreign policy adviser to Mrs Thatcher; King's, Canterbury*
Powell, Dilys - *Film critic; Bournemouth HS and Talbot Heath*
Powell, Rt Hon Enoch - *Former Conservative Minister; King Edward's, Birmingham*
Powell, Jonathan - *Controller BBC 1; Sherborne*
Powell, Philip - *Architect; Epsom College*
Prance, Professor Iain - *Director Kew Gardens; Malvern*
Prashar, Usha - *Direc Nat Councl Voluntary Organisations; Wakefield Girls' HS*
Prescott, John - *Labour MP, Shadow Transport Minister; Ellesmere Port Secondary Modern*
Prescott, Sir Mark - *Racehorse trainer; Harrow*
Preston, Peter - *Editor Guardian; Loughborough GS*
Preston, Rev Prof Ronald - *Professor Theology Manchester University; Caistor GS, Lincolnshire and Borden GS, Sittingbourne*
Preston, Simon - *Organist; Canford*
Price, Christopher - *Director Leeds Polytechnic; Leeds GS*
Price, Margaret - *Opera singer; Pontllanfraith Secondary*
Primarolo, Dawn - *Labour MP; Thomas Bennet Comprehensive*
Pringle, Derek - *Cricketer; Felsted*
Pringle, Lt Gen Sir Steuart - *Commandant General Royal Marines; Sherborne*
Pringle, Margaret - *Head Holland Park Comprehensive; Holton Park Girls' GS*
Prior, Lord - *Chair GEC; Charterhouse*
Pritchett, Sir Victor - *Author; Alleyn's*
Probyn, Jeff - *England rugby player; London Nautical*
Procktor, Patrick - *Painter and designer; Highgate*
Profumo, John - *Chair Toynbee Hall, Former War Minister; Harrow*
Proops, Marjorie - *Agony aunt Daily Mirror; Dalston County Secondary*
Prosser, Ian - *Chair Bass plc; King Edward's, Bath and Watford Boys' GS*
Pryce, Jonathan - *Actor; Holywell GS*
Pryce, Terry - *Chief executive Dalgety; Welshpool GS*
Pryke, Roy - *Chief Education Officer Kent; William Hulme's GS, Manchester*
Pugh, Sir Idwal - *Former Ombudsman; Cowbridge GS*
Purnell QC, Nicholas - *Chair Criminal Bar Association; Oratory*
Purves, Libby - *Radio presenter; Sacred Heart Convent, Tunbridge Wells*
Purvis, Stewart - *Editor ITN; Dulwich*
Puttnam, David - *Film director; Minchenden GS*
Pyke, Dr Magnus - *Nutritionist and broadcaster; St Paul's*
Pym, Lord - *Former Foreign Secretary; Eton*

Quant, Mary - *Fashion designer (13 schools); Unorthodox*
Quick, Diana - *Actress; Dartford GS for Girls*

Quinlan, Sir Michael - *Former Under Secty Min of Defence; Wimbledon College*
Quinton, Lord - *Former Chair Board of British Library; Stowe*
Quinton, Sir John - *Former Chair Barclays Bank plc; Norwich GS*
Quirk, Professor Sir Randolph - *Former President British Academy; Cronk Y Voddy, Isle of Man and Douglas HS, Isle of Man*

Raban, Jonathan - *Travel writer; King's, Worcester*
Race, Steve - *Musician and broadcaster; Christ's Hospital, Lincoln*
Radcliffe, Very Rev Timothy - *Provincial of the Dominicans; Downside*
Radice, Giles - *Labour MP; Winchester*
Rae, Dr John - *Former Headmaster Westminster, Direc Portman Group; Bishop's Stortford College*
Railton, Dame Ruth - *Founder, Mus Direc Nat Youth Orchestra; St Mary's, Wantage*
Raine, Craig - *Poet; Barnard Castle*
Raisman, John - *Dep Chair British Telecom, ex Ch Shell UK; Rugby*
Raison, Rt Hon Timothy - *Former Conservative MP; Eton*
Ramsbotham, Lt Gen Sir David - *Director Army PR Falklands War; Haileybury*
Rand, Mary - *Olympic gold medallist; Millfield*
Randall, Derek - *Cricketer; Sir Frederick Milner, Retford*
Randle, Professor Sir Philip - *Professor Clinical Biochemistry Oxford; King Edward VI GS, Nuneaton*
Rank, Joseph - *President Ranks Hovis McDougall; Loretto*
Rankin, Sir Alick - *Chair Scottish and Newcastle; Eton*
Rankine, Jean - *Deputy Director The British Museum; Central HS, Newcastle*
Rantzen, Esther - *TV presenter That's Life; North London Collegiate*
Raphael, Adam - *Executive Editor Observer; Charterhouse*
Raphael, Frederic - *Writer; Charterhouse*
Ratner, Gerald - *Ratners Group Jewellery; Hendon County GS*
Rattle, Simon - *Conductor; Liverpool College*
Raven, Simon - *Novelist and playwright; Charterhouse*
Rawlins, Peter - *Chief executive The Stock Exchange; St Edward's, Oxford*
Rawlinson QC, Lord - *Former Attorney General; Downside*
Ray, Jane - *Children's book illustrator, designer; Heathcote Junior HS Comprehensive and Highams Park Senior HS Comprehensive*
Ray, Cyril - *Journalist and wine writer; Manchester GS*
Ray, Robin - *Writer and broadcaster; Highgate*
Raymond, Paul - *Publisher, nightclub proprietor; St Francis Xavier's College, Liverpool and Glossop GS, Derbyshire*
Rayne, Sir Edward - *Chair Society London Fashion Designers; Harrow*
Rayner, Lord - *Former Chair Marks and Spencer; City College, Norwich*
Rayner, Claire - *Broadcaster, journalist and agony aunt; City of London Girls'*
Rayner, Rabbi John - *Rabbi; Durham*
Read, Sir John - *Former Chair TSB; Brighton, Hove and Sussex GS*
Read, Miss - *Writer on village life; Bromley County Girls'*
Read, Piers Paul - *Novelist; Ampleforth*
Reader Harris, Dame Diana - *Former Head Sherborne Girls' School; Sherborne Girls'*
Rebuck, Gail - *Head of Random Century publishers; French Lycée, London*
Reddaway, Professor W.B. - *Economist; Oundle*
Redgrave, Lynn - *Actress; Queensgate*

Redgrave, Vanessa - *Actress; Queensgate*
Redhead, Brian - *Broadcaster, presenter* Today *Radio 4; Royal GS, Newcastle upon Tyne*
Redwood MP, John - *Minister of State, Dept of the Environment; Canterbury*
Reece, Sir Gordon - *PR Consultant to Mrs Thatcher; Ratcliffe College*
Reed, Oliver - *Actor; Ewell Castle*
Rees, Angharad - *Actress; Commonweal Lodge, Surrey*
Rees, Brian - *Former HM Merchant Taylors', Charterhouse, Rugby; Bede GS, Sunderland*
Rees, Professor Gwendolen - *Zoologist; Aberdare Girls' GS*
Rees, Lord - *Former Labour Home Secretary; Harrow Weald GS*
Rees, Professor Martin - *Professor Astronomy Cambridge University; Shrewsbury*
Rees-Mogg, Lord - *Chair Broadcasting Standards Council; Charterhouse*
Reeves, Saskia - *Actress; Lady Eleanor Holles*
Reffell, Admiral Sir Derek - *Governor and C in C Gibraltar; Culford and RNC, Dartmouth*
Reger, Janet - *Lingerie designer; Kendrick GS, Reading*
Reid, Beryl - *Actress; Withington Girls' HS, Manchester and Levenshulme Girls' HS*
Reid, Sir Bob - *Former Chair British Railways Board; Malvern*
Reid, Sir Bob - *Chair British Rail; Bell Baxter HS, Cupar, Fife*
Reid Banks, Lynn - *Writer; St Teresa's Convent, Dorking*
Reilly, Malcolm - *England rugby team coach; Ashton Road Secondary, Castleford*
Reisz, Karel - *Film director; Leighton Park*
Relph, Michael - *Film director; Bembridge, Isle of Wight*
Relph, Simon - *Film director; Bryanston*
Rendell, Ruth - *Crime novelist; Loughton County HS*
Renfrew, Lord - *Disney Professor Archaeology Cambridge; St Albans*
Renton MP, Tim - *Former Minister for the Arts; Eton*
Reynolds, Alan - *Painter and printmaker; All Saints C of E, Newmarket*
Reynolds, Gillian - *Radio critic and journalist; Liverpool Institute Girls' HS*
Rhodes, Zandra - *Fashion designer; Medway Girls' Technical, Chatham*
Rhodes James, Sir Robert - *Former Conservative MP; Sedbergh*
Rhys Jones, Griff - *Actor, writer and producer; Brentwood*
Rice, Anneka - *TV presenter; St Michael's, Limpsfield*
Rice, Tim - *Scriptwriter and broadcaster; Lancing*
Rice Jones, Rt Rev Alwyn - *Archbishop of Wales; Llanrwst GS, Denbighshire*
Richard, Cliff - *Pop singer; Riversmead, Cheshunt*
Richard, Wendy - *Actress; Royal Masonic Girls' and Italia Conti Stage*
Richards, Sir Rex - *Director The Leverhulme Trust; Colyton GS, Devon*
Richardson, General Sir Charles - *Former Master-General of Ordnance; Wellington College*
Richardson, Ian - *Actor; Tynecastle, Edinburgh*
Richardson, Joanna - *Writer; Downs, Seaford*
Richardson, Sir Michael - *Corporate financier, stockbroker; Epsom College*
Richardson, Miranda - *Actress; Southport Girls' HS*
Richmond, Rear Admiral Andrew - *Chief Executive RSPCA; King's Bruton and Pangbourne*
Richmond, Sir Mark - *Professor Molecular Microbiology, Vice-Chancellor Manchester University; Epsom College*
Rickett, Sir Raymond - *Director Middlesex Polytechnic; Faversham GS*

Ricks, Professor Christopher - *Professor Eng Lit now at Boston Univ; King Alfred's, Wantage*

Riddell, Sir John - *Equerry to Prince and Princess of Wales; Eton*

Ridley, Lord - *Former Conservative MP, former Sec State Trade/Ind; Eton*

Rifkind MP, Rt Hon Malcolm - *Secretary of State for Defence; George Watson's, Edinburgh*

Rigby, Jean - *Opera singer; Elmslie Girls', Blackpool*

Rigg, Diana - *Actress; Fulneck Girls'*

Riley, Bridget - *Artist; Cheltenham Ladies' College*

Ripley, Andy - *Rugby player; Greenway Comprehensive*

Risk, Sir Thomas - *Governor Bank of Scotland; Kelvinside Academy*

Ritchie, Ian - *Architect; Varndean GS, Brighton*

Rittner, Luke - *Former Arts Council Secretary General; Blackfriars, Northants*

Rix, Lord - *Actor, Chairman MENCAP; Bootham*

Rizzello, Michael - *Sculptor and coin designer; Oratory*

Robens of Woldingham, Lord - *Former Chair National Coal Board; Manchester Secondary*

Roberts, Dr Derek - *Provost University College London; Manchester Central HS*

Roberts, Rt Rev John - *Former Abbot of Downside; Downside*

Roberts, The Ven Raymond - *Former Chaplain of the Fleet; Pontywaun GS, Gwent*

Roberts, Rt. Hon Sir Wyn, MP - *Minister of State, Welsh Office; Harrow*

Robertson MP, George - *Labour Defence spokesman; Dunoon GS*

Robertson, Max - *Sports commentator; Haileybury*

Robertson, Patrick - *Founder The Bruges Group; Dulwich*

Robinson, Ann - *TV presenter and journalist; Farnborough Hill Convent*

Robinson, Bill - *Special Adviser Chancellor; ex-Direc IFS; Bryanston*

Robinson, Jancis - *FT Wine expert; Carlisle County Girls' HS*

Robinson, Robert - *Writer and broadcaster; Raynes Park GS*

Robinson, Tim - *Cricketer; Dunstable GS*

Robinson, Tom - *Singer; Friends', Saffron Walden*

Robson, Bobby - *Footballer, manager England team; Waterhouses Secondary Modern, Co Durham*

Robson, Bryan - *England Football Captain; Birtley Lord Lawson Comprehensive*

Robson, Professor Elizabeth - *Head of Genetics Univers College London; Bishop Auckland Girls' GS*

Rock, Stuart - *Editor Director magazine; Malvern*

Roddick, Anita - *Founder Body Shop; Worthing Girls' GS*

Rodger, Rt Rev Patrick - *Assistant Bishop of Edinburgh; Rugby*

Rodgers, Lord - *Former Vice-President SDP; Quarry Bank HS, Liverpool*

Roebuck, Peter - *Cricketer; Millfield*

Roeg, Nicholas - *Film director; Mercers*

Rogers, Sir Richard - *Architect; St John's, Leatherhead*

Rogers, Martin - *Former Chief Master King Edward's, Birmingham; Oundle*

Romain, Rabbi Jonathan - *Rabbi; University College Sch*

Romsey, Lord - *Film producer; Gordonstoun*

Ronay, Edina - *Knitwear designer; Putney Girls' HS*

Roocroft, Amanda - *Opera singer; Southlands HS, Chorley*

Rooke, Sir Denis - *Chair British Gas; Westminster City and Addey and Stanhope, London*

Rooker, Jeffrey - *Labour MP; Handsworth Technical*

Root, Betty - *Reading and language expert; Newbury Girls'*

Sadie, Stanley - *Editor* Grove Dictionary of Music; *St Paul's*
Sadler, Brent - *ITV Foreign correspondent; Royal Masonic*
Sadler, Joan - *Former Principal Cheltenham Ladies' College; Cambridge Girls' HS*
Sainsbury, Lord - *Chair J. Sainsbury plc; Stowe*
Sainsbury, The Hon Tim - *MP, Minister of State for Trade and Industry; Eton*
Sallis, Peter - *Actor; Minchenden GS*
Sampson, Anthony - *Writer and journalist; Westminster*
Sanders, Peter - *Ch Exec Commission for Racial Equality; Queen Elizabeth's
        GS, Barnet*
Sanderson, Tessa - *Athlete and broadcaster; Wards Bridge
        Comprehensive, Wednesfield*
Sanger, Dr Frederick - *Chemist, first to show protein structure; Bryanston*
Sangster, Robert - *Racehorse owner; Repton*
Santer, Rt Rev Mark - *Bishop of Birmingham; Marlborough*
Sapper, Alan - *Gen Sec Assoc Cinema and TV Trade Union; Latymer Upper*
Saunders, Iain - *Chief executive Robert Fleming Investmt; Radley*
Saunders, Dame Cicely - *Founder The Hospice Movement; Roedean*
Savage, Dr Wendy - *Obstetrician and gynaecologist; Croydon Girls' HS*
Savile, Sir Jimmy - *TV presenter; Elementary school*
Saxton, Robert - *Composer; Bryanston*
Sayeed, Jonathan - *Former Conservative MP; Woolverstone Hall*
Sayle, Alexei - *Comedian; Alsop HS, Liverpool*
Scales, Prunella - *Actress; Moira House, Eastbourne*
Scanlon, Lord - *Former Trade unionist AEUW; Stretford Elementary*
Scarman, Lord - *Former Law Lord; Radley*
Schama, Professor Simon - *Professor of History Harvard University;
        Haberdashers' Aske's*
Schiemann, Hon Mr Justice Konrad - *High Court Judge Queen's Bench Division;
        King Edward's, Birmingham*
Schlesinger, John - *Film director; Uppingham*
Scholey, Sir David - *Investment banker; Chair S.G. Warburg; Wellington College*
Scholey, Sir Robert - *Chair British Steel plc; King Edward VII GS, Sheffield*
Scofield, Paul - *Actor; Hurstpierpoint* and *Varndean GS, Brighton*
Scotland QC, Patricia - *First black woman QC; Walthamstow Senior High School
        for Girls*
Scott, Kenneth - *Assistant Private Secretary HM The Queen; George Watson's,
        Edinburgh*
Scott, Sir Michael - *Former Gen Sec Royal Commonwealth Society; Dame
        Allan's, Newcastle*
Scott, Ronnie - *Jazz musician, nightclub proprietor; Central Foundation
        London*
Scott-James, Anne - *Writer; St Paul's Girls*
Scrivener QC, Anthony - *Barrister; Kent College, Canterbury*
Scruton, Professor Roger - *Professor aesthetics Birkbeck College; The Royal GS,
        High Wycombe*
Scudamore, Peter - *Jockey; Belmont Abbey, Hereford*
Seagrove, Jenny - *Actress; Queen Anne's, Caversham* and *Kirby Lodge,
        Cambridge*
Searle, Graham - *Director ISCO; Plymouth College*
Sebastian, Tim - *BBC correspondent and author; Westminster*
Secombe, Sir Harry - *Comedian and singer; Dynevor GS, Swansea*
Seifert, Richard - *Architect; Central Foundation London*

Selby, Rt Rev Peter - *Suffragan Bishop of Kingston on Thames; Merchant Taylors'*

Sergeant, John - *BBC Parliamentary Correspondent; Millfield*

Sergeant, Sir Patrick - *Chair Euromoney Publications; Beaumont*

Serota, Nicholas - *Director The Tate Gallery; Haberdashers' Aske's*

Service, Alastair - *Gen Secretary Family Planning Association; Westminster*

Sexton, Stuart - *Former adviser Sir Keith Joseph; St Joseph's College, Beulah Hill, London*

Seymour, Jane - *Actress; Arts Educational*

Shackleton, Lord - *Chair RTZ; Radley*

Shaffer, Antony - *Playwright; St Paul's*

Shaffer, Peter - *Playwright; King Edward VII, Lytham* and *St Paul's*

Shah, Eddy - *Founder* Today *newspaper; Gordonstoun*

Shakespeare, Nicholas - *Literary Editor* Daily Telegraph; *Winchester*

Sharpe, Tom - *Novelist; Lancing*

Shaw, Sir Brian - *Company director ANZ, Grindlays Bank; Wrekin College*

Shaw, Henrietta - *First woman Cambridge cox; Harrogate Ladies' College*

Shaw, Neil - *Chair Tate and Lyle plc; Knowlton HS*

Shaw, Sir Roy - *Former Arts Council Secretary General; Firth Park GS, Sheffield*

Shaw, Sandie - *Pop singer; Robert Clack Technical College, Dagenham*

Shawcross QC, Lord - *Chief prosecutor Nuremberg Trials; Dulwich*

Shea, Dr Michael - *Former press secretary to HM The Queen; Gordonstoun*

Sheehy, Patrick - *Chair British Allied Tobacco Industries; Ampleforth*

Sheldon, Mark - *Solicitor Sen Ptnr Linklaters & Paines; Wycliffe College, Gloucester*

Shepard, Giles - *Chief executive The Savoy Hotel Group; Eton*

Shephard, Gillian - *Secretary of State for Employment; North Walsham Girls' HS*

Shepherd, David - *Artist; Stowe*

Shepherd, Sir Peter - *Director Shepherd Building Group; Rossall*

Shepherdson, Isabel - *Former Head Kidbrooke School; Roundhay Girls' HS, Leeds*

Sheppard, Sir Alan - *Chair Grand Metropolitan plc; Ilford County HS*

Sheppard, Rt Rev David - *Bishop of Liverpool; cricketer; Sherborne*

Shepperd, Sir Alfred - *Chair Wellcome Foundation; Archbishop Tenison's GS*

Sheridan, Rabbi Sybil - *Rabbi; Bolton Girls'*

Sherman, Sir Alfred - *Co-founder Centre for Policy Studies; Grocers Company GS, Hackney Down*

Sherrin, Ned - *Radio and TV presenter; Sexey's, Bruton*

Sherrin, Scott - *Presenter* That's Life; *Boswells Comprehensive, Chelmsford*

Shilling, David - *Milliner Royal Ascot; St Paul's*

Shirley, Mrs Steve - *Founder F International Group, IT expert; Sir John Cass College, London*

Shirley-Quirk, John - *Bass-baritone; Holt HS, Liverpool*

Shivas, Mark - *Head of Drama BBC TV; Whitgift, Croydon*

Shock, Sir Maurice - *Rector Lincoln College Oxford; King Edward's, Birmingham*

Shore, Rt Hon Peter - *Labour MP; Quarry Bank HS, Liverpool*

Short, Renee - *Former Labour MP; Nottingham County GS*

Short, Nigel - *Chess champion; Bolton*

Shrimsley, Bernard - *Former editor* News of World, Mail on Sunday; *Kilburn GS*

Sibley, Antoinette - *Prima ballerina; Arts Educational* and *Royal Ballet*

Sieff, Lord - *Hon President Marks and Spencer; Manchester GS* and *St Paul's*

Sieff, The Hon David - *Director Marks and Spencer; Repton*

Sieghart, Mary Ann - *Assistant Editor* The Times; *Cobham Hall* and *Bedales*

Silk, The Ven David - *Archdeacon of Leicester; Gillingham GS*

Silk, Dennis - *Former Warden Radley College; Christ's Hospital*

Silkin, Jon - *Poet; Wycliffe College* and *Dulwich*

Sillitoe, Alan - *Writer, film scriptwriter; Radford Boulevard, Nottingham*

Simmons, Jean - *Actress; Orange Hill* and *Aida Foster Dancing*

Simonds-Gooding, Anthony - *Former Chair and Ch Exec Saatchi and BSB; Ampleforth*

Simpson, Alan - *Scriptwriter; Mitcham GS*

Simpson, John - *Co-Editor* Oxford English Dictionary; *Dean Close, Cheltenham*

Simpson, John - *BBC Foreign News Editor; St. Paul's*

Simpson, N. F. - *Dramatist; Emanuel*

Sims, Monica - *Children's Film and TV Foundation Direc; Gloucester Girls' HS*

Sinclair, Sir Clive - *Chair Sinclair Research; Highgate, Reading* and *St George's, Weybridge*

Singer, Aubrey - *Director Goldcrest Films and TV; Bradford GS*

Singleton, Roger - *Director Barnardos; City GS, Sheffield*

Singleton, Valerie - *TV journalist and broadcaster; Arts Educational*

Sirs, Bill - *Trade unionist; Middleton St John's, Hartlepool*

Sisson, Rosemary Anne - *Novelist and scriptwriter; Cheltenham Ladies' College*

Sissons, Peter - *BBC reporter; Liverpool Institute HS*

Sked, Dr Alan - *Senior lecturer LSE; Bruges Group; Allan Glen's*

Skidelsky, Lord - *Professor International Studies Warwick Univ; Brighton College*

Skinner, Dennis - *Labour MP; Tupton Hall GS*

Skinner, Mick - *England rugby player; Wallbottle GS*

Skipper, David - *Former Head Merchant Taylors' School; Watford Boys' GS*

Skynner, Professor Robin - *Psychiatrist* (Families and How to Survive Them); *Blundell's*

Slade, Julian - *Author and composer; Eton*

Slater, Vice Admiral Sir Jock - *Chief of Fleet Support; Edinburgh Academy* and *Sedbergh*

Slattery, Tony - *Comedian; Catholic GS, London*

Slaughter, Audrey - *Journalist, former Editor* Honey *magazine; Chislehurst HS* and *Stand Girls' GS, Manchester*

Sleep, Wayne - *Ballet dancer; Hartlepool*

Slemen, Michael - *England rugby player; St Edward's, Liverpool*

Slipman, Sue - *Dir National Council One Parent Families; Stockwell Manor Comprehensive*

Sloman, Sir Albert - *Former Vice-Chancellor Essex University; Launceston College, Cornwall*

Smallpelce, Sir Basil - *Former air and sea transport executive; Shrewsbury*

Smets, Pascale - *Fashion designer; Farnborough Hill Convent* and *Alleyn's*

Smith, Alan - *Chief executive TCCB; King Edward's, Birmingham*

Smith, Colin - *Chief Constable Thames Valley Police; Dorking GS*

Smith, Sir Cyril - *Former LD MP; Rochdale Boys' GS*

Smith, Douglas - *Chair ACAS; Leeds Modern GS*

Smith, Professor John - *Emeritus Professor Law Nottingham Univ; St Mary's GS, Darlington*

Smith MP, Rt Hon John - *Opposition spokesman Economic Affairs; Dunoon GS*

Smith, Maggie - *Actress; Oxford HS*

Smith, Mark E. - *Rock singer The Fall; Stand GS, Manchester*

Steedman, Air Chief Marshal Sir Alasdair - *Former Director Defence Operations Staff; Hampton GS*

Steel MP, Sir David - *Former Leader Liberal Party; George Watson's, Edinburgh*

Steele, Tommy - *Pop singer and actor; Bacon's, Bermondsey*

Steele, Vivien - *Dir Nat Assoc Care & Resettlmt Offenders; Kent College, Pembury*

Steele-Bodger, Mickey - *Former England rugby selector; Rugby*

Stephen, Rita - *Trade unionist; Queen's Park, Glasgow*

Stephens, Robert - *Actor; Bradford Civic Theatre Sch*

Stephenson, Professor Hugh - *Professor of journalism City University; Winchester*

Stephenson, John - *Cricketer; Felsted*

Sterling, Lord - *Chair P & O; Reigate GS and Preston Manor County*

Steven, Stewart - *Editor* Mail on Sunday; *Mayfield College, Sussex*

Stevens, Jocelyn - *Former MD, Beaverbrook Newspapers; Eton*

Stevens, Shakin' - *Pop singer; Ysgol Hywel Dda*

Stevens of Ludgate, Lord - *Chairman United Newspapers; Stowe*

Stevenson, Will - *Director British Film Institute; Edinburgh Academy*

Stewart, Alastair - *ITN Newsreader; St Augustine's, Westgate on Sea*

Stewart, Dave - *Pop singer and producer; Bede GS, Sunderland*

Stewart, Jackie - *Racing driver; Dunbarton Academy*

Stewart, Mary - *Novelist; Eden Hall, Penrith and Skellfield, Ripon*

Stilgoe, Richard - *Lyricist; Liverpool College and Monkton Combe*

Stirling, Sir James - *Architect; Quarry Bank HS, Liverpool*

Stirling, Angus - *Director General The National Trust; Eton*

Stockdale, Sir Noel - *Chair ASDA, MFI; Woodhouse Grove, Yorkshire*

Stockton, The Earl of - *Chair Macmillan publishers; Eton*

Stockwood, Rt Rev Mervyn - *Former Bishop of Southwark; Kelly College*

Stoddart, Patrick - *Journalist* Sunday Times; *Watford Boys' GS*

Stokes, Lord - *Company chairman, Dutton Forshaw; Blundell's*

Stone, Carole - *TV interviewer, ex-producer* Any Questions; *Ashford County Girls' GS, Kent*

Stone, Professor Norman - *Professor Modern History Oxford Univ; Glasgow Academy*

Stoppard, Miriam - *Writer and broadcaster; Newcastle upon Tyne Central HS*

Stoppard, Tom - *Playwright and novelist; Pocklington*

Storey, David - *Writer and dramatist; Queen Elizabeth GS, Wakefield*

Storkey, Elaine - *Director, Institute of Contemporary Christianity; Ossett GS, Yorkshire*

Stormonth Darling, Peter - *Head of Mercury Asset Management; Winchester*

Storr, Dr Anthony - *Psychiatrist; Winchester*

Stott, Mary - *Journalist; Wyggeston Girls' GS, Leicester*

Stott, Richard - *Editor* Daily Mirror; *Clifton*

Strachan, Michaela - *TV presenter; Claremont Farm Court, Esher*

Straw MP, Jack - *Shadow Education Secretary; Brentwood*

Strawson, Sir Peter - *Professor Metaphysical Philosophy Oxford; Christ's College, Finchley*

Stride, John - *Actor; Alleyn's*

Strong, Sir Roy - *Former Director Victoria and Albert Museum; Edmonton County GS*

Stuart, Alexander - *Novelist; Bexley GS*

Stubbs, Imogen - *Actress; St Paul's Girls' and Westminster*

Stubbs, Una - *Actress; Baylis Court Secondary Modern, Slough* and *La Roche Dancing, Slough*
Styan, David - *Chair Govt Task Force school management; Ashton under Lyne GS*
Subba Row, Raman - *Chair TCCB; Whitgift, Croydon*
Suchet, David - *Actor; Wellington, Somerset*
Sugar, Alan - *Chair Amstrad plc; Brooke House, London*
Sugden, Mollie - *Actress; Keighley Girls' GS*
Sullivan, David - *Sunday Sport; Abbots Cross County Technical* and *Watford Boys' GS*
Summerscale, David - *Headmaster Westminster, formerly Haileybury; Sherborne*
Sumption QC, Jonathan - *Barrister; Eton*
Surtees, John - *Former racing car driver; Ashburton, Croydon*
Sutch, Screaming Lord - *Professional election candidate; Salisbury Road, Kilburn*
Sutcliffe, Serena - *Head of Sotheby's Wine Department; St Michael's, Limpsfield*
Swann, Donald - *Composer and performer; Westminster*
Swinnerton-Dyer, Professor Sir Peter - *Mathematician; Eton*
Swinton, Tilda - *Actress; Fettes*
Sykes, Dr John - *Lexicographer and translator; Wallasey GS Rochdale HS and St Lawrence College Ramsgate*
Sykes, Rt Rev Stephen - *Bishop of Ely; Bristol GS, Monkton Combe*
Symes, Mary - *First woman coroner; St Mary's Convent, Lowestoft* and *Great Yarmouth HS*
Symons, Julian - *Writer; Wix's Lane, Battersea*

Talbot, Godfrey - *Broadcaster; Leeds GS*
Tarbuck, Jimmy - *Comedian; Rose Lane Secondary*
Tate, Francis - *Vice Chair Tate and Lyle (private tutor); Unorthodox*
Tate, Dr Jeffrey - *Principal conductor Eng Chamber Orch; Farnham GS*
Tavaré, Chris - *Cricketer; Sevenoaks*
Tavener, John - *Composer; Highgate*
Taverne, Dick - *Former Labour Minister, former Indep SD MP; Charterhouse*
Taylor, Ann - *Labour MP; Bolton Girls'*
Taylor, Elizabeth - *Film star; Byron House, Hampstead*
Taylor, Graham - *England Football Team Manager; Scunthorpe GS*
Taylor, Ian - *Hockey goalkeeper; Queen Elizabeth GS, Hartlebury, Worcs*
Taylor, Rt Rev John - *Bishop of St Albans; Watford Boys' GS*
Taylor, Rt Rev John - *Theologian, fmr Bishop of Winchester; St Lawrence College, Ramsgate*
Taylor, Jonathan - *Chief executive Booker plc; Winchester*
Taylor, Kim - *Director Calouste Gulbenkian Trust; Sevenoaks*
Taylor, Professor Laurie - *Sociologist; St Mary's College, Crosby*
Taylor, Matthew - *MP (LD); University College Sch*
Taylor, Rt Hon Sir Peter - *Lord Chief Justice; Newcastle upon Tyne Royal GS*
Taylor, Sir Teddy - *Conservative MP; Glasgow HS*
Taylor, Wendy - *Sculptor; Raine's Foundation Girls'*
Taylor, Prof. Sir William - *Vice Chancellor Hull University; Erith GS*
Taylor Bradford, Barbara - *Novelist; Northcote, Leeds*
Tear, Robert - *Operatic tenor; Barry GS*
Tebbit, Lord - *Former Chair Conservative Party; Edmonton County GS*
Telford, Sir Robert - *Life President Marconi; Quarry Bank HS, Liverpool* and *Queen Elizabeth's GS, Tamworth*

Temple QC, Sir Sanderson - *Recorder of Liverpool; Kendal*
Temple-Morris, Peter - *Conservative MP; Malvern*
Templeman, Lord - *Lord of Appeal; Southall GS*
Tench, David - *Head Legal Dept Consumers' Association; Merchant Taylors'*
Tennant, Sir Anthony J. - *Chair Guinness plc; Eton*
Tennant, Emma - *Writer; St Paul's Girls'*
Terry, David - *Principal Halesowen Tertiary College; Crypt GS, Gloucester*
Terry, Quinlan - *Architect; Bryanston*
Tesler, Brian - *Chair LWT; Chiswick County Boys'*
Tewson, Jane - *Founder Comic Relief Charity; Headington* and *Lord Williams'*
    Comprehensive, Thame
Thacker, David - *RSC director; Wellingborough*
Thatcher, Baroness - *Former Prime Minister; Kesteven and Grantham Girls' GS*
Thatcher, Carol - *Journalist; St Paul's Girls'*
Thatcher, Sir Denis - *Company director; Mill Hill*
Thelwell, Norman - *Artist and cartoonist; Rock Ferry HS, Birkenhead*
Thesiger, Wilfred - *Explorer and writer; Eton*
Thirkettle, Joan - *TV reporter; Bexley GS*
Thoday, Professor John - *Emeritus Professor Genetics Cambridge; Bootham*
Thomas, Harvey - *PR consultant; Westminster*
Thomas, Dr Jean - *Reader in Biochemistry Cambridge Univ; Llwyny Bryn Girls'*
    HS, Swansea
Thomas, Jeremy - *Film producer; Millfield*
Thomas, Sir Keith - *Historian and President, Corpus Christi College, Oxford;*
    Barry GS
Thomas, Leslie - *Author; Kingston Technical College and South West Essex*
    Technical
Thomas, Rosie - *Novelist; Howell's, Denbigh*
Thomas of Swynnerton, Lord - *Chair Centre for Policy Studies; Sherborne*
Thompson, Rt Rev James - *Bishop of Bath & Wells, ex Bishop Stepney; Dean*
    Close, Cheltenham
Thompson, Major General Julian - *Research Fellow in Armed Conflict; Sherborne*
Thomson of Monifieth, Lord - *Former Chair IBA; Grove Academy, Dundee*
Thomson, Sir Adam - *Former Chair British Caledonian; Rutherglen Academy* and
    Coatbridge
Thorn, John - *Former Headmaster Winchester College; St Paul's*
Thorburn, Paul - *Wales rugby captain; Hereford Cathedral*
Thorneycroft, Lord - *Former Chair Conservative Party; Eton*
Thorogood, Alfreda - *Ballerina; Lady Eden's and Royal Ballet*
Thorpe, Jeremy - *Former Leader Liberal Party; Eton*
Thubron, Colin - *Novelist; Eton*
Thwaite, Anthony - *Poet, Director Andre Deutsch publishers; Kingswood, Bath*
Tickell, Sir Crispin - *Former diplomat and environmentalist; Westminster*
Tidmarsh, John - *Presenter* Outlook *BBC World Service; Cotham GS, Bristol*
Tidy, Bill - *Cartoonist; St Margaret's Senior, Anfield, Liverpool*
Tilberis, Elizabeth - *Former Editor* Vogue, *editor US Harpers Bazaar; Malvern*
    Girls'
Tillotson, Professor Kathleen - *Professor Eng Lit London University; Ackworth,*
    Pontefract and Mount, York
Timpson, John - *Writer and former broadcaster Radio 4; Merchant Taylors'*
Tindale, Patricia - *Chief architect Department Environment; Blatchington Court,*
    Seaford

Tushingham, Rita - *Actress; La Sagesse Convent, Liverpool*

Tutin, Dorothy - *Actress; St Catherine's, Bramley, Surrey*

Tuzo, General Sir Harry - *Former Chair Marconi Space and Defence; Wellington College*

Tweedie, Jill - *Journalist and scriptwriter (9 schools); Unorthodox*

Tweedy, Colin - *Chair Assoc Business Sponsorship of Arts; City of Bath*

Twiggy - *Actress, singer, former model; Brondesbury and Kilburn Girls'*

Tyacke, Sarah - *First female keeper Public Record Office; Chelmsford County Girls' HS*

Tyrell, Ann - *Fashion designer; Norwich HS*

Tyzack, Margaret - *Actress; St Angela's Ursuline Convent*

Ullman, Tracy - *Comedienne and singer; Italia Conti Stage*

Underwood, Derek - *Cricketer; Beckenham and Penge GS*

Underwood, Rory - *England rugby player; Barnard Castle*

Ustinov, Sir Peter - *Actor, dramatist and film director; Westminster*

Uttley, Roger - *Rugby player; Director PE Harrow School; Montgomery Secondary Modern and Blackpool GS*

Vaisey, David - *Bodley's Librarian, Oxford; Rendcomb College*

Valin, Reg - *Founder Valin Pollen PR, Chair Business in Community; Emanuel*

Vallance, Iain - *Chair British Telecom; Edinburgh Academy, Dulwich and Glasgow Academy*

Van Straubenzee, Sir William - *Former Conservative Minister of State for Education; Westminster*

Vanneck, Air Commodore Sir Peter - *Former ADC to Her Majesty The Queen; Stowe*

Varah, Rev Dr Chad - *Founder The Samaritans; Worksop College*

Vaughan, Elizabeth - *Operatic soprano; Llanfyllin GS*

Vaughan, Dame Janet - *Authority on blood disorders, Former Principal Somerville College, Oxford; North Foreland Lodge, Basingstoke*

Vaz, Keith - *Labour MP; Latymer Upper*

Veasey, Josephine - *Opera singer; De La Warr, East Grinstead*

Venables, David - *Official Solicitor to Supreme Court; Denstone College*

Verity, Anthony - *Master Dulwich College; Queen Elizabeth's Hospital, Bristol*

Verity, Father Peter - *Director Catholic Media Office; St Michael's College, Kirkby Lonsdale*

Verney, His Honour Judge Laurence - *Recorder of London; Harrow*

Villiers, James - *Actor; Wellington College*

Vincent, General Sir Richard - *Chief of Defence Staff; Aldenham*

Vine, David - *Sports commentator; Barnstaple GS, Devon*

Vinson, Lord - *President Industrial Partnership Assn; Pangbourne*

Vorderman, Carol - *TV presenter Channel 4* Countdown; *Blessed Edward Jones HS, Rhyl*

Waddington, Lord - *Former Lord Privy Seal, and Leader House of Lords; Sedbergh*

Waddle, Chris - *Footballer; Hewarth Grange, Wardley*

Wade, Virginia - *Tennis player, commentator; Tunbridge Wells GS*

Warwick, Diana - *Gen Sec Association University Teachers; St Joseph's College, Bradford*

Wass, Sir Douglas - *Chair Equity and Law Life Assurance Soc; Nottingham HS*

Waterhouse, Keith - *Writer; Osmondthorpe Council, Leeds*

Waterhouse, Dame Rachel - *Former Chair Consumers Association; King Edward VI Girls' HS, Birmingham*

Waterman, Fanny - *Chair Leeds Piano Competition; Allerton HS, Leeds*

Waterman, Pete - *Partner Stock, Aitken, Waterman Music Studio; Frederick Bird Secondary Modern, Coventry*

Waterstone, Tim - *Founder and Chair Waterstones Books; Tonbridge*

Wates, Sir Christopher - *Chief executive Wates Holdings; Stowe*

Watford, Gwen - *Actress; Glenthorne, St Leonards on Sea*

Watkins, Alan - *Political columnist* Observer; *Amman Valley GS*

Watkins, Rt Hon Sir Tasker - *Ld Just Appeal, Counsel Aberfan disaster; Pontypridd GS*

Watson, Angus - *Director of Music Wells Cathedral School; King Edward VI, Norwich*

Watson, James - *Chair National Freight Corporation; Watford Boys' GS*

Waugh, Auberon - *Columnist and Editor* The Literary Review; *Downside*

Waymouth, Lady Victoria - *Interior designer; St Mary's Convent, Ascot*

Weatherall, Sir David - *Geneticist; Calday Grange GS*

Weatherill, Lord - *Former Speaker House of Commons; Malvern*

Webster, Very Rev Alan - *Former Dean of St Paul's; Shrewsbury*

Wedderburn, Professor Dorothy - *Principal Royal Holloway & Bedford Coll; Walthamstow Girls' HS*

Wedderburn of Charlton, Lord - *Professor Commercial Law LSE; Aske's GS, Hatcham and Whitgift, Croydon*

Weighell, Sid - *Trade unionist, Leader Nat Union Railwaymen; Northallerton C of E*

Weinstock, Lord - *MD GEC; Albion Central, North London*

Weldon, Duncan - *Theatre producer; King George V, Southport*

Weldon, Fay - *Writer; South Hampstead Girls' HS*

Welland, Colin - *Actor and playwright; Newton le Willows GS and Bretton Hall College*

Wellington, The Duke of - *Landowner; Eton*

Wells, Doreen - *Dancer Royal Ballet, actress; Walthamstow Girls' HS and Bush Davies*

Wells, John - *Writer, actor, director; Eastbourne College*

Wells, Professor Stanley - *Shakespeare scholar; Kingston HS, Hull*

Wesker, Arnold - *Playwright; Upton House, Hackney*

Wesley, Mary - *Novelist (16 governesses);* Unorthodox *and Queen's College, Harley Street*

West, Peter - *Sports commentator; Cranbrook*

West, Timothy - *Actor; John Lyon, Harrow*

Westall, Robert - *Writer, especially children's books; Tynemouth HS*

Westminster, The Duke of - *Landowner; Harrow*

Weston, Galen - *Chair, President George Weston Toronto; St Paul's*

Weston, Garfield - *Chair Ass British Foods, Fortnum & Mason; Sir William Borlase's, Marlow*

Weston, Dame Margaret - *Former Director The Science Museum; Stroud HS*

Weston, Michael - *British Ambassador in Kuwait; Dover College*

Westwood, Rt Rev Bill - *Bishop of Peterborough; Grove Park GS, Wrexham*

Williams, Michael - *Actor; St Edward's, Liverpool*
Williams, Rev Prof Rowan - *Professor Divinity Oxford University Bishop of Monmouth; Dynevor GS, Swansea*
Williams, Shirley - *Founder SDP (8 schools in UK and USA); Unorthodox*
Williams, Simon - *Actor; Harrow*
Williamson, Marshal of the RAF Sir Keith - *Former Chief of Air Staff; Bancrofts and Market Harborough GS*
Williamson, Rt Rev Roy - *Bishop of Southwark; Elmgrove, Belfast*
Willis, Lord - *Playwright, Labour peer; Downhills Central, Tottenham*
Willis, Norman - *General Secretary TUC; Ashford County GS*
Wilsey, Lt Gen Sir John - *GOC Northern Ireland; Sherborne*
Wilson, AN - *Writer; Rugby*
Wilson, Charles - Daily Mirror, *former editor* The Times; *Eastbank Academy, Glasgow*
Wilson, Colin - *Writer; Gateway Technical, Leicester*
Wilson, Sir David - *Director The British Museum; Kingswood, Bath*
Wilson, Sir David - *Former Governor of Hong Kong; Glenalmond*
Wilson, Sandy - *Composer and lyricist; Harrow*
Wilson, Snoo - *Playwright; Bradfield*
Wilson of Rievaulx, Lord - *Former Prime Minister; Royds Hall, Huddersfield* and *Wirral GS, Cheshire*
Windlesham, Lord - *Director* Observer, WH Smith, ATV; *Ampleforth*
Windsor, Barbara - *Actress; Our Lady's Convent, Stamford Hill*
Winner, Michael - *Film director; St Christopher's, Letchworth*
Winstanley, Alan - *Record producer; St Clement Danes GS*
Winterson, Jeanette - *Novelist; Accrington Girls' HS*
Winterton, Ann - *Conservative MP; Erdington Girls' GS*
Winterton, Nicholas - *Conservative MP; Rugby*
Wintour, Anna - *Editor American* Vogue *magazine; Queen's College, Harley Street* and *North London Collegiate*
Wintour, Charles - *Former editor* Evening Standard; *Oundle*
Wise, Ernie - *Comedian; East Ardsley, Wakefield*
Wisker, Jennifer - *Chief Education Officer Somerset; Kendrick GS, Reading*
Witchell, Nicholas - *TV news presenter BBC Breakfast News; Epsom College*
Wolfendale, Professor Arnold - *Astronomer Royal; Stretford GS*
Wolff, Professor Heinz - *Director Brunel Institute for Bioengineering; City of Oxford*
Wolfson, Sir Brian - *Chair Wembley plc; Liverpool College*
Wolfson, Sir David - *Chair Next plc; Clifton*
Wolfson, Lord - *Chair Wolfson Fndn, Great Universal Stores; King's, Worcester*
Wontner, Sir Hugh - *Chair Claridges and Berkeley Hotels; Oundle*
Wood, Clare - *Tennis player; St Bede's, Hailsham*
Wood, David - *Actor, playwright, composer and producer; Chichester HS*
Wood, John - *Actor; Bedford*
Wood, Rt Rev Maurice - *Former Bishop Norwich; Monkton Combe*
Wood, Victoria - *Comedienne; Bury Girls' GS*
Woodcock, Sir John - *HM Inspector of Constabulary; Preston Technical College*
Woodhead, David - *Director ISIS; Queen Elizabeth GS, Wakefield*
Woodhouse, James - *Headmaster Lancing College; St Edward's, Oxford*
Woodhouse, The Hon Montague - *Greek Resistance organiser; Winchester*
Woodward, Edward - *Actor; Kingston College*

Woodward, Shaun - *Director Communications Conservative Party Former TV producer; Bristol GS*
Wooldridge, Ian - *Sports columnist Daily Mail; Brockenhurst GS*
Woolf, Rt Hon Sir Harry - *Appeal Court Judge, Prisons Enquiry; Fettes*
Woosnam, Ian - *Golfer; St Martin's Modern*
Worcester, Marquess of - *Landowner – Badminton; Eton*
Wormald, Peter - *Head of the Census Office; Doncaster GS*
Worsley-Taylor, Annette - *Organiser London Designer Show; Downham, Hatfield Heath*
Worsthorne, Sir Peregrine - *Former Editor Sunday Telegraph; Stowe*
Wragg, Professor Ted - *Director Exeter Univ School of Education; King Edward VII GS, Sheffield*
Wright, Sir Patrick - *Head of Diplomatic Service; Marlborough*
Wright, Billy - *Footballer, former controller of sport ATV; Madeley Secondary Modern*
Wright, Ben - *CBS Golf commentator; Felsted*
Wyatt, Will - *Former MD BBC TV, now Channel 4; Magdalen College Sch*
Wyatt of Weeford, Lord - *Chair The Tote, former Labour MP; Eastbourne College*
Wyman, Bill - *Rolling Stones; Beckenham and Penge GS*
Wyndham, Francis - *Novelist; Eton*

Yarranton, Sir Peter - *Chair The Sports Council; Willesden Technical College*
Yarrow, Sir Eric - *Chair Clydesdale Bank; Marlborough*
Yarwood, Mike - *Impressionst; Bredbury Secondary Modern, Cheshire*
Yates, Ian - *Chief Executive Press Association; Lancaster Royal GS and Canford*
Yates, Rt Rev John - *Former Bishop of Gloucester; Battersea GS and Blackpool GS*
Yentob, Alan - *Controller BBC 2; King's, Ely*
Yeo, Tim MP - *Health Minister; Charterhouse*
York, Michael - *Actor; Hurstpierpoint and Bromley GS*
York, Susannah - *Actress; Marr College, Troon*
York, HRH The Duke of - *; Gordonstoun*
York, HRH The Duchess of - *; Hurst Lodge, Sunningdale*
Young, Lord - *Former Deputy Chair Conservative Party; Christ's College, Finchley*
Young, Baroness - *Former Minister of State Foreign Office; Headington*
Young, Barbara - *Chief Executive RSPB; Perth Academy*
Young, Sir Brian - *Chair Christian Aid; Eton*
Young, Gavin - *Journalist; Rugby*
Young, Sir George - *Conservative MP; Eton*
Young, Hugo - *Journalist; Ampleforth*
Young, Jimmy - *Presenter Jimmy Young Show Radio 2; East Dean GS, Cinderford*
Young, Sir Richard - *Chair Boosey and Hawkes; Bromsgrove*
Young, Sir Roger - *Former Principal George Watson's College; Westminster*
Young of Dartington, Lord - *Director Institute of Community Studies; Dartington Hall*
Younger, Lord - *Former Secretary State for Defence; Winchester*
Yudkin, Professor John - *Professor of nutrition, broadcaster; Grocers Company GS, Hackney Down*

Index of Schools

Abbey, Malvern Wells
Prunella Stack - *President Women's League Health & Beauty*
Abbey, Reading
Baroness Brigstocke - *Former High Mistress St Paul's Girls'*
Abbey Wood, London
Steve Davis - *Snooker player*
Abbots Cross County Technical
David Sullivan - Sunday Sport
Abbotsfield, Hillingdon
Russell Grant - *TV astrologer*
Abbotsholme, Staffordshire
Jeremy Kemp - *Actor*
Aberdare Girls' GS
Professor Gwendolen Rees - *Zoologist*
Aberdeen GS
Robin Cook MP - *Shadow Health Secretary*
Sir Denys Henderson - *Chair ICI*
Aberdeen Girls' HS
Annie Lennox - *Singer Eurhythmics*
Abergele GS
Ralph Steadman - *Illustrator and cartoonist*
Abersychan GS
Lord Jenkins of Hillhead - *Former Deputy Leader The Labour Party*
Abingdon
The Hon Francis Maude - *Former Financial Secretary to Treasury*
Accrington GS
Graham Fowler - *Cricketer*
Accrington Girls' HS
Jeanette Winterson - *Novelist*
Ackworth, Pontefract
Professor Kathleen Tillotson - *Professor Eng Lit London University*
Acland Burghley Comprehensive
Derek Griffiths - *Actor*
Acton GS
Roger Daltrey - *Singer ex-The Who*
Adam's, Newport, Shropshire
Professor Maurice Stacey -
Mason Professor Emeritus Chemistry Birmingham
Addey and Stanhope, London
Nigel Lowery - *Designer English National Opera*
Sir Denis Rooke - *Chair British Gas*

Aida Foster Dancing
        Jean Simmons - *Actress*
Ainslie Park HS, Edinburgh
        Ron Brown - *Former Labour MP*
Albion Central, North London
        Lord Weinstock - *MD GEC*
Aldenham
        Rt Rev Colin James - *Bishop of Winchester*
        General Sir Richard Vincent - *Chief of Defence Staff*
        Ken Warren - *Former Conservative MP*
Alderman Newton's, Leicester
        Geoffrey Parker - *High Master Manchester GS*
        Sir John Plumb - *Former Master Christ's College Cambridge*
        Sir Alan Walters - *Professor Economics, former adviser Mrs Thatcher*
All Saints C of E, Newmarket
        Alan Reynolds - *Painter and printmaker*
Allan Glen's
        Sir Dirk Bogarde - *Actor*
        Professor Kenneth Calman - *Government Chief Medical Officer*
        Dr Alan Sked - *Senior lecturer LSE; Bruges Group*
        Lord Todd - Former Professor Organic Chemistry Cambridge
Allerton HS, Leeds
        Fanny Waterman - *Chair Leeds Piano Competition*
Allertonshire GS
        Ms Alex Greaves - *Jockey*
Alleyne's GS, Stevenage
        Mike Smith - *Chief executive Argos*
Alleyn's
        Rt Hon the Lord Blanch - *Former Archbishop of York*
        Ray Cooney - *Theatre producer*
        Julian Glover - *Actor*
        John Lanchbery - *Conductor and composer*
        Sir Victor Pritchett - *Author*
        Pascale Smets - *Fashion designer*
        John Stride - *Actor*
        Simon Ward - *Actor*
Allhallows
        Peter Birch - *Chief executive Abbey National*
        Sean Day-Lewis - *Journalist and author*
Alloa Academy
        Lord Forte - *Chair Trusthouse Forte*
Alnwick Secondary Modern
        Ann Burdus - *Marketing director, Olympia & York*
Alperton
        Ron Greenwood - *Former Manager England Assoc Football Team*
Alsop HS, Liverpool
        Alexei Sayle - *Comedian*
Altrincham GS
        Paul Allott - *Cricketer*
        Joanna David - *Actress*
Amberfield
        Maggi Hambling - *1st artist in residence National Gallery*

Amman Valley GS
        Alan Watkins - *Political columnist* Observer
Ampleforth
        Sir Anthony Bamford - *Chair and Managing Director of JCB*
        Rt Rev Patrick Barry - *Former Abbot of Ampleforth*
        Michael Brophy - *Director Charities Aid Foundation*
        S.B. De Ferranti - *Former Chair Ferranti plc*
        Rupert Everett - *Actor*
        Desmond Fennell QC - *High Ct Judge King's Cross Fire report*
        Mark Girouard - *Architectural historian*
        Lord Hesketh - *Government Whip House of Lords*
        Andrew Hugh Smith - *Chair International Stock Exchange*
        Cardinal Basil Hume - *Cardinal Archbishop of Westminster*
        Rev Dominic Milroy - *Headmaster Ampleforth*
        Sir Michael Nolan - *Appeal Court Judge*
        The Duke of Norfolk - *Premier RC layman*
        David Peake - *Chair Kleinwort Benson*
        Sir Antony Pilkington - *Chair Pilkington plc*
        Piers Paul Read - *Novelist*
        Patrick Sheehy - *Chair British Allied Tobacco Industries*
        Anthony Simonds-Gooding -
                Former Chair and Ch Exec Saatchi and BSB
        Sir Christopher Tugendhat - *Chair Civil Aviation Authority*
        Lord Windlesham - *Director* Observer, *W.H. Smith, ATV*
        Hugo Young - *Journalist*
Andover GS
        Lord Denning - *Former Master of the Rolls*
Apsley GS, Hemel Hempstead
        Paul Boateng - *Labour MP, TV presenter*
        Angela Heylin - *Chair, chief executive Charles Barker PR*
Arbroath HS
        Michael Forsyth MP - *Minister of State Employment*
Archbishop Temple
        Barry Fantoni - *Cartoonist and* Private Eye *journalist*
Archbishop Tenison's GS
        Tony Banks - *Labour MP*
        Sir Alfred Shepperd - *Chair Wellcome Foundation*
Ardingly College
        Bill Cotton - *Director Noel Gay TV*
        John Hayes - *Director The National Portrait Gallery*
        Ian Hislop - *Editor* Private Eye, *writer* Spitting Image
        Alan Howard - *Actor*
        Stephen Oliver - *Composer, especially opera*
Ardwyn GS, Aberystwyth
        John Morris QC MP - *Labour Party Spokesman Legal Affairs*
Arnold, Blackpool
        Chris Lowe - *Pop singer Pet Shop Boys*
Arnold Girls HS, Blackpool
        Margaret Maden - *County Education Officer Warwickshire CC*
        Elaine Padmore - *Opera singer, Director Wexford Festival Opera*
Arts Educational
        Beryl Bainbridge - *Writer*

Arts Educational—*contd*
      Claire Bloom - *Actress*
      Darcey Bussell - *Ballerina Royal Ballet*
      Tracy Edwards - *Round the world yachtswoman*
      Liza Goddard - *Actress*
      Nigel Havers - *Actor*
      Cherie Lunghi - *Actress*
      Sarah Miles - *Actress*
      Jane Seymour - *Actress*
      Antoinette Sibley - *Prima ballerina*
      Valerie Singleton - *TV journalist* and *broadcaster*
Ashburton, Croydon
      Harry Carpenter - *Sports commentator*
      John Surtees - *Former racing car driver*
Ashby de la Zouch Girls' HS
      Averil Burgess – *Headmistress South Hampstead Girls' HS*
Ashford County GS
      Norman Willis - *General Secretary TUC*
Ashford County Girls' GS Kent
      Carole Stone - *TV interviewer, ex-producer* Any Questions
Ashford Girls', Kent
      Pamela Armstrong - *ITN newscaster*
Ashleigh House, Belfast
      Heather Harper - *Soprano*
Ashley Secondary
      Maureen Hicks - *Conservative MP*
Ashlyns Secondary Modern, Berkhamsted
      Derek Fowlds - *Actor*
Ashton Road Secondary, Castleford
      Malcolm Reilly - *England rugby team coach*
Ashton under Lyne GS
      David Styan - *Chair Govt Task Force school management*
Ashton-in-Makerfield GS, Nr Wigan
      Sir Eldon Griffiths - *Former Conservative MP*
Ashville College, Harrogate
      Sir Alastair Burnett - *Former ITN newsreader*
      Geoffrey Haslam - *Director Prudential Assurance Co Ltd*
Aske's GS, Hatcham
      Lord Wedderburn of Charlton - *Professor of Commercial Law LSE*
Athelney Street, Bellingham
      Henry Cooper - *Boxer*
Attleborough Secondary, Norfolk
      John Fashanu - *Wimbledon centre forward, Direc Kiss FM*
Austin Friars, Carlisle
      Dr Giles Mercer - *Headmaster Stonyhurst*
Aylesbury GS
      John Junkin - *Actor and scriptwriter*
Ayr Academy
      William Brown - *UK's highest-paid insurance director*
      Sir Andrew Watt Kay - *Regius Professor Surgery Glasgow Univ*
      Lord Perry - *Former Vice Chancellor Open University*

Barry GS—*contd*
      Sir Keith Thomas - *Historian, President, Corpus Christi College, Oxford*
Bath HS
      Lady Howe - *Former Dep Chair Equal Opportunities Cttee*
Battersea GS
      Maurice Cowling MP -
            Fellow, Peterhouse, Cambridge, Conservative historian
      Michael Bryant - *Actor*
      Philip Jones - *Principal Trinity College of Music*
      Rt Rev John Yates - *Former Bishop of Gloucester*
Baylis Court Secondary Modern, Slough
      Una Stubbs - *Actress*
Beal GS, Ilford
      Bill Hagerty - *Editor* The People
Bearsden Academy
      Pam Hogg - *Fashion designer*
Beath HS, Cowdenbeath
      Sir James Black - *Professor of Analytical Pharmacology London*
Beaumont
      Rev Michael Campbell-Johnson - *Provincial Superior British Jesuits*
      Monsignor Alfred Gilbey -
            Former R.C. Chaplain, Cambridge University
      Father Michael Hollings - *Writer, RC parish priest Bayswater*
      Professor Peter Levi - *Poet*
      John Mathew QC - *Barrister*
      Sir Patrick Sergeant - *Chair Euromoney Publications*
Beckenham and Penge GS
      Derek Barron - *Chair and chief executive Ford Motor Co*
      Chris Orr - *Artist and print maker*
      Derek Underwood - *Cricketer*
      Bill Wyman - *Rolling Stones*
Becket GS, Nottingham
      Michael Jayston - *Actor*
Beckfoot Cumbria GS
      Robert Smith - *Show jumper*
Bedales
      Lady Sarah Armstrong-Jones - *Artist*
      Sir Thomas Arnold - *Conservative MP*
      Gyles Brandreth -
            Conservative MP, Author, broadcaster, journalist, producer
      Sir Michael Caine - *Chair Booker*
      Amanda Craig - *Writer*
      Daniel Day-Lewis - *Actor*
      Viscount Linley - *Cabinet maker*
      Tamsin Olivier - *Actress*
      Mary Ann Sieghart - *Assistant Editor* The Times
Bede College, Durham
      Lord Glenamara -
            Former Education Secretary, Chancellor, Newcastle Polytechnic
Bede GS, Sunderland
      James Bolam - *Actor*
      Alan Brien - *Journalist*

Bembridge, Isle of Wight—*contd*
  Lord Foot – *President UK Immigrants Advisory Service*
  Michael Relph - *Film director*
Bemrose, Derby
  James Bolam - *Actor*
Benenden
  HRH Princess Anne
  Liz Forgan - *Director programming Channel 4*
  Joanna Foster - *Chair Equal Opportunities Commission*
  Baroness Ryder - *Fdr Sue Ryder Charitable Foundation*
Berkhamsted
  Sir Colin Buchanan - *Urban planner*
  Professor Alexander Goehr - *Professor Music Cambridge University*
  Tarn Hodder - *Chair Hockey Association*
  Antony Hopkins - *Composer* and *conductor*
  Clive Jacobs - *Broadcaster*
  Robin Knox-Johnston - *Single-handed yachtsman*
  Stuart Lipton - *Chair Stanhope Properties plc*
  Michael Meacher MP - *Shadow Minister for Social Security*
Bexley GS
  Alexander Stuart - *Novelist*
  Joan Thirkettle - *TV reporter*
Bifrons Secondary Modern, Barking
  Most Rev George Carey - *Archbishop of Canterbury*
Bilborough GS
  Rosie Barnes - *Former Liberal Democrat MP*
Bingley GS
  Professor Sir Fred Hoyle - *Astronomer*
  Austin Mitchell - *Labour MP, broadcaster*
Birchfield Road School, Aston, Birmingham
  Ozzy Osbourne - *Singer*
Birkenhead
  Rt Hon Lord Justice Donald Nicholls - *Appeal Court Judge*
  Andreas Whittam-Smith - *Editor* Independent
Birtley Lord Lawson Comprehensive
  Bryan Robson - *England Football Captain*
Bishop Auckland Girls' GS
  Professor Elizabeth Robson -
    Head of Genetics University College London
Bishop Fox's, Taunton
  Sheila Kitzinger - *Writer and birth educator*
Bishop Gore GS, Swansea
  Peter Dawson - *General Scty Prof Association Teachers*
  Lord Flowers - *Former Vice Chancellor Univ of London*
Bishop Vesey's GS, Sutton Coldfield
  Michael Brener - *Director of Music Chetham's Music School*
  John Leese - *Former Editor* Evening Standard
Bishop Wordsworth GS, Salisbury
  Rt Rev Mervyn Alexander - *RC Bishop of Clifton*
  David Boston - *Director Horniman Museum* and *Library*
  Richard Hill - *England rugby scrum half*

Bishop's Stortford College
       John Clement - *Chair Unigate Group*
       Dr John Rae - *Former Head Westminster, Direc Portman Group*
Blackburn GS
       Robert Evans - *Chair British Gas plc*
Blackburn HS
       Audrey Eyton - *Diet writer, F-plan diet*
Blackfriars, Northants
       Luke Rittner - *Former Arts Council Secretary General*
Blackpool GS
       David Atherton - *Conductor*
       Alistair Cooke - *Broadcaster* Letter from America
       Roger Uttley - *Rugby player; Director PE Harrow School*
       Rt Rev John Yates - *Former Bishop of Gloucester*
Blaenavon Secondary
       Joan Lestor - *Labour MP*
Blatchington Court, Seaford
       Patricia Tindale - *Chief architect Department Environment*
Blencathra, Rhyl
       Penelope Mortimer - *Writer*
Blessed Edward Jones HS, Rhyl
       Carol Vorderman - *TV Presenter Channel 4* Countdown
Blessed Sacrament Convent, Sussex
       Yve Newbold - *Company Secretary Hanson plc*
Bloxham
       Ron Hayward - *Former General Secretary Labour Party*
Blundell's
       Hon Sir Alastair Forbes - *President Court of Appeal Falklands Is*
       Robert Fox - *Broadcaster*
       John Gray - *Ambassador to OECD*
       David Jewell - *Head Haileybury, former Chair HMC*
       Professor John Jones - *Professor of Poetry Oxford University*
       Vic Marks - *Cricketer*
       Michael Mates MP - *Minister of State, Northern Ireland*
       Professor Robin Skynner -
              Psychiatrist (Families and How to Survive Them)
       Lord Stokes - *Company chairman, Dutton Forshaw*
       General Sir Walter Walker -
              Former C in C Allied Forces North Europe
Blyth GS, Norwich
       Wendy Cooling - *Head of Children's Book Foundation*
Bolton
       Gordon Clough - *Broadcaster*
       Wade Dooley - *England rugby player*
       Sir Robert Haslam - *Chair British Coal*
       Sir Ian McKellen - *Actor*
       Nigel Short - *Chess champion*
Bolton County GS
       Johnny Ball - *Children's TV presenter*
Bolton Girls'
       Rabbi Sybil Sheridan - *Rabbi*
       Ann Taylor - *Labour MP*

Bootham
        Lord Rix - *Actor, Chairman MENCAP*
        Professor John Thoday - *Emeritus Professor Genetics Cambridge*
Bootle GS
        George Davies - *Former chief executive Next stores*
Borden GS, Sittingbourne
        James Bostock - *Painter and engraver*
        Rev Prof Ronald Preston - *Professor Theology Manchester University*

Boroughmuir, Edinburgh
        Annette Crosbie - *Actress*
Boswells Comprehensive, Chelmsford
        Scott Sherrin - *Presenter* That's Life
Bournemouth GS
        Sir David English - *Editor* Daily Mail
        Sir Paul Fox - *Chair Channel 4*
        Stanley Goodchild - *Chief Education Officer Berkshire*
Bournemouth HS
        Dilys Powell - *Film critic*
Bourneville Boys' Technical, Birmingham
        Ian Lavender - *Actor*
Bracondale, Norwich
        John Edrich - *Cricketer*
Bradfield
        Richard Adams - *Author* Watership Down
        Rev John Drury - *Biblical scholar*
        Walter Merricks - *Assistant Secretary General Law Society*
        Rt Hon Sir John Nott - *Chair Channel Tunnel Commission*
        Professor Desmond Nuttall - *Dir Centre for Educational Research LSE*
        Lord Owen - *Co-founder SDP, former Foreign Secretary*
        Snoo Wilson - *Playwright*
Bradford Civic Theatre School
        Robert Stephens - *Actor*
Bradford GS
        Lord Bullock - *Historian, former Vice Chancellor Oxford*
        Francis Durbridge - *Playwright* and *author*
        Professor H.L.A. Hart - *Law scholar, former Principal BNC Oxford*
        Lord Healey - *Former Deputy Leader Labour Party*
        David Hockney - *Artist*
        Malcolm Laycock - *Head of programming Jazz FM radio*
        Air Vice Marshal Anthony Mason - *Former Air Secretary*
        Adrian Moorhouse - *Swimmer*
        Aubrey Singer - *Director Goldcrest Films* and *TV*
        Michael Wharton - *Former 'Peter Simple' columnist* Daily Telegraph
Bradford Girls' GS
        Baroness Barbara Castle - *MEP, Former Labour Minister*
Braeside, Buckhurst
        Yvette Fielding - *Presenter* Blue Peter *Children's TV*
        Louise Jameson - *Actress*
Breckenbeds Junior HS, Gateshead
        Paul Gascoigne - *Footballer*

Brockenhurst GS—*contd*
>Ian Wooldridge - *Sports columnist* Daily Mail

Brockley County, London
>Alan Brownjohn - *Poet*

Brockworth Comprehensive
>Richard Phelps - *Pentathlete*

Bromley County Girls'
>Miss Read - *Writer on village life*

Bromley GS
>Rt Rev Michael Baughen - *Bishop of Chester*
>Michael York - *Actor*

Bromsgrove
>Lord Boardman - *Director National Westminster Bank*
>Ian Carmichael - *Actor*
>Phil Drabble - *TV commentator*
>Trevor Eve - *Actor*
>Sir Richard Young - *Chair Boosey and Hawkes*

Brondesbury and Kilburn Girls'
>Twiggy - *Actress, singer, former model*

Brooke House, London
>Alan Sugar - *Chair Amstrad plc*

Brooklands College
>Sir Robin Auld - *Judge, Brixton riots enquiry*

Broughton HS
>David Murray - *Chair Murray International; Rangers FC*

Broughton Secondary
>Shelagh Delaney - *Playwright*

Brownhill Road, London
>Alan Brownjohn - *Poet*

Bryanston
>Jasper Conran - *Fashion designer*
>Sir Terence Conran - *Former Chair Storehouse plc*
>Mark Elder - *Musical Director English National Opera*
>John Eliot Gardiner - *Conductor, Founder English Baroque group*
>David Gestetner - *Chair Gestetner Holdings plc*
>Simon Relph - *Film director*
>Bill Robinson - *Special Adviser Chancellor; Ex-direc IFS*
>Dr Frederick Sanger - *Chemist, first to show protein structure*
>Robert Saxton - *Composer*
>Quinlan Terry - *Architect*
>Mark Wigglesworth - *Conductor*

Burford GS, Oxfordshire
>Paul Eddery - *Jockey*

Burlington College
>Sir David Napley - *Solicitor*

Burnage GS, Manchester
>Sir Norman Foster - *Architect*

Bury GS
>Sir David Trippier - *Former Minister for the Environment*

Bury Girls' GS
>Victoria Wood - *Comedienne*

Bush Davies
Doreen Wells - *Dancer Royal Ballet, actress*
Bushmead, Huntingdon
Wayne Larkins - *Cricketer*
Bushey Meads, Herts
George Michael - *Pop singer*
Butler's Mead Secondary
Ian Botham - *Cricketer*
Byron House, Hampstead
Elizabeth Taylor - *Film star*

Caistor GS, Lincolnshire
Rev Prof Ronald Preston - *Professor Theology Manchester University*
Calday Grange GS
Sir David Weatherall - *Geneticist*
Caldecot, Lambeth
Sir Kenneth Oxford - *Former Chief Constable Merseyside*
Cambridge Girls' HS
P.D. James - *Crime novelist*
Joan Sadler - *Former Principal Cheltenham Ladies' College*
Cambridgeshire HS
Malcolm Gill - *Chief Cashier Bank of England*
Camden Girls' HS
Frances Crook - *Director Howard League for Penal Reform*
Campbell College, Belfast
Mark Lambert - *Actor*
Campion, Leamington Spa
Eddie Hemmings - *Cricketer*
Camrose, Edgware
Tommy Nutter - *Savile Row tailor*
Canford
Sir Ashley Bramall - *Ex chair GLC and ILEA, former Labour MP*
Henry Cecil - *Racehorse trainer*
John Drummond - *former controller Music BBC Radio 3*
Derek Hornby - *Chair Rank Xerox UK*
Simon Preston - *Organist*
Stephen Rubin - *Chair Pentland Industries (Reebok shoes)*
Ian Yates - *Chief Executive Press Association*
Cardiff Girls' HS
Bernice Rubens - *Novelist*
Cardiff HS
Geraint Davies - *Controller BBC Wales*
John Humphrys - *Radio 4 presenter*
Professor Josephson - *Physicist*
Cardigan County
Alun Owen - *Playwright* and *screenplay writer*
Carlisle County Girls' HS
Margaret Forster - *Novelist and biographer*
Jancis Robinson - Financial Times *Wine expert*
Carlisle GS
Geoff Cooke - *Manager England Rugby Team*

Carlisle GS—*contd*
      Hunter Davies - *Writer and journalist*
Carrickvale Secondary
      Graeme Souness - *Former Rangers manager, now Liverpool*
Castle Bar, London
      Joan Hickson - *Actress*
Catford Secondary
      Brian Basham - *Founder, MD Broad Street PR company*
Catholic GS, London
      Tony Slattery - *Comedian*
Cavendish
      Robert Smith - *Show jumper*
Cedarhurst, Solihull
      Sir Anthony Beaumont-Dark - *Former Conservative MP*
Central Foundation, London
      Ronnie Scott - *jazz musician, nightclub proprietor*
      Richard Seifert - *Architect*
      Sir Michael Sobell - *Chair GEC*
Central HS, Newcastle
      Jean Rankine - *Deputy Director The British Museum*
Central, Sheffield
      Lord Dainton - *Chemist, Chancellor Sheffield University*
Central Technical, Sheffield
      Tony Mooney - *Head Rutlish School*
Channing, London
      Drusilla Beyfus - *Writer, broadcaster, former editor* Vogue
      Baroness Cox - *Deputy Speaker House of Lords*
Charlton Park Convent, Cheltenham
      Lucy Soutter - *International squash player*
Charterhouse
      Sir John Banham - *Chair CBI*
      Lord Beaverbrook -
            Chair Beaverbrook Fndn; Dep Chair Conservative Party
      Anthony Berry - *Chair Berry Bros Wine Merchants*
      Sir Anthony Caro - *Sculptor*
      Lt Gen Sir Hugh Cunningham - *Former Lieutenant Tower of London*
      Rev Don Cupitt - *Dean Emmanuel Cambridge, divinity lecturer*
      Lord Dacre - *Former Regius Professor of Modern History, and former*
            Master, Peterhouse, Cambridge
      Peter De Savary - *International entrepreneur*
      Jonathan Dimbleby - *Broadcaster, journalist* and *author*
      David Dimbleby - *Broadcaster* and *newspaper proprietor*
      Lord Donaldson of Lymington - *Master of the Rolls*
      Peter Gabriel - *Singer ex-Genesis*
      Rt Hon Lord Justice Ralph Gibson - *Judge of Court of Appeal*
      Sir Allan Green QC - *Former Director of Public Prosecutions*
      Lord Griffiths - *Law Lord*
      Max Hastings - *Editor* Daily Telegraph
      Nicky Henson - *Actor*
      David Hicks - *Interior designer*
      Sir Geoffrey Johnson-Smith - *Conservative MP*
      Sir Timothy Kitson - *Former MP, Director Leeds Building Soc*

Sir David Lees - *Chair GKN plc*
Peter May - *Cricketer*
Sir Robin McAlpine - *Former Chair Robert McAlpine & Sons*
Sir Ronald Millar - *Playwright; former speech writer Mrs Thatcher*
Sir Harry Oppenheimer - *Former Chairman of Anglo-American
        Corporation*
Peter O'Sullevan - *Racing commentator*
Hon Sir Oliver Popplewell - *High Court Judge Queen's Bench Division*
Lord Prior - *Chair GEC*
Adam Raphael - *Executive Editor* Observer
Frederic Raphael - *Writer*
Simon Raven - *Novelist and playwright*
Lord Rees-Mogg - *Chair Broadcasting Standards Council*
Dick Taverne - *Former Labour Minister, former Indep SD MP*
Lord Wakeham MP - *Lord Privy Seal* and *Leader of the House of Lords*
Ian Wallace - *Singer and broadcaster*
Tim Yeo MP - *Health Minister*
Chartesey Secondary Shoreditch
        Frank Johnson - *Associate Editor* Sunday Telegraph
Chatham House, Ramsgate
        Sir Edward Heath - *Former Prime Minister*
        Frank Muir - *Writer and broadcaster*
        Rev Dr Edward Norman - *Dean of Chapel Christchurch Canterbury*
Chelmsford County Girls' HS
        Lady Marre - *Chair Cttee on Future Legal Profession*
        Sarah Tyacke - *First female keeper Public Record Office*
Cheltenham College
        Lindsay Anderson - *Film and theatre director*
        Nigel Davenport - *Actor*
        Vivian Ellis - *Composer*
        Professor H.L.A. Hart -
                Academic laywer, former Principal BNC Oxford
        Rt Hon Michael Jopling - *Former Secretary of State for Agriculture*
        Leonard Manasseh - *Architect*
        Major General Sir Jeremy Moore -
                Commander Land Forces Falklands War
Cheltenham GS
        Desmond Wilcox - *TV reporter, producer* and *presenter*
Cheltenham Ladies' College
        Rosie Boycott - *Writer and feminist, Editor* Esquire
        Katharine Hamnett - *Fashion designer*
        Lady Oppenheimer - *Writer, moral and philosophical theology*
        Bridget Riley - *Artist*
        Rosemary Anne Sisson - *Novelist* and *scriptwriter*
Chester City GS
        Mary Whitehouse - *Gen Sec Nat Viewers & Listeners Assoc*
Chesterfield GS
        Geoff Miller - *Cricketer*
        Sir David Walker - *Chair Securities & Investments Board*
Chetham's
        Peter Donohoe - *Pianist*
        Anna Markland - *Concert pianist*

Chetham's—*contd*

Chichester HS
- A.W. Marsh - *Musical director The Old Vic*

Chichester HS
- Howard Brenton - *Playwright*
- Douglas Bunn - *Chair All Eng Jumping Course Hickstead*
- Adrian Noble - *Director RSC*
- David Wood - *Actor, playwright, composer* and *producer*

Chigwell
- Michael Gough Matthews - *Director Royal College of Music*
- Ian Holm - *Actor*
- Professor Bernard Williams - *Professor of Philosophy Oxford*

Chingford
- ACM Sir Peter Harding - *Chief of Air Staff*
- Leslie Phillips - *Actor*

Chislehurst HS
- Audrey Slaughter - *Journalist, Former Editor* Honey *magazine*

Chiswick County Boys'
- Brian Tesler - *Chair LWT*

Chiswick Polytechnic
- Angela Pleasence - *Actress*

Christian Brothers', Belfast
- Lord Fitt - *former SLDP MP*

Christ's College, Brecon
- Simon Hughes - *LD MP*

Christ College, Finchley
- Professor Malcolm Fraser - *Chair BTEC*
- David Freeman - *Solicitor D.J. Freeman & Co*
- Harvey Goldsmith - *Entrepreneur*
- Stanley Kalms - *Founder, Chair Dixons Stores*
- Sir John Kingman - *Vice Chancellor Bristol University*
- Charles Saatchi - *Founder Saatchi Brothers Advertising*
- Rabbi Jonathan Sacks - *Chief Rabbi*
- Sir Peter Strawson - *Professor Metaphysical Philosophy Oxford*
- Desmond Wilcox - *TV reporter, producer* and *presenter*
- Lord Young - *Former Deputy Chair Conservative Party*

Christ's Hospital
- Sir Colin Davis - *Conductor*
- Patrick Deuchar - *Chief executive Royal Albert Hall*
- John Edmonds - *Trade unionist*
- Clive Exton - *Playwright* and *scriptwriter*
- Sir William Glock - *Music critic, former director Bath Festival*
- Jane Goodsir - *Director RELEASE drugs rehabilitation*
- Professor Margaret Gowing - *Professor History of Science Oxford*
- Stephen Hayklan - *Chair Wiggins Construction Co*
- Robert Heller - *Editor* Finance *magazine*
- Bernard Levin - *Journalist, author and broadcaster*
- Bryan Magee - *TV journalist, author, former Labour MP*
- Michael Marland - *Head North Westminster Community School*
- Dennis Silk - *Former Warden Radley College*
- Francis Warner - *Poet* and *dramatist*

Christ's Hospital, Lincoln
- Steve Race - *Musician* and *broadcaster*

Church Road Secondary Modern, Birmingham
      Moss Evans - *Trade unionist*
City College, Norwich
      Lord Rayner - *Former Chair Marks and Spencer*
City GS, Sheffield
      Roger Singleton - *Director Barnardos*
City, Lincoln
      Roy Sowden - *Former Dir Centre Study Comprehensive Schls*
City of Bath
      Sir Roger Bannister - *4-minute miler; neurologist*
      Sir Gordon Cox - *Chemist*
      Colin Tweedy - *Chair Assoc Business Sponsorship of Arts*
City of Leicester GS
      Stephen Buckley - *Artist*
      Michael Kitchen - *Actor*
      Gary Lineker - *Footballer*
City of London
      Sir Kingsley Amis - *Writer*
      Rev Brian Beck - *Secretary The Methodist Conference*
      Mike Brearley - *Cricketer*
      William Davis - *Author, journalist* and *broadcaster*
      Sir John Davis - *Director The Rank Foundation*
      Victor Hochhauser - *Impresario*
      Lord Judd - *Director OXFAM*
      Anthony Lester QC - *Barrister*
      Sir Peter Levene - *Chman Docklands Light Railway*
      Lord Mishcon - *Labour Spokesman House of Lords*
      Martin Neary - *Master Choristers Westminster Abbey*
      Dennis Norden - *Scriptwriter* and *broadcaster*
City of London Girls'
      Elizabeth Emanuel - *Fashion designer*
      Claire Rayner - *Broadcaster, journalist* and *agony aunt*
      Professor Margaret Turner-Warwick -
              President Royal College of Physicians
City of Norwich HS
      Professor David Holbrook -
              English scholar, Emeritus Fellow Downing College, Cambridge
City of Oxford
      Professor Heinz Wolff - *Director Brunel Institute for Bioengineering*
Claremont Farm Court, Esher
      Michaela Strachan - *TV presenter*
Clifton
      Lord Bernstein - *President Granada Group plc*
      John Cleese - *Actor*
      Roger Cooper - *Businessman* and *Iranian hostage*
      Lord Jenkin - *Former Secretary of State for Energy, Environment*
      Sir John Kendrew - *Molecular biologist*
      Dr Lionel Kopelowitz - *President Board Deputies British Jews*
      The Rt Hon Sir John May -
              Former Lord Justice of Appeal, Enquiry Guildford 4
      Sir Nevill Mott - *Physicist Cavendish Laboratory Cambridge*
      Sir Peter Newsam - *Director London Institute of Education*

Clifton—*contd*
    Stephen Pile - *Journalist*
    Professor Sir Brian Pippard - *Emeritus Professor of Physics Cambridge*
    Richard Stott - *Editor* Daily Mirror
    John Wilkins - *Editor* The Tablet
    Sir David Willcocks - *Musical Director The Bach Choir*
    Sir David Wolfson - *Chair Next plc*
Clifton Comprehensive, Rotherham
    Elizabeth Coldwell - *Editor* Forum *magazine*
Clifton Girls' HS
    Jo Durie - *Tennis player*
    Dame Helen Gardiner - *English literature scholar*
Clydesbank HS
    Gavin Laird - *Trade union Leader Amalgamated Enginrs*
Coatbridge
    David Donaldson - *Portrait painter*
    Sir Adam Thomson - *Former Chair British Caledonian*
Coatham
    Lord Bancroft - *Former Head of The Home Civil Service*
    Sir Rex Hunt - *Former Governor Falklands*
    Lord Pennock - *Director Morgan Grenfell*
Cobham Hall
    Mary Ann Sieghart - *Assistant Editor* The Times
Cockburn HS, Leeds
    Willis Hall - *Playwright*
Colchester Boys' HS
    Tony Gill - *Head of Lucas plc*
Colchester County High School for Girls
    Rachel Kempson - *Actress*
Coleraine Academical Institution
    Ian Langtry - *Education Officer Assoc. of County Councils*
Colfe's GS
    Eric Ambler - *Novelist* and *screenwriter*
    Sir Alan Goodison - *Chair The Wates Foundation*
Colf's GS, Lewisham Hill (destroyed War)
    Norman Hepple - *Portrait painter*
Colne GS
    Jack Rosenthal - *TV dramatist*
Colston's, Bristol
    Chris Broad - *Cricketer*
    John Mason - Daily Telegraph *cricket correspondent*
    Simon Mugglestone - *International athlete*
Colwyn Bay GS
    Her Honour Judge Myrella Cohen QC - *Circuit judge*
Colyton GS, Devon
    Sir Rex Richards - *Director The Leverhulme Trust*
Commonweal Lodge, Surrey
    Angharad Rees - *Actress*
Conv. Immaculate Heart Mary, Billingshurst
    Anna Calder-Marshall - *Actress*
Convent of the Holy Family, Exmouth
    Dame Elisabeth Frink - *Sculptor*

Coopers Company
   Bernard Bresslaw - *Actor*
Copthall GS for Girls, Mill Hill
   Professor Morna Hooker - *Professor Divinity Cambridge University*
Cork GS
   Joss Ackland - *Actor*
Corona Stage
   Judy Geeson - *Actress*
   Susan George - *Actress*
Cotham GS, Bristol
   Leslie Hill - *MD Central TV*
   Philip Jones - *Principal Trinity College of Music*
   Gary Mabbutt - *Footballer Captain Spurs*
   John Tidmarsh - *Presenter* Outlook *BBC World Service*
Cottingley Middle Cumbria
   Robert Smith - *Showjumper*
Council school, left at 13
   Sir Julian Hodge - *Merchant banker*
Coundon Court Comprehensive
   Dr Marjorie Mowlam - *MP Labour front bench City spokesperson*
Coventry GS
   Susan Hill - *Novelist* and *playwright*
Cowbridge GS
   Anthony Hopkins - *Actor*
   Sir Idwal Pugh - *Former Ombudsman*
Cowes Senior, Isle of Wight
   Cliff Michelmore - *Broadcaster*
Craigmount Hawick
   Ferelith Lean - *Founder Glasgow Mayfest*
Cranbrook
   General Sir John Akehurst - *Former NATO Commander*
   Phil Edmonds - *Cricketer*
   Brian Moore - *LWT football commentator*
   Peter West - *Sports commentator*
   Charles Wheeler - *Freelance broadcaster*, Newsnight *etc*
Cranleigh
   Canon Anthony Caesar - *Domestic Chaplain to HM The Queen*
   David Calcutt QC - *Barrister, Master Magdalene Cambridge*
Craven Park, London
   Dennis Norden - *Scriptwriter* and *broadcaster*
Creighton, Carlisle
   Hunter Davies - *Writer and journalist*
Crofton Grange, Herts
   Sarah Miles - *Actress*
   Rose Tremain - *Novelist, radio dramatist*
Cromwell, Chatteris, Cambridgeshire
   Dave 'Boy' Green - *Boxer*
Cronk Y Voddy, Isle of Man
   Professor Sir Randolph Quirk - *Former President British Academy*
Crosby House, Bournemouth
   Peter Alliss - *Golfer* and *TV commentator*

Crouch End Secondary Modern, Hornsey
>Edward Bond - *Playwright* and *director*

Croydon Comprehensive
>Kirsty McColl - *Singer*

Croydon Girls' HS
>Jane Drew - *Architect*
>Penelope Mortimer - *Writer*
>Dr Wendy Savage - *Obstetrician and gynaecologist*

Croydon Secondary Technical
>Roy Hudd - *Actor*

Crypt GS, Gloucester
>David Terry - *Principal Halesowen Tertiary College*

Culford
>Sir David Plastow - *Chair Vickers plc*
>Admiral Sir Derek Reffell - *Governor and C-in-C Gibraltar*

Culverhouse Comprehensive
>Fatima Whitbread - *Javelin champion*

Cumbernauld HS
>Isobel Buchanan - *Soprano*

Dagenham County HS
>Roy Greenslade - *Former editor* Daily Mirror
>Rev Canon Eric James - *Chaplain HM The Queen; Direc Christian Actn*
>Dudley Moore - *Actor* and *composer*

Dalriada GS, Ballymoney, Northern Ireland
>Martyn Lewis - *Newsreader*

Dalston County Secondary
>Marjorie Proops - *Agony aunt* Daily Mirror

Dalziel HS, Motherwell
>Sir Alexander Gibson - *Founder, musical director Scottish Opera*

Dame Alice Harpur, Bedford
>Jean Muir - *Fashion designer*

Dame Alice Owen's
>Joss Ackland - *Actor*
>Dame Beryl Grey - *Former artistic Dir London Festival Ballet*

Dame Allan's, Newcastle
>Professor Arthur Bell - *Biochemist*
>Dr Richard Laws - *Director British Antarctic Survey*
>Sir David Lumsden - *Principal Royal Academy of Music*
>Canon Peter Pilkington -
>>*Former High Master St Paul's: Chair Broadcasting Complaints Commission*
>Sir Michael Scott - *Former Gen Sec Royal Commonwealth Society*

Dane County Secondary, Essex
>John Lever - *Cricketer*

Daniel Stewart's, Edinburgh
>Finlay Calder - *Captain British Lions*
>Andrew Faulds - *Labour MP* and *film actor*
>Renton Laidlaw - *Golf commentator*
>Very Rev James Whyte -
>>*Former Moderator Gen Assembly Church of Scotland*

David Wilkie - *Swimmer*
Darlington GS
    Chapman Pincher - *Journalist*
Darlington Girls' HS
    Elizabeth Esteve-Coll - *Director Victoria and Albert Museum*
Dartford GS
    Terence Frisby - *Playwright, actor, producer*
Dartford GS for Girls
    Sheila Hancock - *Actress*
    Diana Quick - *Actress*
Dartford West Secondary
    Graham Dilley - *Cricketer*
Dartington Hall
    Joanna Drew - *Director The Hayward Gallery*
    Claire Tomalin - *Writer*
    Lord Young of Dartington - *Director Institute of Community Studies*
Darwen GS, Lancashire
    Doreen Massey - *Director Family Planning Association*
Dauntsey's
    Rev Wilbert Awdry - *Author* Thomas the Tank Engine
    David Leach - *Potter*
    John Makepeace - *Furniture designer*
    Adrian Mitchell - *Writer*
    Dr Desmond Morris - *Zoologist and author*
Davenant GS, London
    David Langdon - *Cartoonist* Punch, Sunday Mirror
Dayton and intermediate schools, Guernsey
    Roy Dotrice - *Actor*
De Aston, Lincolnshire
    Lord White - *Chair Hanson Industries*
De La Salle College
    Dr Terry Eagleton - *Professor English Literature Oxford*
    Brian Wildsmith - *Illustrator*
De La Warr, East Grinstead
    Josephine Veasey - *Opera singer*
Deacons, Peterborough
    Leonard Rosoman - *Mural and portrait painter*
Dean Close, Cheltenham
    Francis Bacon - *Artist*
    John Simpson - *Co-Editor Oxford English Dictionary*
    Rt Rev James Thompson - *Bishop of Bath & Wells, ex Bishop Stepney*
Denbigh GS
    Osian Ellis - *Harpist*
Denstone College
    Rear Admiral Peter Hammersley -
        Director Brit Marine Equipment Council
    Dr Tommy Kemp - *Rugby player, physician*
    John Makepeace - *Furniture designer*
    David Venables - *Official Solicitor to Supreme Court*
Dewsbury College of Commerce and Art
    Betty Boothroyd - *Speaker, House of Commons*

Dialystone Lane, Stockport
        Peter Howard - *Editor* Jane's Defence Weekly
Dominican College, Brewood, Staffs
        Elizabeth Appleby QC - *Barrister*
Dominican Convent, Chingford
        Rowanne Pasco - *Religious editor TV AM*
Doncaster GS
        Sir Ron Dearing - *Chair Universities Funding Council*
        Peter Wormald - *Head of the Census Office*
Doncaster Road Secondary Mod, Scunthorpe
        Tony Jacklin - *Golfer*
Dorking GS
        Tom Mangold - *TV reporter* Panorama
        Colin Smith - *Chief Constable Thames Valley Police*
Douai
        Peter Blackburn - *Chief Executive Nestlé UK, Chair Rowntree*
        Brandon Gough - *Chair Coopers and Lybrand accountants*
        P.J. Kavanagh - *Writer*
        Frank Keating - *Sports columnist the* Guardian
Douglas HS, Isle of Man
        Professor Frank Kermode - *Professor English Literature*
        Professor Sir Randolph Quirk - *Former President Royal Academy*
Dover College
        Michael Weston - *British Ambassador in Kuwait*
        Admiral Sir Peter White - *Former Director Fleet Services*
Dover GS
        Hon Mr Justice Mummery - *High Court Judge Chancery Division*
        John Russell-Taylor - *Art critic* The Times
Downe House
        Felicity Clark - *Director Royal Opera House Covent Garden*
        Baroness Jane Ewart-Biggs MP -
                Labour Party spokesperson Home Affairs
        Geraldine James - *Actress*
        Dame Rosemary Murray - *Former Vice Chancellor Cambridge Univ*
        Lady Plowden - *Educationist*
Downham, Hatfield Heath
        Annette Worsley-Taylor - *Organiser London Designer Show*
Downhills Central, Tottenham
        Stan Mendham - *Chief Exec Forum of Private Business*
        Lord Willis - *Playwright, Labour peer*
Downs, Seaford
        Joanna Richardson - *Writer*
Downside
        Rudolph Agnew - *Chair TVS*
        Rupert Allason - *Conservative MP*
        Most Rev Michael Bowen - *RC Archbishop of Southwark*
        Most Rev Maurice Couve de Murville - *RC Archbishop of Birmingham*
        Rocco Forte - *Chief executive Trusthouse Forte*
        Simon Halliday - *Rugby international*
        Dom Philip Jebb - *Former Headmaster Downside*
        Mark Landini - *Joint Managing Director Conran Design*
        Professor Nicholas Lash - *Professor Divinity Cambridge University*

David Mlinaric - *Interior designer*
William Nicholson - *Playwright*
Michael Noakes - *Portrait and landscape painter*
Sir John Pope-Hennessy - *Art historian*
Very Rev Timothy Radcliffe - *Provincial of the Dominicans*
Lord Rawlinson QC - *Former Attorney General*
Rt Rev John Roberts - *Former Abbot of Downside*
Auberon Waugh - *Columnist and Editor* The Literary Review
Christopher White - *Director Ashmolean Museum Oxford*

Dr Morgan's, Bridgwater
Rt Hon John Biffen - *Conservative MP, President of the Council and former Leader, House of Commons*

Duchess County GS, Alnwick
Ann Burdus - *Marketing director, Olympia & York*

Dudley
Lenny Henry - *Comedian*

Dudley Girls' HS, Worcester
Sue Lawley - *Broadcaster*

Duffryn, Conwy
Lord Elis Thomas - *Former Leader Plaid Cymru*

Dulwich
A.C. Abbott - *Senior designer BBC TV*
Roy Amlot QC - *Barrister*
Very Rev Peter Baelz - *Dean Emeritus of Durham*
Simon Brett - *Writer*
Peter Dimmock - *Commentator, Vice President ABC Video*
Alan R. Hacker - *Clarinettist and conductor*
Graham Jenkins - *Musical Direc Glyndebourne Touring Opera*
Bruce Kemble - *Education correspondent* Evening Standard
Rt Hon Peter Lilley MP - *Secretary of State for Social Security*
Bob Monkhouse - *Comedian* and *TV presenter*
Stewart Purvis - *Editor ITN*
Patrick Robertson - *Founder The Bruges Group*
Lord Shawcross QC - *Chief prosecutor Nuremberg Trials*
Jon Silkin - *Poet*
Iain Vallance - *Chair British Telecom*

Dunbarton Academy
Jackie Stewart - *Racing driver*

Dundee HS
Professor Sir Alan Peacock - *Economist*
Lord Perry - *Former Vice Chancellor Open University*

Dunoon GS
George Robertson MP - *Labour Defence Spokesman*
Rt Hon John Smith MP - *Opposition spokesman Economic Affairs*

Dunstable GS
Tim Robinson - *Cricketer*

Durham
John Laws - *First Junior Treasury Counsel*
Rabbi John Rayner - *Rabbi*

Dynevor GS, Swansea
John Beale - *Chief Education Officer West Glamorgan*
Sir Alexander Gordon - *Architect*

Dynevor GS, Swansea—*contd*
        Lord Griffiths - *Former Head No. 10 Policy Unit*
        Sir Harry Secombe - *Comedian and singer*
        Rev Prof Rowan Williams -
                Professor Divinity Oxford University, Bishop of Monmouth

Ealing GS
        R.D.C. Bunker - *Chair West Sussex Education Authority*
        Sir Rick Greenbury - *Chair, chief executive Marks & Spencer*
        Allen Jones - *Artist*
Ealing HS
        Rt Hon Angela Rumbold MP - *Deputy Chair, Conservative Party*
Earl Haig, Guisborough, Yorks
        Bob Champion - *Jockey*
East Ardsley, Wakefield
        Ernie Wise - *Comedian*
East Barnet GS
        Norman Bailey - *Baritone*
        Alan Coren - *Writer* and *broadcaster*
East Dean GS, Cinderford
        Jimmy Young - *Presenter Jimmy Young Show Radio 2*
East Ham GS
        Barrie Keeffe - *Dramatist*
        Wolf Mankowitz - *Author*
East Howe Bilateral
        Stanley Goodchild - *Chief Education Officer Berkshire*
East Lane, Wembley
        Geoffrey Dickens - *Conservative MP*
Eastbank Academy, Glasgow
        Charles Wilson - Daily Mirror, *former editor* The Times
Eastbourne College
        Sir Hugh Casson - *Architect*
        Michael Fish - *Radio* and *TV weather man*
        Professor Sir John Hale - *Historian*
        John Wells - *Writer, actor, director*
        Lord Wyatt of Weeford - *Chair The Tote, former Labour MP*
Eastbourne GS
        John Ingamells - *Director The Wallace Collection*
Ecclesfield GS
        Barry Hines - *Writer*
        Donald Pleasence - *Actor*
Eden Hall, Penrith
        Mary Stewart - *Novelist*
Edgbaston C of E College, Birmingham
        Toyah Wilcox - *Singer* and *actress*
Edgehill Girls' College
        June O'Dell - *Dep Chair Equal Opportunities Commission*
Edinburgh Academy
        Gordon Honeycombe - *TV presenter*
        Lord Keith of Kinkel - *Law Lord*
        Magnus Magnusson - *Presenter* Mastermind *TV Quiz*

Vice Admiral Sir Jock Slater - *Chief of Fleet Support*
Will Stevenson - *Director British Film Institute*
Iain Vallance - *Chair British Telecom*
Edmonton County GS
Sir Roy Strong - *Former Director Victoria and Albert Museum*
Lord Tebbit - *Former Chair Conservative Party*
Elementary School
Sir John Moores - *Founder Littlewoods Pools* and *mail order*
Fred Perry - *Tennis player, now coach and commentator*
Sir Jimmy Savile - *TV presenter*
Elizabeth College, Guernsey
ACM Sir Peter Le Cheminant - *Lt Governor The Bailiwick of Guernsey*
Ellesmere
Bill Beaumont - *Rugby player*
Michael Howard - *Composer* and *conductor*
Peter McEnery - *Actor*
Ellesmere Port Secondary Modern
John Prescott - *Labour MP, Shadow Transport Minister*
Elliott Comprehensive, Putney
Geoffrey Arnold - *Cricketer*
Elmgrove, Belfast
Rt Rev Roy Williamson - *Bishop of Southwark*
Elmhurst Ballet
Jenny Agutter - *Actress*
Val Bourne - *Founder Dance Umbrella dance festival*
Fiona Fullerton - *Actress*
Hayley Mills - *Actress*
Dame Merle Park - *Director Royal Ballet School*
Elmhurst GS
Rev John Polkinghorne - *President Queen's College Cambridge*
Elmore Green, Walsall
Lord Tombs - *Chair Rolls Royce*
Elmslie Girls', Blackpool
Jean Rigby - *Opera singer*
Eltham Secondary
Alan Tuffin - *Trade unionist Communication Workers*
Emanuel
Michael Aspel - *TV presenter*
Professor David Marquand - *Professor Modern History Salford Univ*
Professor Denis Noble - *Professor Cardiovascular Physiology Oxford*
N.F. Simpson - *Dramatist*
Reg Valin - *Founder Valin Pollen PR, Chair Business in Cmty*
Endsleigh, Colchester
David Hemery - *Athlete*
Enfield GS, Middlesex
Terry Lightfoot - *Jazz musician*
Eothen, Caterham
Cicely Berry - *Voice Coach RSC*
Epsom College
Michael Fallon - *Former Under-Secretary of State for Education*
Sir Francis Graham-Smith - *Former Astronomer-Royal*
Stewart Granger - *Actor*

Epsom College—*contd*
>John Piper - *Painter*
>Philip Powell - *Architect*
>Sir Michael Richardson - *Corporate financier, stockbroker*
>Sir Mark Richmond -
>>*Professor Molec Biol, Vice Chancellor Manchester Univ*
>Nicholas Witchell - *TV News presenter BBC Breakfast News*

Epsom County Secondary
>Michael Manser - *Architect*

Erdington Girls' GS
>Ann Winterton - *Conservative MP*

Erith GS
>Professor Sir William Taylor - *Vice Chancellor Hull University*

Ermysted's, Skipton
>Very Rev E.W. Heaton - *Dean of Christ Church Oxford*

Eton
>Sir Antony Acland - *Diplomat, British Ambassador Washington*
>The Earl of Airlie - *Lord Chamberlain The Queen's Household*
>Jonathan Aitken - *Minister of State for Defence*
>The Hon Charles Allsopp - *Chairman Christie's*
>Lord Amery - *Former Conservative MP*
>Lord Annaly - *Stockbroker, director Greenwell Montagu*
>Lord Armstrong - *Former Cabinet Secretary*
>Neal Ascherson - *Journalist* Independent
>The Hon David Astor - *Director, former Editor*, Observer
>The Hon Hugh Astor - *Director Hambro's plc*
>David Waldorf Astor - *Chair Council Protection Rural England*
>Lord Astor of Hever - *Company director*
>The Duke of Atholl - *Landowner*
>Rt Rev Simon Barrington-Ward - *Bishop of Coventry*
>Professor John Bayley - *Literary critic*
>Lord Bearsted - *Deputy Director Hill Samuel, Chair Dylon*
>The Earl Beatty - *Landowner*
>The Duke of Beaufort - *Chair Marlborough Fine Art*
>Michael Beloff QC - *Barrister*
>David Benedictus - *Playwright*
>Michael Bentine - *Comedian* and *author*
>Sir Timothy Bevan - *Former Chair Barclays Bank, Chair BET plc*
>Marcus Binney - *President SAVE Heritage protection*
>Mark Birley - *Nightclub owner Annabel's*
>Rt Rev Ronald Bowlby - *RC Bishop of Southwark*
>Lord Brabourne - *Film and TV producer*
>Field Marshal Lord Bramall - *Former Chief of General Staff*
>Jeremy Brett - *Actor*
>The Duke of Buccleuch - *Landowner*
>Hon Sir Richard Butler - *Former President NFU*
>Sir Adrian Cadbury - *Former chair Cadbury Schweppes plc*
>Dominic Cadbury - *Chief executive Cadbury Schweppes plc*
>The Earl of Carnarvon - *Former racehorse trainer to HM the Queen*
>Lord Carrington - *Diplomat*
>Lord Cayzer - *Financier*
>Christopher Cazenove - *Actor*

Jonathan Cecil - *Actor*
Very Rev Professor Henry Chadwick -
     Master Peterhouse Cambridge
Rt Hon Paul Channon - *Former Secretary of State Transport*
Lord Charteris - *Chair National Heritage Memorial Fund*
The Marquess of Cholmondeley - *Landowner*
Sir George Christie - *Chair Glyndebourne Productions Ltd*
Winston Churchill - *Conservative MP*
The Hon Alan Clark - *Former Minister Defence Procurement; historian*
Nicholas Coleridge - *Editor* Tatler
David Coleridge - *Chair Lloyd's of London*
Robert Compton - *Chair Time-Life International*
Viscount Cowdray - *Landowner*
Martin Cox - *Producer Radio 4 FM*
Viscount Cranborne - *Defence Minister*
Viscount Cranbrook - *Head of Nature Conservancy Council*
Quentin Crewe - *Writer and journalist*
Tam Dalyell - *Labour MP*
Roger De Grey - *President Royal Academy of Arts*
Lord Derby - *Landowner*
The Duke of Devonshire - *Landowner – Chatsworth*
Peter Dickinson - *Author*
Lord James Douglas-Hamilton MP -
     Under Secretary of State Scottish Office
William Douglas Home - *Playwright*
Lord Egremont - *Novelist, landowner – Petworth*
Viscount Esher - *Architect*
Sir Robert Fellows - *Deputy private secretary HM The Queen*
Sir Ranulph Fiennes - *Explorer*
Mark Fisher - *Labour MP*
Anthony Forbes - *Joint Senior Ptner Cazenove Stockbrokers*
Sir Brinsley Ford - *Former Chair National Art Collection*
General Sir David Fraser - *Former ADC General to HM The Queen*
Bamber Gascoigne - *Broadcaster* and *author*
Lt Col Sir Martin Gilliat - *Private secretary HM The Queen Mother*
Lord Glenconner - *Chair Mustique Company Ltd*
HRH The Duke of Gloucester
Lord Goff of Chieveley - *Law Lord*
Sir James Goldsmith - *International businessman*
Sir William Goodhart QC - *Barrister*
The Earl of Gowrie - *Chairman Sotheby's*
Father Benedict Green - *Theologian*
Graham Carleton Greene - *Director Jonathan Cape publishers*
Lord Grimond - *Former leader Liberal Party*
Most Rev Rt Hon John Habgood - *Archbishop of York*
Lord Hailsham - *Former Lord Chancellor*
Charles Hambro - *Chair Hambros plc*
Rupert Hambro - *Banker, director* Daily Telegraph
Rt Hon Archie Hamilton MP - *Minister of State for Defence*
Robin Hanbury-Tenison - *Explorer* and *travel writer*
The Earl of Harewood - *Pres Brit Board of Film Classification*
Andrew Hargreaves - *Conservative MP*

Eton—*contd*

David Hart - *Head of Committee for a Free Britain*
Sir Rupert Hart-Davis - *Publisher*
Nicholas Haslam - *Interior designer*
The Marquess of Hertford - *Landowner – Ragley Hall*
Rt Hon Douglas Hogg MP - *Minister of State, FCO*
Michael Holroyd - *Writer*
Lord Home of the Hirsel - *Former Prime Minister*
Sir Simon Hornby - *Chair W.H. Smith plc*
Philip Howard - *Journalist* The Times
Rt Hon David Howell MP - *Former Secretary of State for Transport*
Rt Hon Douglas Hurd MP - *Foreign Secretary*
Tom Hustler - *Photographer*
Viscount Inchcape - *Life President Inchcape plc*
Sir Martin Jacomb - *Chair Barclays de Zoete Wedd*
Professor Michael Jaffe - *Director Fitzwilliam Museum Cambridge*
David Jessel - *TV journalist*
Brian Johnston - *Cricket commentator*
Ludovic Kennedy - *Broadcaster* and *writer*
HRH The Duke of Kent
HRH Prince Michael of Kent
Sir Kenneth Kleinwort - *Director Kleinwort Benson plc*
Sir David Lane - *Former Chair Commission for Racial Equality*
James Lees-Milne - *Architectural historian*
Sir Hugh Leggatt - *Art dealer*
Sir Robin Leigh-Pemberton - *Governor The Bank of England*
Peter T. Lewis - *Chair John Lewis Partnership*
Magnus Linklater - *Editor* The Scotsman
Rt Hon Lord Justice Anthony Lloyd - *Appeal Court Judge*
Lord Longford - *Writer, former Lord Privy Seal*
Humphrey Lyttelton - *Jazz musician*
Sir Fitzroy Maclean - *Diplomat, soldier and politician*
Patrick Macnee - *Actor*
Derek Malcolm - *Film critic* Guardian
Daniel Massey - *Actor*
Sir Patrick McNair-Wilson - *Conservative MP*
Lord Melchett - *Executive Director Greenpeace*
John Menzies - *Chair John Menzies*
Sir Anthony Meyer - *Former Conservative MP*
Lord Milford - *Painter, Member of Communist Party*
David Money-Coutts - *Chair Coutts Bank*
The Hon David Montagu - *Chair Rothmans International*
Rt Hon Lord Montagu of Beaulieu -
        Conservative peer, founder Beaulieu Motor Museum
Charles Moore - *Deputy Editor* Daily Telegraph
Michael Moore - *Chair NSPCC*
Sir Peter Moores - *Former Chair, Director Littlewoods Pools*
Nicholas Mosley - *Novelist*
Ferdinand Mount - *Editor* Times Literary Supplement
Richard Needham - *Ministry of State, Trade and Industry*
Nigel Nicolson - *Author*
John Julius (Viscount) Norwich - *Writer* and *broadcaster*

Lord Oaksey - *Racing correspondent and commentator*
The Hon Sir Angus Ogilvy - *Company director*
Lord Palumbo - *Chairman The Arts Council*
Nicholas Payne - *Director Opera North*
Rt Rev Simon Phipps - *Former Bishop of Lincoln*
Jonathan Porritt - *Former Director Friends of the Earth*
Lord Portman - *Landowner*
Anthony Powell - *Writer*
Lord Pym - *Former Foreign Secretary*
Rt Hon Timothy Raison - *former Conservative MP*
Sir Alick Rankin - *Chair Scottish and Newcastle*
Tim Renton MP - *Former Minister for the Arts*
Sir John Riddell - *Equerry to Prince and Princess of Wales*
Lord Ridley - *Former Conservative MP Former Sec State Trade/Ind*
Viscount Rothermere - *Chair Daily Mail, Associated Newspapers*
Lord Rothschild - *Financier*
Hon Sir Steven Runciman - *Historian*
Lord Runciman of Doxford -
        Head Royal Commission on Birmingham Six
The Hon Tim Sainsbury MP - *Minister of State for Trade and Industry*
Giles Shepard - *Chief executive The Savoy Hotel Group*
Julian Slade - *Author and composer*
The Earl of Snowdon - *Photographer, artistic adviser* Sunday Times
The Hon Nicholas Soames -
        Minister for Agriculture
The Earl of St Andrews - *Son and heir Duke of Kent*
Rt Hon Lord Justice Staughton - *Appeal Court Judge*
Jocelyn Stephens - *Former MD Beaverbrook Newspapers*
Angus Stirling - *Director General The National Trust*
The Earl of Stockton - *Chair Macmillan publishers*
Jonathan Sumption QC - *Barrister*
Professor Sir Peter Swinnerton-Dyer - *Mathematician*
Sir Anthony J. Tennant - *Chair Guinness plc*
Wilfred Thesiger - *Explorer* and *writer*
Lord Thorneycroft - *Former Chair Conservative Party*
Jeremy Thorpe - *Former Leader Liberal Party*
Colin Thubron - *Novelist*
Rt Hon William Waldegrave MP - *Chancellor of the Duchy of Lancaster*
The Duke of Wellington - *Landowner*
Viscount Weymouth - *Director Longleat*
Samuel Whitbread - *Chair Whitbread & Co Brewers*
Sir William Wilkinson - *Chair Nature Conservancy Council*
Marquess of Worcester - *Landowner − Badminton*
Francis Wyndham - *Novelist*
Sir George Young - *Conservative MP*
Sir Brian Young - *Chair Christian Aid*

Ewell Castle
        Oliver Reed - *Actor*
Exeter
        Sir Anthony Farrar-Hockley - *Defence Consultant and lecturer*
Exmouth GS
        Patricia Beer - *Poet*

Fairfax HS, Sutton Coldfield
    Howard Morgan - *Portrait painter*
Falkirk HS
    Sheila McKechnie - *Director Shelter*
Farmhouse, Wendover
    Laraine Ashton - *Model agent*
Farnborough Hill Convent
    Ann Robinson - *TV presenter* and *journalist*
    Pascale Smets - *Fashion designer*
Farnham GS
    Dr Jeffrey Tate - *Principal conductor Eng Chamber Orch*
Farnham Girls' GS
    Liza Goddard - *Actress*
Farrington HS, Chislehurst
    Wendy Cope - *Poet*
Faversham GS
    Sir Raymond Rickett - *Director Middlesex Polytechnic*
Fawcett Secondary Modern, Brighton
    Michael Heath - *Cartoonist*
Felsted
    Stuart Burge - *Theatre* and *TV director*
    Michael Jackaman - *Chair Allied-Lyons*
    Richard Johnson - *Actor and producer*
    Kenneth Kendall - *Broadcaster*
    Professor Richard Lacey - *Professor Microbiology Leeds University*
    Derek Pringle - *Cricketer*
    John Stephenson - *Cricketer*
    Sam Walters - *Director Orange Tree Theatre, Richmond*
    Ben Wright - *CBS Golf commentator*
Fernhill Manor
    Thea Porter - *Fashion designer*
Fettes
    Tony Blair MP - *Opposition employment spokesman*
    Donald Crichton-Miller -
            Former headmaster of Taunton, Fettes, Stowe
    Ian Findlay - *Former Chair Lloyds*
    David Murray - *Chair Murray International; Rangers FC*
    David Ogilvy - *Chair WPP Advertising*
    Tilda Swinton - *Actress*
    Sir Michael Tippett - *Composer*
    Rt Hon Sir Harry Woolf - *Appeal Court Judge, Prisons Enquiry*
Finchley RC GS
    Dom Aidan Bellenger - *Headmaster Downside*
Firth Park GS, Sheffield
    Bill Hughes - *Chair Scottish CBI, Grampian Holdings*
    Sir Roy Shaw - *Former Arts Council Secretary General*
Fishguard County
    Dillwyn Miles - *Herald Bard National Eisteddfod of Wales*
Fletton GS, Huntingdon
    Geoffrey Dear - *Chief Constable West Midlands Police*
Forest Essex
    Richard Dunn - *Chief Executive Thames TV*

Nickolas Grace - *Actor*

Forfar Academy
Sir Douglas Black - *Physician & Professor Medicine Manchester Un*

Forres, Swanage
Rt Hon Michael Foot - *Former Labour Leader*
Lord Foot - *Presid UK Immigrants Advisory Service*

Framlingham
Brian Aldiss - *Science fiction writer*
General Sir Patrick Howard-Dobson - *Quartermaster-General*

Francis Bacon GS, St Albans
Cheryl Campbell - *Actress*

Francis Holland
The Marchioness of Anglesey - *Chair Broadcasting Complaints Cttee*
Joan Collins - *Actress*
Rosalie Crutchley - *Actress*

Frederick Bird Secondary Modern, Coventry
Peter Waterman - *Ptner Stock, Aitken, Waterman Music Studio*

French Convent, Hull
Ruth Madoc - *Actress*

French Lycée, London
Gyles Brandreth -
      Conservative MP, Author, broadcaster, journalist, producer
Frances De La Tour - *Actress*
Kay Dick - *Writer and critic*
Sir Hugh Lloyd-Jones - *Regius Professor Greek Oxford University*
Lady Olga Maitland MP - *Founder and Chair Families for Defence*
Sophie Mirman - *Founder, MD Sock Shop, Tie Rack*
Gail Rebuck - *Head of Random Century publishers*
Daniel Topolski - *Rowing coach, travel writer*

Frensham Heights
Tom Legg - *Permanent Secretary Lord Chancellor's Dept*
Nick Mason - *Pink Floyd drummer*
Sir Claus Moser - *Warden Wadham College Oxford*

Friends', Saffron Walden
Rt Hon Tony Newton MP -
      Lord President of the Council; Leader of the Commons
Tom Robinson - *Singer*

Friends', Sibford Ferris
Sir John Burgh - *Former Dir Brit Council, Pres Trinity Oxford*
Paul Eddington - *Actor*

Fulham County
Gwyneth Dunwoody - *Labour MP*
Teresa Gorman - *Conservative MP*

Fullbrook County Secondary
Laura Davies - *Golfer*

Fulneck Girls'
Diana Rigg - *Actress*

Garden School, Lane End
Penelope Mortimer - *Writer*

Garth, Morden
      Ray Galton - *Scriptwriter*
Gateshead GS
      Sir George Russell - *Chair, Independent Television Commission*
Gateway Technical, Leicester
      Colin Wilson - *Writer*
Gayton HS, Harrow
      Angus Fraser - *England cricketer*
George Farmer Comprehensive, Holbeach
      Geoff Capes - *Shot putter*
George Heriot's, Edinburgh
      Sir Donald Barron - *Former Chairman Rowntree Trust*
      Andy Irving - *Rugby player*
      Lord Mackay of Clashfern - *Lord Chancellor*
George Watson's, Edinburgh
      Eric Anderson - *Headmaster Eton College*
      Donald Brydon - *Chief executive BZW*
      Sir Robin Cater - *Former Chair Distillers Co*
      Professor David Daiches - *English Literature scholar*
      Gavin Hastings - *Rugby player*
      Sir Ian MacGregor - *Former Chair NCB, Brit Steel; now Hunterprint*
      Rt Hon Malcolm Rifkind MP - *Secretary of State for Defence*
      Kenneth Scott - *Assistant Private Secretary HM The Queen*
      Sir David Steel MP - *Former Leader Liberal Party*
Gidlow Middle, Wigan
      Kay Burley - *Sky News presenter*
Gillingham GS
      David Frost - *TV presenter* and *producer, author*
      The Ven David Silk - *Archdeacon of Leicester*
Glasgow Academy
      Donald Dewar - *Shadow Scottish Secretary*
      Jeremy Isaacs - *General Director Royal Opera House*
      Neil MacGregor - *Director National Gallery*
      Robert Maclennan - *SLD MP*
      Professor Norman Stone - *Professor Modern History Oxford Univ*
      Iain Vallance - *Chair British Telecom*
Glasgow Girls' HS
      Katharine Whitehorn - *Journalist*
Glasgow HS
      Lord Macfarlane - *Chair Macfarlane Group*
      Ron Neil - *Director Regions BBC TV*
      Sir Teddy Taylor - *Conservative MP*
Glenalmond
      Robbie Coltrane - *Comedian*
      Sandy Gall - *Foreign correspondent, newscaster ITN*
      Miles Kington - *Columnist* Independent
      Sir David Wilson - *Former Governor of Hong Kong*
Glenthorne, St Leonards on Sea
      Gwen Watford - *Actress*
Glossop GS, Derbyshire
      Paul Raymond - *Publisher, nightclub proprietor*

Gloucester Girls' HS
Monica Sims - *Children's Film and TV Foundation Direc*
Glyn College, Epsom
David Hemmings - *Actor* and *producer*
Godalming GS
Jenny Topper - *Artistic director Hampstead Theatre*
Godolphin, Salisbury
Jilly Cooper - *Novelist* and *journalist*
Godolphin and Latymer
Sarah Dunnant - *Presenter* The Late Show
Goffs GS, Cheshunt Herts
Richard Lewis - *Tennis player; Nat head of training LTA*
Gordonstoun
Ross Benson - *Gossip columnist*
William Boyd - *Author*
Jason Connery - *Actor*
HRH The Duke of Edinburgh
The Marquess of Huntly - *Heir to Earldom of Aboyne*
The Marquess of Milford Haven - *Landowner*
Lord Romsey - *Film producer*
Eddy Shah - *Founder* Today *newspaper*
Dr Michael Shea - *Former press secretary to HM The Queen*
HRH The Prince of Wales
HRH The Duke of York
Gorringe Park Secondary Modern, Mitcham
Colin Johnson - *Former Pop consultant National Curriculum*
Gosport GS
ACM Sir Robert Freer - *Former Deputy C-in-C Strike Command*
Govan High Senior Secondary
Alex Ferguson - *Manager Manchester United*
Gowerton Comprehensive
Tracy Edwards - *Round the world yachtswoman*
Gowerton GS
Professor Alun Hoddinott - *Composer*
Grange Girls' HS
Billie Whitelaw - *Actress*
Gravesend GS
Peter Jones - *President Racehorse Owners Association*
Professor Sir Richard Southwood -
Professor Zoology, Vice Chancellor Oxford
Gravesend Technical College
Peter Blake - *Painter*
Great Yarmouth GS
Dick Barfield - *Chief Executive Standard Life Assurance*
Sir Kenneth Macmillan - *Principal choreographer Royal Ballet*
Great Yarmouth HS
Mary Symes - *First woman coroner*
Greenhill, Evesham
Sir Keith Speed - *Conservative MP*
Greenock Academy
Linda Gray - *Opera singer*

Greenway Comprehensive
      Andy Ripley - *Rugby player*
Gresham's
      Peter Brook - *Producer*
      Sir Christopher Cockerell - *Inventor of the hovercraft*
      Stephen Frears - *Film director*
      Anthony Habgood - *Chief executive Tootal*
      Sir Alan Hodgkin - *Biophysicist, former Master Trinity Cambridge*
      Sir Robin Ibbs - *Deputy Chair Lloyds Bank*
      His Honour Judge Robert Lymbery - *Commons Serjeant*
      John Tusa - *Managing Director BBC World Service*
Grey Coat Hospital, Westminster
      Ann Goddard QC - *Barrister*
      Sarah Greene - *Actress*
Grimsby Technical
      Donald Kirkham - *Chair Woolwich Building Society*
Grocers Company GS, Hackney Down
      Steven Berkoff - *Actor, director* and *writer*
      Eric Bristow - *Darts player*
      Lord Goodman - *Former Master University College Oxford*
      Harold Pinter - *Playwright, actor* and *director*
      Sir Alfred Sherman - *Co-founder Centre for Policy Studies*
      Professor John Yudkin - *Professor of Nutrition, broadcaster*
Grosvenor HS, Belfast
      George Best - *Footballer*
Grove Academy, Dundee
      Lord Thomson of Monifieth - *Former Chair IBA*
Grove Park GS, Wrexham
      Rt Rev Bill Westwood - *Bishop of Peterborough*
Grove Park Girls' GS, Wrexham
      June Knox-Mawer - *Radio presenter*
Guildford County Girls' GS
      Professor Morna Hooker - *Professor Divinity Cambridge University*
Guildhouse, Pimlico
      Ann Dummett - *Former Director Runnymede Trust*
Gunnersbury GS
      Paul Jackson - *Chair and Chief Executive Noel Gay TV*
      Terry O'Neill - *Photographer*
Guthlaxton GS, Leicestershire
      Adrian Juste - *Presenter Adrian Juste Show Radio 1*
Gwendraeth GS
      Gareth Davies - *Wales rugby player*
      Jonathan Davies - *Wales rugby player*
      Barry John - *Wales rugby player*
      Gascon Edwards - *Wales rugby player*

HMS Conway
      Vice Admiral Sir David Clutterbuck -
            Former Dep Supreme Allied Cdr Atlantic
HMS Worcester
      Roy Boulting - *Film Producer*

Haberdashers' Aske's
> Sir Leon Brittan - *Vice Pres Commission of the EC*
> Paul Daneman - *Actor*
> Chris Dunkley - *Journalist and broadcaster*
> Keith Edelman - *MD Carlton Communications*
> David Elstein - *Director of programmes Thames TV*
> Michael Green - *Chair Carlton Communications*
> Lord McIntosh of Haringey - *Chair SVP UK Ltd*
> Professor Simon Schama - *Professor of History Harvard University*
> Nicholas Serota - *Director The Tate Gallery*
> Rev Rt Hon the Lord Soper - *Methodist leader*
> Martin Sorrell - *Group chief executive WPP Advertising*
> Alan Whicker - *TV broadcaster*

Haberdashers' Aske's Girls
> Fiona Pitt-Kethley - *Poet*

Hadleigh Hall
> Maggi Hambling - *1st artist in residence National Gallery*

Haileybury
> Alan Ayckbourn - *Playwright*
> James Bishop - *Editor* Illustrated London News
> Rt Rev Peter Coleman - *Suffragan Bishop of Crediton*
> Gerald Harper - *Actor*
> Chris Lowe - *BBC newscaster*
> Simon MacCorkindale - *Actor*
> John McCarthy - *Journalist and former hostage*
> Sir John Manduell - *Principal Royal Northern College Music*
> Lord Mayhew - *Liberal Defence spokesman*
> Stirling Moss - *Former racing driver*
> Lt Gen Sir David Ramsbotham - *Director Army PR Falklands War*
> Max Robertson - *Sports commentator*
> Alan Ross - *Author, publisher, editor* London Magazine

Halesowen GS
> Bill Oddie - *Actor*

Hall Green Bilateral
> Nigel Mansell - *Racing driver*

Hammersmith
> Betty Boo - *Pop singer*

Hampshire Sch, London
> Anthony Dowell - *Director The Royal Ballet*
> Susan Hampshire - *Actress*

Hampton GS
> Air Chief Marshal Sir Alasdair Steedman -
> > *Former Director Defence Operations Staff*

Handsworth GS
> Graham Lane - *Vice Chair Newham Education Committee*

Handsworth Technical
> Jeffrey Rooker - *Labour MP*

Hanford, Dorset
> Emma Kirkby - *Soprano*

Hanley HS
> Lord Kearton - *Chemist, Chancellor Bath University*

Hanson, Bradford
        Peter Firth - *Actor*
Harefield, Middlesex
        Russell Grant - *TV astrologer*
Harris Academy, Dundee
        George Galloway - *Labour MP*
        Rt Hon Bruce Millan - *European Commissioner*
Harrogate Ladies' College
        Henrietta Shaw - *First woman Cambridge cox*
Harrow
        John Bentley - *Director Wordnet International*
        Michael Bogdanov - *Artistic Director English Shakespeare* Co
        Lord Brabazon of Tara - *former Minister of State FCO*
        The Marquess of Bristol - *Director Bristol Estates*
        Sir Robin Butler - *Secty to Cabinet, Head of Civil Service*
        Sir John Clark - *Former Chair Plessey*
        Aidan Crawley - *Former Chair LWT*
        Mike D'Abo - *Singer ex-Manfred Mann*
        Gen Sir Peter De La Billière - *Cdr SAS Falklands War, Cdr Gulf War*
        Lord Deedes - *Former editor Daily Telegraph*
        Michael Denison - *Actor*
        Sir John Farr - *Former Conservative MP, Campaigner Birmingham 6*
        Edward Fox - *Actor*
        James Fox - *Actor*
        Sir Peter Green - *Former Chair Lloyd's of London*
        Rt Hon Lord Joseph - *Former Secretary of State for Education*
        Lord Lichfield - *Photographer*
        Rt Rev Michael Mann - *Former Dean Windsor*
        Hugh Montgomery-Massingberd - *Columnist* Daily Telegraph
        John Mortimer QC - *Playwright, author and barrister*
        Rt Hon Cranley Onslow - *Conservative MP*
        The Hon Philip Oppenheim - *Conservative MP*
        Sir Philip Oppenheimer - *Chair The Diamond Trading Company*
        Sir Mark Prescott - *Racehorse trainer*
        John Profumo - *Chair Toynbee Hall, former War Minister*
        Sir Edward Rayne - *Chair Society London Fashion Designers*
        Rt Hon Sir Wyn Roberts MP - *Minister of State, Welsh Office*
        Lord Rootes - *Former Chair Chrysler UK*
        His Honour Judge Laurence Verney - *Recorder of London*
        The Duke of Westminster - *Landowner*
        Simon Williams - *Actor*
        Sandy Wilson - *Composer and lyricist*
Harrow County
        Dr John Beishon - *Chair The Consumers' Association*
        Michael Portillo MP - *Chief Secretary to the Treasury*
Harrow County Girls' GS
        Diane Abbott - *Labour MP*
Harrow Technical College
        Victoria Gillick - *Sec National Assoc Catholic Families*
Harrow Weald GS
        Ken Follett - *Author*
        Lord Rees - *former Labour MP*

Heathfield Senior
        Paul Gascoigne - *Footballer*
Heaton Comprehensive, Newcastle
        Chris Donald - *Founder and editor* Viz *magazine*
Heaton Moor College, Manchester
        Jack Dellal - *Chair Allied Commercial Exporters Ltd*
Hebden Bridge GS, Yorkshire
        Sir Bernard Ingham - *Former press secretary Mrs Thatcher*
Hegginbottom, Ashton under Lyne
        Brian Hitchen - *Editor* Daily Star
Hele's, Exeter
        Sir Anthony Battishill - *Chair Board of Inland Revenue*
Helsby County GS, Cheshire
        Sir Kenneth Green - *Director Manchester Polytechnic*
        Brian MacArthur - *Assistant Editor* The Times
Hemsworth GS Yorks
        Geoffrey Boycott - *Cricketer*
        Leonard Parkin - *Broadcaster*
Hen Lane, Coventry
        David Tindle - *Artist* and *dealer*
Hendon County GS
        Rabbi Lionel Blue - *Writer* and *broadcaster*
        Lord Braine - *Former Father of House of Commons*
        Gerald Ratner - *Ratners Group Jewellery*
Henrietta Barnett, Hampstead
        Joan Burstein - *Owner Browns South Molton Street*
Henry Comprehensive, Fulham
        Linford Christie - *Athlete*
Henry Mellish GS, Nottingham
        Dr Neil Cossons - *Director The Science Museum*
Henry Thornton GS, Clapham
        Hywel Bennett - *Actor*
        Jimmy Hill - *Soccer analyst to BBC, Chair Fulham FC*
        Peter Katin - *Concert pianist*
        Tom Phillips - *Painter, writer and composer*
Henshaw Secondary Modern, Oldham
        Tommy Cannon - *Comedian*
Heolgam Secondary Modern
        Garfield Davies - *Trade unionist Shop Workers*
Herbert Strutt GS, Derbyshire
        Alan Bates - *Actor*
Hereford Cathedral
        Paul Thorburn - *Wales rugby captain*
Herons Ghyll, Horsham
        Virginia McKenna - *Actress*
Hertford GS
        Christopher Brown - *Director NSPCC*
        Michael Dobbs - *Novelist*
        David Gentleman - *Painter* and *designer*
Hewarth Grange, Wardley
        Chris Waddle - *Footballer*

High Oakham, Mansfield, Nottingham
        Carl Toms - *Stage designer*
High Pavement GS, Nottingham
        Peter Bowles - *Actor*
High Possil Secondary
        Kenny Dalglish - *Footballer, former manager Liverpool*
High Storrs GS
        Joe Ashton - *Labour MP*
Highams Park Senior HS Comprehensive
        Jane Ray - *Children's book illustrator, designer*
Highbury GS
        William Dudley - *Stage designer RSC, Royal Opera*
        Lord Matthews - *Former owner Express Newspapers*
Highgate
        Lord Ackner - *Law Lord*
        Geoffrey Archer - *ITN Defence Correspondent*
        Robert Atkins MP - *Minister of State Northern Ireland*
        Rt Rev Stanley Booth-Clibborn - *Bishop of Manchester*
        Dr Alan Bush - *Conductor, Professor Composition Roy Coll Mus*
        Sir Robert Clark - *Chair United Biscuits, Director TSB*
        Dr Alex Comfort - *Physician* and *writer*
        Michael Mansfield QC - *Barrister, Counsel for Birmingham Six*
        Sir Patrick Neill QC - *Warden All Souls Oxford*
        Barry Norman - *TV presenter, journalist* and *author*
        Patrick Procktor - *Painter* and *designer*
        Robin Ray - *Writer* and *broadcaster*
        Sir Clive Sinclair - *Chair Sinclair Research*
        Nicholas Snowman - *Artistic director South Bank Centre*
        John Taverner - *Composer*
Highgate Convent
        Pauline Crabbe - *First black woman magistrate*
Hillcrest GS
        Yvette Fielding - *Presenter* Blue Peter *Children's TV*
Hillhead HS Glasgow
        Menzies Campbell - *Liberal Democrat MP*
        James Herriot - *Writer – Vet books*
        Sir Ian MacGregor - *Former Chair NCB, Brit Steel; now Hunterprint*
Hitchin GS
        Bernard Cotton - *Manager GB hockey team 1992 Olympics*
Hitchin Girls' GS
        Claire Tomalin - *Writer*
Hoddesdon Secondary Modern
        Angela Pleasence - *Actress*
Holland Park Comprehensive
        Polly Toynbee - *Social affairs correspondent BBC TV*
Hollies Convent GS, West Didsbury
        Anne Hobbs - *Tennis player*
Holloway County
        Sir Leslie Porter - *President Tesco*
Holly Lodge GS, Smethwick
        Julie Walters - *Actress*

Hollyfield Road, Surbiton
    Eric Clapton - *Guitarist* and *singer*
Holme Valley GS
    David Bintley - *Principal dancer, choreographer Royal Ballet*
Holt HS, Liverpool
    Ken Dodd - *Comedian*
    John Shirley-Quirk - *Bass-baritone*
Holton Park Girls' GS
    Baroness Mallalieu - *Barrister, 1st woman Pres Cambridge Union*
    Margaret Pringle - *Head Holland Park Comprehensive*
Holy Child Convent, Edgbaston
    Ninivah Khomo - *Fashion designer*
    Noelle Walsh - *Editor* Good Housekeeping
Holy Cross Academy, Edinburgh
    Richard Demarco - *Artist, director Edinburgh Art Gallery*
    Tom Farmer - *Founder* and *Director Kwik Fit Tyres*
    Cardinal Gordon Gray -
    Former Archbishop St Andrews, Edinburgh
    John Junkin - *Actor* and *scriptwriter*
    Sam McCluskie - *Gen Sec National Union of Seamen*
    Sir Eduardo Paolozzi - *Sculptor, RCA tutor in ceramics*
Holyhead Comprehensive
    Glenys Kinnock
Holyrood Senior Secondary, Glasgow
    Helena Kennedy QC - *Barrister*
Holywell GS
    Ann Clwyd - *Labour MP Shadow Minister Overseas Devt*
    Jonathan Pryce - *Actor*
Honley GS, Yorkshire
    Roy Castle - *Entertainer*
Hornsey County
    Ron Moody - *Actor*
Horwell GS
    Charles Causley - *Poet and broadcaster*
Houghton le Spring GS
    Sir Terence Burns - *Permanent Secretary to the Treasury*
Hove College, Sussex
    Peter McEnery - *Actor*
Hove County Girls'
    Eleanor Platt QC - *Barrister*
Hove GS
    Dinsdale Landen - *Actor*
    Don McCrickard - *Chief executive TSB, Chair Hill Samuel*
Howard Gardens, Cardiff
    Lord Cudlipp - *Former Chair IPC*
Howell's, Denbigh
    Nerys Hughes - *Actress*
    Rosie Thomas - *Novelist*
Huish's GS, Taunton
    Arthur C. Clarke - *Science fiction writer*
Hulme GS, Oldham
    Jack Tinker - *Drama critic* Daily Mail

Hulme Girls' GS Oldman
        Enid Castle - *Principal Cheltenham Ladies' College*
Hunmanby Hall
        Fran Bennet - *Director Child Poverty Action Group*
Huntingdon GS
        John Butcher - *Conservative MP*
        Rt Rev Richard Rutt - *Bishop of Leicester*
Huntingdon House, Hindhead
        Zelda West-Meads - *Press Officer RELATE marriage guidance*
Hurst, Baghurst
        Kathy Cook - *Athlete*
Hurst Lodge, Sunningdale
        HRH The Duchess of York
Hurstpierpoint
        Sir Bryan Cartledge - *Principal Linacre College Oxford*
        David Hart - *Gen Sec National Assoc of Head Teachers*
        Ronald Neame - *Film director*
        Paul Scofield - *Actor*
        Michael York - *Actor*
Hutchesons' GS, Glasgow
        Maev Alexander - *Presenter* That's Life
        Duncan Graham - *Chair National Curriculum Council*
        Lord Irvine of Lairg - *Chief Labour Law Spokesman*
        Max Morris - *Former Pres National Union of Teachers*
Hutton GS, Lancs
        Graham Mather - *Former General Director Instit Economic Affairs*
Huyton College
        Mary Arden QC - *Barrister*
Hyde County GS, Cheshire
        Timmy Mallett - *TV AM children's show presenter*
Hymers College, Hull
        Simon Hoggart - Observer *columnist*

Idbury Manor, Oxfordshire
        Lucinda Green - *Three-day eventer*
Ide Hill, Sevenoaks
        Dame Peggy Fenner - *Conservative MP*
Ilford County HS
        Raymond Baxter - *Broadcaster and writer*
        Sir Raymond Lygo - *Former Chief Executive British Aerospace*
        Sir Alan Sheppard - *Chair Grand Metropolitan plc*
Ilford Girls' County HS
        Nina Bawden - *Writer, especially children's books*
        Marion Foale - *Knitwear designer*
Inverkeithing HS
        Stephen Hendry - *Snooker player*
Inverness Academy
        Murdow Fraser - *Chair Young Conservatives*
        Lord Irvine of Lairg - *Chief Labour Law spokesman*
        Donald Macleary - *Principal male dancer Royal Ballet*

Invicta, Sherington
        Jools Holland - *TV presenter, singer*
Ipswich Girls' HS
        Tracy Macleod - *The Late Show*
        Dame Margaret Miles - *Former Head Mayfield School Putney*
Italia Conti Stage
        Naomi Campbell - *Model*
        Bonnie Langford - *Actress*
        Nanette Newman - *Actress and writer*
        Leslie Phillips - *Actor*
        Wendy Richard - *Actress*
        Tracy Ullman - *Comedienne and singer*

James Allen's Girls
        Anita Brookner - *Novelist*
James Gillespie's, Edinburgh
        Ronnie Corbett - *Comedian*
James Gillespie's Girls', Edinburgh
        Muriel Spark - *Writer*
Jarrow GS
        Steve Cram - *Athlete*
        Dr Jack Cunningham - *Labour MP*
Jennings, Swindon
        Lord Marsh - *Chair Newspaper Publishers Association*
John Bright GS, Llandudno
        Sir Gordon Borrie - *Former Director General of Fair Trading*
        Rod Hackney - *Architect*
John Kelly HS, Cricklewood
        Mike Gatting - *Cricketer*
John Lyon, Harrow
        Timothy West - *Actor*
John Ruskin GS
        Bob Phillis - *Chief executive ITN*
Jordanhill College, Glasgow
        Eric Forth MP - *Under Sec State Education and Science*
Judd, Tonbridge
        Humphrey Burton - *Artistic director Barbican, TV producer*
        Admiral of the Fleet Lord Lewin - *Former Chief of Defence Staff*

Keighley GS
        Lord Briggs - *Provost Worcester College*
        Sir Wilfred Cockcroft - *Educationalist (Cockcroft Maths Report)*
Keighley Girls' GS
        Mollie Sugden - *Actress*
Kelham
        Rt Rev Richard Holloway - *Bishop of Edinburgh*
Kelly College
        Sharron Davies - *Swimmer*
        Rt Rev Mervyn Stockwood - *Former Bishop of Southwark*

King Edward VI GS, Nuneaton—*contd*
      Prof Sir Philip Randle - *Professor Clinical Biochemistry Oxford*
King Edward VI Girls' HS Birmingham
      Dame Jill Knight - *Conservative MP*
      Dr Valerie Pearl - *President New Hall Cambridge*
      Dame Rachel Waterhouse - *Former Chair Consumers Association*
King Edward VI, Louth
      Andrew Faulds - *Labour MP and film actor*
King Edward VI, Norwich
      Lord Blake - *Historian*
      Angus Watson - *Director of Music Wells Cathedral School*
King Edward VI, Southampton
      Ian Bruce - *Director Royal Nat Institute for Blind*
      Professor Basil Mitchell -
            Former Professor Philosophy of Christian Religion Oxford
      Rev Professor Dennis Nineham - *Former Warden Keble College Oxford*
King Edward VI, Stratford-upon-Avon
      Dick Tracey - *Conservative MP, Former Minister of Sport*
      Tim Pigott-Smith - *Actor*
      George Tremlett - *Journalist, biographer rock musicians*
King Edward VII GS, Sheffield
      Sir Robert Scholey - *Chair British Steel plc*
      Professor Ted Wragg - *Director Exeter Univ School of Education*
King Edward VII, Lytham
      Peter Shaffer - *Playwright*
King Edward's, Bath
      Ian Prosser - *Chair Bass plc*
King Edward's, Birmingham
      Sir Michael Checkland - *Director General BBC*
      John Copley - *Opera producer*
      Professor Sir Douglas Hague -
            Chair Metapraxis Management Consultants
      Peter Mason - *Former High Master Manchester GS*
      Bill Oddie - *Actor*
      Sir Edward Parkes - *Chair Cttee Vce Chancellors & Principals*
      Rt Hon Enoch Powell - *Former Conservative Minister*
      Hon Mr Justice Konrad Schiemann -
            High Court Judge Queen's Bench Division
      Sir Maurice Shock - *Rector Lincoln College Oxford*
      Alan Smith - *Chief executive TCCB*
      Sir Peter Walters - *Head Midland Bank, ex Chair & MD BP*
      David Willetts -
            Conservative MP, former Director, Centre for Policy Studies
King George V, Southport
      Professor Stanley Runcorn - *Geophysicist*
      Duncan Weldon - *Theatre producer*
King Henry VIII, Coventry
      Paul Daniel - *Musical director Opera North*
      Martin Jacques - *Editor* Marxism Today
      Sir George Turnbull - *Chair Inchcape*
King James I GS, Bishop Auckland
      Dr Keith Hampson - *Conservative MP*

King William's College, Isle of Man
 Geoffrey Maddrell - *Chief executive Tootal*
Kingsbury County, Middlesex
 Professor John Postgate - *Microbiologist*
Kingston College
 Edward Woodward - *Actor*
Kingston GS
 Michael Frayn - *Journalist, playwright, novelist*
 Michael Hepher - *MD British Telecom*
Kingston Girls'
 Sue Douglas - *Journalist* Sunday Times
Kingston HS, Hull
 John Alderton - *Actor*
 Tom Courtney - *Actor*
 Alan Plater - *Playwright*
 Professor Stanley Wells - *Shakespeare scholar*
Kingston Technical College
 Ted Croker - *Former Secretary The Football Association*
 Leslie Thomas - *Author*
Kingswood, Bath
 Sir Nicholas Fenn - *HM Ambassador to Dublin*
 Tom Jaine - *Editor* Good Food Guide
 Sir Bernard Lovell - *Former Director Jodrell Bank Experimtl Stn*
 Jonathan Lynn - *Director and author* Yes Prime Minister
 David Rose - *Head of Drama Channel* 4
 Anthony Thwaite - *Poet, director Andre Deutsch publishers*
 Sir David Wilson - *Director The British Museum*
Kingswood Secondary, Hainault
 Jimmy Greaves - *Former footballer, commentator*
King's, Bruton
 Rear Admiral Andrew Richmond - *Chief Executive RSPCA*
Kings', Canterbury
 Sebastian Barker - *Chair The Poetry Society*
 Very Rev David Edwards - *Provost Southwark Cathedral*
 Patrick Leigh Fermor - *Writer*
 Tristan Garel-Jones - *Minister of State FCO*
 David Gower - *Cricketer*
 Bob Horton - *Chair BP*
 Sir Leslie Joseph - *Vice Chair Trust House Forte*
 Edward Lucie-Smith - *Poet and art critic*
 Very Rev Michael Mayne - *Dean of Westminster*
 Sir Anthony Parsons - *Former HM Ambassador to Iran*
 Sir Charles Powell - *Former foreign policy adviser to Mrs Thatcher*
Kings, Chester
 Nickolas Grace - *Actor*
 George Guest - *University organist Cambridge*
 Ronald Pickup - *Actor*
King's College, Taunton
 Professor Antony Hewish - *Radio astronomer*
 Colonel John Mayo - *Director General Help the Aged*
King's College, Wimbledon
 Professor Peter Moore - *Professor Decision Science London Business Sc*

King's, Ely
      Alan Yentob - *Controller BBC 2*
King's, Macclesfield
      Alan Beith - *Social and Liberal Democrat MP*
      Michael Jackson - *Head of BBC TV Arts and Music*
King's, Rochester
      Peter Gummer - *Founder Chair Shandwick - world's lgst PR co*
      Rt Hon John Selwyn Gummer MP - *Secretary of State for Agriculture*
      Dinsdale Landen - *Actor*
Kings, Wimbledon
      Richard Pasco - *Actor*
King's, Worcester
      Sir Christopher Benson - *Chair Boots the Chemists*
      Nicholas Cleobury - *Conductor*
      Stephen Cleobury - *Director Music King's College Cambridge*
      Rt Rev Edward Knapp-Fisher - *Former Archdeacon Westminster*
      Sir Jack Longland -
            Former Director Education Derbyshire and broadcaster
      Geoffrey Mulcahy - *Chief executive Kingfisher*
      Jonathan Raban - *Travel writer*
      Lord Wolfson - *Chair Wolfson Fndn, Great Universal Stores*
Kinsley Secondary Modern
      Geoffrey Boycott - *Cricketer*
Kirby Lodge, Cambridge
      Jenny Seagrove - *Actress*
Knowlton HS
      Neil Shaw - *Chair Tate and Lyle plc*

LCC Brockley
      Dame Peggy Fenner - *Conservative MP*
La Roche Dancing, Slough
      Una Stubbs - *Actress*
La Sagesse Convent, Liverpool
      Rita Tushingham - *Actress*
La Sainte Union Convent, Bath
      Imelda Staunton - *Actress*
      Ann Widdecombe MP- *Social Security Minister*
Lady Eden's
      Alfreda Thorogood - *Ballerina*
Lady Eleanor Holles
      Lynn Barber - *Columnist* Independent
      Lucy Irvine - *Author* (Castaway)
      Ann Nightingale - *TV presenter*
      Saskia Reeves - *Actress*
Lady Lumley's GS, Pickering, Yorkshire
      Rev Canon Peter Boulton - *Canon Residentiary of Southwell Minster*
Ladybarn House, Manchester
      Dame Kathleen Ollerenshaw - *Educationalist*
Lancaster Royal GS
      Sir Ronald Halstead - *Deputy Chair British Steel*
      Lord Parkinson - *Former Secretary of State for Transport*

Leeds Modern GS
>Alan Bennett - *Dramatist and actor*
>John Craven - *TV presenter*
>Douglas Smith - *Chair ACAS*

Leeds Secondary
>Professor Richard Hoggart -
>>*Professor English Lit, former Warden Goldsmiths*

Leigh GS
>Sir Peter Maxwell Davies - *Composer and conductor*

Leighton Park
>Tony Baldry - *Under Secretary of State, Environment*
>Professor Quentin Bell - *Art historian*
>Richard Rodney Bennett - *Composer*
>Peter Cadbury - *Chair Preston Estates, George Cadbury Trust*
>George Cadbury - *Chair Emer Internat Planned Parenthd Fdn*
>Rt Hon Michael Foot - *Former Labour leader*
>Tom Maschler - *Former Chair Jonathan Cape publishers*
>Karel Reisz - *Film director*
>John Witney - *Theatre director*

Leith Academy
>Edward McWilliam - *Sculptor*

Levenshulme Girls' HS
>Beryl Reid - *Actress*

Leweston Manor Convent, Sherborne
>Erin Pizzey - *Fdr 1st battered women shelter Chiswick*

Lewis, Pengam
>Rt Hon Neil Kinnock MP - *Former Leader of the Labour Party*
>Rev Dewi Morgan - *Rector St Bride's Fleet Street*

Leys, Cambridge
>J. G. Ballard - *Novelist*
>Sir Alastair Burnett - *Former ITN newsreader*
>Lord Hayter - *Deputy Chairman House of Lords*

Leyton County HS
>Derek Jacobi - *Actor*
>John Lill - *Concert pianist*
>Frank Muir - *Writer and broadcaster*
>Jonathan Ross - *Channel 4 broadcaster*

Lincoln
>John Hurt - *Actor*
>Sir Neville Marriner - *Conductor, Director St Martin in the Fields*

Lindisfarne College
>Professor Jim Gower - *Solicitor, Professor Emeritus Southampton*

Liskeard GS
>Sir Roy Harding - *Education consultant*

Littleport Secondary Modern, Isle of Ely
>Roger Law - Spitting Image *puppeteer*

Liverpool College
>Bernard Faulk - *Journalist*
>Rt Hon David Hunt MP - *Secretary of State for Wales*
>Rt Rev Nigel McCullough - *Bishop of Wakefield*
>Simon Rattle - *Conductor*
>Richard Stilgoe - *Lyricist*

Ludlow HS, Shropshire
        Rosemary Leach - *Actress*
Lumley Secondary, Skegness
        Ray Clemence - *Footballer*
Luton GS
        Dennis Farr - *Director The Courtauld Institute*
Lychett Minster, Poole
        Wendy Toms - *Football referee*
Lymm GS
        Neil Fairbrother - *Cricketer*
Lyulph Stanley Central
        Raymond Jackson (Jak) - Evening Standard *cartoonist*

Madeley Secondary Modern
        Billy Wright - *Footballer, former controller of sport ATV*
Madras College, St Andrews
        Rev Professor Duncan Forrester -
                Professor Christian Ethics Edinburgh Univ
Magdalen College Sch
        Sam Mendes - *RSC director*
        Fritz Spiegl - *Musician, writer and broadcaster*
        Will Wyatt - *Former MD BBC TV, now Channel 4*
Magnus GS, Newark
        Sir Godfrey Hounsfield - *Engineer, inventor X-ray scanner*
Maidenhead County Boys'
        Dick Francis - *Novelist*
Maidstone GS
        James Butler - *Sculptor*
        Philip Langridge - *Opera singer English National Opera*
Maidstone Technical College
        Philip Langridge - *Opera singer English National Opera*
Maltby Hall, Modern
        Fred Trueman - *Cricketer, writer and broadcaster*
Malvern
        Rt Hon Lord Justice Stephen Brown - *President of the Family Division*
        Air Marshal Sir Denis Crowley-Milling -
                Former Principal Air Attaché Washington
        Major General Alastair Dennis -
                Secretary Imperial Cancer Research Fund
        Denholm Elliott - *Actor*
        Hon Mr Justice Peter Gibson - *High Court Judge, Ch Law Commission*
        Sir Peter Holmes - *Chair Shell UK*
        Sir Ian MacLaurin - *Chair Tesco*
        General Sir John Mogg - *Adjutant General*
        Jeremy Paxman - *TV presenter and reporter* Newsnight
        Professor Iain Prance - *Director Kew Gardens*
        Sir Bob Reid - *Former Chair British Railways Board*
        Stuart Rock - *Editor* Director *Magazine*
        Peter Temple-Morris - *Conservative MP*
        Lord Weatherill - *Former Speaker House of Commons*

Malvern Girls'
        Deaconess Dr Una Kroll - *Deacon of Church of Wales, Broadcaster*
        Elizabeth Tilberis - *Former Editor* Vogue, *Editor US* Harpers Bazaar
Manchester Central HS
        Dr Derek Roberts - *Provost University College London*
Manchester GS
        Mike Atherton - *England cricketer*
        Sir Michael Atiyah -
                President The Royal Society, Master Trinity, Cambridge
        Sir William Barlow - *Chair BICC plc*
        Robert Bolt - *Playwright*
        Sir Frank Cooper - *Civil Servant and company chairman*
        Howard Davies - *Controller Audit Commission*
        Alan Garner - *Writer, especially children's books*
        Benet Hytner QC - *Barrister*
        Nicholas Hytner - *National Theatre director*
        Sir John Johnson - *Chair The Countryside Commission*
        Sir Brian Kellett - *Chair Port of London Authority*
        Ben Kingsley - *Actor*
        Lord Lever of Manchester - *Former Paymaster General; Labour peer*
        Stephen Pimlott - *RSC director*
        Cyril Ray - *Journalist and wine writer*
        Lord Sieff - *Hon President Marks and Spencer*
        Rt Rev Gordon Wheeler - *RC Bishop Emeritus of Leeds*
Manchester Girls' HS
        Her Honour Judge Myrella Cohen QC - *Circuit judge*
        Kathleen Hale - *Illustrator and author*
Manchester Secondary
        Lord Robens of Woldingham - *Former Chair National Coal Board*
Manor Park, Nuneaton
        Larry Grayson - *TV presenter*
Marist Convent, Paignton
        Sue Barker - *Tennis Player, Commentator Sky Sports Chl*
        Baroness Phillips - *Labour peer House of Lords*
Market Harborough GS
        Marshal of the RAF Sir Keith Williamson - *Former Chief of Air Staff*
Marlborough
        Sir Kingsley Amis - *Writer (5 terms as an evacuee)*
        Rt Rev John Baker - *Bishop of Salisbury*
        Lord Bridge of Harwich - *Law Lord*
        Rt Hon Peter Brooke MP -
                Former Secretary of State for Northern Ireland
        Richard Buckle - *Ballet critic and exhibition designer*
        Christopher Chope - *Former Under Secretary of State for Transport*
        Chris De Burgh - *Pop singer*
        Norman Del Mar - *Conductor*
        Marshal of the RAF Lord Elworthy - *Former Governor Windsor Castle*
        Sir Nicholas Goodison - *Chairman TSB Group plc*
        Derek Hill - *Artist*
        Nicholas Hinton - *Director General Save the Children Fund*
        Sir Christopher Hogg - *Chair Courtaulds*
        Lord Hunt - *Leader of 1952 Everest Expedition*

Marlborough–*contd*

Harriet Jagger - *Senior fashion editor* Vogue *magazine*

Christopher Martin-Jenkins - *Cricket commentator*

Ian Maxwell - *Former Chair Mirror Newspapers*

Kevin Maxwell -
Former Chair Maxwell Communications Corporation plc

Norris McWhirter - *Founder Guinness Book of Records*

Richard Ormond - *Director National Maritime Museum*

Michael Pennington - *Actor and writer*

Julian Pettifer - *Broadcaster*

Captain Mark Phillips - *Olympic horseman*

Rt Rev Mark Santer - *Bishop of Birmingham*

Field Marshal Sir John Stanier - *Former C in C UK Land Forces*

Mark Tully - *Chief of Bureau BBC Delhi*

Sir Patrick Wright - *Head of Diplomatic Service*

Sir Eric Yarrow - *Chair Clydesdale Bank*

Marlborough GS

Sir William Golding - *Novelist*

Marling, Stroud, Gloucestershire

Sir Michael Angus - *Chair Unilever*

Marr College, Troon

Susannah York - *Actress*

Marston Grove, Middlesborough

Brian Clough - *Football Manager Nottingham Forest*

Mayfield College, Sussex

Stewart Steven - *Editor* Mail on Sunday

Mayfield, Putney

Ruth Madoc - *Actress*

Mayfield, Ilford

Kenny Ball - *Jazz trumpeter*

Maynard

Penelope Campbell - *Hockey international*

Rosemary Goodridge - *Hockey international*

Professor Margaret Turner-Warwick -
President Royal College of Physicians

Heather Wakefield - *Hockey international*

Meadway Comprehensive, Reading

Kenneth Branagh - *Actor and director*

Medburn, Hertfordshire

Jack Cardiff - *Film director*

Medway Girls' Technical, Chatham

Zandra Rhodes - *Fashion designer*

Melville College

Finlay Calder - *Captain British Lions*

Mercers

Nicholas Roeg - *Film director*

Merchant Taylors'

Terence Brady - *Playwright, novelist and actor*

Nigel Calder - *Science fiction writer*

Lynn Chadwick - *Sculptor*

Lord Coggan - *Former Archbishop of Canterbury*

Dennis Flanders - *Landscape artist*

Rt Hon John Gilbert – *Labour MP*
Walter Goldsmith - *Former Marketing Director Trusthouse Forte*
Rev Canon Bryan Green - *Evangelical; Canon Emerit B'ham Cathedral*
Sir Christopher Harding - *Chair British Nuclear Fuels*
Very Rev John Lang - *Dean of Lichfield*
Rt Rev Peter Selby - *Suffragan Bishop of Kingston on Thames*
David Tench - *Head Legal Dept Consumers' Association*
John Timpson - *Writer and broadcaster Radio 4*
General Sir Anthony Walker - *Deputy Chief of Defence Staff*

Merchant Taylors', Crosby
Beryl Bainbridge - *Writer*
Lord Runcie - *Former Archbishop of Canterbury*

Merchiston Castle, Edinburgh
Professor Sir Donald Acheson - *Former Chief Medical Officer DHSS*
John Jeffrey - *Scotland rugby player*
Rt Hon John MacGregor MP- *Secretary of State for Transport*
Neil McIntosh - *Director Voluntary Service Overseas*

Merthyr County Secondary
Illtyd Harrington - *Former leader GLC*

Methodist College, Belfast
Most Rev Robert Eames - *Archbishop Armagh, Primate All Ireland*
Richard Ferguson QC - *Barrister*

Mexborough GS
Ted Hughes - *Poet Laureate*

Middlesborough HS
Geoff Cook - *Cricketer*

Middleton St Johns, Hartlepool
Bill Sirs - *Trade unionist*

Midhurst GS
David Gestetner - *Chair Gestetner Holdings plc*

Midsomer Norton
Ken Warren - *Former Conservative MP*

Milford
Ian Botham - *Cricketer*

Mill Hill
Sir Michael Bishop - *Chair British Midland Airways*
Sir Anthony Cox - *Architect*
Professor Francis Crick - *Molecular biologist*
Simon Jenkins - *Editor* The Times
Phillip King - *Sculptor, Professor Sculpture RCA*
Timothy Mo - *Novelist*
Sir Denis Thatcher - *Company director*

Mill Lane Secondary, Sudbury
Godfrey Bradman - *Chair Roseahaugh Estates, property devt*

Millfield
Charles Burton - *World circumnavigator via N and S Poles*
Jason Connery - *Actor*
Mark Cox - *Tennis player*
Gareth Edwards - *Rugby player*
Victoria Glendinning - *Author and journalist*
Duncan Goodhew - *Swimmer*
David Graveney - *Cricketer*

Millfield—*contd*
        Mary Rand - *Olympic gold medallist*
        Peter Roebuck - *Cricketer*
        John Sergeant - *BBC Parliamentary Correspondent*
        Jeremy Thomas - *Film producer*
        J.P.R. Williams - *Former rugby player, orthopaedic surgeon*
Minchenden GS
        Josephine Barstow - *Opera singer*
        David Puttnam - *Film director*
        Peter Sallis - *Actor*
Miss Faunce's PNEU, London
        Countess Mountbatten of Burma - *Vice Patron Burma Star Association*
Miss Ironside's
        Virginia Ironside - *Agony aunt* Sunday Mirror
Miss Lambert's PNEU
        Jane Asher - *Actress and writer*
Mitcham GS
        Alan Simpson - *Scriptwriter*
Moat, Leicester
        Tony Mullett - *Head Nat Criminal Intelligence Service*
Moira House, Eastbourne
        Rumer Godden - *Novelist*
        Prunella Scales - *Actress*
Monkton Combe
        Martin Adeney - *Broadcaster*
        Rt Rev John Bone - *Area Bishop of Reading*
        Rev Canon Gonville Ffrench-Beytagh - *Writer, former Dean of Johannesburg*
        Rt Rev Graham Leonard - *Former Bishop of London*
        Richard Stilgoe - *Lyricist*
        Rt Rev Stephen Sykes - *Bishop of Ely*
        Rt Rev Maurice Wood - *Former Bishop Norwich*
Monmouth
        David Broome - *Show jumper*
        Lord Ezra - *Former Chair National Coal Board*
        The Hon Colin Moynihan - *Former Minister for the Environment*
        Victor Spinetti - *Actor*
Monmouth Girls
        Jane Glover - *Conductor*
Monoux GS
        John Dankworth - *Jazz musician*
Montgomery Secondary Modern
        Roger Uttley - *Rugby Player; Director PE Harrow School*
Monument Hill Secondary, Woking
        Alec Bedser - *Cricketer*
More House, London
        Lady Rachel Billington - *Writer*
Morecambe GS
        John Hayes - *Secretary General The Law Society*
        Hon Mr Justice Christopher Rose -
                High Court Judge Queen's Bench Division

Moreton Hall, Oswestry
        Professor Ruth Lister - *Former Direc Child Poverty Action Group*
        Thea Musgrave - *Composer*
Morley GS
        Michael Whitlam - *DG Brit Red Cross (former DG RNI for Deaf)*
Moseley GS
        Professor Sir Douglas Hague -
                Chair Metapraxis Management Consultants
Mount Grace Comprehensive, Potters Bar
        Dr Pauline Cutting - *Surgeon, Palestine refugee camps*
Mount Pleasant Senior, Hackney
        Derek Jameson - *TV and radio presenter and commentator*
Mount, York
        Kate Bellingham - *Presenter* Tomorrow's World
        Jocelyn Burnell - *Astronomer*
        Antonia Byatt - *Writer*
        Dame Judi Dench - *Actress and producer*
        Margaret Drabble - *Author*
        Professor Kathleen Tillotson - *Professor Eng Lit London University*
Mountcollyer Secondary Modern, Belfast
        James Galway - *Flautist*

Napier, Street, Islington
        David Kossoff - *Actor, author and illustrator*
Neath, County Girls' GS
        Mavis Nicholson - *TV interviewer and presenter*
Neath GS
        Sir David Nicholas - *Former Chair ITN*
Nelson-Thomlinson GS, Wigston
        Melvin Bragg - *Presenter* South Bank Show
New Hall, Chelmsford
        Nadine Beddington - *Architect, former President RIBA*
        Cindy Buxton - *Film maker*
New School, Streatham
        Penelope Mortimer - *Writer*
Newarke Girls' GS, Leicester
        Erica Norton - *Assis Chief Constable Leicester Police*
Newbury Girls'
        Betty Root - *Reading and language expert*
Newcastle under Lyne HS
        John Wain - *Writer, former Oxford Professor Poetry*
Newcastle upon Tyne Central HS
        Miriam Stoppard - *Writer and broadcaster*
Newcastle upon Tyne Royal GS
        Rt Hon Sir Peter Taylor - *Lord Chief Justice*
Newland HS, Hull
        Maureen Lipman - *Actress*
        Elaine Padmore - *Opera singer, Director Wexford Fest Opera*
        Commandant Anne Spencer - *Director WRNS*
Newport GS, Isle of Wight
        AVM Sir Michael Armitage - *Former Head of Defence Intelligence*

Newport HS
    Keith Baxter - *Actor*
Newton le Willows GS
    Fran Cotton - *Sports commentator*
    Colin Welland - *Actor and Playwright*
Norlington HS
    Graham Gooch - *Cricketer*
    Jonathan Ross - *Channel 4 broadcaster*
North Bridge House
    Jane Asher - *Actress and writer*
North Foreland Lodge, Basingstoke
    Dame Janet Vaughan -
        Authority on blood disorders, former Principal, Somerville College, Oxford
North London Collegiate
    Eleanor Bron - *Actress*
    Fenella Fielding - *Actress*
    Susie Orbach - *Feminist writer*
    Esther Rantzen - *TV presenter* That's Life
    Anna Wintour - *Editor American* Vogue *magazine*
North Walsham Girls' HS
    Valerie Packenham - *Director fundraising The Samaritans*
    Gillian Shephard - *Secretary of State for Employment*
Northallerton C of E
    Sid Weighell - *Trade unionist, Leader Nat Un Railwaymen*
Northallerton GS
    Ms Alex Greaves - *Jockey*
Northampton GS
    Bernard Cotton - *Manager GB hockey team 1992 Olympics*
    Lord Donoughue - *Former Labour policy adviser*
    Professor Gerald Fowler - *Rector East London Polytechnic*
Northampton HS
    Lady Falkender - *Columnist*
Northcote, Leeds
    Barbara Taylor Bradford - *Novelist*
Northgate GS, Ipswich
    Brian Cant - *Children's TV presenter*
    Jane Lapotaire - *Actress*
    Trevor Nunn - *Theatre director*
Northside Secondary
    David Jason - *Actor*
Northumberland House, Bristol
    Deborah Kerr - *Actress*
Northwood College
    Dame Margaret Booth - *High Court Judge*
Norwich GS
    Michael Ashcroft - *Head of ADT, UK largest car auction co*
    Sir John Mills - *Actor*
    Sir John Quinton - *Former Chair Barclays Bank plc*
Norwich HS
    Jane Manning - *Soprano*
    Ann Tyrell - *Fashion designer*

Notley Road Secondary Modern, Lowestoft
Michael Foreman - *Illustrator and writer*
Notre Dame Convent, Battersea
Gwyneth Dunwoody - *Labour MP*
Notre Dame Convent GS, Norwich
Margaret Beckett - *Labour MP, Shadow Treasury Minister*
Alison Halford - *Assis Chief Constable Merseyside Police*
Notre Dame HS, Manchester
Margaret Beckett - *Labour MP, Shadow Treasury Minister*
Notre Dame HS, Southwark
Teresa Cahill - *Opera singer*
Notre Dame HS, Wigan
Rosalind Plowright - *Soprano*
Notre Dame Middle, Crawley
Robert Smith - *Rock singer The Cure*
Notting Hill
Rt Hon Angela Rumbold MP - *Deputy Chair, Conservative Party*
Nottingham County GS
Renee Short - *Former Labour MP*
Nottingham Girls' HS
Diana Tuck - *Education, leisure dep Westminster Council*
Nottingham HS
Rt Hon Kenneth Clarke MP - *Home Secretary*
Sir Peter Gregson - *Permanent Secretary DTI*
John Hayes - *Secretary General The Law Society*
Christopher Train - *Former Director General Prison Service*
Sir Douglas Wass - *Chair Equity and Law Life Assurance Soc*

Oak Hall, Haslemere
Tessa Kennedy - *Interior designer*
Oak Hall, Sussex
Frank Bruno - *Boxer*
Oakfield, Dulwich
Michael Crawford - *Actor*
Oakham
Sir John Cope MP - *Paymaster general*
Ogmore GS
Lynn Davies - *Athlete – gold medallist '64 Tokyo Olymp*
Old Know Road, Smallheath, Birmingham
Dennis Amiss - *Cricketer*
Old Swan College, Liverpool
Robert Evans - *Chair British Gas plc*
Oldershaw GS, Wallasey
Dickie Davies - *Sports commentator*
Fred Jarvis - *Gen Sec National Union of Teachers*
Oldfield, Swanage
Joan Hickson - *Actress*
Orange Hill
Angus Fraser - *England cricketer*
Jean Simmons - *Actress*

Oratory
>Simon Callow - *Actor*
>Sir Michael Levey - *Former Director National Gallery*
>Monsignor V. G. J. Morgan - *Former Vicar General to Royal Navy*
>Nicholas Purnell QC - *Chair Criminal Bar Association*
>Michael Rizzello - *Sculptor and coin designer*

Osmondthorpe Council, Leeds
>Keith Waterhouse - *Writer*

Ossett GS, Yorkshire
>Stan Barstow - *Novelist and scriptwriter*
>Elaine Storkey - *Director, Institute of Contemporary Christianity*

Oswestry
>Frank Bough - *Presenter Sky News*

Oswestry Girls' HS
>Rosemary Leach - *Actress*

Oulton HS, Liverpool
>Alun Owen - *Playwright and screenplay writer*

Oundle
>A. Alvarez - *Writer*
>Rt Hon Lord Justice Roy Beldam -
>>*Appeal court judge, former chair Law Commission*
>Peter Benton - *DG British Institute of Management*
>Charles Crichton - *Film Director*
>Bruce Dickinson - *Rock singer Iron Maiden*
>Thomas Faber - *Chair Faber and Faber*
>Anthony Holden - *Journalist and broadcaster*
>Maxwell Hutchinson - *Architect, President RIBA*
>Rt Hon Lord Justice Michael Mustill - *Appeal Court Judge*
>Professor Joseph Needham -
>>*Director Emeritus Needham Research Institute Cambridge*
>Sir Richard O'Brien - *Former Director Manpower Services Commission*
>Professor W.B. Reddaway - *Economist*
>Martin Rogers - *Former Chief Master King Edward's, Birmingham*
>Charles Wintour - *Former editor* Evening Standard
>Sir Hugh Wontner - *Chair Claridges and Berkeley Hotels*

Our Lady's Convent, Stamford Hill
>Barbara Windsor - *Actress*

Our Lady of Lourdes, Southport
>Phil Cooper - *Anti-drugs campaigner*

Our Lady's Priory, Sussex
>Mary Goldring - *Economist and broadcaster*

Owens, London
>Nat Solomon - *Chair Tottenham Hotspur*

Oxford HS
>Dame Josephine Barnes - *Obstetrician and gynaecologist*
>Liz Brooks - *Admin Director The Dyslexia Institute*
>Sian Edwards - *Conductor, Musical director-elect ENO*
>Jane Goodsir - *Director RELEASE drugs rehabilitation*
>Elizabeth Jennings - *Poet*
>Miriam Margolyes - *Actress*
>Maggie Smith - *Actress*

Paisley GS
> Michael Barratt - *Radio and TV Broadcaster*
> Andrew Neil - *Editor* Sunday Times

Pakeman Street LCC, London
> Richard Tompkins - *Founder Green Shield Stamps, Argos*

Palmer's, Grays, Essex
> Sir Bryan Nicholson - *Chair The Post Office*

Pangbourne
> Jeffrey Bernard - Spectator *columnist*
> Rear Admiral Andrew Richmond - *Chief Executive RSPCA*
> Ken Russell - *Film director*
> Lord Vinson - *President Industrial Partnership Assn*

Park HS, Stanmore
> Norman Cowans - *Cricketer*

Park Parade Secondary, Belfast
> Roy Walker - Catchphrase *TV Quiz show presenter*

Park Secondary Modern, Barking, E London
> Billy Bragg - *Rock singer*

Park Senior HS, Swindon
> John Francome - *Jockey, Channel 4 presenter*

Parliament Hill Girls' GS
> Rosy Adriaenssens - *Principal Officer Save the Children Fund*
> Margaret Douglas - *Chief political adviser BBC*

Pate's Girls' GS, Cheltenham
> Felicity Lott - *Soprano*
> Sarah Walker - *Opera singer*
> Professor Anne Warner - *Physiologist*

Peckham
> Owen Luder - *Architect*
> Norma Major

Peckham Manor
> John Emburey - *Cricketer*

Penge Girls'
> Floella Benjamin - *TV presenter*

Penrhos College
> Dianne Hayter - *Chair Alcohol Concern*

Perse, Cambridge
> Mel Calman - *Cartoonist*
> Marius Goring - *Actor*
> Sir Peter Hall - *Director*
> Rev John Polkinghorne - *President Queens College Cambridge*
> Hon Mr Justice Mark Potter -
>> *High Court Judge Queen's Bench Division*

Perse Girls', Cambridge
> Bridget Kendall - *BBC correspondent Moscow*
> Rt Hon Angela Rumbold MP - *Deputy Chair Conservative Party*

Perth Academy
> Alan Calderwood - *Chief Education Officer Cleveland*
> Barbara Young - *Chief Executive RSPB*

Peter Symonds, Winchester
> ACM Sir Patrick Hine - *Commander Gulf War*

Peterborough County GS
        Professor Daphne Jackson - *Professor Physics Surrey University*
Philip Morant, Colchester
        Neil Foster - *Cricketer*
Pinner County GS
        Elton John - *Singer, pianist and composer*
Plaistow County GS
        Terence Stamp - *Actor*
Plaistow Secondary, West Ham
        Fred Jarvis - *Gen Sec National Union of Teachers*
Plymouth College
        Graham Searle - *Director ISCO*
Plymouth Corporation GS
        Rev Prof Gordon Dunstan -
                Emeritus Professor Moral Theology King's London
Plympton GS, Devon
        Jane Drabble - *Deputy MD BBC*
Plymstock Comprehensive
        Sharron Davies - *Swimmer*
Pocklington
        Sir James Cobban - *Former Head Abingdon School*
        Tom Stoppard - *Playwright and novelist*
Poles Convent, Herts
        Sarah Badel - *Actress*
Pontardawe GS
        Gareth Edwards - *Rugby player*
        Gwynne Howell - *Principal bass Covent Garden*
        Sian Phillips - *Actress*
Pontlanfraith Secondary
        Margaret Price - *Opera Singer*
Pontypool Girls' GS
        Joan Ruddock - *Labour MP*
Pontypridd GS
        Rt Hon Sir Tasker Watkins -
                Lord Justice Appeal, Counsel Aberfan disaster
Pontywaun GS, Gwent
        The Ven Raymond Roberts - *Former Chaplain of the Fleet*
Port Talbot Central
        Clive Jenkins - *Trade unionist*
Portadown College, County Armagh
        Mary Peters - *Athlete*
Portadown GS
        Alexander Walker - Evening Standard *theatre critic*
Portree HS, Isle of Skye
        Derek Cooper - *Author, broadcaster and journalist*
        Sir Russell Johnston - *LD MP*
Portsmouth GS
        Roger Black - *Athlete*
        Sir Peter Carey - *Chair Dalgety plc, Direc Morgan Grenfell*
        Paul Jones - *Singer, ex-Manfred Mann; composer, actor*
        Christopher Logue - *Poet*

Queen Anne's, Caversham
>Baroness Brooke of Ystradfelte -
>>*Former Chair The Conservative Party*
>Joanna Kennedy - *Senior engineer Ove Arup*
>Jenny Seagrove - *Actress*

Queen Elizabeth GS, Blackburn
>Sir Kenneth Durham - *Chair Unilever*
>Rt Rev Peter Hall - *Bishop Suffragan of Woolwich*

Queen Elizabeth GS, Carmarthen
>Rt Hon Denzil Davies - *Labour MP*

Queen Elizabeth GS, Darlington
>Sir Geoffrey Cass - *Chair Royal Shakespeare Company*
>Derek Hunt - *Chair MFI furniture stores*

Queen Elizabeth GS, Faversham
>Sir Robert Bunyard - *HM Inspector of Constabulary*

Queen Elizabeth GS, Hartlebury Worcs
>Ian Taylor - *Hockey goalkeeper*

Queen Elizabeth GS, Wakefield
>Peter Dews - *Theatre and TV director*
>Rt Rev David Hope - *Bishop of London*
>Professor Sir Hans Kornberg - *Biochemist*
>David Storey - *Writer and dramatist*
>David Woodhead - *Director ISIS*

Queen Elizabeth's, Crediton
>Bill Giles - *BBC weather man*

Queen Elizabeth's GS, Barnet
>Sir Tim Bell - *PR consultant formerly to Mrs Thatcher*
>Peter Sanders - *Ch Exec Commission for Racial Equality*

Queen Elizabeth's GS, Mansfield
>Lord Butterworth - *Vice Chancellor Warwick University*

Queen Elizabeth's GS, Tamworth
>Sir Robert Telford - *Life President Marconi*

Queen Elizabeth's GS, Wimborne
>Peter Alliss - *Golfer and TV commentator*
>Lionel Jefferies - *Actor*

Queen Elizabeth's Hospital, Bristol
>Anthony Verity - *Master Dulwich College*

Queen Mary's, Basingstoke
>Kathy Cook - *Athlete*

Queen Mary's GS, Walsall
>Lord Ennals - *Chair United Nations Association*
>Sir Harry Hinsley - *Historian, former Master St John's Cambridge*
>Sir Eric Pountain - *Chair Tarmac plc*

Queensgate
>Lynn Redgrave - *Actress*
>Vanessa Redgrave - *Actress*

Queen's, Chester
>Ann Clwyd - *Labour MP Shadow Minister Overseas Devt*
>Ena Evans - *Head King Edward Girls' Birmingham*

Queen's College, Harley Street
>Penelope Gilliatt - *Writer and journalist*
>Mary Wesley - *Novelist*

Anna Wintour - *Editor American* Vogue *magazine*
Queen's Park, Glasgow
Winifred Ewing - *Scottish National Party MP*
Rita Stephen - *Trade unionist*
Quinton, London
Michael Ivens - *Director Aims of Industry*

RNC, Dartmouth
Admiral of the Fleet Sir Edward Ashmore - *Former C-in-C The Fleet*
Vice-Admiral Sir Peter Ashmore - *Chief of Allied Staff NATO*
Admiral Sir Jeremy Black - *Former Deputy Chief of Defence Staff*
Admiral Sir Desmond Cassidi - *Former Flag ADC to HM The Queen*
Sir Robin Chichester-Clark -
Former Minister of State Employment; managmt consultnt
Sir Hugh Cubitt - *Chair Lombard North Central*
Sir Anthony Duff - *Diplomat and intelligence expert*
Admiral Sir James Eberle - *Director Royal Inst Internatl Affairs*
HRH The Duke of Edinburgh -
Admiral of the Fleet Lord Fieldhouse -
Former First Sea Lord, Chf Defence Staff
Sir John Harvey-Jones - *Former Chair ICI, Ch Parallax Enterprise*
Admiral of the Fleet Lord Hill-Norton - *Former First Sea Lord*
Admiral of the Fleet Sir Henry Leach -
Former Chief Naval Staff and First Sea Lord
Admiral Sir Julian Oswald - *First Sea Lord and Chief of Naval Staff*
Admiral Sir Derek Reffell - *Governor and C-in-C Gibraltar*
Rabbinical Sch, Northampton
Mickey Duff - *Boxing promoter*
Radford Boulevard, Nottingham
Alan Sillitoe - *Writer, film scriptwriter*
Radley
Mark Carlisle - *Former Education Secretary*
Major General Richard Clutterbuck - *Writer, lecturer and broadcaster*
Peter Cook - *Entertainer*
Leo Cooper - *Publisher*
Marshal of RAF Sir David Craig - *Former Chief of Defence Staff*
Ted Dexter - *Chair England Committee TCCB*
Sir Timothy Hoare - *Evangelical layman*
Andrew Motion - *Poet, Editor Faber and Faber*
Sir Patrick Nairne - *Chancellor Essex University*
David Pountney - *Production director English Nat Opera*
Rt Hon Richard Ryder MP - *Government Chief Whip*
Iain Saunders - *Chief executive Robert Fleming Investmt*
Lord Scarman - *Former Law Lord*
Lord Shackleton - *Chair RTZ*
Raines Foundation GS, Stepney
Steven Berkoff - *Actor, director and writer*
Raine's Foundation Girls'
Wendy Taylor - *Sculptor*
Raley's, Barnsley
Dickie Bird - *Test match umpire*

Ralph Allen Senior, Bath
        Jeremy Guscott - *England Rugby Centre forward*
Ranelagh, Bracknell
        Sheila Browne - *Principal Newnham College Cambridge*
Rastrick GS
        Sir Larry Lamb - *Former editor* Daily Express
Ratcliffe College
        Ian Bannen - *Actor*
        Sir Gordon Reece - *PR Consultant to Mrs Thatcher*
        Lord St John of Fawsley - *Master, Emmanuel College, Cambridge*
Raynes Park GS
        Derek Cooper - *Author, broadcaster and journalist*
        Robert Robinson - *Writer and broadcaster*
Reading
        Roy Boulting - *Film producer*
        Charles Denton - *Chief executive Zenith Productions*
        Douglas Guest - *Organist Westminster Abbey*
        ACM Sir Douglas Lowe - *Former Director of Ordnance*
        Sir George Pinker - *Former gynaecologist to HM The Queen*
        Sir Clive Sinclair - *Chair Sinclair Research*
Redland HS, Bristol
        Elizabeth Hoodless - *Exec Direc Community Service Volunteers*
Redman's Road, Stepney Green
        Bernard Kops - *Playwright*
Reigate County Girls'
        Joanna Trollope - *Novelist*
Reigate GS
        Vice Admiral Sir Geoffrey Dalton - *Secretary General MENCAP*
        Lord Sterling - *Chair P & O*
Rendcomb College
        David De Peyer - *Direc Gen Cancer Research Campaign*
        Richard Dunwoody - *Jockey, Grand National winner*
        David Vaisey - *Bodley's Librarian Oxford*
Repton
        Sir Ashley Clarke - *Chairman Venice in Peril Fund*
        Graeme Garden - *Actor and scriptwriter*
        Michael Green - *Controller Radio 4*
        Richard Hutton - *Cricketer*
        Sir Desmond Lee -
            Former HM Winchester, President Hughes Hall Cambridge
        Kenneth Rose - *Historian and journalist*
        Hon Mr Justice Christopher Rose -
            High Court Judge Queen's Bench Division
        Robert Sangster - *Racehorse owner*
        The Hon David Sieff - *Director Marks and Spencer*
        Sir Vincent Wigglesworth - *Entomologist*
Rhyl GS
        Lord Williams QC - *Chair The Bar Council*
Ribson Hall Girls' HS, Gloucester
        Dr Clare Burstall - *Director NFER*
Richmond Girls' HS, Yorks
        Professor Brenda Hoggett - *Law Commissioner*

Rowley Regis Sixth Form College
        Josie Lawrence - *Actress*
Royal Ballet
        David Bintley - *Principal dancer, choreog Royal Ballet*
        Darcey Bussell - *Ballerina Royal Ballet*
        Lesley Collier - *Principal ballerina Royal Ballet*
        Clare Francis - *Novelist; round the world yachtswoman*
        Donald Macleary - *Principal male dancer Royal Ballet*
        Monica Mason - *Senior principal dancer Royal Ballet*
        Annette Page - *Ballerina Royal Ballet*
        Antoinette Sibley - *Prima ballerina*
        Alfreda Thorogood - *Ballerina*
        David Wall - *Director Royal Academy of Dancing*
Royal Belfast Academical Institution
        Dr Harry Chasty - *Director of Studies Dyslexia Institute*
        Lord Lowry - *Former Lord Chief Justice N Ireland*
        Dr Brian Mawhinney MP - *Minister of State for Health*
Royal Commercial Travellers'
        Rt Hon Lord Justice Donald Farquharson - *Appeal Court Judge*
Royal GS, Guildford
        Terry Jones - *Actor and* Monty Python *scriptwriter*
Royal GS, High Wycombe
        Richard Hickox - *Conductor, Dir City of London Sinfonia*
        Lord McIntosh of Haringey - *Chair SVP UK Ltd*
        Phil Newport - *Cricketer*
        Professor Roger Scruton - *Professor Aesthetics Birkbeck College*
Royal GS, Newcastle upon Tyne
        Alistair Graham - *Director, The Industrial Society*
        Brian Redhead - *Broadcaster, Presenter Today Radio 4*
Royal GS, Wolverhampton
        Eric Idle - *Actor and writer*
Royal GS, Worcester
        Imram Khan - *Cricketer*
Royal HS, Edinburgh
        Ronnie Corbett - *Comedian*
        Norman MacCaig - *Poet*
Royal Liberty GS, Essex
        Sir Alex Jarratt - *Company Chairman (Prudential, Midland)*
Royal Masonic
        Anthony Andrews - *Actor*
        Brent Sadler - *ITV Foreign correspondent*
Royal Masonic Girls'
        Wendy Richard - *Actress*
Royal National College for the Blind
        David Blunkett - *Labour MP, Shadow Local Govt minister*
Royal Naval, Haslemere
        Drusilla Beyfus - *Writer, broadcaster, former editor* Vogue
Royds Hall, Huddersfield
        Lord Wilson of Rievaulx - *Former Prime Minister*
Rugby
        Sir Campbell Adamson - *Former Director General, the CBI*
        John Aspinall - *Director Howletts Zoo Kent*

Rutlish—*contd*
>Very Rev John Dennis - *Bishop of St Edmundsbury and Ipswich*
>Rt Hon John Major MP - *Prime Minister*

SE London Polytechnic
>Spike Milligan - *Writer, humorist (after schools in India)*
Sacred Heart Convent, Hammersmith
>Pauline Collins - *Actress*
Sacred Heart Convent, Hove
>Yve Newbold - *Company secretary Hanson plc*
Sacred Heart Convent, Roehampton
>Evelyn Anthony - *Novelist*
>Professor Mary Douglas - *Anthropologist*
Sacred Heart Convent, Tunbridge Wells
>Biddy Hayward - *Theatre producer*
>Libby Purves - *Radio presenter*
Sacred Heart Convent, Whetstone
>Stephanie Beacham - *Actress*
Sacred Heart Convent, Woldingham
>Caroline Charles - *Fashion designer*
>Victoria Mather - *Journalist and broadcaster*
Sadler's Wells Ballet
>Christopher Gable - *Artistic direc Northern Ballet Theatre*
>Nadia Nerina - *Ballerina*
Saint: see under 'St'
Sale County GS
>Anne Howells - *Opera and concert singer*
>Dr Eric Midwinter - *Director Centre for Policy on Ageing*
Salford GS
>Albert Finney - *Actor*
>Mike Leigh - *Dramatist, theatre and film director*
Salisbury Road, Kilburn
>Screaming Lord Sutch - *Professional election candidate*
Salt HS, Shipley
>Bob Cryer - *Labour MP*
Saltley GS, Birmingham
>Robert Kilroy-Silk - *TV presenter*
Sandecotes, Parkstone
>Iona Opie - *Folklorist*
Sarah Bonnell HS for Girls
>Maureen Duffy - *Author*
Sarson Secondary Girls'
>Jennifer Pitman - *Racehorse trainer*
Scarborough College
>Ian Carmichael - *Actor*
Scarborough Girls' GS
>Susan Hill - *Novelist and playwright*
Scarborough HS
>Colin Flint - *Principal Solihull College Technology*
>Gilbert Gray QC - *Barrister*

Scunthorpe GS
    Joan Plowright - *Actress*
    David E Plowright - *Former Chair Granada TV*
    Graham Taylor - *England Football Team Manager*
Seaford College
    Sir Louis Blom-Cooper QC - *Former Chair The Press Council*
    Anthony Buckeridge - *Writer, creator* Jennings
Seaham Secondary
    Peter Willey - *Former England cricketer*
Sedbergh
    John Arden - *Playwright*
    Rt Hon Lord Justice Thomas Bingham - *Appeal Court Judge*
    Christopher Bland - *Chair LWT*
    Will Carling - *England rugby captain*
    Sir John Cassels - *Former Director General NEDDY*
    Warwick Hele - *Former High Master St Paul's*
    Sir Robert Rhodes James - *Former Conservative MP*
    Vice Admiral Sir Jock Slater - *Chief of Fleet Support*
    Lord Waddington - *Former Lord Privy Seal and Leader House of Lords*
Selhurst GS
    Harry Carpenter - *Sports commentator*
    Dennis Peach - *Former Chief Charity Commissioner*
Sevenoaks
    Daniel Day-Lewis - *Actor*
    Paul Downton - *Cricketer*
    Chris Tavaré - *Cricketer*
    Kim Taylor - *Director Calouste Gulbenkian Trust*
Sexey's, Bruton
    John Bryant - *Deputy Editor* The Times, *former Editor* The European
    Ned Sherrin - *Radio and TV presenter*
Sheerness Secondary Modern
    Rod Hull - *Entertainer (with Emu)*
Sheffield City GS
    Rt Hon Roy Hattersley MP - *Opposition spokesman on Home Affairs*
    Sir Peter Middleton - *Deputy Chair Barclays de Zoete Wedd*
    Robert Mulvey - *HM Cademuir School for Gifted Children*
Sheffield Girls' HS
    Antonia Byatt - *Writer*
    Baroness Oppenheim-Barnes - *Former Chair Consumer Council*
Sherborne
    Sir Geoffrey Chandler - *Industrial Adviser RSA, former director NEDO*
    Rt Hon Christopher Chataway -
        Former athlete and MP, Company director
    Sir Derman Christopherson -
        Former Master Magdalene College Cambridge
    Timothy Clifford - *Director National Galleries of Scotland*
    Brigadier Patrick Cordingley -
        Commander 7th Armoured Brigade Gulf War
    Nigel Dempster - *Gossip columnist*
    Richard Eyre - *Theatre, film and TV director*
    Robin Field - *Chief Executive Filofax plc*
    David French - *Director RELATE marriage guidance group*

Sherborne—*contd*

Michael Hopkins - *Architect new Glyndebourne concert hall*
Jeremy Irons - *Actor*
John Le Carré - *Novelist*
Michael McCrum - *Former HM Eton, Master Corpus Christi Cambridge*
Sir Alastair Pilkington - *President Pilkington plc*
Jonathan Powell - *Controller BBC 1*
Lt Gen Sir Steuart Pringle - *Commandant General Royal Marines*
Rt Rev David Sheppard - *Bishop of Liverpool; cricketer*
David Summerscale - *Headmaster Westminster, formerly Haileybury*
Lord Thomas of Swynnerton - *Chair Centre for Policy Studies*
Major General Julian Thompson - *Research Fellow in Armed Conflict*
His Hon Mr Justice John Waite - *High Court Judge Family Division*
Lt Gen Sir John Wilsey - *GOC Northern Ireland*

Sherborne Girls'

Maria Aitken - *Actress*
Emma Kirkby - *Soprano*
Dame Diana Reader Harris - *Former Head Sherbourne Girls' School*

Sheredes Comprehensive

Jennie Moncur - *Interior designer*

Shipman County Secondary, East London

David Essex - *Entertainer*

Shooters Hill, Woolwich

Jools Holland - *TV presenter, singer*

Shoreditch Secondary

Frank Johnson - *Associate Editor* Sunday Telegraph

Shoreham GS

Peter Cushing - *Actor*

Shrewsbury

Christopher Booker - *Author and journalist*
Sir Fred Catherwood -
    Industrialist, former Chair British Institute Management
Richard Cobb - *Historian*
Julian Critchley - *Conservative MP, broadcaster, journalist*
Sir John Cuckney - *Chair Royal Insurance, 3i Group plc*
Nigel Forman - *Under Secretary of State Education Science*
Stephen Glover - *Former editor* Independent on Sunday
Hon Mr Justice Denis Henry -
    High Court Judge Queen's Bench Division
Rt Hon Michael Heseltine MP - *President of the Board of Trade*
Rt Hon Sir Brian Hutton - *Lord Chief Justice Northern Ireland*
Richard Ingrams - *Broadcaster, former editor* Private Eye
Stephen Jessel - *Radio 4 Correspondent*
Lord Lane - *Former Lord Chief Justice*
Michael Palin - *Writer and actor*
John Peel - *Disc jockey,* Observer *pop music critic*
Professor Martin Rees - *Professor Astronomy Cambridge University*
Willie Rushton - *Actor, writer* Private Eye
Sir Basil Smallpeice - *Former air and sea transport executive*
Professor Sir William Wade QC -
    Former Master Gonville & Caius Cambridge
Very Rev Alan Webster - *Former Dean of St Paul's*

Shrewsbury local
    Sandy Lyle - *Golfer*
Sidcot
    Deborah Warner - *RSC director, Founder Kick Theatre*
Sidcup Central
    Wally Fawkes - *Cartoonist*
Simon Langton, Canterbury
    Sir Freddie Laker - *Creator Skytrain air passenger services*
Sir Frederick Milner, Retford
    Derek Randall - *Cricketer*
Sir Frederick Osborne, Welwyn
    Nick Faldo - *Golfer*
Sir George Monoux GS
    Peter Plouviez - *General Secretary Equity*
Sir John Cass College, London
    Mrs Steve Shirley - *Founder F International Group, IT expert*
Sir John Leman, Beccles
    Professor Dorothy Hodgkin - *Chemist*
Sir Walter St John's, London
    Paul Bailey - *Novelist and critic*
Sir William Borlase's, Marlow
    Paul Daneman - *Actor*
    Richard Holbrook - *Chair, Board of Management College of Law*
    Garfield Weston - *Chair Ass British Foods, Fortnum & Mason*
Sir William Turner's GS, Coatham, Redcar
    Paul Daniels - *Magician*
Sizewell Hall, Suffolk
    Sheridan Morley - *Author, journalist and broadcaster*
Skellfield, Ripon
    Mary Stewart - *Novelist*
Skinners, Tunbridge Wells
    Phil Edmonds - *Cricketer*
    Alec McCowen - *Actor*
Slough GS
    Ian Curteis - *TV playwright*
Solihull
    Michael Buerk - *TV journalist*
    Lord Butterfield - *Former Master Downing College Cambridge*
    John Curry - *Skater*
    Bert Millichip - *Chair Football Association*
South Hampstead HS
    Helena Bonham-Carter - *Actress*
    Janet Cohen - *Merchant banker and author*
    Miriam Karlin - *Actress*
    Angela Lansbury - *Actress*
    Rabbi Julia Neuberger - *Writer and broadcaster*
South Hampstead HS—*contd*
    Fay Weldon - *Writer*
South London GS
    Bill Keys - *Trade unionist*
South Park Girls' GS, Lincoln
    Jane Eaglen - *Opera singer English National Opera*

South Staffs College
        Sir Kenneth Corfield -
                Industrialist, former President Institute of Directors
South West Essex Technical
        Leslie Thomas - *Author*
South Wigston Girls' GS, Leicester
        Sue Townsend - *Writer* Adrian Mole
Southall GS
        Lord Templeman - *Lord of Appeal*
Southaw Girls' Secondary
        Elaine Paige - *Singer*
Southend HS
        Lord Chilver - *Chair England China Clays*
        Air Marshal Sir Frank Holroyd - *Chief Engineer Royal Air Force*
        Ian Linden - *Gen Sec Catholic Instit Internat Relatns*
        Robert Lloyd - *Opera singer*
        Robert Nye - *Writer*
Southey Green Secondary Modern, Sheffield
        Tony Mooney - *Head Rutlish School*
Southgate County
        Warren Mitchell - *Actor*
        Ron Moody - *Actor*
Southlands HS, Chorley
        Amanda Roocroft - *Opera singer*
Southport Girls' HS
        Miranda Richardson - *Actress*
Spennymoor GS
        Bruce Oldfield - *Fashion designer*
        Lord Walton of Detchant - *Chair National Commission on Education*
Spiers
        Sir James Blyth - *Director and chief executive Boots plc*
Springfield, Elgin
        Rt Rev Mario Conti - *RC Bishop of Aberdeen*
St Agnes Convent, East Grinstead
        Rachel Kempson - *Actress*
St Albans
        Rt Rev Patrick Harris - *Bishop of Southwell*
        Professor Stephen Hawking -
                Cosmologist, author A Brief History of Time
        Lord Renfrew - *Disney Professor Archaeology Cambridge*
        Sir Harry Solomon - *Chairman Hillsdown Holdings*
St Aloysius, London
        Michael Gambon - *Actor*
St Aloysius's, Glasgow
        James Loughran - *Conductor Laureate Hallé Orchestra*
St Angela's Ursuline Convent
        Margaret Tyzack - *Actress*
St Anne's Convent, Ealing
        Dusty Springfield - *Pop singer*
St Anne's Girls College
        Thelma Holt - *Theatre producer*

St Columba's College, Derry
        Brian Friel - *Playwright* Dancing at Lughnasa
        Seamus Heaney - *Oxford Professor of Poetry*
        Very Rev James McGuinness - *RC Bishop of Nottingham*
St Columba's College, St Albans
        Mark Lawson - *Journalist* Independent
St Cuthbert's GS, Newcastle
        Terry Farrell - *Architect*
St Denis Girls', Edinburgh
        Hannah Gordon - *Actress*
St Dunstan's Catford
        Dr David Delvin - *TV, radio and magazine doctor*
        Michael Grade - *Chief executive Channel 4*
        Rt Rev David Jenkins - *Bishop of Durham*
St Dunstan's, Plymouth
        Dawn French - *Comedienne*
St Edmund's, Ware
        Rt Rev David Konstant - *RC Bishop of Leeds*
St Edward's, Liverpool
        Michael Slemen - *England rugby player*
        Michael Williams - *Actor*
St Edward's, Oxford
        Peter Carter-Ruck - *Solicitor*
        William McAlister - *Director ICA*
        Sir Derek Oulton - *Former Permanent Sec Lord Chancellor's Dept*
        Peter Rawlins - *Chief executive The Stock Exchange*
        Jon Snow - *ITN newsreader*
        His Honour Judge Stephen Tumin - *HM Chief Inspector Prisons*
        James Woodhouse - *Headmaster Lancing College*
St Francis Xavier's College, Liverpool
        Sir Bernard Caulfield - *High Court Judge*
        Michael Kenny - *Sculptor*
        Paul Raymond - *Publisher, nightclub proprietor*
St George GS, Bristol
        Diana Moran - *Former Green Goddess TV fitness expert*
St George's, Harpenden
        Sir Christopher Ball - *Founding Fellow Kellogg Foundation*
        Brigadier Anne Field - *Dep Cdt WRAC, Chair W London Lloyds Bank*
        Patrick Heron - *Painter*
St George's, London
        Louis Heren - *Journalist and author*
St George's, Weybridge
        Mark Landini - *Joint Managing Director Conran Design*
        Sir Clive Sinclair - *Chair Sinclair Research*
St Gilda's RC Junior, Hornsey
        Samantha Fox - *Actress*
St Gregory the Great, Farnworth
        Frank Finlay - *Actor*
St Helena's, Colchester
        John Bond - *Soccer mangr fmly Manchester, Shrewsbury*
St Helen's, Northwood
        Julia Allan - *Sculptor*

St Lawrence College, Ramsgate
      Bill Alexander - *Associate Director RSC*
      Sir David Hunt - *Diplomat*
      Martin Laing - *Chairman John Laing plc*
      Sir Maurice Laing - *President John Laing plc*
      Dr John Sykes - *Lexicographer and translator*
      Rt Rev John Taylor - *Theologian, former Bishop of Winchester*
St Leonards Mayfield
      Lady Brook - *Founder Brook Advisory Centre birth control*
      Lindka Cierach - *Fashion designer*
      Ann Leslie - *Journalist and broadcaster*
St Leonards St Andrews
      Dame Kathleen Ollerenshaw - *Educationist*
St Margaret's, Bushey
      Frances Gibb - *Legal Correspondent* The Times
St Margaret's, Middlesex
      Joan Collins - *Actress*
St Margaret's Senior, Anfield, Liverpool
      Bill Tidy - *Cartoonist*
St Marie's Convent, Elgin
      Rt Rev Mario Conti - *RC Bishop of Aberdeen*
St Martin in the Fields Girls' HS
      Carol Barnes - *TV newsreader*
St Martin's Modern
      Ian Woosnam - *Golfer*
St Mary and St Anne, Abbots Bromley
      Lady Olga Maitland MP - *Founder and Chair Families for Defence*
      Katharine Mortimer - *Dir Rothschilds; Securities & Invstmts Bd*
St Marylebone GS
      Marshal of the RAF Sir Michael Beetham - *Former Chief of Air Staff*
      Victor Gauntlett - *Chair Aston Martin Lagonda*
      Benny Green - *Jazz musician, writer and broadcaster*
St Mary's Anglican Convent, Hastings
      Joanna Lumley - *Actress*
St Mary's, Calne
      Dame Jennifer Jenkins - *Chair National Trust*
      Nicola Lefanu - *Composer and lecturer*
St Mary's College, Crosby
      John Birt - *Deputy Director General BBC*
      Roger McGough - *Poet*
      Rt Rev Mgr Vincent Nichols - *Gen Sec RC Bishops' Conference*
      Tom O'Connor - *Comedian*
      Professor Laurie Taylor - *Sociologist*
St Mary's College, Southampton
      Patrick Garland - *Director, producer* and *writer*
St Mary's Convent, Ascot
      Lady Antonia Fraser - *Writer*
      Sarah Hogg - *Head of Number 10 Policy Unit*
      Marina Warner - *Writer* and *critic*
      Lady Victoria Waymouth - *Interior designer*
St Mary's Convent, Lowestoft
      Mary Symes - *First woman coroner*

St Paul's—*contd*
        Sir David Hopkin - *Chief Metropolitan Stipendiary Magistrate*
        The Hon Greville Janner - *Labour MP*
        Sir Anthony Jay - *TV scriptwriter* Yes Prime Minister *etc*
        Very Rev R.M.C. Jeffery - *Dean of Worcester*
        John Lyons - *Trade union leader*
        Lord McColl - *Surgeon*
        Jonathan Miller - *Former Artistic director The Old Vic*
        Nicholas Parsons - *Broadcaster*
        Dr Magnus Pyke - *Nutritionist* and *broadcaster*
        Stanley Sadie - *Editor* Grove Dictionary of Music
        Antony Shaffer - *Playwright*
        Peter Shaffer - *Playwright*
        David Shilling - *Milliner Royal Ascot*
        Lord Sieff - *Hon President Marks and Spencer*
        John Simpson - *BBC Foreign News Editor*
        Jon Speelman - *Chess grandmaster*
        John Thorn - *Former Headmaster Winchester College*
        Galen Weston - *Chair, President George Weston Toronto*
St Paul's Girls'
        Gillian Ayres - *Painter*
        Margaret Bramall - *Vice-Pres Nat Counc One Parent Families*
        Brigid Brophy - *Author*
        Shirley Conran - *Writer*
        Monica Dickens - *Writer, Founder of USA Samaritans*
        Livia Gollancz - *Chair Victor Gollancz publishers*
        Harriet Harman - *Labour MP*
        Lady Selina Hastings - *Writer*
        Patricia Hutchinson - *Diplomat, Former Ambassador Uruguay*
        Deaconess Dr Una Kroll - *Deacon of Church of Wales, Broadcaster*
        Jessica Mann - *Crime novelist*
        Anne Scott-James - *Writer*
        Anne Sofer - *Chief Education Officer Tower Hamlets*
        Imogen Stubbs - *Actress*
        Emma Tennant - *Writer*
        Carol Thatcher - *Journalist*
        Professor Barbara Tizard - *Professor Education, Institute Education*
        Professor Margaret Turner-Warwick -
            President Royal College of Physicians
St Peter's, York
        Professor J.E.C. Hill - *Historian, former Master Balliol College Oxford*
St Saviour's Hall, Knightsbridge
        Anthony Dowell - *Director The Royal Ballet*
St Stephen's, Folkestone
        Margaret Lane - *Novelist* and *biographer*
St Swithun's, Winchester
        Baroness Warnock - *Former Mistress Girton College Cambridge*
St Teresa's Convent, Dorking
        Fay Maschler - *Cookery writer*
        Lynn Reid Banks - *Writer*
St Teresa's Convent, Sunbury
        Margaret Howard - *Radio presenter*

St Thomas More RC Senior, Wood Green
        Samantha Fox - *Actress*
St Vincent's, Belfast
        Mairead Corrigan-Maguire -
            Co-founder The Peace People, Nobel Prize '76
St Wilfrid's RC Comprehensive, Crawley
        Robert Smith - *Rock singer The Cure*
St Winifred's, Eastbourne
        Dame Felicity Peake - *First director WRAF*
St Winifred's, Stockport
        Peter Snape - *Labour MP*
Stamford
        Rt Rev Philip Goodrich - *Bishop of Worcester*
        Mark James - *Golfer*
        Sir Michael Tippett - *Composer*
Stand GS, Manchester
        Mark E. Smith - *Rock singer The Fall*
Stand Girls' GS, Manchester
        Audrey Slaughter - *Journalist, former editor* Honey *magazine*
Stansfield Road, Brixton
        David Bowie - *Rock singer, actor* and *producer*
Stationers' Company
        Professor Alexander Boksenberg -
        Director Royal Greenwich Observatory
Stepney Jewish
        Bernard Kops - *Playwright*
Sternhold College, London
        Roger Moore - *Film star*
        Nanette Newman - *Actress* and *writer*
Steyning GS
        Richard Du Cann QC - *Barrister*
Stirling HS
        Andrew Faulds - *Labour MP* and *film actor*
Stockport GS
        Peter Barkworth - *Actor*
        Victor Blank - *Chair, Chief executive Charterhouse Bank*
Stockport Girls' HS
        Joan Bakewell - *Broadcaster*
Stockwell Manor Comprehensive
        Sue Slipman - *Dir National Council One Parent Families*
Stoneham, Reading
        Robin Lustig - *Radio 4 journalist*
Stonyhurst
        J.C. Bamford - *Inventor JCB excavator*
        Tom Burns - *Journalist, former editor* The Tablet
        Rev John Coventry - *Catholic philosopher*
        Lord Devlin - *Former Law Lord*
        Rt Rev Crispian Hollis - *RC Bishop of Portsmouth*
        Paul Johnson - *Journalist* and *author*
        Bruce Kent - *Vice-President CND*
Stowe
        Lord Annan - *Chairman of Trustees National Gallery*

Stowe—*contd*

Alexander Bernstein - *Chair Granada Group plc*
Richard Branson - *Entrepreneur – Virgin Atlantic, Records*
Sir Nigel Broackes - *Chair Trafalgar House*
Hon Mr Justice Simon Brown -
High Court Judge – Queen's Bench Divisn
Lord Cheshire VC - *Founder of Cheshire Homes for Disabled*
The Earl Haig - *Painter*
Sir Nicholas Henderson -
Diplomat, former Ambassador to Washington
Antony Hichens - *MD Consolidated Goldfields, Chair Caradon*
Sir Brian Hill - *Chair Higgs and Hill Building Co*
Robert Kee - *Author* and *broadcaster*
General Sir Frank Kitson - *Former ADC General HM The Queen*
Sir Nicholas Lyell QC MP - *Attorney General*
Lord McAlpine - *Director Robert McAlpine & Sons*
George Melly - *Jazz musician*
Lord Quinton - *Chair Board of British Library*
The Earl of Rosebery - *Theatre Lighting designer*
Lord Sainsbury - *Chair J Sainsbury plc*
David Shepherd - *Artist*
Lord Stevens of Ludgate - *Chairman United Newspapers*
Air Commodore Sir Peter Vanneck -
Former ADC to Her Majesty the Queen
Sir Christopher Wates - *Chief executive Wates Holdings*
Laurence Whistler - *Glass engraver*
Sir Peregrine Worsthorne - *Journalist* Sunday Telegraph

Strand, Brixton

David Jacobs - *Radio* and *TV broadcaster*
Professor James Lovelock - *Chemist*

Strathclyde, Glasgow

George Chisholm - *Trombonist*

Streatham GS

Sir Phil Harris - *Chair Harris Ventures*

Streatham Girls' HS

June Whitfield - *Actress*

Streatham House

Lynda La Plante - *TV scriptwriter*

Stretford Elementary

Lord Scanlon - *Former trade unionist AEUW*

Stretford GS

John Tomlinson - *Direc Institute Education Warwick Univ*
Professor Arnold Wolfendale - *Astronomer Royal*

Stretford Girls' HS

Brenda Dean - *General Secretary SOGAT*

Strodes, Egham

Sir Stanley Grinstead - *Chair Reed International, ex-Grand Met*

Stroud Central

Laurie Lee - *Poet* and *author*

Stroud Green Secondary, London

Bob Hoskins - *Actor*

The College for Girls, York
> Dame Janet Baker - *Opera singer*

Thetford GS, Norfolk
> Group Captain Niall Irving -
> *Gulf Commander i/c military briefings*

Thomas Bennet Comprehensive
> Dawn Primarolo - *Labour MP*

Thornes House, Wakefield
> Johnny Pearman - *Leader Wakefield Education Committee*

Thornton GS, Bradford
> Billie Whitelaw - *Actress*

Tiffin Boys', Kingston on Thames
> John Bratby - *Painter*
> Sir Gordon Downey - *Chair FIMBRA*

Todmorden GS
> John Kettley - *TV weather man*

Tom Hood Technical
> Bobby Moore - *Footballer, former Director Southend UFC*

Tonbridge
> Rev Professor Owen Chadwick -
> > *Church historian, Chanclr E Anglia Univ*
> Sir Colin Cowdrey - *Cricketer*
> Chris Cowdrey - *Cricketer*
> Richard Ellison - *Cricketer*
> David Emms - *Former Headmaster Dulwich, Director London House*
> Frederick Forsyth - *Novelist*
> Rt Rev Andrew Graham - *Bishop of Newcastle*
> Sir Patrick Mayhew QC - *Secretary of State for Northern Ireland*
> Tim Waterstone - *Founder* and *Chair Waterstones Books*
> Rev Professor Maurice Wiles -
> > *Canon Christ Church Oxford; Professor Divinity*

Tonypandy GS
> Rt Hon The Lord Tonypandy - *Former Speaker House of Commons*

Tonyrefail GS, South Wales
> Cliff Morgan - *Former rugby player, sports commentator*

Tormead
> The Hon Rhiannon Chapman - *1st female director The Industrial Soc*

Tortington Park, Sussex
> Linda Kitson - *Official war artist Falklands War*

Tottenham Commercial College
> Justin De Villeneuve - *Discoverer* and *mentor of model Twiggy*

Tottenham GS
> Sir Archibald Forster - *Chairman Esso UK*
> Lord Harris of High Cross - *Chair Institute of Economic Affairs*
> Mick Newmarch - *Chief executive Prudential Corporation*

Toxteth Technical School
> Jack Jones - *Trade Unionist*

Tregaron Secondary
> Most Rev George Noakes - *Former Archbishop of Wales*

Trinity Academy, Edinburgh
> Martin O'Neill - *Labour MP*

Unorthodox—*contd*
>Francis Tate - *Vice Chair Tate and Lyle (private tutor)*
>Wendy Toye - *Theatre director (left school 3 and half)*
>Jill Tweedie - *Journalist and scriptwriter (9 schools)*
>Mary Wesley - *Novelist (16 governesses)*
>Shirley Williams - *Founder SDP (8 schools in UK and USA)*

Upholland GS
>John Ashcroft - *Former Chair Coloroll*

Uppingham
>Sir Crispin Agnew of Lochnaw - *Explorer* and *Herald*
>Sir Peter Cazalet - *Chair APV, Former Chair BP*
>Sir Richard Francis - *Director General The British Council*
>Stephen Fry - *Comedian* and *scriptwriter*
>Greg Hutchings - *Chief executive Tomkins plc*
>John Schlesinger - *Film director*

Upton House, Hackney
>Arnold Wesker - *Playwright*

Urmston GS
>Rt Hon Lord Justice Patrick Russell - *Judge of Court of Appeal*

Ursuline Convent, Ilford
>Rowanne Pasco - *Religious editor TV AM*

Ursuline Convent, Westgate on Sea
>Rula Lenska - *Actress*

Ursuline Convent, Wimbledon
>Julie Kaufmann - *PR Offr Children in Need, ex-Gingerbread*

Vale of Leven Academy
>Rt Rev Richard Holloway - *Bishop of Edinburgh*

Valentine's, Ilford
>Sir Raymond Lygo - *Former Chief Executive British Aerospace*

Varndean GS, Brighton
>Desmond Lynam - *Sports commentator*
>Ian Ritchie - *Architect*
>Paul Scofield - *Actor*

Victoria College, Jersey CI
>Col John Blashford-Snell - *Explorer, Direc Gen Operation Raleigh*

Vyners GS, Ickenham, Middlesex
>Sue Cook - *TV presenter*

Wade Deacon GS, Widnes
>Alan Bleasdale - *TV scriptwriter*

Wakefield Girls' HS
>Usha Prashar - *Direct Nat Councl Voluntary Organisation*

Wallasey GS
>Dr John Sykes - *Lexicographer* and *translator*

Wallbottle GS
>Mick Skinner - *England rugby player*

Wallingford GS
>General Sir Frank King - *Former ADC General HM The Queen*

Wallington County GS
  Nick Ross - *Broadcaster*
Walthamstow Girls' HS
  Patricia Scotland QC - *First black woman QC*
  Professor Dorothy Wedderburn -
    Principal Royal Holloway & Bedford Coll
  Doreen Wells - *Dancer Royal Ballet, actress*
Walthamstow Hall, Sevenoaks
  Gillian Banks - *Registrar General England and Wales*
  Ann Longley - *Headmistress Roedean*
Wandsworth GS
  Sir Clifford Chetwood - *Chair Wimpey plc*
Wanstead HS
  Nick Berry - *Actor*
Wards Bridge Comprehensive, Wednesfield
  Tessa Sanderson - *Athlete* and *broadcaster*
Ware Girls' GS
  Baroness Blackstone - *Master Birkbeck College*
  Ann Dummett - *Former Director Runnymede Trust*
Warren, Worthing
  Lady Porter - *Former Leader Westminster Council*
Warwick
  Michael Billington - *Drama critic*
Warwick GS
  Harriet Jagger - *Senior Fashion Editor* Vogue
Washington GS, Co Durham
  Bryan Ferry - *Pop musician*
  Willie Hamilton - *Former Labour MP, anti-monarchist*
Waterhouses Secondary Modern, Co Durham
  Bobby Robson - *Footballer, manager England team*
Watford Boys' GS
  Andrew Davis - *Musical Director Glyndebourne Opera*
  Uwe Kitzinger - *President Templeton College Oxford*
  Oliver Knussen - *Composer* and *conductor*
  Ian Prosser - *Chair Bass plc*
  David Skipper - *Former Head Merchant Taylors' School*
  Patrick Stoddart - *Journalist* Sunday Times
  David Sullivan - Sunday Sport
  Rt Rev John Taylor - *Bishop of St Albans*
  James Watson - *Chair National Freight Corporation*
Webber Douglas, London
  Penelope Keith - *Actress*
  Angela Lansbury - *Actress*
Wednesbury Boys' HS
  Lord Archer - *Former Solicitor General, Labour MP*
Wellingborough
  David Frost - *TV presenter and producer, author*
  Roger Levitt - *Ex Chair Levitt Group Financial Services*
  David Thacker - *RSC director*
Wellington College
  Col Sir Michael Ansell - *Director Horse of the Year Show*

Wellington College—*contd*
>Field Marshal Sir Nigel Bagnall -
>>*Former ADC General to HM The Queen*
>General Sir Cecil Blacker - *Former Adjutant General MOD*
>Lord Cockfield - *Former Vice-President, E.C. Commission*
>Lt Gen Sir Napier Crookenden -
>>*Former GOC IN C Western Command*
>Sir Geoffrey De Bellaigue - *Surveyor of the Queen's works of art*
>Sebastian Faulks - *Journalist*
>Nicholas Grimshaw - *Architect*
>Rt Rev Richard Harries - *Bishop of Oxford*
>Professor Sir Michael Howard - *Historian*
>James Hunt - *Racing driver, TV commentator*
>John Keane - *Official war artist Gulf War*
>Peter Kemp - *Second Permanent Sctry Cabinet Office*
>Christopher Lee - *Actor*
>Sir Richard Lloyd - *Chair Hill Samuel*
>Richard Luce - *former Conservative MP*
>Robert Morley - *Actor*
>Robin Oakley - *Political Editor* The Times
>General Sir Charles Richardson -
>>*Former Master-General of Ordnance*
>Sir David Scholey - *Investment banker, Chair S.G. Warburg*
>Peter Snow - *Presenter Newsnight BBC2*
>Michael Spicer MP - *Former Minister for Housing*
>General Sir Harry Tuzo - *Former Chair Marconi Space and Defence*
>James Villiers - *Actor*

Wellington GS, Shropshire
>Lord Murray of Epping Forest - *Former General Secretary TUC*

Wellington Girls' HS, Shropshire
>Rosemary Harthill - *Religious correspondent BBC*

Wellington, Hanbury
>Sir Stanley Matthews - *Former footballer*

Wellington, Somerset
>Lord Archer - *Author* and *politician*
>Keith Floyd - *TV personality*
>David Suchet - *Actor*

Welshpool GS
>Terry Pryce - *Chief executive Dalgety*

Wesley Street, Pudsey, Yorkshire
>Ray Illingworth - *former cricketer, now commentator*

West Bromwich GS
>Brian Walden - *TV presenter* and *journalist*

West Buckland
>Brian Aldiss - *Science fiction writer*

West Ham GS
>Bryan Forbes - *Film director*
>John Junkin - *Actor* and *scriptwriter*
>Michael Kaye - *Director City of London Festival*

West Heath
>HRH The Princess of Wales

West Kirby Girls' GS
      Glenda Jackson - *Actress* and *Labour MP*
West Monmouth
      Lord Chalfont - *Chair The Radio Authority*
Westborough HS
      Christopher Lawrence - *Silversmith*
Westbourne Girls', Glasgow
      Dr Ruth Jarrett - *Head AIDS research unit Glasgow Univ*
      Ferelith Lean - *Founder Glasgow Mayfest*
Westcliff Girls' HS
      Marcelle D'Argy Smith - *Editor* Cosmopolitan *magazine*
Westminster
      Professor Patrick Bateson - *Provost King's College Cambridge*
      Rt Hon Tony Benn - *Labour MP*
      Dr Alan Borg - *Director General Imperial War Museum*
      Peter Bottomley - *Conservative MP*
      Sir Ashley Bramall - *former Labour MP, Ex-chair GLC and ILEA*
      Peter Brook - *Producer*
      John Brown - *Publisher* Viz *magazine*
      The Hon George Bruce - *Portrait painter*
      Lord Crickhowell - *Chair National Rivers Authority*
      Sir Richard Doll - *Medical epidemiologist*
      Rt Hon John Freeman -
          Former Labour MP, journalist, Ch London Weekend
      Sir John Gielgud - *Actor*
      Simon Gray - *Playwright*
      Dominick Harrod - *Economics journalist*
      Colin Hayes - *Painter*
      Anthony Howard - *Political journalist*
      Sir Andrew Huxley - *Physiologist*
      Dominic Lawson - *Editor* Spectator
      Lord Lawson - *Former Chancellor of the Exchequer*
      Sir Andrew Lloyd Webber - *Composer*
      Sir Hugh Lloyd-Jones - *Regius Professor Greek Oxford University*
      David Lloyd-Jones - *Conductor, Artistic director Opera North*
      Rt Rev John Oliver - *Bishop of Hereford*
      Nigel Planer - *Actor*
      Stephen Poliakoff - *Playwright*
      Norman Rosenthal - *Exhibitions Secretary Royal Academy*
      Anthony Sampson - *Writer and journalist*
      Tim Sebastian - *BBC correspondent and author*
      Alastair Service - *Gen Secretary Family Planning Association*
      Imogen Stubbs - *Actress*
      Donald Swann - *Composer* and *performer*
      Harvey Thomas - *PR consultant*
      Sir Crispin Tickell - *Former diplomat, environmentalist*
      Daniel Topolski - *Rowing coach, travel writer*
      Sir Peter Ustinov - *Actor, dramatist* and *film director*
      Sir William van Straubenzee -
          Former Conservative Minister of State for Education
      Sir Roger Young - *Former Principal George Watson's College*

Westminster City
        Rabbi Lionel Blue - *Writer* and *broadcaster*
        Sir Denis Rooke - *Chair British Gas*
Weston Super Mare GS
        Simon Crine - *General Secretary The Fabian Society*
Weymouth GS
        Ronald Allison - *Former press secretary to HM The Queen*
Wheelwright GS, Dewsbury
        Sir Marcus Fox - *Conservative MP*
Whitehaven GS
        Rev Sir Derek Pattinson -
                Former Sec Gen General Synod Church of England
Whitgift, Croydon
        Sir Bernard Ashley - *Chair Laura Ashley Holdings plc*
        Ian Beer - *Former headmaster Harrow School*
        Professor Bernard Crick - *Biographer, lecturer in politics*
        Robert Dougall - *Broadcaster* and *writer*
        Roger Freeman MP - *Minister for Public Transport*
        Donald Frith - *Ex Secretary HMC*
        Martin Jarvis - *Actor*
        Rt Hon Sir Michael Mann - *Lord Justice of Appeal*
        Mark Shivas - *Head of Drama BBC TV*
        Raman Subba Row - *Chair TCCB*
        Lord Wedderburn of Charlton - *Professor Commercial Law LSE*
Whitley HS, Wigan
        Kay Burley - *Sky News presenter*
Widey Technical, Plymouth
        Charles Dance - *Actor*
Wigan GS
        James Anderton - *Chief Constable Greater Manchester*
        Eric Bolton - *Former Senior Chief Inspector of Schools*
        Sir Ian McKellen - *Actor*
Willesden HS, Brent
        Phillip De Freitas - *Cricketer*
        Chris Lewis - *Cricketer*
Willesden Technical College
        Sir Peter Yarranton - *Chair The Sports Council*
William Ellis, Highgate
        Dickie Davies - *Sports commentator*
William Hulme's GS, Manchester
        ACM Sir Joseph Gilbert -
                Former Dpty C-in-C Allied Forces Cen Europe
        Sir Robert Mark - *Former Commissioner Metropolitan Police*
        Roy Pryke - *Chief Education Officer Kent*
William Morris Secondary, Walthamstow
        Joan Lestor - *Labour MP*
Wilmslow & Stockton Heath, Cheshire
        Terry Waite - *Former Archbishop of Canterbury's Special Envoy*
Wilsons GS, Peckham
        Michael Caine - *Actor*
        John Galliano - *Fashion designer*

Wimbledon College
     Sir Patrick Meaney - *Chair Rank Organisation*
     Rt Hon John Patten MP - *Education Secretary*
     Sir Michael Quinlan - *former Under Secty Min of Defence*
     John Walsh - *Literary editor* Sunday Times
Wimbledon Girls' HS
     Professor Marilyn Butler - *Professor English Lit King's Cambridge*
     Valerie Packenham - *Director fundraising The Samaritans*
     Bridget Rosewell - *Deputy Director Economics at CBI*
Wimbledon Technical College
     Eric Porter - *Actor*
Winceby House, Bexhill
     Dame Wendy Hiller - *Actress*
Winchester
     Sir David Barran - *Former Chairman Midland Bank*
     General Sir Hugh Beach - *Former Director Council for Arms Control*
     Sir Jeffrey Bowman - *Senior Partner Price Waterhouse*
     Lord Brandon of Oakbrook - *Law Lord*
     Tim Brooke-Taylor - *Actor* and *comedian*
     Field Marshal Lord Carver - *Former Chief of Defence Staff*
     Robert Conquest - *Writer*
     David Cope - *Master, Marlborough College*
     Professor Michael Dummett - *Wykeham Professor of Logic Oxford Univ*
     Timothy Eggar MP - *Minister of State, Trade & Industry*
     Roger Ellis - *Former Master Marlborough, Chair HMC*
     ACM Sir Christopher Foxley-Norris -
         Chairman Battle of Britain Association
     Lord Gifford QC - *Barrister, Counsel for Birmingham Six*
     Sir Simon Gourlay - *President National Farmers' Union*
     General Sir Michael Gow -
         Former GOC Scotland, Govnr Edinburgh Castle
     Martin Hammond - *Headmaster, Tonbridge School*
     Sir David Hannay - *Ambassador & UK Permanent Repr to EC*
     Richard Hornby - *Former Chair Halifax Building Society*
     Sir John Hoskyns - *Chair Burton Group plc, ex-Director IOD*
     Lord Howe - *Former Deputy PM*
     Peter Jay - *Economics Editor BBC*
     Lord Jay - *Former President Board of Trade*
     Earl Jellicoe - *Chair Medical Research Council*
     Murray Lawrence - *Chair Lloyd's of London*
     Sir James Lighthill - *Mathematics professor*
     John Lucas - *Lay Christian philosopher, Fellow Merton College, Oxford*
     George Medley - *Director Worldwide Fund for Nature UK*
     Alasdair Milne - *Former Director General BBC*
     Julian Mitchell - *Writer, TV playwright*
     Sir John Moberly - *Diplomat*
     Sir Jeremy Morse - *Chair Lloyds Bank*
     Richard Noble - *World land speed record holder*
     Hugh Peppiatt - *Solicitor Senior Partner Freshfields*
     Giles Radice - *Labour MP*
     Lord Roskill - *Former Lord of Appeal in Ordinary*
     James Sabben-Clare - *Headmaster Winchester College*

Winchester—*contd*
 Nicholas Shakespeare - *Literary Editor* Daily Telegraph
 Mark St Giles - *Chair Framlingham Unit Trust, ex-Fimbra*
 Professor Hugh Stephenson - *Professor of journalism City University*
 Peter Stormonth Darling - *Head of Mercury Asset Management*
 Dr Anthony Storr - *Psychiatrist*
 Jonathan Taylor - *Chief executive Booker plc*
 Sir Aubrey Trotman-Dickenson - *Principal University Coll Wales Cardiff*
 Brian Trubshaw - *Former test pilot*
 Sir Anthony Tuke - *Chair Savoy Hotel Group*
 Sir Geoffrey Warnock - *Former Vice Chancellor Oxford University*
 John Whale - *Editor*, Church Times
 Viscount Whitelaw - *Former Leader House of Lords*
 Lord Wilberforce - *Former Law Lord, High Steward Oxford University*
 The Hon Montague Woodhouse - *Greek Resistance organiser*
 Lord Younger - Former Secretary State for Defence
Windsor County Girls'
 Geraldine McEwan - *Actress*
Winston Churchill County Secondary
 Peter Davison - *Actor*
Wintringham Secondary
 Professor Brian Cox - *Professor Eng Lit Manchester University*
Wirral GS, Cheshire
 Lord Wilson of Rievaulx - *Former Prime Minister*
Withington Girls' HS, Manchester
 Judith Chalmers - *TV presenter*
 Sandra Chalmers - *Radio producer*
 Beryl Reid - *Actress*
Wix's Lane, Battersea
 Julian Symons - *Writer*
Woking County GS
 Terry Hands - *Theatre director*
 Kazuo Ishiguro - *Novelist*
Wolstanton GS, Newcastle under Lyne
 Chris Lowe - *Head Oundle Prince William Upper School*
Wolverhampton Girls' HS
 Elizabeth Appleby QC - *Barrister*
 Helene Hayman - *Politician and broadcaster*
 Rachael Heyhoe Flint - *Cricketer*
 Lady Perry - *Director South Bank Polytechnic*
Woodbridge
 Sir Edward Du Cann - *Chair Lonrho plc*
Woodhouse GS
 Dr Robert Anderson - *Director British Museum*
 Linda Kelsey - *Editor* She *magazine*
Woodhouse Grove, Yorkshire
 Alistair Grant - *Head of Safeway Stores*
 Sir Noel Stockdale - *Chair ASDA, MFI*
Woodmill HS, Dunfermline
 Barbara Dickson - *Pop singer*
Woodseats County, Sheffield
 Peter Howard - *Editor* Jane's Defence Weekly

Woodside Senior, Glasgow
> Sir David McNee - *Former Commissioner Metropolitan Police*

Woolverstone Hall
> Ian McEwan - *Novelist*
> Jonathan Sayeed - *former Conservative MP*

Worksop College
> David Naish - *Leader National Farmers Union*
> His Hon Judge James Pickles - *Former circuit Judge*
> Rev Dr Chad Varah - *Founder The Samaritans*

Worth
> Peter Jonas - *Managing Director English National Opera*

Worthing Girls' GS
> Janet Maw - *Actress*
> Anita Roddick - *Founder Body Shop*

Wrekin College
> General Sir Peter Inge - *C-in-C British Army of the Rhine*
> Derek Lewis - *Chief Executive Granada*
> Noel Murless - *Keeper of the Queen's Racehorses*
> Sir Brian Shaw - *Company director ANZ, Grindlays Bank*

Wychwood, Oxford
> Joan Aiken - *Writer, especially children's books*
> Lady Casson - *Architect* and *designer*

Wycliffe College, Gloucester
> Mark Pitman - *Jockey*
> Mark Sheldon - *Solicitor Sen Ptnr Linklaters & Paines*
> Jon Silkin - *Poet*

Wycombe Abbey
> Rt Hon Dame Elizabeth Butler-Sloss - *Lord Justice of Appeal*
> Judith Chaplin MP - *former Political adviser to John Major*
> Penelope Fitzgerald - *Novelist*
> Lady Howe - *Former Dep Chair Equal Opportunities Cttee*
> Her Honour Judge Valerie Pearlman - *Circuit judge*

Wyggeston GS, Leicester
> Sir Richard Attenborough - *Actor, producer* and *director*
> Sir David Attenborough - *Broadcaster* and *naturalist*
> Mark Cox - *Tennis player*
> Anthony Dawson - *Physician to HM The Queen*
> Simon Hoggart - Observer *columnist*
> Bryan Organ - *Painter*
> Tim Pigott-Smith - *Actor*

Wyggeston Girls' GS, Leicester
> Mary Stott - *Journalist*

Wylde Green College
> Francis Durbridge - *Playwright* and *author*

Wyvern Comprehensive, Weston
> Rupert Graves - *Actor*

Xaverian College, Manchester
> Anthony Burgess - *Novelist* and *critic*
> Terry Maher - *Founder, Chair Pentos (Athena, Dillons, Ryman)*

Yarm GS, Yorkshire
    Wendy Craig - *Actress*
Yehudi Menuhin
    Nigel Kennedy - *Violinist*
Yeovil
    Max Hebditch - *Director Museum of London*
Ysgol Hywel Dda
    Shakin' Stevens - *Pop singer*
Ystalyfera GS, Swansea
    Arwel Huw Morgan - *Opera singer English National Opera*
    Thomas Arfon Owen - *Director Welsh Arts Council*